VOLUME·FOUR
DEMOCRACY
IN DEVELOPING COUNTRIES
LATIN AMERICA

Also Available:

Volume 1, Persistence, Failure, and Renewal
Volume 2, Africa
Volume 3, Asia

VOLUME · FOUR
DEMOCRACY
IN DEVELOPING COUNTRIES
LATIN AMERICA

Edited by
Larry Diamond
Juan J. Linz
Seymour Martin Lipset

Lynne Rienner Publishers •
Boulder, Colorado

Adamantine Press Limited •
London, England

Published in the United States of America in 1989 by
Lynne Rienner Publishers, Inc.
1800 30th Street, Boulder, Colorado 80301

and in the United Kingdom by Adamantine Press Limited,
3 Henrietta Street, Covent Garden, London WC2E 8LU

©1989 by Lynne Rienner Publishers, Inc. and the National Endowment for Democracy.
All rights reserved

Library of Congress Cataloging-in-Publication Data
Democracy in developing countries.
    Includes bibliographies and index.
    Contents: — v. 2. Africa — v. 3. Asia — v. 4. Latin America.
    1. Developing countries—Politics and government.
2. Democracy. I. Diamond, Larry Jay. II. Linz, Juan J. (Juan José), 1926-   . III. Lipset, Seymour Martin.
D883.D45   1988   320.9173'4   87-23457
ISBN 1-55587-043-0 (v.4)
ISBN 1-55587-044-9 (pbk. v.4)

British Cataloguing in Publication Data
Democracy in developing countries.—(Adamantine
    studies in international political economy and
    development, ISSN 0954-6065; 4)
    Vol. 4, Latin America
    1. Developing countries. Democracy
    I. Diamond, Larry, 1951-   II. Linz, Juan J. III.
    Lipset, Seymour Martin
    321.8'09172'4
    ISBN 0-7449-0010-7
    ISBN 0-7449-0011-5 pbk

Printed and bound in the United States of America

The paper used in this publication meets the requirements
of the American National Standard for Permanence of
Paper for Printed Library Materials Z39.48-1984.

VOLUME•FOUR
DEMOCRACY
IN DEVELOPING COUNTRIES
LATIN AMERICA

Edited by
Larry Diamond
Juan J. Linz
Seymour Martin Lipset

Lynne Rienner Publishers •
Boulder, Colorado

Adamantine Press Limited •
London, England

Published in the United States of America in 1989 by
Lynne Rienner Publishers, Inc.
1800 30th Street, Boulder, Colorado 80301

and in the United Kingdom by Adamantine Press Limited,
3 Henrietta Street, Covent Garden, London WC2E 8LU

©1989 by Lynne Rienner Publishers, Inc. and the National Endowment for Democracy.
All rights reserved

Library of Congress Cataloging-in-Publication Data
Democracy in developing countries.
  Includes bibliographies and index.
  Contents: — v. 2. Africa — v. 3. Asia — v. 4. Latin
America.
  1. Developing countries—Politics and government.
2. Democracy.   I. Diamond, Larry Jay.   II. Linz,
Juan J. (Juan José), 1926-   .   III. Lipset, Seymour
Martin.
D883.D45   1988   320.9173'4   87-23457
ISBN 1-55587-043-0 (v.4)
ISBN 1-55587-044-9 (pbk. v.4)

British Cataloguing in Publication Data
Democracy in developing countries.—(Adamantine
  studies in international political economy and
  development, ISSN 0954-6065; 4)
  Vol. 4, Latin America
  1. Developing countries. Democracy
  I. Diamond, Larry, 1951-   II. Linz, Juan J. III.
  Lipset, Seymour Martin
  321.8'09172'4
  ISBN 0-7449-0010-7
  ISBN 0-7449-0011-5 pbk

Printed and bound in the United States of America

The paper used in this publication meets the requirements
of the American National Standard for Permanence of
Paper for Printed Library Materials Z39.48-1984.

ERRATUM

Democracy in Developing Countries, v. 4, Latin America
edited by Diamond, Linz, and Lipset

In Chapter 6, two figures have been inadvertently transposed:

Figure 6.2, on page 261, should appear on page 271, and
Figure 6.1, on page 271, should appear on page 261.

Contents

	List of Tables and Figures	vii
	Preface	ix
	Acknowledgments	xxix
1	Introduction: Politics, Society, and Democracy in Latin America *Larry Diamond and Juan J. Linz*	1
2	Argentina: Autarkic Industrialization and Illegitimacy *Carlos H. Waisman*	59
3	Brazil: Inequality Against Democracy *Bolívar Lamounier*	111
4	Chile: Origins, Consolidation, and Breakdown of a Democratic Regime *Arturo Valenzuela*	159
5	Uruguay: The Survival of Old and Autonomous Institutions *Charles Guy Gillespie and Luis Eduardo Gonzalez*	207
6	Venezuela: The Nature, Sources, and Future Prospects of Democracy *Daniel H. Levine*	247
7	Colombia: The Politics of Violence and Accommodation *Jonathan Hartlyn*	291
8	Peru: Precarious Regimes, Authoritarian and Democratic *Cynthia McClintock*	335
9	Costa Rica: The Roots of Democratic Stability *John A. Booth*	387
10	The Dominican Republic: Mirror Legacies of Democracy and Authoritarianism *Howard J. Wiarda*	423
11	Mexico: Sustained Civilian Rule Without Democracy *Daniel C. Levy*	459
	The Contributors	498
	Acronyms	502
	Index	505

· Tables and Figures ·

· TABLES ·

1.1.	Military Expenditures and Strength	34
1.2.	Income Distribution for Selected Latin American Countries	40
1.3.	Selected Development Indicators, 1965–1985	45
3.1.	Socioeconomic Change in Brazil, 1940–1980	131
3.2.	Brazilian Political Structure Since Independence	138
5.1.	Per-Capita GDP at Factor Cost	215
5.2.	Real Wages in Manufacturing Industry, 1930–1972	215
5.3.	Ideological Distribution of Voters by Region, 1971	218
5.4.	Regional Distribution of Voters by Ideology, 1971	218
6.1.	Regimes, Presidents, Central Political Groups, and Basic Political Methods in Twentieth-Century Venezuela	253
6.2.	National Results: Presidential Votes, 1947–1983	262
6.3.	National Results: Legislative Votes, 1946–1983	263
6.4.	Selected Social and Economic Data, 1936–1981	268
6.5.	Competition Between AD and COPEI: Legislative Votes, 1946–1983	274
7.1.	Electoral Results for the Legislature, 1935–1986	296
7.2.	Electoral Results for the Presidency, 1930–1986	298
7.3.	Selected Latin American Countries: Average Growth Rates and Changes in the Consumer Price Index	311
7.4.	Colombia: Demographic and Social Indicators	312
8.1.	Voter Participation, 1945–1985	346
8.2.	Electoral Tallies: 1978, 1980, and 1985	352
8.3.	Attitudes Toward Democracy in Peru, 1982–1988	359

8.4.	Regional Inequalities	365
8.5.	Economic Growth Rates	372
8.6.	U.S. Aid to Peru	375
9.1.	Characteristics of Costa Rican Presidencies, 1824–1986	390
9.2.	Election Results, 1946–1986	396
9.3.	Income Distribution in Costa Rica: 1961, 1971, 1977, 1983	406
9.4.	Selected Indicators of Socioeconomic Change	406
11.1.	Electoral Support for the PRI and the PAN, 1946–1985	475
11.2.	Income Distribution in Mexico, 1950–1977	478

· FIGURES ·

3.1.	Representation, Deconcentration, and Democratization	146
6.1.	National Results: Presidential Votes, 1947–1983	261
6.2.	Expansion of Electorate and Population, 1941–1983	271
6.3.	National Results: Share of Legislative Votes, 1946–1983	275

· Preface ·

This comparative study of democracy in developing countries—encompassing this and three other volumes—was undertaken at a time of tremendous democratic ferment in the developing world. The movement toward democracy that witnessed, in the mid-1970s, the toppling of Western Europe's last three dictatorships, in Greece, Portugal, and Spain, then moved on through Latin America. In the ensuing decade, most Latin American military dictatorships collapsed or withdrew, defying predictions of a longer reign for the "bureaucratic-authoritarian" regimes. Democratic progress was apparent in East Asia as well, in the Philippines, Korea, and even to some extent Taiwan. In the old British South Asian raj, both the more authoritarian states of Pakistan and Bangladesh and the democratic ones, India and Sri Lanka, were facing recurrent tensions and conflicts that could lead to a restoration or revitalization of democracy, or to deeper crisis.

Among the states of Africa, which found it difficult to establish new nationhood and democratic regimes, there have also been signs of democratic emergence or renewal. Uganda, for example, is struggling to put an end to decades of anarchy, tyranny, and civil strife, in order to fulfill its hopes for democracy and human rights. Despite intense repression, the black and coloured peoples of South Africa continue their struggle for a nonracial democracy through an increasingly powerful trade union movement. In Nigeria and Ghana, debate proceeds under military regimes over the constitutional structure for new attempts at democratic government.

These and similar dramas in Asia, Africa, and Latin America form the backdrop for renewed political and intellectual concern with the conditions for democratic government. To be sure, there is no guarantee that the recent and continuing democratic progress will not be reversed. If the past is any guide, many of the new democratic and semidemocratic regimes are likely to fail. Indeed, a number appear to be perched precariously on the precipice of new breakdowns into one-party or military rule or even chaos.

But the 1980s have seen an unprecedented growth of international concern for human rights—including (prominently) the rights to choose democratically the government under which one lives and to express and organize around one's political principles and views. As torture, disappearances, and other grave human rights violations have become more widespread, but also more systematically exposed and denounced around the world, there has developed a renewed and deeper appreciation for the democratic institutions that, with all their procedural messiness and sluggishness, nevertheless protect the integrity of the person and the freedoms of conscience and expression. The growth of democratic norms throughout the world is strikingly evident in the degree to which authoritarian regimes find it necessary to wrap themselves in the rhetoric and constitutional trappings of democracy, or at least to state as their goal the eventual establishment of democracy.

The great competing ideologies of the twentieth century have largely been discredited. Fascism was destroyed as a vital force in World War II. The appeals of Marxism-Leninism have declined with the harsh repressiveness, glaring economic failures, and loss of revolutionary idealism of the existing communist regimes. More limited quasi-socialist or mass mobilizational models—the Mexican, the Yugoslav, the Nasserite—have also lost their aura. Military regimes almost universally lack ideological justification, and legitimacy beyond a temporary intrusion to correct political and social problems. With the important but still indeterminate exception of the Islamic fundamentalist state—for that large portion of the world from Indonesia to West Africa where Islam is a major or dominant religion—democracy is the only model of government with any broad ideological legitimacy and appeal in the world today.

• STUDIES OF THE CONDITIONS FOR DEMOCRACY: A BRIEF INTELLECTUAL HISTORY •

An important element of this new global *zeitgeist* is the renewed proliferation of intellectual concern with the conditions of the democratic order. Beginning perhaps with the four-volume work on *The Breakdown of Democratic Regimes* in Europe and Latin America, edited by Juan Linz and Alfred Stepan,[1] one can trace a growing efflorescence of academic literature on transitions to and from democracy, and the sources of democratic persistence and failure. Studies have focused on varying themes, such as the means for accommodating ethnic or other sectional cleavages within a democratic framework,[2] the role of political institutions and political violence,[3] and the place of competitive elections in the development of democracy.[4] This outpouring of intellectual interest has recently produced a new four-volume study of transitions to democracy,[5] the most prominent in a rich new harvest of literature on the subject. On the more theoretical level of the definition of democracy and the debate surrounding its concepts, relationships, and forms, a stream of stimulating new work is appearing, of which the recent two-volume contribution of Giovanni Sartori should be considered an essential reference.[6]

Of course, intellectual concern with the social requisites, correlates, or conditions for democracy and other types of political systems has a long tradition, dating back at least to the classical Greek thinkers. Aristotle argued that democracy is more likely to occur where the middle strata are large, oligarchy and tyranny where the population is overwhelmingly poor. The Renaissance political theorist, Machiavelli, also placed an emphasis on class distribution in specifying the sources of political systems. The subsequent writings of Hobbes, Locke, and Montesquieu heavily influenced the founding fathers of the American democratic experience in their emphasis on the restraint of state powers through the institutionalization of checks and balances. Turning to the young American republic for clues to the development of democracy, the rule of law, and personal freedom, Alexis de Tocqueville emphasized in his writings the impact of voluntary associations as mediating institutions and contervailing forces to the central government; the division of powers in a federal system; and the relative socioeconomic equality that fostered political participation. In different ways, the role of the middle class in fostering liberty and democracy was also emphasized by the laissez-faire disciples of Adam Smith and by the Marxists.

However, while democracy slowly took root in much of northern Europe, as well as in North America and Australasia, attempts in Southern, Central, and Eastern Europe and in Latin America were generally less successful. These abortive democratic openings unleashed levels of political and social moblization that alarmed established interests such as the aristocracy, the landed elite, the church, and the military. As these groups, often allied with a weaker bourgeoisie, formed reactionary coalitions, the prospects for democracy dimmed. These various trends culminated during the 1920s and 1930s with the establishment of communist dictatorship in the Soviet Union, fascism in Germany and Italy, a host of other rightist dictatorships throughout Europe, and populist autocracies in Argentina, Brazil, and Mexico.

The pessimism about democracy and free institutions occasioned by the events of this period was inverted by the victory of the Allied powers in World War II. Democracy was imposed on Germany, Italy, and Japan, and surprisingly took hold and endured. Beginning with India in 1947, a host of new nations in Asia, Africa, and the Middle East that had been colonies of the Western democracies were granted independence under constitutions and following election procedures modeled on those of their former colonial rulers. The wave of excitement and optimism about the prospects for democracy and rapid development in these newly independent nations spawned a new generation of scholarly thinking and research.

More extensively than ever before, theory and empirical research in political development examined the world outside the West. Employing a multi-dimensional, functionalist framework, *The Politics of the Developing Areas* (1960) was (to quote its coeditor, Gabriel Almond) "the first effort to compare the political systems of the 'developing' areas, and to compare them systematically according to a common set of categories."[7] There followed a wealth of case studies of emerging political systems in the new nations, as well as comparative studies. Almond and Verba's *The Civic Culture* was the first scholarly attempt to apply the methods of modern survey analysis to the comparative analysis of political systems, in this case the relationship between democracy and political attitudes and values in five nations (four of them Western, but also including Mexico).[8] With increasing statistical sophistication, a new style of social science analysis examined quantitatively the relationship between democracy and socioeconomic modernization, or political development more broadly, across nations throughout the developed and developing worlds.[9] Some scholars, such as Samuel Huntington, focused a more skeptical eye on the sources of political disorder and breakdown in the new nations.[10] Also in this period came the ambitious and controversial sociological-historical effort of Barrington Moore to account for the emergence of democracy, authoritarianism, and totalitarianism in the world.[11]

Probably the most ambitious and important project of the decade was the work of the Committee on Comparative Politics of the Social Science Research Council (SSRC), which produced a series of nine volumes (mostly during the 1960s) on the relationship between political development and such social and political subsystems as bureaucracy, education, parties, and political culture. Much of this work was synthesized and distilled theoretically in *Crises and Sequences of Political Development*, which argued that patterns of political development, including the chances for stable democracy, could be explained by the way in which countries encountered and dealt with five characteristic problems of state- and nation-building.[12] The publication that same year (1971) of Robert Dahl's classic study, *Polyarchy*, can be seen as the crowning work on democracy of the political development decade.[13] To this day, it remains one of the most important treatments of the historical, social, economic, cultural, and political factors that foster or obstruct the development of stable democracy, and it has much influenced our own work. Although centered on the European historical experience, the work of Stein Rokkan has also been extremely fruitful for our understanding of the conditions under which states and party systems emerged and the variety of coalitions involved.[14]

The study of democracy was to sag through most of the 1970s. By 1970, critiques of pluralist political development studies as ethnocentric and even reflective of U.S. imperialism were in full cry. Although these criticisms were often based on a superficial and ideologically biased reading of these works,[15] they nevertheless pushed the study of comparative political systems into the background. The fields of comparative politics, political development, and international political sociology became dominated by issues relating to economic dependence and by theories of international dependency—often carrying with them the Marxist assumption that political systems were mere superstructures and "bourgeois democracies" largely illusory and epiphenomenal. To the extent they dealt with the political system explicitly, theories of dependency maintained that political exclusion and repression of popular mobilization were inevitable concomitants of dependent economic development and peripheral status in the world division of labor.¹⁶ Cynicism about political democracy in the developing countries was reflected and deepened by a new cycle of democratic breakdowns in Latin America into particularly harsh, "bureaucratic-authoritarian" dictatorships. This development was interpreted as a consequence of the inherent strains and pressures of economic dependence at a particular, middle stage of development.¹⁷ But the collapse of these and other dictatorships around the world—beginning with the transitions to democracy in southern Europe in the mid-1970s—along with the revalorization of political democracy as an end in itself (partly in response to the extraordinary brutality of many recent authoritarian experiences), has now refocused the attention of the scholarly world on the conditions for liberal democracy.

• THE PROJECT ON DEMOCRACY IN DEVELOPING COUNTRIES •

The growth of political and intellectual interest in democracy in developing countries provided a propitious climate for the study we wanted to launch. Despite the rich profusion of literature, it seemed to us that there remained huge gaps in our understanding of the factors that fostered or obstructed the emergence, instauration, and consolidation of democratic government around the world. All of the existing studies were limited in important ways: to a particular period of time; to particular regions (usually Europe or Latin America); to particular moments or segments of the historical record (such as crises and breakdowns, or transitions); or to a limited range of theoretical variables. While understanding that any one study would inevitably be bound more or less by such limits, we undertook to design a comparative historical analysis that would, nevertheless, reach wider and further than had any previous one.

The resulting four-volume work is, we believe, somewhat unique in several respects. In geographical scope, it is the first study of democracy to compare systematically the historical experiences of individual countries throughout Asia, Africa, and Latin America. In the "developing" world, only the Middle East (for reasons we will later explain) is excluded. In sheer size, it may be the largest comparative study of national political systems to date, with chapters on twenty six different countries. Significantly, these chapters are not the loose collection of varied papers and themes one sometimes encounters. Each was written specifically for this project, in response to a common set of guidelines, definitions, and theoretical concerns. Also we as editors took a broadly inclusive approach theoretically. Rather than pursuing some new, elegant, "parsimonious" model, we deliberately eschewed monocausal and reductionist interpretations in favor of an exhaustive examination of all the historical, cultural, social, economic, political, and international factors that might affect the chances for stable democracy; how they interact; and the conditions that might mediate their salience or their effects.

The contributions to this work are also distinctive in that they deal with the entire history of a country's experience with democracy. This includes the whole range of phenomena: establishment, breakdown, reequilibration, and consolidation of democratic government; periods of democratic persistence, crisis, authoritarianism, and renewal; and all of the ambivalences and oscillations in between. In the process, we consider each country's early cultural traditions, analyze (where relevant) the colonial experience, consider all of its postindependence history, but give special emphasis to post-World War II developments. Whereas most other works cut horizontally through the history of countries to focus on limited time spans and particular processes (usually ignoring the phenomena of democratic consolidation and stability),[18] our study cuts vertically through historical phases in order to explain the overall path of a country's political development.

While it can be enormously fertile, this historical approach is not without certain methodological problems. In particular, it runs the risk of attributing contemporary political patterns to antecedents far removed in time, without clearly demonstrating that those factors (or characteristics resulting from them) are operating at a later time and account for the failure or success of democracy. The past, to be relevant, must in one way or another be present at the time the realities we want to explain happen. We feel, however, that within the constraints of space, the authors of the case studies have generally avoided accounting for events at time t^{20} by reference to factors that appear only at time t^1 or t^5, although sometimes the link with t^{19} might have been made more explicit.

The result is an eclectic, but also very rich, analysis of the opportunities and obstacles for democracy in the developing world today. Indeed, it is the very richness of our study that presents to us, as perhaps it will to many of our readers, the greatest frustration. As our colleague Robert Dahl remarked at a recent scholarly meeting where our work was discussed, a key problem with the previous generation of work on democracy was the paucity of comparative evidence in relation to the abundance of theorizing; on the other hand, the current generation of work, including this comparative study, appears destined to suffer from an abundance of evidence for which there will be a relative dearth of theory. Readers of Volume 1 in this set will find no shortage of theoretical arguments and lessons drawn from this study. But we concede that these are not integrated into a single, all-encompassing theory, and that it will be some time (if ever) before the field produces one.

We began our study by inviting distinguished comparativists and country specialists to write case studies of individual countries' experiences with democratic and authoritarian government. Each of our authors was given the same broad set of guidelines, flexible enough to permit them to do justice to the uniqueness of the society and its history, but structured enough so that each case study would share a common conceptual orientation, analytical purpose, and framework for organizing the material.

The first section of each chapter was to review the country's political history, describing the major experiences with democratic and nondemocratic government, including the structure, nature, and characteristic conflicts and tensions of each regime. The second section would explain the fate of each regime (especially each democratic one), why it persisted or failed or evolved as it did, and why successive ones emerged as and when they did. Alternatively, authors were given the option of combining these tasks of historical review and analysis, which many did. In a third (or second) section, the author was asked to offer a summary theoretical judgment of the factors that have been most important in determining the country's overall degree of success or failure with democratic government—to abstract across the various regimes and events the most consistently significant and salient factors from among the broad inventory of variables in our project outline (and any others we might have neglected). Finally, each author was asked to consider the future prospects for democratic government in the country, along with any policy implications he or she might wish to derive. In addition, each author was asked to assess (somewhere in the chapter) the country's overall experience with democratic government, using our six-point scale (of ideal types ranging from stable and consolidated democratic rule to the failure or absence of democracy).[19]

The task we gave those who wrote our case studies was an imposing one. What made it even forbidding—and sometimes (especially for countries with long and variegated political histories) nearly impossible—was the space constraint we were forced to impose as a result of the economic realities of contemporary book publishing. Thus, each author was compelled to be selective and often painfully brief, both in the treatment of important historical developments and in the analysis of theoretical variables. Although we have sought to make our case studies readily accessible to readers with little or no prior knowledge of the country—in part to encourage the wide reading across regions we feel is essential—we could not avoid giving many key problems and events little or no attention. Our readers are thus cautioned that the case studies provide no more than capsulized surveys of a country's experience, which will, we hope, inspire wider study from among the many other sources they cite.

The theoretical framework for the study grew out of an extensive review of the previous literature, one which appears in Volume 1. The ten theoretical dimensions in this framework covered the gamut of factors that various theoretical and empirical works have associated with democracy: political culture; regime legitimacy and effectiveness; historical development (in particular the colonial experience); class structure and the degree of inequality; national structure (ethnic, racial, regional, and religious cleavage); state structure, centralization, and strength (including the state's role in the economy, the roles of autonomous voluntary associations and the press, federalism, and the role of the armed forces); political and constitutional structure (parties, electoral systems, the judiciary); political leadership; development performance; and international factors.

These broad dimensions encompassed dozens of specific variables and questions, from which we derived forty nine tentative propositions about the likelihood of stable democratic government. Obviously, it would have been foolish to pretend that our study could have "tested" these propositions. In spite of having twenty six countries, we still had the problem of "too many variables, too few cases" to enable us to reach any definitive conclusions about the effects of these variables. But we did believe that the evidence and conclusions from twenty six carefully selected cases, if structured systematically, could shed much light on how these variables affected the democratic prospect, and how these effects might vary with other conditions.

• CONCEPTS, DEFINITIONS, AND CLASSIFICATIONS •

Depending on the individual, ideology, paradigm, culture, or context, the term "democracy" may mean many different things. In fact, it is reflective of the political climate of our time that the word is used to signify the desirable end-state of so many social, economic, and political pursuits, or else to self-designate and thus presumably legitimate so many existing structures. Hence, it is imperative that we be as precise as possible about exactly what it is we are studying.

We use the term "democracy" in this study to signify a political system, separate and apart from the economic and social system to which it is joined. Indeed, a distinctive aspect of our approach is to insist that issues of so-called economic and social democracy be separated from the question of governmental structure. Otherwise, the definitional criteria of democracy will be broadened and the empirical reality narrowed to a degree that may make study of the phenomena very difficult. In addition, unless the economic and social dimensions are kept conceptually distinct from the political, there is no way to analyze how variation on the political dimension is related to variation on the others. But most of all, as we will argue shortly, we distinguish the concept of political democracy out of a clear and frankly expressed conviction that it is worth valuing—and hence worth studying—as an end in itself.

In this study, then, democracy—or what Robert Dahl terms "polyarchy"— denotes a system of government that meets three essential conditions: meaningful and extensive *competition* among individuals and organized groups (especially political parties) for all effective positions of government power, at regular intervals and excluding the use of force; a highly inclusive level of *political participation* in the selection of leaders and policies, at least through regular and fair elections, such that no major (adult) social group is excluded; and a level of *civil and political liberties*—freedom of expression, freedom of the press, freedom to form and join organizations—sufficient to ensure the integrity of political competition and participation.[20]

While this definition is, in itself, relatively straightforward, it presents a number of problems in application. For one, countries that broadly satisfy these criteria nevertheless do so to different degrees. (In fact, none do so perfectly, which is why Dahl prefers to call them polyarchies). The factors that explain this variation at the democratic end of the spectrum in degrees of popular control and freedom is an important intellectual problem. But it is different from the one that concerns us in these four volumes, and so it is one we have had largely to bypass. This study seeks to determine why countries do or do not evolve, consolidate, maintain, lose, and reestablish more or less democratic systems of government.

Even this limited focus leaves us with conceptual problems. The boundary between democratic and nondemocratic is sometimes a blurred and imperfect one, and beyond it lies a much broader range of variation in political systems. We readily concede the difficulties of classification this variation has repeatedly caused us. Even if we look only at the political, legal, and constitutional structure, several of our cases appear to lie somewhere on the boundary between democratic and something less than democratic. The ambiguity is further complicated by the constraints on free political activity, organization, and expression that may often in practice make the system much less democratic than it appears on paper. In all cases, we have tried to pay serious attention to actual practice in assessing and classifying regimes. But, still, this has left us to make difficult and in some ways arbitrary judgements. For countries such as Turkey, Sri Lanka, Malaysia, Colombia, and Zimbabwe, the decision as to whether these may today be considered full democracies is replete with nuance and ambiguity.

We have alleviated the problem somewhat by recognizing various grades of distinction among less-than-democratic systems. While isolated violations of civil liberties or modest and occasional vote-rigging should not disqualify a country from broad classification as a democracy, there is a need to categorize separately those countries that allow greater political competition and freedom than would be found in a true authoritarian regime but less than could justifiably be termed democratic. Hence, we classify as *semidemocratic* those countries where the effective power of elected officials is so limited, or political party competition is so restricted, or the freedom and fairness of elections so compromised that electoral outcomes, while competitive, still deviate significantly from popular preferences; and/or where civil and political liberties are so limited that some political orientations and interests are unable to organize and express themselves. In different ways and to different degrees, Senegal, Zimbabwe, Malaysia, and Thailand fit in this category. Still more restrictive is a *hegemonic party system,* like that of Mexico, in which opposition parties are legal but denied—through pervasive electoral malpractices and frequent state coercion—any real chance to compete for power. Descending further on the scale of classification, *authoritarian* regimes permit even less pluralism, typically banning political parties (or all but the ruling one) and most forms of political organization and competition, while being more repressive than liberal in their level of civil and political freedom. Paying close attention to actual behavior, one may distinguish a subset of authoritarian regimes that we call *pseudodemocracies,* in that the existence of formally democratic political institutions, such as multiparty electoral competition, masks (often, in part, to legitimate) the reality of authoritarian domination. While this regime type overlaps in some ways with the hegemonic regime, it is less institutionalized and typically more personalized, coercive, and unstable. Nevertheless, we prefer not to ignore the democratic facade, because, as we argue in Volume 1, its coexistence with an authoritarian reality may generate distinctive problems for a transition to democracy.

Democratic trappings aside, authoritarian regimes vary widely in the degree to which they permit independent and critical political expression and organization. By the level of what the regime allows, one can distinguish between what O'Donnell and Schmitter call "dictablandas," or liberalized autocracies, and "dictaduras," harsher dictatorships that allow much less space for individual and group action.[21] By the level of what groups in the society recurrently demand (which may or may not overlap with the above), one can distinguish, as we do in Volume 1, between authoritarian situations with strong democratic pressures and those with weak democratic pressures. In selecting cases for this study, our bias was toward the former. Finally, of course, are the *totalitarian* regimes, which not only repress all forms of autonomous social and political organization, denying completely even the most elementary political and civil liberties, but also demand an active commitment by the citizens to the regime.[22] Because our concern in this study was primarily with democracy, these regimes (mainly now the communist ones, although not all of them are totalitarian) were excluded from our analysis.

The "dependent variable" of our study was concerned not only with democracy, but also stability—the persistence and durability of democratic and other regimes over time, particularly through periods of unusually intense conflict, crisis, and strain. A *stable* regime is one that is deeply institutionalized and consolidated, making it likely therefore to enjoy a high level of popular legitimacy. (As we argue in Volume 1, the relationship between stability and legitimacy is an intimate one.) *Partially stable* regimes are neither fully secure nor in imminent danger of collapse. Their institutions have perhaps acquired some measure of depth, flexibility, and value, but not enough to ensure the regime safe passage through severe challenges. *Unstable* regimes are, by definition, highly vulnerable to breakdown or overthrow in periods of acute uncertainty and stress. New regimes, including those that have recently restored democratic government, tend to fall in this category.

• **THE SELECTION OF COUNTRIES** •

One of the limitations, as well as one of the values, of our enterprise is the great heterogeneity of the twenty six countries included. The value is that the country studies provide us with insights into the whole range of factors relevant to our study, rather than limiting us to those variables for which there are data for all

PREFACE   xix

countries of the world (as with the social and economic statistics of the United Nations and the World Bank) or those factors shared by a relatively homogeneous set of countries. The major disadvantage, however, is that—unless we turn to studies and data not included in our volumes—the lack of statistical representativeness (which is, anyhow, dubious in dealing with states) precludes a statistical approach to testing hypotheses. In fact, our introductory volume contains a substantial quantitative analysis, based on data for over eighty countries, of the relationship between socioeconomic development and democracy, a relationship found to be basically positive.[23] Still, for the most part, we believe that the study of twenty six carefully chosen countries, by scholars familiar with each of them, and guided more or less by the concepts and issues suggested, provides us with a better understanding of the complex problems involved.

The criteria for the selection of countries were complex and, although not ad hoc, do not entirely satisfy our plans and ambitions for the well-known reasons encountered in any such large-scale comparative project. The foremost, perhaps debatable, decision was to exclude Western Europe, the North American democracies, Australia, New Zealand, and the most advanced non-Western industrial democracy, Japan—although their historical experiences are analyzed separately in Volume 1. Essentially, these are the OECD countries, members of the Paris-based Organization for Economic Cooperation and Development.[24] All of these countries have been stable democracies since World War II, if not earlier, with the exceptions of Greece, Portugal, and Spain, which joined the club in the mid-1970s and have been stable democracies for over ten years. The southern European experience, however, enters into our thinking and will occasionally be mentioned (if for no other reason than that it is an area of scholarly interest of one of the editors). All in this first group of countries excluded from our study are advanced industrial, capitalist democracies with higher per capita gross national products than the most developed of the countries we included. (The one exception is Portugal, whose per capita GNP is lower than a few of our developing countries, including Argentina and South Korea).

Another basic decision was not to include any communist countries. One of their distinctive characteristics is that, in those with a more or less democratic past (some in Eastern Europe), the absence of democracy is explained more by the power politics of Soviet hegemony than by any internal historical, social, economic, political, or cultural factors (although these might have been important before 1945). Another crucial distinction is that there is little prospect among them of a transition to democracy, but only of liberalization of communist rule. Outside of Eastern Europe, communist countries have little or no past democratic experience, and the present communist rule excludes, for the forseeable future, any real debate about political democracy in the sense defined by us.

Less justifiable, perhaps, is the exclusion of most of the Islamic world from Morocco to Iran, in particular the Arab world. In part, this stemmed from the limits of our resources, which were stretched thin by the scope of the project.

But it was a decision made also in response to theoretical priorities. With the exception perhaps of Egypt, Lebanon, and certainly Turkey (which appears in our Asia volume), the Islamic countries of the Middle East and North Africa generally lack much previous democratic experience, and most appear to have little prospect of transition even to semidemocracy. However, our study does not completely ignore the Islamic world. In addition to the "secularized" Islamic polity of Turkey, we include Pakistan, which shared, until partition, the history of British India and has tried democracy; Malaysia, a multiethnic, multireligious, but predominantly Muslim polity with significant democratic institutions; Senegal, an African Muslim country whose recently evolved semidemocracy is coming under growing challenge from Islamic fundamentalist thinking; and the farthest outpost of Islam, Indonesia, with its syncretic cultural traditions. These five Islamic countries, with their heterogeneity, clearly are not a sample of the world's Islamic polities and, therefore, will not enable us to explore in sufficient depth the complex relationship between Islamic religion and society and democracy.

Otherwise, our twenty six countries are quite representative of the heterogeneous world of those loosely called "Third World" or "developing" countries. These terms are largely misleading, and we want clearly to disassociate ourselves from assuming that such a category is scientifically useful in cross-national comparisons. Certainly, it seems ridiculous to put Argentina or Uruguay or South Korea in the same classification of countries as Ghana, Papua New Guinea, or even India, in terms of economic development, social structure or cultural traditions, and prospects of socioeconomic development. Nevertheless, all twenty six countries included in this study are less developed economically and less stable politically than the established, industrialized democracies of Europe, North America, Australasia, and Japan. And all share the same pressure from within to "develop" economically and socially, to build stable political institutions, and—as we argue in Volume 1—to become democracies, whatever the probabilities of their success in doing so. In this sense, all of these countries may be considered "less developed," or as we most often term them, for lack of a better common label, "developing."

Some readers might feel that all the countries in our study share one characteristic: that they have capitalist economic systems (although some have tried various socialist experiments), but such a characterization again becomes in its vagueness almost meaningless. To what extent can a dynamic, industrial, export-oriented capitalist economy like South Korea be covered by the same term as Uganda, whose population lives largely from subsistence agriculture, with a small native entrepreneurial class based heavily in the informal sector; or as other African countries in which business class formation entails more the access to and abuse of power to attain wealth than it does productive economic activities (which are subject to interference by the state if not extortion by the rulers)? Certainly the term "capitalist economy" covers too much to be meaningful sociologically when it is used simultaneously to describe advanced, industrial, market-oriented economies; state-dominated economies in which much of private enterprise is relegated to the informal sector; and largely subsistence, peasant, agricultural societies with isolated (and often foreign-owned) capitalist enclaves.

For the sake of argument, we might agree that all our countries have nonsocialist economic systems, which, therefore, allows us to ask questions about how "capitalism" in its very different forms may be related to democracy. We start from two obvious facts. First, all democracies (in our sense) are to some degree capitalist. Some are capitalist welfare states, with extensive public sectors and state regulation of the economy; some are capitalist with social democratic governments and more or less mixed economies. But, in all of the world's political democracies, prices, production and distribution of goods are determined mainly by competition in the market, rather than by the state, and there is significant private ownership of the means of production. Second, there are many capitalist countries with nondemocratic governments. But interestingly, among this latter group, those most advanced in their capitalist development (size of market sector of their economy, autonomy of their entrepreneurial class) are also those that have been most exposed to pressures for democracy, leading, in many cases, to the emergence or return of democratic government. This is despite the forceful arguments of some theories that postulated that the authoritarian regimes they suffered were more congruent or functional for their continued capitalist development. In addition, it is not clear how much certain types of nonsocialist authoritarianisms—particularly sultanism[25]—are compatible with the effective functioning of a capitalist economy.

Certainly, our effort can make a contribution to the continuing debate about the relationship between capitalism and democracy, and the even more lively one on the relationship between dependent, peripheral capitalism and democracy. This we seek to do in our theoretical reflections in Volume 1. In doing so, we emphasize that our study did not begin with any *a priori* assumption equating democracy with capitalism. To reiterate an earlier theme, democracy as a system of government must be kept conceptually distinct from capitalism as a system of production and exchange, and socialism as a system of allocation of resources and income. The fact that (to date) one does not find democracy in the absence of some form of capitalism is for us a matter of great theoretical import, but we do not assume that this empirical association must hold inevitably into the future. In our theoretical volume, we suggest why state socialism (which some would insist is only state or statist capitalism) has been so difficult to reconcile with political democracy, and ponder what alternatives to capitalism might potentially be compatible with democracy.

Culturally, our effort includes the Christian societies of Latin America, India with its mosaic of traditions (including the distinctive Hindu culture), five largely Islamic societies, two Buddhist countries, one a mixture of Buddhism, Confucianism, and Christianity, and several African countries that have experienced what Mazrui calls the "triple heritage" of Christianity, Islam, and traditional African religion and culture. Unfortunately, the limited treatment in our country studies does not enable us to deal adequately with the complex issues of the relation between democracy and religious and cultural traditions, although we are unable to ignore them.

One of the most complex and intractable problems in our world is the tension between the model of ethnically, linguistically, and culturally homogeneous societies that satisfy the ideal of the nation-state and the multiethnic, multilingual societies that face the difficult task of nation- or state-building in the absence of the integration and identification we normally associate with the idea of the nation-state. Certainly, even in Europe, before the massive and forced transfers (if not destruction) of populations, most states did not satisfy that ideal, but outside of Europe and Latin America, even fewer do. In our study, only a few Latin American countries—Costa Rica, Venezuela, Argentina, Uruguay, Chile, perhaps Colombia—seem to satisfy that model. Others, like Brazil, the Dominican Republic, Mexico, and above all Peru, include not only descendants of the *conquistadores* and European immigrants, but also substantial populations (intermixed to varying degrees with the above) of Indians and descendants of black slaves. To the list of the relatively homogeneous countries could be added South Korea, Turkey (with some significant minorities), and Botswana (which still has major subtribal divisions). Our remaining cases confront us with the problem of democracy in ethnically and culturally divided societies, some of them, like Sri Lanka, with populations linked culturally with another, neighboring country.

One experience that almost all of the countries in our study share is a previous history of domination by an outside imperial power. Only Turkey and Thailand have been continuously independent countries, and only in the latter do we find a continuity with a premodern traditional monarchy. Our study, therefore, does not cover a sufficient number of countries to deal with the question: does continuous legitimacy of rule by an indigenous state facilitate both modernization and ultimately democratization, by contrast with the historical trauma of conquest and colonial domination?

For those who have raised the question of the relation between size and democracy,[26] our study includes the largest (most populous) democracy, India, and some of the smallest. In each part of the world it includes the largest country and at least some significant smaller ones: Brazil and Costa Rica, Nigeria and Botswana, India and Sri Lanka. Since the major countries—with their political influence and their capacity to serve as models—occupy a special position in their respective areas, where some speak of subimperialisms, we feel our selection on this account is well justified.

In addition to trying, as much as possible, to maximize variation in our independent variables, we have also sought a richly varied pool of cases with regard to our dependent variable, stable democracy. Save for the deliberate exclusion of countries with no prior democratic or semidemocratic experience, or no prospect of a democratic opening, our study encompasses virtually every type of democratic experience in the developing world. Some of our countries are now democratic, some are semidemocratic, some are authoritarian, and one is a hegemonic regime. Some of the democracies have been relatively stable for some time (such as Costa Rica and, so far at least, Botswana and Papua New Guinea); some have persisted in the face of recurrent crises and lapses (India, and now less democratically, Sri Lanka); and some have been renewed after traumatic and, in some cases, repeated breakdowns (e.g., Brazil, Uruguay, and Argentina). Some countries have experienced recurrent cycles of democratic attempts and military interventions, from which Turkey has managed to emerge with a generally longer and more successful democratic experience than Thailand, Ghana, or Nigeria. We have countries in varying stages of transition to democracy at this writing, from the recently completed but still fragile (the Philippines), to the partial or continuing and still undetermined (South Korea, Uganda, Pakistan), to the prospective (Nigeria), to the obstructed (Chile).[27] And, still, we have at least one case (Indonesia) of a failed democracy that seems to have been consolidating a distinctive form of authoritarian rule.

The sheer number of our case studies compelled us to break them up for publication into several volumes. This presented another editorial dilemma. We have opted for the established mode of division into regional volumes, as this follows the dominant organizational logic of scholarship, instruction, and intellectual discourse in the field. But we hasten to underscore our feeling that this is not the most intellectually fruitful or satisfying way of treating such material. It would perhaps have made more sense to group the cases by the characteristic types of regimes and problems they have experienced. But any method of division inevitably breaks the unity of our twenty six cases and disperses the multitude of different comparisons that spring from them. We know of no solution to this problem other than to invite our readers to read widely across the three regional volumes, and to work back and forth between the theory in our introductory volume and the evidence in our cases, as we ourselves have attempted to do over the past three years.

• THE NORMATIVE QUESTION: WHY STUDY DEMOCRACY? •

Finally, we cannot close this introduction to our work without confronting the question (or critical challenge) that is often put to us: Why study political democracy at all? Some critics suggest it is the wrong problem to be studying. They ask: Are there not more pressing issues of survival and justice facing developing societies? Does the limited question of the form of government not conceal more than it reveals? Others contend our choice of topic betrays a value bias for democracy that is misplaced. They ask (or assert): If in some societies democracy in our (liberal) sense has to work against so many odds, as our research unveils, is it worth striving for and encouraging an opposition that purports to establish it, or are there alternatives to democracy that should be considered and whose stability should be supported?

We wish to state quite clearly here our bias for democracy as a system of government. For any democrat, these questions carry serious implications. The former suggest that economic and social rights should be considered more important than civil and political liberties. The latter implies granting to some forms or cases of authoritarian rule the right to use coercive measures, in the name of some higher good, to suppress an opposition that claims to fight for democracy. For ourselves, neither of these normative suppositions is tenable.

If there were many nondemocratic governments (now and in the past) committed to serving collective goals, rather than the interests of the rulers, and ready to respect human rights (to refrain from torture and indiscriminate violence, to offer due process and fair trial in applying laws which, even if antiliberal, are known in advance, to maintain humane conditions of imprisonment, etc.), we might find these questions more difficult to answer. However, nondemocratic regimes satisfying these two requirements are few, and even those that begin with a strong commitment to the collectivity and sensitivity to human rights often become increasingly narrow, autocratic, and repressive (although these trends, too, are subject to reversal).

We emphasize the service of collective goals to exclude those authoritarian systems in which the rulers blatantly serve their own material interests and those of their family, friends, cronies, and clients; and to exclude as well those systems serving a narrowly defined oligarchy, stratum, or a particular ethnic or racial group (which might even be the majority). But even excluding such transparent cases (the majority, unfortunately), who is to define those collective goals, if we disqualify the majority of citizens from doing so? Inevitably, it means a self-appointed minority—a vanguard party, a charismatic leader and his followers, a bureaucracy, army officers, or perhaps intellectuals or "experts" working with them. But why should their definition of societal goals be better than that of any other group with a different concept of the collective good? Only if we were totally certain that one ideological (or religious) concept is the expression of historical reason—true and necessary—would we be forced to accept such an authoritarian alternative as better than democracy. To do so, as we know, justifies any sacrifices and ultimately terrible costs in freedom and human lives. The option between ultimate value choices would inevitably be resolved by force. Thus, democracy—with its relativism and tolerance (so disturbing to those certain of the truth), and its "faith" in the reasonableness and intelligence of the common men and women, including those uneducated and those with "false consciousness" (a concept that assumes others know better their real interests), deciding freely (and with a chance to change their minds every four or five years) and without the use of force—seems still a better option.

Of course, even committed democrats know that the empirical world, and so the normative issue, is full of variation and ambiguity. But this should not lead to intellectual and political confusion. A few authoritarian regimes that manifest commitment to collective goals and human rights might have redeeming qualities, particularly if they are stable and do not require excessive force to stay in power. But that does not make them democracies. Their supporters should be free to argue the positive aspects of their rule, without ignoring or denying the negative ones, but they should not attempt to claim that they are democracies. Not all nondemocracies are totally bad. Nor are all democracies, and especially unstable democracies, good for the people. But, certainly, nondemocracies are not likely to achieve those social and moral goals that require democratic institutions and freedoms. Therefore, from the point of view of a democrat, they will always be undesirable. Moreover, should they turn out to betray the ideals and hopes of their founders (as they have done so repeatedly), there is no easy way to oust them from power by peaceful means. Indeed, the almost law-like inevitability of the abuse and corruption of authoritarian power throughout history constitutes, we believe, one of the most compelling justifications for the institutionalized checks and accountability of a democracy.

For all these reasons, we (along with an increasing proportion of the world's population) value political democracy as an end in itself—without assuming that it is any guarantee of other important values. And we believe that a better understanding of the conditions for it is a worthwhile intellectual endeavor, which does not require us to deny the positive accomplishments of some nondemocratic regimes and the many flaws of democratic governments and societies.

Larry Diamond
Juan J. Linz
Seymour Martin Lipset

· NOTES ·

1. Juan J. Linz and Alfred Stepan, eds., *The Breakdown of Democratic Regimes* (Baltimore: Johns Hopkins University Press, 1978).
2. Arend Lijphart, *Democracy in Plural Societies: A Comparative Exploration* (New Haven: Yale University Press, 1977); Donald L. Horowitz, *Ethnic Groups in Conflict* (Berkeley: University of California Press, 1985).
3. G. Bingham Powell, *Contemporary Democracies: Participation, Stability and Violence* (Cambridge: Harvard University Press, 1982).
4. Myron Weiner and Ergun Ozbudun, eds., *Competitive Elections in Developing Countries* (Washington: American Enterprise Institute, 1987).
5. Guillermo O'Donnell, Philippe C. Schmitter, and Laurence Whitehead, eds., *Transitions from Authoritarian Rule* (Baltimore: Johns Hopkins University Press, 1986).
6. Giovanni Sartori, *The Theory of Democracy Revisited* (Chatham, N.J.: Chatham House Publishers, 1987).
7. Gabriel A. Almond and James S. Coleman, eds., *The Politics of the Developing Areas* (Princeton: Princeton University Press, 1960), p. 3.
8. Gabriel A. Almond and Sidney Verba, *The Civic Culture* (Princeton: Princeton University Press, 1963).
9. Notable early works here were Daniel Lerner, *The Passing of Traditional Society* (Glencoe, Ill.: The Free Press, 1958); Seymour Martin Lipset, "Some Social Requisites of Democracy," *American Political Science Review* 53 (1959): pp. 69–105, and *Political Man* (New York: Doubleday & Co., 1960), pp. 27–63; and Karl W. Deutsch, "Social Mobilization and Democracy," *American Political Science Review* 55 (1961): pp. 493–514.

10. Samuel P. Huntington, *Political Order in Changing Societies* (New Haven: Yale University Press, 1968).

11. Barrington Moore, Jr., *Social Origins of Dictatorship and Democracy* (Cambridge: Harvard University Press, 1966).

12. Leonard Binder, James S. Coleman, Joseph La Palombara, Lucian Pye, Sidney Verba, and Myron Weiner, *Crises and Sequences in Political Development* (Princeton: Princeton University Press, 1971). The work of this committee, and the evolution of political development studies from the 1960s to the present, is surveyed in a sweeping and erudite review by Gabriel Almond, "The Development of Political Development," in Myron Weiner and Samuel P. Huntington, eds., *Understanding Political Development* (Boston: Little, Brown and Co., 1987), pp. 437–490.

13. Robert A. Dahl, *Polyarchy: Participation and Opposition* (New Haven: Yale University Press, 1971).

14. See, for example, Stein Rokkan, *Citizens, Elections, Parties: Approaches to the Comparative Study of the Processes of Development* (Oslo: Universitetsforlaget, 1970).

15. Almond, "The Development of Political Development," pp. 444–450.

16. Peter Evans, *Dependent Development* (Princeton: Princeton University Press, 1979), pp. 25–54.

17. Guillermo O'Donnell, *Modernization and Bureaucratic-Authoritarianism: Studies in South American Politics* (Berkeley: Institute of International Studies, University of California, 1973); see, also, David Collier, ed., *The New Authoritarianism in Latin America* (Princeton: Princeton University Press, 1979).

18. This neglect is, to some extent, overcome in Arend Lijphart's creative and enterprising study, *Democracies: Patterns of Majoritarian and Consensus Government in Twenty-One Countries* (New Haven: Yale University Press, 1984). However, the focus is mainly on political structure, and the comparison is limited to the continuous and stable democracies of the advanced, industrial countries.

19. Specifically, the points on this scale were: (1) *High success*—stable and uninterrupted democratic rule, with democracy now deeply institutionalized and stable; (2) *Progressive success*—the consolidation of relatively stable democracy after one or more breakdowns or serious interruptions; (3) *Mixed success—democratic and unstable* (e.g., democracy has returned following a period of breakdown and authoritarian rule, but has not yet been consolidated); (4) *Mixed success—partial or semidemocracy*; (5) *Failure but promise*—democratic rule has broken down, but there are considerable pressures and prospects for its return; (6) *Failure or absence*—democracy has never functioned for any significant period of time and there is little prospect that it will in the coming years.

20. Dahl, *Polyarchy*, pp. 3–20; Joseph Schumpeter, *Capitalism, Socialism and Democracy* (New York: Harper and Row, 1942); Lipset, *Political Man*, p. 27; Juan Linz, *The Breakdown of Democratic Regimes: Crisis, Breakdown and Reequilibration* (Baltimore: Johns Hopkins University Press, 1978), p. 5.

21. Guillermo O'Donnell and Philippe C. Schmitter, *Transitions from Authoritarian Rule: Tentative Conclusions about Uncertain Democracies* (Baltimore: Johns Hopkins University Press, 1986).

22. The distinction between authoritarian and totalitarian regimes has a long intellectual history predating its fashionable (and in some ways confusing) use by Jeanne Kirkpatrick in "Dictatorships and Double Standards," *Commentary* 68 (1979): pp. 34–45. See Juan J. Linz, "Totalitarian and Authoritarian Regimes," in *Handbook of Political Science*, Fred I. Greenstein and Nelson W. Polsby, eds, (Reading, Mass.: Addison-Wesley, 1975), vol. 3, pp. 175–411.

23. For a review of the literature on the subject from 1960 to 1980, see the expanded and updated edition of Lipset's *Political Man* (Baltimore: Johns Hopkins University Press, 1981), pp. 469–476.

24. In point of fact, the twenty-four-member organization also includes Turkey, but its per capita GNP ($1,160 in 1984) clearly places it among the middle ranks of developing countries (at about the level of Costa Rica or Colombia, for example).

25. Linz, "Totalitarianism and Authoritarianism," pp. 259–263.

26. Robert A. Dahl and Edward Tufte, *Size and Democracy* (Stanford: Stanford University Press, 1973).

27. One of the most important countries in the world now struggling (against increasingly forbidding odds, it appears) to develop a full democracy—South Africa—we reluctantly excluded

from our study not only because it has lacked any previous experience with democracy (beyond its limited functioning among the minority white population), but because the context of pervasive, institutionalized racial domination generates a number of quite distinctive obstacles and complexities. Although we feel our theoretical framework has much to contribute to the study of the conditions and prospects for democracy in South Africa, the unique character of that problem may make it more suitable for exploration through monographic studies, of which there is a proliferating literature. See, for example, Arend Lijphart, *Power-Sharing in South Africa* (Berkeley: Institute of International Studies, University of California, 1985), and Heribert Adam and Kogila Moodley, *South Africa Without Apartheid: Dismantling Racial Domination* (Berkeley: University of California Press, 1986).

· Acknowledgments ·

This comparative study of democracy, and the conference in December 1985 to discuss the first drafts of the case studies, were made possible by a generous grant from the National Endowment for Democracy. The Endowment is a private, nonprofit organization that seeks to encourage and strengthen democratic institutions around the world through nongovernmental efforts. Since its creation in 1983, NED has been an extremely creative and effective institution. The editors and authors gratefully acknowledge the support of the Endowment, and in particular of its President, Carl Gershman, and Director of Program, Marc F. Plattner. The Hoover Institution, with which Diamond and Lipset are affiliated, also contributed in many substantial ways to the project during its more than three years of organization, writing, and production. We wish to thank in particular the Director of the Hoover Institution, W. Glenn Campbell, and the two Principal Associate Directors with whom we have worked, John F. Cogan and John Raisian. The final editing and production of this volume was also assisted by a grant to the Hoover Institution from the MacArthur Foundation for a program of research on democracy in developing countries.

A number of people helped us in arranging the 1985 conference and preparing this volume. We thank in particular Janet Shaw of the Hoover Institution for her excellent editing, typing, and administrative support; Lisa Fuentes, now at UCLA, who was our research and administrant assistant during 1985–1986; Katherine Teghtsoonian, now at the University of Seattle, who produced the proceedings of our conference; Juliet Johnson, for her assistance with indexing, proofreading, and library research; Phyllis Riddle and Connie L. McNeely, for their statistical support; and Nicole S. Barnes, whose efficient and cheerful assistance with typing, indexing, and production has been instrumental to the final completion of this book.

Reprinted from Gary W. Wynia, *The Politics of Latin American Development*, 2d ed., by permission of Cambridge University Press.

• CHAPTER ONE •
Introduction: Politics, Society, and Democracy in Latin America

LARRY DIAMOND
JUAN J. LINZ

Of the "new nations" that have broken free of European colonial rule in the past two centuries (excepting the United States), the countries of Latin America are by far the oldest. Thus, their experiences with alternative regimes—democratic, proto-democratic, semidemocratic, military, populist-authoritarian, bureaucratic-authoritarian, and so on—are considerably longer, more numerous, and more complicated than those of the Asian and African cases examined in this comparative study. Theoretically, this has complicated the quest for causal explanations: There is in each of our ten cases here not only a longer past experience with regimes (and typically more regime change) to explain, but also (therefore) more potential for the past to weigh upon the present in various ways.

This volume also presents us with distinctive opportunities for explaining why democracies emerge, mature, break down, and reemerge; and why some countries have greater overall success with democracy. Because the countries discussed in this volume are more alike in some respects than those we have examined in Asia and Africa, some variables are more or less constant across cases. In addition to their similar age of nationhood (though by no means consolidated statehood), there is the obvious fact that all share a long tradition of Iberic (more specifically, in every case save the Brazilian, Spanish) colonial rule. This common cultural heritage may enable us to evaluate more systematically the thesis that the problems of democratic consolidation in Latin America have a deeply rooted cultural component. In addition, the much greater length of their postindependence political histories enables us to examine time as a potentially important variable in several respects. We are interested to see how the democratic prospect is affected by the sequence of historical developments, the phases or stages of socioeconomic development, the shifting models or pressures in global political culture, and the changing conditions in the world economy. And, as we have already suggested, we want to examine how political struggles, choices, and outcomes at one time may shape, constrain, or facilitate political evolution well into the future.

The cases in this volume include the seven most populous countries in Latin America and three of the most theoretically interesting smaller ones—Uruguay, Costa Rica, and the Dominican Republic. They encompass the most stable, democratic regimes in the region, the most successful cases of democratic development historically, and also the longest standing undemocratic regime—Mexico. But it is important to appreciate that they are not representative of the full range of political historical variation in Latin America, and that this skewing of our sample may give an overly optimistic impression of the future of democracy there.

Our work excludes most countries that have not experienced prolonged periods of at least modestly stable democracy, such as Bolivia, Paraguay, four of the Central American republics, and even Ecuador—areas in which the prospects for democracy are certainly less favorable. Nor have we included Haiti, where for the time being the hopes for redemocratization have been shattered. Cuba would have to be analyzed separately in the broader context of the prospects for liberalization in Communist countries in the Gorbachev era, a task that does not fit into the perspectives used in this volume. There are those who still have serious reservations about the prospects for the creation of democracy in Mexico or for the consolidation of democracy even in such countries as Argentina and Brazil, not to mention Peru, which confronts at this writing a profound socioeconomic and political crisis. Yet, despite their own serious economic problems, the democracies in Costa Rica and Venezuela continue to appear consolidated and stable (for reasons that demand close theoretical attention), and across the ten cases there is sufficient variation in democratic histories and prospects to provide a rich ground for comparative analysis.

• **SOURCES OF DEMOCRATIC PROGRESS AND FAILURE** •

A survey of the theoretical dimensions that have guided our authors may offer the most fruitful introduction to these cases and, we hope, some insights into the question that has motivated this study: What explains the widely varying experiences with democracy of these and other developing countries?[1]

Historical Factors

The ten countries included in this volume share the common legacy of long periods of colonial rule by Spain or Portugal.[2] Many students of Latin American politics attribute to this colonial rule an authoritarian legacy, since the metropolis ruled the colonies through a centralized, bureaucratic state structure as part of a patrimonial monarchical state pursuing mercantilistic policies. The colonial legacies, however, were not uniform. Where mineral resources were particularly abundant and indigenous populations large, as in Peru and Mexico, or where slaves were imported for plantation agriculture, colonial rule was especially harsh and exploitative; steep, severely polarized class divisions developed that would impact on social and political life well into the future. The tremendous inequality that became imbedded in the social and economic structures of these countries remains one of the primary challenges impeding democratic development and consolidation in Mexico, Peru, Brazil, and the Dominican Republic. In Peru, this structural legacy is overlapped and compounded by bitter ethnic cleavage, as the memory of Spanish betrayal of the Incan king and crushing of the Indian rebellions reinforces (four centuries later) the indigenous peoples' feelings of exploitation and exclusion. In general, Chile, Argentina, and Uruguay did not have economies based on a large indigenous labor supply. Costa Rica, too, as a more isolated outpost of the Spanish empire, lacking great agricultural or mineral wealth, bypassed as a site for *hacienda* agriculture, and with a relatively small (and quickly decimated) indigenous population, ultimately benefited from what John Booth terms "the leveling effect of poverty and isolation."

In contrast to the contemporary decolonization of Asia and Africa, independence was not gained by native elites against outside colonial administrators who transferred power to nationalist leaders and returned to the metropolis, but by a Creole, culturally Spanish, or (at the most) Mestizo elite against the officials sent by the crown to rule and administer the Indies. The indigenous population played no role in the struggle for independence, except, perhaps, in Mexico, where a more popular revolution was led by the priest, Hidalgo, succeeded by the soon-to-be-defeated Morelos. These were settler colonies, transplants of European societies in some cases imposed on large Indian or black slave populations, or occupying (as in the Plata region) poorer and emptier outposts. Independence, therefore, was more similar to that of the North American colonies or, in the case of Argentina and Uruguay to that of Australia and New Zealand.

To be sure, the Spanish and Portuguese empires ruled over their overseas territories differently than England ruled over its thirteen North American colonies, with their complex constitutional structures, their charters and assemblies. In continental Europe in the eighteenth century, the liberal revolution had not yet been consolidated, though liberal revolutionary ideas were being received in the colonies from the metropolis. Undoubtedly, the political change in England before its colonies achieved independence left a different legacy from that of continental absolute monarchies with their patrimonial bureaucracies. Yet the local Creoles of Spanish America did participate in government through such institutions as the *cabildos* (city governments), in a way that could be compared to today's participation of the local Hongkong population in the government of the Crown Colony.

The independence of Spanish America coincided with a political change toward liberalism in the metropolis with the approval of the 1812 constitution in Spain, but before its consolidation. Independence was not so much a revolt against the Crown, but the result of a power vacuum generated by Napoleon's occupation of the metropolis and resistance against the rule of his brother, appointed king. Initially, as in the former metropolis, juntas emerged representing the privileged groups of colonial society (with the exception of Mexico) and assuming power in the name of the imprisoned Bourbon king. However, some Creoles, such as Simón Bolívar and Francisco de Miranda, inspired by the U.S. example and the ideas of the French Revolution, made a republic and independence their goal. The occupation in Spain created a legitimacy crisis that in the case of Brazil was avoided, since the king of Portugal moved to the colony until the throne in Lisbon was recovered. Conflicts between liberals and absolutists prevented Spain from sending reinforcements to reassert its authority and support those in the Americas loyal to the crown, such as the authorities in Peru. Independence, therefore, had many elements of a civil war among Creole leaders. In contrast, the Brazilian independence process involved a peaceful transfer of power from the Portuguese king to the new emperor, Don Pedro, thus avoiding a crisis of legitimacy that might have resulted from an abrupt break with existing institutions.[3]

In considering the Spanish colonial legacy, we should not forget that the wars of independence and the subsequent wars between the emerging states destroyed the continuity of most political and administrative institutions. This contrasts sharply with the continuity of institutions and boundaries in the thirteen colonies after the displacement of the British king and his representatives. In fact, it is very likely that in many of the colonies the institutions that provided some minimum protection of the native population against landowners, mine operators, and local oligarchies disappeared or were weakened in the process.

It is also important to appreciate that in the course of the nineteenth century, different countries followed markedly different paths of political development. Chile, Uruguay, Argentina, and Costa Rica all evolved some form of limited, oligarchical semidemocracy. As Arturo Valenzuela notes here for the case of Chile, these institutions were forged by breaking to some considerable degree with the colonial cultural and institutional legacy, rather than by building upon it as was done in the United States and Canada. This attempted break with the past and the range of variation among Latin American countries should give pause to those who would cite the colonial legacy as a decisive factor in explaining Latin America's subsequent experience with democracy.

The prominent role of postindependence immigration raises further questions about the effect of Spanish colonial heritage on political culture. In a number of Latin American countries the descendants of the colonizers are today a minority. For example, Argentina in 1850 had 1,000,000 inhabitants, and between 1857 and 1920 received 5,741,000 immigrants of which only 1,853,000 were Spaniards and 2,718,000 Italians.[4] Nor should we ignore the contribution of immigrants to many countries from other parts of Europe, their prominent place in the elite, nor the number of authoritarian leaders of neither Spanish nor Portuguese descent.

Without denying the importance of the colonial experience, particularly domination over the indigenous people, the different circumstances surrounding the achievement of independence should be taken into account. When one looks for the roots of authoritarianism in at least some Latin American societies, one has to turn to the political, social and economic developments of at least seventy-five years of independence before 1900.

Postindependence politics and state building. The abrupt and violent manner in which Latin American countries seized or gained their independence is of theoretical interest: Not only did these bloody independence wars disrupt existing institutions and heighten the violently conflictual nature of the struggle for power, but in many Latin American countries they also gave rise to long periods of civil war and instability that destroyed the wealth and infrastructure of the colonial period, enervated nascent state structures, and obstructed state building.[5]

The obstacles to state building, and their relationship to democracy, form an important theme in many of our chapters. Our ensuing discussion only highlights the need for further study of how political development in Latin America has been shaped by the many difficulties in the process of creating modern states—establishing law and order, delegitimating private political violence, making constitutional provisions effective, and ensuring honest elections. Latin American countries have had also to contend with the rise of military leaders to political power and the expanding role of armies in politics.

All of the cases in this volume emphasize the political turmoil in the nineteenth century (and in some cases—such as Venezuela—well into the twentieth century) that made a continuous, measured progress toward constitutional, stable government and ultimately toward democratization so difficult in Latin America. Those crises have to be seen in the perspective of a state-building process in countries that initially were artificial in their boundaries. The difficulties in state building and the resort to force in the process show some analogies to decolonization in Africa, with some significant differences owing to the lack of an international guarantee of the existing boundaries, and the much greater difficulties in establishing control given the military and communication resources of the nineteenth century. Shifting the problem from the instability of governments and constitutional rule to an analysis of the difficulties of state building perhaps modifies our thinking about the historical process of democratization in Latin America.

Spanish America—there is a fundamental difference with Brazil—faced the problem of decapitating a legitimate structure of central authority (whatever its limits and weaknesses) represented by the crown in Spain, and the impossibility, given the size and geographic dispersion of its territories, of creating even a weak central authority. The failure of Bolívar's attempt to create a larger confederation of newly independent colonies, and even the failure of his Gran Colombia (which broke up into Venezuela, Ecuador, and Colombia) stands out in contrast with the initial capacity of the thirteen colonies to unify and ultimately create the United States.[6] A look at a map shows the difference in scale of the task: One could speculate on how much more difficult it would have been to unify the United States had its territory included Florida, Louisiana, and the Midwest, not to mention Texas and California, at the turn of the nineteenth century. The geography of Latin America and the importance of a limited number of urban centers of the colonial administration and economy generated a large number of independent states. In addition, some of the key centers, such as Peru, were initially not committed to independence but liberated by outside armies. The military character of the independence process generated a whole new type of leadership—the *caudillos*—and a symbolism, which would not disappear, of the military strongman creating the nation.

The destruction of the centers of authority and the constant conflicts between centers and peripheries in each of the emerging republics complicated the process of state building for decades. The struggles between centralists and federalists dominated the nineteenth century history of Spanish America and very often led to questioning the emerging constitutional structures. Those conflicts were complicated by the fact that within most of the new republics there were relatively few secondary centers outside the coastal capitals or a few urban centers of Spanish administration in the interior. Thus, a strictly equal federal structure like that among the North American colonies was difficult to establish. Federalism did not pit multiple, economically comparable centers of power against each other but rather counterposed a predominantly rural, large landowning interior against coastal cities of commercial elites, who—with the disruption of trade caused by independence—generally had no resources to assert their authority.[7] The answer to this crisis of authority between center and periphery was either efforts to dominate the interior by force, resulting in civil wars and fights among *caudillos,* or in some cases the abdication of central authority to local notables, which undermined the progress of constitutional government and the rule of law.[8]

In addition, the cultural homogeneity among the Spanish colonies made it difficult to define the boundaries between emerging republics. The administrative boundaries between viceroyalties and *audiencias* of the Spanish administration served as a nucleus for the building of new states, but those boundaries were not always well defined and did not respond to the resources of the new states. One of the results was that ever since there have been boundary conflicts leading to a number of wars and to claims that remain unresolved to this day. Some claims were settled only in the twentieth century and left deep scars in the national consciousness. Let us not forget that the War of the Pacific (1879–1884), in which Chile gained large areas of Bolivia and Peru, was not finally resolved by treaty until 1929. Nor can we forget the great Chaco war (between Paraguay and Bolivia, 1932–1935); Paraguay's earlier War of the Triple Alliance (1864–1870) with Brazil, Argentina, and Uruguay; the conflicts among Colombia, Ecuador, and Peru; Bolivia's difficulties in state building in its struggle with

Chile and Peru to maintain access to the sea; and the conflict over Uruguay between Argentina and Brazil until 1851.

These wars (whose cost in human lives, economic destruction, resources, and disruption of political processes deserve more systematic analysis) had consequences for the process of political institutionalization reflected in our chapters. They legitimized the importance of the army in state building and the claim of the armed forces to resources that otherwise would have been devoted to other tasks. They gave popularity to successful army commanders in the victorious countries; and they delegitimized governments and regimes that lost wars. We tend to think of Latin American militarism today almost exclusively in terms of its role in controlling "internal subversion" and social conflict, forgetting both how important armies were in those international wars and the surviving animosity and fear among Latin American republics. It is noteworthy that contemporary Latin American armed forces seek not only adequate equipment for internal war but sophisticated weapons of international warfare—fighter jets, rockets, and battleships, for example. It is easy to think of these weapons as toys or an ideological justification for the military, but we should not ignore the military's real concern, based on the historical legacy of distrust among states, about the security of their borders. It is also significant that those nineteenth century conflicts generated a nationalism that remains politically potent, as became apparent during the Malvinas-Falklands crisis.[9] The nationalism bred by this legacy of insecure statehood and interstate conflict has also facilitated some of the populist mobilization linked today with anti-imperialism and anti–United States leftism. The belief in a strong state—when actually its resources are limited and its institutions weak—leads to a fundamental tension in many Latin American countries.

A very different legacy has been left in Brazil, where the slow evolution and peaceful transition from colonial rule to independence through the imperial period, the avoidance of military secessionist efforts in the nineteenth century, the maintenance of the unity of the vast country by accommodation within a complex set of compromises in the federal structure, and the alliance between Sao Paulo and Minas Gerais, assured the unity of the country. As Lamounier highlights in his chapter, this legacy favored compromise and negotiation among multiple centers of power, particularly between the central government and the powerful governors. In contrast to Spanish America, it yielded notably more peaceful and complex politics, and not merely in the nineteenth century. Even the difference between Brazil's Getúlio Vargas (the politician emerging out of a school of state politics to become dictator) and Argentina's nationalist military dictator Juan Perón, as well as their different legacies, can be partially understood in this perspective.

Historical Sequences. One of the features that distinguishes some of our Latin American cases from the others in this volume and from our Asian and African cases is their evolution during the nineteenth century of competitive, representative political institutions, which became increasingly inclusive and democratic over time. Chile, Argentina, Uruguay and Costa Rica all began, by the mid-nineteenth century, evolving some form of competitive oligarchy. In Colombia this process was delayed and truncated by recurrent civil strife but flowered in the early twentieth century, while in Brazil an even more limited parliamentary monarchy developed during the period of the Empire (1822–1889).

The early development of a partial, elite democracy, however tentative and flawed, contributed to the ultimate development of full democracy. Of those countries in Latin America that have had the most overall success with democracy, or that now have stable democracy, only Venezuela failed to develop an early constitutional system based on elite competition. By contrast, those countries that have had the least success with democracy in the past few decades—notably, in our study, Mexico and the Dominican Republic—are also those that were unable to develop and institutionalize some kind of partial, oligarchical democracy in the nineteenth century.[10]

The protodemocracies of the nineteenth century were hardly exemplary models of free and fair competition for power. Fraud and force figured more or less prominently in each electoral system, diminishing more quickly and substantially in some cases (such as Chile) than in others. But these experiences involved the establishment of important democratic institutions—elected presidents and congresses; political parties—and at least some degree of meaningful competition for and rotation of state power. And the most successful of these experiences—in Chile, Argentina, Uruguay, and Costa Rica—also involved the gradual and continuous expansion of the boundaries of competition, incorporating ever larger proportions of the population (first middle-class groups, then workers and peasants) through peaceful political reforms extending suffrage and access to public office.

This path of political development had several positive implications for democratization. First, even where (as in Brazil) they did not produce lasting democratic institutionalization, elite settlements on peaceful competition for power at least resolved (or preempted) the violent, chaotic conflict of the early postindependence period, permitting state building to proceed.[11] Second, even where (as in Costa Rica) they were frequently interrupted, the oligarchical democracies produced political parties and other democratic institutions that took root in the society and provided the political infrastructure around which democracy could grow and mature. Third, regular elections through constitutional procedures gave competing elites valuable experience with democratic competition and permitted the gradual evolution of trust among contending parties and factions. Over time, the integrity of political competition improved, and its arena widened to incorporate more and more social groups. Fourth, because this process of incorporation was gradual and regulated by elites, mass political participation—signaling the transition to a fuller democracy—could be accommodated, as socioeconomic pressures for it crystalized, without elites fearing mortal damage to their interests. Thus, wider democratic competition, when it came, was more subdued and less polarized than it would otherwise have been. Gillespie and González observe here of the Uruguayan case: "The fact that competitive politics predate mass participation . . . permitted greater institutional continuity and political learning."

Theoretically, then, our evidence strongly supports Robert Dahl's thesis that, historically, the most favorable path to polyarchy was one in which political competition preceded the expansion of participation. The result is that "the rules, the practices, and the culture of competitive politics developed first among a small elite, and the critical transition from nonparty politics to party competition also occurred initially within the restricted group."[12] Similarly, our evidence supports, as Valenzuela observes, theories positing an optimum sequence that begins with the emergence of national identity, followed by the establishment of legitimate and authoritative state structures, only after which does the "crisis" of participation crystalize and find resolution in the expansion of citizenship rights to nonelite elements.[13] Indeed, one of the most crucial historical variables in our Latin American cases is the way in which ruling elites responded to pressures for increasing mass participation in the polity. Where the elite made room gradually for autonomous institutional expressions of new popular interests, democracy developed. Where it resisted incorporation and inclusion, adaptation and political reform, the result was the radicalization and polarization of mass politics, as in Peru.[14] Where reform through brief, democratic experiments failed or was blocked, and elites later pursued strategies of mass incorporation from above in the absence of existing democratic institutions, the result was the most stable undemocratic regime in independent Latin America: Mexico. Where ruling elites panicked in the face of the challenge of mass political incorporation, abandoning democratic institutions for either exclusionary or corporatist strategies, the result, as Carlos Waisman demonstrates in these pages, was the tragic and sweeping reversal of development that plunged Argentina into decades of praetorian instability.

We find, then, that the past does weigh heavily on the present in Latin America, but it is mediated and can be renegotiated by elite strategy and choices. These choices, in turn, may themselves have consequences—positive or negative—for democratization, deep into the future.

Political Culture

Few issues in the study of Latin American political development are more contentious than the role of political culture. Some scholars have insisted, as does Howard Wiarda in his chapter on the Dominican Republic, that the "political culture, inherited from Spain, has been absolutist, elitist, hierarchical, corporatist, and authoritarian," and that this enduring cultural legacy inevitably shapes and constrains the possibilities for democratic development. Wiarda does not rule out democratic development for countries such as the Dominican

Republic (partly because of various changes that have eroded and complicated the Iberian cultural legacy), but he does forcefully maintain that democracy, to be stable, must reconcile liberal, competitive political formulae with the "organic, corporatist, authoritarian" traditions that emphasize strong leadership over mass participation and group over individual interests.

Most scholars of Latin American democracy reject this argument, partly because it implies that liberal, competitive systems in these countries can only be stable if they are less than fully democratic in assuring individual political rights and opportunities. The cultural thesis is rejected on theoretical grounds both by structural determinists, who regard the concept of political culture as epiphenomenal and superfluous (a position that is not taken here by any of our contributors), and by those who find the sources of political culture more varied, its nature more plastic and malleable, and its effects less decisive than the thesis allows. The thesis has also been called into question by recent empirical analyses that do not find evidence of predominantly authoritarian political cultures even in such countries as Mexico and Argentina, which have known stable or recurrent authoritarian rule.[15]

Any assessment of these contending perspectives requires first some delineation of what we mean by the central concept: Political culture involves a number of different psychological orientations, including deeper elements of value and belief about how political authority should be structured and how the self should relate to it, and more temporary and mutable attitudes, sentiments, and evaluations concerning the political system.[16] Although scholars debate the necessary coherence of these dimensions, it is obvious that some dimensions adapt more readily to changes in political reality. It is also clear that different political subcultures may characterize different societal groups, such as the military, intellectuals, or the political elite in general. At some historical junctures, elite values and beliefs may differ sharply from those of the public, and these differences may have crucial implications for democratic development, as we see in several of our chapters. Of particular concern to us here are the two obvious theoretical questions: What determines political cultures (and subcultures) of Latin America? How do these cultural phenomena affect democracy?

Sources of political culture. The cases in this volume strongly suggest a reciprocal relationship between political culture and political system. Democratic culture helps to maintain and press for the return of democracy, but historically, the choice of democracy by political elites clearly preceded, in many of our cases, the presence of democratic values among the general public or other elites. This elite choice of democracy was no doubt influenced by values, including those induced by international diffusion and demonstration effects. Admiration for the political dynamism of the United States was reflected in the degree to which new democracies in Latin America modeled their constitutions after that of the United States. However, to a considerable degree, the option for a democratic regime was a matter of pragmatic, calculated strategy by conservative forces who, to quote Valenzuela on the case of Chile, "correctly perceived that representative institutions were in their best interest and the only real alternative once military solutions to domestic conflicts no longer seemed viable." Even at the elite level, deep normative commitments to democracy appear to have followed these rational choices. In Chile, Uruguay, and Costa Rica (and much later in Venezuela), values of tolerance, participation and commitment to democratic principles and procedures developed as a result of practice and experience with democratic institutions. Rustow refers to this as the "habituation" phase, when "both politicians and citizens learn from the successful resolution of some issues to place their faith in the new rules," and both groups come to internalize democratic norms.[17]

Intellectual and mass public commitment to democracy is deepened by a generally successful performance of democratic systems. The growth in state capacity and effectiveness under democratic rule, the gradual expansion of democracy to incorporate newly mobilized social groups, coupled with the steady expansion of the economy and of education, job opportunities, and social welfare benefits to lower-class groups, produce over time widespread belief in the legitimacy of democracy. Where (proto)democratic regimes performed poorly, as in the Dominican Republic, Peru, and Mexico, no deep cultural commitment to democracy developed. Cynicism about democracy also developed where democratic institutions functioned, as in Somoza's Nicaragua or Stroessner's Paraguay, only as a façade for authoritarian rule.

As suggested by the heavy borrowing from foreign constitutional designs, elite and especially intellectual political thinking has often been strongly influenced by foreign models and ideas. In Latin America, intellectuals play an important role in their societies and are quite open to the world of ideas.[18] Understanding the crisis of democracy in the 1930s in a number of Latin American countries requires, as Waisman shows, some reference to European intellectual, political, and social conflicts. In contrast to the authoritarian regimes born in the 1960s, which lacked intellectual and ideological legitimation, authoritarian ideas were important in the late 1920s and 1930s. Space constraints have prevented an adequate treatment of this aspect, particularly since in Latin America, with the exception of the Brazilian *integralismo,* properly Fascist movements and organizations had limited success.[19] It is obviously much more difficult to refer to the impact of ideas on other political actors, including the military and political parties or movements, not openly identifying themselves as Fascist. However, right-wing nationalism in Argentina cannot be understood without reference to developments in Europe, including the rise of Italian fascism, the intellectual appeal of Charles Maurras and his disciples, and the development of Catholic corporatist conservative thought. Those antidemocratic ideologies of the 1930s had a continued impact at a later date and were not fully irrelevant even for the intellectuals supporting the Pinochet regime, though their loss of global appeal has led him to ignore their proposals in his constitutional designs.

The contemporary weakness of antidemocratic thought on the Right and increasingly on the Left bodes well for democracy in countries where intellectual ideas are important to legitimize political activists.

Political events have also been a source of cultural change, as a result of political learning by Latin American elites and mass publics. In their contributions to this volume, Jonathan Hartlyn and Daniel Levine both heavily attribute democratic changes in political belief and practice to learning from previous disastrous experiences with democracy in the late 1940s, which plunged Colombia into a decade of horrific interparty violence and unleashed a decade of repressive military dictatorship in Venezuela. These painful experiences impressed upon party and group leaders the need for cooperation, compromise, accommodation, moderation, and consensus if democracy was to work. Levine writes of Venezuela: "The experience of being overthrown, and the corrupt and capricious nature of military rule had a sobering effect on democratic leaders in many camps," demonstrating that "there is almost always something left to lose" and that "dictatorship has no virtues." This same lesson of the importance of democracy as an end in itself, and the need for political prudence and accommodation, was driven home to the publics and politicians of Brazil, Argentina, Chile, and Uruguay by the bitter experiences of economic and political stalemate, polarization, and violence, leading to democratic breakdown and repressive, bureaucratic-authoritarian rule during the 1960s, 1970s and early 1980s. The resulting "revalorization" of democracy and moderation of political behavior is one of the most important causes for optimism about the future of democracy in these countries.[20]

Political culture has also been shaped by social structure and reshaped by socioeconomic change. Just as the highly undemocratic elements of political culture in Peru and the Dominican Republic, noted above, were fostered by extreme, cumulative, socioeconomic inequalities, rapid socioeconomic change in these two countries has shifted political values and attitudes in a notably more democratic direction. New business and professional elites, and other educated middle class groups, are more inclined to value democratic participation and to recognize the need for social and political accommodation. As a result of reforms made by the Velasco military regime (1968–1975)—which drew agrarian and urban lower-middle classes into cooperative and self-management experiments while eroding oligarchical power in politics and the national media—and also as a result of dramatically increased access to television and secondary and university education, lower- and middle-class groups in Peru became more politically active, informed, and sophisticated. In Costa Rica, historically low levels of inequality and the absence of feudalistic social relations bred egalitarian social values that were highly conducive to political participation, tolerance, cooperation and support for democratic liberties and procedures.

Effects of political culture. The case histories in this volume give strong support to theories (and to our own hypotheses) that the development and maintenance of democracy is greatly facilitated by values and behavioral dispositions (particularly at the elite level) of compromise, flexibility, tolerance, conciliation, moderation, and restraint. The early development of oligarchical democracy in Chile, Argentina, Uruguay, and Costa Rica clearly was advanced by the evolution of these values among elites. Indeed, it was precisely when violent struggle began to be replaced at the elite level by conciliatory, accommodating behavioral norms that liberal, competitive regimes began to develop and endure. And as these democracies evolved, broad belief in the intrinsic desirability of democracy became an important underpinning of their stability. By the same token, where these beliefs in democratic legitimacy and in compromise and accommodation weakened or were highly contingent on continued elite hegemony, as in Argentina, democracy was much more vulnerable to breakdown.

Just as democratic functioning promotes democratic values, we see in our case studies of Costa Rica and Venezuela that democratic culture contributes to democratic stability. In these two most stable of Latin America's democracies, popular and elite belief in democratic legitimacy remains high, despite prolonged, severe economic crises. Indeed, John Booth argues that it is precisely this high level of diffuse popular support for the democratic system that has enabled Costa Rica to weather the crisis of regime performance in the 1980s. In both countries, pronounced elite dispositions toward compromise, consensus-building, inclusiveness, restraint, and respect for democratic procedures and principles reinforce legitimacy by avoiding political crisis and polarization, focusing political discontent on individual governments rather than the regime, and incorporating new groups into the political process. Democracy in these two countries is also culturally sustained at the mass level by broad and deep normative commitments to tolerance, moderation, and civil liberties, and by unusually high levels of citizen participation in associational life outside the state, motivated and structured by democratic norms.

Recent history also suggests that enduring democratic value commitments make it more difficult to consolidate and perpetuate authoritarian rule. In Uruguay, the military regime's lack of legitimacy hampered its effectiveness, while its need "to justify every action as necessary for the promotion of democracy" showed "the resilience of the democratic political culture permeating even the armed forces, and the inhospitable climate for authoritarian discourse."[21] No less striking has been the concern of the Pinochet regime to construct a constitutional, legal basis for its authoritarian rule and to seek popular validation of its domination through electoral means. In both countries, the resort to plebiscite eventually backfired, leading to stunning electoral defeats for the Uruguayan regime in 1980 and the Chilean in 1988 (after pro-Pinochet plebiscites in 1978 and 1980). Both the fact of the plebiscites and the ultimate popular rejections of the military at the polls reflected the continuing vitality of democratic culture. In addition, they hastened the transition to democracy in Uruguay and the initiation of a transition process in Chile in 1988.[22] Historically in Brazil, political elites have been less committed to democratic values than in Uruguay or Chile, but a similar kind of reverence for legal culture and electoral traditions attenuated the harshness and arbitrariness of authoritarian rule in Vargas' *Estado Novo* and again during military rule in the 1960s and 1970s.

A clear association is also apparent between the absence or disappearance of accommodating norms and democratic values, among elites in particular, and the failure of attempts at democracy. Hierarchical, authoritarian elite norms and values, openly disdainful of lower class aspirations and interests, along with low levels of political efficacy, knowledge, participation, and social trust among the populace, presented an important cultural obstacle to democratic development in Peru and the Dominican Republic through the nineteenth and much of the twentieth centuries. Both Cynthia McClintock, for Peru and Wiarda, for the Dominican Republic, view recent changes in these value configurations as beneficial to democracy. Perhaps the classic case of unraveling of democratic culture in our times occurred in Chile during the years preceding the 1973 military coup, when the commitment to the polarized options of radical change or the status quo came to exceed the commitment to democracy, and the breakdown of accommodative, tolerant norms and practices preceded and accelerated the breakdown of democracy.

Any theoretical conclusions about political culture must inevitably be qualified with many caveats. As we just observed, the development of democratic values and norms is not irreversible, but rather is always liable to erosion. The decay of democratic norms and practices—of communication, cooperation, moderation, and accommodation—in the face of rapid political polarization, escalating stakes, and declining commitment to democracy among key individual and group actors was central to the breakdown of democracy in Uruguay as well as Chile in 1973. Similarly, what is learned politically may also be "unlearned" as a result of generational change or the overwhelming impact of structures and events. At this writing, the renewal of populist leadership formulae and militant political sentiments in Peru, Brazil, and Argentina, with their polarizing implications, is a matter for concern. Finally, a high level of popular commitment to democracy in the abstract does not, in itself, guarantee the maintenance of a democratic regime when, as in Uruguay in the late 1960s and early 1970s, the society is polarizing, the economy collapsing, and politicians are seen as corrupt and ineffective.[23]

Political Leadership

It is already apparent that the skills, values, strategies, and choices of political leaders figure prominently in our explanation of the enormously varied experiences with democracy in Latin America. At a general level, we might reiterate two of our themes: First, the style of political leadership is crucial. A flexible, accommodative, consensual leadership style is more successful in developing and maintaining democracy than a militant, uncompromising, confrontational one (though sometimes at the price of needed reforms). Shifts in political leadership strategies and styles from consensus to confrontation, from accommodation to polarization, are visible in the breakdowns of Latin America's longstanding democratic regimes. Second, the effectiveness of democratically elected or oriented leaders in state building and economic development is clearly associated with the overall success or failure of democracy over time. As Wiarda shows for the Dominican Republic, where democratic or protodemocratic leaders have repeatedly proved weak and inept, especially in contrast to authoritarian rulers, democracy has been unable to develop institutional strength and popular support. Daniel Levy shows that Mexico demonstrates a corollary rule: Sustained skilled and effective leadership that is undemocratic in its values and intentions may contribute to the stability of an undemocratic regime.

More specifically, four elements of political leadership choice and skill stand out in Latin America's political development: (1) the decisions, initiatives and behavioral styles of political leaders in founding or extending democratic regimes; (2) the ability of democratic leaders to adapt and enlarge the political system to satisfy expanding demands for participation; (3) the responses of democratic leaders to economic crises; and (4) the responses of democratic leaders to crises of political polarization and stalemate. The second element is a matter of crisis avoidance and the latter two, which are sometimes closely interrelated, involve the challenge of crisis management and resolution.

Founding democratic leadership. As Lipset has demonstrated for the United States, the period in which a new democratic regime is founded and begins to function provides particularly wide scope for political leadership to shape the character of politics and political institutions.[24] In several of our cases, political leaders stand out, individually or collectively, for choices, initiatives, and strategies that crucially contributed to democratic development at a formative moment. We see in Valenzuela's chapter that the early development of democracy in Chile cannot be understood without appreciating the role of General Manuel Bulnes, who, unlike the *caudillos* of his time, did not use his successful military command to impose a personalistic dictatorship: "Instead, like George Washington in the United States, he insisted on working within the framework of established political institutions and chose to leave office at the end of his term." By refusing to rule autocratically, emphasizing civilian over military authority (in part by reducing the size of the regular army), and respecting the growing autonomy of the legislature and judiciary, Bulnes contributed formatively to the legitimacy and institutional strength of democracy in Chile.

The role of José Figueres in institutionalizing democracy in Costa Rica a century later presents some interesting parallels to the example of Bulnes. After his Army of National Liberation overthrew the fraud-ridden and Communist-influenced electoral regime in 1948 during a six-week civil war, Figueres, in command of a National Liberation junta and the only effective military force in the country, was in a position to do "anything he wanted, including setting up a personal dictatorship."²⁵ Instead, he followed through on his democratic pledges, administering honest Constituent Assembly elections in which his party lost badly, accepting the defeat of his proposed constitution, still achieving some important constitutional reforms (including abolition of the armed forces), and then transferring power in 1949 to the conservative victor in the 1948 elections, whose party had blocked Figueres' social democratic agenda. In so honoring the commitment to democratic procedures over substantive political goals, Figueres and his junta "established precedents of civility and accommodation between opponents which made the establishment of liberal democracy possible after 1949."²⁶ Four decades earlier, Booth notes, political leadership had also been instrumental in the democratization of Costa Rica's Liberal Republic, when González Víquez resisted precedent by tolerating vigorous opposition and then ensuring a free campaign for his successor in 1909.

In Colombia and Venezuela, the critical turns of democratic founding were acts of collective leadership by contending party elites who managed—as a result of the political learning mentioned above—to transcend their rivalries and lay the foundation for stable democracy through the negotiation of elite pacts. In each case, these agreements produced sharing of government power and patronage, limits on political competition and mobilization, and mechanisms emphasizing conciliation, consensus, and mutual guarantees over substantive political goals. The ability of opposing party leaders, so recently locked in bitter conflict, to negotiate creatively and flexibly and to win their followers' consent to these difficult compromises was indispensable to the reconstruction of democracy in these two countries in 1957–1958, and to subsequent democratic consolidation. These wise and skillful acts of statecraft contrast significantly with the brash style and militant, confrontational strategy of Acción Democrática when it ruled in the ill-fated democratic experiment known as the *trienio* (1945–1948).

Adaptation and reform. As we suggested earlier, a common challenge facing the limited democracies of nineteenth- and early twentieth-century Latin America was to reform the political system to make room for newly mobilized social groups demanding political participation and access to power. At times this was accompanied and even superseded by the challenge of social reform. Looking back, the achievement of these reforms takes on an aura of inevitability that was in no way apparent at the time. Invariably—given not only the inertia of existing institutions but the conservatism of established interests—successful reform required shrewd and skillful leadership. Repeatedly, one finds behind reform able and even remarkable efforts of leadership: for example, the interaction between the Radical Party leader Yrigoyen and such opposing Conservative leaders as Saenz Peña, which produced the historic Reform of 1912 in Argentina that expanded the electoral system so far as to enable the middle-class Radicals to win the subsequent presidential election; or the first dramatic expansion of Chile's electorate four decades earlier, championed by conservative leader José Manuel Irarrázaval; or the sweeping political, social, and economic changes wrought in Uruguay by President José Battle y Ordóñez, which laid the foundations of a modern, democratic welfare state in the first decade of the twentieth century; or the political reforms of President Jiménez Oreamuno in Costa Rica (1909–1913), which extended to local peasant leaders access to the structures of municipal power.

That such reforms were not inevitable is suggested by the fact that in many Latin American countries they appeared only much later, after many cycles of political instability, regime breakdown, and crisis. In Peru—where the narrow and powerfully entrenched oligarchy admittedly presented a much stiffer obstacle to reform—the leaders of a briefer experiment in limited democracy concurrent with those above (the Aristocratic Republic of 1895 to 1919) proved unwilling or unable to produce even modest political and social reforms. So did subsequently elected, civilian presidents such as Manuel Prado and Fernando Belaúnde (who promised but never delivered). The only significant socioeconomic reforms were produced by authoritarian rulers—Leguía in the 1920s and more recently Velasco, who laid (if unintentionally) a somewhat more promising foundation for democracy.

Today, we see again that manifest needs for political adaptation and socioeconomic reform call for courageous, creative, determined, and resourceful leadership that may simply not be forthcoming. Thus Hartlyn finds that Colombian "statecraft has recently fallen short" in its failure to respond to changed social and political conditions, which require dismantling the semiconsociational system negotiated a generation ago and opening up the political process. And Levine recognizes that consensus-minded, cautious leadership in Venezuela has not yet found the strategy or will to attack the long-deferred challenge of socioeconomic reform in a society with widespread poverty and deep inequality.

Response to economic crisis. Political leadership assumes particular importance in periods of crisis, strain, vulnerability, and institutional challenge—when it may also face its most severe constraints. Economic crisis represents one of the most common threats to democratic stability. The policy choices and political capacities that democratically elected leaders bring to these crises can greatly affect the survival chances of the democratic regime. Since severe or prolonged economic crisis may call the efficacy of democratic institutions into question, the ability of democratic leaders to implement effective solutions *democratically* is also crucial.

A classic example of effective democratic response to economic crisis was evidenced in Chile during the 1930s, when Arturo Alessandri brought the country out of the Great Depression with firm austerity measures and a strong commitment to democratic institutions, following a period of acute instability. More recently, the administration of Jaime Lusinchi in Venezuela helped to stabilize a disastrous economic situation in the 1980s by negotiating agreements for business and labor to share the costs of necessary economic adjustments. By contrast, the coalition government of Salvador Allende aggravated inflation, destroyed business and middle-class confidence, and deepened Chile's economic crisis by imposing "a host of ill-conceived redistributive and stimulative economic measures,"[27] while a succession of Uruguayan administrations deepened that country's economic stagnation by failing to choose and sustain any kind of coherent economic policies. These blunders contributed significantly to democratic breakdown in each case.

Sadly, the administration of Alan García in Peru has recently added another chapter to the chronicle of democratic leadership failures in Latin America. Like Allende, the impulsive García recklessly pursued short-term economic gains and ignored all kinds of signals of impending economic collapse, which occurred in 1988. García's abrupt attempt at nationalization of financial institutions—characteristic of what McClintock terms his "dangerously wilful decision-making"—enraged the business sector, further alienated the international banking community, polarized the political situation, and deepened the economic crisis.

The response to economic crisis involved a wider element of elite choice with profound implications for the future in Argentina. Waisman traces the reversal of Argentina's democratic evolution and economic development to a series of fateful choices made during the 1930s and 1940s. During the same depression in which Chile reequilibrated its democracy, the Argentine agrarian upper class, fearing for its hegemony, abandoned democracy. Later, in the mid-1940s, an undemocratic leader, Juan Perón, imposed on the country the disastrous choice of radical protectionism *cum* state corporatism that led to decades of stalemate, decay, and praetorianism. A point of Waisman's we wish to emphasize is that this was not a structurally inevitable choice, politically or economically. A different path out of the country's economic morass was offered by selective protection (within a continued long-term strategy of integration into the world economy) and the resumption of inclusionary strategies toward labor.

Response to generalized political crisis. Economic crisis is most dangerous for democracy when it is only one element in a generalized crisis of the democratic system, resulting from political polarization, stalemate, and widespread inefficacy. Such a generalized, systemic crisis characterized both the Chilean and Uruguayan situations in the early 1970s. The times demanded extraordinary efforts of democratic statecraft to bridge yawning divisions and forge pragmatic, coherent policies. But as we have noted, leaders of political parties, groups, and factions insisted on pursuing their own rigid interests and agendas. From a precarious political position, Allende's Unidad Popular government tried to impose its radical program unilaterally, while conservative and business elements sought to sabotage it. Tragically, as Valenzuela notes, "center groups and moderate politicians on both sides of the political divide abdicated their responsibility [to forge a consensus] in favor of narrower group stakes and short-term interests." The descent into polarization and violence in Uruguay was also marked by abandonment of political responsibility, as party and factional leaders failed to adopt or adhere to urgently needed economic stabilization measures, failed to formulate effective policies against terrorism and violence, failed to respect civil liberties and democratic procedures in dealing with escalating protest, and failed to stand firmly against military intervention; rather, they vied with one another for alliance with the military. As Gillespie and González make clear, Uruguay's unique electoral system heavily encouraged this disintegration, but democratic breakdown cannot be understood apart from the miscalculations and the semiloyal, disloyal, and undemocratic acts of democratic politicians, especially the last two presidents, Pacheco and Bordaberry.[28]

As a previous four-volume study has already established, mistakes and inadequacies of political leadership figure prominently in the breakdown of democracy.[29] Goulart's "equivocal behavior" with regard to adherence to constitutional rules was a crucial precipitating factor in Brazil's democratic breakdown. And one cannot ignore Quadros' resignation from the presidency in 1961, which suddenly thrust Goulart into the role while casting doubt on the viability of the democratic system. Historians of Brazil's New Republic will no doubt give much attention to the cruel twist of fate that thrust a vice-president with a weak political base into the presidency in 1985—at the start of a new regime, before the elected Tancredo Neves could ever take office. The mixture of acute political insecurity and weakness with grand political ambition that characterized President José Sarney was no doubt a factor in his choice (and implementation by decree) of a response to economic crisis—the "Cruzado Plan"—that eschewed the necessary, fundamental restructuring for the pursuit of short-term gains (by price freeze) at the cost of medium-term economic chaos.[30]

Political Institutions

The fundamental thread that runs like a silver lining through the political history of Latin America, and consequently through this book, is the early option for an institutional design derived from constitutional thinking: the rule of law; representative institutions; elections; modern legal systems; political freedoms, etc. The dramatic story told in all the chapters is how difficult it was for that commitment to overcome the many obstacles that the social and economic structure, the personalities and ambitions of political leaders, and deep conflicts about the good society, posed to its realization. However, this should not lead us to ignore the fundamental fact that in the last 150 years no other institutional arrangements have been able to gain full legitimacy in Latin America. There have not been and are not now monarchs claiming the divine right to rule. There have not been mass-mobilizing single parties (with the exception of that in Cuba and, in a half-hearted way, in Nicaragua) claiming a revolutionary legitimacy unrelated to democratic procedures (though Mexico did achieve revolutionary legitimacy for decades, largely with one-party dominance and with only marginal dependence on the legitimacy of democracy as defined in this volume). While fascism left its imprint on some of the populist movements in the 1930s and 1940s, particularly in Brazil and Argentina, the leaders of those movements—Vargas and Perón—manipulated and controlled existing institutions, not creating new institutions breaking with Western constitutionalism.[31] More recently, military rulers of Brazil could not, as Bolivar Lamounier shows, ignore the constitutional tradition of two houses and regular elections. Ultimately, the weight of that tradition helped force them to the *distenção* and *abertura,* and ultimately to devolution of power to civilian leaders.

In Uruguay, the tradition of a fair electoral process was able to resist military ambitions to constitutionalize authoritarian rule. Ultimately, restoring democratic institutions and the preexisting party system became unavoidable despite the legitimate criticism that those traditions deserved. Even the most authoritarian of contemporary military rulers—Pinochet—did not talk in a new political institutional language but established the most absolute personal rule legitimized by constant references to a constitution he made and got approved in a referendum, emphasizing his claim of presidential authority over his military base. One can say that the hypocritical and even cynical manipulation of that institutional tradition is the price that vice pays to virtue. It made impossible the institutionalization and legitimation of undemocratic rule.

Thus, the constitutional, liberal, and democratic idea delegitimizes the authoritarian realities of power in Latin America. However, this fact has another side, less promising for democracy. Many countries, particularly some of the Andean and (even more) Central American countries, have become accustomed to brutal, distorted, manipulated, political institutions and pseudo–liberal-democratic regimes. Therefore, *ruptura*—the break with that authoritarian past—cannot be symbolized by discarding authoritarian institutions like those of Italian fascism, Franco's organic democracy, or Salazar's corporatist Estado Novo. It can always be argued by those who are defeated that things do not change when democratization is attempted. Many players have become so distrustful of institutions that they have turned to arms, the guerrilla resistance, or the death squads, rather than trust in the outcome of formal political processes.

Parties and party systems. In several Latin American countries, an important element in the institutional resilience of democracy has been the strength of the party system and the high degree of institutionalization and popular loyalty achieved by the major parties. No one can analyze the political development of Uruguay without reference to Blancos and Colorados, and to the uniqueness and deficiencies of party structure shaped by the complex electoral law. It is not possible to understand Colombian politics without appreciating the depth of popular attachments to the Conservative and Liberal parties. Both the successes and failures of democracy are intimately linked to the history and nature of these parties, which are difficult to fit into contemporary analysis of party structures. Nor would one doubt that the stability of Venezuelan democracy as well as its crises are intimately linked in recent decades with the strength of the party organization, the loyalty it has generated to Acción Democrática, and the stability of the main opposition party COPEI. No one could ignore the capacity for survival of the APRA in Peru through decades of dictatorships and repression, or the central importance of the Radicals and the Peronistas in Argentine politics. Nor can we understand the resistance to and frustration of authoritarian regimes in Colombia, Uruguay, and Chile without appreciating the degree to which established parties continued to occupy organizational space and loyalty in the polity.

Most Latin American parties tend to be heavily clientelistic, contrasting with the mass-membership parties (especially Social and Christian Democratic) of Europe, which tend to be prevalent in only a few Latin American countries, such as Chile and Venezuela.[32] Indeed, our understanding of democracy in many Latin American countries is handicapped by a lack of systematic knowledge of some of the parties. Only the Chilean party system fits into the model of modern and contemporary European politics, a fact that underscores the danger of generalization about Latin American parties and party systems. We caution against trying to measure the institutional strength of Latin American parties by the standard of European ones that became consolidated, and consolidated democracy, in the very different circumstances of late nineteenth- and early twentieth-century (not to mention post–World War II) Europe. The perspective that compares them so and finds them wanting is in our view misleading, contributing to a skepticism about the democratic prospect in Latin America that the recent experience of the new and consolidated democracies of southern Europe suggests is misplaced. With the introduction of television into the political process, public financing of parties and campaigns, and other changes, political parties of the future may lack the mass membership and deep club structure of traditional European parties. Contemporary Spanish democracy, for example, cannot reproduce the model of a large-membership party (the ruling Socialist Party, after obtaining 10 million votes, still has only 250,000 members), but no one doubts its stability.

Weighed against this broader comparative perspective, the historical evidence from our own cases suggests that the crucial consideration for democracy is not the size of party memberships *per se* but the degree of party institutionalization, as well as the number and configuration of parties within the overall system. All of our cases call attention to the institutional strength or weakness of parties as a determinant of success or failure with democracy, and each of them grapples with the problem of institutionalization in terms that inevitably recall Samuel Huntington's classic formula: coherence, complexity, autonomy, and adaptability.[33] Where at least one and eventually two or more parties were able to develop some substantive coherence about policy and program preferences, some organizational coherence and discipline, some complexity of internal structure (with functional groups and linkages and vertical integration down to provincial and local levels), some degree of autonomy from dominance by individual leaders or state or societal interests, and some capacity to adapt to changing conditions—incorporating new generations and newly emergent social groups—Latin American democracy has usually developed considerable durability and vitality. Where one or more of these elements of institutionalization has been missing or has disappeared from the party system, democracy has been unstable.

Democracy in Venezuela since 1958 presents an example of how the deep penetration, permanent organization, vertical and horizontal integration, and continuing, vigorous efforts at renewal and incorporation of two parties with moderate but discernible substantive differences have promoted the consolidation and stable functioning of democracy. A similar generalization could be offered for Costa Rica, though it would better characterize the predominant PLN than the Center-Right coalition that has sometimes captured the presidency. The Chilean party system likewise contributed for many decades to stable democracy, though adaptation depended more heavily on the emergence of new parties to incorporate new social groups and interests. The destabilization of democracy in Chile was caused not by the decline in parties as such but by the polarization of the complex relations between them. The institutional depth of the Liberal and Conservative parties also contributed to democratic development in twentieth-century Colombia—incorporating new social groups and movements, inhibiting class polarization and military domination—but the disastrous polarization of their deep and all-encompassing popular followings again underscores the corollary importance of accommodative interparty relations, while the subsequent ossification of their domination through their rigid, exclusionary National Front agreement emphasizes the importance of continuing adaptation and periodic turnover and renewal in the party system.

Uruguay's two-party system (the core of its democratic stability in the first half of this century) shared some of these features of institutionalization, but with an ultimately fatal flaw that stemmed, as Charles Gillespie and Luis González show, from the unique electoral system of the "double simultaneous vote." This system (reinstituted with the return to democracy in 1984) strongly encouraged factionalism by permitting the presentation of more than one list from each party in the National Assembly elections and more than one candidate for president from each party.[34] The resulting entrenchment of competition among party factions undermined the programmatic, ideological, and organizational coherence of parties while putting a premium on the politics of clientelism and patronage. The latter phenomenon, Gillespie has shown, fostered irresponsible and destabilizing economic policies and a politics of outbidding.[35] The combined effect of party clientelism and incoherence—in an electoral system that gave none of the four administrations of the period an effective parliamentary majority—was the failure to formulate and implement any kind of coherent policies to confront deepening economic crisis in the two decades before 1973. Thus,

Gillespie and González argue persuasively that the double simultaneous vote must be abolished if Uruguay is to produce a more coherent and effective party system.

With the exception of Mexico—where, as Levy shows, the institutionalization of a coherent, structurally complex and elaborate, and shrewdly adaptive but undemocratic party long proved consistent with an undemocratic regime—all of our other cases indicate the costs to democracy of weak, poorly institutionalized political parties. One factor in the instability of competitive politics in Argentina since 1930, Waisman argues, has been the fragile and penetrated character of political parties, relative to powerful, politicized, and autonomous interest groups. The extraordinary incoherence of the Peronist Party, containing numerous mutually contradictory tendencies, has been especially damaging, and its recent evolution of a more democratic structure and commitment is an encouraging sign. The trend toward a more broadly based and settled party system is also cause for hope in the Dominican Republic and Peru, Wiarda and McClintock find.

Lamounier traces the breakdown of democracy in Brazil partly to the "deinstitutionalization" of the party system that began in the mid-1950s, fragmenting or dividing each of the major parties and subjecting the system overall to "increasing radicalization." Decreasing coherence and political capacity diminished the ability of the main parties to implement needed socioeconomic reforms, which failure reduced their popular support at the same time that social change was also eroding traditional political ties. The inability of weak parties to adapt to and harness changing social and economic forces finally proved fatal in 1964. Similarly, in Peru the poor institutionalization of the party system historically made it difficult for democratic regimes to implement policies to reduce socioeconomic inequality. Generally, across our cases, we find that weak parties, lacking in structural depth and excessively dependent on personalities, have made for weak democracy.

We thus find it difficult to quarrel with Lamounier's conclusion that stable democracy in Brazil, and throughout the region, requires the construction of "organized and minimally ideological parties," which have the coherence, strength, and will to institute necessary but politically difficult policies for economic stabilization and reform. At the same time, we should not overlook the importance of the strength of the overall party system.

Our cases convey an additional lesson about the way competing parties relate to one another: Stable democracy requires the avoidance of polarization in the party system. Our evidence suggests two alternative models for this in Latin America. One involves the predominance, as in the United States, of two broad, moderate, multiclass parties that alternate frequently in office and evolve pragmatic working relations, though not at the expense of all substantive distinctions between them. This has been the formula for democratic stability in Costa Rica, Venezuela, and (at times) Colombia and Uruguay, though it carries the risk that the predominant parties will become so alike and cooperative that the necessary element of competition and choice will evaporate, and the system will ossify, as it did in Colombia. The second alternative is a moderate, multiparty system based more on ideological and class divisions, as in Europe historically. Such a system was compatible with stable democracy in Chile for many decades, but only so long as party leaders, especially those in the pivotal center, were able to construct the necessary coalitions. The failure of Chilean democracy in 1973 exposed a crucial vulnerability of this second type of model: Unlike the first, its stability is not fundamentally compatible with a presidential system of government.

Constitutional structure. Among the political institutions common to all Latin American countries, one of the most striking is the almost universal presidential, rather than parliamentary, type of democracy. In comparative terms, this option certainly stands out. Most of the successful European democracies have parliamentary systems, as do Japan, India, and the other democracies of the British Commonwealth. Latin America is, with the United States and a few Asian countries, the only part of the world in which democracy has been institutionalized (or even repeatedly attempted) in the form of presidentialism (and also the only part where presidentialism has been mixed with proportional representation). Surprisingly, however, in the debates about the causes of democratic failure, no attention has been paid until very recently to the role of presidential government, perhaps because it has been so successful in the United States. Latin American republics simply transferred U.S. institutions, so it was tempting to attribute much less successful performance to other political, social, and economic factors. This focus obscured the role of specifically political elements: the presidency; the congress; the relationship between congress and president; federalism; centralism; the role of local governments; and, until recently, even parties and party systems. One of the promising intellectual consequences of the recent authoritarian periods and the search for stable democratic frameworks has been renewed attention (reflected in our chapters) to political institutions, including issues of constitutional structure and efforts at constitutional reform in a number of countries. Unfortunately, however, efforts at rethinking and reform confront the constant invocation of political tradition that has made certain symbolic elements—such as the presidency and the principle of no reelection—almost sacred. The resulting resistance to the kind of institutional innovation that was possible in Western Europe after fascism and authoritarianism is, we think, unfortunate.

We cannot restate here all of Linz's arguments about the problems of presidentialism and the advantages of parliamentarism for a great many polities.[36] But neither can we neglect the considerable evidence from our cases showing how presidentialism has facilitated and exacerbated crises of democracy. Certainly the classic instance, as we have already suggested, was Chile. Valenzuela demonstrates the lack of fit between a highly polarized and competitive multiparty system—which, because it could not generate electoral majorities, necessitated bargaining and coalition making—and a presidential system of centralized authority, zero-sum outcomes, and fixed terms. Presidents, he notes, "felt responsible for the national destiny as the embodiment of popular sovereignty," and yet they represented only a third or so of the electorate and could never count on strong legislative support. In this context, the "fixed terms for both president and Congress contributed to an atmosphere of ungovernability and a feeling of permanent crisis." Increases in presidential power only aggravated the inherent strain in the system and reduced the scope and incentives for accommodation, creating a tendency to polarization and stalemate that finally "came to a tragic head in the Allende years." Valenzuela's counterfactual speculation on the difference a parliamentary system would have made has relevance well beyond the Chilean case and bears recapitulation here:

> A parliamentary system of government would have defused the enormous pressures for structuring high-stakes coalitions around a winner-take-all presidential option, which only reinforced political polarization. At the same time it would have eliminated the stalemate and confrontation in executive-legislative relations. . . . Allende's government might have fallen, but democracy would have survived.

A similar conclusion seems warranted for Uruguay, where in 1971 presidentialism also produced a minority, extremist (in this case rightist) president of dubious democratic commitment. Of course, this outcome was further shaped by the strange electoral system, which produced a minority president lacking even a plurality of electoral support. That the breakdown of democracy was not inevitable is indicated by the majority of the electorate's appearing to favor civil liberties and progressive reform.[37] As we write, the debilitating rigidities of presidentialism have become increasingly manifest in Peru and Brazil, where presidents whose programs have failed catastrophically and whose political support has evaporated must limp through more than a year remaining in their terms with virtually no capacity to respond effectively to the deepening economic and political crises.

The problems of presidentialism are also highlighted when we consider the preoccupation of much of the literature on Latin American politics with the personalization of political leadership, and the appeal of populist and charismatic leaders, which dwarf more institutional political processes (a fact too often and too easily explained in terms of political culture, psychological needs, and personality). Reiterating the importance of a wider comparative analysis, it is useful to recall that the personalization of political leadership has hardly been absent from contemporary European democracies. Even ignoring such leaders as Adenauer and DeGasperi, who were central in the transition to democracy, we have only to look at the roles of Mitterand, Papandreou, and González. In fact, it can be argued that for better or for worse, in the Schumpeterian model of democracy the main objective of the democratic process is the election of a government and its legitimation to rule. In such a model, particularly with the weakening of ideologies, the attention of the voter is likely to focus on the personal qualities of the party leader who assumes the prime ministership. How could we not expect an equally or even more personalized type of political leadership in countries with a presidential system? The writing about personalism in U.S. politics has not given due weight to the fact that presidential elections inevitably focus on individual candidates to the detriment of parties and lower-level leaders.

To be sure, a parliamentary system might introduce difficulties of its own, and its relative value may vary with the social and political context. In many Latin American countries, congressmen's party affiliations may not be sufficiently stable to permit such a system to work as intended. In her research on Peru and Ecuador, McClintock has encountered a strong concern that legislators in a parliamentary system would be continually changing their party for personal advantage, rendering the job of government impossible. The introduction of a parliamentary structure in such situations might require restrictions forbidding a legislator to change party affiliation between elections without first resigning and perhaps might require that a vote of no confidence bring a new election.[38] If a presidential system is retained, one of the most dangerous aspects can be attenuated by providing for a run-off election between the top two presidential candidates, if none receives a majority of the vote. As McClintock indicates, the introduction of this provision in Peru has clearly helped to reduce the number of political parties since 1980 and also to encourage party leaders to stake out more moderate positions (at least relative to their followers).

Our cases offer many other lessons about constitutional structure; we will briefly mention some elementary ones here. A further weakness of democratic experiences in Latin America (not wholly unrelated to the problem of presidentialism) has been the lack of power and effectiveness of legislatures, which often must live in the shadow of extensive presidential decree powers and sharp constraints on legislative authority to budget and investigate. One problem with a presidential system is that when the legislature does become assertive, this may lead to a deadlock between it and the executive, which has been a precipitating factor in several democratic breakdowns (e.g., Colombia in 1949, Brazil in 1964, Peru in 1968, and Chile in 1973).[39] Assertive congresses—as in Brazil in the early 1960s—have often lacked the institutional resources and structures necessary to check and balance executive power and to oversee and monitor expanding and modernizing bureaucracies. A corollary proposition can be offered for the judiciary, which is subject in all but the most institutionalized of Latin America's democracies to political manipulation, corruption, intimidation, and underfinancing. The problem has become particularly acute in Colombia and Peru, where judges (and increasingly the entire legal structure) have become the targets of terrorists and drug traffickers.[40] Stable democracy requires some kind of effective division and balancing of power, and also a rule of law. Only in Costa Rica, and in the partially consolidated democracy of Uruguay, do both of these institutional conditions clearly obtain today in Latin America; that they once did in Chile only underscores the tragic element in that country's democratic breakdown.

Finally, the vertical distribution of power between levels of government is also a matter of concern for democracy, as excessive centralization, particularly in the context of presidential domination of government, has made for a lack of responsiveness and accountability. This issue goes beyond the constitutional design of democracy, however, to the very structure and character of the state.

State Structure and Strength

Democracy encompasses many tensions and seeming contradictions. Prominent among them are those involving the structure of the state. Our cases show quite dramatically what might be termed the tension between "stateness" and statism. Stable democracy requires an authoritative, effective state, but there is often a tension between authority and control, between capacity and domination. In the process of state building in Latin America, there has been a strong tendency on the part of weak and insecure state elites to substitute control for authority, and domination for effective policy. A similar tension arises between the need for the state to maintain order, and the inclination to do so by blunt, violent, repressive, and undemocratic means. Not unrelated to these tensions is the constant tug and pull between the attractions of centralization for a weak, bedeviled state and the need for some vertical distribution of power to ensure democratic vitality and responsiveness.

Historically, as we have already suggested, democracy was more likely to evolve and take root where, as in Chile, early progress was made toward the establishment of an authoritative state, able to maintain order and territorial integrity. Where this challenge persisted unresolved into the twentieth century, it pressed toward centralist, authoritarian, and repressive state-building projects like those of the PRI in Mexico, Gómez in Venezuela, Trujillo in the Dominican Republic, and Leguía in Peru.

The capacity of the state to maintain public order and, at the same time, a rule of law has been an important determinant in democratic stability. Declines in such state capacity, as indicated by growing political violence and terrorism (in some cases by both state and nonstate actors), played a large role in the breakdown of democracy in Colombia in 1949, Uruguay in 1973, and Argentina in 1976. In the late 1980s, such state decay seriously threatens the democratic regimes in Colombia and Peru, where the growth of armed guerilla insurgencies, drug trafficking, terrorism, and anarchic, criminal violence has spawned human rights violations, right-wing death squads, increasing military autonomy and restlessness, and mounting public unease and despair. As Hartlyn shows, the decay has been precipitous and alarming in previously stable Colombia, where the drug traffic has corroded the integrity of every sector of the state and society. Latin America's recent history tells us unambiguously that democracy cannot long survive such increasing ungovernability.

Revolutionary challenges. In view of the inequalities and injustice in Latin American societies we might have expected the overthrow of democracies by revolutionary movements, but in fact—leaving aside the revolutionary tradition of Mexico and the challenge to the pseudo- or semidemocracies in Central America—such movements took power only against undemocratic regimes, as Batista's in Cuba, Somoza's in Nicaragua, and in Bolivia. However, social and economic crisis in South America helped, in the 1960s, to generate revolutionary movements, rural and urban guerrillas, smaller or larger terrorist groups, and much talk about the need for revolutionary action. Such movements and such a climate of opinion was not limited to the poorer and socially disorganized societies but gained considerable strength in some of the more developed, modern, and potentially democratic societies. The Montoneros and the ERP (Ejército Revolucionario del Pueblo) in Argentina challenged not only the authoritarian but the democratically elected government, as did the Tupamaros in Uruguay, while the supporters of some Left parties in Chile and Brazil looked to Cuba as the model.

These revolutionary movements aroused a deep fear and hatred in the armed forces, the bourgeoisie, and even broad sectors of the middle classes. In some cases the government turned to both legal and illegal repression, as in Argentina, so that the support of the military became more important, even as it assumed more and more power and ultimately responded by erecting brutal counterrevolutionary regimes. The paranoia of the armed forces was reflected in their national security doctrine, their conception of a dirty war, and their turn to lawless repression on a scale that affected not only those involved in radical activities, but sectors sympathetic to them, intellectuals and clergymen critical of the social order, their families, and innocent bystanders or witnesses of illegal repressive acts.

Democracies or the possibility of democratic political development were not destroyed by revolution, but unviable revolutionary dreams and violent acts of minority groups generated, as in interwar Europe, antidemocratic counterrevolutionary responses that have left a terrible legacy for the restored democracies. The previous democratic governments cannot be blamed for those developments, though a clear stand against loose revolutionary talk, a maintenance of their authority within the law, and assertion of authority over the security forces and the army might have avoided the counterrevolutionary breakdown, as illustrated by comparison between Venezuela and Argentina.

State expansion and economic intervention. Another important dimension of state structure is its degree of economic intervention and control. Certainly the European experience shows that democracy can be compatible with a sizable welfare state and extensive state intervention in and regulation of the economy. But the effect of such state expansion on democracy seems to depend significantly on historical timing. Where representative institutions became entrenched and strong, and autonomous structures of civil society developed before (or at least concurrently with) the construction of a large state bureaucracy for public welfare and economic production and regulation, state expansion does not appear to have damaged democracy (at least not directly). Rather, as in Chile, Uruguay, and Costa Rica, strong political and social institutions were able to subject the expanding state to democratic accountability and control, and different social groups were able to articulate their interests autonomously. But as Valenzuela observes, where such democratic infrastructure was not in place, the expansion and bureaucratization of state power tended to produce authoritarian and corporatist patterns of interest representation. Dismantling the institutional structure of state corporatism is vital to the democratic prospect in Argentina and Mexico. And reducing economic control by bureaucratic forces not accountable to public opinion is important for Argentina, Mexico, and Brazil as well.

There is another reason why statism is a problem for democracy in Latin America, independent of the sequence of historical development. Throughout the region (and indeed the world), evidence is mounting that extensive state ownership and huge state bureaucracies are hampering economic efficiency and may even constitute a major obstacle to the renewal of economic dynamism. In Argentina in 1988, the losses of the thirteen largest state enterprises accounted for 51 percent of the government's fiscal deficit (which jumped to 7.2 percent of GDP).[41] The swelling of civil service and public sector employment as a result of patronage-intensive politics was, Gillespie has argued, "a major cause of the mounting inflation and slumping investment" that plunged Uruguay into economic crisis after 1957.[42] In Costa Rica, there is, from both the Right and the Left, growing criticism of statism for fostering inefficiency, corruption, and inequality, and for hindering investment and growth. Such concerns are heard now throughout the region. Even the Mexican government under President Salinas de Gortari could well take significant steps in the coming years to dismantle the state corporatism that has been crucial to regime stability for decades but may be detrimental to it now.

The problem is particularly stark in Peru, where the state expanded tremendously during the 1968–1980 military regime. Frequently porous instruments of corruption and patronage, state corporations have been an unprofitable drag on the national economy. Hopelessly swollen with employees and regulations, the bureaucracy has become a major impediment to private investment while informal workers and enterprises now dominate many sectors.[43] The Peruvian state is large but weak, venal, unresponsive, and ineffective, feeding public disillusionment and violent insurgency. A rationalized, streamlined, and more accountable state is crucial to the consolidation of democracy in Peru, as it is in the Dominican Republic, which was left in 1961, after three decades of Trujillo's sultanistic dictatorship, with the second largest state sector in Latin America (after Cuba).

Centralization and federalism. An important contemporary issue in the crisis of Latin American democracy is the extent to which those republics want to have a powerful central government that will produce economic growth, redistribute resources, relieve the huge social and economic problems accumulating in the mushrooming cities; and at the same time, respond to the need for some devolution and distribution of resources on a territorial basis.

Historically, intellectual and political thinking has leaned heavily toward the imperatives for centralism. It is standard in many analyses to focus on the negative consequences of clientelistic networks and of the unwillingness of the legislature—representing narrow local interests, against the rationality of the presidential central government and its teams of expert advisers linked with international planning agencies—to relinquish its influence on policies. Some of that debate, however, ignores the role that conservative provincial, notable networks can and have played in distributing resources, not necessarily to the most needy, but certainly to the periphery. The delegitimation of those non-modern forces by much of the democratic progressive perspective in Latin America ignores their latent functions in the democratic process. Centralists argue that a more rational central government can do more for the development of the interior than can those backward political forces, but one might question that perspective when one thinks of the pressures from the masses of impoverished people in the big urban centers, which threaten public order. To what extent can any Mexican president pay attention to the periphery when he faces the monster of Mexico City demanding public services—unless there is more devolution to democratic or oligarchic forces in the periphery?

In several of our cases, including Mexico, Colombia, Venezuela, and Peru, opposition to the extreme centralization of state power is increasing along with recognition of its costs to equity and democracy. Despite the role that centralized power has played in subordinating the military and consolidating civilian, hegemonic-party rule in Mexico, a new wave of government leaders sees that some degree of political decentralization is essential to restoring the system's legitimacy and effectiveness. Colombia and Peru have launched a process of limited, decentralizing reforms. In Colombia, these involve not only some fiscal decentralization but the popular election of mayors, which, when first carried out in 1988, did show signs of bringing new political forces into the electoral arena while also dispersing the stakes in electoral competition.[44] In Peru, mayors have been popularly elected for some time, but they have been dependent on funds from the center to be politically active. Under President García, a regionalization program was initiated to address this specific problem and to decentralize further, but the program lagged with the crumbling of García's mandate and effectiveness. Modestly decentralizing reforms in 1979 gave greater independence to cities in Venezuela, but despite the formality of federalism, democracy continued to be diminished by what Levine calls the "overwhelming centralization of administrative and political life." However, the work of the COPRE (Commission for the Reform of the State) may produce significant reforms in the near future, including the plan to begin choosing governors by popular election in 1989.

The Military

All the authors of the country chapters inevitably refer to civil-military relations in the historical past, to the military regimes that interrupted the evolutionary process of democracy, to the military doctrines and role expansion that established the armed forces as "privileged definers and guardians of the national interest" (to quote Waisman on Argentina), and to the current legacy of military rule and the problems facing democratically elected governments in achieving a proper relationship with the military, and its subordination to civil authority. The problem is central and goes beyond the limits of this introduction. The very different responses of the military in different countries to the crises of democracy and authoritarianism show the need for more systematic comparative analysis of Latin American militaries, in spite of the very valuable works published in recent years. More research is needed on civil-military relations in the nineteenth century and the role they played in the development of democracy. Valenzuela argues, for example, that successful democratic consolidation in 19th-century Chile was aided by civilian, democratic control over armed institutions.

It is important to emphasize that our volume does not include the cases of full praetorianization of politics (such as Bolivia and some Central American republics), where the army as an institution is divided into politicized factions, which in turn have strong ties and alliances with political and social forces, and where it becomes very difficult to talk about civil-military relations, or about periods of civilian or military rule. It is also important to keep in mind the distinction between a military presence in the political process—the exercise of influence and even veto power over certain decisions—and a military regime, in which the leadership of the armed forces collectively and in the name of the institution exercises power. In many of the countries included in this volume, the military have long cast their shadow over democratic politics, but periods of strictly military rule have been limited and, one could argue, exceptional.

We further emphasize the difference between a military regime and a regime led or inaugurated by a military officer. A military officer at the head of the regime does not always mean that the military as an *institution* exercises power.[45] Neither Perón's first nor his second presidency can be understood as a military dictatorship or regime. In fact, there was a radical break between him and his comrades in arms, and much of the army leadership was ready to veto even by force his access to power. In a very different way one can ask if the power of Trujillo in the Dominican Republic was based on the army as an institution or if (like Somoza in Nicaragua) he had created a praetorian guard, which could not be identified with the normal armed forces, in his sultanistic type of regime.[46] As Valenzuela highlights in his chapter, General Pinochet has developed a personal power base and a tight control over the armed forces, which make it doubtful that the army as an institution is ruling today in Chile. In fact, Pinochet attempted to reduce the political role of the armed forces by continuously emphasizing his authority as president according to the 1980 constitution, and the need for depoliticization of the armed forces. Of course, this does not necessarily mean that the armed forces and those who were involved in the coup and the repression do not identify with him and sustain his power.

Strictly military regimes are in essence transitory. In fact, as Alain Rouquié notes, "A permanent system of military rule is almost a contradiction in terms. The army cannot govern directly and durably without ceasing to be an army. And it is precisely the subsequent government, the successor regime that legitimates the prior military usurpation."[47] That is why military rule in Brazil represented more an authoritarian situation than a distinctively military regime, increasingly leading to a separation between the military as government and the military as an institution, with the former thinking in political terms and attempting to create a broader basis of support in civil society, initiating a process of regime transformation that ultimately would lead to redemocratization.

The contributors to our volume avoid, we think, two dangerous temptations that Rouquié rightly notes, both of which involve ignoring the strictly military dimension in the authoritarian situations and regimes to which they refer. They do not think "that contemporary militarism is merely a culturally determined anachronism offering transitory resistance to the ultimate political good—that is representative democracy."[48] They are conscious that military intervention in politics is not exclusive to Latin America or the developing countries. And they do not fall into the alternative functionalist determinism that tends to establish "a more or less instrumental correspondence between dominant economic actors and regime types."[49] None of them sees the military as merely an expression or instrument of exogenous socioeconomic factors. Unfortunately, space does not allow them to analyze in more depth how the military developed its propensity to intervene in politics, how the prerogatives gained in the society facilitated its exercise of voice in and exit from the constitutional political system, and the particular historical political circumstances that facilitated or triggered its assumption of political power.[50]

While the military factor in Latin American politics is certainly a confining condition, and in many countries one that cannot be ignored by democratic rulers, a military threat to democratic rule is not inevitable. However, repeated interventions in politics over decades have shaped the mentality of many officers, and the formal role conception and organization of the armed forces, in ways that generate a higher probability of such intervention. Argentina, which experienced four serious military revolts against civilian, democratic authority during 1987–1988, is a case in point. It underscores the need for democratic leaders to move at an early stage to circumscribe and professionalize the military role. Purging disloyal elements among the officer corps, as in Venezuela after 1958 and Mexico during the 1920s, would seem to be a necessary element in an overall strategy of subordinating the military. So would terminating military control over important economic and administrative institutions not strictly related to national defense. But it is difficult to generalize about how far and fast democratic leaders should move toward these goals, or how much (if at all) military funding should be cut, or to what extent amnesty or accountability is the best policy for past military crimes and abuses against society.

Part of the dilemma is that where subordination and even punishment of the military are most needed, decisive moves by democratic leaders would be most likely to precipitate a military coup. Soon after taking power in Argentina, the new democratic administration of Raúl Alfonsín retired most top officers, reduced the military budget significantly, removed many firms and agencies from military jurisdiction, and tried the top leaders of the military regime for human rights abuses. But military rebellion and intimidation forced granting an amnesty to lower-level officers and, no doubt, postponing further reform measures.[51] Waisman argues for a "thorough reorganization" of the armed forces into "a small but highly professional military organization, focused on defense against external armed threats, better equipped, and socialized into a doctrine of subordination to constitutional authorities." But could the civilian regime survive the military's reaction to such drastic reduction in its size and prerogatives?

As Stepan has observed, the challenge for new democratic leaders is certainly easier where, as in Brazil, the departing military regime had already reduced military expenditures to a reasonable and politically acceptable level, thus removing an important area of potential civil-military contestation.[52] As Table 1.1 shows, Brazilian military expenditures were by 1980 among the lowest, proportionally, of major Latin American nations. Argentina, Uruguay, and Peru were left (proportionally) with among the highest military expenditures and largest military establishments in the region around the time of their transitions to democracy, and only in Argentina—where the military was discredited by its defeat in the Falklands-Malvinas war—was the new, civilian regime able to reduce military expenditures substantially. The data in Table 1.1 suggest a relationship between stable civilian (but not necessarily democratic) rule and small military establishments; Costa Rica, Venezuela, and Mexico have, proportionally, the smallest military expenditures and armed forces. Unfortunately, the data provide little counsel about how to arrive at this enviable point. Just as civilian institutionalization and circumscribed militaries may tend to reinforce one another, so do civilian instability and large, costly, and interventionist military establishments.

The tension between the military and democracy has to be seen as a result of a broader set of problems in the consolidation of democratic regimes. The conflicts derived from the legacies of the past are likely to generate serious crisis, but as the case of Argentina has shown, until now military regimes have suffered, over the decades and particularly in recent times, considerable delegitimation, and otherwise successful (effective and legitimate) democratic regimes should be able to prevent a renewed military takeover. Certainly this ap-

Table 1.1. Military Expenditures and Strength

	Military Expenditures					Armed Forces	
	as a percent of GDP		as a percent of Central Government Expenditures			per 1000 People	
	1976	1980	1972	1980	1986	1972	1980
Argentina	2.4	2.6	10.0	11.8	5.2	5.7	5.6
Brazil	1.3	0.5	8.3	4.3	3.1	4.1	3.7
Chile	6.1	7.4	6.1	—	10.7	7.7	10.5
Uruguay	2.2	2.6	5.6	11.6	10.2	7.1	9.7
Venezuela	2.2	2.7	10.3	5.9	4.9	3.9	3.2
Colombia	1.2*	2.0	NA	NA	NA	2.2	2.4
Peru	8.0	5.7*	14.8	12.5	NA	5.2	8.6
Costa Rica	0.7	0.7	2.8	2.6	2.2	1.1	1.3
Dominican Republic	1.7	1.5	8.5	10.3	8.1	3.5	4.2
Mexico	0.6	0.6	4.2	2.3	2.5	1.5	2.1

Sources: Stockholm Institute of Peace Research, *World Armaments and Disarmament, SIPRI Yearbook 1986* (New York: Oxford University Press, 1986); World Bank, *World Development Report 1983, 1988* (New York: Oxford University Press, 1983, 1988); and United States Arms Control and Disarmament Agency, "World Military Expenditures and Arms Transfers," Washington, DC, April 1984.

*Uncertain data

pears true in Uruguay, Brazil, even Peru, and especially Venezuela (where the authoritarian rules of Gómez and Pérez Jiménez were more personal dictatorships than the exercise of power by the armed forces as an institution).

The incapacity of democratic regimes to deal successfully with widespread violence, guerrilla warfare, urban terrorism, and other forms of violence makes the military a much more relevant political actor than it is in more pacified and stable societies. As Stepan has shown, once the expansion of institutional mission and prerogatives occurs, it tends to endure and advance, diminishing not only the stability but also the authenticity of democracy, as numerous areas of public policy pass from elected civilian to unaccountable military control. It is thus imperative that newly restored democracies in Latin America (and elsewhere) reorient the military role around external defense, reduce military prerogatives to control or influence vast reaches (military and nonmilitary) of the state, the political system, and even civil society, and assert civilian control and oversight even over strictly military functions. At the same time, the legitimacy, effectiveness, and stability of democracy requires achieving reasonable cooperation from the armed forces. This implies a difficult and delicate process of reform and restructuring that may take considerable time to effect. The key to this process, Stepan forcefully argues, is "democratic empowerment"— through which civilian scholars and policy specialists acquire credible expertise in military and intelligence affairs, legislatures develop the institutional capacity effectively, responsibly, and routinely to monitor military and intelligence systems, and democratic state leaders implement "a well conceived, *politically led* strategy toward the military" that "narrows their involvement in state regulation of conflict, builds effective procedures for civilian control, seeks to increase military professional capacities, and lessens the risks—for the polity and for the military—of further military intervention."[53] An important part of this strategy, we think, is the development of a responsible and competent police, under civilian control, which would further reduce the need and justification for military intervention in political and social conflicts.

Civil Society and Associational Life

The cases in this volume give strong support to a corollary proposition about the relationship between state and society: Just as democracy requires an effective but limited state, so it needs a pluralistic, autonomously organized civil society to check the power of the state and give expression democratically to popular interests. Among our Latin American cases, there is a strong correlation between the strength and autonomy of associational life and the presence and vitality of democracy. We have already noted that two of the region's most stable and vibrant democracies, Costa Rica and Venezuela, have notably rich arrays of voluntary organizations, as does Uruguay. Booth's data indicates an average of one and a half organizational memberships per family head in Costa Rica, and high levels of citizen participation within these various economic, professional, civic, and cultural organizations.

Levine's study of voluntary associations in Venezuela and McClintock's analysis of the self-managed cooperatives in Peru suggest some reasons why these organizations contribute to democracy. By modeling their operational norms on those common in the political system (e.g., competitive elections, opposition rights, proportional representation), voluntary associations reinforce democratic principles and practices. Further, they foster participatory orientations and political awareness, elicit "new leaders from hitherto passive populations," and draw out "untapped capacities for organization and self-expression," in Levine's words. Thus they are important instruments of democratic socialization and renewal.

As Gillespie and González find for Uruguay, the early development of active, independent popular organizations, especially trade unions, may benefit democracy by preempting the "political space" that could otherwise be occupied by authoritarian populist and state corporatist strategies of mobilization and inclusion. Such mobilization and inclusion in Argentina and Mexico certainly figures prominently in those countries' failure to develop stable democracy in the past half-century. Levy shows how the early, forceful incorporation of popular groups from above, by the state, promoted the stability of the undemocratic regime in Mexico by giving it a broad base, while co-opting, preempting, constraining, or neutralizing the most serious sources of potential challenge to its domination. At the same time, in a mirror image of the democratic reinforcement that occurs within Costa Rican and Venezuelan organizations, the hierarchical, authoritarian structures of governance inside Mexico's mass organizations discourage autonomous political participation, depress citizen efficacy, and so buttress the cultural and social foundation of authoritarianism. A less sophisticated and stable strategy is simply to repress the development of trade unions and other popular and even middle-class organizations. As the histories of Peru and the Dominican Republic suggest, this may seriously weaken the prospect for democracy, but in the process it also undercuts the possibility of a stable, long-term authoritarian regime.

It is clear (almost by definition) that autonomous interest groups and civic associations are freer to develop and prosper in a democracy. The fact of this association, however, leaves open the question of causation. Booth shows that such groups began to develop very early in Costa Rica, to some extent preceding and certainly propelling the development and expansion of democracy. The effect of growth in the number, variety, and vitality of organizations—trade unions, community groups, cooperatives, professional associations, school groups, etc.—was to mobilize ever increasing numbers of people into the political arena and to multiply political and socioeconomic demands in ways that could not be easily satisfied short of fundamental democratization. Something of the same process occurred in Peru during the 1970s: Socioeconomic reform under General Velasco spawned a dramatic growth in both the number and memberships of autonomous popular organizations, which in turn (ironically) provided the basis for the popular mobilization against military rule under his successor, General Morales Bermúdez, in the late 1970s.

The presence or growth of independent organizational life has also been a factor in frustrating authoritarian regimes and pressing for termination or transition. Hartlyn observes that independent labor organization (along with established political parties) helped to frustrate General Rojas's effort to create a Peronist-style, corporatist labor organization and a "Third Force" political movement. The growth or resurgence of independent associational activity—what Schmitter and O'Donnell call "the resurrection of civil society"—has been a key factor in the escalating pressure for democratization that has culminated in the transition from authoritarianism of numerous Latin American countries in the past decade.[54] The growth of autonomous associational activity was partly the result of rapid socioeconomic modernization under authoritarian regimes. In Brazil, Lamounier finds, this phenomenon gave rise to new, more autonomous types of entrepreneurial associations that pulled "out of the traditional corporatist framework," more authentic and independent trade union leadership, rural labor unions encouraged by the military to undermine traditional political bosses, and politicized urban middle class groups such as white collar unions and neighborhood organizations.

The mass media. Both logic and theory should warn us against neglecting the role of the mass media in shaping the democratic prospect. As an important source of political values and information, and a potential check on the abuse of state power, we would expect the mass media, and perhaps especially the print media, to contribute to the emergence and maintenance of democracy to the extent they are autonomous, pluralistic, vigorous and democratic in editorial orientation. Certainly, the obvious correlation seems to hold in Latin America: The press appears more vigorous, critical, pluralistic and independent of state control in democratic countries (though the electronic media, especially television, tend to lag well behind in this regard). But our case studies tell us little about the historical process by which free and independent media emerge, and about the particular and sometimes more subtle components of journalistic ownership structure, editorializing, and reportage that contribute to the strength of democracy.

It is interesting that a critical and pluralistic press may emerge rather quickly even out of a very authoritarian situation. Wiarda notes that since the 1961 demise of Trujillo—a dictator so ruthless he eliminated all independent forms of social and political organization—"the Dominican press has been remarkably free," vigorous, and pluralistic. This independence and vitality of the media (including an extraordinary number of independent radio and even television stations), "has been one of the great bulwarks of Dominican democracy in recent years." Similarly, in Peru since 1980, the press has, quite rapidly, developed diverse ownership, political vigor, and relative independence. But with such rapid growth of a liberal press can come an open, free-swinging journalistic style that borders on the irresponsible or downright scandalous. Intense partisanship is one element of this phenomenon, as McClintock notes of Peru, where television news "tends to be less partisan and less prone to emphasize petty scandals than the press."[55] The impact of often intense partisanship on the otherwise democratic character of the press is a factor also mentioned in our studies of Colombia and Uruguay, and one that deserves more systematic comparative analysis.

It seems that our understanding of the role of the press in democracy is sufficient to permit us to see some current of hope for democratization in its growing pluralism and autonomy (at least at the level of elite publications) in Mexico and to view with alarm the deepening intimidation and fear surrounding the exercise of independent and especially investigative and critical journalism in Colombia. But we lack, in the social sciences, a good understanding of how a democratic press develops over time and articulates with other social and political institutions.[56]

Inequality, Class and other Cleavages

Issues of socioeconomic inequality and class structure figure prominently in the experiences with democracy of many of our cases. This is not surprising, given the well known levels of inequality in Latin America. But our analyses suggest that the relationship between inequality and democracy is considerably more complex than a simple negative correlation.

Historically, countries with the most rigidly stratified and severely unequal class structures proved least successful in developing any kind of democratic polity in the nineteenth and early twentieth centuries. Quasi-feudalistic patterns of land tenure and labor exploitation, and enormous concentrations of land and other forms of wealth, were forbidding obstacles. The failure to implement even moderate redistributive reforms heightened political instability, giving rise to violent revolution in Mexico and to polarized, politicized class cleavage in Peru. However, the impact of inequality on the possibility of democracy was mediated significantly, as we have argued, by political leadership and choice. As Valenzuela notes, agrarian society in Chile during the nineteenth century was also rigidly stratified, with great concentrations of land ownership and semifeudalistic landlord-peasant relations, persisting well into the twentieth century. What was most different in Chile was that economically privileged elites judged a gradual opening and democratization of the political system (and later, socioeconomic reform) to be in their interest. A similar judgment by the landed upper class in Argentina also led to experimental democratization, despite substantial inequality in land ownership; this political reform was made "cheaper," as Waisman notes, by the large numbers of recent immigrants lacking citizenship rights.

While substantial inequality was not necessarily incompatible with the development of democracy, it can certainly be argued that it was *less* conducive to democracy than was a more egalitarian social structure. The historic absence of *hacienda* agriculture and large landholdings in Costa Rica, and the shortage of agricultural labor that kept rural wages high, bred an egalitarian social culture and what Booth terms an "interdependence among classes" that clearly helped to foster the development of democratic political institutions. As the political system continued to open in the late nineteenth and twentieth centuries, social reform attenuated the effects of newly increasing inequality and so enhanced democratic legitimacy. In Colombia, Uruguay, and Costa Rica, the absence of a large class of landless laborers diminished the potential for radical class mobilization, just as the control of the major export crop (coffee) by an indigenous agrarian bourgeoisie reduced the potential for radical nationalist mobilization; both trends facilitated the emergence of oligarchical democracy.

The role of an emergent bourgeoisie in pressing for democratization and the limitation of state power in Latin America is an obvious and important issue for investigation. The case of Chile cautions against any simplistic analogies between the rise of democracy in Europe and its development in Latin America: In Chile, as elsewhere in the region, democratization preceded the emergence of a substantial urban bourgeoisie and was spawned instead by landed elites. In some cases, however, the rural elites who pushed forward democratization were not really aristocrats but more properly an agrarian bourgeoisie, as were the coffee planters in Costa Rica.

An equally rich area for comparative analysis concerns the rise of the working class and the way in which it became excluded from or incorporated into the political process. We have already cited the response to new social mobilization as a crucial factor in shaping the trajectory of political development in Latin America; the response to working class mobilization was often the most fateful. In Chile, open politics combined with repressive employment circumstances to produce class-based parties, the Communists and the Socialists, oriented to the electoral process. A similar development was probably aborted in Argentina by the 1930 coup, and subsequently by Perón's drastic reordering of the whole class structure through his dual strategy of state corporatism and radical protectionism. But the failure of his policies turned his strategy on its head, creating a highly mobilized and organized labor movement with great political autonomy and an undemocratic character. With its political role crystalized in this way, labor became a major player in the political and economic stalemate and instability that bedeviled Argentina during the 1950s, 1960s and 1970s. By contrast, in Colombia and Uruguay, with their established two-party structures, initial organization of the working class did not lead either to a corporatist or an independent unified labor organization, facilitating the tendency of the party system to cut across and diminish class cleavage. It was only later, as real wages declined precipitously during the 1960s and radical ideology flourished, that labor militancy and government repression polarized into a crisis that contributed to democratic breakdown in Uruguay.[57]

It is notable that the major political parties in Venezuela and Costa Rica also tend to cross-cut and soften class cleavages. To the extent this does not result in the effective exclusion of strategic social forces from the political process, it seems to be conducive to democracy. We do not wish to advance the proposition that more clearly class-based parties, as in Chile and Peru, are incompatible with democracy, but (to return to an earlier theme) the tendency of such party systems to fractionalization and polarization argues strongly for the flexibility and coalition-inducing features of a parliamentary system.

To conclude with some more contemporary evidence, our cases suggest a tension between extreme inequality and (or) class polarization on the one hand, and stable democracy on the other. The urgent need for "deconcentration" is a crucial element in Lamounier's analysis of the democratic prospect in Brazil, where inequality became especially severe and politically destabilizing during the country's rapid, post–World War II transformation from a predominantly rural and agricultural to a predominantly urban, industrial, and service economy. The marked failure to reduce inequality, Lamounier argues, was an important structural factor underlying the breakdown of democracy in 1964, as it denied the established parties strong bases of popular support and eroded the overall legitimacy of the political system, while at the same time subjecting that weakened system to a combination of pressures—tenacious rural clientelism and emerging urban radicalism and populism—that it could not manage. As Brazil has become even more urbanized and socially mobilized in the past two decades—while income inequality and, by some accounts, even absolute poverty have worsened despite the stunning economic growth under military rule—

deconcentration for democratic consolidation has become imperative. And yet policies to reduce inequality, such as land reform, carry serious political risks in the short run, while the reduction of absolute poverty requires sustained policy commitment over the long term that may be equally difficult to achieve politically. This, Lamounier maintains, is the inescapable structural dilemma facing Brazil's New Republic. The strains are evident, as we write, in the growth of urban labor militancy and strife, violent rural land conflicts, and growing electoral support for populist and Marxist parties and candidates.

Although quantitative data on income distribution in developing countries are difficult to come by and still riskier to assess and compare, World Bank evidence (from the 1970s) illustrates our general point. Table 1.2 shows that Peru and Brazil had the most unequal distributions of the seven cases for which we have data. Indeed, with the top tenth of households controlling half the total household income, Brazil's distribution was the most highly skewed at the top of the forty-six countries for which income distribution data are available. Looking at the percentage of household income accruing to the poorest 20 percent, Peru's income distribution stands out as the most unequal at the base of any of those forty-six countries, with Brazil (and Panama) next. With the apparent, notable exception of Uruguay, none of the other five countries in Table 1.2 ranks among the more equitable income distributions in the developing world, though income inequality is slightly more moderate in the other two democracies, Costa Rica and Venezuela. What is perhaps more telling is that in both of these cases, and Colombia as well, our authors identify substantial, persistent and even increasing inequalities of wealth and income as serious challenges to the maintenance (or for Colombia, reconsolidation) of stable democracy. Similarly, Wiarda finds the enduring legacy of extreme inequality one of the most

Table 1.2. Income Distribution for Selected Latin American Countries

		Percentage share of household income, by percentile groups of households					
	Year	Lowest 20 percent	Second quintile	Third quintile	Fourth quintile	Highest 20 percent	Highest 10 percent
Peru	1972	1.9	5.1	11.0	21.0	61.0	42.9
Costa Rica	1971	3.3	8.7	13.3	19.8	54.8	39.5
Brazil	1972	2.0	5.0	9.4	17.0	66.6	50.6
Mexico	1977	2.9	7.0	12.0	20.4	57.7	40.6
Argentina	1970	4.4	9.7	14.1	21.5	50.3	35.2
Venezuela	1970	3.0	7.3	12.9	22.8	54.0	35.7
Uruguay[a]	1976	4.8	10.5	15.6	22.8	46.4	30.1

Sources: *World Development Report 1988* (New York: Oxford University Press, 1988), Table 26, pp. 272–273; for Uruguay: Alberto Bensión and Jorge Caumont, *Política Económica y Distribución del Ingreso en el Uruguay 1970–76* (Montevideo: Acali, 1979), pp. 70 and 73.

[a] Average of the income distribution figures for Montevideo (which contains roughly half of Uruguay's population) and for four interior cities. Figures for the two population groups are similar.

disturbing obstacles to democratic consolidation in the Dominican Republic.

The overall degree of inequality is not the only measure of the problem; our cases also urge attention to two other, interrelated factors. First, there is some indication that expansion of the educated middle classes may also improve the social and cultural base for democracy, while softening and even perhaps mediating between the extremes of wealth and poverty. Our studies of Peru and the Dominican Republic suggest that the growth of urban professional and business classes, and even a middle peasantry in Peru, has shifted values and perceived interests in a democratic direction. At the same time, however, the cases of Argentina and Uruguay call for careful attention to the actual and perceived interests of middle-class groups, and to the rate of social mobility. The dependence of the industrial bourgeoisie on state protection from competition has vitiated much of its potential democratic character in Argentina, Waisman concludes. Lack of political autonomy is, in fact, a general problem for the industrial bourgeoisie (and for many other middle-class groups) throughout much of Latin America. Moreover, non-elite groups in general and perhaps middle-class groups in particular may assess social equity not so much in terms of equality of outcome as equality of opportunity. Where mobility aspirations become blocked by prolonged economic stagnation, this may result in radicalization of strategic groups, such as the intelligentsia, and sapping of legitimacy among the middle classes and the more well-to-do elements of the working class. This is the argument Waisman makes, we think persuasively, for Argentina, and it seems to apply to Uruguay as well. It also points to the fluidity in Brazil's class structure, and its high rate of spatial mobility among the lower classes, as safety valves that relieve somewhat the pressure of acute inequality.[58]

Ethnic and regional cleavage. Within the so-called "Third World," Latin America stands out for its high degree of cultural and linguistic homogeneity. Although racial divisions exist in Brazil and the Dominican Republic and correlate with socioeconomic inequality, they are not invested with the feelings of enmity and exclusion that have polarized political and social life in so many other multiracial societies. And though Argentina and Uruguay both absorbed large immigrant populations in the nineteenth and early twentieth centuries, these ethnic differences did not crystalize into separate identities but softened over time. Generally, the common bonds of Spanish language and Catholic faith provide a substantial degree of cultural homogeneity that is conducive to (at least in that it removes one potential obstacle to) democracy.

This generalization, however, must be qualified. As we observed earlier, regional cleavages have been historically important in many Latin American countries, and the balance of power and resources between center and periphery remains a contentious and difficult issue. Particularly in the Andean region, where the rugged topography has impeded integration, regional cleavages remain important. The problem is especially serious in Peru, where acute and deeply imbedded inequality has contributed to political polarization, producing not only growing support for the Marxist Left but also escalating guerrilla insurgency. As McClintock points out, a particular problem in Peru is that class, regional, and ethnic inequalities cumulate and overlap, even more so than in Brazil and to a degree that is unparalleled in South America. Although socioeconomic reform under the military regime did help middle- and lower-middle-class groups, it did not relieve the immense problems of land inequality, resource scarcity, and agonizing poverty in the remote southern highlands—the historic base of rebel movements, including Sendero Luminoso, and the home of indigenous Indian peoples whose culture, language, and folk religion separate them from white, urban, and middle-class Peru. As McClintock shows, the enduring instability of Peruvian politics, not to mention the immense difficulty of consolidating the new democracy, only come into focus when one appreciates the depth and cumulative nature of the divisions that separate the Indian peoples from the advantaged white minority—that eighth of the population descended from the Spanish conquerors that resides on the coast and controls the wealth and power of the country.

Socioeconomic Development

A central theme in much social science research on democracy has been the effort to link the stability and instability of democratic institutions to levels and patterns of economic development. Today even the wealthiest of Latin American countries lag behind most of the less developed European and some of the East Asian countries in economic development. This fact, however, should not lead to the simplistic conclusion that the breakdown of democracy can always be attributed in some way to underdevelopment. The chapters by Waisman and by Gillespie and González show how the two Plata countries achieved in the first decades of this century a high level of wealth, organization, education, social mobility, and, in the case of Uruguay, welfare state institutions. Argentina was ahead of a number of Southern European countries and was among the most privileged in the world when its democratic system was overthrown in 1930. Chile also enjoyed a period of prosperity, though based on a more precarious export mining base, yet it began to develop democratic institutions in the first half of the nineteenth century, when it was overwhelmingly rural and preindustrial, with low levels of literacy. Certainly these three countries of the Southern Cone were not and are not like the typical economically and socially less developed countries of Africa and Asia; they are even fundamentally different from a number of Andean (not to mention Central American) republics.

Argentina is perhaps the prime case of a country experiencing a prolonged period of stagnation, even periods of regression, and in this sense the title of our series, *Democracy in Developing Countries,* is misleading. Nor should we think that all Latin American countries have been lagging in economic development, as examination of the absolute rates of economic growth shows. Some of the explanation of the difference with non-American countries in their economic and social development has to be found in the rates of population growth. For example, at some point Spain and Mexico had almost the same population and identical growth rates of GDP and industrial production. But the radical difference in the rates of population growth contributed to different social conditions and, consequently, difficult problems.[59]

Although *latifundia* are an important factor in the agrarian structure of a number of countries, labor-intensive plantations, large holdings rented to poor tenants, and large cattle-raising estates represent different social structures with widely different political implications. We should be wary of aggregate economic explanations of the difficulties encountered in the process of democratization.

With this caution in mind, and with the assumption of a linear relationship between socioeconomic development and democracy quite obviously ruled out, what, if anything, can we conclude about the effect of socioeconomic development on democracy in Latin America? First, economic performance—in terms of steady, broadly distributed growth—is probably more important for democracy than a high level of socioeconomic development (measured either by per-capita income or productive structure).[60] We have noted repeatedly how prolonged economic stagnation and widespread frustration of mobility expectations undermined democracy in Argentina and Uruguay, and, through more sudden crisis, in Chile. On the other hand, democracy began taking shape at modest levels of development (compared to Europe) in these and other countries, such as Costa Rica.

Second, the process of socioeconomic development generates social changes that can potentially facilitate democratization, but this depends on how political elites respond to them. Urbanization, industrialization, educational expansion, increasing literacy, communication and transportation linkages, and so forth alter the social structure and the configuration of political actors and expectations. New classes and other functional groups arise, traditional political attachments erode, and new political interests demand expression and representation, partly as a means to pry rewards from the political system. These changes generate the basis, potentially, for a broader, more inclusive, legitimate, and stable democracy, but only if the newly mobilized social groups are meaningfully included. Such inclusion seems to involve two elements: access to political power, as a result of institutional expansion and adaptation, especially in the party system; and access to economic opportunity and rewards—more land, better jobs, health care, consumption goods, etc. *Ceteris paribus,* democracy has fared better in such countries as Venezuela and Costa Rica, where socioeconomic development has coincided with greater real political and social inclusion, than in other countries—such as Brazil and Peru, where inclusion (especially socioeconomic) has been much more limited.

Third, socioeconomic development does promote other changes that are conducive to democratization. Most notable here may be the growth of all types of social organizations and of the middle class, both of which, over time, appear to have helped to generate pressure for democratization in Mexico.[61] But again, the real contribution to democracy depends on many other factors: the political autonomy, productive base, and economic security of new middle-class groups; and the autonomy and internal governance of new social organizations. Where democracy is already in place, as in Costa Rica, Venezuela, and Chile at different times, socioeconomic development may at once generate these new social forces and shape them democratically, while also increasing the legitimacy of the system. But one need only cite the case of Chile to appreciate that such gains are not irreversible.

In summary, the contribution of socioeconomic development to democracy illustrates again the powerful and indeed inescapable mediating role of political leadership, choice, and institutionalization.

A brief examination of the development indicators in Table 1.3 illustrates some of our points. There is no striking relationship between our ten countries' (1985) per-capita GNP and their democratic status. Two of the highest income countries in Latin America—Argentina and Mexico—have respectively been highly unstable and stably authoritarian. Costa Rica, whose per-capita income is only slightly above the median for Latin American countries, has been the most stable democracy. Oil income, lifting Venezuela to unprecedented wealth in regional terms, has facilitated—but as Levine shows, by no means predetermined—that country's consolidation of democratic rule since 1958. Virtually all of our cases are by now predominantly urban societies and nonagricultural economies, and it is again democratic Costa Rica that is the least urban. A measure that reinforces our observations about inequality is the infant mortality rate. Not surprisingly, it is the countries with the greatest inequality—Peru, Brazil, the Dominican Republic, and Mexico—that have the highest infant mortality rates among our ten cases, and that also have had generally the least success with democracy in recent decades.

Economic Policies and Performance

From the varied experiences in Latin America, few would question the assumption that democratic regimes are stable only to the extent that there is broad and deep popular belief in their legitimacy. The salient question is what accounts for the presence of this system support, and for its erosion or disappearance. A primary factor, our authors repeatedly indicate, is the performance of the regime over time in delivering what people want and expect from government. A crucial (though by no means exclusive) dimension of this performance is economic.

Our cases suggest a strong correlation between the economic performance of democratic regimes in Latin America and their consolidation and persistence. As our chapters show, long-term economic expansions contributed significantly to the development and consolidation of democracy during the later nineteenth and early twentieth centuries in Chile, Argentina, and Uruguay. Sustained growth and high rates of social mobility helped to legitimate the emerging democratic order among a wide variety of social groups, including relatively

Table 1.3. Selected Development Indicators, 1965–1985

	Argentina 1965	Argentina 1985	Brazil 1965	Brazil 1985	Chile 1965	Chile 1985	Uruguay 1965	Uruguay 1985	Venezuela 1965	Venezuela 1985	Colombia 1965	Colombia 1985	Peru 1965	Peru 1985	Costa Rica 1965	Costa Rica 1985	Dominican Republic 1965	Dominican Republic 1985	Mexico 1965	Mexico 1985
Civil and Political Liberties, 1975 & 1987[a]	6	3	8	4	12	11	10	4	4	3	4	5	12	5	2	2	6	4	7	8
Population in Millions, 1966 & 1985	22.6	30.5	86.5	135.6	8.7	12.1	2.7	3.0	9.3	17.3	19.3	28.4	11.5	18.6	1.5	2.6	3.9	6.4	44.9	78.8
Population Growth Rate, 1973–1984		1.6		2.3		1.7		0.5		3.3		2.0		2.4		2.9		2.4		2.9
GNP per Capita in US Dollars,[b] 1966 & 1985	1010	2130	280	1640	740	1430	530	1650	880	3080	320	1320	470	1010	420	1300	260	790	490	2080
Average Annual Growth Rate, GNP per Capita, in Percent, 1965–1985		0.2		4.3		−0.2		1.4		0.5		2.9		0.2		1.4		2.9		2.7
Average Annual Rate of Inflation, 1965–1980, 1980–1985	78.5	342.8	31.6	147.7	129.9	19.3	57.7	44.6	8.7	9.2	17.5	22.5	20.5	98.6	11.2	36.4	6.6	14.6	13.2	62.6
Percent of Labor Force in Agriculture, 1965 & 1980	18	13	49	31	27	17	20	16	30	16	45	34	50	40	47	31	59	46	50	37
Life Expectancy at Birth Male	63	67	55	62	57	67	65	70	61	66	54	63	49	57	63	71	53	63	58	64
Life Expectancy at Birth Female	69	74	59	67	62	74	72	75	65	73	59	67	52	60	66	76	56	66	61	69
Infant Mortality Rate per 1000 Births	58	34	104	67	107	22	47	29	65	37	96	48	131	94	72	19	102	70	82	50
Adult Literacy Rate, 1960–1980	91	93	61	76	84	—	—	94	63	82	63	81	61	80	—	90	65	67	65	83
Percent Enrolled in Primary School	101	108	108	104	124	109	106	110	94	108	84	117	99	122	106	101	87	124	92	115
Percent Enrolled in Secondary School	28	70	16	35	34	69	44	70	27	45	17	50	25	65	24	41	12	50	17	55
Urban Population as Percent of Total	76	84	50	73	72	83	81	85	72	85	54	67	52	68	38	45	35	56	55	69
Total External Public Debt as Percentage of GNP, 1970 & 1986	8.4	46.2	8.2	31.9	25.8	101.2	11.3	46.4	6.6	50.5	18.5	36.6	12.3	45.0	13.8	90.1	15.7	52.5	9.1	62.6

[a] Combined score of civil and political liberties, each rated on a 1 to 7 scale with 1 being freest and 7 least free. A score of 5 or less (with a 2 on political rights) is regarded as "free," 6 to 11 as partly free, and 12 to 14 as "not free."
[b] GNP per capita is expressed in current U.S. dollars for each year. Comparison between 1966 and 1985 figures therefore is not controlled for (U.S.) inflation.
Sources: World Bank, *World Development Report 1983, 1987, 1988* (New York, Oxford University Press, 1983, 1987, 1988); World Bank, *World Tables 1987*, 4th ed. (Washington, DC: World Bank, 1987)

disadvantaged ones. Steady and broad improvement in popular well-being made an important contribution to the consolidation of a secure and popular democracy from 1948 in Costa Rica (with particularly impressive gains in quality of life measures) and from 1958 in Venezuela, until the economic crises of the 1980s.

The recurrent, now again current, nature of economic crisis in Latin America raises the question of how exactly economic performance is related to legitimacy over time. We find the evidence in this volume to be consistent with the argument that a long record of successful performance tends to build a large reservoir of legitimacy that can be drawn on in times of temporary crisis.[62] The case of Argentina casts some doubt in this regard, but as Waisman notes, the 1930 depression came at a time when democratic norms were still being institutionalized, and the abandonment of democracy then was an elite rather than mass phenomenon. In Uruguay, democratic breakdown followed two decades of continuous economic stagnation, decline, and crisis, over four successive administrations. And as we have seen, the democratic breakdowns in both Uruguay and Chile were not solely the product of economic crises, but, perhaps even more preeminently, of political polarization and decay brought on by disastrous leadership and deeply flawed political institutions.

As the new democracies of the Andes and the Southern Cone wind their way through one of their worst periods of economic crisis in this century, it is useful to keep in mind a corollary proposition about legitimacy and performance: New regimes are more vulnerable precisely because they lack a record of past achievements to which they may "point as proof of the regime's efficacy in the face of their presumably temporary failures."[63] The high stakes, the feeling of a need to produce quick and dramatic results, may help to explain the dramatic policy gambles of new democratic leaders like Alfonsín, García, and Sarney. These new democracies seem to have less time to ease and reverse the economic crisis than consolidated democracies such as Costa Rica and Venezuela. No one should dismiss casually McClintock's warning that the glaring economic failure of both of Peru's first two administrations risks a general discrediting of its new democratic regime, by associating democracy with economic disaster.

Economic policies. Although it is obviously beyond our scope here to treat in any depth the complex relationship among democracy, economic policy, and economic performance, a few generalizations merit attention. Moderation, prudence, and consistency appear to contribute to democratic success as much in economics as in politics. As Hartlyn emphasizes, Colombia has achieved one of the highest economic growth rates in the region over the past two decades, with relatively low inflation (see Table 1.3), by pursuing a moderate, stable mix of policies emphasizing simultaneously steady (but not spectacular) growth and the limitation of fiscal deficits and inflation. Countries following such a policy approach (including pre–oil boom Mexico and Venezuela), he notes, "have generally avoided extreme populist policies—with high inflation, extreme protectionism, dramatic wage increases and extensive fiscal deficits—or radical neoliberal ones—brusquely eliminating state subsidies and fiscal deficits, imposing massive devaluations, sharply curtailing wage increases, clamping down on the money supply, and slashing tariffs."

Many of our cases—notably Argentina, Chile, Peru, Uruguay, and, recently, Brazil—show the high costs to long-term economic vitality and political stability of abrupt and repeated swings between such policy extremes. Populist and radical protectionist economic policies, by ignoring the imperatives of fiscal responsibility and economic competitiveness and by confronting rather quickly (given the small domestic markets in most Latin American countries) the limits and contradictions of import-substituting industrialization, eventually make inevitable a swing toward radical austerity and liberalization measures. To the extent that the latter policies are pursued single-mindedly, however, they may depress popular wage levels and welfare to a degree that builds up irresistible pressure for a new burst of economic populism. As Waisman shows, once competing sets of economic interests and political actors converge around these policy extremes, it may be very difficult to break the debilitating pattern of cyclical alternation between them.

A related lesson of policy and strategy, only more recently being appreciated in the region, is the cost of excessive state expansion, employment, and regulation. As we suggested earlier, the tension between statism and democracy in Latin America derives not just from the intrinsically illiberal features of a domineering state but also from its economically stultifying consequences: inefficient use of capital and labor; unprofitable public enterprises; persistent fiscal deficits; corruption, inflation, and massive indebtedness. The shift toward leaner, more efficient state sectors and more competitive, export-oriented economies thus seems to be an important dimension of the democratic project in Latin America.

International Factors

Those who assume that the source of Latin America's political turmoil and democratic failures is primarily external—U.S. intervention and manipulation; economic dependence—may be disappointed with the historical analyses in this volume. Without exception, each of our authors attributes the course of political development and regime change primarily to internal structures and actions, while acknowledging the way structures have been shaped historically by international factors, such as the struggle for independence against the metropolis and the relations with the former motherlands. Nevertheless, international factors have had an impact, and at times a crucial one, on the experience of different regimes in Latin America.

We have already mentioned the role of international demonstration and diffusion. Successful democratic models in Europe and the United States influenced the choice of regimes, and even constitutions, among many Latin American elites during the nineteenth and early twentieth centuries. Waisman sees the growth of democracy in Argentina during this time partly as a conscious strategy by elites to attract West European capital and immigrants and to become integrated into a world economy dominated by democratic powers. Later, however, Argentine elites misunderstood and drew the wrong lessons from the experiences of the Spanish Civil War and Italian fascism, exaggerating the danger of revolution and the need for state corporatist controls.

Demonstration effects have perhaps been especially potent among Latin American countries. The Cuban revolution reverberated powerfully throughout the entire region, inspiring other leftist, revolutionary movements and escalating the Right's fear of revolutionary, Marxist movements and parties. Similarly, the Brazilian military coup of 1964 and the subsequent technocratic-repressive "economic miracle" may have helped to inspire other right-wing, technocratic military interventions, especially in Uruguay and Chile. Alternatively, one may view the overall context of political trends in the region as a salient influence for or against democracy. Gillespie speaks of "the continent-wide contagion of military intervention" as one factor promoting military role expansion in Uruguay in the early 1970s,[64] while the current regional context of "democratic contagion" appears to exert at least some modest pressure for the perpetuation of democracy in such unstable settings as Peru, for the return to democracy in Chile, and for the inauguration of democracy in Paraguay.

Our case studies do not reveal economic dependence to be a primary factor behind the lack of success with democracy in Latin America. To be sure, Latin American countries do have high levels of economic dependence, as reflected in the degree to which their prospects for economic growth are externally determined. Given the relationship between economic performance and democratic (or regime) stability, this can have important political consequences. The economies of Latin America are acutely vulnerable to the cycles in the global economy, and particularly in their largest trading partner, the United States. In stressing the role of the Great Depression in Uruguay's 1933 coup, Gillespie and González observe, "Between 1930 and 1936 only *two* countries managed to retain their political stability in Latin America." Moreover, several countries are highly dependent on the export earnings of one or two commodities whose prices on world markets are notoriously volatile: Colombia and Costa Rica (coffee), the Dominican Republic (sugar), Chile (copper), Venezuela and Mexico (oil). The new export commodity boom in cocaine and marijuana has not yet seen the same price collapse, but it has distorted the social and political structures of Colombia and Peru, and, increasingly, other Latin American countries, in devastating ways. Such factors do not make democracy impossible, but they certainly complicate the task of political leaders who seek to consolidate and maintain democratic rule.

Today, the steepest international challenge to democracy emanates from a different form of economic dependence: external indebtedness. During the

1970s and early 1980s, external public debt in our ten cases exploded from about 10–15 percent of GNP to 35, 50, even 90 percent in the case of Costa Rica (see Table 1.3). Total external debt in Latin America mushroomed from $27 billion in 1970 to $370 billion by the end of 1984.[65] After four more years of debt crisis management and renegotiation, that figure had reached $401 billion by the end of 1988. Virtually all of the new democracies in Latin America, and most of the existing ones, have been suffering a prolonged economic crisis throughout the 1980s, as huge debt service payments (representing a third to a half of export earnings in many cases) have diverted the resources needed to finance new investment and even to maintain the existing levels of health and education. Lamounier's observation for Brazil is broadly relevant throughout the region: "Massive transfer of real resources abroad to meet disproportionate debt obligations strangles the country's effort to promote growth and aggravates already intractable political problems at home." Certainly no one can assess the prospect for the new democracies of Argentina, Brazil, Uruguay, Peru, and the Dominican Republic (along with others not represented in this volume) without giving due weight to the tremendously destabilizing implications of the debt crisis, and the general economic depression throughout the region. Whether these debts are restructured or relieved in a way that provides democratic leaders more scope for policy maneuver and their countries more opportunity for economic growth may have much to do with whether the new democracies become consolidated, and whether stable democracies like Costa Rica remain stable.

U.S. policy. Almost two centuries of conflict, tension, intervention, and even in some cases invasion and occupation have left Latin Americans extremely wary of their giant neighbor to the north and inclined to see behind every political and economic debacle in their countries the hand of "Yankee imperialism." This suspicion is as exaggerated as it may be unavoidable. With the exception of direct, military interventions—for example, the 1965 invasion of the Dominican Republic to quash a democratic revolution (which sought to restore the elected reformer, Juan Bosch, to the presidency after a military coup)—the United States has typically been able to do no more than influence events. Historically, U.S. influence and control has been greatest in Central America and the Caribbean, but even there it is waning (witness the stunning failure of the Reagan administration's efforts to force General Manuel Noriega from power in Panama).

In assessing the effect of deliberate U.S. policies on democracy in Latin America, one must consider both their direction and their effectiveness. With few exceptions, most U.S. presidents have been quite comfortable with and supportive of such pro–U.S. dictators as Trujillo, Somoza, and Pérez Jiménez, and have even been willing to conspire against or sabotage popularly elected regimes that seemed threatening.[66] The Kennedy administration failed to produce the moderate democratic regime it had sought in the Dominican Republic, but substantial U.S. assistance was instrumental in helping the vulnerable young democracy in Colombia stay afloat economically during the early 1960s, while in Venezuela strong U.S. political and diplomatic support "helped allay conservative fears and restrain potential military conspirators."[67] Elsewhere, until the late 1970s, U.S. policy did little to support democracy in Latin America, abiding and abetting military regimes in Brazil, Argentina, Uruguay, and Chile, and withholding needed economic assistance from the elected government of Belaúnde in Peru during the mid-1960s because of commercial disputes.

More recently, U.S. policy has seemed to tilt more decisively toward promotion of democracy. Human rights pressure from the Carter administration (as well as several European democracies) did not in itself bring down authoritarian rule in Argentina, but Waisman judges that it "saved many victims of indiscriminate repression in the late 1970s and was a factor in the international isolation of the regime." Perhaps much more crucial was the forceful role the Carter administration played in 1978 in preempting electoral fraud by the armed forces of the Dominican Republic—against the presidential candidate of the same (albeit now more moderate) democratic, populist PRD whom U.S. troops had stopped from returning to power in 1965! More recently, massive economic assistance from the United States has helped Costa Rica's democracy to wade through and recover from the severe recession of the 1980s while easing the harsh effects of economic adjustment policies.

The U.S. impact on democracy in Latin America has thus varied with the policy intentions and priorities of administrations. When it has wanted to, the United States has been able to assist the cause of democracy in the region, but only when there have been democratic forces and institutions able to make effective use of that assistance.

• THE DEMOCRATIC PROSPECT •

Democracy has returned to Latin America in less than auspicious circumstances. The 1980s have seen the entire region mired in the most profound and prolonged period of economic and social decline since the Great Depression of the 1930s. Abraham Lowenthal has observed:

> The statistics on Latin America's distress are stark. Production per capita has fallen about 7 to 8 percent since 1980 and real income per capita has dropped by as much as 10 percent, if the terms of trade effects are considered. Individual income has regressed to 1977 levels; a full decade of growth has been lost. In many countries—including Argentina, Bolivia, Chile and Peru—per capita income has declined to levels of the early to mid-1960's. As petroleum exporters, Mexico, Venezuela and Ecuador benefited from the oil-fueled expansion of the 1970s, but all three countries were then severely affected by the drop in oil prices. Of the 20 largest countries in Latin America, only Brazil and Colombia avoided an economic disaster in the mid 1980's, and Brazil's strong economic recovery faltered badly in 1987.
>
> Rates of unemployment and underemployment remain high in many countries, upward of 40 percent in some. Hardships caused by unemployment and low wages have been compounded by deep cuts in public expenditures for health, housing, education and social security. Malnutrition is worsening in some nations, and infant mortality is on the rise.[68]

Such levels of decline, distress, and suffering cannot persist indefinitely without gravely damaging democratic institutions and norms.[69] As economic misery deepens, pressure increases from democratic interest groups and publics for some kind of solution, and the temptations of a short-term populist fix become difficult to resist. Among the most ominous economic statistics for Latin America in the 1980s was the doubling of inflation during 1988 to a staggering regional average of 470 percent, what the UN Economic Commission for Latin America (ECLA) termed "a new historical high in the region."[70] Newly restored democracies have been particularly hard hit: Peru's inflation rate reached 1,300%, Brazil's 800%, Argentina's 370%. Regional economic growth slowed to 0.7%, falling behind population growth for the first time in six years. A central factor in both trends, ECLA observed, was the crippling burden of foreign debt service obligations, which ate up record export earnings for the region while also inducing many governments to run up inflationary fiscal deficits to make debt payments.[71]

The devastating effects of foreign indebtedness underscore the need for international assistance and flexibility if Latin American countries are to renew economic growth and consolidate and maintain democratic government. Initiatives—transformation of short-term obligations into very long-term ones, swapping of debt for equity, reduction in interest rates—are needed from creditor countries and institutions that will diminish debt service obligations and enable countries to begin investing resources again in human and physical capital.[72] At the same time, the United States and other industrialized nations must move to reduce trade barriers and maintain open markets if new strategies of export-oriented growth are to have any chance of succeeding in Latin America.

This is not to ignore, however, the large and predominant responsibility for the democratic prospect in the region that lies with Latin Americans themselves, at all levels. Throughout this introduction, we have noted numerous institutional deficiencies that threaten the stability of democracy. Streamlining of state structures, reassertion of state authority and the rule of law, subordination of the military, administrative decentralization, party building, invigoration of legislative and judicial institutions, and constitutional reform are essentially political challenges. Whether they are met effectively will depend on the capacity, courage, judgment, and values of domestic political actors. Even those sociopolitical challenges complicated by international economic crisis—reduction of inequality, incorporation of marginal groups, management of class conflict, defeat of insurgency, and reduction of still very high rates of population growth—cannot be resolved without effective political leadership and action. And of course, whatever international economic actors may do, the resumption of economic growth in Latin America will also heavily depend on domestic policy choices and implementation.

At this juncture, democracy in Latin America is everywhere in pain. In Colombia—where the reconstruction of state coherence, judicial integrity, and the rule of law is, as Hartlyn notes, an urgent imperative—the agonizing quest for pacification has rarely seemed more unlikely and more illusive," and the stability of democracy has declined to the point where its collapse is not inconceivable.[73] All of the newly restored democracies remain vulnerable. Peru's is particularly so, and the further economic and security deterioration during the term of Alan García could make the 1990 presidential election the last chance for democrats to produce an effective response. Even as the world awaits with renewed hope the end of authoritarian rule in Chile, the prospect of new democratic breakdowns in Latin America during the 1990s cannot be dismissed.

Yet, there are also reasons for cautious optimism about the prospects for new democracies such as Argentina, Uruguay, Brazil, and (prospectively) Chile.[74] The performance of the authoritarian regimes, particularly in Argentina, has weakened the potential appeal of military rule. In contrast with that rule, democracy has gained renewed legitimacy, even when it confronts serious unsolvable problems and shows low efficacy. At the same time, the hopes for revolutionary change kindled by the Cuban revolution and even by the far away model of China—so disturbing in the 1960s to democracies and appealing to certain intellectuals, students and younger generations—have faded.[75] In addition, one should not discount the positive effect on the momentum and strength of democracy in Latin America that would derive from the development of democracy in Mexico—a prospect that, while it would be unprecedented, must no longer be dismissed. And democratic spirits in the region may also be boosted by the overthrow in February 1989 of the hemisphere's longest serving dictator, General Alfredo Stroessner of Paraguay.

Democracy might not be the ideal regime and it might not be able to solve all problems, but we suspect the fate of most of the new democracies of Latin America will be to make their present democratic institutions work as well as possible. Our perspective, which is probabilistic, assumes that people have the opportunity and the choice to make institutions work, to improve them, and to make necessary social changes within a peaceful democratic framework. However, we should stress once more that politics is only part of the life of a society, and that its success in facing the economic and social problems and the technological and scientific revolution in changing societies depends ultimately on the society, not exclusively on political institutions. Neither the state nor the political process—nor, obviously, democracy—can assure a good life for everyone. That sobering realization should contribute to the stability of democracy in the Iberoamerican world.

INTRODUCTION   53

• NOTES •

We are deeply indebted to our coeditor, Seymour Martin Lipset, and the authors of the case studies in this volume for their numerous detailed and very valuable comments and suggestions on an earlier draft of this introduction.
    1. It is beyond our scope here to offer a thorough theoretical interpretation of the enormous quantity of evidence and analysis in our ten case studies. For a treatment of the evidence in a wider and more systematic theoretical and comparative perspective, we refer the reader to Volume 1 in this series, which examines the evidence from all twenty-six of our cases.
    2. In fact, some scholars, such as Octavio Paz and Richard Morse, argue that the Spanish period cannot strictly be considered colonial since the "kingdoms" of the Indies were part of the crown with the same status as those of Castile and Leon, and only the French-inspired administrative reforms of Charles III around 1760 introduced a centralized "colonial" system. Independence for the Indians deprived them of the tutelage of the church and state, giving the landowning oligarchies a measure of absolute power that would exceed even the dreams of the conquistadors. See for example Richard M. Morse, "The Heritage of Latin America," in Louis Hartz, ed., *The Founding of New Societies,* (New York: Harcourt, Brace & World, 1964), pp. 123–177.
    3. On the role of the monarchy in helping to avoid a "crisis of legitimacy" during periods of democratization in Europe, see Seymour Martin Lipset, *Political Man* (Baltimore: Johns Hopkins University Press, 1981), pp. 65–66.
    4. Data are from Alejandro Bunge and Carlos Muta, quoted by M. Hernandez Sanchez-Barba, "Los Estados de America en los Siglos XIX y XX," in Jaime Vicens Vives, *Historia Social y Economica de España y America* (Barcelona, Teide, 1959) vol. IV, p. 532.
    5. Carlos A. Floria and Cesar A. Garcia Belsunce, *Historia Politica de la Argentina contemporanea 1880-1983* (Madrid: Alianza, 1988), devote many pages to the difficulties due to geopolitical, economic, ideological and international factors in consolidating Argentine statehood. The reading of this historical record is fundamental to understand the building of civil political institutions, and the role of the military, in the period from independence to modern democracy.
    6. Richard Morse puts it very well: "In one case 'e pluribus unum' in the other 'ex uno plures,'" ("The Heritage of Latin America," p. 161).
    7. In a few countries, however, such as Colombia and Brazil, power was less concentrated in a single center or capital.
    8. The complex relationship between federalism and centralism in the building of democracies in large territorial expanses like the United States and Australia has not been incorporated sufficiently into analyses (including perhaps our own) of Latin American politics, though there is an extensive literature on the problem, especially in Brazil.
    9. See, for example, Carlos Escudé, *La Argentina vs. Las Grandes Potencias* (Buenos Aires: Editorial Belgrano, 1986); "Argentine Territorial Nationalism," *Journal of Latin American Studies* 20: 139–165; and "Contenido nacionalista de la enseñanza de la geografía en le República Argentina 1879-1986." Paper presented at a seminar organized by EURAL and the University of Warwick, on "Las Relaciones Anglo-Argentinas despues del Conflicto de Atlántico Sur," Buenos Aires; April 19–21, 1988.
    10. Peru may merit mention in this regard; it did develop an elite democracy, the Aristocratic Republic, at the turn of the century (1895–1919) but failed to institutionalize it.
    11. For a theoretical and wider comparative treatment of elite settlements as a route to stable democracy, see Michael G. Burton and John Higley, "Elite Settlements," *American Sociological Review* 52 (June 1987): 295–307.
    12. Robert Dahl, *Polyarchy: Participation and Opposition* (New Haven: Yale University Press, 1971), pp. 33–36.
    13. See in particular Leonard Binder, et al., *Crises and Sequences in Political Development* (Princeton: Princeton University Press, 1971). Our Latin American cases also fit substantially (though not perfectly) Rustow's model of the historical process of transition to democracy, which presumes a background condition of national unity, then "is set off by a prolonged and inconclusive political struggle," which in turn is concluded or resolved by "a deliberate decision on the part of political leaders . . . to institutionalize some crucial aspect of democratic procedure," marking the start of a democratization process that is consolidated in a "habituation" phase. The correspondence of this sequence to the historical development of oligarchical democracies in Latin America is especially striking given that Rustow developed his model with reference to the experiences of Europe,

North America, and Turkey. See Dankwart Rustow, "Transitions to Democracy: Toward a Dynamic Model," *Comparative Politics* 2, no. 3 (April 1970): 337–363.

14. Our evidence thus strongly supports Lipset's early argument that "easy access to the *legitimate* political institutions tends to win the loyalty of the new groups to the system," but "political systems which deny new strata access to power except by revolution inhibit the growth of legitimacy by introducing millennial hopes into the political arena." *Political Man*, p. 67.

15. John A. Booth and Mitchell A. Seligson, "The Political Culture of Authoritarianism in Mexico: A Reexamination," *Latin American Research Review* 19, no. 1 (1984): 106–124; and Susan Tiano, "Authoritarianism and Political Culture in Argentina and Chile in the Mid-1960s," *Latin American Research Review* 21, no. 1 (1986): 73–98.

16. See, for example, Gabriel A. Almond and Sidney Verba, *The Civic Culture* (Princeton: Princeton University Press, 1963), p. 14.

17. Rustow, "Transition to Democracy," p. 360.

18. Our brief reference to political culture would be incomplete if we were to ignore the impact on the elites in the last hundred years of the Ibero-American thinkers—the ensayistas Sarmiento, Martí, Rodó, Vasconcelos, Mariátegui, Martinez Estrada, Eyzaguirre, Zea, and Octavio Paz among others—who have attempted to answer the questions derived from the confrontation of their societies with modernity, industrialism, capitalism, science, and positivism, the diffusion of political institutions and values from Europe and Anglo-Saxon America. In what ways this rich intellectual output has contributed to the crisis or success of political change toward democracy is too complex a problem to be discussed here but certainly deserves serious attention. Sol Serrano, "America latina y el mundo moderno en alguno ensayistas latinoamericanos," *Opciones* (Septiembre-Diciembre 1984), pp. 56–100, presents an overview of this literature with useful bibliographic references.

19. Juan J. Linz, "O Integralismo e o fascismo internacional," *Revista do Instituto de Filosofia e Ciencias Humanas,* Universidad Federal de Rio Grande do Sul (1977): 136–143.

20. For an analysis of the "revalorization of politics and of democracy" and the "demystification of the myth of revolution" on the intellectual Left in Latin America, and contending perspectives, see Robert Barros, "The Left and Democracy: Recent Debates in Latin America," *Telos* 68 (1986): 49–70.

21. Charles G. Gillespie and Luis Eduardo González, "Uruguay: The Survival of Old and Autonomous Institutions," in this volume.

22. For a detailed analysis of the 1988 Chilean plebiscite and its political implications, see Pamela Constable and Arturo Valenzuela, "The Chilean Plebiscite: Defeat of a Dictatorship," *Current History* 89, no. 536 (March 1989).

23. This phenomenon has been demonstrated in some detail by Charles Gillespie in "The Breakdown of Democracy in Uruguay: Alternative Political Models," Working Paper No. 143, Latin American Program, The Wilson Center, Washington, DC, 1984 (see especially pp. 27–28).

24. Seymour Martin Lipset, *The First New Nation: The United States in Comparative and Historical Perspective* (New York: W.W. Norton, 1979), especially pp. 16–23.

25. John A. Peeler, *Latin American Democracies: Colombia, Costa Rica, Venezuela* (Chapel Hill: University of North Carolina Press, 1985), p. 73.

26. Ibid., p. 74.

27. Arturo Valenzuela, "Chile: Origins, Consolidation, and Breakdown of a Democratic Regime," in this volume.

28. Again, for a detailed account and analysis of this breakdown, see Gillespie, "Breakdown of Democracy in Uruguay."

29. Juan J. Linz and Alfred Stepan, eds., *The Breakdown of Democratic Regimes* (Baltimore: Johns Hopkins University Press, 1978).

30. See, for example, Charles G. Gillespie, "Prospects for Democratic Consolidation in Brazil and the Southern Cone: Beyond Political Disarticulation," *Third World Quarterly* 11, no. 2 (April 1989). Riordan Roett similarly attributes the failure to relieve Brazil's deepening internal economic crisis in 1988 to the weakness of political leadership: "There is no one willing or able to make the tough decisions required to confront the entrenched economic interests who wield tremendous clout in Brazil's byzantine political system." Roett, "Brazil's Transition to Democracy," *Current History* 89, no. 536 (March 1989): 149.

31. Vargas did introduce constitutional reforms including corporatist components in an authoritarian framework, but his abandonment of the Estado Novo ultimately showed that the constitutional traditions were too strong to displace.

32. Chilean parties and party system are the most similar to the European in ideology and organization.

33. Samuel P. Huntington, *Political Order in Changing Societies* (New Haven: Yale University Press, 1968), pp. 12–24.

34. Legislative seats are allotted by proportional representation, first between parties and then among rival factions within parties. In the presidential election, the winner is the candidate with the most votes from the party with the most votes, even if that candidate—like Bordaberry in 1971—fails to win a plurality (much less a majority) of the overall vote.

35. Gillespie, "Breakdown of Democracy in Uruguay," pp. 23–26. As Hartlyn observes comparatively, and Valenzuela emphasizes for the case of Chile, "Clientelism and patronage are an essential 'glue' in otherwise ideologically polarized party systems, but when they become entrenched at a national level in countries without such ideological parties, they can lead to devastating consequences, as in Colombia, Uruguay, and the Dominican Republic." Private communication from Jonathan Hartlyn.

36. Juan J. Linz, *The Breakdown of Democratic Regimes: Crises, Breakdowns and Reequilibrations* (Baltimore: Johns Hopkins University Press, 1978), pp. 71–74; and Linz, "Democracy: Presidential or Parliamentary. Does It Make a Difference?" Paper presented to the Workshop on "Political Parties in the Southern Cone," Wilson Center, Washington, DC, 1984.

37. Gillespie, "Breakdown of Democracy in Uruguay," p. 19.

38. At the same time, however, it could be argued that the often-noted weakness of these parties may be in part the *result* of the presidential system, which does not force legislators to realize the consequences of their actions. Further, it should be emphasized that we have in mind here precisely those modern forms of parliamentarism that have introduced innovations (like the constructive vote of no confidence of the German and Spanish constitutions) that compel legislators to behave more responsibly.

39. We are grateful to Jonathan Hartlyn for emphasizing this point to us.

40. See, for example, William R. Long, "'Law of Gun' Endangers Colombian Justice System," *Los Angeles Times,* February 5, 1989, pp. 1, 14–15. Long concludes: "Colombian courts are a shambles. Murder, threats, bribery, inefficiency and under-funding have broken down the justice system, virtually giving legal immunity to growing hordes of killers and drug traffickers and other criminals." In addition to the eleven Supreme Court justices killed in a 1985 terrorist assault, thirty-six judges have been assassinated since the late 1970s. Judges are poorly trained, overburdened with heavy caseloads, and "desperately short on clerical and investigative help." A constitutional amendment expected to pass in 1989 would establish, for the first time, a public prosecutor's office; a new judicial police corps was created in 1987 to help judges with criminal investigations, but pervasive intimidation has effectively prevented any of the murderous drug lords from being brought to justice. Another recent analysis thus concludes: "Restoring the judicial system and reviving popular faith in it is the only way Colombia can save itself—not only from the mafia but from all the forms of violence that are destroying the country." Tina Rosenberg, "Colombia, Murder City," *The Atlantic,* November 1988, p. 30.

41. Gary W. Wynia, "Campaigning for President in Argentina," *Current History* 89, no. 536 (March 1989): 133.

42. Gillespie, "Breakdown of Democracy in Uruguay," p. 25.

43. Hernando De Soto has shown this in detail in *El Otro Sendero* (Lima: El Barranco, 1986).

44. The March 1988 local elections brought 55 percent of the 11 million eligible voters to the polls to select 1,009 mayors and 10,000 municipal representatives. The democratic significance of this development was seriously marred, however, by escalating political violence, directed in particular at the left-wing Unión Patriótica. Twenty-nine of the UP's 87 mayoral candidates and over 100 UP candidates for municipal councils were killed during the six months before the election. John D. Martz, "Colombia's Search for Peace," *Current History* 88, no. 536 (March 1989): 145. See also the discussion in Hartlyn's chapter.

45. On this important distinction between the military as government and the military institution, see Alfred Stepan, *Rethinking Military Politics: Brazil and the Southern Cone* (Princeton: Princeton University Press), p. 30.

46. For an analysis of "sultanistic regimes" as a particular, personalistic form of authoritarian rule, see Juan J. Linz, "Totalitarian and Authoritarian Regimes," *Handbook of Political Science, Vol. 3: Macropolitical Theory,* Fred I. Greenstein and Nelson W. Polsby, eds. (Reading, Mass.: Addison-Wesley, 1975), pp. 259–263.

47. Alain Rouquié, "Democratization and the Institutionalization of Military-dominated

Polities in Latin America," in Guillermo O'Donnell, Philippe C. Schmitter, and Laurence Whitehead, eds., *Transitions From Authoritarian Rule: Comparative Perspectives* (Baltimore: Johns Hopkins University Press, 1986), p. 111.

48. Ibid., p. 108.

49. Ibid.

50. For some theoretical insights into those processes, we refer the reader to S. E. Finer's classic *The Man on Horseback: The Role of the Military in Politics* (New York: Frederick A. Praeger, 1962), and the seminal analysis of the new professionalism by Stepan, *Rethinking Military Politics*. See also Alain Rouquie, *L'etat militaire en Amerique latine* (Paris: Editions du Seuil, 1982), Gianfranco Pasquino, *Militari e Potere in America Latina* (Bologna: Il Mulino, 1974), Genaro Arriagada, *El pensamiento politico de los militares* (Santiago de Chile: Centro de Investigaciones Socioeconomicas (CISEC) de la Compañia de Jesus, private edition, 1981), and by the same author, *La Politica Militar de Pinochet* (Santiago de Chile, n.p., 1985).

51. Wynia, "Campaigning for President in Argentina," pp. 136, 144. About the December 1988 military rebellion, Wynia observes, "Alfonsín insisted that no concessions had been made, but a week later (after the rebellion ended) military wages were increased by 20 percent" (p. 144).

52. Stepan, *Rethinking Military Politics*, pp. 72–75.

53. Stepan, *Rethinking Military Politics*, especially Chapter 8. Quoted passages are from pages 138 (emphasis in the original) and 139.

54. Philippe Schmitter and Guillermo O'Donnell, *Transitions From Authoritarian Rule: Tentative Conclusions about Uncertain Democracies* (Baltimore: Johns Hopkins University Press, 1986).

55. Private communication from Cynthia McClintock, who stated, "Although television is more vulnerable to economic pressures in Peru than the press is, both from large businessmen and the state—and thereby tends to exclude the Marxist Left more than the print media (where the Marxist Left and until recently Sendero Luminoso had their own newspapers)—overall, television has been a tremendous asset to democracy in Peru, playing a crucial role in getting key information out to the lower classes."

56. Much is being written, however, on the role of the press in particular democracies. See, for example, Kenneth Maxwell, ed., *The Press and the Rebirth of Iberian Democracy* (Westport, CT: Greenwood Press, 1983), and Helmut Bischoff, *Die Spanische Presse in Redemokratisierungsprozess* (Bochum, Germany: Dr. N. Brockmeyer, 1986).

57. Gillespie, "Breakdown of Democracy in Uruguay," p. 8. For a detailed, comparative historical analysis of the initial incorporation of labor and its implications for subsequent political development in eight Latin American countries, see Ruth Berins Collier and David Collier, *Shaping the Political Arena: Critical Junctures, the Labor Movement, and Regime Dynamics in Latin America* (Princeton: Princeton University Press, forthcoming). We regret that our own book on Latin America was completed before we were able to consider the extraordinarily rich analysis and findings of the Colliers' pathbreaking work.

58. To put it another way, as long as there is rapid economic progress inequality might not have destructive political consequences. On this point see Albert O. Hirschman, "The Changing Tolerance for Income Inequality in the Course of Economic Development," in *Essays in Trespassing: Economics to Politics and Beyond* (Cambridge: Cambridge University Press, 1981), pp. 39–58.

59. The following figures illustrate what we mean: In 1900 the population of Spain was 18.6 million, that of Mexico 13.6; in 1930 in Spain 23.7 million and in 1937 in Mexico 18.7 million (the slow growth was due to the terrible toll of the revolutionary wars). In subsequent years the populations of Spain and Mexico were, respectively, 28.1 and 25.7 million in 1950, 33.9 and 48.2 million in 1970, and 37.9 and 73.1 million in 1982. The crude birth rate (births per 1000) in Spain was 34.9 in 1901 and 15.1 in 1980, while the Mexican figure for 1980 was 35.3. The fecundity (live births per 1000 women in the age group 15-49) in 1970 was 81 in Spain and 223 in Mexico. Data from the National Statistical Yearbooks.

60. There is little relationship among our ten cases between stability of democracy and level of development. This may in part be an artifact of our excluding the poorest and least democratic countries of the region from our selection of cases. However, a recent statistical analysis across numerous measures of democracy and over several points in time shows that the relationship between socioeconomic development and democracy holds much more strongly for the subset of advanced industrial countries than for Latin American countries (among which the association is often

INTRODUCTION 57

not statistically significant, and substantially more of the variance in levels of democracy is left unexplained by economic development variables). Glaúcio Ary Dillon Soares, "Economic Development and Democracy in Latin America." Paper presented at the Fourteenth World Congress of the International Political Science Association, August 28–September 1, 1988, Washington, DC.

61. The Mexican case is distinctive, as Levy shows, in that many of the factors we may associate theoretically with democracy have been supportive of undemocratic stability in Mexico, while producing societal modernization that, in the long run, has built pressure for democratization.

62. Lipset, *Political Man,* pp. 61–71.

63. Linz, *Breakdown of Democratic Regimes,* p. 21.

64. Gillespie, "Breakdown of Democracy in Uruguay," p. 29.

65. Abraham F. Lowenthal, *Partners in Conflict: The United States and Latin America* (Baltimore: Johns Hopkins University Press, 1987), p. 11.

66. For an analysis of "political development doctrines" in U.S. foreign policy between 1947 and 1968, and the frequent conflict between the goals of fighting the expansion of communism and promoting democracy abroad, see Robert Packenham, *Liberal America and the Third World: Political Development Ideas in Foreign Aid and Social Science* (Princeton: Princeton University Press, 1973). On the evolution of the Kennedy administration's foreign policy concerns with democracy, see especially pp. 69–75. For a broad survey of U.S.-Latin American relations since the 1950s and consideration of possible new directions, see Lowenthal, *Partners in Conflict.* For an innovative analysis of how a shift in U.S. policy toward "realistic multilateralism" could help promote democracy in Latin America, see Robert A. Pastor, "Securing a Democratic Hemisphere," *Foreign Policy* no. 73 (Winter 1988–89), pp. 41–59.

67. Daniel Levine, "Venezuela: The Nature, Sources, and Future Prospects of Democracy," in this volume.

68. Abraham F. Lowenthal, "The United States and South America," *Current History* 87, no. 525 (January 1988): 2–3.

69. As this chapter was going to press, the explosive political implications of Latin America's prolonged, debt-related economic crises were vividly demonstrated in Venezuela, one of the region's oldest and most stable democracies. At the end of February 1989, newly elected President Carlos Andrés Pérez's announcement of stiff austerity measures (sharply increasing fuel and public transportation prices) ignited widespread rioting and looting that left over 300 people dead and hundreds more wounded and led Pérez to impose emergency measures suspending constitutional rights regarding arrest and arraignment. The protests appear to have been fed both by pent-up frustration of many Venezuelans, who have seen average real wages fall 38 percent since 1983, and by the perception that the I.M.F. was dictating the new austerity policies. See the articles by Alan Riding and Mark A. Uhlig in the *New York Times,* especially March 1, pp. 1 and 6.

70. "Latin Inflation Hits 470%," *Los Angeles Times,* December 21, 1988, part 4, p. 5.

71. Ibid. The ECLA report, released December 20, 1988, reported an increase in the region's exports from $90 billion in 1987 to a record $102 billion in 1988. The low combined growth rate for the region, it said, was most heavily influenced by virtual stagnation in Brazil, Mexico, and Argentina. The combined effect of stagnation and inflation led to a decline in the purchasing power of the minimum wage in nine of the eleven countries for which data was available.

72. Among the recent penetrating studies of the debt crisis in Latin America, its relationship to democracy, and possible policy alternatives are Robert A. Pastor, ed., *Latin America's Debt Crisis: Adjusting to the Past or Planning for the Future?* (Boulder: Lynne Rienner Publishers, 1987); Pedro-Pablo Kuczynski, *Latin American Debt* (Baltimore: Johns Hopkins University Press, 1988); Robert Wesson, ed., *Coping with the Latin American Debt* (New York: Praeger, 1988); and Barbara Stallings and Robert Kaufman, eds., *Debt and Democracy in Latin America* (Boulder: Westview Press, 1989).

73. Martz, "Colombia's Search for Peace," p. 147. Particularly ominous in Colombia have been the rise of right-wing death squads, the expansion of the military's role conception, and growing links between elements of these two groups and the drug traffickers. Martz reports that leading military figures have of late been openly advocating a military solution as the only course of action. "Few Colombians," Martz concludes, believed by the end of 1988 "that the armed forces were on the brink of overturning the constitutional system," but the growing "violence underlined the fragility of civilian rule, the restiveness of the military, and the prospects that the government and the guerillas might be facing another decade of killings" (pp. 127, 147).

74. At the time of this writing, the complex process of transition from authoritarianism to

democracy in Chile has only hopefully begun with the defeat of Pinochet in the plebiscite.

75. Revolutionary faith has by no means completely disappeared, however, as evidenced by the active insurgencies in El Salvador, Peru, and Colombia.

• CHAPTER TWO •
Argentina: Autarkic Industrialization and Illegitimacy

CARLOS H. WAISMAN

Argentina fits the "mixed success: democratic and unstable" category in the summary scale used in this book.[1] An administration committed to an inclusive level of political participation, meaningful competition for office, and the institutionalization of civil and political liberties has been in power since the end of 1983. For the past half-century, one or more of these three criteria of liberal democracy were absent or severely restricted. Obviously, democratic rule is not deeply established, and serious threats to it remain.

• HISTORICAL ANALYSIS •

There is an "Argentine question": Why did this country fail to become an industrial democracy?[2] The pattern of political development of Argentina is problematic for two reasons, theoretical and empirical. Argentina, rich in agrarian resources and with a population consisting mostly of Europeans who immigrated at the turn of the century, resembles the "new countries" or "lands of recent settlement," such as Australia, Canada, New Zealand, and, to some extent, the United States. There is a line of theoretical argument in the social sciences, which includes convergent theses by Adam Smith, Tocqueville, Marx, and others, predicting that agrarian countries with a high land-labor ratio and a labor shortage will develop dynamic capitalist economies and liberal democratic polities. These nations would differ from standard undeveloped ones, characterized by a low land-labor ratio and a labor surplus, whose evolution would couple nondynamic economies and undemocratic types of state.[3]

Argentina deviates from this tradition, for the country's social structure at the end of the nineteenth century fits the "new country" type. Export agriculture, based on the coastal and central regions—the littoral—was organized into large landholdings, as in Australia. As for importation of labor, Argentina was second only to the United States as a recipient of the "great migration" from Europe.

ARGENTINA

Five characteristics of this process are important for our analysis.[4] First, the ratio of immigrants to the pre-existing population was, in 1914, 30 percent foreign-born, twice the ratio in the United States at the time of maximum foreign impact. Second, most newcomers settled in the littoral, deepening the social and cultural cleavage between it and the less-populated interior. Third, unlike the United States, land in Argentina was not available for ownership by settlers; it was monopolized by the agrarian upper class. Many immigrants became tenant farmers, but most went to the cities. Fourth, foreign impact on urban class structure was very strong. In 1914, immigrants accounted for about a third of the active population in agriculture, but they were two-thirds of industrial proprietors, three-fourths of merchants, and half of industrial workers and employees. (The balance included native children of immigrants, for by that time mass immigration had been going on for four decades.) Fifth, unlike all lands of recent settlement (except the United States), most emigrants to Argentina originated in countries other than its original colonizer, Spain. A third were Spanish; almost half were Italian.

The second, empirical, reason for the problematic nature of the Argentine case is its curvilinear pattern of economic and political development. The period from around 1880 to the present can be divided into halves, with radically different traits. Up to the Great Depression, Argentina combined a very dynamic economy and an expanding and relatively stable liberal democracy. Constitutional legality was interrupted by a military coup in 1930; from that year to 1983, Argentine politics was an unstable succession of military, populist-corporatist, and restricted democratic regimes. The economy expanded until the end of the 1940s, then became sluggish for most of the subsequent period. There was a switch of developmental tracks: From behaving like a "new country," Argentina changed into a typical underdeveloped society.

In the second half of the nineteenth century, Argentina was fully incorporated into the international division of labor as a supplier of grains, beef, and wool to Europe, especially to England. The period from the 1870s up to the depression was one of rapid economic and social change. The population was 1.7 million in 1869, but from 1870 to 1930 it swelled by over 6 million immigrants. By the turn of the century, Argentina had attained a relatively high level of per-capita income, comparable to Germany and Belgium and higher than southern Europe and Scandinavia.[5] Rapid growth of exports propelled Argentina to "compete with Japan for the title of fastest growing country in the world between 1870 and 1913."[6] From the beginning of the century up to the depression, gross domestic product (GDP) grew at a rate of 4.6 percent per annum.[7] The economy slowed after World War I: from an annual growth rate of 6.3 during 1900–1914 to 3.5 percent during 1914–1929. However, Argentina's per-capita GDP at the outbreak of World War I was higher than Sweden's or France's. When the depression hit, GDP was still much higher than that of Austria or Italy.[8]

The economy not only grew, it diversified. Manufacturing, which began in the late nineteenth century as a forward linkage of agriculture, expanded—in the 1920s as a result of foreign investment; in the 1930s and 1940s, as a consequence of the automatic protection that followed the depression and the war. In 1938, the contributions of manufacturing and agriculture to GDP were similar.[9] In the early 1940s, the labor force in the secondary sector was larger than that in the primary sector.[10] In the mid-1940s, Argentina was more highly urbanized than the United States and most of Europe.[11]

Economic growth and diversification allowed a relatively high standard of living. At the outbreak of the depression, indicators of nutrition, health, consumption, and access to higher education placed Argentina ahead of most of Europe, and it ranked ahead of Britain in per-capita number of automotive vehicles.[12] At the beginning of World War II, Argentina had more physicians per capita than any country in Europe except Switzerland and Hungary.[13] Such facts are not easy to reconcile with the image of Argentina as a typical Latin American society.

Before the turning point, the political system can be characterized as an expanding elite democracy. Competition and, more specifically, toleration of peaceful opposition existed, but participation was severely restricted by electoral practices and the large proportion of foreigners. Power was monopolized by the landed upper class, labeled "the oligarchy" by its opponents. Pressures for participation by the large middle class led to an electoral reform that established secret and universal manhood suffrage—but only for natives. At the time of World War I, power was peacefully transferred by the Conservatives to the opposition Radicals.

Economic and political evolution after the depression and World War II has been a sharp reversal. Standards of living continued to be relatively high: Life expectancy in the late 1970s was in the same range as in the United States and Europe.[14] Enrolment in higher education was higher in the mid-1960s than in any European nation except the Netherlands.[15] But well-being was deteriorating or stagnant in many areas, while European and other Latin American countries continued to improve. Steady economic growth came to a halt after a spectacular upsurge immediately after World War II. Per-capita GDP grew at an annual rate of only .9 percent in the 1950s; it jumped to 2.8 percent in the 1960s; was 2.3 percent in the first half of the 1970s; fell to almost zero (.3 percent) during the rest of the decade; and was negative in the early 1980s.[16] Argentina was not literally stagnant after World War II, but its economy was characterized by sharp fluctuations—stop/go cycles—so that good and bad years almost cancelled out. The overall growth rate of per-capita GDP during 1950–1983 was 1 percent. As a result of this sluggishness, Argentina is now closer to Latin American development levels than it is to those of Europe or lands of recent settlement. If, in 1913, Argentine per-capita GDP was comparable to that of Switzerland, twice as large as Italy's, and almost half Canada's, in the early 1980s the corresponding proportions were less than a sixth, a third, and a fifth. Further, the Argentine per-capita GDP was only slightly higher than those of Chile, Brazil, and Mexico.

The political transformation has been total. Since 1930, Argentina has wavered among three types of polity: military dictatorship, populist-corporatist regime, and restrictive democracy. From 1930 to the reestablishment of liberal democracy in 1983, there were six major military coups (1930, 1943, 1955, 1962, 1966, and 1976) and countless minor ones. In that period, there were twenty-five presidents; though one administration (Juan D. Perón's) lasted for ten years (1946–1955). There were twenty-two years of military rule (1930–1931, 1943–1946, 1955–1958, 1966–1973, and 1976–1983); thirteen years of Peronism, a regime with a populist-corporatist ideology; and nineteen years of restrictive democracy (1932–1943 and 1958–1966), an intermediate type that preserved constitutional forms but banned the majority parties (the Radicals in the 1930s and the Peronists in the 1960s). From 1955 to 1983, political instability reached critical levels. There were eighteen presidents, and all those elected were overthrown except one, Perón, who died less than a year after his election.

The Rise and Fall of Democracy

In the second half of the nineteenth century, Argentina seemed an unlikely place for the emergence of a stable liberal democracy. As in most of Europe and the whole of Latin America, social and cultural institutions such as family, education, and religion were strongly authoritarian. Argentina, like the rest of the Hispanic world, lacked traditions of participation, contestation, and toleration of dissent, in both the political and cultural spheres. Moreover, the country had just overcome decades of internal strife; the national state had begun to be reorganized in the middle of the nineteenth century. Also, Argentina was split between the littoral and the interior. Landed property—the central source of wealth, power, and prestige—was highly concentrated. Finally, large-scale immigration began soon after the national state was reconstituted, so that the new and fragile political institutions were in danger of being overwhelmed by the flow of new inhabitants, most of whom originated in countries with weak democratic traditions.

Three centuries of Spanish rule had left as a political legacy the norm of absolute authority, a highly centralized state, and the antiliberal ideology of the Counterreformation. The settler revolt known as the "revolution of independence" was the local repercussion of the Atlantic revolutionary wave initiated in France and the United States. The leaders of the independence movement were liberals seeking to transform the backward periphery of a backward empire into a modern nation with a capitalist economy, a democratic polity, and the culture of the Enlightenment. These plans foundered on the inhospitable reality of the new nation. Democratic schemes proved unfeasible; so did unified government. The state collapsed after independence in the early nineteenth century. Power was grabbed by provincial governors—autocratic chieftains who were the Bonapartist representatives of the local landed elites. For most of the fifty years following independence, Argentina lacked an effective central government. Several civil wars reflected economic, social, and cultural tensions among the provinces. Civil strife did not correspond precisely to the main line of regional cleavage, that between the littoral (centered in the city and province of Buenos Aires) and the interior (which in the nineteenth century meant the center and north). The littoral was the area that exported to Europe and through which European commodities, immigrants, and ideas entered Argentina, as well as where trade taxes were levied. The interior had mostly native populations, traditional Hispanic culture, and subsistence or regional economies that were threatened by European imports and did not generate much revenue.

The national state was reestablished in the 1850s on the basis of a constitution adapted from that of the United States. The consolidation of democracy was facilitated by three factors—political, ideological, and economic—which overcame the weight of the legacy of Spanish rule.

First, as a result of the long and inconclusive period of civil wars, the economic and political elites developed support for a political formula that sought reconciliation among the different provincial elites and political factions, and sharing of power on the basis of consensus. Such a formula conduced more to an elite democracy than to any alternative. Electoral laws (which established public voting and representation based on the "winner takes all" principle) and tolerance for fraudulent practices guaranteed the provincial elites continued control of their territories, while a federal constitution and the development of the norm of government by agreement allowed institutionalization of the political formula. Only at the verge of World War I did the Electoral Reform provide for the secret ballot, minority representation, and guarantees against electoral fraud.

Second, the elite was determined to carry out the project that liberal Argentine intellectuals had conceived in previous decades: to transform the country into a modern nation by integrating it into the world economy and importing Western European capital, immigrants, and institutions. They believed that Argentina could hope to attract English, French, and other European capital and population only if its institutions were similar; i.e., based on economic and political liberalism. That the progress of the country owed in part to implementing this project sets Argentina apart from other Latin American nations.[17]

Third, there is no question that Argentine economic and political development was externally induced. European industrialization and urbanization created a large-scale demand for Argentine products and a large-scale supply of capital and immigrants. But Argentina's conversion into major agrarian producer, recipient of immigrants, and democratic nation was more the result of the internal processes noted above than of the opportunity provided by European expansion. However, once the country was strongly integrated into international trade, the development of the export economy was a powerful determinant of institutionalizing the democratic state. Sustained economic growth and the ensuing high rates of social mobility cushioned the effect of inequality and regional differences. Urbanization, industrialization, and an expanding educational system facilitated both the legitimation of the new political order among all social classes and absorption of the immigrant inflow.

The Argentine polity, when the country became a major exporter, was similar in its basic traits to Whig democracies in many agrarian societies in Europe and Latin America. First, the mass of the population was not mobilized; the upper class and some sectors of the middle classes were the only participants. Second, given that the various factions or parties represented different segments of the elite, competition embraced a relatively narrow range of contending interests.

What distinguishes evolving liberal democracies from preindustrial exclusionary regimes is not their level of participation, but their response to mobilization. The development of capitalism and the industrial and educational revolutions bring new political forces to the fore: the industrial bourgeoisie, other urban middle-class sectors, and the working class. Elite responses can be triggered by the mere formation of these new classes, or they can be a reaction to their mobilization. Elsewhere, I have classified these responses as three elite strategies: inclusion, which is the extension of the right to participate in the polity as an independent political force; exclusion, the denial of that right; and co-optation, an intermediate form consisting of participation controlled by the elite or the state apparatus, usually on the basis of corporatist mechanisms.[18]

In Argentina, the inclusionary response to the mobilization of the middle and working classes before 1930 is indicated by the tolerance for peaceful opposition from the Radical and Socialist parties, which represented these new social forces; by the Reform of 1912, which enfranchised the native middle classes; and by the transfer of political power to the Radicals in 1916. Exclusion existed as a secondary aspect, triggered by the violent activities of the Anarchists and mainly directed against them.[19] Policies such as suspending constitutional guarantees through the state of siege and persecuting terrorists (but also labor militants and dissenters in general) were applied, but sparingly; only a few hundred foreigners, for instance, were deported under the residence law.[20] In fact, it would be the Radicals rather than the administrations representing the Conservative oligarchy who responded to labor mobilization, in isolated instances, with large-scale repression.

Participation was restricted by the initially low level of mobilization among nonelite groups, but also by fraudulent electoral practices—which covered the whole range from buying votes to falsifying results.[21] These practices disappeared or were minimized, however, with the Reform of 1912.

Mobilization of the middle and lower classes presented challenges that, for different reasons, could be met by the landed upper class without altering the existing distribution of wealth and power. The Radicals, with an elite leadership and a mass base including large segments of the middle classes, staged several armed revolts at the turn of the century. Their demands, however, were totally consistent with continued oligarchic rule. Their central goal was to extend electoral participation through the "universal" and secret manhood suffrage; nothing in their diffuse economic and social doctrine could be construed as antagonistic to the status quo.

Labor mobilization was intense in the first decade of the twentieth century and, because of the Anarchist presence, was coupled with significant violence. However, mobilizing labor did not represent a high level of threat to elite rule for three reasons. First, the central themes of workers' protests were conventional bread-and-butter issues and opposition to repression. As such, they could be controlled by political reform and by institutionalizing the labor conflict, two measures that were feasible in the existing economic and political structure. Second, the distribution of forces in the labor movement—Socialists and Anarchists—presented an ideal combination for applying elite carrot-and-stick strategies. Including the Socialists, who were convinced supporters of free trade and liberal democracy, could only strengthen existing institutions. And excluding the Anarchists was facilitated by two traits of their ideology: their concentration on immediate demands and their rejection of participation in the existing state. Finally, most workers were foreign, a fact that facilitated elite strategies, as we shall see below. Thus, Socialists and Radicals were incorporated into the system, and government intervention in labor disputes grew during this period, especially after power was transferred to the Radicals. The use of force by this party (there were two major incidents in the first postwar period) was more a reflection of panic and a lack of capability for riot control than a systematic policy of persecuting the labor movement.

This regime has to be evaluated in comparative perspective. Certainly, the regime did not rank very high on the democratic scale, but it does not make any sense to compare it with contemporary authoritarian polities such as Bismarckian Germany or the extreme case of czarist Russia. The crucial issue is that the Argentine elite did extend participation to the new classes generated by development and was willing to abide by the norms of the liberal democratic game—which included losing control of the government—as long as their basic economic interests were not endangered. Elites in many late industrializing nations were not so inclined.

The peculiarities of Argentine political evolution are related to two distinctive traits. Unlike other lands of recent settlement, it had a landed upper class that controlled the state apparatus, and unlike the modal Latin American setting, its population included a high proportion of immigrants. In the specific conditions of Argentina, the second trait was conducive to democracy, while the first one was not.

The immigrant presence contributed to democratic development not because of the culture they carried, but because their sheer weight and social marginality allowed the elite to reconcile its control of the state with the ideal norms of democracy. Two traits of this immigrant contingent in the beginning of the century indicate how "cheap" political reform was for the elite. In the littoral, where the bulk of the population was concentrated, 50 to 70 percent of males over twenty were foreign-born, and in the whole country, only 1.4 percent of immigrants had become Argentine citizens by 1914. These peculiarities of the immigrant contingent permitted the elite to legitimize the exclusionary aspects of its response to mobilization of the lower classes. Since most industrial workers were foreign-born, agitators and organizers could be deported. Also, the immigrant presence allowed the elite to live up to the ideal of universal manhood representation without, as Smith notes, enfranchising the lower classes.[22] The Reform of 1912 established a universal, secret, and compulsory ballot on the basis of new and complete rolls. However, in the 1916 election won by the opposition Radicals, voters were, in the most important districts, no more than 9 percent of the total population and only 30 percent of males over eighteen.[23]

This is not to imply that the reform was meaningless. It is true that the elite yielded to mobilization because it expected to win by the new rules. It is also true that in supporting the reform, some elite leaders had a hidden agenda: They expected, very reasonably, that participation would deflect labor militancy. Finally, there was some apprehension about Radical revolts, even though it would be an overstatement to claim that the 1912 law was a fearful reaction to the mobilized masses.[24] In spite of all these factors, the reform was a genuine, even if deferred, leap in the dark. The elite was aware that, in one or two decades, the children of immigrants would join the electorate; the whole male population would then be enfranchised.

The other Argentine peculiarity vis-à-vis lands of recent settlement was the existence of the landowning upper class itself. The local elites, both in the littoral and the interior, were constituted as political forces and had laboriously developed norms for their interaction before the constitution was adopted and applied. The half-century from independence to national organization is usually seen as "anarchic," but the counterpart of the protracted conflict among the provinces was the gradual development of consensus about the institutions of the new nation. In social terms, this meant the emergence of a relatively homogeneous national elite out of a fractious set of local ones.

The massive and swift transformation in all spheres of life following the establishment of democratic institutions had contradictory effects on legitimacy. The organization of the export economy, foreign investment, and mass immigration showed the effectiveness of the elite (enhancing the legitimacy of the social order) and rendered the upper class hegemonic. In the long run, however, the transformation undermined political legitimacy, in that it triggered mobilization before the new political institutions could attain a high level of legitimacy among the different social groups, the upper class in particular. A high level of legitimacy implies an acceptance that is automatic rather than deliberate, emotional rather than rational. Only then do social and political forces, and especially elites, develop a stable conception of the general interest as a product of impersonal institutions, binding on all social groups even when it contradicts particular interests. Attaining this sort of legitimacy presupposes at least two conditions: efficacy and time.[25] Time was missing in the Argentine case.

The Argentine elite was not deeply committed to democratic norms.[26] Such commitment is not an intrinsic attribute of a social group, or the product of explicit socialization provided by the educational system. The lapse of time between the establishment of the new institutions and the appearance of fresh claimants to power was so brief that the outcome was natural. As long as it had no intense conflicts with these new forces, the agrarian upper class was willing to enfranchise the middle classes and even transfer power to the party representing them. It could also tolerate peaceful labor opposition. But, once its basic interests were in danger, the landed elite revoked its support for liberal democracy and seized control of the state.

Until 1930, all social and political forces, except the anarchist faction of the working class, coincided to support the basic characteristics of Argentine society and its position in the world economy. Conflicts involving interest groups and political parties were exclusively of a secondary or unantagonistic nature. Since most manufacturing was a forward linkage of agriculture, there was no conflict between agriculture and industry. Foreign capital was combined or allied with domestic rural and urban capital, so there was no contradiction between them. Also, since the well-being of the middle and working classes depended on the export economy, vertical cleavages were moderate in content despite the occasional violent action. Thus, the oppositions between littoral and interior upper classes, domestic and foreign capital, landowners and tenant farmers, elite and urban middle class, capitalists and workers, and Conservatives and Radicals or Socialists were all consistent with the hegemony of the dominant class. These were conflicts over participation in decisionmaking or distribution of surplus rather than over property or the nature of political institutions.

When the Radicals were in power from 1916 to 1930, their opposition to the Conservatives was exclusively political. As Smith points out, the Radicals departed from the Conservative tradition of government by consensus and moved toward competitive decisionmaking.[27] In addition, they aimed at weakening the Conservatives' local power base through the systematic intervention of the federal government in provincial administrations.[28] Nevertheless, as Rock argues, the Radicals limited themselves to administering the existing economic and social order. They did not attempt to introduce any major changes in the structure of Argentine society or in its location in the international economy.[29] However, when the depression hit, the hegemony of the dominant classes was endangered. Not only did the position of the country in the international system have to be renegotiated, but the consent of subordinate classes could erode as domestic conflict took the appearance of a zero-sum game. The agrarian upper class turned way from democracy, more in order to face the critical situation than to restore the premobilization oligarchic state.

There is no question that the depression was followed by an oligarchic restoration, but this does not mean that the depression was the main cause of the 1930 coup that marked the end of democratization. This is still a debated issue. Smith challenged the traditional interpretation, according to which there was a direct link between the economic crisis and the coup. He argued that the depression's important repercussions appeared only after the coup and explained the coup by the Radicals' refusal to abide by the Conservative tradition of power-sharing. The ensuing separation between economic and political power led the agrarian elite to withdraw legitimacy from democratic institutions and seize power by force.[30] Opposing Smith, Rock and Solberg restated the conventional thesis, arguing that even before the overthrow of the Radical government, the economic situation had deteriorated significantly, and that the seriousness of the situation was already manifest to the economic and political elites.[31]

My own view is that regardless of the specific determinants of the coup, there was a causal connection between the depression and the establishment of non-democratic regimes after the coup. The breakdown of democracy was not caused by the depression, but by its timing; the crisis took place when the norms of liberal democracy were being institutionalized. Power had been transferred from the Conservatives to the Radicals, but the different social and political forces were just beginning to develop norms for interaction. These groups granted legitimacy to the social order and the political system, but it was still a pragmatic, tentative, contingent legitimacy. In such a situation, the depression, which affected the basic interests of all groups, ended democratization. Delegitimation did not begin at the bottom of the social structure, but at the top. Apprehensive about the effectiveness of democratic rules to protect its economic interests and its hegemony over other social forces, the agrarian upper class and its Conservative Party inaugurated a period of rule based on force, fraud, and proscription.

The Non-Democratic State

From 1930 to 1983, the Argentine polity had three types of non-democratic regime. The first was what I have called restrictive democracy. The president and other executive officials were elected; Congress and other representative assemblies functioned, but the largest party (Radicals in the 1940s, Peronists in the late 1950s and early 1960s) was excluded from electoral participation and otherwise restricted in its activity. So, typically, was the extreme Left. Usually there was significant toleration of dissent by other parties and groups, and considerable freedom of the press, assembly, and of interest and political organizations.

In the corporatist-populist regime—the Peronist administrations of 1946–1955—there was an inclusive level of political participation and majority rule, but power was centralized by the leader. Congress and the judiciary became rubber stamps for the executive. Moreover, regard for political competition and for civil and political liberties was not systematic. Respect for liberal democracy by large sectors of Peronism, and probably by Perón himself, was purely pragmatic. Their ideal polity was hierarchical and corporatist, rather than representative and pluralistic.

Military regimes conformed to the authoritarian and bureaucratic-authoritarian models: The military ruled as an institution; representative assemblies were dissolved; political parties and political activity in general were restricted (occasionally banned altogether); and there was limited freedom of the press, assembly, and organization.

The coup of 1930 did not lead to a stable authoritarian regime. The military faction, which in Argentina's Orwellian political discourse is called "liberal," prevailed over the "nationalist"; proscriptive democracy was inaugurated. The organizations and procedures established by the constitution were reinstated, but the Radicals were excluded from elections. The means employed were not only conventional electoral fraud, but outright banning. Communists and other leftists were repressed. Nevertheless, the regime that existed until 1943 was a limited democracy, for there was a significant degree of pluralism and, in general, of political and ideological contestation.[32]

Given the contradiction between the ideal norms of democracy and the actual operation of the regime, political legitimacy foundered—this period is commonly called "the infamous decade"—but social legitimacy declined more slowly. Despite the cumulative impacts of the political and economic crises, and of the polarization in world politics, mass-based radicalism did not develop. The revolutionary Left remained small; right-wing radicalism grew considerably but did not acquire a base among the subordinate classes. The social order preserved its legitimacy because it could still borrow from the "capital of trust," to use Blondel's expression, accumulated over two generations of satisfactory performance.[33] This capital was "well distributed," for its had reached precisely the potential mass base for radicalism: the immigrant working class. The Anarchist rhetoric of a large segment of the labor movement up to World War I had reflected more the strains of transition into the industrial world and assimilation into the new society than an articulate opposition to the social order. Such opposition would have been surprising, given the intense social mobility in Argentina. In fact, with the decline of anarchism and the growth of syndicalism, the labor movement became more moderate. With the new stage of industrialization after the depression, communism began to make some inroads in the industrial unions, a development that would be arrested by Peronism.

However, social legitimacy would eventually be undermined by the commitment, in the 1930s and 1940s, of a large proportion of the country's capital and labor to a noncompetitive form of manufacturing. Import substitution—begun in the 1930s in response to the depression and made permanent in the 1940s as a consequence of absolute protectionism—sapped legitimacy for two reasons. First, it generated two new classes, whose interests were incompatible with the hegemony of the agrarian upper class: a new industrial bourgeoisie, large but weak; and what would become (in the 1940s and 1950s) a powerful labor movement. Both were oriented to the internal market but needed the foreign exchange generated by agriculture. Second, absolute protectionism eroded legitimacy because it eventually led to lower growth rates and thus decreased the perceived efficacy of the social and political order. The new bourgeoisie was recruited from the middle and working classes, and the new proletariat from the rural lower class. The industrial sector was fragmented along economic and cultural lines. Old and new bourgeoisie were mostly of immigrant origin, but the old segment included a larger proportion of older Argentines, controlled larger and more efficient firms, and was tied to the agrarian upper class and foreign capital. In the working class, there was a cultural gulf between the older immigrant segment and the new Creole one.[34]

These new fractions constituted an available mass. The essence of Peronism was precisely the attempt and failure to incorporate these social forces through a corporatist state.[35]

The military coup of 1943, out of which Peronism sprang, is the watershed in Argentine economic and political development. The regime that came to power in 1930 had modified the nature of the polity, and the economic policies followed by the agrarian elite after it regained control of the state had led to significant changes. The authoritarian regime established in 1943, and its successor constitutional administration headed by Perón, reoriented the economy inward and the state downward, i.e., in a corporatist direction. These transformations led Argentina to switch developmental tracks and veer toward the Latin American type of society.

For the first time in its history, Argentina's polity in 1943–1946 fit the authoritarian model fully.[36] As in 1930, participation through elections and representative bodies was interrupted, but civil and political liberties were severely restricted as well. The dominant faction in the military was a coalition of neutralists, right-wing nationalists, and Fascists. The policies of the regime went beyond cultural fundamentalism and political exclusion. It banned all political parties, severely restricted freedom of the press, and persecuted leftist and pro-Allied organizations. It also initiated lasting changes in the economy and the society. The regime extended protection and credits to new industries and granted wage increases and favorable legislation to the working class. Perón, the secretary of labor, mounted a massive organizational drive and established a system of labor organization and collective bargaining under government control. At the same time, leftists and other uncooperative unionists were repressed. And benefits, of course, were contingent on support for the regime.[37]

The initial social base of Peronism comprised not only the new urban sectors, but also segments of the old working and rural classes. Perón's central goal was to mobilize, from above, the working class and the bourgeoisie. This distinguishes Peronism from European fascism, whose social base was the petty bourgeoisie and whose enemy was the labor movement, and also from Latin American populism, whose working-class component was usually weaker.

Cleavage lines were clear: Labor and the new bourgeoisie were Perón's initial social base, along with the armed forces, the church hierarchy, and the antiliberal Right; against the regime were most of the agrarian upper class and the "older" bourgeoisie, and most of the middle classes, together with liberal and leftist parties and organizations.[38]

The economic policies of the regime corresponded to this cleavage. Perón transferred surplus from agriculture to manufacturing by nationalizing exports and controlling domestic terms of trade. He also nationalized railroads and utilities and further improved the working class's standard of living through protective legislation and wage increases. Agriculture was reoriented toward the domestic market; noncompetitive manufacturing was not only preserved, but expanded. The regime's central goal was employment; thus the long-term viability of industries geared toward captive markets and kept alive by impregnable tariff barriers was not a consideration.[39] However, these policies had limits. There were no significant expropriations of land or industrial capital, and Perón shifted to a more moderate course when it became clear—after a few years—that his anti-agrarian policies were leading to a reduction of output and exports.

The failure of Peronism was the consequence of what I have called the intrinsic weakness of state corporatism.[40] It can be more properly considered its contradiction. In order to control them, Perón had to organize the new bourgeoisie and the working class. His expectation was, of course, that the new organizations would be a transmission belt for state power. But such a plan, to be workable, would have required continuous redistribution; i.e., the steady transfer of surplus to these urban sectors. When stagnating tendencies appeared toward the end of the 1940s, the conflict between the powerful labor movement and the weak bourgeoisie surfaced; the latter distanced itself and finally left the coalition. Perón attempted to divert attention by provoking a conflict with the church over the issues of divorce and disestablishment, but this maneuver expanded and strengthened agrarian and middle-class opposition to his rule. Eventually, he was overthrown by a military coup with substantial civilian support.

Workers accepted corporatist controls for as long as their incomes increased but became an autonomous political force after redistribution stopped. Thus, following the failure of the corporatist attempt, labor became a much stronger power contender than it would have been without state-controlled organization.

How Argentina Became an Ungovernable Society

Conflict in post-Peronist Argentina has largely been a contest for the distribution of surplus, the main players being labor, industrialists, agrarians, and the armed forces. The labor movement's power is a function of the trait that distinguishes Argentina from the Latin American modal pattern: the absence of a large labor reserve. In countries such as Mexico or Brazil, corporatist-populist regimes did not have similar political consequences. Import substitution has been as inefficient a lever for self-sustained economic growth as in Argentina, but its development has not produced a social stalemate. One central reason for this is a rural and urban labor reserve, which prevents the working class from becoming a central political actor.

In Argentina, no social force could replace the agrarian upper class as the hegemonic group. With strong interest organizations contending in an unstable and sluggish economy, the country became the perfect embodiment of Huntington's praetorian society.[41] The prevailing interpretation of the post-Peronist period has seen political instability as the consequence of stalemate among the different social and political forces.[42] Since no contender, or coalition of contenders, could accumulate enough power to overcome and dominate the others, illegitimacy and praetorianism resulted.[43]

Agrarian interests and the fraction of the industrial bourgeoisie linked to them (such as international capital and the domestic capital less dependent on protection) made up one coalition. The opposing coalition consisted of the bulk of the domestic bourgeoisie—particularly its weaker segment, which is highly dependent on tariffs—and the labor movement. Besides this major line of cleavage, there were secondary conflicts within each bloc; there was also a latent cleavage between labor and the bourgeoisie as a whole. The interrelationship among the groups, interacting with the political parties representing some of them, was thus very complex: Different alliances, with varying degrees of mobilization among their constituent members, were formed in particular circumstances or in relation to specific issues. The state, and especially the armed forces, intervened as a moderator or arbiter of the conflict, or as the political representative of the pro-agrarian coalition.

In this conflict, success could only be limited and temporary, and it was reversed quickly. Whenever one of the coalitions prevailed and seized control of the government, it carried out policies that protected or advanced the interests of its members. But it could not drastically alter the power position of the opposing bloc. Applying government programs led to economic or political outcomes that triggered mobilization of the other coalition, which eventually accumulated enough power to block policy implementation, force a retreat, or even capture the government.

Economic policies thus protected the basic or immediate interests of the two blocs in sequence, wavering, as Diamand puts it, like a pendulum between two poles: conservative or—in Argentine vocabulary—"liberal" policies (such as floating currency, incentives to agriculture, lower tariffs, wage controls, and reduced government spending) and "populist" policies (exchange controls, lower prices for agricultural commodities, higher tariffs and other manufacturing incentives, higher wages, and increased government spending).[44]

The pendulum's range of oscillation was determined by the power of the social forces. The barriers to conservative measures were mainly political. Mobilization of the labor movement, segments of the middle classes, and those of the bourgeoisie hurt by these policies raised the specter of popular revolt. In this situation, the big bourgeoisie and the agrarians yielded power. The obstacles to populist strategies, on the other hand, were mainly economic. Their implementation led to declines in agrarian output and crises in the balance of payments. When that happened, labor and the less competitive segments of the bourgeoisie were paralyzed by the inefficacy of their program, and a segment of the middle class usually moved to the right, thus supporting the reinstatement of conservative policies—often as a consequence of military intervention and the establishment of an authoritarian regime.[45]

This description of Argentine political dynamics suggests an institutionalization model, and two causes. The stalemate was the consequence of the structural linkages of the two policies—radical protectionism for manufacturing and a state corporatist strategy toward the working class—followed by the Peronist regime in the postwar period. Their effects on the social structure were similar and cumulative: economic growth and legitimacy in the short run; a sluggish economy and political illegitimacy in the long run.

After the war, Argentina abandoned the model of industrialization based on integration into the world economy. Instead, autarkic policies, which the depression and the war had forced on the country, were intensified when the world economy was reorganized. These policies gave rise to a noncompetitive manufacturing sector, whose existence was made possible only by the automatic and unlimited protection granted to import-substituting industries without regard to current or prospective competitiveness.[46]

Thus, the internationally efficient agrarian sector co-exists with a manufacturing sector tied to a captive market and operating behind effective protection barriers that are among the highest in the world.[47] This situation has been aptly characterized as a new form of dualism by Mallon and Sorrouille.[48] As in the old form, though, the connections between the sectors are more important than the differences; the survival of manufacturing depends on the surplus generated by agriculture. Manufacturers can import machinery and other necessary inputs only with the foreign exchange generated by agriculture. This is the root of the stalemate described above: the conflict between the two sectors is coupled with a unilateral dependency of manufacturing on agriculture. Agrarians and their allies have retained a veto power despite the fact that the majority of the country's capital and nonservice labor force has been committed to manufacturing, and that the wave of foreign investment in the 1960s and the growth of finance capital in the 1970s have increased the weight of the nonagrarian sector of the economic elite.

The economic consequences of hothouse capitalism are well known: high rates of growth until the captive market is saturated, and sluggishness thereafter. The size of the internal market limits the possibility of "deepening" industrialization, and the large-scale export of manufactured goods is not possible without subsidies. The political effects of radical protectionism have also varied with time. In the short run, expanding employment and income produced a satisfied working class, which consented to the state's control of the labor movement. In the long run, the working class generated by this type of industrialization became the foremost delegitimating force. Large-scale industrialization in an economy averse to adopting technological innovation and in a society without a large labor reserve generated a highly mobilized and organized labor movement. The demands made by labor and by other social forces, including the large middle class, were likely to lead at times to situations that contenders perceived as a zero-sum game. This was not necessarily due to actual stagnation, but to a large gap between the size of the surplus and the combined demands made by the different strata. This situation could only lead to illegitimacy and political instability.

Integrating the working class into the political system through a corporatist strategy (i.e., a strategy presupposing both participation and control by the state) had similar political effects: a positive relationship with legitimacy in the short run, and a negative one in the long run. It also had similar economic long-term effects: It contributed to the low and unstable rate of growth. These consequences follow from the contradiction of corporatism: Perón's utilization of the working class as a political base required a powerful labor movement, albeit under state control.

Redistribution was a precondition for the stability of the corporatist arrangement. When radical protectionism led to an economic slowdown, and the regime collapsed, the labor movement became an autonomous political force, much more powerful than it would have been without organization from above. Thus, the Argentine crisis is the long-term result of Peronist policies that, on the one hand, allocated economic and human resources inefficiently and, on the other, increased the level of mobilization and organization of the labor movement.

I consider the 1943 coup the turning point in modern Argentine history because, thereafter, both radical protectionism and corporatism began to be institutionalized. Despite antecedents for these industrial and labor policies, it is with Peronism that they began to be implemented officially and systematically. In about a decade, they changed Argentina's social structure, economy, and polity.

Post-1943 industrial and labor policies were a sharp departure from the past. Up to that point, the industries Argentina was forced to develop in response to the depression and the war had usually been classified by the government into two categories: "emergency industries" (which would be dismantled when the world economy was reorganized) and "genuine industries" (which were compatible with reintegrating the country into the world economy and which would continue being protected).[49] This distinction disappeared with Perón, who granted blanket protection to manufacturing. As for labor policy, inclusion and exclusion were practiced in different mixes until the early 1940s, but it was with the military coup of 1943 that the attempt to incorporate labor on the basis of a state corporatist mechanism became government policy.

It is important to understand the options available to the Argentine elites in the postwar years. The alternative to blanket protectionism would have been selective protection, in a few cases for welfare or defense considerations, but more generally on the basis of the "infant industry" argument. The alternative to state corporatism would have been to resume the inclusionary strategies toward the labor movement followed prior to the depression. This latter course would not have led to stalemate, and thus it would have allowed for different long-term economic and political outcomes.

Neither radical protectionism for manufacturing nor a corporatist strategy toward labor were carried out by the state as a response to demands made by the economic elite, for both policies were against elite interests. Agrarians could not support the perpetuation of noncompetitive manufacturing financed by taxes on agricultural exports; the older industrial bourgeoisie, linked to agriculture and foreign capital, could survive without radical protectionism, as it had done in the past. Further, corporatism entailed not only a strong state controlling the society, but also a setting in which the economic interests of the lower classes would loom larger than in the liberal inclusionary and authoritarian exclusionary arrangements the elites were familiar with.[50]

The shift to radical protectionism and state corporatism was not determined by external constraints either. It is true that in the postwar period Europe could not buy Argentine products, and the United States boycotted Argentine trade as a consequence of the country's pro-Axis orientation during the war.[51] In those conditions, a partial closure of the economy may have appeared reasonable. These obstacles, however, were temporary, for by the end of the 1940s the Europeans economies had regained their dynamism, and the U.S. boycott had ended. Resuming the open industrialization model would then have been entirely feasible. As for state corporatism, it is impossible to identify any postwar external economic or political process or constraint of which corporatism in Argentina would have been a direct consequence. In fact, it is difficult to imagine a system of government-labor relations more at variance with the West's ideological climate at that time.

If the new industrial and labor policies were determined neither by the interests of the economic elites nor by external constraints, then their institutionalization was an instance of the state's autonomy. In fact, both radical protectionism and state corporatism were implemented by an administration whose main opponents were precisely the agrarian upper class and the big capitalists.

The economic and social stalemate that led Argentina to switch developmental tracks was the delayed effect of a process of differentiation between the state and the balance of interests in civil society. This process began with the depression and intensified during the war. The depression triggered the period of military rule and restrictive democracy of 1930–1943, but these regimes still corresponded to the interests of the agrarian upper class, whose leaders and representatives remained in control of the state apparatus.[52] The agrarians gradually lost their hegemony as a consequence of the crisis of the export economy brought about by the depression, and of the fact that in the 1930s they ruled by coercion and fraud. The decline of agrarian hegemony, however, was a precondition for state autonomy, not a cause in itself.

In my view, there were two determinants of state autonomy in the early 1940s. There were external constraints: British and U.S. pressures in relation to Argentine participation in the war, and military competition with Brazil, Argentina's traditional rival for regional power. Britain favored Argentine neutrality, for this would facilitate continuing trade. The United States pushed Argentina to enter the war and began to treat the country as a quasi enemy when it refused. Regionally, the balance of power began to shift in Brazil's favor when Brazil joined the war and received large amounts of U.S. economic and military aid.[53]

The second factor was the fragmentation of the dominant class. Capitalists were split in the early 1940s by several cleavages, some of which predated the depression but were intensified by it. Others emerged as a consequence of changes associated with the depression and the war: breeders versus fatteners within the agrarian elite; agrarians versus industrialists; the agrarian and the "older" bourgeoisie alliance versus the new manufacturing class generated by import substitution; pro-Allied versus neutralist factions.[54] Factionalism, coupled with the decline of hegemony that had followed the depression, rendered the elite ineffective. It was at this point that the military captured the state and began implementing policies that were at variance with the interests of the dominant sectors.

State autonomy, however, does not determine the content of state policies: The fateful choice of radical protectionism and corporatism by the group controlling the state after 1943 does not follow from the state's relative independence from the dominant class. These industrial and labor policies were consistent with the right-wing nationalist and fascist ideologies then in circulation, but a regress from Peronist doctrines to nationalist or fascist ideology is not a satisfactory explanation.[55] The problem is to understand why all these related ideas were influential, why radical protectionism and corporatism made sense to the sectors of the state elite supporting Perón.

A key to this question can be found in the response of different segments of the established elites to Peronism. The election if 1946, which brought Perón to power as a constitutional president, was a crucial juncture: Perón was supported by the military, the church hierarchy (to the dismay of the many liberal Catholics), and what could be called the new Right (antiliberal Conservatives and right-wing nationalists). He was opposed by the established economic elites, agrarian and industrial, and by most Conservatives. The sector supporting Perón was obsessed by the fear of communism and revolution, and he focused on this issue in his discourse to the elites from the 1943 coup onwards.

Perón was a Marxist in reverse, in the sense that he was a passionate anticommunist who nevertheless accepted the validity of basic Marxist propositions; e.g., that the working class is intrinsically a revolutionary actor, or that the central content of our epoch is the spread of the revolutionary wave that began in Russia. More specifically, he argued that the immediate danger to

Argentina was that the postwar reorganization of the international economy would produce mass unemployment, increasing the revolutionary menace. He proposed as remedies not only authoritarian corporatism, whereby the state would take control of labor, but also radical protectionism, for this was the only means by which mass unemployment could be prevented. Perón argued, then, that dismantling the emergency industries developed during the war, and the possible contraction of other industries as a consequence of reestablishing normal international trade, would produce a political cataclysm in the country.[56] It is irrelevant whether he was sincere when making such a forecast. A competent political entrepreneur, Perón told different audiences what he thought they wanted to hear. Eventually, he was rebuffed by the established economic elites, who thought, very accurately, that Perón was more a cause than a solution of the labor question. This was dramatically shown in October 1945, when a mass workers' demonstration reinstated Perón in government leadership, after he was displaced by fellow officers disgruntled by his ascendancy.[57] The sectors of the state elite accepting Perón's proposals, on the other hand, were guided by ideological considerations rather than by the protection or advancement of their interests, for the instrumental or organizational interests of the military or the church could have been safeguarded under the coalition opposing Perón.

The important point is that the postwar fear of communism was totally unrealistic: The level of class polarization was not very high, and the forecast that it would increase if Argentine manufacturing were reconverted was not reasonable. First, the Communist Party—the only substantial revolutionary organization—was small, and its influence limited by several factors: the repression it had suffered in the previous decades; the cultural cleavage between the party's European organizers and the "new" working class produced by import substitution since the depression (whose members were mostly recent rural migrants of non-European origin); and the wide gyrations of the party line (which, for instance, impelled the Communists to oppose strikes against firms owned by Allied corporations during the war). Second, not only were there no signs of increased radicalization in the labor movement, but the facts point to the growth of moderate and pragmatic trade unionism.[58]

Finally, and most importantly, the fear of mass unemployment should emergency or "artificial" industries be dismantled after the war was unfounded. According to the best estimates, phasing out the exposed industries would have produced an unemployment rate of 2 percent, which was very manageable. The absolute number of unemployed would have been small (about 80,000) and concentrated in a small geographical area; the government had ample resources for public-works or reconversion programs, which would have been accepted by large segments of the labor movement.[59]

This inordinate fear of communism was grounded in distorted political knowledge: The sectors of the elite supporting Perón's diagnosis and remedies had an erroneous image of the working class, and they inaccurately understood and derived lessons from the Spanish Civil War and Italian fascism, to whose demonstration effects Argentina was uniquely sensitive.

First, these sectors of the elite viewed the working class as intrinsically dangerous. This inaccurate evaluation of the current labor movement was the product of the recollection—by the military, the antiliberal clergy, and the new Right—of experiences the Argentine elite had had with labor during the intense mobilization in the early 1900s and after World War I. That was a different working class and a different elite, but the image of the working class as an inherently menacing actor was ingrained in the Right's collective memory and determined by the foreign and diverse origins of most workers.[60] The very fact that, at the beginning of the century, half the active population consisted of individuals imperfectly integrated into the national political community and the dominant culture, who were nevertheless pursuing individual mobility within the society, was easily translated as meaning these foreigners were a threat. In addition, while it is true that most immigrants' cultural background was close to that of the older Argentines, there were important dissimilarities. Only one-third came from Spain and thus spoke the same language as the Argentines. Moreover, all foreigners (Spaniards included) carried political traditions, experience, and ideologies that differed from local ones.

Nevertheless, the Argentine elite in the early 1900s dealt with the lower classes pragmatically, and its strategy toward them was mainly inclusionary. It is paradoxical that this image of the dangerous lower classes was activated in the 1940s by bureaucratic elites such as the military, few of whom were of upper-class origin, and most of whom were the children of immigrants. The large-scale rural-urban migration of the 1930s and 1940s contributed to the reappearance of this image: In the early 1940s, at least a third of the working class were recent migrants and, as was the case earlier, imperfectly integrated into Argentine society.

Second, the sectors of the state elite supporting Perón were strongly affected, as was Argentine society generally, by the demonstration effects emanating from Italy and Spain, the countries from which the large majority of Argentines had emigrated in the previous two generations. The strength of personal and cultural networks tying Argentina with Italy and Spain meant that developments in these countries were lived as domestic ones by the mass of Argentines. The impact of Italian fascism and the Spanish Civil War was much wider than in most of Latin America and the United States, where they affected mainly the political and intellectual elites and the relatively smaller immigrant communities. Demonstration effects were facilitated by the perceived generalizability of these examples. The Argentine antiliberal Right interpreted the Spanish case as a model of democratic development, as if it showed that democracy and the ascent of labor necessarily lead to chaos and then to communism (a proposition still popular among supporters of military regimes in Latin America). Fascism, on the other hand, was understood as an equitable solution to the unrest brought about by industrialization and liberal democracy.

The depression, the spread of communism, the Spanish Civil War, and, later, World War II, were interpreted as showing that liberalism—in both its economic and political senses—was no longer a viable form of social organization.

Communism and fascism were seen as efficacious alternatives, for both Russia and Italy had developed stable political institutions. For the Argentine counter-revolutionaries, it made sense to think that at least one mechanism of fascism, control of interest groups and arbitration of conflict by the state, was an effective response to the danger of revolution.[61]

The depression was therefore only an indirect determinant of the Argentine decline. In the final analysis, the switch of developmental tracks was the product of the interaction among the depression, the characteristics of the social structure of the country, and political choice. The depression led to the decline of the agrarian upper class's hegemony, to structural changes that resulted in fragmenting the economic elites in general, and ultimately to state autonomy. But it was the "modernity" of the Argentine social structure, the fact that the country had land and labor endowments that corresponded to the lands of recent settlement, that produced an inordinate fear of revolution among sectors of the state elite and rendered Perón's success possible.

Finally, radical protectionism and corporatism had the consequences they did because Argentina was a "new country" rather than an underdeveloped one. Radical protectionism would have led to stagnation anyway, but the absence of a large labor reserve was a powerful determinant of the failure of state corporatism and of the subsequent economic and social stalemate.

From the Overthrow of Perón to the Re-establishment of Democracy

The overthrow of Perón by a broad military-civilian coalition in 1955 split Argentine society down the middle. In the following decades, the country gradually became ungovernable.[62] The process of delegitimation ended in the 1970s, in large-scale terrorism and repression. Paradoxically, the prospect of chaos brought the different social and political forces to their senses and was conducive to restoring constitutional rule.

The coup that overthrew Perón was an attempt to restore the power of the agrarian upper class, but the structural changes that had taken place in the 1940s and 1950s rendered this unworkable. From 1958 to 1966, weak regimes of restrictive democracy tried vainly to govern in the face of continuous opposition by labor (which represented the excluded Peronist movement), and of military intervention whenever social unrest mounted or there was a possibility of reintegrating Peronism into the political system.[63] A military regime came to power in 1966, with the explicit goal of ending the economic and political stalemate.[64] The means to that end would be orthodox economic policies aimed at furthering efficient industrialization, and the control of labor mobilization through coercion. The expectation was that resuming sustained economic growth would allow a subsequent "reopening" of the political system. O'Donnell has argued that the emergence of this regime was caused by the need to expand import substitution from the consumer goods to the capital goods stage, through foreign investment and the importation of advanced technology.⁶⁵ There has been considerable debate as to whether this need was a causal factor, but there is no question that such restructuring of the economy was a central programmatic goal of the regime.⁶⁶ Hirschman has pointed out the clear fact that installing this regime was a part of the authoritarian wave that swept Latin America following the Cuban Revolution.⁶⁷

The new economic policies, and the futile attempt to suppress political activity through banning parties and restricting trade unions, led to an erosion of whatever passive acceptance the regime had in the beginning. The consequence was the eruption of mass mobilization and riots, whose protagonists were labor and the middle classes. Mobilization of these two classes was a function of political exclusion, and of economic dissatisfaction derived from perceiving competition for surplus as a zero-sum game. There was significant economic growth in the 1960s, but the combined demands by intensely mobilized groups could not be satisfied in the context of the economic and social stalemate described above.

Mobilization of the middle classes was still anomic, due to their fragmentation. A crucial segment was the intelligentsia, which constituted the social base of the guerrilla organizations that were forming inside Peronism and the extreme Left. The radicalization of the intelligentsia, which entailed an ideological shift in this traditionally anti-Peronist group, sprang from two specific factors, in addition to disappointment with the economic and political performance of post-Peronist Argentina that affected all social groups. A large intelligentsia and an unstable and, for most of the time, sluggish economy made an explosive combination. Argentina had more university students relative to its population than most West European countries, and these students expected rates of social mobility comparable to those their parents and grandparents had experienced in the first half of the century. Large segments of the intelligentsia reacted to social frustration in a typical manner, by wishing to change the society through identifying with "the people"; i.e., the working class, which was the backbone of Peronism.

As a consequence of this shift in a segment of the middle classes, a large left wing appeared in the movement, along with its traditional components, bread-and-butter unionism and centrist and rightist political factions. This heterogeneous coalition resembled original Peronism very little, and Perón's role as absolute leader eroded. Nevertheless, he came to be seen by all social forces, the economic elites and the military included, as the only one who could contain the mobilization of the lower and middle classes, and especially a new phenomenon in Argentine society, the guerrillas.⁶⁸

The military regime recognized its defeat when it called for elections in which all parties could participate. This was tantamount to transferring power to the Peronists. In fact, elites were calling Perón's bluff: For thirty years, he had presented himself to them as the only effective bulwark against revolution. He was not believed in the 1940s, for there was no realistic revolutionary danger. The situation was different in the 1970s, and Perón was finally cast in the role he had defined for himself a generation before.

The Peronist administrations of 1973–1976 were spectacular failures, for the old corporatist design was of no use with an autonomous working class and industrial bourgeoisie, and without a surplus available for redistribution. Moreover, Perón had no control over the leftists masquerading as Peronists, the guerrilla groups in particular.[69] When he died in 1974, guerrilla action escalated, right-wing terrorism sponsored by the government developed, and praetorian mobilization intensified. The government, led by the ineffectual Isabel Perón and her corrupt circle, was paralyzed. The coup of 1976 was a forgone conclusion.

The military resumed rule as an institution, and political parties and political activity in general were banned. The new regime's central goal was military rather than political: to destroy the guerrilla organizations and what the armed forces considered to be their social base, i.e., the political Left and considerable segments of the intelligentsia. Left-wing terrorism had triggered a new phenomenon on the Argentine political scene—state terrorism. Large-scale repression in the late 1970s, in which thousands disappeared, was directed not only against the actual terrorists and guerrillas, but also against left-wing political and trade-union activists and considerable segments of the intelligentsia. State violence was disproportionate and arbitrary, but guerrilla groups and their surface organizations were wiped out.[70]

Underlying this military conflict, the stalemate between industrial and nonindustrial coalitions was continuing. The coup replaced Isabel Perón's populist government, whose base of support was labor and the industrial bourgeoisie producing for the domestic market, and whose economic policies favored industrial expansion and higher wages, both at the expense of agrarian exporters.[71] The new regime pushed the economic policy pendulum toward the interests of the agrarian bourgeoisie, manufacturers not dependent on domestic mass consumption, and finance capital. It carried out the most systematic offensive against the industrial coalition in the post-Peronist period. Overvaluation of the currency and lowering of tariffs led to massive bankruptcies, the fall of real wages, the growth of the informal sector of the economy, and open unemployment. From 1976 to 1981, the size of the industrial working class decreased by 26 percent.[72]

It has been argued that this was a deliberate policy aimed at weakening the social base of the populist coalition.[73] In any case, the combined effects of coercion and the reopening of the Argentine economy undermined the economic and social power of labor and the noncompetitive manufacturers. This does not mean, however, that these policies produced conditions favorable to resuming economic growth. First, few Argentine capitalists took advantage of the new economic policy to develop competitive manufacturing. In a context of high uncertainty about the future of economic policy, and of national politics in general, most reacted to the inflow of imports and the contraction of domestic demand by reducing output or by transferring capital to unproductive activities or to foreign countries. Thus, deindustrialization ensued. Second, the military regime contracted a massive foreign debt, equal to over five years of exports and the third largest in Latin America, which still constitutes a very effective brake on the country's development.

Another long-lasting consequence of this regime is the delegitimation of the military, both as a professional organization and as a political actor. This was, paradoxically, a result of using force in both the domestic and the international arenas. Internally, indiscriminate repression of many sectors of the population not involved in terrorism or guerrilla activities undermined the legitimacy of the military as a player in the praetorian game, at least among labor and in the political center. Finally, the defeat in the Malvinas/Falklands War with Britain in 1982 was the most important blow to the legitimacy of the armed forces, for it showed both recklessness—provoking a war with a more powerful nation over a minor territorial dispute in order to divert attention from the difficult economic situation and to redeem their image, tarnished by domestic repression—and limited competence (the air force excepted) when confronting professional opponents, rather than civilians and irregulars.

The combined economic and political failure of the regime resulted in collapse of whatever residual consent it had. In the face of the mass mobilization of the middle and lower classes that followed its defeat, the military called elections at the end of 1983. Military dictatorship, revolution, and Peronism had been tried, and all had failed. These experiences produced a new moderation in all political forces. The Radicals, the only mass party with a liberal democratic ideology, were the only possible beneficiaries of this cultural change.

• **THEORETICAL ANALYSIS** •

The rise of liberal democracy in the nineteenth century was caused by three factors: (1) the development of a consensus, among the different factions of the economic and political elites, that the only possible political formula for creating a national state was power-sharing, and that the principles of Whig democracy were most appropriate to institutionalize this political formula; (2) the demonstration effects of the advanced capitalist democracies, especially Britain, the United States, and the other lands of recent settlement (the U.S. example—a country of immigration, on the American continent, and from which Argentina borrowed its constitution—was central); (3) the opportunity to integrate Argentina into the world economy as an exporter of foodstuffs and an importer of European immigrants, capital, and manufactures; i.e., as a "new country." This opportunity, in turn, had two determinants: (1) internal, the land and labor endowments of Argentina; and (2) external, European industrialization and urbanization. These factors led to sustained economic growth.

The stability of liberal democracy up to the depression was the result of two causes, one economic and the other political. First, a high and sustained rate of growth, which allowed for absorption of mass immigration, rapid urbanization and industrialization, expansion of education, and high standards of living for the lower classes (relative to the countries of origin of the immigrants). These processes produced very high rates of social mobility. Second, the elite responded to middle-class pressures for participation and to intense labor mobilization with inclusionary strategies. The expansion of liberal democracy was facilitated by two facts: As a result of the efficacy of the economic and social order over which it presided, the agrarian upper class was hegemonic, so that integrating the middle classes and labor did not represent a threat to its power; and a large foreign population cushioned the effects of extending the franchise, for it meant that middle and lower classes would be incorporated very gradually, as immigrants were replaced by natives. Thus, the overall conclusion is that the Argentine case confirms the general proposition linking efficacy (both political and economic) with legitimacy, and thus stability.

The fall of liberal democracy and the shift to unstable, non-democratic, forms was a more complex process. The depression had two direct consequences. First, it led to import-substituting industrialization, producing two new class segments: a noncompetitive bourgeoisie of small capitalists, many of them foreign; and a working class formed mostly by recent migrants of Creole (i.e., nonimmigrant) background. Second, the depression prompted the agrarian upper class to abandon its commitment to liberal democracy.

The coup of 1943 was the turning point in Argentine development, for it signaled the emergence of a state, independent of economic elites, and later to carry out policies antagonistic to elite interests. For the first time, power was seized by the military as an institution. State autonomy was made possible by the need to face external constraints derived from World War II and the fragmentation of the agrarian and industrial elites along economic and political lines.

At the end of World War II, the agrarian and industrial upper classes rejected Perón's forecast that resuming imports could cause a revolutionary upheaval, and his prescription to deal with the threat. But a sector of the state elites (the military and the church hierarchy) supported him. This fear of revolution was unrealistic, for neither the characteristics of the labor movement or the revolutionary Left, nor the reasonable estimates of postwar unemployment in case imports were resumed were consistent with that forecast.

The failure of liberal democracy in postwar Argentina was the result of institutionalizing the new industrial and labor policies. Radical protectionism for manufacturing and the failed attempt to establish a corporatist relationship between state and labor led, because of the peculiarities of Argentine social structure, to an economic and social stalemate, which eventually produced stagnation and instability. Radical protectionism and the expansion of noncompetitive agriculture led to a low-growth economy. Since the availability of a surplus for redistribution is a precondition for the stability of state corporatism, stagnation caused labor to become an autonomous actor. The strength of labor was due to the absence of a large labor reserve, and to the corporatist episode itself, for the

Peronist regime, in order to use the working class as a power base, had to increase its degree of unionization.

From the 1950s to the 1980s, two unstable coalitions competed for power: labor and the noncompetitive manufacturers on the one hand; and the agrarians and the industrial sectors less committed to radical protectionism on the other. The characteristics of these groups changed over time, but their stalemate underlay the extreme instability of the period and the role of the military as arbiter of the conflict. Mass praetorianism was gradually established, and Argentina became an ungovernable society when different segments of the middle classes and the intelligentsia radicalized in the 1960s and 1970s.

Finally, the reestablishment of liberal democracy in 1983 was the consequence of three processes that took place during the military regime that began in 1976. First, the populist coalition was considerably weakened by the anti-labor and anti-industrial policies of this regime, so that the economic and social stalemate may have been broken. Second, the military lost legitimacy as a player of the praetorian game as a consequence of their reckless use of force against the guerrillas and domestic opposition in general, and of their defeat in the war they provoked against Britain over a minor territorial dispute. Third, the Peronists were fragmented, leaderless, and discredited by their past performance.

Thus, the success or failure of democracy was the result of a complex interaction among an evolving social structure, the opportunities and constraints derived from the international system, and political choice.

Some factors had different consequences for democracy at different times. The country's peculiar land and labor endowments were conducive to democratization before the Depression, but they also led to economic and social stalemate in the post-Peronist period. International demonstration effects contributed to the establishment of liberal democratic institutions in the nineteenth century, and to the demise of these institutions in the 1930s and 1940s.

It is tempting to isolate three relationships that have general validity throughout Argentina's political development: (1) a positive correlation between sustained economic growth and liberal democracy; (2) a negative relationship between the autonomy of the state vis-à-vis economic elites and liberal democracy; (3) a positive correlation between a realistic evaluation, by elites in control of the state, of threats to their power, from below and from without, and liberal democracy. These relationships were part of complex causal chains. Sustained economic development depended on the ability to establish a "virtuous" relationship with the world economy, and this in turn was a function of characteristics of European and Argentine societies at different points in time. These economies were complementary up to the depression, but the relationship turned "vicious" when the Argentine economy turned inward after the war. Likewise, the growth in state autonomy after the depression was the product of the confluence of external and domestic economic and political processes.

Finally, the unrealistic assessment by state elites of external as well as internal threats in the 1930s and 1940s was caused by the heterogeneity of the Argentine population, and by demonstration effects at a time of very high uncertainty. Evaluation had been much more realistic in the nineteenth century, when the Argentine state successfully engineered integrating the country into the world economy and developing democratic institutions, and in the early twentieth century, when the contentious middle and working classes were integrated into the political system. These realistic evaluations had been carried out by politicians who represented the upper classes, and in a context of both high certainty about the economic and political characteristics of the international system and Argentina's position in that system.

I will now situate the Argentine case in relation to the theoretical framework of this project.

Political Culture

The Argentine experience supports our hypotheses that link democratic government with two determinants: institutionalization of democratic beliefs and values in the society and, in particular, the depth of the elite's commitment to democratic values. Throughout Argentine history, acceptance of democratic institutions and practices by the most important social groups has been contingent and partial. Before 1930, the agrarian upper class and its Conservative Party were more committed to pluralism than to the extension of participation to nonelites, but they did eventually integrate the middle and lower classes into the political system, as well as transfer power to the Radicals. Support for democracy in the elites, however, was a function of the fact that they were hegemonic. After 1930, economic elites and their political parties were the social base of restrictive democracy and of authoritarian regimes.

The middle classes and the Radical Party had a stronger commitment to constitutional rule up to World War II, but they participated, in the 1950s and 1960s, in restrictive democratic regimes that excluded labor and the largest political party, the Peronists. Peronism was also partially democratic: It was committed to majority rule, but its support for pluralism was not systematic. There was, nevertheless, a difference between the Peronists and the Conservatives or the Radicals: The former never claimed to support, as an ideal, political liberalism, while the latter maintained a theoretical commitment to majority rule, the aspect of democracy they were in fact denying to their opponents. This tension between theory and practice contributed, after World War II, to the collapse of the Conservative Party, and in the 1970s to the gradual acceptance of the legitimacy of Peronism by the Radicals, who wanted to avoid a similar fate. From the 1950s onward, the experience of economic and political stalemate, with its sequels of stagnation and violence, taught the different social and political forces the virtues of peaceful competition for power. Elites in the post-Peronist period thus replicated the experience of their nineteenth century predecessors, among whom acceptance of the democratic formula had evolved slowly, as a product of their long, costly, and inconclusive conflict.

Historical Development

Our hypotheses in the area of historical development relate democratic government to experience with democratic institutions prior to a country's independence, to the development of political competition prior to the extension of participation, and to the compatibility between democratic institutions and the country's conditions and traditions. Even though the Argentine case does not falsify these relationships, neither the development of democracy in the nineteenth century nor its demise in the twentieth century is entirely consistent with them.

First, Argentina did not have the opportunity to acquire experience with democratic institutions prior to independence, yet stable liberal democracy did develop, albeit after a half-century of internal conflict. Second, political competition began and competitive institutions developed before there was mass political participation, yet there was a correlation between mass participation since the second postwar period and the decline of democracy. This decline was not, however, due to a crisis of participation: The problem was not that the system was overwhelmed by new participants. Democracy foundered because a segment of the elite in control of the state turned the country's economy inward and its state downward, and changed the social structure in such a way that stable government became impossible.

Third, though it is obvious that the U.S.-style constitution superimposed on nineteenth-century Argentina was not very congruent with the nation's conditions or with its cultural and historical traditions, it worked until the depression. Both Peronism and military rule appear *a priori* as much more compatible with the country's culture than does liberal democracy: the former because of its personalism, organic definition of the nation, and communitarian conception of economy and polity; the latter because of its emphasis on hierarchy and intolerance for dissent. Yet, these regimes emerged only *after* at least two generations of stable liberal democracy. It is tempting to argue that Argentine "Latin" or "Latin American" identity was latent throughout the constitutional period, but in any case this underlying culture was not incompatible with liberal democratic institutions.

Class Structure

The Argentine case contradicts assumptions that democracy is more likely if there is limited economic inequality, and if the distribution of land is relatively egalitarian. The pattern of economic and social development throughout the century (continuous urbanization, industrialization, growth of professional and commercial middle classes) indicates that inequality has been decreasing throughout the century; i.e., it was higher during the period of stable democracy than after the depression and the war, when the Argentine polity became nondemocratic.

Land was always highly concentrated in Argentina. In 1914, the average farm was 8.4 times larger than in the United States and 1.8 times larger than in Australia, another agrarian exporter with large-scale agriculture.[74] Also, most farmers were tenants. The economic and political significance of land ownership declined after the war because of the lower returns consequent on Perón's antiagrarian policies, the growth of industry and other urban sources of wealth, and the displacement of the agrarian upper class from control of the state. Land was continuously subdivided, and the proportion of tenants declined sharply. In 1960, the Gini index of concentration of land ownership in Argentina was only 1.2 times greater than in the United States and about the same as in Australia.[75]

In terms of income concentration, Argentina occupies, like the United States, an intermediate category between the most egalitarian European nations and the highly inegalitarian Latin American countries. In the 1970s, the highest decile of households received 35 percent of household income (versus 33 percent in the United States, 23 percent in Britain, and 51 percent in Brazil), while the lowest quintile received 4 percent of the income (versus 5 percent in the United States, 7 percent in Britain, and 2 percent in Brazil).[76] There are few data on the evolution of income distribution, but there is no doubt that Argentina is more egalitarian now than before the depression, when it had stable democracy.

I think that the question of the relationship between equality and democracy should be reformulated. The Argentine case shows that it is equality of opportunity, rather than equality of outcome, that is a critical condition of legitimacy and hence of the stability of democracy. Up to World War II, sustained economic growth allowed for very high rates of social mobility in Argentina: Wages were higher than in much of Europe, and the growth of industry, trade, and higher education permitted a large proportion of immigrants to reach non-manual occupations, and a large proportion of their children to enter the professions. Germani has estimated that, in 1914, two-thirds of the already large middle class was of manual origin.[77] After the economic slippage, mobility aspirations continued unabated, but the chances for realizing expectations became slim. The incidence of frustration was aggravated by the expansion of university enrolments in the post-Peronist period: from 11 percent of the population aged 20–24 in 1960 to 25 percent in 1981. This expansion was similar to that which took place in France, Italy, West Germany, and other European countries in the same period.[78] The resulting blockage sapped legitimacy among the middle classes and the upper reaches of the proletariat.

The relationship between the intensity of class polarization and democracy has not been consistent in Argentina: There were periods of relatively intense conflict between workers and capitalists both under liberal democracy (early in the century, before World War I, and in the first postwar period) and under nondemocratic regimes (in the restrictive democracies of the late 1930s, late 1950s, and early 1960s, and in the final stages of the military governments in the post-Peronist period).

Polarization, however, was never high in absolute terms (let us say, a revolutionary situation). Only in the beginning of the century was a large segment of the working class under revolutionary (anarchist) leadership, but the level of unionization was then low, and the predominant orientation among the rank and file was toward individual mobility. The Communist Party was an important force in the late 1930s, but its influence waned as a consequence of repression, state corporatism, cultural changes in the working class, and the ineffectiveness of the party line. For the remainder of the period, labor was under moderate leadership, and its demands were either the standard economic ones or integration into the political system (in the post-Peronist period). Polarization after the slippage, then, was due more to the unsatisfactory rate of economic growth than to the radicalism of labor.

Argentina has both a substantial indigenous industrial bourgeoisie and a substantial educated middle class, but there is no positive correlation between the size or power of these classes and the stability of democratic institutions. In the case of the industrial bourgeoisie, the relationship is negative. Throughout the twentieth century, there was a large stratum of small manufacturers, but before the depression the only economically and politically significant segment of the bourgeoisie was big business, which was allied to the agrarian upper class (e.g., in industries that were a forward linkage of agriculture), and foreign capital (mostly British and U.S.). After the depression and World War II, the bourgeoisie mushroomed as a consequence first of import substitution and later of radical protectionism. Since the new class of small and medium-sized manufacturers was exclusively oriented toward the internal market, noncompetitive internationally, and dependent on the state for financing and tariff protection, it had a sharp conflict of interest with the old bourgeoisie. While the latter opposed Perón, as did the agrarian upper class, the former became, together with labor, the social base of the new movement. Over time, concentration and centralization of capital differentiated the new class in terms of size, competitiveness, and relation with foreign capital, but there is no evidence of a particular commitment for democratic options by any fraction of the bourgeoisie in the post-Peronist period. Big capitalists, both old and new, usually supported "liberal" policies, and that meant in many cases support for military rule, while the small and middle bourgeoisie briefly reconstituted the old Peronist coalition with labor in the mid-1970s.

However, it is important to note that, since the transformation of the Argentine social structure on the basis of radical protectionism and state corporatism, the bourgeoisie has hardly been autonomous. Most of it is, for all practical purposes, a creature of the state and continuously dependent on state economic and political support. For this reason, the fact that the bourgeoisie has not been inherently prone to democracy does not disprove the Marxist proposition that "bourgeoisie = liberal democracy, except when there is a revolutionary situation." In any case, the general validity of the equation is dubious. A typology of situations should be developed; the Argentine case points to the need to be especially sensitive to horizontal cleavages within the bourgeoisie, and to vertical coalitions involving segments of the bourgeoisie and labor or other "nonpossessing" classes.

We know that the parties representing the middle classes (mainly the Radicals) supported democracy before Peronism but opted for restrictive regimes in the post-Peronist period. There is, then, no consistent relationship. Like their counterparts in the cases of fascism in Europe and authoritarianism in Brazil or Chile, the Argentine middle classes supported antiliberal regimes of the Right whenever they felt threatened by a mobilized working class.

National Structure

In terms of cultural integration, twentieth-century Argentina could be ranked "medium" or "medium high": Its population is more diverse than that of homogeneous and relatively isolated nations, but the cultural differences among the main components are not very significant and have not led to enduring communal cleavages. The vast majority of the current population of Argentina descends from Italian and Spanish immigrants who arrived there between 1870 and 1930. There is a significant component of pre-immigration origin. In the 1960s, Lambert estimated that 86 percent of the population was "white" and the remainder was "*Mestizo* or Indian."[79] Half the immigrants were Italian, one-third were Spanish, and the remainder were mostly from other places in Europe (French, German, East European Jews, etc.). Except for these latter groups, differences among the various components were significant but not major. Cultural, religious, and linguistic congruity between Italians and Spaniards, and between them and the native population, was considerable.

Nonwhites had been acculturated during three centuries of Spanish rule. Unlike the English, the Spaniards practiced racial inclusion in their colonies. This led to the forced assimilation of native populations into the dominant culture, to widespread intermarriage, to the ethnic integration of most social classes and strata, and to the dampening of native identities. This process went very far in Argentina, whose Indian population was small, fragmented, and economically and politically less advanced than those of Peru or Mexico. Moreover, unintegrated tribes were decimated in the Indian wars of the nineteenth century.

As a result, ethnic differences did not crystalize into separate identities, there was little segregation along nationality lines among the three major groups (Italians, Spaniards, and Creoles), and Argentina never developed ethnic politics. The process of cultural integration among these three segments was relatively rapid. Given the size of the groups, however, this was not a process of assimilation into the majority culture, as in the United States, but one of amalgamation and development of a new, common culture, under the impact of interaction among Italians, Spaniards, and Creoles, continuous migration from the interior to the littoral, and generalization of public elementary education in the early 1900s.

Over the past century, the correlation between variations in the level of cultural integration and the presence or stability of democracy was negative, but this does not mean, of course, that there was a causal link in this direction. Cultural integration was relatively low in the first half of the twentieth century, and this had different consequences for democracy according to whether the economic elite controlled the state, and whether the external environment was threatening and uncertain. Before World War I, in a state controlled by a hegemonic and secure economic elite, the foreign origin of much of the population actually facilitated extending the franchise by diluting its impact; during World War II, under an autonomous state insulated from economic elites and in a context of high uncertainty, the ethnic heterogeneity of the working class, and the networks that still tied much of the Argentine population to Latin Europe, facilitated a distorted image of the working class and demonstration effects not conducive to democracy.

The consolidation of democratic institutions throughout the constitutional period supports the proposition that democracy will be more likely if a civil war has been decisively resolved and followed by reconciliation. The establishment of the democratic state was part of a policy of reconciliation among provincial elites after decades of indecisive conflict. Thereafter, the gap between the littoral and the interior intensified, for the benefits of the export economy, immigration, urbanization, expansion of education, and growth of the state were concentrated in the former region, especially in its core, the city and province of Buenos Aires. By the turn of the century, there was no question that the civil wars had been decisively resolved. Thus, the cleavages between the regions were cumulative, but their impact was controlled initially through federal mechanisms and the norm of rule by agreement, and later through the growth of the national state. Most interior provinces were eliminated as significant power contenders because they were economically peripheral to the littoral.

Although there is a cumulation of class and ethnicity, in that Creoles are overrepresented in the lower classes, this did not intensify social conflict in a lasting manner, even though there was an ethnic dimension in the antilabor and anti-Peronist attitude of the middle and upper classes during the large-scale migration of the 1940s and 1950s. Two factors mitigated the salience of ethnic cleavages: (1) the blurring of ethnic identities (and especially the weakness of the Mestizo and Indian ones); and (2) the fact that the correlation between class and ethnicity is still specified by region of residence or origin (most poor Creoles live either in interior provinces, where Creoles are represented in all social classes, or they are migrants into the big littoral cities, in which case their class status is attributed by them and others to their migrant origin rather than to their ethnicity).

State Structure and Strength

Our hypotheses postulate that democracy is more likely where state authority is effective, state power is not highly centralized, state control of the economy is limited, and autonomous intermediate groups limit state power.

The authority of the Argentine national state was effectively established in the nineteenth century, and this was without any doubt a precondition for democratization. The level of centralization was medium in the period of constitutional rule prior to the depression. There was a federal structure, but it was undermined when the Radicals resorted extensively to the constitutional procedure of federal intervention (by which the central government was empowered to replace provincial authorities in loosely defined critical situations) in order to weaken the Conservatives' power bases. The state also departed from the nightwatchman type in that it controlled public education and also, under the Radicals, began to develop government enterprises (the oil monopoly, in particular).

The level of centralization increased, as could be expected, in the non-democratic period; this supports the above proposition. Under military rule, and also under Peronism, provincial and local administrations, Congress (when it existed), and the judiciary were subordinate to the national executive. State control of the economy grew with the antidepression policies of the 1930s, but it leaped qualitatively after the turning point of 1943, with the new industrial and labor policies. Moreover, the Peronist government nationalized foreign trade, railroads, utilities, and a large share of banking. Eventually, a big public sector came into being. It included steel, military industries, and other activities ranging from meat-packing to hotels. In the 1960s and 1970s, many bankrupt firms in all areas were taken over by the state in order to prevent their liquidation and to save jobs (an original "Argentine road to socialism"). In the early 1980s, public investment was about half of gross domestic investment, and currently the state employs about 17 percent of the active population of the country.[80]

This triumphal march of the state over the society in the non-democratic period is consistent with the propositions under discussion, but it is important to note, first, that the expansion of the state was more an effect than a cause of the breakdown of liberal democracy; and second, that a large state sector, independently of its effectiveness in purely economic terms, is compatible with stable liberal democracy, as the European experience shows. The power of the state was always limited to some extent by organizations such as business groups, unions, the Catholic church, universities, and professional associations. Even under military regimes, there was limited pluralism. The strength and freedom of these organizations, however, varied during the non-democratic period that started in 1930.

Probably the church was the most immune to government control, except for the brief conflict between church and government toward the end of Peronism. It is, however, a semi-established institution, anchored in both state and society. (The church is financed by the government and, until the early

1960s, the government participated in appointing bishops; this is why, in my analysis, I have included the hierarchy within the state elite in the 1940s.) Business organizations have also been autonomous, except for the Peronist period, in which government intervened in the manufacturers' association and created another organization under government control. Unions have been subject to positive state control during Peronism, and to negative controls of different types, including intervention, freezing of assets, and imprisonment of leaders, during much of the post-Peronist period. Labor, however, always retained a significant degree of autonomy, because of a structural factor: In a society without a large labor reserve, unions had, for most of the post-Peronist period, effective control of labor markets. In any case, the autonomy of business associations and unions since World War II was limited by governmental control of every aspect of economic activity, and by government participation in collective bargaining. Finally, there was, since the University Reform, a tradition of autonomy in public universities, but it was severely restricted or canceled under Peronism and most military regimes.

Thus, the autonomy of intermediate groups has been generally lower under non-democratic regimes, but in any case the consequences for democracy of the activity of large and politically involved intermediate groups are not necessarily positive. These consequences vary according to the groups' ideologies and objectives, and to the degree to which they become channels for noninstitutionalized participation. In Argentina, most of these organizations have backed undemocratic options at different times, and all have been agents of mass praetorian conflict in the post-Peronist period.

The armed forces are the key sector of the state apparatus for analyzing the relationship between state and democracy. Our hypotheses postulate that democracy is more likely when the military is committed to democratic principles and civilian control, and where it is not dominated by any particular class (a reference, I assume, to the dominant classes). The Argentine case bears out both propositions, with some qualifications in regard to the latter. The Argentine military was subordinate to constitutional authorities up to the depression and during most of the Peronist regime and was the central component of what I have called the autonomous state in the rest of the period 1930–1983.

In the coup of 1930, the military clearly represented the interests of the dominant classes, and all the subsequent coups except that in 1943 shifted economic policies toward the interests of these classes. However, calling the military an instrument, or representative, of the dominant classes would be a gross simplification, except in the trivial sense that the military always had as its central objective containing revolution, and thus maintaining the status quo. This commitment, after the decline of the hegemony of the agrarian upper class, led the armed forces to develop doctrines that presented them as the central institution of society, not just as the core of the state but also of the nation, and consequently as the privileged definers and guardians of the national interest. This mentality has guided the military bureaucracy since the 1940s, regardless of the ideological differences between "liberals" (supporters of a measure of economic *laissez faire* and of authoritarian rule, at least in current conditions) and "nationalists" (committed to economic autarky, and to rightist antidemocratic political formulae).

This definition of their role led the armed forces, at different times, to support or to steer the state toward policies that were sometimes at variance with, and even contradicted the interests of different segments of the economic elites. In fact, the military has shifted between two poles: the simple role of arbiter, which led to coups whenever elected governments were seen as ineffective or illegitimate (e.g., in 1955 and 1958), and an "activist" posture, in which it sought, beyond replacing a weak government and responding to real or alleged revolutionary threats, to restructure the economy or the society (in 1966 and 1976).

The counterrevolutionary orientation of the Argentine military is paradoxical for two reasons. First, I have already argued that their panic in the 1940s, which had fateful consequences for Argentine society, was unfounded, and the same was true in the post-Peronist period, until the late 1960s.[81] The revolutionary threat was real enough in the 1970s, but the tradition of military intervention itself was one cause of guerrilla action: The choice of violence by a sector of the radicalized intelligentsia was determined by the system of mass praetorianism, one of whose central players was the military. They were the first ones to show that power grows out of the barrel of a gun. Second, this one time that the threat was realistic, the policy followed by the armed forces (basically, the use of violence disproportionately and quite indiscriminately) was politically counterproductive, for it led to the decline of their legitimacy, both as professionals and as players of the praetorian game.

Political Structure

The Argentine case is generally consistent with hypotheses that expect democracy to be more likely where the major parties have been moderate and nonideological; extreme parties are not significant; the ideological and social distance between parties has been limited, and parties have not sponsored or condoned violence or coups.

Argentina has had, throughout the twentieth century, two major parties (Conservative and Radical up to the turning point in the 1940s, Radical and Peronist thereafter) and several smaller ones whose significance was a function of their regional weight, or their ability to enter coalitions with the major parties (Socialist and Progressive Democrat up to the 1940s, and several regionally based conservative parties, the left-wing Intransigent, and small parties on the Center and Left in the post-Peronist period).

In the presidential elections held in the post-Peronist period, the two major parties together polled between 71 percent (in 1973) and 92 percent (in 1983) of the vote. Their social base and ideology are in a state of transition. From the 1940s to the 1960s, the lines were clear. The Radicals represented the middle classes, and their ideology was liberal-democratic in politics and diffusely populist, with some nationalist overtones, on economic issues. The Peronists represented a coalition based on labor, small manufacturers, and the antiliberal segment of the middle classes, while their economic ideology was strongly populist and nationalist, and their political ideology combined majority rule with antiliberalism and state corporatism.

The two parties were moderate, but their divergent social bases and significant ideological differences, both aggravated by stagnating tendencies and sharp cyclical fluctuations in the economy, were in themselves factors of instability. Extreme parties were not important, but both Peronists and Radicals were antisystem, the former because of their ideology and the latter because of their willingness to condone restrictive democracy, and even to support military intervention (at least once, when Perón was overthrown in 1955; a courtesy returned by the Peronists in 1966, when they acquiesced to the coup that deposed a Radical president, Illia).

Both parties changed in the 1970s and 1980s. I have already referred to the causes of the rise and fall of Peronism in these years: the entry of a segment of the intelligentsia, the appearance of a left wing, the emergence of guerrillas and their military defeat, the weakening of labor because of repression and the anti-industrial policies of the late 1970s, the leadership crisis after Perón's death, and the disastrous performance of the Peronist administration of 1973–1976. As a result, the Left is no longer a significant factor, the Right is less powerful than in the past, and a substantial liberal-democratic segment (the Renovating wing) has developed within the party.

Radicalism has also changed. With the failure of Peronism, the party made modest inroads among the lower classes, labor included. The experiences of the past two decades rendered the Radicals more democratic, and the experience of governing a society with a stagnated economy is turning them away from populist and nationalist formulae. Thus, social and ideological polarization between the two major parties may be weakening, a development that would be conducive to strengthening democracy.

Since the loss of a mass base by the Conservatives following Peronism, no major party has represented the interests of the dominant classes, so they have entered their demands into the political system through their associations (Sociedad Rural Argentina and Unión Industrial Argentina, which represent the large agrarian producers and the big manufacturers), and through their support for regimes, usually military ones, that applied "liberal" economic policies. Since there is a correlation between the eclipse of the Conservatives and the breakdown of democracy, the Argentine case would seem to support the proposition that democracy is more likely to persist if no major interest is excluded from representation in the political system. In fact, several authors have argued that the absence of a large party representing the economic elites and the subsequent discontinuity between economic and political power is the key to political instability after World War II.[82]

My view in this connection is that this discontinuity is more an effect than a determinant of the breakdown of democracy. Before the turning point, the Conservative Party was a coalition of provincial notables, while the Radicals had a stronger organization and urban political machines. The Conservatives did not change their structure in order to compete with the Radicals, for the latter, even though their following was mostly middle class, focused their demands on political reform (basically, the secret ballot), and nothing in their ideology was incompatible with the hegemony of the agrarian upper class. In fact, this party could be easily penetrated by that class.

After the turning point, there could not be a party representing the unified interests of the economic elite. First, the economic elite was not unified: its two segments, the agrarians and the "old" forward-linkage and foreign manufacturers on the one hand, and the new industrialists who expanded under radical protectionism (some of whom became large capitalists) on the other, could not co-exist in the same party, for their interests collided. Each segment joined a different coalition. Second, after World War II, the two support classes available in Argentine society—the middle class and labor—had already been captured by the Radicals and Peronists, respectively.

So far, all attempts to reconstitute a mass Conservative Party at the national level in the post-Peronist period have failed. There have been "populist" schemes such as that of the Federal Party, as well as more doctrinaire liberal projects like the current one led by the Union of the Democratic Center. The problem is that such a party would have to take a major segment of the middle classes away from the Radicals, which could happen only if the current Radical administration fails dramatically. In any case, consolidation of a significant conservative party committed to the principles of liberal democracy is still one of the prerequisites for institutionalizing competitive politics.

Finally, a hypothesis links democratic government with a strong and independent judiciary and with an independent press. The Argentine judiciary has never been strongly independent (the Supreme Court generally acquiesced to military coups, judges routinely accepted the validity of decisions made by technically illegal regimes, etc.), and the press, though seldom a mouthpiece for the rulers, has only rarely been vigorously free and independent when it was risky to be so, a rather frequent occurrence in the past four decades. In any case, autonomous judiciary and press are conditions for maintaining democracy, rather than causes of its establishment.

Political Leadership

There is a tradition of personalistic leadership in Argentine politics. Since the organization of the modern state, strong leaders have been central in the emergence of all the major parties: Julio A. Roca in what became the Conservative Party, Hipólito Yrigoyen in the Radical Party, and Juan Perón in Peronism. Personalized leadership, however, did not become a permanent trait: The Conservative and Radical parties developed as competitive political organizations, and the current crisis of Peronism is one of routinization of the founder's charisma. These and other leaders have been, in many situations, very skillful practitioners of coalition, compromise, and the resolution of conflict on the basis of complex strategies. Often in the twentieth century, leadership was a significant independent variable in major political processes, but its effect on democracy varied according to the nature of political institutions.

Before 1930, the Reform of 1912 stands out as an event in which skillful leadership was conducive to democracy. This reform was the product of interaction between Yrigoyen and his Conservative opponents, especially Roque Saenz Peña (the intellectual author of the reform law). After the breakdown, there were many instances in which leadership made a major difference, but one that was not conducive to liberal democracy. Perón, for example, was the most capable political leader in the century, as shown by the disparate political coalition he wove in the 1940s, and by his comeback in the 1970s, after having been overthrown and repudiated by the elites and a large segment of the citizenry. But he was a political entrepreneur rather than a statesman, and the consequences of his leadership exercises were always destabilizing. In the 1940s, his industrial and labor policies led to stagnation and illegitimacy; in the early 1970s, he condoned guerrilla activities first and right-wing violence later; when reelected, he presided over a chaotic administration; finally, his emphasis on the "leadership principle" plunged his own movement into a major succession crisis after his death.

But irresponsible leadership was the general norm after the turning point: Other leaders called for military intervention or did their best to provoke situations that would trigger such intervention. Only in the early 1980s, as a result of overall moderation and the growing acceptance of pluralism, is responsible and democratically oriented leadership reemerging in all the significant parties and interest groups.

Development Performance

The Argentine experience strongly confirms the proposition that links democracy with sustained and well-distributed economic growth. As I argued, development performance, which was in turn determined by changes in Argentine economic and political policies, was one central cause of the consolidation of democracy after the organization of the national state, and of the stalemate that prevented democracy in the post-Peronist period.

International Factors

The hypothesis that democracy is more likely if sources of potential diffusion have had democratic governments is borne out by the Argentine case. I have discussed the consequences for democracy of international demonstration effects that were salient at different times: positive influence of English and U.S. examples from the organization of the national state up to the depression, and negative influence of Italian fascism and the Spanish Civil War in the 1930s and 1940s. In addition other demonstration effects shaped the behavior of different social forces in the post-Peronist period. The Cuban Revolution had a powerful impact on both the Left and the Right: Its example, locally interpreted, led to guerrilla attempts and preemptive coups throughout Latin America, Argentina included. The example of Brazil, Argentina's traditional rival for regional hegemony, was also significant: The Brazilian coup of 1964 and the subsequent industrialization spurt was one of the factors that prompted the coup in Argentina in 1966 and inspired the economic policies of the new regime. In the early 1970s, finally, the experience of the Allende government in Chile and its overthrow by the armed forces was also followed closely by the Left and by the military in Argentina. The former confirmed their belief that a peaceful revolution was impossible, and the latter assimilated the fact that an actual revolutionary threat could be effectively controlled by large-scale application of force.

The relevance of these demonstration effects was a function of three factors: (1) the existence of cultural networks between recipient and sender countries; (2) the degree of applicability of the foreign experiences as defined by locals; and (3) the perceived efficacy of foreign models as positive examples (to be copied) or negative ones (to be avoided). Political development theory needs a more systematic analysis of how demonstration effects travel in the international system. A key actor in this process is the local intelligentsia, which selects, interprets, and disseminates demonstration effects.[83]

Propositions that democracy is more likely if the nation has not undergone exogenous subversive activities, and if it has received assistance, in times of stress, from other democratic polities have little relevance to the Argentine case. I do not think that the development of guerrilla groups in the 1960s was a result of Soviet or Cuban intervention. Such was the claim made by the military regimes, under the so-called national security doctrine. The Argentine guerrillas may have received, in addition to ideological inspiration, some training, arms, and funds from these and other foreign sources, but the emergence and activities of guerrilla organizations can be fully explained on the basis of domestic processes. The Soviet or Cuban governments may have taken some advantage of opportunities to spread their influence, but their participation in producing these opportunities was minor at best.

I am not aware of any specific action by other democratic nations that would have contributed directly to preserving or reestablishing democratic institutions in Argentina. However, there is no question that the human-rights policy of the Carter administration, as well as similar policies in France, Italy, and other European countries, saved many victims of indiscriminate repression in the late 1970s and was a factor in the international isolation of the military regime. On the other hand, the Argentine Left saw U.S. intervention behind the coup of 1930, and behind every coup and military regime in the post-Peronist period. No adequate evidence has been produced, and in any case it is very difficult to support claims of this type. There is no reason to assume that destabilizing these elected regimes was in the U.S. interest, but this is not an appropriate answer to these claims. Such an answer takes for granted what should be ascertained empirically; i.e., the long-term rationality of U.S. foreign policy.

As with the symmetric allegations about Soviet involvement in the development of guerrillas in the 1960s and early 1970s, it is more productive to ask whether these coups can be fully explained on the basis of domestic factors, and this happens to be the case. This conclusion does not exempt the United States and some European nations from indirect responsibility in two typical situations. First is the support by advanced industrial countries for International Monetary Fund (IMF)–style austerity plans in the face of balance-of-payment difficulties. Applying these plans in Argentina in the 1960s was one cause of labor unrest and the general social polarization that triggered military coups. Second, the United States supported, with economic assistance and political recognition, military governments once they were in place (in Argentina, I have noted the exception of the military regime in the late 1970s). In these two situations, narrow and even misleading considerations of short-term advantage were at work: concern for the interests of domestic creditors, even at the risk of provoking turmoil in countries of strategic significance for the United States; and the search for stability and for anti-Communist allies, which prevented U.S. policymakers from realizing how illusory is the apparent legitimacy of authoritarian regimes, and to what extent allegations about revolutionary danger could be more a justification for a military takeover than a reality.

• PROSPECTS •

Reestablishing constitutional rule in 1983 took place in an inauspicious context: an economy characterized by stagnation, three-digit inflation, and a staggering debt; and a polity shaped by decades of mass praetorianism and authoritarian rule.[84] There were, however, two favorable factors: The sincere commitment by the Alfonsín administration and the Radical Party to institutionalizing liberal democracy, and the shift toward moderation and tolerance that the recent traumatic experiences produced in most interest groups and political parties. But these democratic orientations in the polity and in civil society are so incompatible with the underlying economic and political structure that there is a clear danger that they might weaken as different social groups pursue their interests.

First, mass praetorianism may reassert itself because its determinant, the co-existence of a large noncompetitive manufacturing sector and a society characterized by highly mobilized social forces, is still there. Such a combination can produce only a low-growth economy and a high propensity for social and political conflict. Stagnating tendencies are aggravated by the new factor of a large foreign debt. Instead of the sharp cyclical fluctuations that characterized it in the past, the Argentine economy is likely to remain in a protracted recession, as a large share of the gains from agrarian exports is allocated to debt service.

Second, the institutional infrastructure of mass praetorianism and corporatism has not been broken. As long as the party system is relatively weak, and interest groups and bureaucratic organizations such as the unions, the military, business, and others are strong, politicized, and independent from parties, there is a danger that an explosion of demands could trigger the destabilization mechanism that destroyed elected governments in the past: Balance-of-payment difficulties forced the government to implement recessionary policies; these spawned intense mobilization by labor and other groups, which eventually produced hyperinflation and a high level of social polarization. The result was panic by the bourgeoisie and a sector of the middle classes, the paralysis of government, and eventually a military coup aimed at demobilizing labor and other social forces.

Consolidating democracy would be facilitated by the resumption of economic growth and would require dismantling the institutional infrastructure of corporatism. These two changes amount, in short, to the undoing of the wrong choices made in the 1940s. The first change presupposes the reconversion of the manufacturing sector, or at least of an important part of it. The second entails transforming Peronism into a party that would be strong vis-à-vis the unions (and thus capable of representing their interests in a nondestabilizing manner) and that would be committed to preserving constitutional rule; and subordinating the armed forces to the government. These are complex processes, and the full realization of the goal requires minimally satisfactory outcomes in all. The issues are interrelated, and the results depend on many factors, but in two instances—the resumption of economic growth and the subordination of the military to civilian rule—responsibility lies primarily with the government; the transformation of Peronism depends more on processes that take place within that movement.

Economic policy was, in the beginning of the new administration, dominated by negotiations over debt. In its dealings with the IMF, the major leading banks, and the creditor governments, the Alfonsín administration tried to thread a difficult path between recessive stabilization policies and a unilateral moratorium, or other confrontational strategies. For the first year and a half, the government endeavored to obtain foreign support for gradual adjustment policies. In 1985, in the face of four-digit annual inflation, there was a drastic shift toward a shock treatment, what came to be known as the Austral Plan. Stabilization policies, after considerable initial success, proved incapable of controlling inflation, which is, in early 1988, back at the three-digit level. In any case, policies of this sort, regardless of their effectiveness in reducing inflation and helping with debt negotiations, do not deal with the structural problem of the Argentine economy: A large share of capital, labor, and the foreign exchange obtained through agrarian exports, is committed to noncompetitive manufacturing. With or without the debt, this is the issue Argentina has to face if the country is to resume sustained economic growth.

Substantially reconverting the economy is a major challenge for any political system, but it is especially unmanageable in a democracy, particularly in a recently established one. For reconversion is obviously inconsistent with the interests of a large share of workers and capitalists, of the managers of the inefficient public sector, and also of the broad segment of the middle classes that is hired by, sells to, or provides services for noncompetitive manufacturing. Even a military regime like that of Argentina in the late 1970s succeeded only partially in its attempt to reorient the economy outwards through trade liberalization (an attempt that was part of an irrational economic policy that did little to promote reindustrialization: Its only consequence was a massive wave of bankruptcies and layoffs).

Reconverting through foreign investment is not a viable option either. There can be a significant flow of capital to Argentina, but it is unlikely to be large. After all, there are more profitable opportunities around the world than those offered by a country that has no strategic raw materials, an inefficient infrastructure, a medium-size market far away from major consumption centers, a militant working class, a large foreign debt, and a history of hyperinflation and political instability.

The only feasible policy is a gradual reconversion. Rather than an across-the-board cut in effective protection, a step-by-step program of industrial transformation could be politically feasible. Such a program would cushion the impact of transition for both capitalists and workers. Government agencies could provide economic and technological support to selected industries or firms and retrain workers who are laid off. But a reconversion of this type would still antagonize the business sector and the unions and would require a long-term policy horizon, something lacking in the Radical administration.

The policies of advanced industrial countries might make a major difference in the economic issue. This applies most obviously to negotiations over the debt: Some steps by the creditors, such as transforming short-term obligations into very long-term ones, guaranteed by all the governments involved, would remove the brake on the economies of debtor nations such as Argentina. Trade policy would be a second area: eliminating restrictions on imports into the U.S. and European markets and facilitating transfer of equipment and technology in areas of manufacturing in which Argentina and other debtor nations have an export potential could contribute to reconverting these countries' economies, and also to their ability to service the debt.

The government has been more decisive on the military front, but here, also, a major structural transformation still needs to be undertaken. The reason for the greater decisiveness is that Alfonsín had no choice in dealing with the armed forces: Either he moved fast and tried to bring them back to their legal role within the state, or he soon would be at their mercy. Paradoxically, it is in relation to this issue, which was untouchable for two generations, that the constitutional administration has the best chance for success, because of the military's loss of legitimacy.

In the beginning of the new government, most leading officers were retired, the military budget was significantly reduced, and many of the firms and agencies controlled by the military were removed from its jurisdiction. But the most important action was the trial of the leaders of the military regime and of various officers who ran the torture and illegal detention centers. Some of the defendants have been found guilty of massive violations of human rights, and the two most important leaders were given life sentences. This is the first time since the breakdown of democracy in 1930 that authoritarian rulers must answer for their actions before a court of law. This is immensely significant for institutionalizing democracy, even though, it should be noted, these officers were prosecuted for kidnapping, torture, and murder, not for having carried out a coup or for having usurped the power of the state.

Initially, the armed forces absorbed this offensive, even though there was a great deal of discontent among them. However, when army officers on active duty began to be summoned by the courts, localized rebellions broke out in 1987. Parties, labor, and other interest groups immediately mobilized to defend the constitutional order, but the government avoided a confrontation by granting an amnesty to officers who had violated the law while complying with orders, thus effectively blocking prosecution of all but a handful of leaders of the military regime. This policy obtained the support of the most moderate or professional segment of the armed forces, and the most extremist elements were isolated. Many of the rebellious officers were disciplined, but the antiliberal cluster within the military is still, because of its strategic location in the state apparatus, the major immediate threat to the stability of constitutional rule.

The precondition for placing the armed forces firmly under civilian control is a thorough reorganization of the military. Instead of a large and unwieldy apparatus geared to controlling the domestic population, operated by poorly trained and equipped officers, and run on the basis of rationalizing ideologies such as the national security doctrine, the country should have a small but highly professional military organization, focused on defense against external armed threats, better equipped, and socialized into a doctrine of subordination to constitutional authorities. A transformation of this type would, of course, antagonize officers even in the lower ranks, since it would involve a drastic reduction in the size of the services, a new emphasis on the development of technical skills, and major changes in military lifestyles (e.g., many officers would have to move from cities to border posts).

The key to the dissolution of the praetorian polity, however, lies with the labor unions and Peronism. If they are thoroughly integrated into the democratic system, constitutional rule could be strengthened, even in the absence of a fully satisfactory military reform. Conversely, a very high level of social polarization caused by an explosion of labor discontent, and a destabilizing offensive led by the opposition, are likely to produce a coup in any case.

At the beginning of the new administration, the labor movement had been weakened not only by deindustrialization and the repression it had experienced under the military, but also by the electoral defeat suffered by the Peronists, and by the questionable legitimacy of many of the union leaders. Since 1983, labor had been revitalized by the resurgence of the trade-union federation and the renovation of leadership in many of the unions. The behavior of the labor movement has been more moderate than in past civilian regimes. The stabilization policy followed by the government has caused a significant drop in real wages, the rate of unemployment has been rising, and the informal sector of the economy keeps growing. There have been important strikes, including, as of this writing, eleven general ones, and isolated factory takeovers, but on the whole the labor response has not been destabilizing. There are two reasons for this pragmatism: (1) growing unemployment, be it open or disguised, which produces insecurity among workers still employed and deters their mobilization; and (2) the memory of repression and deindustrialization under the previous military regime, which induces workers to think that their situation would be even harsher under renewed military rule.

The potential for mass mobilization remains, as real wages keep falling and discontent grows, and as the memories of distress under the military blur with time. Moreover, the political conditions of liberal democracy are more conducive than those of authoritarianism to forming a large stratum of activists and of social-movement organizations. However, the possibility that this discontent might be canalized by a large and effective political organization bent on destabilizing the government is not very high, for neither the Left nor the Peronist Right appear as likely agents for such a process.

The growth of the revolutionary Left is probable in the near future, but it is likely to be a middle-class Left, with a base in a segment of the students and the intelligentsia. The Left, whose combined strength is about 10 percent of the electorate, includes the Intransigent Party, a heterogeneous combination of former left-wing Radicals and Marxists; a small Communist Party, which polls 1–2 percent of the votes and is in ideological and organizational turmoil; and several other Marxist and socialist groups. The Peronist Left has been decimated by repression, and only small circles remain.

All these organizations have tried to develop a labor base, but their success has been limited so far, despite the adverse economic conditions. What is most important, the overall trend toward moderation in the middle classes includes the intelligentsia, students, and the professional strata; i.e., the social base of the Argentine Left. The causes of this shift are several: the defeat of the guerrillas in the 1970s; the failure of the revolutionary strategies in neighboring Chile and Uruguay; the waning of the revolutionary glamor of the countries of "real socialism," Cuba included; and the demonstration effect of the disenchantment of the European Left with Marxism. Thus, the blocked and frustrated middle class is more likely to orient its discontent toward liberal-democratic left-wing options rather than toward the Communist Party or other revolutionary groups.

As for the Peronist Right, its influence receded as democratic practices and beliefs strengthened, both within Peronism and in the political system as a whole. Overall, the sectors behaving as a loyal opposition to the Radicals, both in the labor movement and in the party organization, are the winners in this process of differentiation. However, Peronism is still in transition from a diffuse "movement" into a social-democratic or Christian-democratic party. A successful shift of this type is necessary to consolidate democracy, for democracy requires, in addition to a democratic governing party, a democratic opposition. For the Peronists to become such a party, they should develop a competitive, pluralistic organization, and an ideology that explicitly accepts liberal institutions. If these changes take place, Peronists would become, like Democrats in the United States, a party representing labor and the country's periphery.

Such a transformation in Peronism could lead to the Radicals' shifting to a Center-Right party; i.e., a party that would represent not only the middle classes, but also business interests. This prospect is buttressed by the new "economic realism" shown by the Radicals but would nevertheless run counter to the social-democratic leanings of their most articulate leaders. The representation of business interests is more likely to be based on a coalition among the Union of the Democratic Center and several small conservative parties. Thus, the Argentine party system could be consolidated into four significant units: the two large parties (Radicals and Peronists) each getting 30–50 percent of the vote, and smaller coalitions on the Left and Right, each having about 10–15 percent of the electorate.

These are the issues the country faces. This still-fragile democracy will be submitted to a crucial test should the Peronists, who are in the middle of their own uncertain transition, win the next presidential election. In any case, students of Argentina will look back at the transfer of office by President Alfonsín to an elected successor in 1989 as a milestone in the process of democratization. The last time that such a transfer took place between two different persons in the context of a liberal-democratic regime was in 1928.

• NOTES •

1. Most of this section draws from chs. 1 and 3 of Carlos H. Waisman, *Reversal of Development in Argentina: Postwar Counterrevolutionary Policies and Their Structural Consequences* (Princeton, NJ: Princeton University Press, 1987). I was completing my work on that book when I wrote this chapter, and the two projects merged.

2. For some historical interpretations of Argentina, see Juan E. Corradi, *The Fitful Republic: Economy, Society, and Politics in Argentina* (Boulder, CO: Westview Press, 1985); James R. Scobie, *Argentina: A City and a Nation* (New York: Oxford University Press, 1964); David Rock, *Argentina 1516–1982: From Spanish Colonization to the Falklands War* (Berkeley: University of California Press, 1985); Peter Smith, *Argentina and the Failure of Democracy* (Madison: Univer-

sity of Wisconsin Press, 1974); and Waisman, *Reversal of Development,* especially ch. 4.
   3. For a summary of these arguments, see Waisman, *Reversal of Development,* ch. 2.
   4. See Roberto Cortés Conde, *El progreso argentino, 1880–1914* (Buenos Aires: Sudamericana, 1979), ch. 4; Gino Germani, *Política y sociedad en una época de transición* (Buenos Aires: Paidós, 1962), ch. 7; Carl Solberg, *Immigration and Nationalism: Argentina and Chile, 1890–1914* (Austin: University of Texas Press, 1970), ch. 6; and Waisman, *Reversal of Development,* ch. 3.
   5. Carlos F. Díaz Alejandro, *Essays on the Economic History of the Argentine Republic* (New Haven, CT: Yale University Press, 1970), p. 1n.
   6. W. Arthur Lewis, *Growth and Fluctuations, 1870–1913* (London: George Allen and Unwin, 1978), p. 197.
   7. Naciones Unidas, *El desarrollo económico de la Argentina,* vol. 1 (Mexico D.F.: Naciones Unidas, 1959), p. 15.
   8. Alfred Maizels, *Industrial Growth and World Trade* (Cambridge: Cambridge University Press, 1963).
   9. Estimates of the Central Bank of the Argentine Republic, in Díaz Alejandro, *Economic History,* p. 406.
   10. The secondary sector includes manufacturing, construction, transport, and utilities. Naciones Unidas, *Desarrollo económico,* vol. 1, p. 37.
   11. W. S. Wyotinsky and E. S. Wyotinsky, *World Population and Production, Trends, and Outlook* (New York: Twentieth Century Fund, 1953), p. 117.
   12. Díaz Alejandro, *Economic History,* p. 56.
   13. As measured by the proportion of the population living in cities over 100,000. See Wyotinsky and Wyotinsky, *World Population,* p. 229.
   14. World Bank, *Poverty and Human Development* (New York: Oxford University Press, 1980), pp. 68–69.
   15. Charles L. Taylor and Michael C. Hudson, *World Handbook of Political and Social Indicators,* 2d ed. (New Haven, CT: Yale University Press, 1972), pp. 229–231.
   16. United Nations Economic Commission for Latin America, *Statistical Yearbook for Latin America 1984* (Santiago: United Nations, 1985), p. 146.
   17. Tulio Halperin Donghi, "Prólogo." In *Proyecto y construcción de una nación (Argentina, 1846–1880),* ed. Tulio Halperin Donghi (Caracas: Biblioteca Ayacucho, 1980), p. xii.
   18. Carlos H. Waisman, *Modernization and the Working Class: The Politics of Legitimacy* (Austin: University of Texas Press, 1982), chs. 2 and 5.
   19. For general discussions of the oligarchic state, see Natalio Botana, *El orden conservador* (Buenos Aires: Sudamericana, 1977); see also two classical works: José N. Matienzo, *El gobierno representativo federal en la République Argentina* (Madrid: Editorial América, 1917); and Rodolfo Rivarola, *Del Régimen federativo al unitario* (Buenos Aires: n.p., 1908). For the process of state construction, see Oscar Oszlak, *La formación del estado argentino* (Buenos Aires: Editorial de Belgrano, 1982).
   20. David Rock, *Politics in Argentina, 1890–1930: The Rise and Fall of Radicalism* (Cambridge: Cambridge University Press, 1975), p. 83.
   21. See Botana, *Orden conservador,* pp. 174–189; Darío Canton, *Elecciones y partidos políticos en la Argentina* (Buenos Aires: Siglo XXI, 1973), ch. 1.
   22. Peter H. Smith, "The Breakdown of Democracy in Argentina." In *The Breakdown of Democratic Regimes: Latin America,* ed. Juan J. Linz and Albert Stepan (Baltimore, MD: Johns Hopkins University Press, 1978); and Smith, *Failure of Democracy,* pp. 16, 23, 90–92.
   23. Botana, *Orden conservador,* p. 328. See also Canton, *Elecciones y partidos,* ch. 2.
   24. On the Reform of 1912, see Botana, *Orden conservador;* Canton, *Elecciones y partidos;* Rock, *Politics in Argentina;* Miguel Angel Cárcano, *Saenz Peña: La revolución por los comicios* Buenos Aires, 1963).
   25. See Samuel P. Huntington, *Political Order in Changing Societies* (New Haven, CT: Yale University Press, 1968), ch. 1; Juan J. Linz, *Crisis, Breakdown, and Re-equilibration* (Baltimore, MD: Johns Hopkins University Press, 1978), ch. 2; Seymour M. Lipset, *Political Man: The Social Bases of Politics* (Garden City, NY: Doubleday, 1960), ch. 3.
   26. Canton, *Elecciones y partidos;* Robert A. Dahl, *Polyarchy: Participation and Opposition* (New Haven, CT: Yale University Press, 1971), pp. 133–136.
   27. Smith, *Failure of Democracy,* pp. 93–94; and, "Breakdown."
   28. Smith, "Breakdown": Anne L. Potter, *Political Institutions, Political Decay, and the*

Argentine Crisis of 1930 (Ph.D. diss., Stanford University, Stanford, CA, 1978).
29. Rock, *Politics in Argentina.*
30. Smith, "Breakdown."
31. Rock, *Politics in Argentina,* ch. 11; Carl E. Solberg, *Oil and Nationalism in Argentina* (Stanford, CA: Stanford University Press, 1979), ch. 5; Carlos A. Mayo et al., *Diplomacia política y petróleo en la Argentina* (Buenos Aires: Rincón, 1976).
32. On this period, see Alberto Ciria, *Partidos y poder en la Argentina moderna, 1930–1946* (Buenos Aires: Jorge Alvarez, 1964); and Mark Falcoff and Ronald H. Dolkart, eds., *Prologue to Perón: Argentina in Depression and War, 1930–1943* (Berkeley: University of California Press, 1975).
33. Jacques Blondel, *Comparing Political Systems* (New York: Praeger, 1972), ch. 4. See also the discussion of legitimacy as capital in Waisman, *Modernization and the Working Class,* ch. 2.
34. See Miguel Murmis and Juan Carlos Portantiero, *Estudios sobre los orígenes del peronismo* (Buenos Aires: Siglo XXI, 1971); Gino Germani, "El surgimiento del peronismo: El rol de los obreros y de los migrantes internos" and Tulio Halperin Donghi, "Algunas observaciones sobre Germani, el surgimiento del peronismo, y los migrantes internos." In *El voto peronista,* ed. Manuel Mora y Araujo and Ignacio Llorente (Buenos Aires: Sudamericana, 1980); Hiroschi Matsushita, *Movimiento obrero argentino, 1930–1945* (Buenos Aires: Siglo Veinte, 1983); and David Tamarin, *The Argentine Labor Movement, 1930–1945* (Albuquerque: University of New Mexico Press, 1985).
35. For interpretations of Peronism, see Eldon Kenworthy, "The Function of the Little-known Case in Theory Formation, or What Peronism Wasn't," *Comparative Politics* 6 (October 1973): 1–35, and his "Interpretaciones ortodoxas y revisionistas del apoyo inicial del peronismo," in Mora y Araujo and Llorente, *Voto peronista.*
36. For analyses of this regime, see Ciria, *Partidos y poder;* Enrique Díaz Araujo, *La conspiración del 43* (Buenos Aires: La Bastilla, 1971); Ruth and Leonard Greenup, *Revolution Before Breakfast: Argentina, 1941–1946* (Chapel Hill: University of North Carolina Press, 1947); Robert A. Potash, *The Army and Politics in Argentina, 1928–1945: Yrigoyen to Perón* (Stanford, CA: Stanford University Press, 1969); and Alain Rouquié, *Pouvoir militaire et société politique en Republique Argentine* (Paris: Presses de la Fondation Nationale des Sciences Politiques, 1978).
37. See Germani, "Surgimiento del peronismo"; Felix Luna, *El 45: Crónica de un año decisivo* (Buenos Aires: Jorge Alvarez, 1969); Murmis and Portantiero, *Orígenes del peronismo;* Waisman, *Modernization and the Working Class,* ch. 4.
38. See George I. Blanksten, *Perón's Argentina* (Chicago: University of Chicago Press, 1953); Corradi, *Fitful Republic,* ch. 5; Peter Waldmann, *El peronismo, 1943–1955* (Buenos Aires: Sudamericana, 1981).
39. On Perón's economic policies, see Díaz Alejandro, *Economic History,* ch. 2; Aldo Ferrer, *The Argentine Economy* (Berkeley: University of California Press, 1967), ch. 15–17; Aldo Ferrer, *Crisis y alternativas de la política económica argentina* (Buenos Aires: Fondo de Cultura Económica, 1980); Gary W. Wynia, *Argentina in the Post-War Era: Politics and Economic Policymaking in a Divided Society* (Albuquerque: University of New Mexico Press, 1978), ch. 3.
40. Waisman, *Modernization and the Working Class,* pp. 22–23, 65–66; Waisman, *Reversal of Development,* pp. 121–124.
41. Huntington, *Political Order.*
42. See Torcuato S. Di Tella, "Stalemate or Coexistence in Argentina." In *Latin America: Reform or Revolution?,* ed. James Petras and Maurice Zeitlin (Greenwich, CT: Fawcett, 1968); and Guillermo A. O'Donnell, *Modernization and Bureaucratic Authoritarianism: Studies in South American Politics* (Berkeley: University of California, Institute of International Studies, 1973).
43. The relation of forces underlying this conflict has been described by several authors. See Mario Brodersohn, "Conflicto entre los objetivos de política económica de corto plazo de la economía argentina" (Buenos Aires: Instituto Di Tella, 1977); Marcelo Diamand, *Doctrinas económicas, desarrollo e independencia* (Buenos Aires: Paidos, 1973); Marcelo Diamand, "El péndulo argentino: Empate político o fracasos económicos?" (Buenos Aires: Mimeo, 1976); Aldo Ferrer, *Crisis y alternativas;* Gilbert W. Merkx, "Sectoral Clashes and Political Change: The Argentine Experience," *Latin American Research Review* 4 (1969): pp. 89–114; Guillermo A. O'Donnell, "Estado y alianzas en la Argentina, 1956–1976," *Desarrollo económico* 16, no. 64 (1977): pp. 523–554; Lars Schoultz, *The Populist Challenge: Argentine Electoral Behavior in the Postwar Era*

(Chapel Hill: University of North Carolina Press, 1983), pp. 85–95; and Gary W. Wynia, *Argentina in the Post-War Era* (Albuquerque: University of New Mexico Press, 1978).

44. Diamand, *Doctrinas económicas,* and "El péndulo argentino."
45. Ferrer, *Crisis y alternativas;* O'Donnell, "Estado y alianzas."
46. Díaz Alejandro, *Economic History;* Richard D. Mallon and Juan V. Sorrouille, *Economic Policymaking in a Conflict Society: The Argentine Case* (Cambridge, MA: Harvard University Press, 1975); see also Adalbert Krieger Vasena and Javier Pazos, *Latin America: A Broader World Role* (Totowa, NJ: Rowan and Littlefield, 1976).
47. See Santiago Macario, "Protectionism and Industrialization in Latin America," *Economic Bulletin for Latin America* 9, no. 1 (1964); Díaz Alejandro, *Economic History,* pp. 255–276; Julio Berlinski and Daniel M. Schydlowsky, "Incentives for Industrialization in Argentina," (Washington, D.C.: International Bank for Reconstruction and Development, 1977).
48. Mallon and Sorrouille, *Economic Policymaking,* p. 159.
49. Javier Villanueva, "Aspectos de la estrategia de industrialización argentina." In *Los fragmentos de poder,* ed. Torcuato S. Di Tella and Tulio Halperin Donghi (Buenos Aires: Jorge Alvarez, 1969), pp. 339–350; and his "Economic Development." In Falcoff and Dolkart, *Prologue to Perón,* pp. 72–79; Eduardo F. Jorge, *Industria y concentración económica* (Buenos Aires: Siglo XXI, 1971), pp. 67, 131–132; Waisman, *Reversal of Development,* chs. 5–6.
50. These issues are discussed in Waisman, *Reversal of Development,* chs. 5–7.
51. Jorge Fodor, "Perón's Policies for Agricultural Exports, 1946–1948: Dogmatism or Commonsense?" In *Argentina in the Twentieth Century,* ed. David Rock (Pittsburgh: University of Pittsburgh Press, 1975); Carlos Escudé, *Gran Bretaña, Estados Unidos, y la declinación argentina* (Buenos Aires: Editorial del Belgrano, 1983).
52. Díaz Alejandro, *Economic History,* pp. 104–105; Murmis and Portantiero, *Orígenes del peronismo,* pp. 3–48; Villanueva, "Aspectos," pp. 329–330; and his "Economic Development," p. 65.
53. See Ciria, *Partidos y poder,* pp. 132–139; Alberto Conil Paz and Gustavo Ferrari, *Política exterior argentina, 1930–1962* (Buenos Aires: Editorial Huemul, 1964), pp. 65–161; Díaz Araujo, *Conspiración del 43,* passim; Escudé, *Gran Bretaña,* pp. 23–162; Potash, *Army and Politics, 1928–1945,* pp. 131–237; Mario Rapoport, *Gran Bretaña, Estados Unidos y las clases dirigentes argentinas, 1940–1945* (Buenos Aires: Editorial de Belgrano, 1980), pp. 239–292.
54. Peter Smith, *Politics and Beef in Argentina* (New York: Columbia University Press, 1969), pp. 32–56; Oscar Cornblitt, "Inmigrantes y empresarios en la política Argentina" in Torcuato S. Di Tella and Tulio Halperin Donghi, eds. *Los fragmentos del poder* (Buenos Aires: Jorge Alvarez, 1969); Jorge, *Industria y concentración económica,* pp. 34, 151–152; Ciria, *Partidos y poder,* pp. 110–147; Díaz Araujo, *Conspiración del 43,* pp. 11–201; Tulio Halperin Donghi, *Argentina: La democracia de masas* (Buenos Aires: Paidós, 1972), ch. 1; Potash, *Army and Politics 1928–1945,* pp. 182–200; Rapoport, *Gran Bretaña,* passim; Alain Rouquié, *Pouvoir militaire et société politique,* pp. 275–317.
55. On Argentine right-wing nationalism, see Cristian Buchrucker, *Nacionalismo y peronismo* (Buenos Aires: Sudamericana, 1987); Marysa Navarro Gerassi, *Los nacionalistas* (Buenos Aires: Jorge Alvarez, 1969); and Enrique Zulueta Alvarez, *El nacionalismo argentino,* 2 vols. (Buenos Aires: Editorial La Bastilla, 1975).
56. Waisman, *Reversal of Development,* ch. 6; Perón's speeches 1943–1946 are collected in Juan Perón, *El pueblo quiere saber de qué se trata* (Buenos Aires, n.p., 1944) and *El pueblo ya sabe de qué se trata: Discursos* (Buenos Aires, n.p., n.d.).
57. Waisman, *Reversal of Development.*
58. Matsushita, *Movimiento obrero;* Murmis and Portantiero, *Orígenes del perónismo;* Tamarin, *Argentine Labor Movement.*
59. See Banco Central de la República Argentina, Departamento de Investigaciones Económicas, *Informe preliminar sobre los efectos que tendría en las actividades industriales internas la libre reanudación de las importaciones* (Buenos Aires, Banco Central de la Republica Argentina, 1945); Waisman, *Reversal of Development,* ch. 6.
60. The image of the intrinsically dangerous working class recurs in the writings of right-wing nationalists and other antiliberals in the interwar period. For the labor movement in the beginning of the century, see Hobart Spalding, ed., *La clase trabajadora argentina: Documentos para su historia, 1890–1912* (Buenos Aires: Editorial Galerna, 1970); Samuel L. Baily, *Labor, Nationalism, and Politics in Argentina* (New Brunswick, NJ: Rutgers University Press, 1967), ch.

1; Julio Godio, *Historia del movimiento obrero argentino: Inmigrantes, asalariados, y lucha de clases, 1880–1910* (Buenos Aires: Editorial Tiempo Contemporáneo, 1973); Rubens Iscaro, *Origen y desarrollo del movimiento sindical argentino* (Buenos Aires: Editorial Anteo, 1958), ch. 5; Alfredo López, *Historia del movimiento social y la clase obrera argentina* (Buenos Aires: Editorial Programa, n.d.), ch. 20–27; Sebastián Marotta, *El movimiento sindical argentino*, vol. 2 (Buenos Aires: Ediciones Lacio, 1961); Jacinto Oddone, *Gremialismo proletario argentino* (Buenos Aires: Editorial La Vanguardia, 1949), ch. 16–36; Panettieri, *Los trabajadores* (Buenos Aires: Jorge Alvarez, 1967), ch. 6–7; Ruben Rotondaro, *Realidad y cambio en el sindicalismo* (Buenos Aires: Editorial Pleamar, 1971), ch. 2. On the Socialists, see Oddone, *Gremialismo proletario argentino;* Nicolas Repetto, *Mi paso por la política: de Roca a Yrigoyen* (Buenos Aires: Santiago Rueda, 1957); José Vazeilles, *Los socialistas,* (Buenos Aires: Jorge Alvarez, 1967); Richard J. Walter, *The Socialist Party of Argentina, 1890–1930* (Austin: University of Texas Press, 1977). On the Anarchists, see Diego Abad de Santillán, *El movimiento anarquista en la Argentina* (Buenos Aires: Argonauta, 1930); and *La FORA: Ideología y trayectoria,* 2d ed. (Buenos Aires: Editorial Proyección, 1971); Iaacov Oved, *El anarquismo y el movimiento obrero en Argentina* (Mexico: Siglo XXI, 1978). On labor conflicts after World War I, see Julio Godio, *La semana trágica de enero de 1919* (Buenos Aires: Granica Editor, 1972); Marotta, *Movimiento sindical argentino,* ch. 16; David Rock, "Lucha civil en la Argentina: La Semana trágica de enero de 1919," *Desarrollo económico* 11, no. 42 (1972): pp. 165–215, and his *Politics in Argentina,* ch. 7; and Osvaldo Bayer, *La Patagonia rebelde* (Mexico: Editorial Nueva Imagen, 1980).

61. The strength of the Spanish and Italian demonstration effects is obvious in the political writings of the antiliberal Right. For a representative example of the impact of fascism in the work of a prominent mainstream intellectual, see Leopoldo Lugones, *El estado equitativo* (Buenos Aires: La Editora Argentina, 1932). See also Carlos Ibarguren, *La historia que he vivido* (Buenos Aires: Editorial Peuser, 1955) and Mario Amadeo, *Ayer, hoy, y mañana* (Buenos Aires: Editorial Gure, 1956). For general discussions, see Ciria, *Partidos y poder;* John J. Kennedy, *Catholicism, Nationalism, and Democracy in Argentina* (Notre Dame, IN: University of Notre Dame Press, 1958); Mark Falcoff, "Argentina." In *The Spanish Civil War, 1936–1939; American Hemispheric Perspectives,* ed. Mark Falcoff and Frederick B. Pike (Lincoln: University of Nebraska Press, 1982); and Waisman, *Reversal of Development,* ch. 7.

62. For general discussions of the period, see Marcelo Cavarozzi, *Autoritarismo y democracia, 1955–1983* (Buenos Aires: Centro Editor de América Latina, 1983); Corradi, *Fitful Republic;* and Félix Luna, *De Perón a Lanusse, 1943–1973* (Buenos Aires: Editorial Planeta, 1973).

63. See Robert A. Potash, *The Army and Politics in Argentina, 1945–1962* (Stanford, CA: Stanford University Press, 1980).

64. On this regime, which pompously called itself "the Argentine revolution," see Guillermo O'Donnell, *1966–1973: El estado burocrático-autoritario* (Buenos Aires: Editorial del Belgrano, 1982); and Rubén M. Perina, *Onganía, Levingston, Lanusse: Los militares en la política argentina* (Buenos Aires: Ediciones de Belgrano, 1983).

65. O'Donnell, *Modernization and Bureaucratic Authoritarianism;* O'Donnell, "Modernization and Military Coups: Theory, Comparisons, and the Argentine Case." In *Armies and Politics in Latin America,* ed. Abraham F. Lowenthal (New York: Homes and Meier, 1976); O'Donnell, *1966–1973: El estado burocrático-autoritario.*

66. See Albert O. Hirschman, "The Turn to Authoritarianism in Latin America;" Robert R. Kaufman, "Industrial Change and Authoritarian Rule in Latin America: A Concrete Review of the Bureaucratic-Authoritarian Model;" and José Serra, "Three Mistaken Theses Regarding the Connection Between Industrialization and Authoritarian Regimes." In *The New Authoritarianism in Latin America,* ed. David Collier (Princeton, NJ: Princeton University Press, 1979).

67. Hirschman, "Turn to Authoritarianism," p. 71.

68. See Donald C. Hodges, *Argentina, 1943–1976: The National Revolution and Resistance* (Albuquerque: University of New Mexico Press, 1976); Richard Gillespie, *Soldiers of Perón: Argentina's Montoneros* (New York: Oxford University Press, 1982); Pablo Giussani, *Montoneros: La soberbia armada* (Buenos Aires: Sudamericana Planeta, 1984).

69. On this regime, see Liliana De Riz, *Retorno y derrumbe: El último gobierno peronista* (Mexico: Folios, 1981); Guido Di Tella, *Perón-Perón, 1973–1976* (Buenos Aires: Sudamericana, 1983).

70. See the report by the official commission of inquiry on the disappearance of persons: Comisión Nacional sobre la Desaparición de Personas, *Nunca más* (Buenos Aires: EUDEBA, 1984).

71. Di Tella, *Perón-Perón*.

72. Adolfo Canitrot, "Teoría y práctica del liberalismo: Politica anti-inflacionaria y apertura económica en la Argentina, 1976–1981," *Estudios CEDES* 3, no. 10 (1981); on the economic policies of the regime, see also Alejandro Foxley, *Latin American Experiments in Neoconservative Economics* (Berkeley: University of California Press, 1983).

73. Canitrot, "Liberalismo"; Juan M. Villarreal, "Changes in Argentine Society: The Heritage of the Dictatorship." In *From Military Rule to Liberal Democracy in Argentina*, ed. Mónica Peralta Ramos and Carlos H. Waisman (Boulder, CO: Westview Press, 1987).

74. Computed on the basis of data in Wyotinsky and Wyotinsky, *World Population and Production*.

75. Computed on the basis of data in Taylor and Hudson, *World Handbook*.

76. World Bank, *World Development Report 1984* (New York: Oxford University Press, 1984).

77. Gino Germani, "Movilidad social en la Argentina." In Seymour Martin Lipset and Reinhard Bendix, *Movilidad social en la sociedad industrial* (Buenos Aires: EUDEBA, 1963), p. 325.

78. World Bank, *World Development Report 1984*.

79. Jacques Lambert, *Latin America: Social Structures and Political Institutions* (Berkeley: University of California Press, 1967), p. 29. Lambert did not specify his sources or the procedures he followed, but the proportions seem reasonable, even though he may have underestimated the "non-white" segment somewhat.

80. Jorge Schvarzer, *Expansión económica del estado subsidiario, 1976–1981* (Buenos Aires: CISEA, 1981), pp. 16, 38; World Bank, *World Development Report 1984*, p. 225; and *Clarin Económico* (Buenos Aires, August 4, 1985), pp. 4–5.

81. Rouquié's expression "anti-Communism without Communists" is very appropriate in this regard. See Rouquié, *Pouvoir militaire*, p. 670.

82. Torcuato S. Di Tella, "La búsqueda de la fórmula política argentina," *Desarrollo económico* 11, no. 42–44 (1972): pp. 327–325; Oscar Cornblitt, "La opción conservadora en la política argentina," *Desarrollo económico* 14, no. 56 (1975): pp. 599–639.

83. See Waisman, *Reversal of Development*, ch. 7.

84. This section draws from Carlos H. Waisman, "The Legitimation of Democracy under Adverse Conditions: The Case of Argentina." In *From Military Rule to Liberal Democracy in Argentina*, ed. Mónica Peralta-Ramos and Carlos H. Waisman; and from Waisman, *Reversal of Development*, ch. 8.

BRAZIL

• CHAPTER THREE •
Brazil: Inequality Against Democracy
BOLÍVAR LAMOUNIER

Political scientists have repeatedly emphasized the advantages of viewing democracy as a political subsystem rather than as a total pattern of society. The study of democratic breakdowns has given them every reason to insist on that view, since it has showed that in many cases dictatorship could have been avoided through institutional change and conscious political effort. Observing processes of "opening" (*abertura*) or "decompression" in authoritarian regimes has certainly reinforced that preference, not least because the importance of prior institution-building came clearly to light during some of these processes. Democracy, then, is a political subsystem, not a total pattern of social organization. But how sharply can we draw the line between the development of political institutions and the substantive democratization of society? How should we approach the fact that enormous tensions develop between these concepts—especially when we move from the dilemmas of democratic opening to those of democratic consolidation?

The Brazilian case is certainly worth examining in this connection. Recall that on March 31, 1964, a military coup overthrew President Goulart and inaugurated the longest period of ostensible authoritarian rule in Brazil's history. More than two decades later, on January 15, 1985, the Electoral College instituted by the military to ratify their presidential nominations elected Tancredo Neves—a civilian and a moderate oppositionist since 1964—to the presidency of the republic. The Brazilian authoritarian regime was ending by peaceful means. Quite obviously, this is not the kind of change that takes place in countries without a fair degree of institutional development. Protest and popular resistance played an important role, of course, but there was also an element of flexibility among power holders and a weight of their own among traditional representative institutions.

Can we then say that the Brazilian Nova República is fully democratic or fully consolidated? The answer to this question transcends the Brazilian case. It depends on our evaluation of the historical record, but also on our conceptualization of democracy and on our models of consolidation. Our first step here should be an attempt to determine Brazil's position on the scale of democracy employed in this book. Few would have major doubts about Brazil's position; it is clearly not a case of high success or of extreme failure. The optimist would think of Brazil as a "mixed success," noting that we have some democratic tradition, despite many interruptions, and that civilian rule is again in place after twenty years of ostensible military domination. The pessimist will prefer to speak of "partial development," rejecting the view that democracy has been the dominant pattern. Mixed or partial, both will agree that we are a case of unstable democracy, since the democratic system cannot be said to be fully institutionalized in Brazil.

Facing sharp inequality and major social strains, a political system—democratic or authoritarian—can hardly be said to be institutionalized completely. In some cases, democracy succeeds in becoming accepted as a framework for an endless series of substantive changes. Not every contender accepts it as an end in itself, but all or at least the key ones trust that its continuing practice will make substantive outcomes more compatible at some future date. The distinction between state and democratic institutions properly so called is not as simple as it seems when one is still close to the historical process of state-building. Brazilian history can be told as a series of steps toward state formation or toward democracy, depending on one's viewpoint. This has an important bearing on the evaluation of democratic development and seems to demand some conceptual refinement.

• FROM GEISEL TO TANCREDO: OPENING THROUGH ELECTIONS •

Gradual and peaceful, the Brazilian *abertura* seems unique by virtue of a third characteristic: It was essentially an opening through elections. It was not a result of sharp mass mobilization and was not precipitated by dramatic or external events, as in Portugal, Greece, and Argentina. In this sense, Brazil must be distinguished even from Spain, if we consider that the death of Franco brought the Spanish political system to an inevitable moment of restructuring. The Brazilian process had no such moment. Here, a gradual accumulation of pressures was channeled through the electoral process. Election results functioned as indicators of the degree to which the authoritarian regime was losing legitimacy and, in turn, helped to aggregate further pressures against it.[1]

Taking the period 1964–1984 as a whole and ignoring for a while certain moments of authoritarian exacerbation, three important democratic formalisms seem to have been at work, channeling the opening process in the direction just described: (1) an element of self-restraint on the part of military institutions; (2) electoral rules and practices kept at an acceptable level of credibility, despite some manipulations; and (3) a clear (and after 1974 virtually unanimous) preference on the part of the opposition to play the electoral game and to avoid violent confrontation.

The Brazilian opening has a strong element of deliberate decompression, starting with the Geisel administration (1974–1978). It amounted, from this point of view, to recognition among the regime's power holders that an indefinite monopoly of power, or even "Mexicanization" by means of a hegemonic party, would not be viable. The opposition seems on the whole to have evaluated the situation correctly and to have sought to explore the political spaces that appeared at each moment. The formidable impact of the 1974 elections helped it to organize under the label of the Partido do Movimento Democrático Brasileiro (PMDB) for electoral purposes, while at the same time establishing bridges among a variety of social movements and associations then increasingly (re)politicizing.

It would be naive to gloss over the tensions inherent in these changes, as if the actors were simply following a previously conceived blueprint. The point is rather that both sides, government and opposition, found enough space to redefine their respective roles through several stages, since each perceived what it stood to gain from the continuity of the process. The opposition was capable of extracting important concessions while at the same time organizing itself as a powerful electoral force. The government also benefited in many ways. Most importantly, it saw a gradual reduction in the costs of coercion. Decompression helped it to contain the growing autonomy of the repressive apparatus, which had seriously compromised, as is well known, the country's image abroad. In short, the government could capitalize on the political benefits of an atmosphere of progressive "normalcy," as if exchanging losses of legitimacy arising from discontent with its past for gains based on the increasing credibility of its intentions as to the future. Paradoxically, the erosion of authoritarian legitimacy since 1974 amounted to a revitalization of governmental authority—since such authority was thus invested in the role of conductor of the decompression (later rebaptized normalization and eventually redemocratization).

We have said that the electoral game was the institutional expression of an implicit negotiation between the parliamentary opposition and the liberal sectors of the military—or of the regime as a whole. Three examples will make these arguments more concrete. All three refer to the legitimation, in practice, of a congressional majority that the government would hardly be capable of putting together if it did not have semidictatorial powers. The first is the so-called Pacote de Abril (April Package) of 1977. Using the "revolutionary" powers of the Institutional Act 5, President Geisel decreed several measures designed to preserve a majority for the Aliança Renovadora Nacional (ARENA, the government party) in the Senate, to make an oppositionist victory for the lower chamber unlikely, and to postpone the return to direct state gubernatorial elections from 1978 to 1982.[2] Despite the incredibly massive and arbitrary nature of this intervention, the opposition chose not to reject the electoral process and went confidently to the polls. In so doing it legitimized the new authoritarian parameters; the actual election results confirmed ARENA's majority, though by a small margin. This meant that the government, with an absolute majority in both houses and controlling all but one of the twenty-three states, kept a complete monopoly of the presidential succession and of the political initiative. On the other hand, because it had such a monopoly, the government agreed to relinquish the supraconstitutional powers of Act 5 in December 1978, and negotiated a fairly comprehensive amnesty law, finally approved the following August.

The second example is the party reform of 1979, which ended the compulsory two-party structure established by the first "revolutionary" government in 1965. Knowing that the continuity of the electoral disputes within the two-party framework would inevitably lead to a major defeat, perhaps forcing the regime to violate its own rules, the Figueiredo government (1979–1984) resorted to its majority in both houses and changed the party legislation, precipitating the return to a multiparty system. The ambiguity of the opening process was again brought to the surface. On one hand, the procedure was formally impeccable, since the government did have the majority, and the reform was demanded even by some sectors of the opposition; on the other, the evident intention was to break up the opposition party, the PMDB, in order to keep the agenda under control for a more extended period of time and to set the conditions under which the new party structure would be formed.

The third example is the imposition, in November 1981, of a new set of electoral rules, requiring a straight party vote at all levels (councilman, mayor, state and federal deputy, governor, and senator). This effectively prohibited any kind of alliance among the opposition parties in the 1982 elections. Care was thus taken to avoid a serious defeat for the government, since that election would affect the composition of the Electoral College that would choose the next president, in January 1985. Again, though the straight ticket helped the government's party in the overall count, many thought that it would (and certainly did) help the opposition in some key states. Also, despite its manipulative intent, this new set of rules was approved by a congressional majority that had, just a month before, broken up over two bills deemed essential to the government's interests.[3]

Although our focus in this chapter is mainly political and institutional, we must note as well the economic legitimation of the authoritarian governments up to 1984. With the exception of the first three years (1964–1966), the post-1964 governments gave an enormous impetus to modernization and economic growth. The rapid internationalization of the economy and the heavily regressive effect of government policies on income distribution eventually alienated many sectors initially favorable to the authoritarian experiment. However, during most of the post-1964 period, growth rates were high enough to grant the regime an important claim to legitimacy. Under the Médici administration, which was the most repressive and culturally stagnant, such rates were extremely high (the Brazilian "economic miracle").

Geisel, chosen for the presidency in 1973, started the decompression project exactly when the international environment began to become severely adverse. However, his economic policies were designed not only to sustain high rates of growth but, through an ambitious strategy of import substitution in basic sectors, to reduce Brazil's external dependency significantly. With the help of hindsight, it is not difficult to question some of these measures, which aggravated our external debt intolerably. However, this was not an authoritarian government lost in its internal contradictions and without any semblance of a project. On the contrary: in addition to engaging the opposition in gradual political decompression, Geisel's administration was sometimes praised by representatives of the opposition, who perceived his economic policies as nationalistic and antirecessionist.[4]

The first two years of Figueiredo's administration (1979–1980) can be regarded as a continuation of Geisel's strategy, but 1981 was a clear dividing line. On the economic side, sustaining high rates of growth became clearly impossible, after the second oil and the interest-rate shocks of 1979. Politically, Figueiredo's unwillingness to support a thorough investigation of a terrorist attempt against a May 1 artistic show in Rio de Janeiro struck a heavy blow to the credibility of the *abertura*. The attempt was seemingly planned by the information and security agencies. The lack of a thorough investigation thus brought to the surface with stunning clarity the suspicion that the whole process was subject to a military veto, regardless of electoral results or of public-opinion trends.

The election of 1982 inaugurated a fundamentally different situation. Together, the opposition parties made a majority (albeit small) in the lower chamber. Even more important, gaining a large number of local and ten of the twenty-three state governments, including São Paulo and Rio de Janeiro, the opposition now had significant bases of power. The only secure institutional instruments of containment at the disposal of the regime were now the Senate and the Electoral College, both severely questioned in their legitimacy.[5] This strange "diarchy," pitting the military-bureaucratic system against state governments and a lower chamber enjoying stronger popular legitimacy, was bound to affect the presidential succession, and thereby the fate of the regime. A proposed amendment to the Constitution, determining that Figueiredo's successor would be chosen by direct election, set the stage for a major popular campaign, led by the opposition parties and supported by the oppositionist state governments. This was the *diretas já* (direct elections now), marked by a series of impressive popular rallies, which not only revealed the further loss of regime legitimacy but also paved the way for a formal dissidence (the Frente Liberal) within the government party, the Partido Democrático Social (PDS). The proposed amendment failed to get the two-thirds majority in the Chamber, but after the vote the situation was close to irreversible. Combined, the Frente Liberal and the largest of the opposition parties, the PMDB, established the Democratic Alliance and led Tancredo Neves to victory in the Electoral College in January 1985. Tancredo died without taking office and was succeeded in the presidency by José Sarney, a PDS dissident who had been nominated for vice-president.

It can thus be said that the outcome of the opening process became clear only when the moving horizon that guided it during ten years became completely exhausted. Deep recession and the succession crisis combined to make the implicit negotiation virtually impossible after 1982; or rather, to make it possible only insofar as it was embodied in the already existing institutional rules, without further manipulation. The presidency, as an expression of military tutelage over the political system, was forced to stay neutral in the succession struggle.

This rather peculiar process of decompression was made possible because, in the initial stages, the opposition party was fighting for institutional positions almost totally emptied of real power. Up to 1982, the state governments were chosen indirectly, in effect appointed by the federal government. Congress had completely lost its main functions and prerogatives. The docility of the government party (ARENA) and of the (indirectly elected) "bionic" senators, one-third of the upper house, made it hopelessly weak. Hence, the return to civilian rule did not amount to a clear-cut return to a preexisting order. Congress, political parties, the federation: all of these regained some prestige and strength but did not automatically invest themselves in their traditional roles, first because the traditions themselves were modest, and second because the country had changed immensely under authoritarian rule. To understand the prospects for democracy in Brazil, one must appreciate these historical traditions and legacies.

· INSTITUTIONAL HISTORY: AN OVERVIEW ·

Our interpretation of the Brazilian *abertura* stressed that the electoral process and conventional representative institutions had preserved their potential as vehicles for an orderly and peaceful transition. This element seems to have been missed by some academic theories and pieces of journalistic analysis that depicted a far more petrified authoritarian regime. Linz, one of the few scholars who did pay attention to this problem, correctly observed that the Brazilian authoritarian rulers would have a hard time if they had seriously decided to search for an alternative and durable legitimacy formula.

Our reconstruction of Brazilian institutional history starts with a view of the nineteenth-century empire as an extremely difficult and slow process of state-building. In fact, we look at that process as a Hobbesian construction, not in the vulgar sense of violent or tyrannical domination, but just the opposite way, meaning that certain legal fictions had to be established lest naked force become imperative—and even then, it might not be available in the requisite amount. Stretching it a little further, the empire will be regarded as a political system that developed in order to build a state, not the other way around.[6]

The concept of representation will help us bring the process of state-building into the analysis. In fact, the original or Hobbesian meaning of representation is simply formal authorization: It is the fiction that creates the state as an institution. It is prior to Dahl's legitimate contestation, since it corresponds to establishing the state framework within which contestation may later take place.[7] The democratic components of the concept appear at a more advanced stage. Social conflict and participation demands give rise to the descriptive image of representation; i.e., the notion that representative bodies should be like a sample or miniature, reflecting society's diversity. Increasing conflict and cultural strains may at the same time give rise to a demand for symbolic representation; i.e., institutions or charismatic leaders embodying a collective self-image of the nation. A fourth concept eventually emerges, focusing on the behavior of representatives. It expresses itself in the demand for faithfulness and relevance, for greater coherence in the party system, greater independence for unions and other associations, and the like. It corresponds, in short, to a more watchful state of public opinion. Let us now see what these ideas look like in historical perspective.[8]

The Empire: Hobbesian State Building

The only Portuguese colony in the New World, Brazil's political path after independence was completely different from that followed by her Spanish-speaking neighbors. Independence, obtained in 1822, was already marked by a unique feature: It came without a war against the Portuguese metropolis. A proclamation by the regent prince effected the separation and turned Brazil into an independent monarchy. After some years of instability, the monarchical form of government succeeded in establishing a stable political order and in keeping the integrity of the national territory.

The key factor accounting for stability during most of the nineteenth century was the existence of a cohesive political elite entrusted with the legal control of the country. The political system, considered more broadly, was a coalition of the rural aristocracy with the bureaucratic elite, but at the top these two sectors became strongly integrated. Recruited among landowners, urban merchants, and miners, this political elite was trained in the spirit of Roman law, Portuguese absolutism, and mercantilism.[9] The ideological unity of the elite helped it cope with threats to territorial integrity, despite the centrifugal tendencies inherent in our continental size, inadequate means of communication and transportation, the thinness of the economic linkages among provinces and regions, and the absence of a strong sense of national identity. Another important factor, in contrast with the old Spanish colonies, lies in the field of civil-military relations. During the empire, there was no threat to civil hegemony in Brazil. A parliamentary monarchy thus developed. The whole arrangement was elitist, no doubt, but the fact is that cabinets were elected and governed, liberals and conservatives rotated in office, and representative practices thus developed to some extent.

The "artificial" character of this political system has been frequently pointed out. Constitutional arrangements gave the emperor the so-called moderating power, which placed him above parties and factions, in fact allowing him to make and unmake majorities when he decided to dissolve parliament and call new elections. The two parties hardly differed, it is said, and had no significant roots in society. Elections not only tended to return the same people but were frequently fraudulent. This account is as correct as it is anachronic; it completely misses the fact that here we are not talking about descriptive representation in a highly differentiated society, but rather about Hobbesian authorization in the course of state-building. In order to understand this, we must take a broader look at the function of elections and at the way in which they were regulated up to 1930.[10]

The endless series of electoral reforms and the constant accusations of fraud were due primarily to the fact that there was no independent judicial organization to manage elections. The whole process, from voter registration (or rather, recognition) to counting ballots and proclaiming results was, in one way or another, subject to the interference of those involved and especially of police authorities subject to the provincial governors. To this extent, the importance of elections was indeed reduced. But local councils did affect the choice of state and national deputies. The government was thus constantly concerned with elections at all levels; in fact, it is said that the main function of the provincial governor, under the empire, was to win elections. From our Hobbesian standpoint, it may be deduced that losing them too frequently would force the central government to resort to its *ultima ratio*; i.e., open intervention.

Not a few observers have gone as far as to say that in Brazil, elections were totally farcical, and that more "authentic" results would have been achieved through a plain recognition of whomever held power in a given region or locality; or, on the other extreme, through complete centralization. The argument seems persuasive simply because it skips the difficult step. If recognition in this sense means granting a legal title to rule (as elections do), at that time it would have been tantamount to unleashing an endless series of small civil wars, since in each case public authority would be bestowed on a specifically named individual or faction, to the exclusion of others. The central government would thus be multiplying the conflicts it was seeking to avoid.

It is equally evident that the imperial government did not possess material capabilities to intervene everywhere and "centralize" power, as the recipe goes. Centralization did occur, but in a different sense. The representative mechanism of the empire operated by means of a highly aristocratic two-party system. Rotation between the two was partly a matter of elections, but it also had a lot to do with imperial inducement. The whole point of this courtly and apparently alien system was actually to control the processes of party formation. Monarchical government meant that, contrary to the United States, we did not have the formative impact of presidential elections. Formation through class conflict was out of the question, given the rudimentary state of the productive structure and the low level of social mobilization. But two other alternatives can still be imagined, and the empire carefully controlled both. One was parties of principle, in Burkean language; i.e., parties based on religious or otherwise doctrinal views. Some initiatives of this kind appeared toward the end of the century and were adequately controlled or repressed. The other, certainly more significant, was a gradual evolution from kinship groups (with their private armies) toward nationally organized parties. Something of this sort happened in Uruguay, for example. Brazil's territorial extension made it far less likely, but, in any case, it was prevented exactly by the flexible rotation allowed at the top of the pyramid and managed by the emperor.

The nineteenth-century constitutional monarchy was clearly not a democratic system. Its equilibrium rested largely on the bureaucracy, but this arrangement worked well only as long as it was attractive to a few key actors. When it ceased to be attractive to landowners and slave owners, and when new interests, most notably the military, became more differentiated, it fell without anyone to defend it and without violence.

The First Republic: Hobbes II

When Marshall Deodoro da Fonseca marched before the troops in Rio de Janeiro, on November 15, 1889, signaling the change of the regime, military discontent with the monarchy had already gone a long way. During most of the nineteenth century, the military had played virtually no role in Brazilian politics. The Paraguayan war (1865–1870), however, led to the development of a strong professional army. Victorious, the military decided to claim a share in power and greater respect from society. This was also the time when Comtean positivism and republican ideas began to penetrate military circles, starting a military circles, starting a long tradition of military politicization.[11]

Another major source of opposition to the political system of the empire were the São Paulo coffee growers. One of the links between the bureaucratic elite and the landowners under the empire was the underlying agreement to preserve slavery. But the coffee plantations of São Paulo, which developed rapidly during the last decades of the century, depended on wage labor, and indeed on the free labor of European migrants. Republican ideas thus became clearly linked to economic modernization. But the republic was, at the beginning, just as bad for the coffee growers; first because an inexperienced military exerted decisive influence and made the system potentially very unstable, and second because the unitary monarchy gave way to extreme federative decentralization. The republican Constitution of 1891, closely inspired by the U.S. model, gave a great deal of autonomy to the states, including extensive fiscal rights. The country thus faced a precocious "ungovernability" syndrome. The weakness of the central government affected, very adversely, the interests of the more dynamic sectors of the economy, which were exactly those located in São Paulo. For the *paulista* coffee growers, the fiscal and exchange policies were vital.

These elements do not exhaust the picture but go a long way to explain the changes that took place in the political system of the First Republic, producing a generalized feeling that the "real" Brazil had little to do with its liberal Constitution. First, the political leaders of the two major states, São Paulo and Minas Gerais, decided to establish between themselves the backbone of a functioning polity. A key aspect of the pact was that they would alternate controlling the federal executive. From this vantage point, they went on to develop a new "doctrine", called politics of the governors: They would support whichever oligarchy was dominant in each of the other states, in exchange for support for their arrangement at the federal level. The central government thus refrained from passing judgment on the quality of the political practices of each state.[12] This was the new guise of the Hobbesian construction. Needless to say, it went rather far to making liberal "formalities" indeed a farce. The legislative and judicial branches were decisively reduced to a secondary role; Congress became increasingly docile and lost its potential as a locus of party formation; and opposition was curbed in most of the states, so much so that statewide single parties became the rule.

The end of slavery and the extension of voting rights to large numbers of town dwellers and rural workers made it imperative for the federal government to be sure it would gain these votes. The governor's role thus became one of disciplining an extended electoral base, which he did by granting extensive extralegal authority to local bosses, in exchange for electoral support. This is the root of the phenomenon of *coronelismo,* which did so much to demoralize the electoral process in the eyes of the urban middle class up to 1930 and to generalize the notion that electoral institutions were somehow "alien" to Brazilian soil. Another result of this process of state-building was to make the relationship between political and private power—the latter based on land ownership—extremely transparent and resilient to change.

In exchange for the votes they garnered, the *coronéis* (backland bosses) received support from the oligarchy in control of the state machinery, thus reproducing further down the scale the arrangement between the states and the federal government. Control of the state machinery thus became rather literally a matter of life and death, since in addition to hiring and firing it could easily arrest or release.

Hobbes III: Getúlio Vargas

It is in many ways astounding that the political system of the First Republic did, after all, last forty-one years. In addition to the modest development of the urban middle strata and to the very incipient advances toward forming an industrial working class, that longevity was facilitated by the hierarchical character of nonurban politics, which was the real center of gravity of the whole construction. The votes of the peasants and other lower strata were controlled by rival factions of *coronéis*, who tended to be unified in a single pyramid because of the fied in a single pyramid because of the single-party structures in the states.

In October 1930, the First Republic was terminated by a revolutionary movement led by Getúlio Vargas, who until then was a rather conventional politician from the southernmost state, Rio Grande do Sul. The Revolution of 1930 cannot be described by a single set of causes. It was a reflection of regional cleavages as well as of urban middle-class and military discontent. It was made possible by the obsolescence of the political pact between the two major states, Minas Gerais and São Paulo. The rapid development of the latter toward modern capitalist agriculture and even toward industrialization gradually unbalanced the initial arrangements. However, São Paulo was hit hardest by the international crisis of 1929; other important states, Minas Gerais included, thus made a bid for greater power and influence.[13]

The main institutional result of the movement headed by Getúlio Vargas was an irreversible increase in central authority: The federative excesses of the First Republic were curtailed; government intervention in the economy was legitimized to a far greater degree; and, last but not least, important changes in representation concepts and practices were quickly introduced. Descriptive and symbolic meanings of representation finally made headway into the legal and political culture.

Descriptive representation is based on the notion that representative bodies ought somehow to look like a sample of society. It is therefore a demand that the Hobbesian process of formal authorization be enriched, in order to bring the diversity of social cleavages into those bodies. Perhaps we should stress the word *enriched*, since, for the 1930s, it is not always possible to speak of an articulate demand on the part of autonomous and identifiable social groups. A great deal of the legislation adopted must be understood as having a preemptive character (as was clearly the case of corporatism in the field of labor organization). In the electoral field, the introduction of a comprehensive scheme of proportional representation (through the Electoral Code of 1932), the design of which remains basically the same today, was intimately linked to other changes, in an overall design intended to enhance governmental authority. Indeed, the revolution rapidly moved to lower the voting age to eighteen, to extend the right to vote to women, to introduce the secret ballot, and to create an Electoral Court in charge of the whole process, from voter registration to certifying the victor.

These advances beg the question of how efficacious voting rights could be at that moment. But the point is that the First Republic had seriously degraded parliamentary and electoral institutions. To recover them would, of course, have a democratizing impact in the long run; but there was a pressing problem of reorganizing and reasserting authority in the short run. The revolution, after all, had decisively strengthened the federal executive vis-à-vis states and regions; signs of Left/Right polarization and especially resistance to a quick return to institutional normalcy were quite visible.

The provisional government was thus obliged to meet, and drew a great deal of legitimacy from meeting, the prior demand for "moralization of electoral practices." What most attracted Assis Brasil (the main author of the Electoral Code of 1932) to proportional representation (PR) was the enhancement he thought it would give to government legitimacy and stability, rather than the faithful representation of social diversity. Because it represented the (electoral) minority, PR strengthened its involvement with the state system and its acceptance of the majority. Also, PR was based on larger geographical divisions (actually, the states), thus making the mandate truly independent, in the Burkean sense, instead of the almost imperative mandate that resulted from small districts under the direct influence of landowners and local potentates. It should also be noted that Assis Brasil's model prevails even today insofar as the representation of the different states in the federal Chamber is concerned. The latter is based on the overrepresentation of the smaller and on the underrepresentation of the very large states (especially São Paulo), thus introducing considerations of federative equilibrium, and not simply of electoral justice, in the composition of the lower chamber. In recent years this has been much criticized, but at that time the logic was clearly the same that underlies Assis Brasil's reference to minority support.

It was also thought that PR on a broad geographical basis would practically force the consolidation of the other elements of the electoral reform, such as the secret ballot and administration of the electoral process by an independent Electoral Court. It is noteworthy that one of the most capable analysts of Brazilian institutional history, Nunes Leal, hardly emphasizes the element of proportionality when he discusses the reform of the early 1930s. The important aspect for him is the advance toward "moralization"; i.e., the Electoral Court. This is also remarkable in that Nunes Leal was deeply skeptical about the development of representative democracy in Brazil without a major change in the agrarian structure. Even so, he wrote, in 1948,

> despite the excesses and frauds that may have occurred here and there, most testimonies have been favorable to the electoral laws of the early thirties. The gravest accusations against our system of political representation ended simply as a consequence of the fact that those laws withdrew the prerogative of certifying who was elected from the chambers themselves. The *ins* ended up defeated in some states and a numerous opposition, later reinforced by contestation in the presidential election, found its way even to the Federal Chamber.[14]

One irony of modern Brazil is that these initial and decisive advances toward Dahlsian democratization were in part instrumental to the new Hobbesian/Getúlian thrust. Moreover, they were in part effected under the auspices of protofascist thinking.[15] The forty-one years of the first republican Constitution had given rise to a deep strain in political culture: Liberal forms had come to be regarded as an alien factor, distorting or corrupting the "true" nature of Brazilian society. There arose a demand for "authentic" representation, for an institutional structure truly adapted to Brazilian reality. For some, this meant an improvement, but for others it meant the suppression of electoral, party, and parliamentary institutions. The Constitutional Congress of 1934 included a section of "corporatist" deputies, an experiment that did not take root and would never be repeated. But corporatist views of representation were widely propagated and became in fact the framework within which so-called social rights were extended to the urban working class.[16] Such views were part and parcel of the Getúlian thrust toward an authoritarian (as distinguished from totalitarian) integration of the political order. Under Getúlio Vargas' guidance, protofascist thinking quickly became *anti*fascist; i.e., an edge against the further development of mobilizational fascism. More than that, it became an ideological framework helping him effectively to repress the two extremes, *integralistas* and Communists, starting in 1935 and leading to the formal announcement of the dictatorial Estado Novo (1937–1945).

The two pillars of this move toward a far more centralized state structure must be considered, since they embody the presence, apparently for the first time in Brazilian history, of a comprehensive experiment in symbolic representation. One was the increasingly charismatic nature of the presidential office, with Getúlio Vargas in the role of founding father. At the time, however, this was a limited and cautious change, if we compare it with the more portentous events that would soon take place in Argentina with Perón. In Brazil, the charismatic presidency developed without a confrontation with the system's element of limited pluralism (in Linz's sense): A *de facto* federation continued to exist, with strongly oligarchical features within each state; the church's traditional legitimacy went on receiving a great deal of deference; and the elite (strange as this may sound) did not give up its reverence for legal culture and for the Brazilian legal tradition.

Another pillar in the emergence of Getúlian representation was the reinforcement, if not, indeed, a considered invention of certain symbols of national identity. It is surely possible to assert that at this time we witness the emergence of culture policy; that such policy was closely associated with a process of nation- (as opposed to state-) building; and finally that both would have long-range effects in crystallizing a whole new notion of representation in Brazilian political culture. This cultural construction vigorously asserted that zero-sum conflict cannot reasonably emerge in Brazilian society. This view became truly encompassing and persuasive in part because it was espoused by leading intellectuals and artists, but also because it reflected important historical and social traits. It was, first, a celebration of past success in keeping together such a vast territory; this in turn always associated with the notion of unlimited opportunity. Second, it suggested that Brazilian social structure had indeed evolved in the direction of increased equality and mobility, not least in the field of race relations.[17] Third, it was a view of Brazilian politics; it effectively retrieved the experience of the early empire, especially Conciliation, when elite restraint and skill put an end to regional and factional struggles. But in the 1930s, a subtle turn seems to have occurred: Instead of reinforcing its nascent negative image as oligarchical, intra-elite behavior, this cultural construction came to regard political flexibility and realism as an emanation of similar traits in the social system, implying that Brazilian politics at its best would always be flexible. Finally, it was a reassertion, on a grand scale, of the conservative (patriarchal) view of conflict as childish behavior: an image that could only be persuasive in a country that had virtually no experience with principled politics and that felt threatened by its emergence in the guise of communism and mobilizational fascism.

The Failure to Consolidate: 1945–1964

Getúlio Vargas was forced to resign on October 29, 1945. His fall and the subsequent developments had a lot to do with the changed international environment. The defeat of the Axis had discredited the Estado Novo internally and externally, despite the fact that it did not belong to the family of mobilizational fascism. At least at first sight, the democratic "experiment" that followed the fall of the Estado Novo had very favorable conditions to prosper and succeed. The international environment was certainly favorable; the domestic economy was not under unusual strain; the armed forces had developed a high decree of organization and an antipersonalistic outlook as a result of their close attention to the weakness of Italian fascism; and the Getúlian dictatorship had led to the emergence of a vigorous liberal opposition, with outstanding parliamentary leadership: the União Democrática Nacional (UDN). The deepest of all Brazilian evils, in the eyes of Nunes Leal, the sin of *governismo*, seemed to have ended.[18] The transition had once again been peaceful: If the lack of a clear break with the Estado Novo made further democratization more difficult later on, it is also true that the absence of bloody cleavages could have made it easier.

Why did the democratic system then fail to consolidate itself in the next twenty years? The first difficulty that comes to mind is the important institutional contradiction that had developed after 1930 and as a consequence of the Estado Novo. Authority now seemed to bifurcate in a truly charismatic image of the presidency on one side, and an enormous assertion of the parliamentary institution—not least because of the formation of the UDN in the struggle against Vargas—on the other. This was not an immediate threat, since Vargas withdrew to a silent role after his downfall, but became extremely serious when he came back, riding the tide of a direct presidential election in 1950. The political system was now torn between an executive with strong Caesarist overtones, and a parliamentary center of gravity that pulled toward some sort of congressional or party government. Needless to say, Vargas' second presidency was extremely tense, and the contradiction was aggravated instead of diluted by his suicide in August 1954.[19]

Second, this newly assertive and formally powerful Congress was essentially made up of notables. It understandably had not developed a technical substructure to speak of and was not supported by a modern party system. In order to appreciate this difficulty, it is necessary to recall that the scope of government intervention had been enormously enlarged since 1930. The bureaucracy, traditionally large by virtue of the patrimonial origins of the Brazilian state, had again been expanded and modernized after the revolution. The legislature had constitutional powers but lacked everything else it needed to supervise and check this massive amount of policymaking.[20]

Interpretations of the 1964 breakdown have diverged a great deal. Stating his preference for those that stress the "internal sociopolitical situation" rather than "causes exogenous to the polity," Merquior aptly summarizes this literature:

> government instability, the disintegration of the party system, virtual paralysis of legislative decision-making, equivocal attitudes on the part of President Goulart, not least with regard to his own succession; the threat of an ill-defined agrarian reform; military concern with government-blessed sergeants' mutinies; and mounting radicalism on both the right and the left . . . all of this compounded by soaring inflation and, of course, by the haunting ghost of the Cuban revolution.[21]

The fate of the party system should be specifically noted. We have suggested that from 1945 onward we had for the first time some basic conditions to develop a competitive party structure. Most observers seem to agree that the start was promising, but that the new party system underwent a sharp deinstitutionalization from the second half of the 1950s up to 1964. Some impute this to sheer erosion; i.e., rapid social mobilization in the wake of industrialization and urbanization, decreasing efficacy of traditional control mechanisms of the patron-client type, and so forth. Others place greater emphasis on institutional regulations, especially the electoral system based on PR and on the preferential vote (open party lists). The fact, however, is that from Jânio Quadros' presidential resignation (August 1961) to the military takeover (March 1964), the party system was overpowered by the worst of all worlds. It became highly factionalized and subject to increasing radicalization at the same time that each of the major parties was internally divided; the tide of antiparty populism became truly exponential (the election of Jânio Quadros to the presidency in 1960 being an example); and the party traditionally identified with moderation and equilibrium, the Partido Social Democrático (PDS) became fragmented.[22]

However, we must guard against an overly "politicistic" interpretation. On a broader canvas, the fragmentation of the party system was itself associated with the overall process of economic and social change. This relationship operated in two ways. On one hand, urbanization and social mobilization eroded traditional attachments and social-control mechanisms. On the other, the lack of substantial advance toward deconcentration (reduction of social inequality) left the parties, individually and as a system, without strong bases of popular support. This was the structural framework within which older ideological and institutional conflicts were acted out, setting the stage for the military takeover. On March 31, 1964, the incumbent president, João Goulart, Getúlio Vargas' political heir, was ousted from office and sent to exile.

It would thus seem that Brazil moved rapidly toward instituting the form of democracy—political contestation and participation—but failed to consolidate democracy by reducing socioeconomic inequality. Unable to channel social conflict toward concrete policies, the party system entered a cycle of deinstitutionalization, rather than of consolidation in the new democratic mold. Had there been substantial advances toward reducing inequality, we might have had major conflict among the parties and along class lines, but not the combination of radicalism and populism that took place in big cities, plus survival or even reassertion of basically clientelistic structures in the less developed areas of the country. The crisis of the party system was thus rather telling and cannot be understood simply in terms of the traditional view of those parties as being premodern, preideological, or otherwise not ripe for serious representative democracy. It was more in the nature of an induced suicide, by means of which the society seems to have expelled an extraneous body: a trend toward stronger political representation in the absence of any substantial deconcentration.

An Overview of the Overview

Brazilian institutional development was, so to speak, preeminently state-centered. It must be understood in terms of the prolonged process of state-building and the cautious strategies on which it was based, since a small central elite and state structure were confronted with the challenge of preserving territorial unity in a country of continental dimensions. Today's heavy bureaucratic machinery; the ponderous legalistic ethos, despite the fact that legal norms are frequently bypassed; the continuing weight of clientelism and of conservative interests based on land ownership, not to speak of the increasingly tutelary role of the military since the Estado Novo—all these can be traced to or partly explained by that fundamental thrust of our state formation. These aspects of state-building have also been held responsible for what is felt to be an absence of public authority, or a lack of differentiation of the political system vis-à-vis societal structures. This is often phrased as an absence of political institutions properly so-called. This chapter has argued, to the contrary, that there has been significant institution-building, though not necessarily of a formally democratic character. Certain aspects of the post-1964 regime, which are surely relevant for understanding the *abertura* process of the last decade, are clearly related to that prior institutional development.

The literature on the recent authoritarian experiment rightly stresses that its economic project was one of capitalist modernization and greater integration in the world capitalist system; and further, that this led, from 1967 on, to a strategy of accelerated industrial growth rather than of income redistribution or of reduction of absolute poverty. It is also correctly said that the initial perceptions led policymakers to curb labor unions and "progressive" organizations; and finally, that this overall thrust, combined with the need to repress guerilla activities, ended up engaging the regime, from 1968 to 1974, in a highly repressive phase, with very high costs in terms of human rights. Yet, two features of the post-1964 regime helped preserve institutional continuity, which in this context meant a chance for a peaceful resumption of democracy. The first is the impersonal concept of government, which materialized in: (a) tighter rules to contain politicization among the military; (b) conservation of the presidency as an elective office, at least through an Electoral College; and (c) keeping the traditional limits pertaining to the duration of the presidential mandate and the norm against reelection.[23]

The second feature was the preservation of the representative system. Needless to say, representation here meant formal authorization, in the Hobbesian sense; but it now took place within institutional parameters that not even the military could afford to ignore or distort completely. It is interesting to note, in this context, that the pre-1964 party structure was not immediately suppressed. The decision to terminate the old parties was made only in October 1965, one and one-half years after the coup, and was immediately followed by the creation of at least a "provisional" party structure; i.e., the two-party system that was to remain until 1979. The military governments obviously manipulated the conditions under which elections were held in the ensuing twenty years but did not try to do away with the electoral mechanism as such or replace it by a totally different doctrine of representation.

• THEORETICAL REVIEW •

State-building in Brazil left a highly contradictory legacy for contemporary democratic development. As a skillful extension of central regulatory capabilities, it was constantly oriented toward keeping intra-elite conflict at a low level and preventing the eruption of large-scale political violence. But this preemptive pattern of growth undoubtedly made Brazilian society too "backward" from the standpoint of autonomous associational participation. This, in turn, gave the elites and the bureaucracy an excessive latitude to define policy priorities, crystalized unjustifiable income differentials, and left the political system constantly exposed to a dangerous legitimacy gap.

Overall Historical Pattern

Brazil was a part of the Portuguese Empire from 1500 to 1822. During those three centuries, it was in essence a commercial (as opposed to a settlement) colony: mining and large-scale plantations based on slave labor. Even the colonizers were few, since the Portuguese population was pathetically small compared to the vast world empire it tried to build. These are some of the reasons why the colonial system left neither a powerful central authority nor an integrated national community in its wake.

The comparative question with respect to Brazil's colonial past, then, is not so much one of democratic tradition, imported or indigenous.[24] It is rather the relatively smooth transition to a process of political development that we see as consciously oriented toward long-range goals. Political competition and the appropriate institutions began to develop under the empire, at a time when mass political participation was totally absent. From then on, political changes became comparatively nonviolent, allowing enough room for the contending groups to accommodate their differences afterwards. Since the nineteenth century, large-scale violence has been increasingly controlled, and bitter memories have not accumulated, at least not among the political elite.

The theoretical judgment according to which democracy is better off when peaceful contestation among elites precedes mass participation may be accepted, but requires some qualifications in the Brazilian case. First, there is a matter of degree, since that process finally led to a state structure that seems excessively strong vis-à-vis civil society: too large and clientelistic to be effectively controlled by the citizenry and constantly reinforced by the constraints of so-called late industrialization. Second, the Dahlsian sequence seems to have left serious strains in terms of legitimacy and political culture, as indicated by the alleged excess of conciliation and elitist character of the political system.

State Structure and Strength

Historians who see a strong state in Brazil in the nineteenth century normally stress that the empire kept the country's territorial integrity, though compelled to use force against important separatist movements. Other analyses attempt to trace the bureaucratic organization of the Brazilian government directly back to the Portuguese absolutist state. But these arguments overstate the case, since they overlook the fact that state structures never became entirely distinguished *qua* public authority. Symbiotic arrangements with private power (e.g., landed wealth) were part and parcel of a gradual extension of regulatory capabilities. The effectiveness of the central authority in keeping public order and eventually in undertaking social changes is, then, recent in Brazilian history. It is difficult to see how it could exist at a time when the national army hardly existed, or even before it developed organizational responses to its own internal divisions.[25]

The organizational "maturity" of the army would appear only after the Revolution of 1930. From the 1930s onward, the armed forces developed an increasingly tutelary conception of their role vis-à-vis civilian institutions and society as a whole. Thus, in 1945 they pressured Getúlio Vargas out of office, on the understanding that the days of the Estado Novo were gone. Friction with elected presidents or with their ministers was evident throughout the 1950s and early 1960s. In 1961, following Jânio Quadros' resignation from the presidency, the military ministers actually vetoed the transfer of power to the elected vice-president, João Goulart. This move brought the country to the brink of civil war and was defeated only because the military ministers failed to achieve unitary backing for their position among the regional commanders. In 1964, with substantial popular support, the military overthrew Goulart and took power.

However, this tutelary role should not be taken to mean that the Brazilian military is quintessentially opposed to democratic principles and institutions. The tutelary self-conception clearly belongs to the broader authoritarian ideology that presided over the last phase of state-building; i.e., the Getúlian thrust of the 1930s. That ideology includes elements that, paradoxically, help sustain some of the institutional mechanisms of representative democracy. Being, at root, antipopulist and nonmobilizational, it stresses the distinction between private and public roles—hence the limits on the duration of mandates, the electoral calendar, and, more generally, the importance of keeping the legislature, at least as an institution, capable of being reactivated—all of these clearly practiced by the post-1964 regime.

Brazil's political development has also benefited from the fact that instances of direct armed challenge to the state have been few in this century and have been effectively repressed since the 1930s. Ethnic separatism has been virtually nonexistent in modern Brazil. From this point of view, too, state-building was brought to a conclusion that certainly favors democracy.

On the other hand, the procedures and justifications used to repress armed challenges, in the 1930s and again after 1964, led to threatening precedents. In both cases, those challenges were treated in terms of "internal war," far more than as unlawful behavior that perhaps could be dealt with by judicial or political means. The legislature, political parties, the judiciary: all of these came out clearly weakened vis-à-vis the executive (which in fact meant the military). With the military directly in power after 1964, this trend became far more serious. First there came the arrests, proscriptions, and similar measures designed to curb opposition and promote societal demobilization. From 1968 to 1974, confronting armed underground movements, the regime adopted widespread censorship and all sorts of cover-up repressive practices. The cost of this phase in terms of human rights was not as high as that faced by Argentina shortly afterwards, but it cannot be underestimated as a negative effect for democratic prospects. As argued in our first section, some of the military seem to have recognized that they had gone too far, when they opted (circa 1973) for a gradual "opening from above."

The description of the Brazilian military as exerting a tutelary role and as having directly established an authoritarian regime that would last for twenty-one years obviously does not square well with the emerging image of a vigorous "civil society." In fact, we think that there have been exaggerations in applying the latter concept to the Brazilian case. It is true, of course, that Brazilian society has not become highly differentiated and complex. Combined with resistance to the military regime, this has led to a rapid increase in associational politicization. But a more appropriate reading of this trend would be that of updating a society marked by unusually low participation and predominantly organized along corporatist, rather than along consociational, lines. The latter term refers to autonomous subcultures or subsocieties, which hardly exist in Brazil. Corporatist political organization, in contrast, is organization stemming from occupational criteria, directly controlled by the state (as in the case of labor unions) or, more frequently, aiming to keep differential privileges among professions, the gradient of such differences being guaranteed by the state.

After twenty years of military-authoritarian rule (1964–1984), no one will doubt that the Brazilian state is highly centralized vis-à-vis the federation, or that it directly controls a large proportion of the economy. Since the nineteenth century, the predominant concern with state-building, and the high degree of cohesion of the political elite contrasting with the dispersion and abysmal poverty of the general populace, meant that the central authorities enjoyed a wide margin of discretion to make choices in economic policy.

Development Performance

Disregarding redistributive issues for a moment, there can be no question that Brazilian governments have been consistently seeking to promote economic growth for a long time, and that their record is fairly impressive. The Brazilian economy now belongs among the ten or twelve largest in the world, roughly on a level with Italy and Canada. This rank is the result of continuously high rates of growth since the early 1930s, and especially of steady advances toward industrialization. The average growth rate of GDP during this whole period has been of the order of 6 to 7 percent a year, with a peak of 10 percent a year from 1968 to 1974. Industrial growth rates have been twice or thrice that of agriculture; in 1968, ten times higher. This growth pattern accounts for the vast scale of the structural changes the country has undergone (see Table 3.1), which Santos finds at least as impressive as that promoted by Meiji restoration in Japan or by the Soviet government in its initial two decades.[26]

Some structural aspects of Brazil's "late-developer" pattern of growth must be underlined if we are to understand its political implications. Far from deconcentrating state power, the growth record mentioned above has greatly reinforced it. Reacting to the constraints brought by World War I and by the crisis of 1929, subsequent governments assumed an increasingly direct role in the economic sphere. Starting with the Volta Redonda steel complex, in 1942, state and mixed enterprises were created to foster industrial infrastructure. Foreign trade was regulated not only through fiscal and exchange policies, but also through government entities specifically designed to supervise the commercialization of coffee, sugar, and other commodities. Four decades later, Hewlett could aptly describe the Brazilian state as "a significant producer of basic industrial goods and infra-structural items, an important agent of protection and subsidy, a powerful regulator of economic activity, and *the* determiner of the direction of national economic development."[27]

Needless to say, this record of growth underlies the proven ability of the Brazilian political system to avoid the generalization of zero-sum perceptions and expectations. But these successes have not been sufficient to dilute the illegitimacy syndrome that permanently surrounds the political system, if not authorities in general. In fact, the Brazilian state, having relied heavily on economic growth for legitimacy, has been reasonably successful in promoting growth but seems rather far from overcoming its legitimacy deficit. In theory,

Table 3.1. Socioeconomic Change in Brazil, 1940–1980

	1940	1950	1960	1970	1980
Population (in millions)	41.2	51.9	70.1	93.1	119.1
Percent of population in urban areas	31.2	35.1	45.1	55.9	67.6
Percent of population in metropolitan areas (nine largest cities)	15.2	17.9	21.5	25.5	29.0
Percentage of the labor force in:					
Agriculture	67.4	60.2	54.5	44.6	30.5
Industry	12.6	13.3	12.4	18.1	24.9
Services	19.9	26.4	33.1	37.8	44.6
Per-capita gross national product (GNP) (in U.S. dollars)	391[a]	444	640	960	1,708

Sources: For population data: *Fundação IBGE* (Censos Demográficos e Tabulações Avançadas de 1980). For GNP: *Conjuntura Econômica* 26, no. 11 (1972), and *Gazeta Mercantil* (1970–1985).

[a] Data for 1947.

the state can manipulate the supply of key inputs and thus start altering the many perverse aspects of the growth pattern, but it cannot readily do that in practice, as Hewlett points out, since interfering with the market conditions toward which major enterprises are oriented would often mean reducing the rate of growth—hence, losing legitimacy. Moreover, insufficient domestic savings, technological dependence, and other imbalances have increasingly led the country, since the 1950s, to a strategy of growth-*cum*-debt and inflationary financing. In the 1970s and early 1980s, as is well known, foreign debt skyrocketed to over $100 billion and inflation rapidly moved to the three-digit altitude.

In conclusion, Brazilian development can thus be said to have very positive and very negative aspects. High rates of growth (hence variable-sum perceptions among different strata of society) co-exist with dramatic imbalances—regionally, against the northeast; sectorally, against small-scale agriculture and rural labor; by class, against the poor in general. But there is no persuasive evidence that those positive or negative aspects are predominantly associated by the mass public with either democratic or authoritarian governments. Memories of high growth flash back on democratic (e.g., Kubitschek, 1955–1960) as well as on extreme authoritarian (e.g., Médici, 1969–1973) administrations.

A significant distinction emerged in the 1970s and early 1980s among the educated, urban middle class. In this segment, there undoubtedly was an increase in the proportion of those thinking that the military-authoritarian regime achieved growth at an unacceptable social cost: income concentration; neglect of welfare investments; denationalization of economy and culture; damage to the environment; corruption. This change was crucially important for the Brazilian political *abertura*, expressing itself in electoral mobilization as well as in the political activation of professional and civic associations of numerous types. How lasting this realignment will be is a moot question. Disappointment with the "New Republic" may induce further changes in the political value system of this segment.

A final word on corruption: up to 1964, corruption was clearly perceived in a patrimonial rather than in a capitalistic framework. The widespread feeling that politicians are corrupt was then primarily focused on clientelistic (patronage) practices. Undue use of public funds for private enrichment was not unknown, of course, but it was perceived as associated with only a few practices (e.g., dubious credits to landowners and co-optation of union leaders). Under the military governments, the context and, therefore, the whole perception of corruption underwent an enormous change—perhaps we should say that both moved to an exponential scale. Accelerated industrialization, increasing internationalization of the economy, the whole strategy of growth-*cum*-debt—all of these took place, we must recall, without any effective parliamentary oversight and often under the protection of pervasive press censorship. No wonder, then, that the idea of corruption became associated with financial scandals, alleged "commissions" in foreign dealings and so on; the number of known cases being sufficient, needless to say, to lend credence to the most extravagant generalizations.

The gradual and negotiated nature of Brazilian redemocratization made the exemplary investigation and punishment of major instances of corruption politically very difficult. The "new republic" thus failed to capitalize on one of the most potent sources of popular discontent with the previous authoritarian regime. Worse, it was quickly affected by a resurrection of the older "patrimonial" perception, since critics of the huge public deficit readily seized on patronage (*empreguismo*) as a target. Against a background of poverty and inequality, insufficient governability, and a political culture strongly affected by pervasive images of corruption, it comes as no surprise that even as remarkable a record of growth as the Brazilian may fall short of full legitimation for a democratic regime.

Class Structure, Income Distribution, and Social Organization

No matter how one measures them, levels of income inequality and mass poverty in Brazil are among the worst in the world. The main determinants of present income differentials and class structure undoubtedly have their roots in the pattern of land appropriation inherited from the colonial past. Concentration of landed wealth and use of the best land to produce export commodities have always been the major "push" factors behind the enormous supply of cheap labor constantly flocking to the cities.[28] Rapid industrial growth oriented toward a predominantly middle-class market, high rates of population growth, and the insufficiency of investment in basic welfare services have combined to maintain extreme inequalities and indeed to make a mockery of the "trickle-down" theory of indirect redistribution.[29] Needless to say, the full implications of Brazilian-size poverty and inequality for democratic prospects must also take into account that the country has now become highly urbanized and "mobilized" (in Deutsch's sense).

Throughout the empire and the First Republic, both working class and urban middle strata were numerically unimportant. The vast majority of the population lived in rural areas or in very small villages and towns, where society was steeply stratified. Here, there was no middle class worth speaking of. At the bottom were the peasants, a sprinkling of very poor independent farmers, and similar strata in the towns. At that time, a crisis in the coffee business was tantamount to economic recession, but it did not necessarily mean that a large number of laborers lost their jobs. From World War II onward, the picture started changing dramatically. Total population grew from 41 million in 1940 to 119 million in 1980; urban population, from 13 to 70 million; and metropolitan population (i.e., residents of the nine largest urban centers) from 6.3 to 35 million. These changes were accompanied by major shifts in the labor force out of agriculture and into industry and services (see Table 3.1).

Despite the impressive overall rates of economic growth during the "economic miracle" period of the military regime (the late 1960s and early 1970s), there is ample evidence that income differentials and some telling indicators of basic welfare (such as infant mortality) went on worsening. By the early 1970s, several studies were showing that income inequality had increased relative to the early 1960s. Writing in 1976, Graham offered the following summary of the evidence:

> (a) income concentration (as measured by the standard Gini index) increased overall, and in all regions, during the sixties; (b) the rates of concentration were more pronounced in the more developed (and most rapidly growing) areas like Sao Paulo and the south than in the lesser developed regions; (c) real income increased in all areas; (d) average monthly real income per urban worker increased much more rapidly (43 percent) than income per agricultural worker (14 percent), thereby increasing the intersectoral income differentials during the decade; (e) these intersectoral income differentials stood out much more dramatically in the northeast than in Sao Paulo and the center and south.[30]

World Bank data on forty-four countries, including twenty-six less developed countries, shows Brazil to have the worst income inequality, as evidenced in the share of national income received in 1972 by the highest 20 percent and 10 percent of the population.[31] Using data from 1960 to 1980, Serra reports that concentration was still going on in the 1970s. The lowest 20% of the economically active population had gone from 3.9% of total income in 1960 to 3.4% in 1970, to 2.8% in 1980; the top 10%, from 39.6% to 46.7%, to 50.9%.[32] This means that the governmental policies practiced throughout this period, at best, did not counteract structural forces making for greater inequality; at worst they aggravated their effect. Combined with the massive character of absolute poverty that prevails in the northeast and in the outskirts of all major cities, this degree of income concentration is undoubtedly one of the steepest challenges to democratic consolidation.

Let us now look at this picture in terms of class structure, rather than of income distribution. The starting point here must be the corporatist order imposed from above in the 1930s.[33] This system can be seen as a highly successful attempt to control, not to say petrify, the process of class formation, by which we mean development of differentiated collective identities and autonomous political organization. The lowest extremity of the class structure, made up of landless peasants and very poor small farmers, was not regulated in a strict sense, since they lacked the occupational differentiation that formed the basis of the whole system; rather, they were excluded from it. The upper extremity, made up of large landowners, provided another parameter—untouchable property rights. But this should not be confounded with total political autonomy, much less with monolithic control of the state: The political sphere (embodied in the military, the bureaucracy, and in the political "class") retained considerable decisional discretion.

Between these two extremes, a corporatist gradient was imposed on the rest of society; i.e., on urban wage labor and middle-class independent occupations in general. The privilege of "representing" a given sector was thoroughly subjected to state (legal) control, as well as to effective means to circumscribe each sector's agenda-building and other overt political moves. This pattern applied even to industrial and commercial entrepreneurs, through corporatist pyramids exactly paralleling those of urban labor. As Santos points out, this whole structure remained virtually unchanged through the "democratic experiment" based on the Constitution of 1946. Attempts at self-organization on the part of rural labor, in the early 1960s, were quickly repressed by the post-1964 regime, obviously with full applause and cooperation from the landowners, who saw such attempts as outright subversion.

Ironically enough, serious and lasting "subversion" of the regulated order would occur, first as the result of the scale of the economic changes induced by the military governments; second, as an unintended by-product of some of their "modernizing" reforms; and finally, in that context of large-scale structural change, from the reactivation of "civil society" during the political opening. Development of large-scale industry led entrepreneurs, especially in the heaviest and most dynamic sectors, to organize in new types of associations, pulling themselves out of the traditional corporatist framework. Ousted, as it were, from the administration of social-security funds, labor leaders found themselves with nothing to offer their constituencies; nothing but more authentic leadership. This was the origin of so-called new unionism, which thrived in the most dynamic sectors of the economy and struck a major blow against the old corporatist structure. Trying to sidestep political clientelism in their attempt to extend social security to the rural areas, the military governments stimulated the formation of rural labor unions. From 1976 to 1983, unionized rural labor increased from slightly over 3 to more than 8 million, accounting now for more than half of total union membership in the country, even though rural labor accounts for only 30 percent of the economically active population. Needless to say, rural unions did not conform to the passive blueprint that the government probably conceived for them. In less than two decades, they had a national leadership, undertook successful strikes, and indeed placed land reform firmly on their agenda. The politicization of the urban middle strata has not lagged behind. White-collar unions, neighborhood organizations, and associations of numerous types quickly emerged, undoubtedly reflecting the increasing complexity and, in many ways the increasing technical and professional sophistication of Brazilian urban life.

The conclusion, then, is that, in Brazil, medieval economic inequalities exist side-by-side with a dynamic and increasingly sophisticated society. Heavy external dependency does not mean that an indigenous bourgeoisie failed to develop. There is, in fact, a modern entrepreneurial class, in industry as well as agriculture. This class has become much more affirmative in the last decade, profiting from the process of political opening. Perceiving that it could not unconditionally count on the military or on elected politicians, it became highly and autonomously organized. This process in fact underwent a remarkable acceleration under the new republic, first in view of the Constitutional Congress (elected in November 1986); and second, and perhaps more important, because the economic reforms of the Sarney government (the Cruzado Plan) politicized the economy to a far greater extent; for example, introducing generalized price controls.

We have so far emphasized the economic bases and the organizational aspects of class formation. Needless to say, the picture becomes much less politicized when we look at the rank-and-file and especially at class consciousness. A very large proportion of the urban working class is young, politically inexperienced, indeed made up of recent migrants. Wage strikes can be mobilized without much difficulty, but both unions and political parties must reckon with a great deal of instability, indeed of volatility, when it comes to broader electoral or ideological disputes.

Brazilian development, as we have repeatedly stressed, has been able to create a basically non–zero-sum perception of social conflict. Spatial mobility has been extremely high and has, in fact, meant better life chances for poor migrants. The belief in upward social mobility is probably not as deep today as it was in the 1950s, but access to education and to consumption has increased considerably with increases in total income. Some fashionable descriptions of Brazilian society as being rigidly hierarchical must, then, be taken with a grain of salt. The concentration of property, twenty-one years of authoritarian rule, and huge income inequalities have not meant petrification of status inequality.

On the other hand, socioeconomic inequalities do tend to cumulate to some extent. Although extremely high correlation among education, occupation, income, and, say, "honor," certainly does not exist, the overall structure of inequalities has an evident regional component. The southeast (where São Paulo is located) and the extreme south are "rich" regions, whereas the northeast, with 35 million inhabitants, is one of the major examples of mass poverty in the world. This regional disparity has an important overlap with the country's ethnic differentiation. Blacks and *pardoes* account for well over two-thirds of the northern and northeastern states, while the reverse proportion obtains in the southeast and the south. These definitions are known to be very imprecise in Brazilian population statistics, but the difference is large enough to merit attention.

Nationality and Ethnic Cleavages

Political conflict among language or religious groups is virtually nonexistent in Brazil. On these two dimensions, let alone nationality, the country is comparatively very homogeneous. The picture is much more complex in the field of race relations. Interpretations range from the belief in a genuinely "peaceful" evolution to the notion that underprivileged minorities (especially blacks) lack collective identity and organization as a consequence of white economic and political domination. The extremes do seem to agree that overt ethnic strife is not prevalent. There can be no doubt, however, that poverty and color are significantly correlated.[34] Blacks, and especially black women, are disproportionately locked in low-status and low-income occupations. The proportion of white men earning less than three minimum wages per month was 66% in 1976, while the comparable proportion was 82% for white women, 87% for black men, and 95% for black women. Educational data also show important differences (though not significantly between men and women). The proportion of illiterates among white men declined from 44% in 1950 to 24% in 1980; among black men, from 74% to 47%.[35] These figures clearly indicate diffuse racial barriers to social mobility.

But the country does have an overarching national identity. Living generations have virtually no memory of separatist movements or politically relevant subcultures, whether based on language, race, or religion. It can, of course, be said that this high degree of cultural uniformity reflects a process of authoritarian state-building under colonial and then imperial government. The fact, however, is that Brazil is not presently confronted with serious ethnic or cultural strife. Given the immense burden that socioeconomic cleavages place on the political agenda, this relative homogeneity is clearly a positive factor for democratic development.

Political Structure

The formal structure of the Brazilian state has varied a great deal since independence (see Table 3.2), but the concentration of power in the national executive has been a constant. Accepted as a hallmark of state-building and, more recently, as necessary for the sake of economic development and national security, that concentration was often carried out at the expense of state and local governments, of legislative and judicial powers, and even more clearly of the party system.[36]

The First Republic (1889–1930) tried to adapt the U.S. model, providing for a popularly elected president and granting extensive autonomy to the provinces, now called states, of the old unitary empire. The result was full of perverse effects, as the "politics of the governors" decisively weakened the national legislature and judiciary and seriously compromised elections and party competition. In practice, the government became as oligarchical and probably far less legitimate than the empire, in the eyes of the relevant strata. This process of political decay eventually led to the Revolution of 1930 (and, in 1937, to Vargas' Estado Novo), which again concentrated federal power, but now within a framework of nonmobilizational, partyless authoritarian rule.

The Revolution of 1930 is undoubtedly the "founding" mark of the modern Brazilian political system, but again with contradictory effects in terms of democratic prospects. In the short run, advances in "state-ness" (bureaucratic reach, military complexity, greater regulation of economy) were certainly favorable, since they reduced the scope of private power and made purely praetorian involution thenceforth unlikely. In the long run, however, some of those advances seem to have outlived their function. The corporatist system of labor

Table 3.2. Brazilian Political Structure Since Independence

Regimes	Form of Government	Party System	Civil/Military Relations	Social Mobilization	Demise
EMPIRE (1822–1889)	Unitary state; parliamentary monarchy cum "moderating power"	Two parties (Liberal and Conservative) since the 1830s; district voting (very unstable rules)	Civil hegemony through National Guard; weak army	Extremely low	Republican military coup; no resistance
FIRST REPUBLIC (1889–1930)	Directly elected president; highly decentralized federation	One-party systems at state level; multimember district voting; unstable rules	Increasing tension between military (especially young officers) and politicians	Very low	Revolutionary movement headed by Getúlio Vargas; three weeks fighting
REVOLUTION OF 1930 (1930–1937)	Provisional government headed by Vargas; in 1934, Weimar-inspired constitution with strong corporatist leanings	Numerous, unstable party groupings; growing Fascist/Communist polarization	Army becoming dominant national institution	Growing significantly in urban areas	Vargas' coup, with military backing, leads to Estado Novo
ESTADO NOVO (1937–1945)	Authoritarian, non-mobilizational regime; Getúlio Vargas dictator	None; all parties and elections suppressed	Army identified with regime through national security ideology	Growing rapidly; population 31% urban in 1940	Senior army officers force Vargas to resign; 1945: controlled redemocratization

Table 3.2. Brazilian Political Structure Since Independence, cont.

DEMOCRATIC REGIME (1946–1964)	Directly elected president; weak federation and powerful national legislature	Multiparty system with 13 parties; increasing polarization at end of period; PR electoral system	Frequent friction between military factions and civilian governments; threats of military intervention	Fairly high, increasing even in rural areas; population 45% urban in 1960	Military coup with substantial popular backing in middle strata ousts President Goulart
MILITARY REGIME (1964–1985)	Republican form; presidency *de facto* monopoly of the military; nominations ratified by Electoral College only up to 1985; federation severely weakened	Compulsory two-party system from 1965 on; partial return to pluralism in 1979, still barring Communist parties; PR electoral system	Unmistakable hegemony of military as institution, guaranteeing "technocratic" governments	Very high; population 67% urban in 1980	Very gradual, negotiated transition culminating in election of Tancredo Neves (civilian, oppositionist) through Electoral College
NEW REPUBLIC (1985–)	Direct election of president reestablished as constitutional principle; growing influence of states and legislature; Constitutional Congress, 1987	Multiparty system; no legal restrictions on Marxist parties; moderates (PMDB) control both chambers, early 1987; PR electoral system	Civilian control formally guaranteed; military influence remains strong	(Very high)	

relations has certainly been detrimental to the political organization of the working class. The conventional PR electoral system then established has clearly not contributed to developing a stable party system. Worse still, the presidential office became overloaded with contradictory expectations. For professional politicians, it became the ultimate distributor of patronage, credits, and public investments, and the arbiter among regional interests. For the newly mobilized urban masses, after 1945, it was the focal point of demands for better wages and improvements in living conditions. From the viewpoint of the military establishment, it came to be the very embodiment of national security, implying containment of both "oligarchical" and "mob" rule.

These cross-pressures and institutional deficiencies were clearly operative in the 1964 breakdown. The democratic experiment initiated in 1945 was based, in comparison with the earlier periods, on a far stronger representative system. The national legislature and the main political parties started as fundamental political actors. However, growing social mobilization and persistent inflation made it impossible for the two major parties (UDN and PSD) to retain their initially safe electoral advantage. As a typical "institutional" party, the PSD became increasingly vulnerable to a bipolar (Left and Right) opposition, roughly as suggested by Sartori's "polarized pluralism" model.[37]

The erosion of party and congressional support meant that Goulart (1961–1964) had to carry the full burden of maintaining institutional equilibrium exactly when the Caesarist ghost that surrounds Latin American presidentialism came, full-bodied, to the fore. The Caesarist dilemma stems from the need to cope with stringent and clearly defined contradictory situational constraints. Frustrating mass demands in the name of austerity or economic rationality alienates diffuse support and thus deprives the president of the one resource that makes him strong vis-à-vis elected politicians. If, on the contrary, he chooses to court those demands too closely, the specter of a mob-based dictatorship is immediately raised by the propertied classes and, often, by the military organization. The middle course is often unavailable because of the very weakness and inconsistency of the party system. When the difficulties inherent in these situational constraints are compounded by ambiguous personal behavior, as was evidently the case in the Goulart presidency, the breaking point is near.

Leadership

From 1961 to 1964, President Goulart proved unable to escape the Caesarist trap. He in fact made it more inexorable by allowing too much room for doubt as to his intention to abide by the constitutional rules that would govern his succession. Few analysts would dispute that Goulart's equivocal behavior was a crucial precipitating factor in the democratic breakdown.[38] The important question, then, is how does it come about that a country with an important institutional history and a fairly impersonal conception of governing falls prey to that sort of populistic retrogression and thence to breakdown.

Part of the answer may indeed be an oversupply of leaders willing to violate the rules of the game. The pattern was set by Getúlio Vargas, in 1930 and especially with the Estado Novo coup of 1937. Liberal opposition to the *varguista* tradition, after 1945, often displayed the same ambiguous behavior of which Goulart was later accused. Prominent UDN leaders, like Carlos Lacerda, were not only *golpistas* but, in fact, strongly inclined to (and skillful at) impassioned demagogic rhetoric.

Yet, personalistic leadership has not been as successful as implied in the common lore. Getúlio Vargas did not establish a personality cult comparable to that of Perón in Argentina. Former president Juscelino Kubitschek (1955–1960) is remembered as a modernizer and a "nice guy," not as a power-seeking *caudillo*. Jânio Quadros ascended to the presidency in 1960, riding a protest vote that he cleverly mobilized by means of a rancorous, theatrical style. In August 1961, he resigned, claiming that the country was ungovernable (in his terms, of course). His decision was fateful in the ensuing years, but is it not a blessing for our hypothesis that the Brazilian political system has developed antibodies against wild personalism? His successful comeback as the elected mayor of São Paulo in 1985 would seem to deny our view, but it is noteworthy that Quadros has carefully confined his Poujade-like, protofascist appeal to the electoral arena, never daring to establish some sort of paramilitary apparatus.

The leadership problem cannot therefore be considered simply as a lack of men with the appropriate skills and civic virtues, and not even as an absence of antibodies against irresponsible demagogs. It is rather the inherent instability of democracy amid rapid social mobilization and extreme inequality, trying to escape the Scylla of Caesarist *caudillismo* and the Charybdis of uninspiring, clientelistic politics. A proper understanding of the leadership problem must then consider, in addition to the already cited situational constraints, some underlying cultural elements that contribute to shaping them.

Political Culture

Brazilian political culture is sometimes said to embody an unchanging Iberian propensity toward monolithism, and thus to be irreducibly inimical to democratic development. We argue that, on balance, the effects of political culture may indeed be negative, but hardly for that reason. The views that do operate in the political system (i.e., those put forward by influential writers, journalists, and the like) show a pervasive and persistent concern, indeed an obsession, with the alleged incongruence between elite and mass culture. Since the early decades of this century, outstanding writers of different persuasions have insisted that powerful cultural strains tend to undermine the idea of a Western-style democracy in Brazil. Alberto Torres was only one among hundreds who emphasized the discrepancy between the "legal" Brazil, expressed in political institutions, and the "real" one, embodied in actual social behavior.

Somehow, popular culture came to be seen as the only real thing, while political institutions became irremediably artificial. What is certainly disturbing in this dichotomous approach is that through it, we may be unconsciously demanding a degree of congruence among different spheres of society and especially between "center" and "periphery," which does not in fact exist anywhere among advanced democracies. The starting point is the Aristotelian ideal that social institutions (familial, educational, religious) must buttress and reinforce the overarching principle of legitimacy. But that ideal, petrified in a simplistic dichotomy, gradually comes to imply that democratic political principles are irrelevant or illegitimate when they fail to mold each and every subsystem. Even in the advanced democracies, we find, as in Brazil, that knowledge of and support for democratic rules of the game are undoubtedly correlated with education and other indicators of social status. In Brazil, this is hardly surprising, if we consider that elite political socialization has been closely associated, since the nineteenth century, with the law schools (hence with a reverence for legal culture) as well as with a free press and more recently with a sizable and reasonably cosmopolitan academic community.[39]

The dichotomous view just described derives historically from the state-centered pattern of political development and from the fact that elite contestation preceded, by far, the expansion of participation. In fact, elite culture became political at a time when the bulk of the populace, poor and widely dispersed over a large territory, was totally excluded from the system. In 1900, the illiteracy rate among the population over fifteen was 75 percent. There thus arose an excessive predominance of state over societal development and hence a deep anxiety, among opinion makers, that liberal-democratic development would not be viable under such conditions.

However, this picture has changed in surprising ways during the decompression process of the 1970s and now under the new republic. The Aristotelian craving for congruence remains, but its contents and ideas to correct incongruence have become more complex. Under the impact of high social mobilization (see Table 3.1), of repoliticization and, of course, of protest against income inequality, there appeared an Augustinian strand, according to which the people are good and the state is evil. Stimulated by religious movements and by abundant leadership coming from the now much larger wage-earning middle sectors, the implied correction is no longer to replace liberal by authoritarian politics, as in the 1920s, but rather to substitute some sort of Rousseauan "participatory" for representative democracy.

The historical sequence of institutional development, combined with persistently wide income differentials and other factors, thus seemed to have produced very negative cultural conditions for representative democracy. These negative effects do not derive from a would-be unitary worldview, but rather from a pervasive utopian standard against which democratic development is constantly measured by the leadership of some popular movements and by influential opinion makers. The impact of these trends on parliamentary politics has been so far modest, but may increase through the Workers' Party or even through the left wing of the PMDB.

The usual pessimistic account of Brazilian political culture must be qualified in many ways. Consideration of some positive developments that took place despite distant Iberian origins and recent authoritarian experiences may be useful as an antidote. First, since the establishment of the Electoral Court, in 1932, there has been unmistakable progress toward orderliness and fairness in administering the electoral process. On the side of the voters, sheer size (now about 75 million registered voters) allied to social mobilization have made the assumption of individual autonomy increasingly realistic. Despite abysmal poverty and the prevalence of patron-client relationships in many regions, there can be no doubt that the electoral process now operates with the requisite quantum of aggregate uncertainty.

Second, there is no monolithic domination, not even at the local level. This is in part a consequence of the overall changes in the electoral process and in part of local rivalries even among landowners. The image of monolithism has been frequently maintained by students of Brazilian social structure, but they tend to underestimate the impact of political and electoral competition when it is not linked to ideological or class cleavages.

Third, as we noted earlier, even the authoritarian ideology of the 1920s and 1930s (and hence the idea of military tutelage) has been tempered by antipopulist elements that help sustain some democratic institutions and practices. Hence, the limits on the duration of mandates, the electoral calendar, and, more generally, the importance of keeping the legislature as an institution capable of being reactivated—all these are clearly practiced by the post-1964 regime.

Fourth, as noted above, a significant degree of social mobility exists, despite severe income inequality. Here, the cultural process of modernization does seem to have an impact of its own, judging from the increasingly informal character of social relationships. Urban living and mass communications work massively in the direction of an egalitarian culture.

Finally, the development of representative institutions, in a general way, clearly implies that primitive *caudillismo* and unitary blueprints are not deemed desirable or realistic by the political elite—not even by authoritarian (military) elites. Three features seem to characterize the Brazilian "doctrine" of representation. One is the recognition of diversity among the elite. This should not be understood primarily in ideological terms and even less in terms of cultural or ethnic segmentation. It is rather an acceptance of the fact that politics involves constant division and disagreement, making monolithic rule inconceivable. This recognition is deeply rooted in the country's cultural and legal system because, if for no other reason, it was historically a *sine qua non* for holding the provinces and local governments together.

The second feature is the electoral process. Countless writers have seen a puzzle, or worse, a mimetic disease, in the Brazilian tendency to import such profoundly "alien" liberal institutions. But the fact is that electoral mechanisms, with many of the classical provisions for fair competition, have strong roots in Brazil. Despite the equally countless instances of violence, fraud, and manipulation that can be cited, it is perfectly legitimate to speak of a

Brazilian electoral tradition, and even more to recognize that the recent struggle against authoritarian rule has reinforced it.

The third feature, which has the military institution as its main guardian, is the notion that the government must be an impersonal entity. Hence the military's fundamental dislike for any kind of plebiscitarian *caudillismo* and their (reluctant, no doubt) understanding that elections are the ultimate safeguard against some sort of personalistic appropriation of the state.

Do these three features amount to "democratic" representation? Not quite: one indication that they do not are the powerful cultural strains that constantly delegitimize the representative process. Public debate is full of references to the "elitist" character of such institutions. The image of politicians is incessantly associated with clientelism, co-optation, and conciliation—the last being a reference to the early nineteenth century, but also a way of saying that our pluralism is still oligarchical, without substantive meaning for the average citizen. Indeed, what we can assume, in the Brazilian case, is the existence of strong state institutions, which are not necessarily democratic and which in many ways belong in the category of structural resistances in need of "deconcentration."

International Factors

The international environment is a positive factor for representative democracy in political, military, and cultural terms, but it is also an overwhelmingly negative condition on the economic dimension. Brazil is a fully Western nation in cultural terms, and a dependent (if you will) part of the world capitalist system. One (oft-neglected) consequence of this is that Brazilian elites, including the military, do not ignore the risks involved in toying with fundamentally different principles of political organization. Brazil's territory acquired its present shape a long time ago. Nature provided most of the solution to Brazil's frontier problem. Diplomatic efforts polished it up early in this century. Participation in foreign wars and military readiness are unknown to the vast majority of Brazilians. Were it otherwise, the weight of the military vis-à-vis civilian institutions would undoubtedly be much greater than it has been. Proper understanding of the negative effects of the economic dimension requires a broad historical perspective. Dependency on export commodities, with its attendant instability, was extremely high until the 1950s at least. Import-substituting industrialization began during World War I, but was until recently insufficient to alter that basic link to the external world.

An important change took place in the 1950s. Under Juscelino Kubitschek, the Brazilian government gave up its formerly cautious strategy and started emphasizing durable consumer goods as a means to accelerate industrial growth. The automobile industry was the driving force of that new phase. The impact of industrialization on the overall social structure became thenceforth much greater. A rapidly expanding population, large cities, and the demonstration effect of foreign consumption patterns now made for permanent tension, leaving no option but constantly high rates of growth. Major inflationary pressures, the need to increase exports at any price, and, of course, to attract investments and credits now became permanent features of the economic system. Internationalization had come to stay.

This, in a rough sketch, is the background of Brazil's deep involvement in the international debt crisis. Having again accelerated growth in the late 1960s and early 1970s, the military governments, especially under President Geisel (1974–1978), undertook major new steps toward import substitution, this time in basic or "difficult" sectors.[40] The premise of that effort, needless to say, was the easy credit situation of that decade. The oil- and interest-rate shocks of the late 1970s and early 1980s thus caught Brazil in an extremely vulnerable position.

Our judgment that the present international environment is negative for the consolidation of democracy goes far beyond the "normal" pattern of external dependency. When the country depended on export crops, the urban population was so small that even a sharp decline in economic activity did not affect the majority immediately and dramatically. Now it does. Massive transfer of real resources abroad to meet disproportionate debt obligations strangles the country's efforts to promote growth and aggravates already intractable political problems at home.

• PROSPECTS FOR DEMOCRATIC CONSOLIDATION •

Reconceptualizing Democratic Consolidation

Liberalization and participation are described by Dahl as distinct theoretical dimensions of democratization. However, when we think about consolidating democracies recently reinstated as a consequence of authoritarian demise, socioeconomic conditions must be incorporated more effectively into our models. It is a trivial observation that a large amount of genuine political democracy tends to be incompatible with a rigid or unequal society, or even with a low rate of change toward greater mobility and equality. Thus, when we think about consolidation, social and economic conditions cannot remain in the category of purely external correlates or prerequisites. They must be "politicized"; i.e., brought into the model, and this for two important reasons. The first is that, like liberalization and participation, those conditions will necessarily appear to political actors as objects of decision, and therefore as so many choices they will be forced to make. Land reform is the obvious example in Third World countries. Whether and how such choices are faced may make the difference between keeping and losing support; the loss may transcend individual leaders and parties and extend to the newly constituted democratic system as a whole. The second reason has to do with the change from procedural to substantive demands in the course of redemocratization. Cast in a different theoretical language, this means that, once achieved, formal democracy becomes an Olsonian collective good. Since it already exists and benefits everyone, the incentive to defend and protect it decreases sharply.[41] In Third World countries, the implications of this fact are obviously more dramatic, since elites have not completely consolidated pluralism among themselves, frequently perceive conflicts as zero-sum, and are vastly more threatened by the substantive demands of the masses.

If the assumptions just stated are correct, it seems clear that we need, not two, but three dimensions. The graphic representation of democratic consolidation would thus be a cube made up of Dahl's liberalization and participation plus another dimension referring to policy advances toward structural deconcentration, which means greater equality, social mobility, and the like. Taking all three dimensions at once, the dilemmas of democratic consolidation will, we believe, appear in a more realistic light. If our questions about the democratic character of the Brazilian new republic were to deal only with Dahl's two-dimensional scheme, the answer should probably be positive. Looking at the "liberalization" axis, we would find that most legal restrictions on political competition have been removed. If difficulties remain, they are somehow produced by hidden vetoes (e.g., expectations concerning military behavior), by the sheer weight of certain resources (e.g., bureaucratic power), and by other, "nonpolitical" determinants (e.g., those determining the concentration of power in the societal environment of the political system).

Probing somewhat further, it seems possible to compact Dahl's liberalization and participation into a single dimension, which would be representation; i.e., strength of the representative system. Where contestation becomes the nor-

Figure 3.1 Representation, Deconcentration, and Democratization

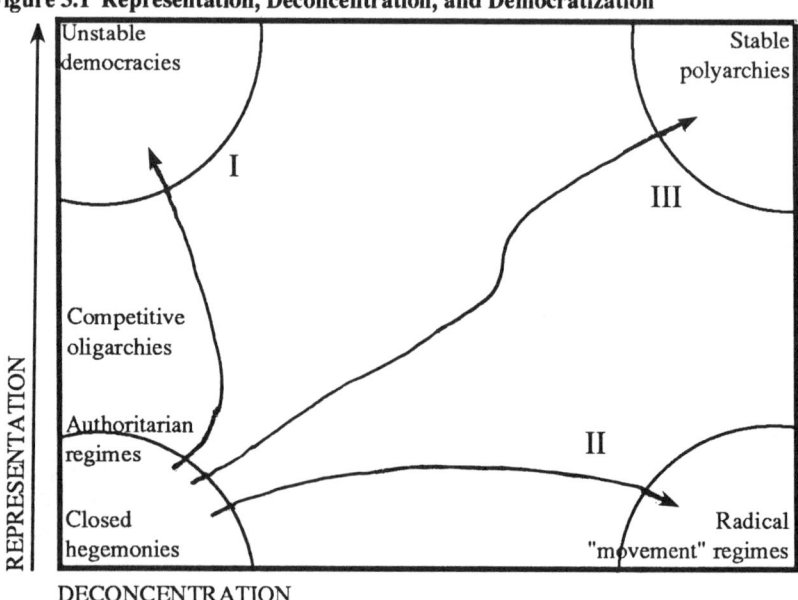

mal way of doing things among political elites and where such elites are regarded as adequate foci for support or as spokesmen for demands arising from participation, what we have is a strong representative system. We can thus come back to a two-dimensional space, with strength of the representative system on one axis and advances toward social change, or deconcentration, on the other (see Figure 3.1).

The first two years of the new republic have shown very clearly that the reinstatement of formal democracy is a far cry from real consolidation. On the horizontal axis of Figure 3.1, the new civilian government was faced with what might be called the vicious circle of transition. The prior authoritarian suppression of politics and the prolonged struggle for redemocratization dammed up enormous (substantive) expectations, which could not (in fact cannot) be met in the short run. Not meeting them at an adequate rate, the government quickly loses the support it needs in order to undertake more forceful policies, the lack of which reinforces the circle. The "moving horizon" that worked so well during the decompression process at the institutional level (i.e., on the vertical axis) thus seems far more difficult to sustain when it comes to our horizontal axis.

Toward Deconcentration?

The proposition that greater equality helps sustain democracy is certainly correct in the long run, but the concrete steps and policies that will reduce inequality may also undermine support for the democratic system in the short run. This is evident enough when we speak of deconcentrating income and wealth, and especially land ownership. Virtually any policy intended to achieve deconcentration produces visible and immediate losses and thus tends to change the basis of political support, often in the direction of undemocratic forces. But there is, in addition, the worst face of inequality, so-called absolute poverty. The problem here is that a truly substantial effort would have to be sustained over many years; this presupposes a degree of consistency in political support and implementation that seems unlikely in fragile, underdeveloped democracies. There is thus a tendency to avoid sweeping commitments of this kind, not least because they may raise expectations beyond a realistic level and eventually cause an antidemocratic backlash. And yet, the circle is truly demonic, because without a major effort, duly announced and symbolized, such basic welfare measures may not gain the allegiance of disadvantaged groups to the point of compensating losses of support among the well-to-do. Or they may compensate, but produce at the same time a threatening effect on the latter. In order to consolidate itself, a functioning democratic system should be capable not only of undertaking substantial measures to reduce inequality but, also, of conveying to the deprived majority that such measures are serious efforts undertaken on their behalf; and at the same time, that underdevelopment and the pattern of inequalities traditionally associated with it cannot be overcome on short notice.

The "new republic" clearly did not find a consistent answer to these problems in its first two years. The initial idea was to launch an "emergency program" of assistance (while at the same time designing alternative economic policies and starting a moderate, long-range land-reform project). There would be, for example, a milk program directed toward groups known to have a desperate nutritional deficit. The results of this phase could not have been more disastrous. Insufficient production, inadequate implementation networks, and political disputes all combined to paralyze such initiatives. Toward the end of 1985, these difficulties were compounded by the ghosts of hyperinflation and an unprecedented strike wave in the subsequent few months. The "illegitimate" origins of Sarney's presidency (i.e., the fact that he was the conservative side of the ticket, as Tancredo Neves' running mate, and that both had been elected indirectly) began to be recalled. Support for the government rapidly dwindled.

It is therefore probably correct to infer that the so-called Cruzado Plan had political as well as economic objectives. The stabilization plan and monetary reform introduced by President Sarney on February 28, 1986, were decisive in stopping a dangerous erosion of authority. Popular acquiescence to the plan immediately reinforced presidential leadership. But, clearly, such acquiescence was entirely due to the price freeze, the difficulties of which began to appear rather soon. In a country with tremendous income inequalities, the redistribution of money income implicit in the price freeze quickly led to an explosive demand for consumer goods of all kinds. Entrepreneurs responded to the price freeze by reducing supply and enhancing their political organization. To make things worse, a decisive election was scheduled to take place in November (state deputies and governors, and federal deputies and senators, the latter two making up the Constitutional Congress). Sarney's enormous popularity after the economic reforms of February was the one big asset of the governing Democratic Alliance, hence the enormous pressures to go on with the price freeze, despite the evident distortions to which it was giving rise. Confronted with an enlarged demand and a reduced internal supply, the government resorted to massive imports of food products. The result was that reserves fell sharply. By early 1987, readjustment measures had proved insufficient and the country had no alternative but to declare a partial default on foreign-interest payments.

The irony, or tragedy, is that the Cruzado Plan was the closest thing to actual income redistribution in several decades; it was also the one moment in which the government seemed capable of gaining widespread support. But short-run euphoria should not obscure the dark contours of the broader picture. To begin with, bold measures like the Cruzado Plan reflect the institutional weakness of the political system, not its sources of institutional strength. Presidential authority was reinforced by the populist, indeed Caesarist components of the situation, not by the denser substrata of the country's power structure. It is perhaps unnecessary to point out that not every government faces such an opportunity; that the gains were short-lived; and indeed that such a sweeping reform was introduced through a decree-law, and not by means of a prior amalgamation of party and congressional support.

On the economic side, a recovery of sorts, after three years of recession, had been taking place since 1984. The transition to civilian rule, in early 1985, thus began in a moment of relative relief. But, on a broader canvas, the country is clearly confronted with severe economic constraints. The balance sheet of twenty years of authoritarian rule includes, on the negative side, a staggering external debt that demands massive remittance of real resources abroad and internal debt that rivals in magnitude the external one. The Brazilian economy is thus besieged by multiple and contradictory requirements. It is imperative to grow, but growth constantly leads to perverse results in the balance of payments; it is necessary to promote exports, but that takes away some of the goods required for domestic consumption and refuels inflation; expanding imports to curb inflation quickly reduces reserves to a dangerous low point.

So far we have dealt with deconcentration of income and wealth, but the concept also involves the dimension of power, and particularly of bureaucratic power. In a country like Brazil, where the weight of the state is said to be a barrier to democratic development, welfare or antipoverty programs are often included among structures to be deconcentrated. However, the parts of the state that pose truly difficult problems of democratic control seem to be neither the traditional public service not the more modern welfare programs. It is, rather, the so-called entrepreneurial public sector, made up of state companies that directly control large economic assets and thus exert substantial influence in economic policymaking.[42] In order to understand the institutional problem involved here, it will be necessary to make a short theoretical detour.

Among the conceptual schemes presently available, one of the most appropriate to the problem at hand seems to be Lowi's distinction among three decisional arenas—the redistributive, regulatory, and distributive.[43] But it is not entirely clear how sensitive this scheme is to the political structure of societies like Brazil's, which have long had an inclusive and interventionist public sector—an "entrepreneurial state," as it is sometimes described. From this standpoint, Lowi's threefold classification seems incomplete, in fact truncated at the top, since it does not distinguish for separate treatment what might be called an accumulative arena; i.e., the locus par excellence of the main investment decisions, which ends up being responsible for the rate and for the overall direction of economic growth. This arena has not been and cannot easily be subject to "pluralistic" political competition—at least not as long as parliamentary and party structures remain fragmented and ineffectual as they have been in Brazil. Despite their broad disagreement on everything else, neoconservative entrepreneurs demanding "de-statization" and left-wing parties demanding "democratic control" over this arena seem to agree that a problem does in fact exist. Needless to say, this autonomous power, of vast proportions, was the technocratic spine of the post-1964 military regime. The idea of dismantling or deconcentrating it can be considered largely lyrical, since it embodies the model of economic growth that, for good or evil, changed the face of Brazil during the last thirty to forty years.

Dahl identifies the "centralized direction of the economy," regardless of the form of ownership, as a negative condition for democracy. He also says that "where the military is relatively large, centralized and hierarchical, polyarchy is of course impossible, unless the military is sufficiently depoliticized to permit civilian rule."[44] It is doubtful whether the Brazilian military is "sufficiently depoliticized"; and there is little doubt but that they keep a close watch on what we have called the accumulative arena. This leads to a particularly complex situation. Purely "praetorian" political decay seems unlikely, given the sheer weight of the military institution and its modern pattern of organization. But it is not certain how adaptable the institution is to open competitive politics, taking into account not only past ideological propensities but also the strategic links that bind it to these major economic concerns, deemed essential to economic growth and national security. This may be called a "Huntingtonian" weakness of the Brazilian political system, if we consider that political development has to do not only with the strength but also with the adaptability of organizations; and further, with the primacy of specialized political institutions, such as parliaments and political parties.

Institutional Options

The dualistic expression "state versus civil society" became quite common in Brazil, by virtue of the struggle against authoritarian rule during the 1970s. "State" became virtually synonymous with authoritarian mechanisms, in the mind of the intellectualized or militant opposition; "civil society" was sometimes understood as the opposition as a whole, but more often the ensemble of professional, university, religious, and other associations. The factual political importance of this distinction is undeniable, but if a dualistic characterization is necessary, it does not seem to run exactly along those lines. It is probably more appropriate to say that the completion of state-building and increasing social mobilization have made the Brazilian political system diarchical, the division running between state and democratic institutions properly so-called. The former has clearly identifiable clusters—the bureaucracy, public and semipublic economic concerns, and, of course, the military. These are not necessarily authoritarian in an absolute or doctrinaire sense, but they do certainly conceive of their role primarily in terms of ensuring stability, preventing an exaggerated escalation of social conflict, controlling the effort toward economic growth in its fundamental lines, promoting industrialization and technological development, and protecting national security.

The democratic half of the diarchy can be said to have comparable clusters in a purely formal sense—Congress, political parties, the press, universities, churches, and labor unions—but it is far from certain that all of these share a core conception of what democracy is about or what should be its long-range goals, mechanisms, and practices. For one thing, it is here above all that one feels the tensions between formal and substantive views of democracy. The latter often appear associated with more or less utopian conceptions of "participatory" democracy, aiming to replace or subordinate representation to a more "authentic" expression of the people's will. Part of the problem confronting the Constitutional Congress involves benefiting from this increased participation at the level of civil society as a means to enhance the democratic half. Can it realistically be done? An adequate answer must consider at least three levels: (*a*) the overall conception of democracy deemed viable for Brazil; (*b*) the form of government (i.e., presidential or parliamentary); and (*c*) the inability of the party structure to provide intermediation between the two halves of the diarchy.

A convenient starting point for the discussion of the overall conception is the contrast between consociational and majoritarian models of representative democracy. The majoritarian model can be described as a pattern of institutional organization that consistently leads to excluding minorities (sometimes large ones) from governing; the consociational model forces coparticipation in that process. In the Brazilian case, there can be little doubt that a pure majoritarian model would be disastrous. Brazil is not nearly as segmented culturally and religiously as the societies studied by Lijphart, but the depth of socioeconomic differences perhaps makes majoritarian organization even less advisable. If legitimizing the political system is difficult through more inclusive mechanisms, it can be easily surmised that the typical Westminster model, as Lijphart calls it, would simply not work in Brazil.

This is not to say, however, that the pure consociational model would work. The amount of decentralization and fragmentation of power that this idea implies can hardly be imagined in a country without consociational traditions, just recently emerged from a long-drawn process of state-building, and deeply confronted with the dilemmas of economic growth, income redistribution, and basic welfare.[45] Instead of collaboration among a myriad of autonomous subcommunities, the consociational model would more likely produce an exacerbation of corporatism, clientelism, regionalism, and the like—thus opening the breach for a major reassertion of authoritarian rule in the usual guise of the imperial presidency, bureaucratic power, and military tutelage.

Historically, the Brazilian political system can be described as standing somewhere half-way between Lijphart's two poles. If the preceding remarks make sense, the route to follow now is not a sharper inclination toward either of these broad models. It is rather a need for another major step toward institutionalization. In practice, this means reducing the distance and the potential for conflict between underlying and equally viable models of government. Since the 1930s, Brazil has been deeply torn between a hyperpresidential (virtually Caesarist) and a more typically parliamentary conception of what the political center of gravity should be. These two often conflict, and it is not inconceivable that they may develop into true *weltanschauungen*, since they are in many ways implicated with the substantive versus formal disagreement as to the nature of democracy. That is why further institutionalization will require reexamination of the form of government. Quite obviously, we cannot go from a hyperpresidential to a classical (i.e., British-type) parliamentary system. The latter would clash with the political culture and prevailing structures on many points. Assuming that the Constitutional Congress retains direct election of the president, we would have the additional difficulty of investing a head of state, elected by fifty or sixty million voters, in the role of the queen of England; not to speak of the proverbially weak party system that would be operating such a parliamentary system.

The search for a "mixed" formula is thus inevitable, and it must be conscious of the risks inherent, for example, in the French system, now facing the difficult issue of "cohabitation." The most promising lines would then seem to be either a slight attenuation of the separation of powers, as in the letter of the Finnish Constitution, where the prime minister is clearly submitted to the president; or a more clearly parliamentary system, where the cabinet is in fact responsible before the legislature, even though the president is elected directly and keeps substantial powers and prerogatives.[46]

Strengthening the party system is important in itself but becomes imperative in the parliamentary or semiparliamentary hypothesis. There can be little question that this will require a great deal of institutional "engineering," if we consider that Brazil has not known the historical processes that typically led to the crystalization of party systems. In Europe, such systems resulted either from class cleavages, which did not emerge as sharply in Brazil until recently, or from cultural, linguistic, or religious cleavages that simply do not have a Brazilian equivalent, and that were decidedly controlled by the central authority when they did come up in embryo. Anxiety over the need to assert central authority also explains why Brazil did not have strong nationwide parties based on an articulation among regional oligarchies—quite aside from the fact that federation and continental size made such parties unlikely. Brazil also lacked, except during the democratic experiment of 1945–1964, the formative impact of direct presidential elections.

This is to say that strong parties, in Brazil, will of necessity be a "work of art." The main instrument to bring them about will be the party and electoral legislation and other regulations pertaining to political representation. Given the inappropriateness for Brazil of the extreme Lijphartian models, such regulations should avoid the extreme majoritarian as well as the looser forms of proportional representation. The promising suggestion, here, would seem to be the electoral system practiced in West Germany, which attempts to combine the PR representative principle with the participatory principle of majoritarian elections.[47]

These hypotheses, as stated before, start from the notion that democratic consolidation in Brazil will depend on a major increase in institutionalization, which in turn will require deliberate efforts to enhance the party and parliamentary gravitation of the political system.[48] So-called participatory proposals, inspired by the new vigor brought to the political arena by labor, religious, and professional organizations, are here seen as a healthy updating of Brazilian politics, the overall trajectory of which was unusually oligarchical and/or concerned with the basic issue of state-building. It is, however, hardly realistic to conceive of a functioning democracy, on the Brazilian scale, in terms of a Rousseauan ideology. Carried to an extreme, such proposals will end up diluting rather than reinforcing political representation. Seeking Rousseau, we may again find Hobbes.

Conclusion

From 1986 to 1988, Brazil moved from an extreme of wild optimism to extreme pessimism. The dream of rapid growth without inflation gave way to virtual stagnation and severe inflation (20 percent a month during the first quarter of 1988); with these came a deep sensation that the country is rapidly losing its developmental edge and becoming ungovernable. If the final note we have struck was already a bit pessimistic, no improvement could be expected under such circumstances.

Yet, the real battle is the one the country is now fighting on the economic front, in the short run. The political and ideological "reading" of this crisis will probably be adapted *ex post factum* to success or failure in the attempt to curb inflation, and resume growth—and thus avoid another democratic breakdown. If we succeed, we will probably hear an ode to prudence. The gradual path to redemocratization will again be hailed as the best, or as the only one available; the politician's low prestige will be seen as inevitable or as a temporary phenomenon; even the signs of a "populistic revival" in the elections of 1985 and 1986 and wild clientelism in the federal government in 1987–1988 may be interpreted as the price to pay for mass democracy: our Jacksonian age?

If, on the contrary, hyperinflation leads the country into convulsion and thereby into another cycle of authoritarian rule, all "obvious" hypotheses will have been thoroughly confirmed. As in Jorge Luis Borge's story, Kafka's existence will lead to the discovery of an infinite chain of Kafka's "precursors." We will again discover that excessive gradualism does undermine legitimacy; that a large-scale democracy will not become stable in Brazil until we have strong political parties; that without organized and minimally ideological parties, we should not have embarked on a competitive process of constitution-making; that the Constitutional Congress showed the enormous strength of an obsolete set of institutions by keeping the presidential system, an overly permissive electoral system, nationalist rhetoric, paternalistic welfare provisions—and even confirmed, in the democratic way, with strong support from the labor unions, the corporatist system established by Vargas in the 1930s, which had been branded as "fascist" for over forty years!

The Constitutional Congress did confirm, as expected, a five-year term for President Sarney. Those who supported this decision believe it will give the country the stability it needs to face the economic crisis; those who didn't are convinced that we will face that crisis with a very weak president, recently confirmed in office, throughout 1989.

· NOTES ·

Note: This chapter was largely written before the Constitutional Congress, which met during 1987 and 1988.
I am grateful to Luis Aureliano Gama Andrade for his collaboration in the initial version of this chapter. Wanderley G. Santas, Amavry de Sovzar, and my colleagues at IDESP also made very valuable suggestions.

1. The Movimento Democrático Brasileiro (opposition) elected sixteen of the twenty-two senators in 1974 (renovating one-third of the Senate), with a strong showing in the more urban and modernized states. An extended discussion of the structure of electoral competition as a factor capable of preventing authoritarian consolidation in Brazil can be found in Bolívar Lamounier, "Authoritarian Brasil Revisited." In *Democratizing Brazil,* ed. Alfred Stepan (Princeton, NJ: Princeton University Press, forthcoming).

2. One of these measures was the introduction of indirect elections for one-third of the senators. These senators were quickly nicknamed "bionic" and were never accepted as legitimate by public opinion. Another measure was the severe curtailing of electoral propaganda through radio and television, generalizing restrictions previously applied only in the municipal election of 1976.

3. One of these bills aimed at increasing contributions to finance the social-security system; the other attempted to extend the *sublegendas* (triple candidacies in each party) to the gubernatorial elections.

4. Cardoso was probably the first scholar to stress that the Brazilian authoritarian regime did not pursue stagnant economic policies; that it was, on the contrary, decidedly modernizing. See Fernando H. Cardoso, "Dependent-Associated Development: Theoretical and Practical Implications." In *Authoritarian Brazil: Origins, Outputs, Future,* ed. Alfred Stepan (New Haven, CT: Yale University Press, 1973). On economic policy in the 1970s, see Bolívar Lamounier and Alkimar R. Moura, "Economic Policy and Political Opening in Brazil." In *Latin American Political Economy: Financial Crisis and Political Change* ed. Jonathan Hartlyn and Samuel A. Morley (Boulder, CO: Westview Press, 1986); and Antônio Barros de Castro and Francisco E. Pires de Souza, *A Economia Brasileira em Marcha Forçada* (Rio de Janeiro: Editora Paz e Terra, 1985)

5. In addition to the "bionic" senators, created in 1977, the government majority increased the weight of the smaller states in the Electoral College through Constitutional Amendment 22 of 1982. The traditional but now controversial overrepresentation that those states enjoy in the federal chamber was thus unacceptably extended to the presidential succession. It is worth noting that the opposition assimilated even this change when it decided to present Tancredo Neves to the Electoral College as a presidential candidate.

6. Bureaucratic continuity has led many historians to accept the naive idea that Brazil inherited a ready-made state from the Portuguese at the time of independence in 1822. The more cautious view that Brazilian state-building was "completed" by 1860 or 1870 may be accepted, but even this with important qualifications. See J. G. Merquior, "Patterns of State-Building in Brazil and Argentina." In *States in History* ed. John A. Hall (London: Blackwell, 1986).

7. On the formation of a central power as a precondition for peaceful competition, see the excellent treatment of the English case in Harvey Mansfield, Jr., "Party Government and the Settlement of 1688," *American Political Science Review* 63, no. 4 (1964): pp. ; on the U.S. case, see Richard Hofstadter, *The Idea of a Party System* (Berkeley and Los Angeles: University of California Press, 1972).

8. Our treatment of these questions is evidently inspired by Hannah Pitkin's now-classic work. However, searching for different images of representation in the Brazilian case, we placed them in a historical sequence she may not have intended, at least not as a general rule. See Hannah Pitkin, *The Concept of Representation* (Berkeley and Los Angeles: University of California Press, 1972).

9. See José Murilo de Carvalho, *A Construção da Ordem* (Rio de Janeiro: Editora Campus, 1980).

10. The classic here is Victor Nunes Leal, *Coronelismo, Enxada e Voto: O Município e o Regime Representativo no Brasil* (Rio de Janeiro: Editora Forense, 1948). For a quick introduction to the history of electoral legislation in Brazil, see Toshio Mukai, *Sistemas Eleitorais no Brasil* (São Paulo: Instituto dos Advogados, 1985).

11. On the evolution of military institutions, see Edmundo Campos Coelho, *Em Busca da Identidade: O Exército e a Política na Sociedade Brasileira* (Rio de Janeiro: Editora Forense,

1976); José Murilo de Carvalho, "As Forças Armadas na Primeira República: O Poder Desestabilizador." Belo Horizonte, UFMG, *Cadernos do Departamento de Ciência Política* no. 1, March 1974. On the nineteenth-century National Guard, see Fernando Uricoechea, *O Minotauro Imperial* (São Paulo: Difel, 1978).

12. Control of the credentials commission (Comissão de Verificação de Poderes) of the federal chamber was the key to the system, since through it undesirable deputies eventually elected in the states would not be allowed to take up their position. This became popularly known as *degola* (beheading). Souza provides an excellent treatment of this question: "If the sedimentation of the [state] oligarchies was essential to consolidate the federation, it was also the reason for its future weakness. Contrary to the imperial framework, rotation in power among state oligarchies now became impossible." See Maria do Carmo Campello de Souza, "O Processo Político-Partidário na Velha República." In *Brasil em Perspectiva,* ed. Carlos Guilherme Mota (São Paulo: Difel, 1971), p. 203.

13. There is an extensive literature on the Revolution of 1930. Especially useful for our purposes is Campello de Souza, "Processo Político-Partidário". See also Boris Fausto, ed., *O Brasil Republicano,* 3 vols. (São Paulo: Difel, 1978, 1982, and 1983); Hélio Silva, *A Revolucão Traída* (Rio de Janeiro: Civilização Brasileira, 1966); and two volumes of conference proceedings: UFRGS, *Simpósio sobre a Revolução de 1930* (Porto Alegre: Universidade do Rio Grande do Sul, 1982); and UnB, *A Revolução de 1930: Seminário Internacional* (Brasília: Editora da Universidade, 1982).

14. Nunes Leal, *Coronelismo,* p. 170–171.

15. Protofascism is used here in the same sense given to it by James Gregor, *The Ideology of Fascism* (New York: Free Press, 1969), Ch. 2. He deals with important theoretical precursors, such as Gumplowicz, Pareto, and Mosca, stressing their antiparliamentarianism, their view on the relation between elite and mass, on the function of political myths, and the like.

16. On the corporatist "regulation" of citizenship, see Wanderley Guilherme dos Santos, *Cidadania e Justiça* (Rio de Janeiro: Editora Campus, 1979). Comprehensive accounts of the corporatist features of the labor relations system can be found in P. Schmitter, *Interest Conflict and Political Change in Brazil* (Stanford, CA: Stanford University Press, 1971); and Amaury de Souza, *The Nature of Corporatist Representation: Leaders and Members of Organized Labor in Brazil* (Ph.D. Diss., Massachusetts Institute of Technology, 1978).

17. The name of Gilberto Freyre comes readily to mind in connection with race relations and nationality in Brazil. On these themes, see T. Skidmore, *Black into White* (New York: Oxford University Press, 1974). The impact of these developments in Brazilian political culture was of course enormous in the 1930s and as a support to the Estado Novo. The factual importance of these core beliefs has been recognized quite broadly in the ideological spectrum since then. On intellectuals and culture policy in that period, see Simon Schwartzman et al., *Tempos de Capanema* (Rio de Janeiro: Paz e Terra, 1984); Sérgio Miceli, *Intelectuais e Classe Dirigente no Brasil (1920–1945)* (São Paulo: Difel, 1979); Lúcia Lippi de Oliveira, *Estado Novo—Ideologia e Poder* (Rio de Janeiro: Zahar Editores, 1982).

18. On the downfall of the *Estado Novo,* see Mario do Carmo Campello de Souza, *Estado e Partidos no Brasil* (São Paulo: Editora Alfa-Ômega, 1976): T. Skidmore, *Politics in Brazil: An Experiment in Democracy* (New York: Oxford University Press, 1968); Peter Flynn, *Brazil: A Political Analysis* (Boulder, CO: Westview Press, 1975). On the UDN, see Maria Vitória Benevides, *UDN e Udenismo* (Rio de Janeiro: Paz e Terra, 1981).

19. The literature on Vargas' second government is surprisingly small. In addition to the works of Flynn and Skidmore, already cited, see Maria Celina Soares D'Araujo, *O Segundo Governo Vargas, 1951–1954* (Rio de Janeiro: Zahar Editores, 1982); and Edgard Carone, *A República Liberal II* (São Paulo: Difel, 1985).

20. Useful data on bureaucratic growth under the Estado Novo can be found in Maria do Carmo Campello de Souza, *Estado e Partidos Políticos.* On economic policymaking from the 1930s to the mid-1950s, see John Wirth, *The Politics of Brazilian Development, 1930–1954* (Stanford, CA: Stanford University Press, 1970); and Luciano Martins, *Pouvoir et développement économique au Brésil* (Paris: Éditions Anthropos, 1976).

21. J. G. Merquior, "Patterns of State-Building," p. 284.

22. An overview of these hypotheses and of the relevant literature can be found in Bolívar Lamounier and Rachel Meneguello, *Partidos Políticos e Consolidação Democrática: O Caso Brasileiro* (São Paulo: Editora Brasiliense, 1986), sect. 4. Rigorous analysis of the crisis leading to 1964 was pioneered by Wanderley Guilherme dos Santos, *The Calculus of Conflict: Impasse in*

Brazilian Politics (Ph.D. Diss., Stanford University, 1974). Important works for the understanding of executive-legislative relations in the 1950s and early 1960s include: Celso Lafer, *The Planning Process and the Political System in Brazil* (Ph.D. Diss., Cornell University, 1970); Maria Vitória Benevides, *O Governo Kubitschek* (Rio de Janeiro: Paz e Terra, 1976): and Lúcia Hippolito, *PSD: De Raposas e Reformistas* (Rio de Janeiro: Paz e Terra, 1984).

23. On the ambiguities of military-directed institution-building after 1964, see Juan Linz, "The Future of an Authoritarian Situation or the Institutionalization of an Authoritarian Regime: The Case of Brazil." In Stepan, *Authoritarian Brazil;* Bolívar Lamounier, "*Authoritarian Brazil* revisited"; Wanderley Guilherme dos Santos, *Poder e Política: Crônica do Autoritarismo Brasileiro* (Rio de Janeiro: Forense, 1978). Roett synthesized those ambiguities as follows: "In Brazil, although the latitude given to the civilian political process is severely compromised, it does exist. The commitment to political participation—limited, elitist, and manipulable as it is—is strongly rooted in Brazilian constitutional history. Geisel's efforts at decompression were part of that historical belief that there should be a more open system". See Riordan Roett, "The Political Future of Brazil." In *The Future of Brazil,* ed. William Overholt (Boulder, CO: Westview Press, 1978).

24. Before independence and especially before the intensification of mining, in the early eighteenth century, the local chambers (*câmaras municipais*) were almost exclusively made up of landowners and had virtually unlimited authority, concentrating executive, legislative, and judiciary functions. Their members were chosen by means of a crude electoral system set forth in the *ordenações* of the Portuguese Crown. During the nineteenth century, detailed regulations were established to control local and statewide elections. Needless to say, the franchise was limited and voting was not secret. In addition, the empire kept the tradition of not allowing a clear distinction between legislative and executive functions at the local level; an elected local executive would appear only under the republic, and especially after 1930.

25. On bureaucratic continuity, see Raimundo Faoro, *Os donos do Poder* (Porto Alegre: Editora Globo, 1958); for a comparative analysis, see Merquior, "Patterns of State-Building"; on the military organization, see Coelho, *Em Busca da Identidade*

26. See Wanderley Guilherme dos Santos, "A Pós-'Revolução' Brasileira." In *Brasil: Sociedade Democrática,* ed. Hélio Jaguaribe (Rio de Janeiro: José Olympio Editora, 1985).

27. Sylvia A. Hewlett, "The State and Brazilian Economic Development." In Overholt, *Future of Brazil,* p. 150.

28. Russet calculated Gini coefficients for inequality in land tenure circa 1960 in forty-seven countries and found Brazil to be the thirty sixth from low to high concentration. See Bruce M. Russet, "Inequality and Instability: The Relation of Land Tenure to Politics." In *Readings in Modern Political Analysis,* ed. Robert A. Dahl and Deanne E. Neubauer (Englewood Cliffs, NJ: Prentice-Hall, 1968), pp. 150–162. There is no reason to assume that landed property is less concentrated today than in the 1960s. What did happen was that agrarian social relations became thoroughly capitalist. Landed property in Brazil was never "feudal" in a technical sense. Land was essentially used for capitalist purposes; i.e., to produce for a market or to function as a reserve of value in a highly inflationary economy. True, social relations were often paternalistic and exploitative, but this, too, is now undergoing rapid change.

29. The literature on growth and income distribution in this period is, of course, voluminous. A convenient starting point is Ricardo Tolipan and Artur Carlos Tinelli, eds., *A Controvérsia sobre Distribuição de Renda e Desenvolvimento* (Rio de Janeiro: Zahar Editores, 1975); see also Edmar Bacha, *Os Mitos de uma Década* (Rio de Janeiro: Editora Paz e Terra, 1976); Clarence Zuvekas, Jr., "Income Distribution in Latin America: A Survey of Recent Research." Center Essay no. 6, Center for Latin America, University of Wisconsin, Milwaukee, July 1975; and World Bank, *World Development Report 1983* and *World Development Report 1986* (New York: Oxford University Press, 1986).

30. Douglas H. Graham, "The Brazilian Economy: Structural Legacies and Future Prospects." In Overholt, *Future of Brazil,* p. 122.

31. World Bank, *World Development Report 1986,* Table 24, pp. 226–227.

32. See José Serra, "Ciclo e Mudanças Estruturais na Economia Brasileira do Pós-Guerra." In *Desenvolvimento Capitalista no Brasil—Ensaios sobre a Crise,* no. 2, ed. L. G. Belluzzo and Renata Coutinho (São Paulo: Editora Brasiliense, 1983), p. 64.

33. The following account of class structure in relation to the corporatist system draws heavily on dos Santos' important essay, "Pós-'Revolução' Brasileira."

34. See dos Santos, "Pós-'Revolução' Brasileira," p. 258; see also Carlos A. Hasenbalg, *Discriminação e Desigualdades Raciais no Brasil* (Rio de Janeiro: Edições Graal, 1979).

35. Data from an unpublished paper by Carlos A. Hasenbalg and Nelson do Valle e Silva, as quoted in dos Santos, "Pós-'Revolução' Brasileira," pp. 258, 264.

36. On Brazilian party history, see Lamounier and Meneguello, *Partidos Políticos*.

37. See works cited in n. 22, above.

38. Alfred Stepan, "Political Leadership and Regime Breakdown: Brazil." In *The Breakdown of Democracies,* ed. Juan Linz and Alfred Stepan (Baltimore, MD: Johns Hopkins University Press, 1978).

39. The importance of law schools throughout the nineteenth century and up to 1945 is beyond dispute. Resistance to Vargas' Estado Novo and again to the post-1964 military governments gave them a new lease on life. The Brazilian Lawyers Association was a basic reference point for the opposition during the decompression period.

40. A detailed analysis of Geisel's economic and political strategies can be found in Lamounier and Moura, "Economic Policy and Political Opening".

41. Perhaps we can interpret in this light the familiar finding that support for the democratic "rules of the game" is often more a matter of elite ethos than of mass attitudes. On "collective goods" as a tool in political analysis, see Mancur Olson, Jr., *The Logic of Collective Action* (New York: Schocken Books, 1968).

42. Even more serious than the influence exerted by such companies is perhaps the lack of coordination that results from their autonomous power, which leads several authors to talk about Balcanization, or feudalization. See dos Santos, *Poder e Política,* p. 123; and Luciano Martins, *Estado Capitalista e Burocracia no Brasil Pós-64* (Rio de Janeiro: Paz e Terra, 1985), p. 81.

43. The redistributive arena affects income and wealth, consequently producing very visible and highly organized contenders; the regulatory deals with the conditions under which certain activities will be exercised; finally, the distributive is what, broadly, one would call clientelistic politics, based on highly divisible and thus rather invisible decisions. Theodore Lowi, "American Business, Public Policy, Case Studies and Political Theory," *World Politics* 16 (1964): pp.

44. Robert A. Dahl, *Polyarchy; Participation and Opposition* (New Haven, CT: Yale University Press, 1971); p. 50.

45. The important critique of Lijphart's consociational model by A. O. Cintra and Plínio Dentzien, In *A Ciência Política nos Anos 80,* ed. Bolívar Lamounier (Brasília: Editora da Universidade, 1982).

46. Article 2 of the Constitutional Act of Finland states that the legislative power shall be exercised by Parliament together with the president and that the supreme executive power is vested in the president of the republic.

47. The West German system is clearly proportional, but the principle has been operationalized so as to allow for a "personalized" (majoritarian) choice of half the seats allocated to each party. No less important from our point of view is the choice of the other half by means of closed lists, in order to enhance the authority of the party as such over individual candidates.

48. Of course, we are here discussing long-run prospects. The new Constitution (October 5, 1988) has lifted the restrictions that the military had imposed on congressional powers—including those pertaining to economic and budgetary matters. But a full appreciation of the new Constitutional structure and its possible impact on democratic development requires another essay.

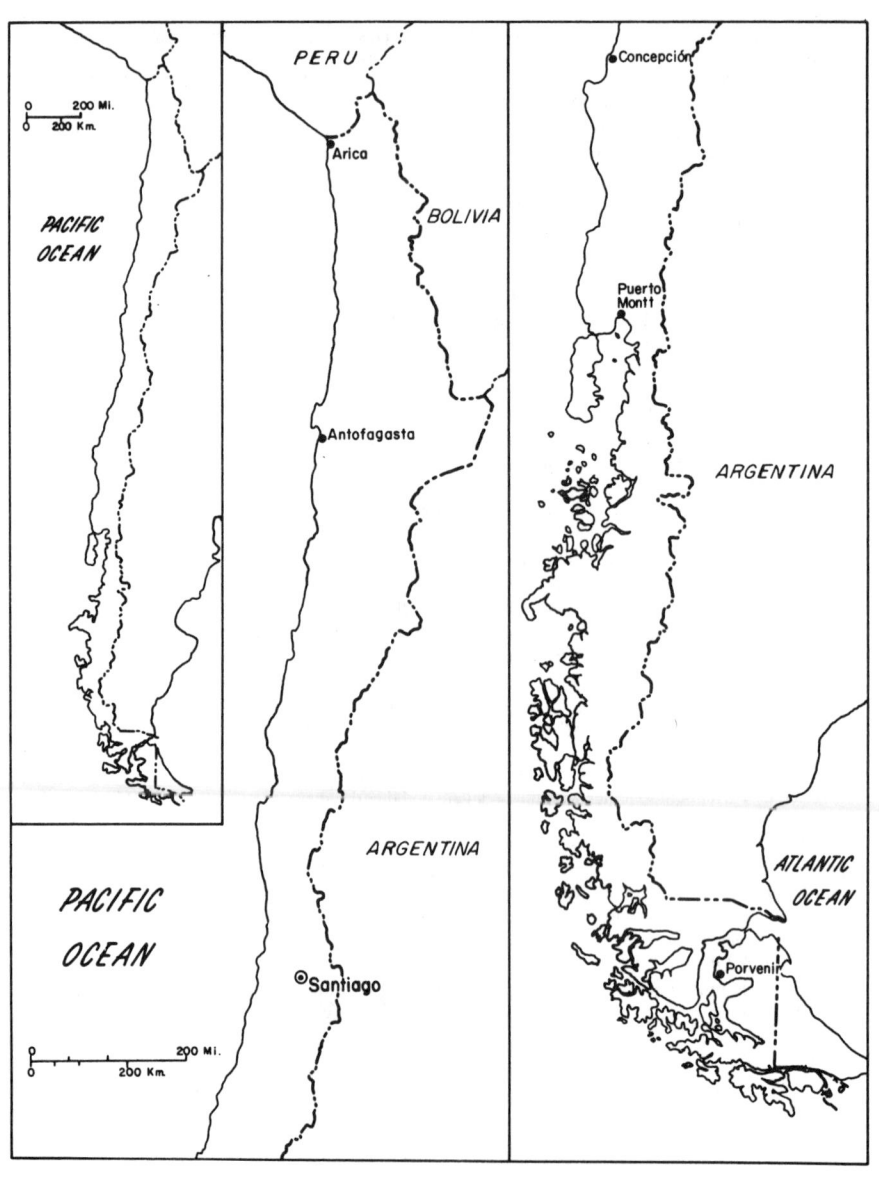

CHILE

• CHAPTER FOUR •
Chile: Origins, Consolidation, and Breakdown of a Democratic Regime

ARTURO VALENZUELA

Chile, under the rule of General Augusto Pinochet Ugarte, experienced the longest single government in the nation's history and one of the harshest dictatorships of the contemporary world. For years after the military coup of September 11, 1973, elections for public office, and even elections within private organizations and associations were circumscribed or monitored by the authorities. The doors of Congress were closed, and all major public decisions were made by the general, officials appointed by him, or a junta consisting of the commanders of the four military services.

Elected local governments, which had dated back to colonial times, were replaced by mayors who served at the pleasure of the commander-in-chief of the army and president of the republic. Even the nation's universities were not spared. Soon after the coup, high-ranking army officers were appointed to head both private and public institutions of higher education, with a mandate to purge government opponents and administer with an iron hand. Political parties were banned or dismantled, and their leaders persecuted. Rights of assembly and free speech were restricted. The press was severely censored, while the authorities made ample use of television to project their own vision of the world. An elaborate security apparatus operating with broad formal and informal powers sent regime opponents into internal and external exile without trial. Thousands were arrested, "disappeared," or killed.[1]

Despite serious economic difficulties and international isolation, Chile's authoritarian regime resisted the trend in Latin America back to democratic forms of government. A new constitution, written by a handful of government advisers and ratified in a highly suspect plebiscite in 1980, extended Pinochet's term until 1989 and made it legally possible for him to continue in office until 1997 or beyond. Although the constitutional framework specified the return to elective politics in 1989, the document contained many features that sharply restricted democratic practices and the accountability of government authorities to popular will. It created a powerful executive and a weak Congress and gave the commanders-in-chief of the armed forces veto power over public-policy issues. The Constitution also declared illegal all political parties that advocate philosophical doctrines based on class struggle.[2]

This state of affairs, though not uncommon in the Third World, was a sharp and historic departure for Chile. Before the 1973 breakdown, the country would have been classified, following the criteria used in this book, as a high success, a stable and uninterrupted case of democratic rule. For most of the preceding one hundred years, Chilean politics had been characterized by a high level of party competition and popular participation, open and fair elections, and strong respect for democratic freedoms. Indeed, Bollen, in one of the most comprehensive cross-national efforts to rank countries on a scale of political democracy, placed Chile in the top 15 percent in 1965, a score higher than that of the United States, France, Italy, or West Germany. For 1960, Chile's score was higher than that of Britain.[3]

However, synchronic studies such as Bollen's fail to account for the fact that Chile's democratic tradition was not a recent phenomenon but goes back several generations. In the nineteenth century, Chile developed democratic institutions and procedures, setting the country apart from many of its European counterparts, as well as its Latin American neighbors. As Epstein has noted, in Europe "political power was not often effectively transferred from hereditary rulers to representative assemblies no matter how narrow their electorates until late in the nineteenth century."[4] By contrast, Chile had, by the turn of the century, experienced several decades in which political authority was vested in elected presidents, and Congress wielded substantial influence over the formulation of public policy.[5] Indeed, from 1830 until 1973, all Chilean presidents were followed in office by their duly elected successors. Deviations to this pattern occurred only in 1891, in the aftermath of a brief civil war, and in the turbulent period between 1924 and 1932, when four chief executives felt pressured to resign in an atmosphere of political and social unrest and military involvement in politics. In 143 years, Chile experienced only thirteen months of unconstitutional rule under some form of junta, and only four months under a junta dominated exclusively by the military. And, though the executive was preeminent in the decades after independence, Congress gradually increased its prerogatives, becoming an important arena for national debate and one of the most powerful legislatures in the world.

Dahl has noted that the development of democracy entails not only establishing institutions for public contestation and leadership renewal, but also popular sovereignty.[6] In nineteenth-century Chile, citizenship was sharply restricted, first to men who owned property and later to those who were literate. Thus, Chile was only a partial democracy, according to the definition used here, until well into the twentieth century, when women's suffrage was established, the literacy requirement abolished, and 18-year-olds given the right to vote.[7] It must be stressed, however, that Chile did not deviate substantially from other nascent democracies in extending citizenship. In 1846, only 2 percent of the Chilean population voted, but this figure was comparable to that in Britain in

1830, Luxembourg in 1848, the Netherlands in 1851, and Italy in 1871. In 1876, two years after it had abolished the property requirement, Chile had 106,000 registered voters, compared to 84,000 in Norway for a comparable adult male population. Secret voting was established in Chile shortly after its adoption in Britain, Sweden, and Germany, and before its adoption in Belgium, Denmark, France, Prussia, and Norway.[8]

Reflecting the profound social changes brought about by urbanization, incipient industrialization, and a booming export economy, Chile's middle- and then working-class groups were incorporated into the democratic political game by the second decade of the twentieth century. With the rise of an organized Left, Chilean politics became sharply polarized between vastly different conceptions of what the country's future should be. This division, articulated by powerful and institutionalized parties functioning within the framework of Chile's presidential system, placed increasing strains on democracy. In the 1970s, these strains contributed to the the breakdown of democracy soon after the first leftist candidate in Chilean history had been elected to the nation's highest office.

In the aftermath of the defeat of President Pinochet in a plebiscite prescribed by his own constitution, Chile can be characterized as a democratic failure with promise according to the terminology employed by the editors of this volume. Ironically, though authoritarian rule and the sharp divisions that persist in Chilean politics, and the complexities of partisan relationships, have made the transition to democracy unusually difficult, there is reason to believe that because of Chile's long history of democratic practices, once a transition is instituted it may be more durable than in many other countries of the Third World.

The historical overview provides a sketch of the major trends in Chilean politics. It is not intended to cover all periods in equal depth; rather, it gives disproportionate attention to those historical developments that are especially important to making analytical arguments about the development and breakdown of Chilean democracy. Following this is a theoretical assessment of the applicability to the Chilean case of several leading hypotheses generated by social scientists to account for the emergence of democratic politics. The third part analyzes the breakdown of democracy, highlighting those variables that best explain the complex process resulting in the 1973 military coup. The fourth gives an overview of military rule in Chile, explaining how authoritarian politics was first institutionalized and why the transition back to democracy was so slow and painful. It ends by speculating about the future course of Chilean democracy.

• HISTORICAL OVERVIEW •

Origins and Consolidation of Chilean Democracy, 1830s-1960s

As in the rest of Latin America, attempts in Chile to inaugurate republican institutions, based on democratic principles inspired by the framers of the U.S. Constitution, met with resounding failure.[9] For a quarter-century after Chile's declaration of independence from Spain in 1810, the new nation alternated between dictatorship and anarchy. The war of independence was a prolonged and bloody civil "war to the death," as much as a war to end colonial rule, as many Chileans supported the royalist cause. The final defeat of Spanish forces left the territory's administrative and governing institutions in shambles, and local elites bitterly divided by regional, family, ideological, and personal disputes. Gone were the complex, far-flung patrimonial bureaucracy and the mediating power of the crown, which for centuries had imposed a traditional style of political authority over a distant colony. In 1830, the clear military victory of one coalition of forces permitted the inauguration of a concerted effort to institute political order and encourage economic progress. However, despite the able leadership of Cabinet Minister Diego Portales and military President Joaquín Prieto, and the establishment of a new constitution in 1833, coup attempts and conspiracies continued to plague Chile; Portales himself was assassinated in 1837 by troops he had thought loyal.

Portales' death was widely, though probably erroneously, blamed on interference in Chilean affairs by General Andrés Santa Cruz, the ruler of the Peru-Bolivia Confederation and a powerful rival for hegemony in Pacific commerce. The Bolivian dictator, after gaining control over Peru, had made no secret of his ambition to extend his empire southward. In response, Portales engineered, in 1836, a declaration of war, an unpopular move widely condemned in political circles. Ironically, Portales' death helped galvanize support for the war among disparate Chilean political factions; incensed at foreign intervention, several groups agreed to back an expeditionary force to Peru.

The war effort and the resounding victory achieved by the Chilean military had a profound impact. Individuals of all stations enthusiastically welcomed home the returning expeditionary force. The victory ball at the presidential palace was attended by rival families who had not spoken to each other in years, helping to heal long-standing wounds and forge a sense of common purpose. In the wake of triumph, authorities decreed a broad amnesty and the restitution of military ranks and pensions for those defeated in the civil war of 1830. As historian Encina notes, defeat of the Chilean forces would have magnified political divisions and seriously imperiled the already tenuous governmental stability. Military success gave the Prieto government and Chile's fledgling institutions a new lease on life.[10]

The 1837-1838 war had another, equally important consequence for Chile's political development. It created a national hero, the first Chilean leader to rise unambiguously above factional disputes. General Manuel Bulnes, the embodiment of national unity, was easily able to succeed Prieto in the presidential elections of 1840, a transition facilitated by Prieto's willingness to leave office in favor of his nephew. In his two terms, Bulnes took two important steps to implement the principles set forth in the nation's republican Constitution, principles that were nothing less than revolutionary at the time.[11]

In the first place, Bulnes refused to rule autocratically, giving substantial authority to a designated cabinet carefully balanced to represent some of the most important factions of the loose governing coalition. And though executive power was paramount, Bulnes permitted growing autonomy of the courts and the legislature. In time, Congress became increasingly more assertive, delaying approval of budget laws in exchange for modifications in cabinet policy. The cabinet's response to growing congressional activism was not to silence the institution but to capture it by manipulating the electoral process. Ironically, while this practice was condemned by opponents as a perversion of suffrage, it contributed to reinforcing the legitimacy of the legislature as a full-fledged branch of government. Eventually, as presidents changed ministers or as political coalitions shifted, even legislatures originally elected through fraud became centers for the expression of opposition sentiments, reinforcing presidential accountability to legislative majorities.

In the second place, Bulnes firmly exchanged his role as commander-in-chief of the armed forces for that of civilian president. Under his guidance, the professional military was sharply cut back, its personnel thinned out, and many of its assets sold. Instead, and to the dismay of his former military colleagues, Bulnes poured resources into the National Guard, a force of citizen soldiers closely tied to the government patronage network, who served as a ready pool of voters for government-sponsored candidates. In his last presidential address to the nation, Bulnes proudly described the reduction of the regular army and the expansion of the militia as the most convincing evidence of his administration's fidelity to republican institutions.[12]

The transition to a new president, however, was not easy. Many of the country's elites rejected the candidacy of Manuel Montt, a civil servant and cabinet minister of middle-class extraction, to succeed Bulnes. His candidacy was also rejected by elements in the professional army, who believed Bulnes would support a revolt to prevent Montt's accession to power and thus ensure the continuity of leadership from his native area of Concepción. When a revolt was attempted, however, Bulnes personally led the National Guard to defeat the rebel forces.

With the mid-nineteenth–century development of a new class of government functionaries and political leaders who espoused the liberal creed, the state gained substantial autonomy from the traditional landed elite, the pillar of social and economic power. State autonomy was reinforced by the government's success in promoting economic progress, particularly the booming export trade in wheat and minerals, which encouraged economic elites to give the authorities substantial leeway in policy formulation and implementation. Just as important, however, the export-import trade gave the authorities a ready and expanding source of income from customs duties, without their having to make the politically risky decision to tax property or income. Ironically, had the Chilean economy been more balanced and less dependent on foreign trade, the state would have been much more vulnerable to the immediate and direct pressures of economic elites. In Chile, economic dependency contributed to strengthening, not weakening, the state.[13] From 1830 to 1860, customs revenues, which represented 60 percent of all revenues, increased sevenfold, enabling the Chilean state to undertake extensive public-works projects, including constructing Latin America's second railroad, and to invest large sums of money in education, which officials believed to be the key to prosperity and national greatness.

In time, however, the state, rapidly extending its administrative jurisdiction and public-works projects throughout the national territory and actively promoting domestic programs in education and civil registries, clashed sharply with landowners, the church, and regional interests. Discontent in the ranks of the conservative landed elite was such that it led to the formation of the country's first real party, the Conservative Party, in direct opposition to Montt's administration. The Conservatives were committed to preserving the traditional order, and defending the values and interests of the church. At the same time, and also in opposition to the state, a group of ideological liberals, influenced by the Revolution of 1848 in France, pressed to accelerate secularization and decentralization and to expand suffrage and democratization. The secular-religious issue, with state elites taking a middle ground, would become the most salient political cleavage in nineteenth-century Chile, and the basis for crystalizing partisan alignments.

By 1859, discontent with the government from various quarters was such that a disparate coalition, composed of aristocratic Conservatives, regional groups, and the newly formed Radical Party representing the anticlerical and mining interests, challenged the government by force. In particular, the dissidents objected to the widespread state intervention in the 1858 congressional election, in which the government obtained a large majority in the Chamber of Deputies. Once again, however, state officials, with strong support from provincial interests and urban groups, were able to make use of the National Guard to put down the revolt. In the process, they put to rest the lingering center-periphery cleavages that had challenged central authority from the days of independence. The new president, following earlier precedents, granted a national amnesty and incorporated many dissidents into policymaking positions. Even the Radical Party obtained congressional representation in the next election.

The monopoly that the government had obtained over the country's most effective fighting forces made it difficult for Conservatives and other opposition elements to contemplate victory through armed challenge. Because of official intervention in the electoral process, moreover, opponents were unable to wrest control of the state from incumbents. Ironically, Conservatives soon realized that they had no choice but to push for expanded suffrage if they were to succeed in capturing the state. Even more oddly, in opposing the government they structured alliances of convenience in Congress with their nemeses, the staunchly ideological liberals, who were worried about electoral intervention and the authorities' refusal to press for increased democratization. This strategic adoption of a "liberal" creed by Conservative forces in a traditional society explains one of the most extraordinary paradoxes of Chilean history: the legislative alliance of ultramontane Catholics and radical liberals, both seeking for different reasons the fulfilment of democratic ideals.

Clearly, the Conservatives did not become democrats because of an ideological conversion, though many with close ties to England had come to believe that parliamentary government was a requirement for any civilized nation-state. But they correctly perceived that representative institutions were in their best interest, and the only real alternative once military solutions to domestic conflicts no longer seemed viable. Conservatives were forced to make the liberal creed their own precisely because they had lost ground to a new political class, which had gained strength by dominating the state. In turn, the pragmatic "liberals" (known as the Montt-Varistas) were not acting irrationally when they resisted attempts to expand suffrage and bar official manipulation of the electoral process. They fully realized that in an overwhelmingly rural society, with traditional landlord-peasant relationships, the Conservatives would beat them at the polls and challenge their monopoly of power.[14]

Under the leadership of Conservative José Manuel Irarrazaval, who became a champion of electoral reform, the Right sought to advance its interests through the democratic electoral process, rather than through military conspiracies or direct ties with elements of the central bureaucracy, as was the case in many other countries at the time. As a result, the church, hostile to electoral democracy in much of Latin Europe, also came to accept the legitimacy of suffrage in generating public officials. From a position of strength in Congress, the Conservatives, together with Radicals and ideological liberals and over the objections of the executive, successfully pressed for a series of reforms that restricted presidential power. The president was limited to a single 5-year term, and his veto power was restricted. The adoption of the Electoral Reform Act in 1874 tripled the electorate from 50,000 to 150,000 voters over the 1872 total.[15]

Nevertheless, official intervention in the electoral process did not end with electoral reform, and the stakes in controlling the state continued to increase. With its victory in the War of the Pacific (1879–1883), Chile gained vast new territory and rich nitrate deposits. Customs duties climbed to over 70 percent of government income, eliminating the need for property taxes and swelling state coffers. President José Manuel Balmaceda (1886–1891) refused to give in to congressional demands that ministers serve with congressional approval. He also balked at proposals that local governments be given substantial autonomy from the central administration, and that local notables be given control of the electoral process. When his cabinet was censured, Balmaceda sought to govern without congressional approval, adopting the national budget by decree. Finally, a civil war broke out between Congress, backed by the navy, and the president, backed by the army; Balmaceda was defeated in August 1891 and committed suicide.

With the country in disarray and the president dead, a junta headed by a navy captain, the vice-president of the Senate, and the president of the Chamber of Deputies assumed control of the government for three months. This marked the first time since 1830 that political power had been exercised in a manner not prescribed by the Constitution. But the brief period of unconstitutional rule did not involve imposing an authoritarian regime, nor did the military as an institution involve itself in politics except to take orders from civilian leaders. The cabinet continued to be a civilian cabinet, and Congress remained in session with virtually no interruption.

The victory of the congressional forces ushered in almost four decades of parliamentary government (1891–1927), in which the center of gravity of the political system shifted from the executive to the legislature, from the capital to local areas, and from state officials and their agents to local party leaders and political brokers. Politics became an elaborate log-rolling game centered in Congress, in which national resources were divided for the benefit of local constituents. Democratization, implied by these changes, had important effects on the political system. With the expansion of suffrage and local control of elections, parliamentary parties expanded beyond the confines of congressional corridors and became national networks with grassroots organizations.

Just as significant, however, was the emergence of parties outside the congressional arena (in Duverger's terms) in response to increased democratization and to other dramatic changes taking place in Chilean society.[16] While the Conservatives initially gained from electoral reform and were able to dominate the politics of the Parliamentary Republic, they did not foresee that the country's social structure would change so quickly in a quarter-century, and that electoral reform would soon benefit a new group of parties with far different agendas. The urban population, which accounted for 26 percent of the total in 1875, had soared to 45 percent by 1900. Nitrate production, employing between 10 and 15 percent of the population, spawned a host of ancillary industries and created a new working class, which soon found expression in new political parties when the traditional parties, particularly the modern Radicals, failed to provide the leadership required to address its grievances.

Both the state and private employers were slow to recognize the legitimacy of working-class demands and often brutally repressed the infant labor movement. But the openness of the political system, and the sharp competition among traditional parties searching for alliances to maximize electoral gain, permitted the development of electorally oriented class-based parties. By 1921, the year the Chilean Communist Party was officially founded, it had elected two members to Congress; four years later, it achieved representation in the Senate. Thus, to the secular-religious cleavage of the nineteenth century was added the worker-employer cleavage of the early twentieth century—generative cleavages that would shape the basic physiognomy of Chile's contemporary party system.

The 1920s were years of considerable political upheaval. The invention of synthetic nitrates during World War I led to the collapse of the Chilean nitrate industry, with far-reaching ramifications for the whole economy. The cumbersome and venal Parliamentary Republic fell increasingly into disrepute, criticized by the Right for allowing politics to become corrupt and overly democratic; denounced by the Center and Left for its inability to address national problems. President Arturo Alessandri (1920–1924) violated political norms by becoming an activist president and pressing for change in the face of congressional inaction and opposition. In September 1924, a group of young military officers unsheathed their swords in the congressional galleries, demanding reforms and the defeat of a congressional pay increase. Bowing to the unprecedented pressure, Alessandri resigned his post and left the country in the hands of a military junta—the first time in over 100 years that military men had played a direct role in governing the nation.

Senior officers, however, objected to the reform agenda of their younger colleagues; uncomfortable with the responsibility of governing, they soon began to defer to civilian leaders of the Right. This prompted a national movement to have Alessandri return, backed by younger officers who identified with the September *pronunciamiento*. In January 1925, the president resumed his position, marking the end of the first extraconstitutional government since 1891. During Alessandri's term, the 1925 Constitution was adopted with the expectation that it would increase the power of the president. It was the first full reform of the basic document since the Constitution of 1833, but it also embodied many elements of continuity.

Alessandri's elected successor, Emiliano Figueroa, proved unable to stand up to political pressures and the growing influence of Minister of War Colonel Carlos Ibañez, a military officer who had participated in the 1924 movement. In 1927 Figueroa resigned, and Ibañez was elected with broad support from all major parties, who sensed the country's and the military's demand for a "nonpolitical" and forceful chief executive. During his administration, Ibañez sought to alter fundamentally Chilean politics by introducing "efficient and modern" administrative practices, disdaining the role of Congress in cabinet appointments and resorting to emergency and executive measures, such as forced exile, in attempting to crush labor and opposition political parties. It is important to stress, however, that Ibañez's government was not a military dictatorship. While his authority derived in large measure from support in the barracks, army officers did not govern. The vast majority of cabinet officials were civilians, though most were newcomers to politics who criticized the intrigues of the traditional political class.

Ibañez soon discovered that he, too, could run out of political capital. His inability to curb the influence of parties, and his growing isolation, combined with the catastrophic effects of the Great Depression (in which Chilean exports dropped to a fifth of their former value) and mounting street unrest, finally led the demoralized president to submit his resignation in July 1931. After a period of political instability, which included the resignation of yet another president and the 90-day "Socialist Republic" proclaimed by a civil/military junta that attempted to press for social change, elections were scheduled in 1932. Once again, Arturo Alessandri was elected to a full constitutional term, thereby restoring the continuity of Chile's institutional system. During his second administration, Alessandri was far more cautious than during his first, successfully bringing the country out of the depression with firm austerity measures and reaffirming the value of institutions based on democratic values and procedures at a time when they were under profound attack in Europe.

The 1938 presidential election represented another major turning point in Chilean politics and a vivid confirmation of the extent to which ordinary citizens had become the fundamental source of political authority. In an extremely close election, the Center, in an alliance with the Marxist Left called the Popular Front, captured the presidency, and Radical Pedro Aguirre Cerda was elected. Despite the often-bitter opposition of the Right, the government for a decade expanded social-welfare policies, encouraged the rise of legal unionism, and actively pursued import-substituting industrialization through a new Corporación de Fomento de la Producción (Corporation for the Development of Production). The trend toward urbanization continued: in 1940, 53 percent of the population lived in cities; by 1970, that figure had increased to 76 percent.

By 1948, the new Cold War climate abroad and the increased local electoral successes of the Communist Party were making both Socialists and Radicals increasingly uneasy. Encouraged by Radical leaders, President Gabriel González Videla dissolved the Popular Front, outlawed the Communist Party, and sent many of its members to detention camps. These actions, combined with the wear of incumbency and general dissatisfaction with the opportunistic Radicals, contributed to the election of Carlos Ibañez as president in 1952 on an antiparty platform. But Ibañez, unable to govern without party support, was forced to shift his initial populist programs to a severe austerity plan that contributed to wage and salary declines. He was succeeded in 1958 by Conservative businessman Jorge Alessandri, the former president's son, who edged out Socialist Salvador Allende by only 2.7 percent of the vote. Alessandri applied more austerity measures, provoking cries for profound reform from a populace tired of spiraling inflation and economic stagnation. In the 1964 presidential elections, fear of the growing strength of the Left led Chile's traditional rightist parties to reluctantly support Eduardo Frei, the candidate of the new Christian Democratic Party, which had replaced the Radicals as the largest party in Chile and the most powerful party of the Center. With massive financial assistance from the United States, the Frei government attempted to implement far-reaching reforms, but after dissolving their tacit alliance with the Right, the Christian Democrats were unable to increase their share of the vote. In 1970, claiming to have been betrayed by Frei's reformist policies, the Right refused to support Christian Democratic candidate Radomiro Tomic, making possible the election of leftist candidate Salvador Allende and his Popular Unity coalition, with only 36.2 percent of the vote. The Christian Democratic and Popular Unity governments are treated in more detail in the discussion of the breakdown of Chilean democracy, below.

Characteristics of Chilean Politics at Mid-Century[17]

By the 1930s, with the rise of Marxist parties at a time of electoral expansion, the Chilean party system, in Lipset and Rokkan's terms, had become complete.[18] In addition to the traditional Conservative and Liberal parties that had emerged from church-state cleavages in the early nineteenth century, and the Radical Party that had developed later in that century out of similar divisions, Communist and Socialist parties had now developed in response to a growing class cleavage. The only new party to emerge after the 1930s, the Christian Democratic Party, was an offshoot of the Conservatives, which sought to address social and economic issues from the vantage point of reform Catholicism.

Yet this "complete" system was characterized by sharp social polarizations in which the organized electorate was divided almost equally among the three political tendencies. Although numerous small parties appeared after 1932, the six major parties continued to dominate politics, commanding over 80 percent of the vote by the 1960s. Elections and politics became a national "sport," as parties became so deeply ingrained in the nation's social fabric that Chileans would refer to a Radical or a Communist or a Christian Democratic "subculture." Parties helped to structure people's friendships and social life. Partisan affiliation continued to be reinforced by both class and religion, so that Christian Democratic elites were more likely to go to Catholic schools and universities and come from upper-middle-class backgrounds, while Socialist elites went to public schools and state universities and came from lower-middle-class backgrounds. Communist strength was heavily concentrated in mining communities and industrial areas, Christian Democrats appealed to middle-class and women voters, while the Right retained substantial support in rural Chile.

The major parties framed political options not only in municipal and congressional elections but also in private and secondary associations. The penetration of parties into Chilean society was such that even high school student associations, community groups, universities, and professional societies selected leaders on party slates. Political democracy helped democratize social groups and erode historic patterns of authoritarian social relations.

It is crucial to stress that there were no giants in the Chilean political system. No single party or tendency could win a majority and impose its will. This pattern had clear implications for the functioning of Chile's presidential system.

Since majorities were impossible to achieve, Chilean presidents were invariably elected by coalitions or were forced to build governing coalitions with opposing parties in Congress after the election. However, because preelection coalitions were constituted primarily for electoral reasons, in an atmosphere of considerable political uncertainty, they tended to disintegrate after a few months of the new administration.

Ideological disputes were often at the root of coalition changes, as partisans of one formula would resist the proposals of opponents. But narrow political considerations were also important. Since a president could not succeed himself, leaders of other parties in his coalition often realized they could best improve their fortunes in succeeding municipal and congressional elections by disassociating themselves from the difficulties of incumbency in a society fraught with economic problems. In the final analysis, only by proving their independent electoral strength in nonpresidential elections could parties demonstrate their value to future presidential coalitions.

Since Chilean presidents could not dissolve Congress in case of an impasse or loss of congressional support, they needed to build alternative alliances in order to govern. Parties assured their influence by requiring that candidates nominated for cabinet posts seek their party's permission (*pase*) to serve in office. Presidents, required continually to forge working coalitions, were repeatedly frustrated by the sense of instability and permanent crisis that this bargaining process gave Chilean politics.

An image of Chile's party system as excessively competitive and polarized, however, is incomplete and inaccurate. The collapse of party agreements, the censure of ministers, and the sharp disagreement over major policy issues captured the headlines and inflamed people's passions. But the vast majority of political transactions were characterized by compromise, flexibility, and respect for the institutions and procedures of constitutional democracy. Over the years, working agreements among political rivals led to implementing far-reaching policies, including state-sponsored industrialization; comprehensive national health, welfare, and educational systems; agrarian reform; and copper nationalization. Agreements were also structured around the more mundane aspects of politics. Congressmen and party leaders of different stripes would join in efforts to promote a particular region or to provide special benefits to constituency groups and individuals.[19]

This pattern of give-and-take can be attributed to three mutually reinforcing factors: a pragmatic center; the viability of representative arenas of decision-making and neutrality of public institutions; and the imperatives of electoral politics. Compromise would have been difficult without the flexibility provided by Center parties, notably the Radical Party, which inherited the role of the nineteenth-century Liberals as the fulcrum of coalition politics. The Radicals supported, at one time or another, the rightist presidencies of the two Alessandris in the 1930s and 1960s and governed with support of the Right in the late 1940s. In the late 1930s and through most of the 1940s, however, they allied with the Left to form Popular Front governments under a Radical president, and in the 1970s, a substantial portion of the party supported Salvador Allende, though by then the party's strength had been severely eroded.

Accommodation and compromise were also the hallmarks of democratic institutions such as the Chilean Congress, whose law-making, budgetary, and investigatory powers provided incentives for party leaders to set aside disagreements in matters of mutual benefit. Indeed, the folkways of the legislative institution, stemming from years of close working relationships in committees and on the floor, contributed to the development of legendary private friendships among leaders who were strong public antagonists. Just as significant, however, were such prestigious institutions as the armed forces, the judiciary, and the comptroller general, respected for their "neutrality" and remoteness from the clamor of everyday politics. These institutions provided an important safety valve from the hyperpoliticization of most of public life. The legitimacy of public institutions was further reinforced by a strong commitment to public service, which extended from the presidential palace to the rural police station. Although electoral fraud and vote-buying by political party machines were common, financial corruption remained very rare in Chilean public life, and the vigilance of the Congress and the courts helped prevent wrongdoing for personal gain by public office–holders.

Finally, the press of continuous elections forced political leaders to turn away from ideological pursuits and attend to the more mundane side of politics, such as personal favors and other particularistic tasks inherent in a representative system. Congressmen and senators had to look after their party brokers in municipalities and neighborhoods, making sure to provide public funds for a local bridge or jobs for constituents. Often political leaders from different parties joined in advancing the common interests of their constituencies, setting aside acrimonious, abstract debates over the role of the state in the economy or Soviet policy in Asia. In Chile, the politics of ideology, rooted in strong social inequalities, was counterbalanced by the clientelistic politics of electoral accountability reinforced by that same inequality. As will be noted below, many of these elements disappeared during the later 1960s and early 1970s, putting the democratic system under great strain and ultimately contributing to its total collapse.

• ORIGINS OF CHILEAN DEMOCRACY: A THEORETICAL ASSESSMENT •

Because it is one of the few cases in which a democratic government was successfully established in the mid-nineteenth century, and an especially dramatic example of democratic failure, Chile constitutes a valuable paradigmatic case in the effort to construct theoretical propositions explaining the origins, consolidation, and breakdown of democratic regimes. Its theoretical utility is enhanced by the fact that there are no comparable cases of democratic development outside the Western European–North American context, or among primarily Catholic or export-oriented countries. As a deviant case, which has been largely neglected in scholarly literature, Chile can serve as a useful test for the validity of theoretical propositions generated by observing the experience of other countries, primarily European.[20]

The most prominent theses aimed at explaining the development of democracy assume that political practices and institutions can be understood by reference to a series of historical, cultural, or economic determinants. It is the central argument of this chapter that such approaches fall short in accounting for Chilean exceptionality, and that the Chilean case can be best explained by considering political factors as independent variables in their own right. This section will review the "determinants" of democracy embodied in what can be called the colonial-continuity thesis, the political-culture thesis, and the economic–class-structure thesis.[21] It will then turn to an analysis of those political variables that are most helpful in understanding Chile's political evolution, variables that can add to the development of theoretical propositions to be tested in other contexts.

Naturally, any hypotheses derived from the Chilean case or any single case will remain tentative until subjected to systematic comparative analysis drawing on a broader sample of carefully chosen observations. Without comparative evidence it would be difficult to identify those factors that are generalizable and constitute necessary conditions for the development of democratic practices and institutions, and those that are unique to and ultimately incorrect for explaining the single case.

The Colonial-Continuity Thesis

According to the colonial-continuity thesis, democratic practices will flourish in postcolonial regimes if institutions for self-rule, even if limited, were in place for several generations during colonial times, and if the transition from colony to independent state was accomplished without too much violence and destruction of those institutions. Both these conditions figure prominently in accounts of the outcome of the British decolonization experiences of the eighteenth and twentieth centuries.[22] It is clear that this thesis cannot account for the Chilean case. Although Chile was a more isolated colony than the major centers of Spanish rule in the new world, there is no evidence that the colony was able to gain the necessary autonomy to develop institutions of self-rule that would carry it into the postindependence period. Chile was subject to the same patrimonial administration and mercantilistic policies that discouraged expressions of political or economic independence and frowned on participatory institutions as contrary to the fundamental conception of monarchical rule. The colonies were the personal property of the king, subject to his direct control. Moreover, the Chilean wars of independence were profoundly disruptive of the previous political order, plunging the nation into a fratricidal conflict that tore asunder institutions and political practices that had been in place for generations. Although Chileans later established democratic rule, this accomplishment had little to do with the political experiences gained in colonial times.[23]

There is, however, a variant of the continuity thesis that must be addressed because it constitutes the principal explanation found in the historiographical literature dealing with Chilean exceptionality. According to this thesis, Chile deviated from the pattern that held sway in nineteenth-century Latin America not because its colonial institutions were more liberal, but because its postindependence institutions were more conservative. This argument holds that Diego Portales, the cabinet minister who dominated the government of President Prieto during the 1830s, helped to establish firm and authoritarian rule equivalent to that of the Spanish crown during the colonial era, thus rescuing Chile from misguided liberals enamored with unrealistic federal formulae and excessive freedoms.[24] Chile succeeded not because it broke from the colonial past, this argument holds, but because it reimposed that past. Morse articulates the point:

> Chile was an example perhaps unparalleled of a Spanish American country which managed, after a twelve-year transitional period, to avoid the extremes of tyranny and anarchy with a political system unencumbered by the mechanisms and party rhetoric of exotic liberalism. . . . [T]he structure of the Spanish patrimonial state was recreated with only those minimum concessions to Anglo-French constitutionalism that were necessary for a nineteenth century republic which had just rejected monarchical rule.[25]

It is disingenuous to argue, as most Chileans do, that Portales forged Chile's institutions singlehandedly. The minister was in office for only a total of three years, had little to do with drafting the 1833 Constitution, and died in office at a time when his government was under serious challenge.[26] Regardless of Portales' role, it is also profoundly mistaken to argue that Chile's concessions to Anglo-French constitutionalism were minimal. The political system established by the Constitution of 1833 was qualitatively different from the colonial system of the past, bearing far greater resemblance to the institutions and practices followed in the North American colonies, and the compromises struck at the constitutional convention in Philadelphia, than to the institutions set up by the Castilian rulers.

In Weberian terms, Chile's new constitutional formula substituted rational-legal authority for traditional authority; that is, it replaced the authority of an hereditary monarch, whose power was inherent in his person by virtue of divinely ordained practices going back generations, with the authority of an elected president whose power derived from the office as defined by law. Moreover, rather than recreating colonial patterns of political domination, nineteenth-century Chilean politics from the outset expanded the concept of citizenship (a radical notion at the time) and affirmed the legitimacy of elected assemblies to claim political sovereignty equally with the chief executive.

When viewed in this light, the achievements of the forgers of Chilean institutionality are very significant in contrast to those of their North American counterparts, who fashioned their institutions and practices by drawing on generations of experience with self-rule within the political framework of Tudor England.[27]

The Political-Culture Thesis

Perhaps the most influential set of propositions associated with the development of democratic institutions are those that hold that democracy requires a country's citizens, or at the very least its politically active elites, to share the liberal beliefs and values that are the hallmark of the Enlightenment. These include values conducive to accepting the equality of all people and their fundamental worth, values tolerating opposition and the free expression of ideas, and values celebrating the legitimacy of moderation and compromise. In short, they are the values associated with participatory politics as opposed to authoritarian patterns of governance. These political-culture variables have figured prominently in efforts to explain the general failure of democracy in Latin America and in Latin Europe, and the success of democracy in Protestant Europe and the United States. Democracy succeeded in the United States, this argument holds, because the British colonies were populated by settlers already imbued with more egalitarian values stemming from the Enlightenment and the Protestant Reformation. By contrast, the colonizers of Latin America brought aristocratic and feudal values reinforced by a Catholic faith stressing the importance of hierarchy, authority, corporativism, and the immutability of the traditional social order.[28]

But if the absence of democracy in Latin America is explained by the lack of appropriate beliefs, how can we account for the Chilean case? Were Chileans, located in one of the most remote colonies of the empire and dominated by an aristocracy of Basque descent, less tied to royal institutions? Or was the Chilean church more liberal or less influential in the social and political life of the colony? None of the historical evidence supports these contentions. To the contrary, Chile's isolation had made the colony one of the most traditional on the continent. Royalist sentiment was as strong in Chile as anywhere else, and troops who fought with the Spaniards to suppress the insurrection were recruited locally. Similarly, the church was as conservative as in other countries and retained the strong backing of the local aristocracy despite its close ties with the colonial power. Chilean elites were no less Catholic than the political elites of other former colonies.[29]

A variant of the political-culture thesis holds that it is not so much the religious traditions or political practices of the past that condition political beliefs and attitudes, but the authority relations found in secondary spheres of society: the workplace, the family, or the educational system.[30] Of particular importance in a predominantly agricultural society are the social relations of production resulting from the country's land-tenure system. Where land is concentrated in a small number of estates with traditional patron-client authority relations, this thesis argues, political values will be hierarchical and authoritarian. Where land is divided more equally and exploited by family farmers and contract labor, political values will be more egalitarian and democratic, facilitating the development of democratic politics. This is the argument that Booth makes in attempting to account for democratic development in Costa Rica.[31] Dahl echoes this approach when he suggests that the Chilean case can be explained by "considerable equality in distribution of land and instruments of coercion, reinforced by norms favoring social and political equality."[32]

However, Dahl's argument also fails to stand up to historical scrutiny. Chile's system of social relations and stratification was one of the most rigid and traditional on the continent, based on large landed estates and semifeudal relationships of authority between landlord and peasant. Authority relations in the family and in the educational system, still under church tutelage, were also authoritarian and hierarchical.[33] The wars of independence disrupted the country's social structure less than they did elsewhere. As Dominguez notes, "Chile lagged behind the other colonies, although it had experienced economic growth and mobilization. Its society had been transformed the least. The social bonds within it remained strong. Centralization had not been advanced nor had society been pluralized. Traditional elites remained strong, and traditional orientations prevailed."[34] Throughout the nineteenth and well into the twentieth century, the traditional nature of social relations in the countryside remained one of the most striking features of the Chilean social structure. Despite the rise of an urban working class and the democratization of other spheres of social life, rural social relations were not significantly altered until the 1960s, when agrarian reform was finally undertaken as national policy.[35]

There is no reason to assume that the evolution of democratic politics in Chile in the nineteenth century was due to more "favorable" political-culture variables. The failure of cultural explanations to account for the Chilean case raises serious questions about the underlying assumption that there is a direct fit between societal values and political institutions. It is very unlikely that Chile had societal values comparable to those of Norway, Australia, or the United States (though they may not have been too dissimilar to those found in class-concious Britain), yet the political outcomes were not dissimilar. Several students of democracy have argued that "stable" democracy is the product not only of liberal and participatory values, but of a mixture of participatory and deferential ones. However, in the absence of a clearly defined set of values that relate to democracy, it is difficult to ascertain which mix is appropriate. As a result, there is a real temptation to engage in circular reasoning: If a particular regime was stable or had the requisite democratic characteristics, it was assumed it had *ipso facto* the appropriate value structure.

Although egalitarian and democratic values were not necessary to structure democratic institutions and procedures, the Chilean case suggests that the exercise of democratic practices over a period of time encourages the development of certain norms of political conduct and reinforces belief in the legitimacy of the rules of the game. As early as the 1850s, Chilean political elites of different ideological persuasions worked together in Congress to advance common objectives, thus developing habits of flexibility and compromise. The Radicals, who were excluded from decisionmaking roles in Argentina until after the 1912 Saenz Peña law, were invited to serve in cabinets fifty years earlier in Chile.

As an industrial working class developed, moreover, Chilean elites, despite serious objections to accepting the principle of collective bargaining at the workplace and brutal repression of the incipient labor movement, accepted the legitimate role of working-class parties in the arena of electoral competition and eventually in the corridors of power. Democratic institutions came to be accepted by most Chileans as the best way to resolve disagreements and set national policy. By mid-twentieth century, ordinary Chileans took great pride in their civic duties, participating enthusiastically in an electoral process that made Chile distinctive among Third World nations. In sum, Chilean democracy emerged without strongly held democratic values. But the practice of democracy itself instilled norms of give-and-take, tolerance, and respect for fundamental liberties that were widely shared by the population as a whole.[36]

This does not mean that democratic politics in Chile were centrist-oriented and devoid of sharp conflict. In 1891, after thirty years of domestic tranquility, the strongly felt political anatagonisms generated by the executive-congressional impasse spilled onto the battlefield, a conflict that nonetheless pales by comparison with the U.S. Civil War, which also took place eighty years after the Declaration of Independence. The deep ideological disagreements of twentieth-century Chile continuously challenged the country's institutions and practices. The Chilean case and those of other highly polarized political systems like Italy, France, and Finland show that consensus on the fundamentals of public policy can be relatively low, while consensus on the rules and procedures for arriving at policy decisions can be high.

It was not moderation that made Chilean democracy function; It was Chilean democracy that helped moderate political passions and manage deep-seated divisions. A democratic political culture is not an abstract set of beliefs or psychological predispositions governing interpersonal relations in the body politic, but practical and ingrained traditions and working relations based on regularized patterns of political interaction in the context of representative institutions. As will be noted below, with the breakdown of democracy, Chile lost not only representative rule, but the institutional fabric that helped define many of the values of democratic human conduct.

The Economic–Class-Structure Thesis

While there is broad variation in studies emphasizing the economic determinants of democracy, they can be divided into two categories: those relating democracy to overall levels of economic development; and those focusing on the contribution to the creation of democratic institutions of particular groups or classes that emerge as a result of economic transformations in society.

The first group draws on the insights of "modernization" theory, arguing that economic development leads to more complex, differentiated, secularized, and educated societies, opening the way for the rise of new groups and institutions that find expression in democratic practices.[37] In addition, economic growth is said to provide channels for upward mobility and for ameliorating the sharp social disparities found in poor societies, disparities that undermine democratic performance. Empirical evidence for these propositions was advanced in a host of cross-national studies conducted in the late 1960s, inspired by Lipset's classic article on the "economic correlates of democracy."[38] The main difficulty with these studies in explaining the Chilean case is that they are ahistorical. Chile in the nineteenth century, like most incipient democracies of the time, was a rural, pre-industrial society with very low levels of personal wealth and literacy, yet it met many of the criteria for democratic performance. In the twentieth century, as several authors have noted, Chile was clearly an outlier, exhibiting many of the characteristics of economic underdevelopment while boasting high scores on democratic performance.[39] As Linz has argued, explanations that draw on levels of economic development do not contribute much to our understanding of the origins and development of democratic politics.[40]

Scholars writing in a Marxist tradition have argued that the most important variable is not overall economic development, but the rise of rural and urban middle classes capable of challenging the monopoly of landed elites and breaking their political power. Based on his reflections on the European case, Therborn attributes the rise of democracy to the emergence of agrarian bourgeois groups, giving particular emphasis to "the strength of these agrarian classes and the degree of their independence from the landowning aristocracy and urban big capital."[41] Moore goes further, presenting a more complex argument. For Moore, as for Therborn, the development of a bourgeoisie was central to the development of democracy. However, whether a country actually followed a democratic path depended on how agriculture was commercialized, whether or not it became "labor repressive" or "market commercial."[42]

As with the political-culture thesis, it is difficult to accept the applicability of the economic–class-structure thesis to the Chilean case. As noted earlier, Chilean agriculture remained "labor repressive" well into the twentieth century, retaining a high concentration of land ownership. And though, as Dominguez notes, Chilean agriculture was geared by the eighteenth century to the export of wheat, wheat production was never commercialized as in North America. As in czarist Russia, it was expanded with only minimal modifications to the traditional manorial system.[43] By the same token, and despite some interpretations of Chilean history that stress the rise of an urban bourgeoisie as the key liberalizing force, Chile did not develop a strong and independent urban-based bourgeoisie before the development of democratic rules and procedures. Although mining interests became powerful and some of the most prominent mine owners were identified with the Radical Party, it is mistaken to identify Chilean mining interests as representatives of a new and differentiated bourgeois class. Other, equally prominent mine owners had close ties to the Conservative Party, and many members of the Chilean elite had both mining and agricultural interests.[44]

However, the most telling argument against the economic–class-structure thesis has already been anticipated in the historical discussion at the beginning of this chapter. The rise of democracy in Chile—including the limitations on presidential authority, the expansion of legislative prerogatives, and the extension of suffrage—took place not over the objections of the conservative landed elites but, as in Britain, at their instigation. If the traditional landowning class, which championed the Roman Catholic church, decided to support suffrage expansion and the development of democratic institutions, then theoretical explanations that hold that democracy emerges only with the destruction of that class are less than adequate. This is a central point, to which we will return.

The Political-Determinants Thesis

An examination of various theses dealing with the historical, cultural, and economic "determinants" of democracy suggests that they are not particularly useful in explaining the Chilean case. What is more, the Chilean case, as one of successful democratic development that does not conform to the principal arguments of those theses, raises serious questions about their overall validity. However, from this evidence alone it would be clearly mistaken to argue that these factors play no substantial role in democratic development. A "liberal" colonial tradition, egalitarian values, economic development, and a variegated social structure are undoubtedly conducive to the implementation and acceptance of institutions of self-governance. Indeed, a perspective such as the one advocated here, the political-determinants thesis, which stresses the importance of discrete political variables and even historical accidents as independent variables, need not eschew the economic and cultural constants nor shy away from developing generalizations that relate socioeconomic to political variables. The point is that these cultural and economic variables are hardly determinants of democratic practices. They may very well be important contributory or even sufficient conditions; but they are not necessary ones.

A historical review of the development of Chilean political institutions immediately suggests the utility of the "political-crisis" literature developed by political scientists. According to this literature, all countries face severe challenges in developing democratic institutions and, depending on the timing and sequence of those challenges, have greater or lesser success in achieving democratic stability.[45] Although the challenges vary in kind and number, most authors view the crises of national identity (creating a sense of national community over parochial loyalties), authority (establishing viable state structures), and participation (incorporating the citizenry into the political system) as crucial.

In addition, the sequence and timing of the appearance of these problems on the historical scene can seriously affect the political outcome. As Nordlinger puts it, "the probabilities of a political system developing in a nonviolent, nonauthoritarian, and eventually democratically viable manner are maximized when a national identity emerges first, followed by the institutionalization of the central government, and then the emergence of mass parties and mass electorate."[46] It can be argued that Chile followed this "optimal" sequence and that the timing was also favorable, particularly with respect to the emergence of the participation crisis, which did not become a critical issue until after central authority structures had been consolidated.[47]

National identity. It is doubtful that Chileans considered themselves a nation before independence, because there were far fewer mechanisms of social communication and exchange than in North America and a far more ubiquitous set of colonial authority structures.[48] However, the clear-cut military victory in the war against the Peru-Bolivia Confederation, a victory without parallel in Latin America, gave the small, divided nation a powerful new sense of confidence and purpose, creating tangible symbols of patriotism and nationality. These feelings were reinforced with the victory of Chilean forces in the War of the Pacific, which led to the incorporation of large portions of Peruvian and Bolivian territory into national boundaries.

Political authority. Rustow has noted the importance of distinguishing between establishing and consolidating institutions of democracy. Consolidation involves a lengthy process of "habituation," which is not necessarily unilinear; there can be reversals and even breakdown.[49] In consolidating political authority in Chile, five factors were critically important: leadership; state autonomy; government efficacy; civilian control of the armed forces; and conservative support for democratic rules.

The first important element was leadership. General Bulnes, drawing on his command of the most powerful armed forces in the country and his widespread popularity, could have easily used his position to establish personal rule, following the pattern of notable Latin American *caudillos* such as Paez in Venezuela, Rosas in Argentina, or Santa Ana in Mexico. Instead, like Washington in the United States, he insisted on working within the framework of established political institutions and chose to leave office at the end of his term, making way for his successor. His willingness while in office to underscore the autonomy of the courts, accept the role of Congress in policy, and allow ministerial cabinets to formulate the government's program set a precedent for his successor and future administrations, and helped to establish the legitimacy of democratic institutions.[50]

The second important factor was state autonomy. A crucial legacy of Bulnes' and, later, Montt's respect for constitutionally mandated institutions was the development of politics and government service as a vocation. An impressive group of functionaries and legislators emerged who were committed to strengthening and expanding the secular state. By 1860, more than 2,500 people worked for the state, not including local officials, construction workers, and members of the armed forces. All of Chile's nineteenth-century presidents save one had extensive congressional experience before being elected to office, and five who took office before 1886 began their careers in the Bulnes administration. Between Bulnes and Pinochet, only two of Chile's twenty-two presidents were career military officers, and both of those were freely elected with political-party support in moments of political crisis.[51]

The third element was governmental efficacy. Under the leadership of the first three presidents to serve after 1830, the Chilean economy performed relatively well. This not only brought credit to the new institutions and leaders of the independent nation, but more importantly, it gave the government elites time and autonomy to begin state consolidation. By the time important interests sought to stop the expansion of the secular state, it had garnered significant political, financial, and military strength.[52]

The fourth factor was control of the armed forces by civilian governmental leaders. By deliberately refusing until after the War of the Pacific to create a professional military establishment, while retaining close political control over an effective national militia, Chilean officials were able to establish a monopoly over the control of force and a tradition of civilian supremacy over the military. The military challenges of 1851 and 1859 were defeated, discouraging dissident elites from gathering their own military force to challenge national authority structures.

The fifth factor was conservative support for democratic rules. This factor is directly related to the development of state autonomy and control of the military. Control of the military prevented aggrieved sectors of the elites from resorting to insurrectionary movements in order to prevent state action or to capture the state by force. Thus such elites, including conservative landholders, were forced to turn to democratic procedures already in place, and indeed to seek their expansion, in order to preserve and advance their interests. Far from being a minor footnote in history, this support of the Chilean conservatives for liberal rules was of central importance. It led to the creation of a Conservative Party, committed to representative institutions, which had no exact parallel in Latin America or Latin Europe.

This leads to a basic proposition: that the origins and evolution of democratic institutions and procedures are determined more by the choices made by key elites seeking to maximize their interests within the framework of specific structural and political parameters, than they are by abstract cultural or economic factors. Chilean elites, initially hostile to democracy, came to embrace democratic rules as a conscious choice for political survival, in the process contributing to the strengthening of those institutions over the years.[53] Where political elites have fewer incentives to support democratic institutions, and, in particular, where resorting to force to prevent the distribution of power through the expansion of citizenship is a viable option for those elites, the consolidation of democratic authority structures is seriously jeopardized.

Participation. Perhaps the greatest challenge to the consolidation of stable democracy is the expansion of citizenship rights to nonelite elements, and the incorporation into the political process of new groups and classes. Like Britain and Norway, but unlike Latin Europe, the consolidation of democratic institutions in Chile benefited from a gradual extension of suffrage, less in response to pressures from below than as a consequence of interelite rivalries and strategies to maximize electoral gain. Like Britain, but unlike Latin Europe, Chile found in the elites of the Conservative Party the driving force in the first pivotal extension of suffrage in 1874. This took place a dozen years before the French Third Republic teetered on the brink of collapse with Boulangisme, and twenty-five years before the French Right, still resisting republicanism and democracy, became embroiled in the Dreyfus Affair. It also took place forty years before the pope lifted the *non-expedit* that barred Catholics from participating in Italian elections.

The extension of suffrage in Chile clearly benefited the Conservatives who controlled the countryside, but it also benefited middle-class sectors who identified with the growing urban-based Radical Party. Forty-two years before the adoption of the Saenz Peña Law in Argentina, which forced reluctant Conservatives to suddenly expand the electoral system to permit the Radical Party's eruption on the political stage, Chile had initiated the gradual expansion of suffrage, permitting middle-class sectors to become full participants in ministerial and congressional politics.

In a classic case of what Merton calls the unanticipated consequences of purposive social action, the expansion of suffrage in Chile also soon benefited the growing working class.[54] But the entry of the working class into politics in Chile was also gradual, coming both after the consolidation of parliamentary institutions and after middle-class parties had become full actors in the political process. Indeed, in the 1910s, suffrage expansion was actually limited by complex electoral rules and byzantine electoral pacts in which the working-class parties became full participants.

The gradual expansion of suffrage and incorporation of new groups in Chile had some clear implications for the country's democratic development. Had the pressure for full participation coincided with attempts to set up democratic institutions, it is difficult to see how these could have survived. At the same time, however, it is important to stress that in Chile, suffrage expansion and party development occurred prior to the growth of a powerful and centralized state bureaucracy. The growth of the public sector was consequently shaped by organizations whose primary goals were electoral success and accountability. This reinforced the viability of representative institutions. Where strong bureaucracies emerged before strong parties or legislatures, as in Brazil or Argentina, informal or officially sponsored linkage networks without popular representation were much more likely to develop, encouraging corporatist and authoritarian patterns of interest representation.[55]

In sum, the political-determinants thesis suggests that the development of democracy must be understood as a complex process that owes much to fortuitous events and variables, such as leadership, that defy quantification and precise definition. It is a long and difficult course, subject to challenges and reversals as societal conditions and the correlations of political forces change. Its chances of success are better in some contexts than others and may depend on the timing and sequence of fundamental societal challenges.

In the final analysis, however, democracy involves human choice by competing groups and leaders who must determine whether peaceful mechanisms for the resolution of conflict, based on the concept of popular sovereignty, provide them with the best possible guarantees under the circumstances. More often than not, this choice may stem from an inconclusive struggle for power; a situation of stalemate where there are no clear winners. That being so, democracy can be understood as resulting from a set of compromises—second-preference choices—in which the concurrence of nondemocrats may be as important as the support of democrats. Once democracy is structured, it provides the key rules of the game, defining the parameters for action and the strategies to be pursued by relevant actors. In time, democratic rules may be accepted as the only proper norms for political conduct, but only if democracy continues to provide guarantees to all players, even if it is not the preferred system of all.

• **THE BREAKDOWN OF CHILEAN DEMOCRACY** •

Chilean Politics and the Dialectic of Regime Breakdown

The breakdown of Chilean democracy did not occur overnight. Several developments contributed to the erosion of the country's system of political compromise and accommodation, even before the 1970 election of President Salvador Allende. These included the adoption of a series of reforms aimed at making Chilean politics more "efficient," and the rise of a new and more ideological Center, less willing to play the game of political give-and-take.[56]

In 1958, a coalition of the Center and Left joined in enacting a series of electoral reforms aimed at abolishing what were considered corrupt electoral practices. Among the measures was the abolition of joint lists, a long-established tradition of political pacts that permitted parties of opposing ideological persuasions to structure agreements for mutual electoral benefit. While this reform succeeded in making preelection arrangements less "political," it also eliminated an important tool for cross-party bargaining. More important were reforms aimed at curbing congressional authority, promulgated in the guise of strengthening the executive's ability to deal with Chile's chronic economic troubles. Congressional politics were viewed by chief executives and party elites of various political persuasions as excessively incremental and old-fashioned; the antithesis of modern administrative practices. In the name of modernity, the executive was given control of the budgetary process in 1959, and Congress was restricted in its ability to allocate fiscal resources. Indeed, under the Christian Democratic administration (1964–1970), government technocrats pushed strongly to restrict entirely congressional allocations of funds for small patronage projects, even though these represented an infinitesimal portion of the total budget.

The most serious blow to congressional authority came with the constitutional reforms enacted in 1970, this time through a coalition of the Right and Center. Among other provisions, the reforms prohibited amendments not germane to a given piece of legislation and sanctioned the use of executive decrees to implement programs approved by the legislature in very broad terms. More significantly, it barred Congress from matters dealing with social security, salary adjustments, and pensions in the private and public sectors—the heart of legislative bargaining in an inflation-ridden society.[57]

These reforms went a long way toward cutting back on many of the traditional sources of patronage and log-rolling, reducing the most important political arena for compromise in Chilean politics. Again, the principal motivation was to strengthen executive efficiency. It is clear, however, that the 1960 reformers were also convinced they would be able to win the 1970 presidential election and did not want to have to deal with a difficult Congress in which the Left had a strong presence. Ironically, it was the Left that won the presidency, leaving a legislature with reduced powers in the hands of the Right and Center.

Although these changes were significant, they were symptomatic of other far-reaching changes in Chilean politics, the most notable of which was the rise in the 1960s of a new Center party with a markedly different political style. Unlike their predecessor, the pragmatic Radicals, the Chilean Christian Democrats conceived of themselves as a new and vital ideological force in Chilean politics, a middle road between Marxist transformation and preservation of the status quo. The Christian Democrats believed they would be capable of capturing the allegiance of large portions of the electorate from both sides of the political divide, and become a new majority force. In the early 1960s, they began an unprecedented effort at popular mobilization, appealing to women and middle-class voters, as well as factory workers and especially shanty-town dwellers. Their determination to transform the physiognomy of Chilean politics was strengthened by their success in capturing the presidency under the leadership of Eduardo Frei in 1964, in an electoral coalition with the Right, and by their impressive victory in the 1965 congressional race, the best showing by a single party in Chile's modern history. Their success presented a serious challenge to the parties of both the Right and Left. The Right was practically obliterated in the 1965 election, while the Left redoubled its efforts to maintain its constituents and to appeal with a more militant cry to Chile's most destitute citizens.

Once in office and heartened by their electoral success, the Christian Democrats sought to implement their "revolution in liberty" by disdaining the traditional coalition politics of the past. They were particularly hard on the now-diminished Radicals, refusing any overtures for collaboration. Unlike the Radicals, they were unwilling to tolerate clientelistic and log-rolling politics or to serve as an effective bridge across parties and groups. Although they enacted critical copper "Chileanization" legislation in concert with the Right, and agrarian reform in coalition with the Left, the Christian Democrats went out of their way to govern as a single party and refused to deal with opponents unless they had to. At the same time, they expended large amounts of state resources and vast amounts of U.S. foreign-aid funds on programs that were clearly designed to enhance their electoral superiority at the expense of both Right and Left.[58]

The Christian Democrats' rigid posture added to the growing radicalization of elites on the Left (particularly the Socialist Party), who feared the electoral challenge of the Center party, and to profound resentment among elites on the Right, who felt betrayed by the reforms, especially in land redistribution, enacted by their erstwhile coalition partners. Radicalization of the Left was also profoundly affected by international events, notably the Cuban Revolution, which set a new standard for the Latin American Left to emulate.

Had the Christian Democrats succeeded in becoming a genuine Center majority, the increased ideological tension would not have had such serious institutional repercussions. But despite vast organizational efforts and extraordinary levels of foreign aid from the Johnson administration in Washington, which was anxious to promote Chile as a showcase of democracy on a continent fascinated by Cuba, they did not succeed in breaking the tripartite deadlock of Chilean politics.

As a result, even when it became apparent that the Christian Democrats would not be able to win the 1970 presidential election in their own right, they were unable to structure preelection coalitions with either the Right or the Left. The bulk of the Radical Party joined in supporting Salvador Allende, who stunned most observers by edging out rightist Jorge Alessandri by a plurality of 36.2 percent to 34.9 percent of the vote. Christian Democratic candidate Radomiro Tomic received only 27.8 percent of the vote.

The election of Allende was not the result of growing radicalization or political mobilization. Nor was it due, in Huntington's terms, to the inability of Chile's political institutions to channel societal demands. Allende won even though he received a smaller percentage of the vote than he had received in his loss to Frei in the two-way race of 1964. Electoral analysis suggests that a greater percentage of newly mobilized voters voted for the Right than for the Left. The election results simply underscored the repercussions of the failure of the Right and Center to structure a preelection coalition.[59]

Because no candidate received an absolute majority, the election had to be decided in Congress, forcing the creation of a postelection coalition. Christian Democrats joined legislators of the Left in confirming Allende's accession to the highest office in the nation. But the president's minority status, and his lack of majority support in Congress, meant that like other presidents before him, he would have to tailor his program to the realities of coalition politics in order to succeed, even though the very reforms that the Right and the Christian Democrats had enacted made such compromises more difficult. But compromise was easier said than done. Important elements in the Unidad Popular (Popular Unity, UP) coalition, including Allende's own Socialist Party, were openly committed to a revolutionary transformation in the socioeconomic order and the institutional framework of Chilean politics. Furthermore, the coalition was unwieldy and fractious, with parties and groups competing as much with one another for spoils and popular support as with the opposition.

At the same time, Allende's election touched off an extraordinary reaction from other sectors of Chilean society, who feared a pro-Moscow, Marxist-Leninist system might be established in Chile, to their detriment. They encouraged sabotage, subversion, and foreign intrigue. On both sides of Chile's divided party system, the commitment to change or preservation of the status quo now exceeded the commitment to the principles and practices of Chile's historic democracy.

Under these circumstances, structuring a Center coalition committed to social change within the framework of traditional liberties and democratic guarantees was crucial to the system's survival. However, like the Christian Democrats before them, many leaders of the UP coalition became convinced that bold use of state power could break the political deadlock and swing the balance to the Left. This misconception led them to enact a host of ill-conceived redistributive and stimulative economic measures, which aggravated inflation and generated serious economic difficulties. When combined with measures of questionable legality to bring private business under state control, these policies alienated not only Chile's corporate elite, but also small businessmen and much of Chile's middle class.

In an atmosphere of growing suspicion and violence, the lines of communication between leaders and followers of opposing parties eroded, accentuating the polarization of Chilean politics. At several key junctures, and despite pressures from both sides, attempts were made to forge a Center consensus and structure the necessary compromises that would have saved the regime. But Center groups and moderate politicians on both sides of the political divide abdicated their responsibility in favor of narrower group stakes and short-term interests. The involvement of "neutral" powers, such as the courts and the military, only served to politicize those institutions and pave the way for the military coup—a coup that undermined the very institutions of compromise and accommodation moderate leaders had professed to defend. With the failure of Congress, parties, the courts, and other state institutions to serve as viable arenas to resolve conflict, politics became more and more confrontational; contending groups resorted to mobilizing ever greater numbers of their followers to "prove" their power capabilities. Politics spilled out of the chambers of government onto the streets, exacerbating an atmosphere of fear and confrontation.[60]

The Chilean breakdown was a complex and dialectical process, in which time-tested patterns of accommodation were eroded by the rise of a Center unwilling to bridge the gap between extremes, by the decline of institutional arenas of accommodation in the name of technical efficiency, and by the hardening of ideological distance between leaders with radically different conceptions of a good society. It was also the product of gross miscalculations, extremism, narrow group stakes, and the lack of courage in key circumstances. Breakdown was not inevitable. While human action was severely circumscribed by the structural characteristics of Chilean politics and by the course of events, there was still room for choice for a leadership willing to prevent the final denouement. Nor did most Chileans want a military solution to the country's problems. Surveys taken in the weeks before the coup indicated an overwhelming support for democracy and a peaceful outcome of the political crisis.[61]

Political Structures and Regime Breakdown:
A Critique of Presidentialism

Although it was not inevitable, the breakdown of Chilean democracy raises serious questions about the viability of particular institutional forms of governance in democratic regimes. It is a premise of this chapter that in Chile there was an inadequate fit between the country's highly polarized and competitive party system, which was incapable of generating majorities, and a presidential system of centralized authority.[62]

The starting point for this argument must be a recognition that through much of the twentieth century, presidentialism in Chile was in crisis. By definition, a presidential election is a zero-sum game that freezes the outcome for a fixed period of time. In Chile, the winner invariably represented only a third of the electorate, and yet, as the head of government and head of state, he felt responsible for the national destiny as the embodiment of popular sovereignty. As minority presidents, however, Chilean chief executives received weak legislative support or outright congressional opposition. And since they could not seek reelection, there was little incentive for parties, including the president's, to support him beyond mid-term. The fixed terms for both president and Congress contributed to an atmosphere of ungovernability and a feeling of permanent crisis, alleviated only by the willingness of centrist parties or politicians to provide last minute reprieves to beleaguered presidents in exchange for ambassadorial appointments or concessions on policy.

Paradoxically, the response to this problem of governance was to seek an increase in presidential power. The resolution of the country's pressing social and economic problems required strong leadership, it was argued, and such leadership should not be thwarted by ideological wrangling and the narrow partisan interest of the parties and the legislature. However, increased presidential power only aggravated the problem by further reducing arenas for accommodation and by making executive-legislative relations more bitter. Indeed, the stronger the power of the presidency as a separate constitutional actor, the greater were the disincentives for structuring presidential support among parties and groups jealous of their autonomy and future electoral prospects.

In Chile, there was an inverse correlation between the power of the presidency and the success of presidential government. The stronger the president, the weaker the presidential system—a perverse logic that came to a tragic head in the Allende years. A parliamentary system of government would have defused the enormous pressures for structuring high-stakes coalitions around a winner-take-all presidential option, which only reinforced political polarization. At the same time, it would have eliminated the stalemate and confrontation in executive-legislative relations. Had Chile had a parliamentary regime in the early 1970s, Allende's government might have fallen, but democracy would have survived. The working majority in Congress that elected Allende to the presidential post would have had to continue for him to have retained his position. This was not out of the question. The Christian Democrats were close to the UP government on many key points of substance, as attested by the near-agreements at several key junctures of the unfolding drama of the UP years. And, had the coalition collapsed, it is quite likely that a Christian Democrat, or perhaps a member of the small Leftist Radical Party, would have formed a new government with support from elements on the Right.

It is important to stress that parliamentary politics would have had the opposite effect of presidential politics on party distance. It would have contributed to moderating Chilean politics by reinforcing the time-honored traditions of give-and-take honed by generations of politicians. Moderate leaders on both sides of the congressional aisle would have gained strength, encouraging centripetal drives toward coalition and compromise, rather than being outclassed by maximalist leaders who thrived in the public arenas of high-stakes electoral battles. Moreover, legislators of all parties would have thought twice about abandoning hard-fought coalition arrangements if they had faced the prospect of immediate reelection, and the greater accountability of having been part of an agreement to structure executive authority.

The considerations should be borne in mind by political leaders of both Right and Left in discussing the transition back to democracy after military rule. Ironically, as will be noted in the next section, the very prospect of a presidential election is one of the principal obstacles in structuring a return to democracy in Chile.

• MILITARY RULE IN CHILE AND THE PROSPECTS FOR REDEMOCRATIZATION •

With the collapse of democracy, Chile was abruptly tranformed from an open and participatory political system into a repressive and authoritarian one. Few

Chileans could have imagined in September 1973 that military intervention would lead to a government so alien to institutions and traditions dating from the nation's founding. Fewer still would have believed that Chile would produce an authoritarian regime capable of outlasting other contemporary military governments on the continent, or that General Pinochet, the obedient commander who assured President Allende of his undivided loyalty, would achieve a degree of personal power rare in the annals of modern dictatorship. How could this transformation have taken place? What has happened to Chilean institutions under military rule? What are the prospects for transition back to stable democracy?

Soon after the coup, it became clear that Chile's military commanders, with no personal experience of direct involvement in politics, were not about to turn power back to civilian leaders after a brief interregnum. From the outset, they articulated two basic aims.[63] The first was to destroy the parties of the Left and their collaborators. The Chilean military did not interpret its intervention as a simple military coup aimed at replacing a government, but as an all-out war to crush an enemy that it believed had infiltrated close to half the population. However, military leaders were convinced that it was not only foreign Marxists who were to blame for Chile's predicament. They thought the Left had been able to make inroads because of the inherent weaknesses of liberal democracy, which they saw as encouraging corruption and demagoguery. Thus, their second objective was to engineer a fundamental restructuring of Chilean political institutions and political life, aimed at "cleaning" impurities from the body politic while creating a new political order of committed and patriotic citizens, dedicated to modernizing the country and projecting its grandeur to a hostile world.

The junta had a clear idea of how to pursue its first objective; it simply took the years of training, awesome firepower, and many contingency plans that had been developed to protect the constitutional government, and applied them to the new task of finding and neutralizing the enemy. Military units moved in to "clean up" neighborhoods that were strongholds of the Left, as if they were securing enemy territory during wartime.[64] Thousands of party leaders, trade-union officials, and community activists associated with the parties of the Left were "neutralized" through arrests, exile, and, in some cases, death. Labor unions were sharply circumscribed, parties were banned or declared in "recess," and internal elections were prohibited or closely monitored in all private organizations including professional associations and nonprofit agencies. Citizens, who during the Allende years and before had been repeatedly enlisted for one cause or another, now turned inward and avoided public affairs entirely, either out of fear of reprisals or outright support for military rule. Politics, which for generations had revolved around parties and interest groups that penetrated all levels of society, was now confined to small groups of individuals and cabals in the inner corridors of power. One of the most highly mobilized societies in the world became one of the most demobilized.

The junta, however, had a much hazier conception of how political power should be structured, no experience in governing, and no precise blueprint for its foundational program. In the first months and years, the military governed in an *ad hoc* and arbitrary fashion, at times racked by internal tension. Gradually, however, the commanders succeeded in establishing a degree of national political authority rare among Latin American military regimes. Ironically, a major reason for this achievement was that, in contrast to other bureaucratic authoritarian regimes in the Southern Cone, the Chilean military successfully invoked Chile's tradition of political stability and concern for legality to reinforce its own political control. By drawing on the ubiquitous power of the Chilean state and utilizing constitutional principles from Chile's presidentialist tradition, while, at the same time, restoring the principle of military obedience to constituted authority, Chile's commanders were able to structure efficient, if not fully legitimate, governing institutions. An important ingredient of this process was elevating General Pinochet to the role of president of the republic, while he retained his posts as commander-in-chief of the army and a voting member of the four-man junta. Further aiding the consolidation of political rule by Pinochet and his colleagues was the successful effort to implement far-reaching socioeconomic transformations of a more revolutionary nature than those attempted by their elected predecessors.[65]

It should be stressed that Pinochet did not resort to populist or charismatic rule, as did Juan Perón in Argentina and Getúlio Vargas of Brazil, nor was power based on developing a corrupt political machine like those of Paraguay's Alfredo Stroessner or the Somoza clan of Nicaragua. In Chile, the consolidation of political power and one-man rule was due to four fundamental factors. First, Pinochet and his advisers were able to draw on the framework of traditional constitutional legality to justify one-man rule. Second, they could rely on the disciplined and hierarchical nature of the armed forces and the growing power of the secret police. Third, they enjoyed the strong and uncritical support of much of the business community and sectors of the middle class. And fourth, they were able to take advantage of continued sharp divisions in the opposition, which continued to fuel widespread fear among influential Chileans that an end to military rule would permit the Left to resurge and once again challenge the socioeconomic status quo.

Constitutional Tradition and the Rise of Pinochet

In the immediate aftermath of the coup, the commanders of the army, navy, and air force, and the director general of the Carabineros (Chile's paramilitary police) constituted themselves as a governmental junta, which would exercise executive, legislative, and constitutional authority through unanimous agreement of its members. General Pinochet was selected to be junta president by virtue of his position as leader of the oldest military branch. He argued initially, however, that the junta presidency would rotate on a periodic basis among the commanders. Junta members also agreed to divide up policy areas so that each of the services would handle the affairs of different ministries. Even the appointment of university presidents was parceled out among the services, so that Pinochet named the army general who became president of the University of Chile, while Admiral Merino appointed one of his own colleagues to the top post at the Catholic University.

Pinochet, however, moved swiftly to assert his position as more than *primus inter pares*. Although Air Force General Gustavo Leigh was, in the early days, the most articulate, visible, and hardline member of the junta, Pinochet proved to be more politically skillful and ambitious.[66] But, Pinochet owed his ascendancy to more than his personal qualities. Ministers and other governmental officials automatically turned to the junta leader for direction, as they had always done to Chile's constitutional presidents. Soon, Pinochet was far better informed than the other junta members about government issues and began to make day-to-day decisions, including top government appointments, without consulting his colleagues. The growing junta staff, which he "generously" provided the junta from the ranks of the army, and the increasingly assertive secret police, both reported directly to Pinochet.

At the same time, key Conservative civilian and military legal advisers, even some of those who worked for other junta members, became increasingly uncomfortable with the concept of collegial rule, fearing that divided authority would lead to incoherent policies and regime instability. Ironically, they were profoundly influenced by Chilean constitutional law and the traditional practices of a strong presidential system. They could not conceive of a system of authority that did not reproduce the structure of Chile's presidential constitution, with its clear separation of powers between executive, legislative, and judicial branches. Working directly with Pinochet, they gradually proposed to the junta, which was overwhelmed by legislative detail and legal and policy complexities, the adoption of several measures aimed at "rationalizing" military rule in conformity with constitutional doctrine.

The most important of these was Decree Law 527 of June 26, 1974, which directly took the constitutional framework of the 1925 Constitution and applied it to the military government. It specified that the junta would exercise legislative and constitutional powers, while the junta president would have executive power as "Supreme Chief of the Nation."[67] The judiciary, which had shown a strong willingness to support the coup and defer to the armed forces on issues of personal liberties, would remain independent though subject to funding authorizations provided by the junta. Although the other commanders objected to Pinochet's new title, they went along with the measure, persuaded that it was necessary for the efficient administration of a country whose legal corpus was designed for a presidential regime. They were startled and displeased when Pinochet unexpectedly called a ceremony in which he donned the presidential sash.

Although the new statute was designed to institutionalize military authority by providing it with the legitimacy of Chile's presidentialist constitution, it failed to institute a genuine separation of powers. While Pinochet became the nation's chief executive, he continued to serve as one of the four junta members. Since all junta measures required a unanimous vote for adoption, any junta member could block legislation he did not approve of. Because Pinochet could resort to widespread executive authority to implement policy initiatives, the unanimity rule clearly worked in his favor. He could either work with the junta or ignore it; but the junta could not function without his consent. As the chief executive to whom ministers, government officials, and an expanding presidential staff reported, Pinochet had incomparably better information than did his colleagues. The junta soon became a weak legislature overwhelmed by initiatives from a large and complex state, ably administered by political and economic advisers and a growing secret police—all of whom owed exclusive loyalty to the president.

As Pinochet's powers grew, his relationship with the junta became more and more conflictive. General Leigh in particular bitterly opposed Pinochet's ambitions and growing prerogatives, as well as the growing influence over public and economic policy of a group of free-market economists protected by Pinochet. Leigh blocked, in mid-1977, Pinochet's proposal to have junta laws approved by a majority rather than by unanimity. At the end of that year, he also blocked Pinochet's request for junta approval of a referendum endorsing "President Pinochet in his defense of the dignity of Chile" in the face of widespread international criticisms of Chilean human-rights policy. Leigh perceived this as a move on the president's part to gain popular legitimacy for his mandate and to increase further his supremacy over the junta. Pinochet, in the face of junta objections, called the referendum anyway, invoking executive authority.

The tension between Pinochet and Leigh worsened as the two men continued to clash. But the president, making use of his now-considerable powers of persuasion, was able to get the other junta members to side with him against General Leigh. On July 28, 1978, with the support of the other two junta members, he forcibly and illegally removed General Leigh from office, risking an open and armed confrontation with the air force in order to accomplish his ends.[68] With this coup within the coup, Pinochet resolved his principal obstacle to unipersonal control of the Chilean state, control that was formally embodied in a legal foundation that reflected the constitutional practices of the past and gave the general the authority of Chile's traditional presidents without the constraints of a democratic political order.

With the defeat of opposition within the government, Pinochet moved with more confidence to design a new constitutional framework for the country's and his own future. In early 1980, a group of conservative legal advisers sent a constitutional draft to the Council of State for approval and revision. The draft, though based on the 1925 Constitution, called for a further increase in presidential authority, including a provision that reduced the autonomy of legislative bodies, and another that enabled the president to appoint several members of the Senate. The Constitution also created a National Security Council, composed primarily of the armed forces commanders, with the authority to rebuke any governmental institution, elected or nonelected, if its actions were deemed to be a threat to the national security. Finally, it outlawed parties and politically banned individuals for supporting doctrines that are based on the notion of "class struggle" or that "violate the integrity of the family."[69]

The Council of State also proposed a number of transitional provisions, calling for a return to democracy and open presidential elections by 1985. Although a Congress would be named before then, Pinochet would be allowed to continue as president until that date. However, Pinochet rejected these proposals. He made it clear to his advisers that he wanted a document that would enable him to stay in office at least until 1997, or through two more 8-year "constitutional" terms. When his advisers hesitated on the grounds that such a formula would be widely rejected even by the political Right, Pinochet agreed to a compromise whereby the four armed forces commanders (including himself) would select his successor in late 1988 or early 1989, subject to ratification in a popular plebiscite. But he managed to alter the Constitution in one way that made it easier for him to remain in office: The document specifically exempts him, by name, from the provision barring Chilean presidents from succeeding themselves in office.[70] In a 1980 plebiscite, held without electoral registration and in a climate that gave opponents few opportunities to challenge the government publicly, the new Constitution was approved by the voters, establishing Pinochet *de jure* as the most powerful leader in Chilean history.

Military Obedience to Authority

Ironically, military obedience to governmental authority, a second important factor in Chile's long democratic tradition, also abetted Pinochet's efforts at consolidating dictatorial supremacy. During the UP years, Chile's armed forces had become increasingly politicized, as officers openly called for the resignation of commanders unwilling to move to overthrow the constitutional government. Pinochet himself was forced to shift at the last minute from a position of loyalty to the elected government to support for a coup when he realized that "his" generals were in open revolt. In the immediate aftermath of the coup, military leaders moved quickly to reestablish the lines of authority within the institution and to stress the professional and "nondeliberative" character of the armed forces.

Pinochet proved his shrewdness by retiring those members of his cohort who had led in planning the coup, while at the same time promoting officers who had remained loyal to the institutional chain of command. He thus eliminated potential rivals among officers who had, ironically, forced the military to intervene, while seeking to mold the officer corps into a loyal group of followers completely beholden to Pinochet for their careers. All colonels promoted to the rank of generals were required to provide the army commander with a signed letter of resignation, which Pinochet could use at any moment to end a general's career.

But, loyalty was assured with more than the threat of sanctions. Under military rule, officers enjoyed privileges that they had never dreamed of. In addition to increases in pay and fringe benefits, officers could look forward to attractive rewards such as ambassadorships or membership on boards of public and semipublic corporations. Government service provided military men with responsibility and status they had never before enjoyed in the nation's history.[71]

More important for regime stability than the privileges accorded officers was the reestablishment of traditional norms of obedience to authority and hierarchy of rank, practices that had eroded in the turbulent final months of the Allende government. This meant that to a degree unheard of in other military regimes the Chilean authorities were able to establish a sharp separation between the military as institution and the military as government.[72] High-ranking officers were often brought into governmental positions that ranged from cabinet posts, heads of state agencies, and ambassadorships, to university presidencies and local governorships.[73]

However, once in government service, officers no longer took orders from their immediate military superiors but reported instead to their superiors in government, either military or civilian. As government officials, they could discuss policy with their military and civilian counterparts but were barred from discussing these matters with military colleagues serving a strictly military command. Indeed, officers in the military line of duty could be dismissed from the services for discussing politics or policy with fellow officers or with civilians. And for the duration of the Pinochet years, military men were not allowed to remain for long periods of time in governmental duties, continuously being rotated back to military command. Officers who were not deemed to be completely reliable found that their careers were terminated, cutting short a chance for a lucrative and prestigious post and retirement with high pensions. By serving both as president and commander-in-chief of the army with direct responsibility over the institution, and by strictly observing the separation of the military as government from the military as institution, Pinochet avoided the inherent tensions that develop in military regimes between officers occupying government positions and those serving in the institution itself.[74]

Aiding the general's ascendancy and ability to control the armed forces in the early years was the growing power of the secret police. The DINA (Dirección de Inteligencia Nacional or National Bureau of Intelligence), under the direction of Colonel Manuel Contreras, a close friend of the Pinochet family, soon became a law unto itself. It eliminated with efficient brutality the clandestine leadership of leftist parties in Chile and carried out with impunity a series of high-risk political assassinations abroad, aimed at silencing prominent critics of the regime. But DINA's power extended beyond its role in fighting the resistance movement. The secret organization came to be feared in military and governmental circles as DINA agents reported on the personal lives and political proclivities of prominent officers and advisers. It soon developed its own cadres of experts in fields including economic policy, as DINA officers sought to take control of sectors of the Chilean state, particularly the nationalized industries. Pinochet made use of Contreras' services to counter other advisory groups and to strengthen his hand vis-à-vis the junta and the military.[75]

Regime Support in the Business Community

The durability of Chile's military regime cannot be understood without underscoring the strong support for the military in key sectors of Chilean society. Business groups have been profoundly affected by economic policies that have transformed the Chilean economy from a state-supported, import-substituting industrialization model to an export-oriented economy with low tariff barriers and few government subsidies. Although many Chilean businessmen went bankrupt because of these policies and became bitter opponents of the regime, the bulk of the business community remained a strong pillar of the military government. In particular, the government gained powerful new supporters in a new breed of dynamic business leaders who flourished with the opening of Chile's economy to the world market. For Chile's business leaders, democracy had meant the electoral triumph of political forces bent on destroying them. No matter how objectionable the Pinochet government was, it remained a far preferable alternative to the uncertainties of democratic politics. Many people in Chile's middle classes, despite serious reverses, shared these views.

It should be stressed that the business community, while supporting the government, had little direct influence in the formulation of public policy. Policies were made by an economic team that had the complete confidence of the president, and substantial latitude to implement policies without consulting affected groups. The use of a group of neutral technocrats with no strong constituency support, but with a clear and sophisticated understanding of economic policy, helped insulate the president from societal pressures and demands, contributing further to state autonomy and to his increasing powers.

Political Polarization and a Fragmented Opposition

The coup that ended Chile's long trajectory of democratic politics was applauded by many sectors of society, while condemned by others. Chile's rightist parties welcomed the new authorities and soon agreed to disband, confident that the military would represent their interests. The Christian Democrats, Chile's largest party, reluctantly accepted the coup as the inevitable result of the Popular Unity government's policies. However, Christian Democrats were not prepared to accept the diagnosis of the country's new rulers that democracy was also at fault and that military rule should be maintained for an indefinite period of time. Soon, the Christian Democrats began to join the parties of the Left in strong criticisms of the regime's human-rights abuses and its redrafting of the nation's institutional structures. By the late 1970s, Christian Democrats were able to begin a dialogue with elements on the Left, as both groups attempted to come to terms with their collective responsibility in the failure of Chile's political order.

It was not until 1983, however, that Chile's political parties reasserted themselves, signaling that the regime's efforts to obliterate them from national life had failed.[76] The spontaneous protest movement, begun at the urging of a group of labor leaders, surprised the party leadership as much as it surprised the regime. The government's swift repressive measures against labor, rendered vulnerable by high levels of unemployment, opened the door for the party leadership to gain control over the burgeoning opposition movement. In the moderate opposition, the Christian Democrats sought to create a broad alliance with small groups on the Right and Left in order to structure a proposal for an alternative government that would press the armed forces to negotiate. On the Left, the Communist Party, which had countenanced an armed strategy against the regime, sought to mobilize popular discontent through increasingly militant protests in the expectation that the regime would capitulate.

This division, between those that sought peaceful mobilization in order to engage in negotiations with the authorities and those that sought sharp and even violent confrontations in order to render the country ungovernable, is the key to understanding the paralysis of Chile's opposition after 1983.[77] When the regime's intransigence led important sectors on the Right to join with the center and moderate Left and sign a National Accord for Transition to Democracy in 1985, calling for free elections and significant modifications in the 1980 Constitution, the fragile alliance failed. Some groups accused the Right of trying to halt political mobilization in Pinochet's favor; others accused the Left of trying to undermine possible negotiations with the armed forces while alienating middle-class support for the opposition.

At the root of this division is the continued polarization of Chilean politics between a strong Marxist Left, which advocates far-reaching socioeconomic reforms, and a rejuvenated Right, which refuses to have any of the economic gains of authoritarianism threatened. While significant political learning took place in broad quarters of Chilean party life, with Socialists embracing democratic practices as important ends in their own right, and Christian Democrats vowing not to pursue single-party strategies for their own gain, mistrust remains high as elements on both extremes press for radically divergent solutions.

Antidemocrats on both sides made it difficult for centrist forces to pursue concerted policies. Moderate Socialists feared that too many concessions to the regime would lead to a loss of support among the faithful, who might be attracted by the more militant line of the Communist Party or socialist groups affiliated with them. Democratic rightists have feared that they would be isolated and outflanked by Pinochet supporters who argued that any compromise with the opposition is nothing but an opening to the Communist Party. The Christian Democrats, in turn, were immobilized by sharp internal divisions over fears that the party might move too close to either the Left or the Right. The same logic of polarization that made it difficult to maintain a Center consensus and finally helped bring Chilean democracy crashing down in 1973 conspired against structuring a broad and coherent opposition movement to force the military from power. Widespread rejection of the Pinochet regime as illegitimate could not translate into an early return to democracy for lack of a clear alternative.[78]

• PROSPECTS FOR REDEMOCRATIZATION •

Paradoxically, it was the regime that provided the opposition with a rationale for unity and a means to define the transition process in its favor. Although no opposition leader accepted the legitimacy of the plebiscite formula spelled out in the 1980 Constitution, calling instead for open and fair presidential elections as soon as possible, by 1987 most seemed resigned to accepting the plebiscite as a fact of political life. At first, opposition leaders called on Chileans to register in the electoral roles, while still pressing for open presidential elections. Gradually and reluctantly, they began to call on their followers to register to vote NO in the plebiscite that would ratify the individual chosen by the armed forces chiefs to serve the next 8-year presidential term beginning on March 11, 1989.[79]

The Communist Party and sectors of the socialist Left strongly objected to this "participation in the legality of the regime." They were convinced that registering and voting would simply serve further to legitimize the regime, since they felt that the authorities would not permit a negative result and would resort to fraud if necessary to impose their candidate.

Moderate opposition leaders, on the other hand, argued that the plebiscite represented a valuable tool for popular mobilization and an important opportunity to try to defeat the regime at its own game—the only viable alternative for an opposition that had not succeeded in overthrowing the dictatorship through other means. Reluctantly they agreed to go further than asking citizens to vote: They also proceeded to register their political parties according to government regulations, which limited in several ways the autonomy of party organizations and forced them to engage in a national campaign to collect signatures from potential members, many of whom feared committing themselves publicly to a particular party or movement. Party registration was necessary to entitle opposition groups to name poll watchers to monitor the fairness of the election. The principal groups to register were the Christian Democrats and a loose coalition of Left-of-Center groups that called itself the Party for Democracy.

By December 1987 it became clear Chileans were prepared to register and vote in large numbers, forcing party leaders to structure a united effort in an attempt to win the NO vote in the plebiscite. A massive television campaign on the part of the authorities and growing evidence of the use of public resources to bolster the official candidate helped further to galvanize opposition groups into action. The Communist Party soon became isolated as its allies on the Left decided to join the NO command.

In governmental circles there was considerable speculation that Pinochet might not be the candidate selected by the four commanders-in-chief (including Pinochet as commander of the army). Many leaders on the Right felt that the government needed to project its institutions into the future without being tied to the figure of one man. They also feared that Pinochet was too controversial a leader, one around whom the opposition could unite in a simple zero-sum decision. An alternative candidate, preferably a civilian, would contribute to dividing the opposition and depersonalizing the regime. Two of the four commanders shared this view.

In late August 1988, however, Pinochet was named the candidate. He was determined to be selected and used the force of his personality and the weight of his office to obtain the designation. Leaders on the Right had not been willing to go too far in proposing an alternative for fear of antagonizing the chief executive. Businessmen who were still heavily indebted to the state were not about to jeopardize key loans by coming out publicly for an alternative. Without strong vocal support from the Right for another candidate, the dissenting commanders were not able to press for an alternative, particularly since Pinochet's supporters argued effectively that he was the country's most prominent figure and could win popular support.

Government and military leaders were confident that an improved economy, a massive housing and public-works program, and a saturation television campaign would tip the balance in favor of the regime. In particular, they felt that most Chileans did not want uncertainty and the fear of a return to a Marxist government; that television and other media could effectively remind them of the dangers of not supporting the regime. Furthermore, key government officials and advisers in both the military and civilian sectors repeatedly stressed that their evidence pointed to a strong victory for Pinochet as the only candidate to appear on the ballot. They noted that the disarray and divisions in the opposition would only strengthen the government's position.

The Chilean authorities came under considerable pressure internally and internationally to stage a fair contest, even though the plebiscite formula was widely criticized as undemocratic. Chile's tradition of fair and free elections, combined with the military regime's own desire to assert its legitimacy, contributed to the structuring of virtually fraud-proof voting procedures. The contest was unequal, however, because the government used substantial resources for media efforts on behalf of its "record" and made ample use of the authority of provincial leaders and mayors to give an advantage to the YES campaign. The opposition was able to turn to television only in the last month, after Pinochet had been officially nominated, and then was restricted to fifteen minutes of free air time a day, to be shared in equal amounts with the YES campaign.

To the surprise of most people, particularly in the government, the opposition groups mounted an extraordinarily successful media and door-to-door campaign in the last few weeks before the elections. With limited resources and relying on volunteer workers, they successfully countered the "fear" campaign of the government by stressing a positive and upbeat message. NO came to denote happiness and the future, while the YES campaign remained mired in the past. The drive to produce advertisements, recruit poll watchers, to set up an effective parallel vote count, and to conduct door-to-door campaigns cemented further the unity of the sixteen parties that formed the NO command. International support, particularly through the U.S. National Endowment for Democracy, channeled through the National Democratic Institute for International Affairs, contributed important resources for the media campaign and for the computer system designed to monitor the electoral count.

The victory of opposition forces by a 12-percent margin was a stunning achievement. Ninety-seven percent of the registered voters (representing 92 percent of the eligible population) went to the polls, and the opposition won in all but two of the country's twelve regions. Pinochet lost among most categories of voters, including women and provincial dwellers.

Two elements were critical in making it possible for the NO vote to win and to derail plans by some elements close to Pinochet to create a climate of violence that they hoped would lead to canceling the plebiscite. First, elements in the military and in the civilian political Right expected a fair contest and would not have tolerated any disruption of the process. Pinochet was the most powerful person in the country, but Chile's institutions were not "personalized." Even in the army, institutional loyalties and respect for "legality" were more important factors than allegiance to the ambitions of the commander-in-chief. Second, opposition leaders were successful in persuading voters to stay home, waiting calmly for results on election night, and to celebrate peacefully the next day. The violence that some elements in the regime had expected simply did not materialize. The Communist Party played an important role by insisting that its own militants refrain from organizing street demonstrations.

The election showed clearly how easy it is for an authoritarian regime to engage in collective self-delusion. Countless polls and newspaper accounts suggested that once the voters got over their skepticism about the election's fairness, the NO vote stood a good chance of winning. And yet, Pinochet, his advisers, and his supporters in the military and the business community were absolutely convinced that the government could not lose. All the information transmitted up the chain of command was designed to reinforce the president's wishes, to the point that negative information was filtered out. Often, however, it was difficult for the authorities to perceive such information; citizens were for the most part not forthcoming when asked their views by individuals with official credentials. A generalized contempt for politics and politicians, even those supporting the regime, made it difficult for officials to sense the mood of the country.

The victory of the NO vote in the plebiscite augurs well for Chile's democratic future. Had Pinochet been ratified for another 8-year term the country might have become ungovernable. A large percentage of the population would not have accepted the plebiscite as legitimate, and some sectors, in the aftermath of the opposition failure, would have renewed their calls for violence. At the same time, Pinochet would have had to govern with an elected Congress, one in which the opposition would have played a substantial role. The evolution of Pinochet from military commander and authoritarian leader to civilian president, albeit with strong executive powers, would not have been easy.

With the opposition victory, the country will hold open presidential elections at the end of 1989. What is unclear at this writing is whether, before the election, opposition leaders and government officials will be able to agree on some fundamental changes in a Constitution that is not accepted as democratic by opposition leaders. Although opposition leaders hope to obtain those changes, arguing that the victory represents not only a defeat for Pinochet but also for his "constitutional itinerary," fundamental changes are unlikely precisely because the military sees the Constitution as one of its principal legacies to the country. Changes will come only with the election of a democratic president and a Congress with constituent powers, and provided that the opposition is able to gain majorities in those elections. An opposition majority is more likely if the parties that structured the NO campaign can agree on a presidential candidate and a transition formula. Such an opposition, which would represent the reconstruction of a Center consensus in Chilean politics, would permit a return to democratic practices with broad majority support.

Should the coalition of the Center-Left, which supported the NO vote in the plebiscite, fail to present a common program and candidate, Chileans will face a presidential contest with candidates representing each of the traditional "thirds" of Chilean politics: a Marxist Left, a social democratic Center, and a pro-business Right. The country would thus run the risk of being governed once again by a president without majority support, facing hostile majorities in the Congress—a formula that might lead to decisional paralysis and political confrontation and place significant pressures on the armed forces to resolve the conflict through extraconstitutional measures. Given the strength of the three political tendencies of the Chilean electorate, constitutional experts should seriously entertain the option of creating a parliamentary form of government, where Center coalitions can more easily be formed and where the country's future is not at the mercy of a president who was either elected for a fixed term without a majority mandate or who has lost a majority mandate.

Despite the continued polarization of Chilean politics, the transition may be easier than that of other countries for several reasons. In the first place, the strong tradition of democratic rule that existed before the regime breakdown and was so eloquently manifested in the plebiscite will help Chileans return to democratic practices. Institutions of democratic governance in Chile do not have be new-forged as they do in many other Latin American countries; they need to be restored. Second, Chile's armed forces, even after a decade and a half of military rule, have not become politicized. The sharp separation of the political from the institutional roles of the military under Pinochet makes it possible for the institution to return to its professional pursuits without becoming involved in the daily political tug of war of a democratic regime. This does not mean that the Chilean armed forces would be reluctant to intervene in politics again should they feel that "national security" is threatened. There is strong evidence that the Chilean officer corps is less committed than in the past to respecting democratic rules and procedures. However, the institution itself is not fragmented and politicized and is likely to intervene only in a serious crisis. Third, the Chilean armed forces retain substantial prestige despite deep resentment against the authorities in some sectors. Of particular importance is the fact that the institution was not directly compromised by the "dirty war" of the security police that led to the most flagrant human-rights abuses. Demands for an accounting for human-rights abuses and justice for the guilty will not create a serious rift between civilian authorities and military leaders. Finally, Chile begins its transition with a relatively good economic picture compared to that of its neighbors. Chilean economic planners succeeded in reordering the Chilean state so that it operates more efficiently. They have also encouraged an impressive new class of entrepreneurs able to compete in world markets. Although these economic successes were made possible by strong authoritarian practices, including curbing labor rights and imposing policies with strong regressive tendencies, planners under a democratic regime will not face the same intractable economic problems that their Argentine neighbors faced when coming to power. The challenge to maintain growth and efficiency, while at the same time tending to the real demands for greater social justice, will tax the abilities of the most skilled leaders. But, Chileans in the aftermath of the 1988 plebiscite seem determined to return to their historic democratic practices with a renewed realism and hope for the future.

• NOTES •

1. There are few general treatments of the military regime in Chile. The best single study is Manuel Antonio Garretón, *El proceso político chileno* (Santiago: Facultad Latinoamericana de Ciencias Sociales, 1983). Useful edited volumes are those by Manuel A. Garretón et al., *Chile: 1973–198?* (Santiago: Facultad Latinoamericana de Ciencias Sociales, 1980); and J. Samuel Valenzuela and Arturo Valenzuela, eds., *Military Rule in Chile: Dictatorship and Oppositions* (Baltimore, MD: Johns Hopkins University Press, 1986). The literature on the human-rights situation under the Chilean military government is voluminous. The most complete record is that provided by the publications of the Vicaría de la Solidaridad, dependent on the Archbishopric of Santiago (see the annual reports). The most comprehensive and authoritative overview of the human-rights record of the Chilean government is provided by the Commission on Human Rights, Organization of American States, in its *Informe sobre la situación de los derechos humanos en Chile* (Washington, DC: Organization of American States, 1985). The commission estimates that approximately 1,500 people were killed after the coup (see *Informe*, p. 54). The Vicaría has documented 668 cases of individuals who disappeared after being arrested in the period 1973–1985. The number killed in Chile may be closer to 3,500, as many deaths and disappearances may not have been reported, particularly in rural areas. Most rural towns visited by the author appear to have lost a few people after the coup, in some cases because of private feuds or reprisals on the part of landowners.

2. A valuable sourcebook on the 1980 Constitution is Luz Bulnes Aldunate, *Constitución política de la República de Chile: Concordancias, anotaciones y fuentes* (Santiago: Editorial Jurídica de Chile, 1981). For a "legislative history" of the Constitution see Sergio Carrasco Delgado, *Génesis y vigencia de los textos constitucionales chilenos* (Santiago: Editorial Jurídica de Chile, 1980).

3. Kenneth A. Bollen, "Comparative Measurement of Political Democracy," *American Sociological Review* 45, no. 3 (June 1980): pp. 370–390. See also Robert W. Jackman, "On the Relations of Economic Development to Democratic Performance," *American Journal of Political Science* 17, no. 3 (August 1973): pp. 611–621; and his "Political Democracy and Social Equality: A Comparative Analysis," *American Sociological Review* 39, no. 1 (February 1974): pp. 29–44.

4. Leon Epstein, *Political Parties in Western Democracies* (New York: Praeger, 1967), p. 192. For a discussion of the rise of parliamentary opposition in Western Europe, see the excellent collection in Robert Dahl, ed., *Political Oppositions in Western Democracies* (New Haven, CT: Yale University Press, 1966). See also Dahl's *Polyarchy: Participation and Opposition* (New Haven, CT: Yale University Press, 1971).

5. Some countries, including Britain and Norway, developed political contestation with parliamentary responsibility before Chile did. Others, such as Belgium and the Netherlands, began to develop parliamentary influence at around the same time. The Swedish king was able to choose ministers without regard to parliamentary majorities until 1917, though the parliament's views were taken into consideration earlier. Italy was not unified until the 1860s and did not establish a system of parliamentary rule until the 1880s. Republican France dates from 1871, and many observers, noting the importance of the Napoleonic bureaucracy, question the degree of authority wielded by the French parliament. Because of the importance of the monarchies in Europe, Chile comes closer to the United States in the origins and evolution of its political institutions. For historical discussions of these issues, see Dahl, *Political Oppositions;* and Stein Rokkan, *Citizens, Elections, Parties* (Oslo: Universitetsforlaget, 1970).

6. See Dahl, *Polyarchy,* ch. 1. Dahl's definition informs the discussion of democracy in Chapter 1 of this volume.

7. Women were able to vote in national elections for the first time in 1952. The voting age was reduced from 21 to 18 and illiterates were given the right to vote with the constitutional reforms of 1970. The best discussion of Chilean electoral practices can be found in Federico Gil, *The Political System of Chile* (Boston: Houghton Mifflin, 1966). The 1970 reforms are discussed in Guillermo Piedrabuena Richards, *La reforma constitucional* (Santiago: Ediciones Encina, 1970). The intricacies of the electoral system are described in Mario Bernaschina G., *Cartilla electoral* (Santiago: Editorial Jurídica de Chile, 1958). For an overview of electoral participation, see Atilio Borón, "La evolución del régimen electoral y sus efectos en la representación de los intereses populares: El caso de Chile." Estudio no. 24 (Santiago: Escuela Latinoamericana de Ciencia Política y Administración Pública, FLACSO, April 1971).

8. Voting data for Europe can be found in Stein Rokkan, *Citizens*. Voting data on Chile is found in J. Samuel Valenzuela, *Democratización vía reforma: La expansión del sufragio en Chile* (Buenos Aires: Ediciones del IDES, 1985). This is the best study of the critical decisions that led to suffrage expansion in Chile in the nineteenth century, underscoring the important role of the Conservatives in that process. As such, it is an important revisionary study in Chilean historiography.

9. This section draws extensively from J. Samuel Valenzuela and Arturo Valenzuela, "Chile and the Breakdown of Democracy." In *Latin American Politics and Development,* ed. Howard J. Wiarda and Harvey F. Kline (Boston: Houghton Mifflin, 1979), pp. 234–249. The author is grateful to J. Samuel Valenzuela for his contribution to this work and to much of the thinking that is reflected in this chapter. See also Arturo Valenzuela, *Political Brokers in Chile: Local Government in a Centralized Polity* (Durham, NC: Duke University Press, 1977), ch. 8.

10. Francisco Antonio Encina, *Historia de Chile,* vol. 9 (Santiago: Editorial Nacimiento, 1941–1942), p. 493; cited in Arturo Valenzuela, *Political Brokers,* p. 175.

11. This thesis is at variance with standard interpretations that attribute to Diego Portales a pivotal role in forming the Chilean institutional system. See Arturo Valenzuela, *Political Brokers,* ch. 8; and his "El mito de Portales: La institucionalización del régimen político chileno en el siglo XIX." In *La transición a la democracia en América Latina,* ed. Fernando Molina (Santiago: Universidad Católica de Chile, forthcoming).

12. Chile, *Documentos parlamentarios correspondientes al segundo quinquenio de la administración Bulnes, 1846–1850,* vol. 3 (Santiago: Imprenta del Ferrocarril, 1858), p. 795.

13. Some of the generalizations from the "world-system" and "dependency" literature to the effect that dependent capitalist development leads to weak states does not fully apply to the Chilean case.

14. This section draws heavily on Arturo Valenzuela and J. Samuel Valenzuela "Los orígenes de la democracia: Reflexiones teóricas sobre el caso de Chile," *Estudios públicos* 12 (Spring 1983): pp. 3–39; and J. S. Valenzuela, *Democratización*.

15. In 1863, the total electorate was about 22,000. By 1878, the electorate had expanded sevenfold. See J. S. Valenzuela, *Democratización*, pp. 118–119.

16. Maurice Duverger, *Political Parties* (New York: John Wiley, 1965), pp. xxiii–xxxvii.

17. This section draws heavily on Arturo Valenzuela, *The Breakdown of Democratic Regimes: Chile* (Baltimore, MD: Johns Hopkins University Press, 1978), ch. 1.

18. Seymour Martin Lipset and Stein Rokkan, *Party Systems and Voter Alignments* (New York: Free Press, 1967), pp. 50–56.

19. For a discussion of this, see Valenzuela, *Political Brokers*.

20. An exception to this generalization is Dahl's *Polyarchy*. Not only has Chile been neglected in the broader literature, Latin America in general has been left out. The volumes of the Committee on Comparative Politics of the Social Science Research Council had only a few studies dealing with Latin America, and Latin America did not figure prominently in the theoretical efforts of the 1960s. In his excellent study of parties in Western democracies, Epstein acknowledges that a few Latin American countries meet his criteria for inclusion but leaves them out "mainly because the whole of Latin America is *customarily* treated along with developing nations" (emphasis added). See Epstein, *Political Parties*, p. 4. For a discussion of the place of Latin America in the literature on comparative politics, see Arturo Valenzuela, "Political Science and the Study of Latin America." In *Windows on Latin America: Perspectives from Six Disciplines*, ed. Christopher Mitchell (Stanford, CA: Stanford University Press, forthcoming).

21. These terms are designed to group in analytically similar categories propositions that are sometimes advanced in more discrete fashion. They are drawn from previous work of the author on the subject, some of which has been done in collaboration with J. Samuel Valenzuela. I have attempted to address within each category the relevant variables advanced in this book. I do not treat what can be called the national-cohesiveness thesis because it is not as relevant to the Chilean case. Ethnic, regional, and center-periphery cleavages were defused in the early half of the nineteenth century.

22. The importance of gradual evolution without significant upheaval is stressed by Dahl in *Polyarchy*, pp. 40–47. The continuity of institutions from the colonial period is one of the points advanced by Seymour Martin Lipset in his provocative study of the United States, *The First New Nation* (New York: Doubleday, 1967), pp. 106–107. For a discussion of differences in the colonial experience, see Rupert Emerson's classic *From Empire to Nation* (Boston: Beacon Press, 1960).

23. Chile inaugurated a polyarchy through a struggle for independence that led to the collapse of the remnants of the old colonial regime, and not, as Dahl holds, through an evolutionary process comparable to that of England or Sweden. In this sense, the Chilean case is closer to that of France than England. See Dahl, *Polyarchy*, p. 42.

24. See Frederick Pike, *Chile and the United States, 1880–1962* (Notre Dame, IN: University of Notre Dame Press, 1963), p. 11. The literature on Portales is voluminous. An influential work that argues this thesis is Alberto Edwards Vives, *La Fronda aristocrática* (Santiago: Ediciones Ercilla, 1936), pp. 50–51. For a sampling of views, see B. Vicuña Mackenna, J. Victorino Lastarria, and R. Sotomayor Valdés, *Portales: Juicio histórico* (Santiago: Editorial del Pacífico, 1973).

25. Richard Morse, "The Heritage of Latin America." In *The Founding of New Societies*, ed. Louis Hartz (New York: Harcourt, Brace and World, 1964), pp. 163–164. See also Hartz's comments on the Chilean case on p. 88 of that work.

26. For an elaboration of this argument see Valenzuela, *Political Brokers*, ch. 8.

27. See Samuel P. Huntington, *Political Order in Changing Societies* (New Haven, CT: Yale University Press, 1968), ch. 2.

28. David Martin argues that "the incidence of pluralism and democracy is related to the incidence of those religious bodies which are themselves inherently pluralistic and democratic. . . . Such bodies . . . are much more prevalent in the Anglo-American situation than elsewhere. . . . In Russia and Latin America democratic and individualistic Protestantism arrived late in the process and could not have an important effect." See his *A General Theory of Secularization* (New York: Harper and Row, 1978), p. 25. For an influential essay dealing with Latin America along these same lines, see Seymour Martin Lipset, "Values, Education and Entrepreneurship." In *Elites in Latin America*, ed. Seymour Martin Lipset and Aldo Solari (New York: Oxford University Press, 1963). See also Howard Wiarda, "Toward a Framework for the Study of Political Change in the Iberic-Latin Tradition: The Corporative Model," *World Politics*, 25, no. 2 (January 1973): pp. 206–235. For a classic work that links liberal values stemming from the Protestant tradition with the growth of democracy in the United States, see Louis Hartz, *The Liberal Tradition in America* (New York: Harcourt, Brace and World, 1955).

29. See Jorge I. Dominguez, *Insurrection or Loyalty* (Cambridge, MA: Harvard University Press, 1979) for a discussion of some of these points.

30. Harry Eckstein, *Division and Cohesion in a Democracy: A Study of Norway* (Princeton, NJ: Princeton University Press, 1966).

31. See Booth's chapter on Costa Rica in this volume.

32. Dahl, *Polyarchy*, p. 140.

33. For a description of Chile's *hacienda* system, see George M. McBride, *Chile: Land and Society* (New York: American Geographical Society, 1936). For the origins, the classic study is Mario Góngora, *Origen de los inquilinos del Valle Central* (Santiago: Editorial Universitaria, 1960). See also Arnold J. Bauer, *Chilean Rural Society from the Spanish Conquest to 1930* (New York: Cambridge University Press, 1975).

34. Dominguez, *Insurrection*, p. 141.

35. See Robert Kaufman, *The Politics of Land Reform in Chile, 1950–1970* (Cambridge, MA: Harvard University Press, 1972); and Brian Loveman, *Struggle in the Countryside: Politics and Rural Labor in Chile, 1919–1973)* (Bloomington: Indiana University Press, 1976).

36. Chile is a good illustration of Dankwart Rustow's argument that democracies must go through a "habituation" phase before they are consolidated. See his "Transitions to Democracy: Toward a Dynamic Model," *Comparative Politics* 2, no. 3 (April 1970): pp. 337–363.

37. See Daniel Lerner, *The Passing of Traditional Society* (New York: Free Press, 1958). See also S. N. Eisenstadt, "Social Change, Differentiation and Evolution," *American Sociological Review* 29 (June 1964): pp. 375–387.

38. Seymour Martin Lipset, "Some Social Requisites of Democracy: Economic Development and Political Legitimacy," *American Political Science Review* 53, no. 1 (March 1959): pp. 69–105. For collections of articles on "empirical democratic theory," see J. V. Gillespie and B. A. Nesvold, eds., *Macroquantitative Analysis: Conflict, Development and Democratization* (Beverly Hills, CA: Sage Publications, 1971); and Charles Cnudde and Deane Neubauer, eds., *Empirical Democratic Theory* (Chicago: Markham, 1969). For an excellent review of this literature, see Leonardo Morlino, "Misure di Democrazia e di Libertá: Discusione di Alcune Analisi Empiriche," *Rivista Italiana di Scienza Política* 5, no. 1 (April 1975): pp. 131–166.

39. See, for example, Phillips Cutright, "National Political Development: Measurement and Analysis," *American Sociological Review* 28, no. 2 (April 1963): pp. 253–264; and Bollen, "Comparative Measurement of Political Democracy."

40. Juan Linz, "Totalitarian and Authoritarian Regimes." In *Handbook of Political Science*, vol. 3, ed. Fred I. Greenstein and Nelson W. Polsby (Reading, MA: Addison Wesley, 1975), p. 182. As Dahl notes, the United States in the nineteenth century did not meet the development criteria but met the political criteria. See Dahl, *Polyarchy*, p. 72.

41. Goran Therborn, "The Rule of Capital and the Rise of Democracy," *New Left Review* 103 (May-June 1977): p. 3–41. Therborn adds that the rarity of bourgeois democracy in capitalist Third World countries is due to the vulnerability of commodity-oriented economies, which give the "indigenous bourgeoisie little room for manoeuvre vis-à-vis the exploited classes." In such contexts there is an "intertwining of capitalist with feudal, slave or other pre-capitalist modes of exploitations . . . impeding the development of impersonal rule of capital and free labormarket, thereby seriously limiting the growth of both the labor movement and an agrarian petty bourgeoisie." Ibid., pp. 1, 32. Although he is not dealing with the development of democracy *per se*, Immanuel Wallerstein argues that peripheral states in the world system were much weaker in part because the social structure of export economies did not permit the development of bourgeois sectors. See his *The Modern World System*, 2 vols. (New York: Academic Press, 1974, 1980.)

42. Barrington Moore, *Social Origins of Dictatorship and Democracy: Lord and Peasant in the Making of the Modern World* (Boston: Beacon Press, 1966). As he notes, for democracy to emerge, "the political hegemony of the landed upper class had to be broken or transformed. The peasant had to be turned into a farmer producing for the market instead of for his own consumption and that of the overlord. In this process the landed upper class either became an important part of the capitalist and democratic tide, as in England, or, if they came to oppose it, they were swept aside in the convulsions of revolutions (France) or civil war (U.S.). In a word the landed upper classes either helped to make the bourgeois revolution or were destroyed by it." Ibid., p. 429–430. Moore's analysis, though brilliant in scope, leaves much to be desired in terms of clarity. For a valuable critique, see Theda Skocpol, "A Critical Review of Barrington Moore's Social Origins of Dictatorship and Democracy," *Politics and Society* 4 (Fall 1973): pp. 1–34. See also Joseph V. Femia, "Barrington Moore and the Preconditions for Democracy," *British Journal of Political Science* 2 (Janu-

ary 1972): pp. 21–46; and Ronald Dore, "Making Sense of History," *Archive Européenes de Sociology* 10 (1969): pp. 295–305.

43. See Dominguez, *Insurrection*, p. 131.

44. Influential works of Chilean historians in this vein include Julio César Jobet, *Ensayo crítico del desarrollo económico-social de Chile* (Santiago: Editorial Latinoamericana, 1965); and Hernán Ramirez Necochea, *Historia del movimiento obrero en Chile, antecedentes siglo XIX* (Santiago: Editorial Austral, 1956). The most fully developed version of this thesis is in Luis Vitale, *Interpretación marxista de la historia de Chile* (Frankfurt: Verlag Jugend und Politik, 1975). Maurice Zeitlin's *The Civil Wars in Chile: 1851 and 1859* (Princeton, NJ: Princeton University Press, 1984) draws uncritically from the work of Vitale and others.

45. See Leonard Binder et al., *Crises and Sequences in Political Development* (Princeton, NJ: Princeton University Press, 1971). For a volume of essays applying the framework to particular cases, see Raymond Grew, ed., *Crises of Political Development in Europe and the United States* (Princeton, NJ: Princeton University Press, 1978). Influential earlier studies that anticipate the arguments in these books include Dankwart Rustow, *A World of Nations* (Washington, DC: Brookings Institution, 1967); Lipset and Rokkan, eds., *Party Systems and Voter Alignments;* and Gabriel Almond, Scott Flanigan, and Roger Mundt, eds., *Crisis, Choice and Change: Historical Studies of Political Development* (Boston: Little, Brown, 1973). Although some of these works focus on political development more generally, and not on the development of democracy as such, their framework is oriented toward democratic regimes rather than other regime types.

46. Eric Nordlinger, "Political Development, Time Sequences and Rates of Change. In *Political Development and Social Change*, 2d ed., ed. Jason L. Finkle and Robert W. Gable (New York: John Wiley, 1971), p. 458. This argument is made in Rustow, *World of Nations*, pp. 120–123.

47. Of the three crises, the most difficult to deal with is that of national identity. Its definition is imprecise and in the absence of survey-research data it is virtually impossible to find empirical evidence to document its relative strength. Much of this analysis has to be speculative and informed by general historical accounts. Particularly useful in capturing the mood of Chile in the early period is the work of Diego Barros Arana, which is also an eyewitness account. In particular, see his *Un decenio de la historia de Chile*, 2 vols. (Santiago: Imprenta Universitaria, 1906.)

48. See Richard Merritt, "Nation-Building in America: the Colonial Years." In *Nation-Building*, ed. Karl W. Deutsch and William J. Foltz (New York: Atherton Press, 1966; and Karl Deutch, *Nationalism and Social Communication: An Inquiry into the Foundations of Nationality*, 2d ed. (Cambridge, MA: MIT Press, 1966). Lipset discusses the question of national identity in the United States in his *First New Nation*, ch. 2.

49. See Rustow, "Transitions to Democracy."

50. For a discussion of Washington's impact, see Lipset, *First New Nation*, pp. 18–23.

51. For lists of all Chilean presidents, cabinet officials, and members of Congress from independence until the 1940s, see Luis Valencia Avaria, *Anales de la república*, 2 vols. (Santiago: Imprenta Universitaria, 1951). Most presidents had extensive parliamentary experience.

52. On the question of efficacy, see the arguments of Juan J. Linz in *The Breakdown of Democratic Regimes: Crisis, Breakdown and Reequilibration* (Baltimore, MD: Johns Hopkins University Press, 1978), pp. 20–21.

53. For an elaboration of this argument, see Valenzuela and Valenzuela, "Orígenes de la democracia."

54. R. K. Merton, "The Unanticipated Consequences of Purposive Social Action," *American Sociological Review* 1936, 1: pp. 894–904.

55. This point is made in Arturo Valenzuela and Alexander Wilde, "Presidentialist Politics and the Decline of the Chilean Congress." In *Legislatures in Development: Dynamics of Change in New and Old States*, ed. Joel Smith and Lloyd Musolf (Durham, NC: Duke University Press, 1979), p. 194.

56. The material in this section is taken from the author's *Breakdown*. For other books on the Chilean breakdown, see Paul Sigmund, *The Overthrow of Allende and the Politics of Chile* (Pittsburgh, PA: Pittsburgh University Press, 1977); Ian Roxborough, Phil O'Brien, and Jackie Roddick, *Chile: The State and Revolution* (New York: Holmes and Meier, 1977); and Manuel A. Garretón and Tomás Moulian, *Análisis coyuntural y proceso político: Las fases del conflicto en Chile (1970–73)* (San José, Costa Rica: Editorial Universitaria Centro-Americana, 1978). The last-named is drawn from the comprehensive and detailed daily account of the most important events of the Allende administration, published in Manuel Antonio Garretón et al., *Cronología del período*

1970–73, 9 vols. (Santiago: Facultad Latinoamericana de Ciencias Sociales, 1978); an invaluable publication including extensive indices to parties, individuals, and events. In the immediate aftermath of the coup, a host of primarily more polemical works were published. For a review essay of thirty-one books, see Arturo Valenzuela and J. Samuel Valenzuela, "Visions of Chile," *Latin American Research Review* 10 (Fall 1975): pp. 155–176.

57. See Valenzuela and Wilde, "Presidentialism and Decline of Congress," pp. 204–210.

58. The most comprehensive study of U.S. involvement was conducted by the U.S. Select Committee to Study Govermental Operations with respect to Intelligence Activities (Church Committee) of the 94th Congress, 1st Session. See its *Covert Action in Chile 1963–1973* (Washington, DC: Government Printing, 1975).

59. The fact that Allende received fewer votes in 1970 than in 1964 suggests that his victory was not due to an increase in popular discontent and mobilization fueled by a worsening socioeconomic crisis. An examination of socioeconomic indicators in the late 1960s does not support the argument that the lot of the average Chilean was becoming worse or that political mobilization was exceeding historic levels. Survey data also supports the view that a majority of voters would have preferred a Center-Right to a Center-Left coalition. Huntington's thesis, in *Political Order*, that political order collapses when political institutions are too weak, is not supported by the Chilean case. Chile's parties prior to the election of Allende were very strong (perhaps too dominant), and political mobilization was the product of deliberate strategies on the part of the parties and the government to bring people into the political process, rather than the product of widespread discontent or anomic behavior. In Chile, the election of Allende and the economic and social crisis of the Allende years was more the product of the sharp political crisis rather than vice-versa. For a full elaboration of this argument, see my *Breakdown*, ch. 3. An article that argues that mobilization in Chile became excessive is Henry Landberger and Tim McDaniel, "Hypermobilization in Chile, 1970–73," *World Politics* 28, no. 4 (July 1976): pp. 502–543.

60. For the concept of neutral powers, see Linz, *Breakdown*, pp. 76–80. For a discussion of the growing confrontation, suggesting that mobilization was more the result of political crisis rather than its cause, see Valenzuela, *Breakdown*, p. 34.

61. Seventy-two percent of those polled thought Chile was living through extraordinary times, but only 27 percent of the respondents felt the military should be involved in the political process. See Valenzuela, *Breakdown*, p. 65. The Chilean case suggests that even where democratic norms are widespread and deeply rooted in a society, political crisis resulting from institutional struggles and competing claims can seriously erode democratic practices. A democratic political culture is no guarantee for the maintenance of democratic institutions.

62. This argument is elaborated in Arturo Valenzuela, "Orígenes y características del sistema de partidos políticos en Chile: Una proposición para un gobierno parlamentario," *Estudios Públicos* 18 (Fall 1985): pp. 87–154; and my "Hacia una democracia estable: la opción parlamentaria para Chile," *Revista de Ciencia Política* 7, no. 2 (1985): pp. 129–140. The author is grateful to Juan Linz for his reflections on this subject. See the suggestive discussion in Linz, *Breakdown*, pp. 71–74; and his "Democracy, Presidential or Parliamentary: Does It Make a Difference?" Paper presented at the 83rd Annual Meeting of the American Political Science Association, Chicago, IL, September 3–6, 1987.

63. This section draws on the author's forthcoming book with Pamela Constable, *By Reason or By Force: Pinochet's Chile*.

64. This section is based on interviews, conducted in August 1987, with high-ranking military officers who commanded troops during the coup and were responsible for "cleaning up" or "neutralizing" Santiago neighborhoods.

65. A valuable discussion of the neoconservative economic policies applied by the Chilean military regime is Pilar Vergara, *Auge y caída del neoliberalismo en Chile* (Santiago: FLACSO, 1985).

66. This section is based on extensive interviews with advisers close to the junta and General Pinochet in 1973–1978.

67. For the text of Decree Law 527, see Eduardo Soto Kloss, *Ordenamiento constitucional* (Santiago: Editorial Jurídica de Chile, 1980), pp. 145–153.

68. These observations are based on interviews conducted with General Leigh in Santiago, Chile, during November 1985. An excellent published interview is in Florencia Varas, *Gustavo Leigh: El general disidente* (Santiago: Editorial Aconcagua, 1979). Pinochet retired eighteen air force generals before finding one who would accept his action and replace Leigh on the junta. Had

Leigh had better intelligence, the conflict might have been much more dramatic.

69. See Chile, *Constitución de la República de Chile 1980* (Santiago: Editorial Jurídica, 1981). See Article 8, p. 13, for that language.

70. See transitional articles 16 and 27 in *Constitución*.

71. For an excellent study that gives a picture of rising military expenditures for personnel, see Jorge Marshall, "Gasto público en Chile 1969–1979," *Colección estudios cieplan* 5 (July 1981): pp. 53–84.

72. As such, the Chilean military regime was of the military, but not by the military. I am indebted to the excellent work of Genaro Arriagada for this insight. See his *La política militar de Pinochet* (Santiago: Salesianos, 1985).

73. For an article detailing the service of military men in government positions, see Carlos Huneeus and Jorge Olave, "Autoritarismo, militares y transición a la democracia: Chile en una perspectiva comparada" (Santiago: CERC, mimeo, 1986).

74. See Alfred Stepan's now classic elaboration of this problem in his *The Military in Politics: Changing Patterns in Brazil* (Princeton, NJ: Princeton University Press, 1971).

75. Senior officers such as General Oscar Bonilla, perhaps the most powerful general at the time of the coup, were not successful in their attempts to control Contreras. Bonilla died in an accident of suspicious nature. Many civilian advisers came to fear that Contreras could come to threaten Pinochet, though the general succeeded in playing various groups off against each other. Contreras was finally fired and the DINA restructured as relations between the United States and Chile deteriorated following U.S. demands for extradition of Contreras to the United States for his alleged involvement in the assassination of Orlando Letelier, Allende's foreign minister, in the streets of Washington. For studies that deal with the Letelier case and provide insights into the DINA, see John Dinges and Saul Landau, *Assassination on Embassy Row* (New York: Pantheon, 1980); and Taylor Branch and Eugene M. Propper, *Labyrinth* (New York: Viking, 1982).

76. For a discussion of political parties under authoritarianism, see Arturo Valenzuela and J. Samuel Valenzuela, "Political Oppositions under the Chilean Authoritarian Regime." In *Military Rule in Chile: Dictatorship and Oppositions*, J. Samuel Valenzuela and Arturo Valenzuela (Baltimore, MD: Johns Hopkins University Press, 1986).

77. See Pamela Constable and Arturo Valenzuela, "Is Chile Next?" *Foreign Policy* 63 (Summer 1986): pp. 58–75.

78. See Adam Przeworski's persuasive critique of the notion that the lack of legitimacy is a sufficient condition for the breakdown of a regime in his "Some Problems in the Study of the Transition to Democracy." In *Transitions from Authoritarian Rule*, ed. Guillermo O'Donnell, Philippe C. Schmitter, and Laurence Whitehead (Baltimore, MD: Johns Hopkins University Press, 1986).

79. This section is based on field research conducted by the author in Chile in 1987 and 1988. For a more detailed description of the events leading up to the plebiscite, see Pamela Constable and Arturo Valenzuela, "Plebiscite in Chile: End of the Pinochet Era?" *Current History* 87 (January 1988): pp. 29–33, 41; and Pamela Constable and Arturo Valenzuela, "The Victory of the No Vote in Chile: Implications for Democratic Transitions" *Current History* (forthcoming, 1989).

• CHAPTER FIVE •
Uruguay: The Survival of Old and Autonomous Institutions

CHARLES GUY GILLESPIE
and
LUIS EDUARDO GONZÁLEZ

• LATIN AMERICA'S MOST SUCCESSFUL POLYARCHY •

Although there is ultimately little to be gained from arguments as to which Latin American country has had the most enviable democratic record during this century, available evidence suggests that Uruguay merits just such an accolade. A survey of experts undertaken by Taylor every five years (using the "Delphi" principle) continuously ranked Uruguay as the most democratic nation on the continent through 1965.[1] Uruguay's level of development was similarly advanced. In fact, one socioeconomic index ranks it fourth in the world by the late 1880s among countries independent by 1869. This was the period of major migration to Uruguay from Italy and Spain, precisely because the standard of living was so high. On the previous measure, Uruguay was not overtaken by Japan and the Soviet Union in level of development until 1963, by Spain until 1968, nor by Romania, Greece, Portugal, or Venezuela until 1973.[2] Along with Argentina, Uruguay's levels of education, nutrition, and life expectancy are the highest on the continent. The same is true with respect to per-capita ownership of radios, televisions, and telephones, as well as newspaper readership.[3]

Prior to the inauguration of an authoritarian regime in 1973, competition among individuals and groups for major positions of government power had, apart from just one interruption, been based on peaceful electoral competition ever since the end of the last Civil War (1904).[4] With regard to the level of inclusion and participation in selecting leaders and policies, universal male suffrage and secret ballots have been in force since 1918. Although elections were not held under the 1973–1984 authoritarian regime, universal suffrage, secret ballot, and a decentralized and fair method of vote-counting remained in force for the 1980 plebiscite and the 1982 party primaries.[5] Historically, civil and political liberties have been widely respected in Uruguay, which many times served as a haven for political refugees from neighboring countries. Almost until 1973, and again since 1984, it has maintained a flourishing and varied press that, if often partisan, was certainly not controlled by the government. Uruguayan interest groups were also highly developed, and, despite the relatively small

URUGUAY

industrial proletariat, this was equally true of labor unions. Although some have seen a "corporatist" flavor in Uruguay's interest-group politics, unions were entirely autonomous and free from state control, unlike their counterparts in most of Latin America.[6] Finally, leaving aside politicometric approaches, Luis González has argued that Uruguay's democratic record was superior to that of Chile, given subordination of the military to civilian politicians until 1973, far earlier extension of the franchise (18–21-year-olds and illiterates acquiring the vote fifty-two years sooner), and greater freedom of action for the opposition.[7]

The harshest criticism of Uruguayan democracy came from the Left. Some critics believed—and perhaps still believe—that what they call democracy cannot exist within a capitalistic social order. Others seem to have thought simply that Uruguayan democracy was particularly flawed. With regard to the first kind of criticism, the problem is simply definitional. With regard to the latter, it seems to us that Uruguay was as much a "democracy" as many advanced capitalist nations. Those who argued that the country remained under the tutelage of an "oligarchy" were using a form of rhetoric on account of their political aims—and perhaps their lack of electoral headway as well—rather than making an objective statement.

Despite such an impressive record, at least by Latin American standards, the 1973 coup was followed by more than a decade of authoritarian rule. Having returned to democracy in 1985, Uruguay does not fall easily into the categories developed in this book regarding degree of "democratic success." We shall argue in this chapter that democracy in Uruguay *is* very highly institutionalized, particularly when compared to other Latin American cases. Such a view is borne out by available survey data on public opinion, the difficulties the military experienced in legitimating their rule, and the survival of the prior political elite. It can be argued that the survival of democracy until the 1970s, following nearly two decades of declining national income, mounting inflation, paralyzing strike waves, and one of Latin America's most successful urban guerrilla movements (the Tupamaros), precisely demonstrates the deep roots and resilience of democracy in Uruguay. Yet, serious threats to democracy's existence also remain. These include the country's long-term relative economic decline, the more recent related acquisition of $5 billion in foreign debts, and post-1972 problems of military role expansion.

• **HISTORICAL ANALYSIS** •

Emergence and Consolidation of Democracy

Carved from what had once been Argentina's eastern province, Uruguay has been a republic ever since 1828, when it came into existence as a nation with the help of the British, who were eager to create a client and buffer state between Buenos Aires and Brazil. As could be expected, however, Uruguay only achieved a degree of democracy matching the conditions laid out in Dahl's

Polyarchy in this century. The nineteenth century saw repeated civil wars and foreign intervention. In the last quarter of that century, modernizing dictatorships and simultaneous technological advances (such as wire fencing) coupled with rapid export-led economic growth permitted the consolidation of state formation and the introduction of the rule of law to the sparsely populated prairie hinterland. This process was completed at the beginning of the present century. The invention of refrigerated ships then produced a renewed economic spurt, which saved the large-scale cattle ranchers from eclipse by the smaller sheep farmers, creating the country's unusual rural structure, which has survived to this day.[8] Uruguay has almost no peasantry, apart from a ring of very small market-garden farmers around Montevideo, the only large city in the country. As late as World War I, Uruguay remained a prosperous corner of Britain's "informal empire," equal in level of development to, say, New Zealand. As with other primary-product–exporting countries lucky enough to lie in temperate zones, incorporation in the world economy produced a reasonable degree of sustained development, as the terms of trade between manufactured imports and exports of beef and wool did not deteriorate.[9]

It is by no means easy to explain the distinctive traits and endurance of the major cleavage of Uruguayan political society, that between Colorados and Blancos. One pro-Colorado historian has said: "From the beginning of the century until the Centenary of the Republic (1930) one was cosmopolitan and reformist under Batlle; the other patrician, nationalist and conservative with Luis Alberto de Herrera."[10] Zum Felde's simplified account is nevertheless useful for portraying the flavor of the traditional parties. In the conclusion to his most famous book, he wrote:

> In examining the birth, genesis and character of the traditional parties we have shown that one represented the force of Europeanist innovation, the other the force of conservative nationalism. . . . The Colorado Party is never still but rather malleable and changing; it is constantly undergoing internal renovation; it is of a more heterogeneous and cosmopolitan substance; it presents a variety of attitudes and orientations in the course of time, according to circumstances and social and political conditions. The Blanco Party keeps itself more homogeneous, identical, *castizo* [pure-bred Spanish], stable; offering the same leadership throughout history. . . . [I]ts leading elite is composed of the same traditionally hispanic and "criollo" social elements, with a certain patrician, "distinguished" tone. . . . [T]he Colorado Party of 1920 is different from that of 1890, that of 1880, that of 1865, that of 1830. It has successively been "caudillistic," militarist, civilian, semisocialist. . . . Its leadership elite is composed of elements *de origen popular* [of common extraction] to a large extent descendents of the Italian immigration, as in 1890 lawyers and members of the Athenaeum [a liberal club of Montevideo], in 1880 military chiefs, in 1865 near *gaucho* caudillos.[11]

Being a small, ethnically and linguistically homogeneous country, Uruguay's politics were not marked by the regional and communal rivalries that rent most of Latin America. Many have seen the Blancos as the party of the hinterland, the Colorados of Montevideo's commercial and financial interests.

Although both parties encompassed a broad spectrum of liberal and conservative ideologies, the Colorados tended toward a more paternalist and reformist version of liberalism,[12] while the Blancos, particularly because they were almost always in the opposition, tended toward a more antistatist and libertarian line. They also claimed to be the more nationalistic party and adopted the formal title, National Party.

One of the most interesting features of Uruguayan government was the pattern of conflict regulation that recurred from the late nineteenth century onward. The word "consociational" has been applied to this pattern, but we would not go so far as to use that term.[13] In some periods, conflict regulation took the form of an agreement that the Blancos might run certain interior regions, unchallenged by the Colorados, who controlled national government. From 1918 to 1933, under the influence of former President José Batlle y Ordoñez, who admired Switzerland's form of government, Uruguay attempted to divide executive authority between a president and a nine-man Council of Government.[14] From 1952 to 1966, a fully collegial executive ran the country. Both these collegial governments included guaranteed minority representation for the largest opposition party.

One feature of Uruguayan politics that strongly contrasts with Lijphart's model of "consociational democracy" has been the extreme internal fluidity and factionalism of Uruguayan parties. This has permitted fractions of one party to ally with fractions of the opposition at critical junctures, such as the coup of 1933. Although some have seen this as evidence of consociation, it was actually an unusual form of majoritarianism, insofar as important minorities of both parties opposed such constitutional revisions as abolishing the collegial executive branch and permanently splitting the Senate seats. More consociational was the practice known as coparticipation, by which opposition parties obtained a share of the seats on boards running supposedly decentralized public agencies. These were known as *entes autónomos* and began to proliferate rapidly, as utilities and infrastructural industries were nationalized during the 1930s and 1940s. In fact, they were not autonomous at all but became the fiefdoms of party factions and a source of patronage, which personalist leaders could call on to win voters.[15]

Once Uruguay had enacted its impressive array of liberal and social reforms during the first third of this century (divorce, separation of church and state, nationalization of monopolies, secondary education, votes for women, and an 8-hour working day, to name only the most notable examples), politics settled into a relatively calm and more or less routine struggle till the 1960s. Although exporting ranchers grumbled at exchange-rate and tariff policies, designed at first to generate state revenues and later to promote import-substituting industrialization, so long as prosperity continued they could afford the burden. This was particularly true once the progressive Colorados abandoned hopes of land reform. Similarly, fiscal conservatives might be apprehensive at the growth of public-sector employment and the creation of nationalized industries, but they only mobilized their opposition during depressions, such as that which hit Uruguay following the Wall Street crash of 1929 or the end of the Korean War boom in beef and wool prices. The basis of competition between Colorados and Blancos, and indeed between their various fractions, was thus not very ideological. In this respect, Uruguay resembled the United States.

Some authors have suggested that the clientelist dimension of electoral politics, whereby political bosses (*caudillos*) acted as patrons, in particular to the lower classes, was the central characteristic of Uruguayan politics. From a comparative perspective, however, Uruguayan clientelism does not look especially distinctive, and it is certainly not a "defining" characteristic of Uruguayan politics. Solari pointed out more than twenty years ago that in the Uruguayan context of a half-century of secret-ballot voting and welfare programs, clientelism is a self-defeating practice.[16] Besides, distributive politics at the group level might just as easily motivate the broad lines of public policy as the particularist benefits doled out by the members of the political class in neighborhood clubs. In addition, there were genuine political differences between leaders over the best form of constitutional arrangements and over foreign policy.[17] The National Party (Blancos) advocated neutrality. The Colorados were pro-Allied and in subsequent decades have often strongly supported U.S. policy in Latin America.[18]

No discussion of Uruguayan politics is possible without an elementary understanding of the country's somewhat unique electoral system, in force now for sixty years and known as the "double simultaneous vote" (DSV). Under this system, parties present more than one list in each election, and the number of seats for each party as a whole is first calculated using a modified d'Hondt form of proportional representation. Then, seats are distributed between the rival fractions of each party by the same method. Sometimes two or more lists within the same party ally to form an intermediate electoral cartel known as a *sublema* in order to improve their chances of winning a seat. Seat allocation therefore becomes a three-stage process. The practical working of the DSV becomes clearer if we consider the presidential election, which is held at the same time. Each party may field more than one candidate, the competing lists lining up behind whomever they favor. The candidate with the most votes from the party with the most votes is declared the winner.[19] For example, in 1971 the Colorados had 13,000 more votes than the Blancos and therefore won the presidency, even though the Blancos had the most-voted single candidate. Some people consider this system analogous to holding a primary election simultaneously with the general election. This is debatable, however, since there is a degree of voter uncertainty as to precisely what effect their votes will have.

Many have argued that introducing the DSV was merely a maneuver by Uruguay's established political elite to try to maintain the unity and dominant role of the traditional Colorado and Blanco parties in the face of their factional splits.[20] Recently, however, Luis González has challenged the view that the DSV has prevented a multiplication of parties or helped maintain Uruguay's normally two-party system. He has stressed, rather, the ban on ticket-splitting, which is also a firm canon of Uruguayan electoral law, as the source of party-system stability. There is no way to vote for a Colorado presidential candidate and a Blanco congressional list (or vice versa) for the simple reason that the parties preprint their ballots, and they are not allowed to entertain such an alliance. Furthermore, local elections are held on the same day as the general election, and voters who put the municipal ballot of one party with the national ballot of another in their voters' envelope will have their votes annulled when they are counted.

One piece of evidence that would tend to support González's dismissal of DSV as favoring two-partyism is that since 1971 the Left—which in Uruguay is made up of various formerly separate parties none of which had been able to poll more than about 5 percent—has formed an alliance known as the Frente Amplio (Broad Front). This achieved over 18 percent of the vote in 1971 and 21 percent in 1984, effectively challenging the future of the two-party system (unless one of the other parties is eventually displaced, as occurred in Britain between the wars). It is hard to believe that the Broad Front—which includes Communists, ultraleftists, Socialists, Christian Democrats, and moderate Social Democrats—would have survived without the DSV. Consider, on the other hand, that former supporters of the military regime remained a sizable faction within the Colorado Party with their own candidate, former President Jorge Pacheco Areco. Had the DSV not existed, they would have been forced to reach agreement with the centrist and even left-wing Colorados on joint electoral lists. It is very unlikely that any agreement could have been reached that would have satisfied all concerned; hence the plausible hypothesis that small-to-middling fractions might have broken away to form separate parties (as happened to the Blanco Party in the 1930s). In sum: though many agree that straight-ticket voting favors the larger parties (and even two-partyism), and that the DSV favors fractionalism within parties—there is less agreement over the question of whether the DSV also favors reducing the tendency of proportional representation to produce a multi-party system.[21]

Whatever the ultimate reason for the stability of Uruguay's two-party system, there can be little doubt that it constituted the core of Uruguay's democratic stability as well. A major explanation of both would seem to be the combination of two factors. First, a "path to polyarchy" that allowed experience of expanded competition among conflicting elites for some time before mass extension of the franchise is more favorable, as Dahl argues.[22] Second, rather than being a purely "transformist" process, similar to the Chilean one, the development of Uruguayan polyarchy during the first third of the century was able to achieve a level of democratic participation and popular inclusion unique to Latin America.[23] As late as 1970, Alisky was to subtitle an essay on Uruguay, "Economic Turmoil and Political Stability."[24] By the time his essay appeared, however, this optimistic judgment was no longer applicable.

Breakdown of Democracy

The social and economic crisis that made the 1973 coup possible had much in common with the parallel crisis that developed in Argentina.[25] Our account of the political economy of Uruguay's crisis therefore mirrors O'Donnell's synthesis of Argentina's stagnation and cyclical instability.[26] Both Argentina and Uruguay are recently colonized nations of transplanted citizens.[27] This is particularly true of Uruguay, where immigration started at the beginning of the eighteenth century. Cattle-raising, the source of national prosperity, developed on the basis of an organizational type, the *estancia,* peculiar to the region. Compared to plantations, enclaves, or *haciendas,* it was less intensive in labor, capital, and technology. This in turn allowed the principal productive resource to become the property of an "early domestic agrarian bourgeoisie" (or national bourgeoisie) with their own important basis for accumulation, rather than a scarcely capitalist oligarchy. Furthermore, this gave rise to prosperous urban, commercial, and even industrial development, outstripping the rest of the subcontinent, all of which formed a relatively wealthy and fully capitalist urban market. Concretely, this meant that the 1930s were not the first period of industrialization either in Argentina or Uruguay.[28]

The economic results of this regional accumulation of circumstances were already significant at the end of the last century. If, by regional standards, the prosperity of the River Plate was relatively more impressive then than now, the lead it gained by the end of the nineteenth century in terms of social development has, in many respects, perpetuated itself until today. The consequences, as we now, are "European" parameters of demographic growth, life expectancy at birth, nutrition, urbanization, and education. Yet, cracks in the edifice were soon visible in both countries. From about 1930, "output per productive unit [ranch] in Uruguay and Argentina [was] rapidly left behind," primarily because of the increasingly capital-intensive characteristics that cattle-rearing took on in the international context.[29] With stagnating productivity, and taking into account the fact that import-substituting industrialization altered the structure of imports and in the long run even increased their value while promoting the domestic consumption of exportable goods,[30] growth was inexorably strangled.

Table 5.1 shows the effects of the Great Depression on Uruguay's growth trends, the ascent toward the ceiling of 1951–1955, and subsequent sustained deterioration, returning the situation to that of the immediate postwar period, twenty years earlier. Even admitting that the figures for the final periods may be underestimated because of the volume of emigration (which later grew enormously), per-capita national income must have been falling.[31] The conceivable correction would not be sufficient to offset the downward trend, let alone reverse it. International comparisons underline the singularity of the case: Of the 135 nations whose per capita GDP and growth rates between 1961 and 1965 are included in the *World Handbook of Political and Social Indicators,* only two (Malawi at -1.5 and Dominican Republic at -2.0) experienced more serious negative growth than did Uruguay (-0.9). Indeed, only one other country had

URUGUAY 215

Table 5.1. Per-Capita GDP at Factor Cost (Constant 1961 Prices)

Year	U.S. $ (1961)	Index (1951:55 = 100)
1930	430.2	77.2
1935	378.3	67.9
1936–1940	410.8	73.7
1941–1945	402.4	72.2
1946–1950	491.8	88.3
1951–1955	556.9	100.0
1956–1960	552.6	99.2
1961–1965	525.7	94.4
1966–1968	499.8	89.7

Source: Julio Millot et al., *Desarrollo industrial* (Montevideo: Universidad de la República, 1973); and Instituto de Economía, *Uruguay: Estadísticas Básicas* (Montevideo: Universidad de la República, 1969).

negative growth in the same period (North Vietnam at -0.8).[32] Given the cumulative trade deficit of $494 million from 1950 to 1964, it was to be expected that Uruguay's foreign-exchange reserves would be exhausted, while its foreign debt climbed to hitherto unimagined levels. Although the net assets of the country were positive until 1958 (taking into account monetary gold, foreign currencies, and the debts of other countries, minus Uruguay's foreign debts), by 1970 they had reached the negative sum of $280 million.

To complete the picture, gross domestic fixed-capital formation during 1955–1966 represented just 12.9 percent of GDP, and in 1967 it was 11.4 percent. The significance of these figures is best understood in relation to the comparative ratios for Europe's market economies. In 1960, they invested an average 20 percent of their domestic products, while centrally planned economies invested as much as 25 percent. Table 5.2 shows the consequences of the crisis on real wages in manufacturing industry.

From 1945 onward the figures refer to manufacturing industry in Montevideo only, but the series is representative of the average of the industrial sector for the country as a whole, if only because most industry is located in the capi-

Table 5.2. Real Wages in Manufacturing Industry, 1930–1972

Year	Index (1955: 59 = 100)
1930	65.5
1935–1939	65.1
1940–1944	67.9
1945–1949	78.8
1950–1954	98.5
1955–1959	100.0
1960–1964	99.6
1965–1969	95.1
1970–1972	87.1

Source: Millot et al., *Desarrollo industrial;* and Instituto de Economía, "Un reajuste conservador," *Estudios y Coyuntura* 3 (1973).

tal. The table clearly shows the peak of 1955–1959 (midpoint of the most prosperous fifteen years, 1950–1964) as well as the magnitude of the decline, which brought real wages to less than their 1950 level. Those sectors with the least mobile resources were the worst affected. The real salary of Montevideo shopworkers, for example, slid to 79.3 percent of its 1961–1963 level in 1970–1972. Rural workers were in even worse circumstances.

Such developments began gradually to translate themselves into social agitation and growing political polarization. How would different social actors react? In terms of the traditionally heterogeneous middle classes, a series of contradictory responses were to be expected. The rural middle classes reacted against the political polarization by reaffirming their traditional loyalties, given the stability of rural society and its demonstrated political conservatism. The only minor exceptions, perhaps, were those sectors engaged in urban occupations while physically (ecologically) located in rural areas. The urban middle classes, for their part, found themselves the victims of cross-pressures. On the one hand, their loss of purchasing power, made more severe by an occupational structure that afforded fewer and fewer opportunities for social advancement, conflicted with predominantly conformist values that were repeatedly shown to oppose change.[33] It was therefore no surprise that "certain signs of rightwing authoritarianism" appeared in the middle sectors,[34] in some ways following the pattern of the interwar years in Europe.

Among the dependent middle classes including civil servants, an attitudinal pattern typical of an "anti–status quo configuration with authoritarian content and, presumably, poor chances for ideological structuration" appeared.[35] "The inconsistency between attitudes and voting, which reflect[ed] a questioning of the ultimate sources of economic power . . . without affecting support for the existing political system" was reaffirmed. The predisposition of this group "as a political potential seem[ed] to orient itself more towards forms . . . with nationalistic and moralistic content, a search for legitimacy outside the political system requiring forms of charismatic leadership as a substitute for highly structured ideologies."[36]

Acting on the same social sector, the potential effects of the devaluation of qualifications for the highly educated are well known. In the Uruguayan case, as early as the 1950s, "the University show[ed] itself ever more systematically opposed to the traditional parties; intellectuals become radicalized . . . an important institutional sphere is politically dominated by groups which, in terms of society as a whole, are a minority."[37] Other well-known phenomena were: (a) the overrepresentation of the highly educated among the extreme Left, as argued by D'Oliveira;[38] and, (b) opinion-poll data showing that in urban areas formal education was the best predictor of the Left's vote.[39] Matching these patterns was the militancy of the typically white-collar unions (such as the bankworkers), whose radical positions situated them to the left of the bulk of the trade-union movement.

The political responses of less affluent working people to the crisis were also heterogeneous. With regard to the urban working class, though its trade-union history began as early as the last century, it was only during the economic downturn and crisis that it was able to consolidate its organizations. The first really united national federation of unions was created only in 1964. Given that, even today, the manual labor of the secondary (industrial) sector includes an important segment of semiskilled craftsmen, it would seem reasonable to distinguish these from the proletariat in the traditional sense of the term. With regard to the political attitudes of the "artisan" element, it is hard to go beyond more or less risky and dubious generalizations. With regard to the proletariat proper, however, we are on firmer ground: The most reasonable hypothesis is that these workers supported the traditional Left, the Communist Party (PCU) achieving an increasing preponderance. In fact, the PCU managed to control practically the entire workers' movement (to a far greater extent, no doubt, than it did student activism).

For rural laborers, excepting workers in crops with intensive patterns of cultivation, the most plausible hypothesis is the same as the argument put forth with respect to the rural middle classes.[40] The offspring of the poorest and most "submerged" rural sectors (it is difficult to speak of marginality in the Uruguayan context without a long conceptual excursus) often join the ranks of the army.[41] Their urban counterparts also often seek either to enter the army or, possibly to a greater extent, the police force and seem disposed to follow right-wing charismatic leaders.

From this all-too-brief synthesis, it may be deduced that potential support for the "traditional" parties of the Left (i.e., the Communists and Socialists) was relatively restricted in the 1960s. It was limited to the organized working class plus a difficult-to-quantify fraction of the middle sectors, including a good part of the country's intelligentsia. In this sense, the famous slogan that grew out of the conflicts of 1958, *"obreros y estudiantes, unidos y adelante"* (workers and students, unite and go forward) inadvertently reflected the limits to the proposed action. A superficial inspection was enough to show how narrow was this base.

The 1971 elections were a decisive moment. The Left achieved its electoral unity under the protection of Uruguay's peculiar DSV voting legislation. Even the urban guerrillas—the Tupamaros—allowed their hopes to rise in the face of the massive growth that was predicted by the Broad Front. Few felt that the Left would win the national contest, but a clear victory was seen as automatic in Montevideo, which includes almost one-half of the electorate. Nevertheless, the ruling Colorado Party won, both nationally and in the capital. Examination of the election results according to the position of different political fractions in the ideological spectrum corroborates our analysis. The options were:

(*a*) Right: Bordaberry (Colorado winner) and Aguerrondo (Blanco minority)
(*b*) Center-Right: Jorge Batlle (Colorado minority)

Table 5.3. Ideological Distribution of Voters by Region, 1971

	Right	Center-Right	Center-Left	Left	Total[a]
Montevideo	29	12	27	30	100%
Interior	42	16	31	10	100%
Nationwide Total	37	15	29	18	100%

[a] Entries are row percentages. Percentages shown may not total 100% due to rounding.

Table 5.4. Regional Distribution of Voters by Ideology, 1971

	Right	Center-Right	Center-Left	Left	All[a]
Montevideo	33	36	40	70	42%
Interior	67	64	60	30	58%
Total	100%	100%	100%	100%	100%

Source: Julio Fabregat, *Elecciones uruguayas* (Montevideo: Cámara de Senadores, 1972).

[a] Entries are column percentages.

(c) Center-Left: Ferreira Aldunate (Blanco majority) and Vasconcellos (small Colorado sector)

(d) Left: Líber Seregni (Broad Front)

These options were distinguished by the candidates' platforms, the issues and "tone" of the campaign, and their political personalities. They cut across the divide between the traditional Colorado and Blanco parties. Taking into account the massive electoral turnout of 1971, Table 5.3 gives eloquent testimony to the restricted foundations of support for the Left. In Montevideo, the Broad Front showed a very slight plurality, though not even reaching one-third of the electorate; in the rest of the country, it had just 10 percent. The correlation between the respective strengths of the Left and Right and the urban-rural cleavage is brought out in Table 5.4. The election accelerated the already advanced process of political polarization. The Right and the extreme Right considered that the results had confirmed their perceptions of the situation and legitimized their authoritarian remedies.

The effect on the armed forces was perhaps even more important. The agitation resulting from prolonged economic stagnation was seen as the product of the action of minorities manipulated, or at least encouraged, from abroad. Economic and social problems could therefore be defined as basically problems of law and public order, and therefore a matter for the police. On the other hand, part of the Left, above all the extreme Left, ended up convincing themselves of the alleged futility and "trickery" of what they called "formal democracy." The electoral road to socialism was dead, in their eyes. In the face of social and economic deterioration, the results were held to signify not their own political weakness, but rather the capacity of an "oligarchic" minority to distort and use the system for its own exclusive interests.

Uruguay's difficulties in "reinserting itself in the world economy" after the end of the Korean War boom must not be seen as the only cause of democracy's breakdown almost two decades later. Nor does it suffice to label such symptoms of the crisis as violence, extremism, or military-role expansion as causes in themselves. These were rather the deadly challenges that the political elites needed to face while maintaining a democratic polity. They attempted to do so, for, when finally confronted by the military takeover, about two-thirds of the members of the legislature were against it. Yet, this majority was unable to take proper action to avoid the coup. The central problem was the fractionalism and poor organization of the two major parties. This was compounded by declining state resources and increasing polarization. The previously successful model of a relatively autonomous state that acted as arbiter between classes and as distributor of resources was threatened by increasing fiscal crisis and social mobilization. Political failures clearly accelerated the spiral of inflation, declining revenues, and trade deficits, while policies compounded the loss of export markets, breeding speculation, and capital flight. On two occasions, Uruguay unsuccessfully attempted to adhere to IMF–imposed austerity, each time the political pressures becoming too great to bear.[42]

Concerning what in the short run was the most pressing problem after 1968—that of military-role expansion—the failure of politicians was even worse: Leaders were hardly able even to discuss policies on the military and the antiguerrilla effort, much less to agree on them. The survival of the traditional parties was thus increasingly accompanied by turmoil and a loss of "ascriptive" legitimacy by their leaders.[43] After 1967, there was a new and growing tendency for ministers to be chosen from technocratic sectors or relevant interest associations. The last president, Bordaberry, was not even a "real" Colorado, but rather a right-wing former Blanco Senator who had emerged from a rural "Poujadist" movement known as "ruralism."

Uruguay was ultimately no exception to the rule that all armed forces require a minimally favorable climate of national opinion before they can carry out a coup. Although opinion data did not show any declining abstract belief among Montevideans in the merits of democracy as a system, they did show a severe loss of confidence in most traditional politicians.[44] One indicator of this was the increasing number of retired military officers who ran for president (including Aguerrondo on the Right and Seregni on the Left). The Tupamaros conducted a devastating campaign against alleged corruption among politicians and turned over much of their evidence to the military, both before and after their imprisonment. Corruption was a major theme subsequently used by the military to justify their seizure of power. Early in 1972, the urban guerrillas launched a renewed offensive against the armed forces. In less than a year, they were militarily destroyed by means of a "dirty war." Yet, by the time the strictly military aspects were over and political leaders tried to put a brake on the rapid expansion of the military's power, it was too late to save democracy in Uruguay.

One major incident testified to the political paralysis of Uruguayan polyarchy: the February 1973 mutiny of the army and air force. Refusing to accept the new minister of defense, the military issued communiqués calling for radical measures, including land reform, to break out of the crisis of inflationary economic stagnation. Although the navy remained loyal to the president, his call for citizens to rally outside Government House to defend the Constitution was met by total apathy. Even within the Left—which was to be the authoritarian regime's main victim—many believed in the possibility of a "progressive coup." The level of mistrust among political leaders was such that they allowed power to fall into the hands of the military, who set up the new National Security Council (COSENA) to oversee the government.

Failure of Authoritarianism

Faced with an additional mutiny of naval officers supporting Communiqués Four and Seven, in which the rebels had announced their demands, Rear Admiral Zorilla resigned in February 1973. The following day, President Bordaberry accepted the creation of a National Security Council under military control, with wide-ranging executive powers. In the ensuing months, a final showdown occurred when the National Assembly refused to lift the immunity from prosecution of Senator Erro, whom the military accused of links with the terrorists. On June 27, the army occupied the National Assembly, and Bordaberry issued a decree dissolving it "for grave violations of the principles of the constitution."[45]

Despite hopes among sectors of the Left that the coup might bring to power progressive generals similar to those who had seized power in Peru five years previously, the immediate response to the dissolution of parliament from labor was the declaration of an indefinite general strike by the Convención Nacional de los Trabajadores (CNT) union federation.[46] Two weeks of factory occupations, sabotage, and economic paralysis were broken only by a combination of wage rises, mass arrests, and failed talks with the Left and students, held essentially to exhaust the strikers. Soon after the coup, Bordaberry said that the traditional parties remained the "essence of democracy and the formation of our nationality." One year later, however, his response to an open letter signed by hundreds of congressmen was to insist they give up hope of once more "using their perverted political apparatuses."[47] By that time, the parties of the Broad Front had been systematically dismantled, their presses confiscated and leaders arrested, while the traditional parties remained merely "suspended."

The first three years of the authoritarian regime have been characterized as a relatively pure form of "commissary dictatorship" based on a self-proclaimed "state of exception."[48] The new regime appeared close to O'Donnell's model of "bureaucratic-authoritarianism,'" vindicating a number of his predictions.[49] It should be emphasized that the prognosis was by no means obvious, at least for contemporary observers. Even after the coup, a good part of the Uruguayan intelligentsia continued to speculate as to the relative strength of different factions within the army, such as the supposed progressive Peruvianists.[50] Left opposition, which was the most intellectually and politically active, was divided among a majority who argued that the "principal contradiction" was between the "oligarchy" and the "people," and a minority who argued that the most pressing need was to sustain civilian power in the face of the military takeover. With hindsight, the latter group has been shown to have been all too correct.

Perhaps the most important caveat regarding the applicability of the bureaucratic-authoritarian model to Uruguay's military regime was the absence of what O'Donnell foresaw as "deepening" (the development of capital-goods industries and so-called "backward linkages"). This was of little relevance, as the size of the domestic market was such that heavy industry was an unrealistic goal. The early years of economic policy were in fact characterized by a heterodox model emphasizing export promotion and relative price adjustments, as well as market liberalization.[51] High interest rates and the liberalization of banking laws designed to promote Uruguay as the "Switzerland of Latin America" in a rather newer sense of the term led to speculative inflows of foreign capital during the 1970s and the purchase of most remaining private banks by foreign conglomerates.

From 1978, an all-out war was waged against inflation by means of preannounced exchange-rate devaluations far below the rate of inflation. This policy led to massive foreign-debt accumulation and the bankruptcy of most producers of any tradable commodity.[52] Brazil was less taken with the model, with the result that unlike what happened in the other bureaucratic-authoritarian regimes, much of its inflow of foreign capital was in fact productively invested rather than consumed or squirreled away overseas.[53] It is hard to see how Uruguay's quite different (and nearly suicidal) anti-inflation policy can have been "imposed" by the ruling classes. Rather, it seems to have been adopted as a result of the appeal of Mundellian international monetarism to some technocratic circles in the Southern Cone.[54] The inference that regimes that allegedly favor certain class factions automatically represent direct rule by those classes is dubious at best. Accounts of the hegemonic influence of finance capital over the military are thus misleadingly simplistic.[55]

Certain class-based analyses of the evolution and eventual crises of bureaucratic-authoritarian regimes tend to assume the existence of some preordained and almost rigid "geometry" of class alliances. More successful in explaining elite opposition to Uruguay's authoritarian regime are simpler models based on opposition to authoritarianism *tout court* and opposition to specific policy choices made by technocrats, such a the decision deliberately to overvalue the currency after 1978. To some extent, discontent may also have been rooted in resentment at the usurpation of power by a formerly marginal and not particularly prestigious or educated group of parvenus such as the military.[56]

After 1976, the Uruguayan military regime entered a phase of attempted institutionalization. President Bordaberry was ousted shortly before his term expired because he proposed the permanent abolition of political parties and an experiment in no-party corporatist rule. On the one hand, the military were unwilling to break with the line that they were cleaning up democracy—curing it of the disease of subversion, rather than killing it. On the other hand, the unwelcome proposal that they withdraw from administration clashed with their prevailing assumptions as to the breadth of issues affecting national security. It also came precisely at the time when senior officers had begun to enjoy the power and rewards of running Uruguay's many state agencies and enterprises. After a struggle, the collegiality of military rule was maintained by installing a new civilian figurehead, Aparicio Méndez, and a timetable of sorts was announced for a return to a new "strengthened" model of democracy. Institutional acts inspired by those of the Brazilian regime were promulgated, banning most existing politicians from all political activity for fifteen years, while the nonelected Council of State began to meet in joint session with the Junta de Oficiales Generales (consisting of all generals) as the Council of the Nation to consider a new constitution. In essence, the plan was to set up a democradura—that is, a plebiscitarian "democracy" with limits on which parties and candidates might run for office, and a continued and dominant role for the military-controlled National Security Council in the executive. Whereas in Brazil, about 500 citizens (only some of them politicians) were selectively deprived of their political rights, in Uruguay, 15,000 citizens were affected: proportionately more than 1,000 times more. Other institutional acts abolished civil servants' immunity from being fired (a preliminary to major purges), subordinated the judiciary to the executive, and intervened in the machinery for future elections.

One of the central characteristics of the Democradura plan was the attempt to "decapitate" the traditional political parties, many of whose leaders retained personal prestige. Unlike Brazil's officialist ARENA Party, the military made few attempts to co-opt notable conservative civilian allies or build a party to mobilize support for the regime. In structural terms, the possibility of using state patronage to take over an existing party, launch a new one, and/or combine this with some form of corporatist institutionalization was highly circumscribed. Unlike Brazil, Uruguay lacked the large rural population, previously marginal to political participation, and therefore "available" to be incorporated from above in alliance with traditional elites, as in ARENA. Furthermore, it is widely agreed that the crisis preceding the instauration of the authoritarian regime did not produce the level of polarization seen, for example, in Chile. Put simply, the new regime never achieved the same degree of initial legitimation in Uruguay, as can be seen in the duration of the general strike, the support of that strike by middle-class professionals, and the relatively minor support for the coup from politicians.

Even if building an ARENA–like entity was impossible, the military could have attempted to make more politically conscious use of the resources they administered. In fact, a combination of ambitious development projects and bureaucratic momentum, along with the militarization of public administration, tended to jeopardize plans to cut government spending. Yet, the regime made no attempt directly to mobilize citizens. This is somewhat surprising, given the very large size of Uruguay's public sector and the number of civil-service jobs to be filled as alleged "subversives" were fired. The real obstacle was not simply a lack of resources, but the more complex problem that welfare-state programs could not easily be exchanged for votes when sophisticated Uruguayans had already come to see these as their birthright. Furthermore, the military were perhaps influenced by their own rhetoric of "house-cleaning," and the common military aversion to "dirty" party politics. They were also probably hampered by the lack of any definite preponderance of ties to either traditional party among the officer corps.

In any case, most of the military's civilian collaborators were "has-beens." Nor did the military themselves benefit from the personal prestige afforded by a single leader such as Pinochet in Chile. By default, the traditional parties were allowed to survive in "suspended animation," while the brunt of repression on the left was born by the Communists. Explanations for the parties' survival inevitably tend to be either negative or almost circular: They survived because they were so central to Uruguay's political culture (this culture arising from their longevity), and they also survived because of the absence of any military project to displace them. Nevertheless, their survival demonstrated that their appeal was not purely based on patronage and clientelism, as state resources were obviously denied to the opposition fractions that took control of both parties.

The fact that the military constantly had to justify every action as necessary for promoting democracy and eliminating its enemies shows the resilience of the democratic political culture permeating even the armed forces, and the inhospitable climate for authoritarian discourse. The military were anxious to win electoral support for the new institutional order they had decreed, but they refused to countenance any input from the traditional politicians of the moderate opposition. The first attempt to break out of isolation from electoral legitimation with the 1980 plebiscite was initiated without any liberalization. A real "transition" would not even be on the horizon until this attempt at controlled re-institutionalization had failed.

The announcement that the draft constitution had been defeated, 57.2 percent to 42.8 percent on a turnout of 87 percent, stunned the military as much as the opposition. It was surprising that the parties had been able to organize adequately in the very limited time available to counter the regime's publicity. Yet, it was inevitable that the military would not win the support of politicians whom they had banned until 1991. Two major leaders called for a Yes vote: right-wingers Pacheco among the Colorados and Gallinal among the Blancos. The rest called for a No vote, and even though they were banned, surrogates sprang up, leaving little ambiguity as to whom they represented. It was not true that only the heartland of the Left had voted No (as investigation of the ecological pattern of voting shows), and, of course, the total No vote was over three times higher than the Left vote in 1971. It was also found that young and first-time voters had voted No overwhelmingly (they were distinguishable by their higher voter-registration numbers).[57]

Until 1980, the regime could compensate for its lack of legitimacy via the revival of economic growth after two decades of stagnation and decline. Following the second oil shock and the disastrous slump brought on by currency overvaluation, they lost that surrogate. The high costs of the economic strategy in terms of living standards and income distribution became more apparent, though free-market policies were, if anything, heightened. Within the military, the struggle intensified between those who argued that redemocratization should continue with more input from "valid interlocutors" in the traditional parties, and those who thought democracy should be taken off the agenda. Out of this bitter conflict, retired General Gregorio Alvarez finally achieved his goal of becoming the regime's first noncivilian president—but only by ruthlessly exposing the corrupt dealings of his opponents.

One month after Alvarez's September 1981 inauguration, it was announced that the traditional parties would be allowed to choose new leaders by means of primary elections the following year. These new leaders would then negotiate the constitutional revisions the military continued to demand. The draft of a new Statute of Parties was submitted to the Council of State in January 1982. It forbade parties "with foreign links" and those "advocating violence" and stipulated that in order to register for elections, parties had to be internally democratic. The terms were further manipulated, but the opposition leaders within the traditional parties felt they had no choice but to participate and hope to win another electoral victory, this time over proregime factions. In fact, the turnout of 60.5 percent in the November 1982 primaries was not as low as it might have been given the silence of the media, the confusion surrounding the new lists' names, and the abolition of absentee voting.[58] Nor can there be any doubt that, this time, economic conditions played an important role in the regime's defeat; just forty-eight hours before voters went to the polls, the government was forced to announce the free-floating of the Uruguayan peso, undoing at a stroke the centerpiece of their anti-inflation policy since 1978.

The Left entered the poll in some disarray, with the Communists committed to their alliance with exiled Blanco leader Wilson Ferreira in the Convergencia Democrática, and imprisoned Broad Front leader, General Líber Seregni, favoring a blank ballot. The Christian Democrats and the Socialists (under José Pedro Cardoso) agreed with Seregni. In practice, a call to endorse the most ardent opponents of the regime would largely have meant voting for the Wilsonistas inside the Blanco Party, as the leaders of the exiled Convergencia Democrática had calculated. Some former leftists probably did opt for the latter strategy, and the Communists' support for the blank ballot was probably half-hearted. The other Left parties, however, were determined to protest their exclusion from the primaries and to avoid any charge that they were attempting to take over the traditional parties. Nevertheless, in Montevideo the Wilsonista "ACF" (Adelante con fé) list won in every district, while nationally the blank vote was

7 percent, well down from the 18.2 percent of the Broad Front in 1971. Furthermore, in all but four departments of Uruguay's interior, the Blancos outpolled the Colorados, nationally attaining 49.2 percent to 42.1 percent. The clear message of the primaries was an even greater rejection of the regime than in the plebiscite of two years previously.[59]

The 1983 talks in the Parque Hotel were deadlocked from the beginning, with the parties unable to detect any willingness to compromise on the military's part. Resistance on both sides was heightened by the first important labor demonstration since the coup. On May 1, over 100,000 demonstrators marched in the capital, under the organization of a new federation called the Plenario Intersindical de Trabajadores (PIT). The reason that the talks failed was not just that the military insisted on such points as the future authority of the National Security Council, the right to search homes, and the right to declare a "state of subversion" and to hold suspects for fifteen days without trial. What strengthened the position of opposition intransigents was that the demands of the Armed Forces Political Affairs Commission (COMASPO) were accompanied by the stepped up government policy of arrests and censorship, so that opinion in the moderate sectors of the traditional parties was utterly alienated. In June, the fifteen-man Directorio of the Blanco Party voted twelve to three against pulling out of the talks; late on July 4, it voted fourteen to one in favor.

Although the stalemate and confrontation was very real between the traditional parties and the regime, the military as an institution became increasingly concerned to achieve an understanding with moderate politicians for a peaceful return to democracy. Their major dilemma was that their main opponent, Wilson Ferreira, might win a presidential election, given the strong showing of his supporters in the primaries.[60] The logic of Uruguay's party system remained unavoidably clear: If the military were to defeat Wilson with his charismatic appeal to youth and deliberate strategy of courting radicals, they would have to divide the opposition by rehabilitating at least part of the Left. This was not an easy step, by any means, given that the regime had based its entire *raison d'être* on an anti-Communist discourse. Nevertheless, the essence of the Naval Club Pact that was eventually reached at the beginning of August 1984, a year after the previous talks had broken down, was legalization of the Broad Front. The military obtained very few concessions regarding the Constitution, but their major victory was successfully to ensure electoral participation by the Colorados, the Left, and, eventually, the Blancos—even though Blanco leader Wilson Ferreira (who had returned to the country amid a blaze of publicity) remained securely in jail until one week after the elections.[61]

The military's entire strategy was predicated on the gamble that the Blancos would not win enough votes as a result of the "martyrdom" of their leader to upset plans and overtake the Colorados. In the event, the Blanco campaign was dogged by a number of disasters and strategic mistakes (compounded by the absence of their leader) and their vote share actually fell compared to 1971. The electorate of the Left proved particularly loyal and resistant to Wilsonism despite their leaders' sudden moderation. The vote share of the Colorados was almost exactly unchanged, though it was more heavily rural than in 1971. The Broad Front achieved a modest increase in support but again narrowly missed winning control of Montevideo's city government, which had been one of the major risks of the military's strategy.[62]

In sum: the economic crisis was clearly a contributing factor to the military's needs to reach a negotiated way out from power. Yet, their attempted institutionalization had failed decisively in the 1980 plebiscite, a moment in which the economy was still experiencing an artificial boom, and business elites were particularly favored. Thus, the economic slump determined neither the transition nor its manner and timing. Neither was pressure from social and political movements an overriding factor in the ultimate course of the transition. It was one element in the military's calculations, and a force that the parties (especially the Left) attempted to keep under control, in order to avoid any damaging "Chileanization" of the situation. The single most important internal difficulty faced by the regime was its lack of legitimacy. In the long run, given the Uruguayan context, this meant the military would eventually be forced to abandon government. But this still left open to negotiation many of the details governing the transition. In this regard, the political elites were able to pursue a subtle and ultimately more complementary strategy than at first sight appeared the case. Of course, the Blancos charged the Left and the Colorados with betrayal, yet by opposing the Naval Club Pact, they had strengthened the bargaining position of those parties that were willing to reach a deal and thus forced the military to make greater concessions.

• **THEORETICAL INTERPRETATION** •

From a comparative perspective, there are two processes of theoretical significance in the Uruguayan democratic experience. Uruguay was capable of constructing the most clearly democratic political order in South America, and this in a continent where democracy has been the exception and not the rule up to now. Yet, democratic institutions have ruptured on two occasions, in 1933 and in 1973. Theoretically, the original process of democratic construction is as significant and relevant to our analysis as are its later failures.

Explaining Democratic Emergence and Restoration

Our two most general conclusions regarding the development of democracy are: First (and quite obviously), the process cannot be reduced to socioeconomic factors. Argentina is socially very similar to Uruguay, and—though historically even more prosperous—the broad stages of its development during the past century have been parallel. Yet the differences in the historical record of democracy in the two countries are striking. Had socioeconomic factors been decisive,

Argentina would have had a more democratic record than Uruguay, or at least one that was comparable. Second, since Uruguay was in the democratic vanguard of Latin America, regional-diffusion effects can not explain its success.[63] Even a superficial analysis of Uruguayan history is sufficient to show how political institutions developed as a direct result of internal conflicts. External influences undoubtedly existed and may have been important at the ideological level, but the dynamics acquired by Uruguay's institutional structure were unequivocally local.[64] Electoral legislation had a deliberately chosen foreign inspiration eighty years ago, for example, but nobody emphasizes this today, either inside or outside the country. When the Hondurans employed some of the characteristics of the DSV in 1985, they baptized the system *canasta uruguaya* (Uruguayan basket). The Brazilians also looked to the Uruguayan practice in creating their *sublegendas*. Even Uruguay's state enterprises, or *entes autónomos*, served as a model for other countries before World War II.

The importance of endogenous factors in Uruguayan politics may also be appreciated in the recent democratic restoration; external political factors were at most secondary to the resolution of the Uruguayan transition. Few would deny that external economic "shocks" and structural constraints contributed to the crisis of the authoritarian regime, but this is quite a different thing to saying that they determined the course and manner of the eventual transition to democracy. Perhaps the most interesting external phenomena revolved around demonstration effects and the deliberate evocation of foreign models and antimodels by political leaders. The Colorados, for instance, repeatedly stressed that their desire to compromise with the military was based on the need to avoid "Chilean-ization." The Spanish transition was equally mentioned by those members of the political elite who approved the 1984 Naval Club Pact between the Colorados, the Left, and the military. Far from evoking a simple "domino process," the overriding importance of international events lay in their deliberate appropriation and manipulation for symbolic purposes by domestic politicians.

Political culture. Uruguayans' historic aversion to extremism and preference for compromise tends to confirm the vital role of political culture in the emergence of democracy. The authoritarian interlude of the 1930s was mild by regional standards, while democracy survived under severe strains during the 1960s. In the especially difficult circumstances of the 1980 plebiscite, both civilian elites and electors showed their commitment to the democratic ethos. Furthermore, it was the popular vote in the 1982 primaries that chose the (opposition) political leaders of the transition until the 1985 inauguration of the Sanguinetti administration.

In the recent democratic transition, not only the political leaders and voters demonstrated their democratic commitment: During the 1980 plebiscite, the behavior of entrepreneurial elites was strikingly different than in Chile, where Pinochet "won" a similar but admittedly more dubious referendum.[65] Chilean entrepreneurial groups backed Pinochet massively, none of them declaring against his new constitution, which in effect called for prolonging his personalist rule. In Uruguay, the opposite occurred: While no interest associations backed the military's proposed new constitution, some individuals of high standing in the business community expressed their personal reservations about the text. One of the most criticized provisions was the stipulation that there be a single, military-approved candidate in the first elections. Indeed, the voice of the large ranchers, in particular the Rural Federation, had been critical of the military regime and its policies from an earlier stage.[66]

Civil society. The Uruguayan class structure, however much social mobility has been blocked by economic stagnation, remains among the most open in South America, and its income distribution is even today one of the most egalitarian. The middle strata remain numerous and influential, as much in urban as in rural areas, having been so since the beginning of this century. Uruguay never has had a peasantry in the sense in which the term is typically employed in Latin America. Although land tenure is significantly more unequal than in New Zealand (a country to which Uruguay is often compared), this is due, at least in part, to different production conditions (i.e., to the importance of stock-rearing in natural pasture, with relatively poor and "unimproved" soils). Hence, even quite large holdings in Uruguay produce less, and the income thus afforded provides a correspondingly more "middle-class" way of life for their owners.

What of the institutional expression of this comparatively equal society in terms of a plurality of autonomous nonstate groups? In marked distinction to most of Latin America, Uruguay's labor movement has always retained a significant degree of independence from the state, slowly evolving from its anarchist and socialist roots at the beginning of this century. Precisely because Uruguay achieved such high levels of democratic political participation early on, there was no "political space" for populism. Such a form of political mobilization of previously unincorporated masses by charismatic leaders as was to occur in Argentina under Perón, Brazil under Vargas and, indeed, in many Latin American countries, was quite simply irrelevant to Uruguay.[67] We do not find characterizing Batllism as a form of populism to be ultimately helpful, since it requires a definition of populism purely as an ideology of social compromise, without any of the political mechanisms of mobilization and incorporation by a charismatic and often authoritarian leader.[68] Neither do we see truly corporatist characteristics in Uruguay's system of pluralist interest-group representation or the militant trade-union movement.[69] Wages councils were set up for tripartite bargaining between capital, labor, and the state after 1942, yet these were based on the relative autonomy and independence of each sector. This system was possibly "neocorporatist" in the more European sense of the term, but had none of the typical Latin American characteristics of subordinate incorporation of labor into a state-created union bureaucracy by means of privileges and coercion.[70] Coherently with this interpretation, the anti-inflation policies of the increasingly authoritarian government of President Pacheco led to the abolition of the wages councils in 1968, and their replacement by avowedly technocratic wage-price fixing.

It has been stated that, in terms of ethnic and religious cleavages, Uruguay is undoubtedly the most homogeneous country in South America. Many citizens are nominally Catholic, but rather few practice their faith. Conflicts over such issues as divorce, which have only recently been solved (and not without pain) in Italy and Spain, were settled in Uruguay in the early decades of this century. On the other hand, the last civil war gave way to a tradition of tolerance and reconciliation toward the defeated. Perhaps the most delicate issue regarding this reconciliation was recently the question of the amnesty. Shortly after the inauguration of President Sanguinetti in March 1985, the National Assembly enacted legislation that permitted the immediate release of all political prisoners.

The issue of whether members of the security forces should be tried for their part in human-rights violations, however, has more recently led to great controversy. Some alleged that the military demanded immunity from prosecution at the secret talks held in the Naval Club prior to the 1984 transition; after long discussions, a law that amounts to a general amnesty was finally passed. Human-rights organizations estimate that twenty-six Uruguayans disappeared during the authoritarian regime (and perhaps five times as many Uruguayans who were living in Argentina, some of whom were probably kidnapped in internationally coordinated operations).[71] In any case, the number is sufficient to create serious tensions and bitter resentments at what many see as the lack of justice for those involved and as an unacceptable precedent that endangers democratic consolidation.

The state and political society. With regard to the structure and force of the state, Uruguay tends to constitute an ambiguous case. It is not easy to decide whether the Uruguayan state is "strongly" centralized, or its control over the economy "limited" without reference to specific criteria for comparison. The state *is* relatively centralized, perhaps not more so than those of many states of comparably modest size, or even of European democracies such as France. Recently, there have been calls for more power and resources to be allocated to local authorities. Yet, the lack of a professional bureaucratic corps and the accompanying penetration of agencies and state enterprises by almost all political parties and factions on the basis of the spoils system creates a far from monolithic structure. Needless to say, it also hampers efficiency. Similarly conflicting reflections apply to the question of state control over the economy, which *prima facie* is rather highly developed, particularly when the numbers of state employees are added to the number of citizens deriving all or part of their income from transfer payments. Tentative examination would suggest that if the state really was "excessively" centralist (which is not obvious) and its control over the economy overwhelming, the result did not seem to weaken democracy.

It should be remembered that the present size of the state and its role in the economy emerged at the same time as, or soon after, the achievement of democracy at the beginning of this century.[72] There may have been effective advantages for democracy given that the authority of the state over the national territory has been imposed since 1904,[73] and that there exist numerous intermediate social and political groups with a capacity to negotiate with the state.[74]

Party system. The country has had, until a short time ago, a two-party system with the same dominant parties: Colorados and Blancos. In the 1984 elections, their combined vote totalled 75 percent of the poll. The remaining major "party," the Broad Front, is a coalition with some of the characteristics of a political movement and would probably find it even harder to survive without the peculiarity of Uruguay's electoral legislation than would the traditional parties. There was a pronounced movement toward the Center in terms of the electoral strategies of both Colorados and the Left in the most recent and crucial elections. They were rewarded by the voters, who also showed strong support for the most centrist fractions within each party.

Both the Colorados and Blancos have been typically catch-all parties, with little ideological distance between them, and strong civic roots. In the last eighty years, they have eschewed violence as a means to resolve political conflicts; in the past fifty, they have not resorted to it even in words. The failed attempt to rise up against the 1933 institutional coup (which did not involve the military but the dissolution of Parliament by the elected president, who proceeded to rewrite the Constitution after a pact with one wing of the Blanco Party) had no equivalent in 1973 or afterward.[75] The independence of the judiciary was an obvious casualty of the authoritarian regime but has in normal times been assured in Uruguay. The press, on the other hand, is highly partisan, but independent from the state.

Political leadership. The political class has given historical proof of its abilities. César Aguiar has emphasized that, as late as 1903, the remarkable group of social, political, and economic transformations that were to dominate the first third of the century—the "first" Batllism, as it is somewhat inaccurately referred to by many—would have been impossible to predict. The masses certainly did not foresee anything like it, nor did many of the Colorados whose lukewarm acquiescence allowed Batlle to ascend to the leadership of the Colorado Party.[76] However, the balance sheet has been less positive in recent years, particularly in light of the fact that most Uruguayans did not regard the military takeover of 1973 as inevitable, but rather the product of politicians' mistakes.[77] There are no signs of a definite end to the economic stagnation that began three decades ago and has led to massive emigration.[78] This period embraces a whole generation, and as yet there are no dynamic policy innovations or even proposals addressed to reversing the trend.

Explaining Democratic Breakdowns

As we seek to explain the two democratic breakdowns, these latter two issues, stagnation and the problems of overcoming it, were present in both 1933 and 1973, albeit in different forms and intensities. The relationship between socioeconomic factors and the crisis of the democratic order is the reverse of the links between those same factors and the construction of the democratic order. Patterns of economic development do not determine the emergence of polyarchy, but rather a certain threshold below which a democratic order becomes unlikely. In other words, they are necessary but not sufficient conditions. Uruguay, in particular, appears to have had no problem in satisfying them in the period of polyarchic emergence. In a similar vein, our argument has been that social and economic factors were also necessary but not sufficient conditions for the democratic breakdown.

Apart from socioeconomic factors, our second conclusion, that of the endogenous nature of democratic development in Uruguay, must be compared to the external shocks at work in both the 1933 and 1973 crises. The former was the more clear-cut: Uruguay's 1933 coup was one of a long line following the 1929 Wall Street crash. Between 1930 and 1936, only two Latin American countries managed to retain political stability: Colombia and Costa Rica.[79] The depression was so destabilizing that in some authoritarian regimes it led to transitions to radical and democratic republics (for example, in Chile and Spain, though neither was to survive very long). The connection between the world economy and the political crisis that led to the 1973 coup is less clear in Uruguay than in some of the other Southern Cone cases of bureaucratic-authoritarianism. Yet, insofar as O'Donnell is right to see the crisis of import-substituting industrialization (which certainly did occur in Uruguay) as a function of the crisis in the forms of economic relationships between Latin America's more advanced nations and the developed world, then the economic crisis might be viewed as externally driven.[80]

The well-known argument concerning the diffusion of the ideology of national security among the armies of the hemisphere, and training by the United States at the Panama Army School of the Americas also points to the role of external factors in the breakdown of democracy.[81] Less plausible is the argument that subversion was promoted from outside (allegedly by Cuba as a Soviet proxy). Far more important than eventual supplies of arms, politicomilitary training, or money was simply the ideological impact of *guevarismo,* which did not need external organization. The real explanation for Left radicalism was rather the paroxysm of discontent, criticism, and alienation of a generation, as becomes clear on reading authors such as Costa Bonino. Whatever the precise importance of each of these external factors, the proximity in time and family resemblances of the Brazilian coup of 1964, the Argentine coups of 1966 and 1976, as well as the Chilean coup of 1973, all point to common processes rather than coincidences.[82]

In sum, the following factors, closely reflecting the analytic framework of this volume, were central to the democratic breakdown (in 1973 especially):

1. The state's failure to maintain order by democratic means
2. Ideological changes in the discourse of the military
3. Growing ideological polarization and an abandonment of belief in democracy by both Left and Right
4. Failures of political leadership and the high level of mistrust among politicians, which led the majority to act in "semiloyal" ways with regard to the democratic constitution during the crisis
5. Increasing "defensive" union militancy and mobilization, unequivocally linked, however, to the minoritarian and semiloyal Left—part of which was definitely antisystem

• SUMMARY THEORETICAL ANALYSIS •

Let us now confront the tentative propositions on democracy offered throughout this volume with the Uruguayan evidence. Those propositions state a series of conditions whose fulfilment helps "to *develop* and *sustain* democratic government" (our emphasis). "Development" and "sustenance" may be parts of a single process following the same logic, but this is not always necessarily so. If the essentials of our argument are right, by the 1950s Uruguay was a reasonably stable democratic polity. The development of Uruguayan democracy was a long process, which took about a half-century—approximately from the revolution of 1870 to the 1918 Constitution that established universal male suffrage and the secret vote. The 1933 coup appears as a mild step back at a relatively early stage of democratic consolidation. In Linz's terms, what followed the coup was reequilibration rather than restoration. The 1973 coup was an entirely different matter. It was not mild, it did not happen at an early stage of democratic consolidation, and it did not leave any democracy to reequilibrate; what came later was a real restoration. Thus, the events that led to the 1973 coup are not related to the development of democracy but to the capacity to sustain it. We have then two sources of evidence by which to test the guiding propositions of this volume: The first process was long, relatively gradual, and mainly endogenous; the second process was relatively short (its visible phase no longer than five years, 1968–1973), with an important exogenous component, and it began fifty years after the completion of the first.

Conditions favoring one of these processes do not necessarily favor the other. For example, the fractionalization of parties played a positive role in certain crucial respects during the first twenty years of the century, but a negative one in the twenty years preceding the coup. This adds further importance to the separate consideration of the two processes. Accordingly, we will proceed as follows: (1) we will consider the presence of each condition discussed below as favoring the development of democracy and first assess it with regard to the original process of democratic emergence; and (2) we will consider the opposite of each condition as favoring democratic failures and assess it with regard to the eventual breakdown of democracy. Given the nature of the evidence, we will often be forced to assess trends in variables rather than their values at any given moment. For each proposition, we will judge that it has been: (*a*) strongly supported (contradicted) if both assessments support (contradict) it; (*b*) supported (contradicted) if one of the processes supports (contradicts) it and the other does not contradict (support) it; and(*c*) ambiguous otherwise. A few of the conditions are not applicable.[83]

Political Beliefs and Motivations

The guiding hypotheses of this book regarding the role of ideas in democratic systems are borne out by this chapter. The proposition that democracy is strongest when democratic beliefs and values are shared by major social groups and strata was confirmed for the development stage. Uruguay's political culture is profoundly democratic, and there is good evidence that this contributed to the emergence of democracy. However, deeply rooted democratic values were not enough to save democracy from crisis by 1973. Nevertheless, the view that democratic values should be especially deep among the political elite was strongly confirmed by the evidence from both periods: Whereas political leaders formerly demonstrated significant commitment to democracy, there was a notable deterioration in their attitudes prior to the democratic breakdown. The importance of cultural and social institutions that reflect democratic authority patterns also emerges for the period of democratic development. On the whole, Uruguayans are not very deferential citizens and favor political participation, though again this characteristic did not prevent the apathetic acquiescence of many in the advent of military rule. The value of an ethic of public service in which corrupt personal accumulation is not a motive for political action seems to have operated historically in Uruguay and survives relatively intact. Allegations of political corruption made by the Left and the military against the traditional parties have rarely been proved, at least not at the national level. Above all, the evidence strongly confirms that the democratic system long had elite and mass legitimacy, and this cushioned it from adverse environmental shocks over many years. However, by the time of the military intervention, this legitimacy was precisely what was being exhausted.

Historical Sequences and Authenticity

Uruguay has been independent since 1828, so its form of government prior to independence is not really a relevant variable. However, two other historical factors do seem to have been important, one concerning sequence, the other authenticity. In the first place, the establishment of a competitive oligarchy in the nineteenth century gave the country valuable experience with political contestation. The fact that competitive politics predated mass participation, for example, permitted greater institutional continuity and political learning. Furthermore, Uruguay evolved many unique laws and customs, and this meant that its institutions were successfully adapted to national conditions.

Stratification

A strongly supported hypothesis of this book is that limited social inequality favors democratic development and its maintenance: A major component of the democratic breakdown was precisely the emergence of increasing inequalities and social tensions in Uruguayan society. Most of the other hypotheses regarding inequality are also supported: Economic differences are dispersed, at least in Latin American terms, while Uruguayan classes have not been polarized and have historically benefited from a rather mobile society, in which there was a comparatively large educated middle class and a strong local bourgeoisie, particularly of ranchers and merchants. By contrast, frustrated mobility aspirations and middle-class discontent seem to have played a major part in the crisis of democracy. Finally, the impact of Uruguayan land-tenure patterns is ambiguous: One cannot say that land is very evenly distributed, particularly by North American standards. Yet, despite the fact that holdings are large, landless peasants are few—largely because the past century of ranching development has led to very sparse rural settlement. Consequently, Uruguay has very few peasants at all.

Pluralism Versus Cohesion

In many ways, Uruguay exhibits a rather ideal balance between social homogeneity and civil diversity, and our hypotheses in this regard are also supported, where relevant. To take an important example, and one that distinguishes Uruguay from many other Latin American countries: Unions and other interest-articulating organizations are not state-controlled, and so-called "state corporatism" has never existed in Uruguay. Rather, there is a rich tradition of independent voluntary association among citizens in all spheres of national life, and this has often been linked to the country's democratic heritage. Cultural homogeneity appears also to have contributed to national integration, the country possessing only very small minority groups: hence, the inapplicability of those hypotheses concerning balance among subcultures, and mechanisms to provide security to segmented polities. On the other hand, Uruguay's multiclass integrative parties have often shown the value of crosscutting social cleavages in defusing political conflict. Violence and separatism ceased to be problems after the turn of this century. The fact that the last civil war was settled decisively, bringing conciliation of the defeated Blancos, clearly contributed to democratic development.

The Democratic State: Strong But Small?

The counterpart to conciliation after the civil wars was the effective establishment of state authority and capacity over the entire national territory and, interestingly, the emergence of a very centralist form of government. In Latin American terms, Uruguay developed a reasonably capable bureaucracy, though partisanship among civil servants was often blamed for inefficiency during the crisis of democracy. However, a major hypothesis of this book, regarding the value of limited state control over the economy, is not supported. There really seems no evidence that Uruguay's interventionist welfare state and venerable nationalized industries have ever sapped pluralism (however inefficient they may have been). Indeed, the hypothesis positing that state power should not be heavily centralized comes up against ambiguous evidence in Uruguay. Local authorities are formally quite weak; on the other hand, the country has been viewed by some as in effect akin to a city-state. We have already alluded to the evidence that highly developed interest group activity provided the autonomous intermediate groups that limited the overconcentration of state power.

Civilian Authority

The Uruguayan record strongly underlines the importance of ensuring that order and security be maintained by democratic means. The failure of politicians to reconcile legality and peace was a major syndrome of the crisis of democracy, in our view. The value of ensuring that the armed forces remain committed to democracy and civilian control is also strongly confirmed: This military commitment evaporated between 1968 and 1973. On the other hand, the hypothesis that the armed forces should not be dominated by one class or group is ambiguously supported by events in Uruguay. Although never elitist, the military did tend historically to be Colorados in the formative democratic period.

Avoiding Polarized Pluralism

The fundamental importance of the existence of moderate major parties is strongly supported by Uruguay's historical success with democracy, as well as by the tragic process of polarization prior to the 1973 coup. Although historically marginal, extremist parties took on much greater importance in the period of democratic crisis: At this point, the value of limited ideological and social distance among parties (which some had questioned) was also strongly confirmed. So, too, was the importance of having parties that do not sponsor or condone violence and coups, a historical blessing that also began to disappear. The positive effect of having only a moderate number of parties is also confirmed by the Uruguayan experience, and, despite the recent challenge to the two-party system, this factor continues to hold to some extent.

Representation and Respect for Law

More strongly supported is the hypothesis that no major interest should be excluded from influence in national affairs: High party "porosity" to civil society was a historic virtue of Uruguayan democracy, though unions were essentially excluded until very recently. The value of institutionalized parties is also sustained, though in Uruguay they benefit from their embedded cultural roots rather than from developed organizational capacities. Similarly sustained are the importance of lively, independent judges and a strong, democratic press—both of which were suppressed by the military.

Skilled Leaders

Uruguayan evidence strongly supports this book's emphasis on honest leadership as a crucial democratic resource. Uruguay's political leaders are skilled at forging consensus and solving problems—though they have long been more adept at building consensus than at implementing reforms. The necessity that loyal oppositions be consulted is also strongly confirmed, while the abandonment of the consensual tradition and deficiencies of leadership constituted ominous trends prior to the 1973 coup. Correspondingly, Uruguayan leaders have traditionally forsworn subversion, though again this was less true of the precoup period. Above all, Uruguayan leaders appear historically to have learnt from their errors, and this virtue would appear to have been revived by the experience of military rule.

Economic Development

Developmental stagnation has been the Achilles' heel of Uruguayan democracy, strongly bearing out the importance of sustained and well-distributed economic growth. Inability to achieve this fundamental requirement had exhausted much of the democratic system's strength by 1973. The fact that Uruguay has had few periods of authoritarian rule make the hypothesis that authoritarian regimes should ideally bequeath a healthy economy hardly applicable (though, for what it is worth, the recent experience has been the opposite).

International Factors

The hypothetical impact of external subversion is not a variable that can be tested in the Uruguayan case, in our view, since, despite military suggestions to the contrary, the democratic breakdown was almost exclusively the product of domestic processes. Uruguay also violates the dictum that countries exerting diffusion effects be democratic: Uruguay's powerful neighbors have much less history of democracy. Nor does the variable of assistance from other democracies during crises apply: Quite simply, Uruguay stood out as a democratic beacon on the continent on the basis of its own efforts. When democracy was under assault from 1968 to 1973, foreign security assistance was either irrelevant or counterproductive.

• THE DEMOCRATIC CHALLENGE OF REFORM •

Our conclusions briefly address two groups of problems that seem particularly important for the consolidation of Uruguayan democracy. In the first place, let us analyze internal factors and processes. Perhaps the most prominent feature of the twenty years preceding the 1973 coup was the failure to choose and sustain a coherent group of policies aimed at confronting the crisis, no matter what ideological sign they followed. None of the four administrations that preceded the coup could achieve this imperative.

There seems to be a certain agreement among observers—both Uruguayan and foreign—as to the fact that the principal responsibility for this state of affairs lay in the structure of the party system. The great internal fractionalization of the parties had several negative consequences. On the one hand, none of the four administrations—that is, none of the corresponding principal factions of the winning parties—attained a parliamentary majority. Apart from investing considerable time and energy trying to reach elusive legislative majorities and ward off votes of censure, governments found that the price normally consisted of diluting their policies. This was an inevitable consequence of the catch-all character of the dominant parties, and of the relatively broad ideological spectrum that both of them embraced.

These same factors usually give rise to fractions from different parties that are closer to each other in relation to the main problems of the moment than to other fractions of their respective parties. Yet, the logic of electoral competition impedes stable coalitions between fractions from different parties. It may be possible, therefore, that electoral majorities potentially capable of implementing (and legitimating) coherent policies exist, while in practice they cannot crystalize because of the intrinsic mechanics of the system. This logic would affect not only the traditional parties but the Left, too. In 1971, the Frente Amplio united groups that were decidedly antisystem and others that had social-democratic tinges, together with the Communist Party, which straddled the frontier between the two extremes. A hypothetical victory of the Frente Amplio would have probably led to a crisis not unlike that which met Chile's Popular Unity administration under Allende.

If this analysis is accurate, it is necessary to curb the fragmentation of the parties and perhaps facilitate the structural possibilities for coalitions as well.[84] A drastic way to obtain this last result, as Linz has recently pointed out, would consist of establishing a parliamentary regime.[85] This, nevertheless, seems difficult to achieve in a country with 150 years of presidentialist tradition. Sartori has suggested that electoral legislation is the main instrument to overcome the fragmentation of parties.[86] The first step in the Uruguayan case would be to eliminate the DSV.[87] What other measures could (or should) accompany this step might be open to discussion, but it seems clear that abolishing the DSV is necessarily the fundamental nucleus of any reforms.

The second group of problems to underline here concerns external factors. The magnitude of the present social and economic crisis in Uruguay is only comparable to that which led to the 1933 coup. The authoritarian regime left almost $5 billion of external debt (in a country of 3 million inhabitants and $1,800 GNP per capita), a distribution of income considerably more unequal than it was fifteen years earlier, and real wages that are approximately 60 percent of their 1968 level.[88] Which policies of the industrialized nations might contribute to strengthening the prospects for democratic restoration? In the first place, a major priority is to eliminate, or at least mitigate policies that limit exports: quotas, tariff barriers, and subsidies to competitive products. Uruguay is a much more efficient producer of meat, leather, and wool than the European Economic Community, for example, but community subsidies depress prices. European products also compete in third markets by dumping. The so-called Uruguay round of General Agreements on Tariffs and Trade (GATT) negotiations, which emerged from the Punta del Este conference, will attempt to liberalize world trade in agricultural products, though progress will be slow at best. As for U.S. protectionism, typical examples of unfortunate policies are the quotas for shoes and textiles.

Another crucial economic problem is the related one of the external debt. Only recently has it been admitted explicitly by industrialized countries that this problem has political aspects. Nobody seems to believe seriously that Uruguay can pay its debt on the present terms and with the present interest rates. Nevertheless, reasonable ways forward from the crisis have yet to appear, more than three years after the return to democracy. The ill-fated Baker plan was—at least in this sense—a step in the right direction. From a Uruguayan perspective, however, it did not look promising, in part because of the proposed linkage of rescheduling to free-market economic policies. Compared to its historical tendencies, Uruguay remains more economically *laissez faire* and noninterventionist than it was before the crisis. This is an issue on which the government already faces serious opposition in the National Assembly, making the orthodox free-market message all the less appropriate. Recently there have been signs that multilateral lending agencies are coming round to the idea of "adjustment with a human face," but the likelihood of a foreign "rescue" remains low. The most Uruguay can hope for is no further protectionism in advanced countries, and improving terms of trade. However, it may also benefit from efforts to boost regional trade flows.

What should our prognosis for the future stability of polyarchy be in a country where it is clearly highly institutionalized, but nevertheless faces very severe challenges? All of the objective social and economic problems of the 1960s have been worsened by the authoritarian regime. The failure both of radicals and the military to transform Uruguay's politics has led to the restoration of the institutional status quo ante. Already there have been serious cases of executive-legislative conflict. The military are still a force to be reckoned with, not having been defeated in the manner of their Argentine counterparts, for example. During the first year of the restored democracy, a wave of strikes paralyzed almost every sector of the economy at some point, though this was hardly surprising given the persistent, accumulated deterioration of wages. Nevertheless, we are cautiously optimistic. We do not know whether Uruguayan democracy will be able to strengthen and consolidate itself in spite of its current problems, but we do believe this is an attainable goal. A major revalorization of democracy as a necessary component of civilized life has taken place on all sides. Little else has changed in Uruguay, except for experience; but that may be enough.

• NOTES •

Charles Gillespie's research for this paper began in David Mayhew and Robert Lane's seminar at Yale in the fall of 1981. They are owed an overdue debt of gratitude for their comments. Luis González's unpublished M.A. Thesis, "La transformación del sistema político uruguayo" (Bariloche, Argentina, 1976) constitutes an even earlier source that we have drawn on in this joint effort. Our subsequent work has benefited greatly from the help of Juan Linz, Alfred Stepan, and Robert Dahl. Our field work was made possible by fellowships from the Inter-American Foundation and the Social Science Research Council.

    1. Although such measures may be criticised from a variety of viewpoints, unless they are all systematically biased in same way, the fact that they tend always to rate Uruguay highly is of some consolation. See Kenneth F. Johnson, "Research Perspectives on the Revised Fitzgibbon-Johnson Index of the Image of Political Democracy in Latin America." In *Quantitative Latin American Studies, Statistical Abstracts of Latin America*, Supplement 6, ed. James W. Wilkie and Kenneth Ruddle (Los Angeles: University of California Latin America Center Publications, 1977). Johnson favors a pure measure of political democracy, leaving out such factors as equality or development included in the original measure that he calls measures of "social democracy." Given Chile's socioeconomic handicaps, Johnson's index puts it in a more favorable light, allowing it to tie with Uruguay, in 1965, for second place behind Costa Rica. In the postscript to his book, *Polyarchy: Participation and Opposition* (New Haven, CT: Yale University Press, 1971), Robert Dahl estimated Uruguay to be a stable case of "polyarchy" as it had been operationalized. Finally, Tatu Vanhanen's more recent study awards Uruguay a similarly high score; see Vanhanen, *The Emergence of Democracy*, Commentationes Scientiarum Socialum 24 (Helsinki: Finnish Society of Sciences and Letters, 1984).

    2. Arthur S. Banks, "An Index of Socio-Economic Development, 1869–1975," *Journal of Politics* 43, no. 2 (May 1981): pp. 390–411. Other evidence of Uruguay's advanced level of development is brought out in statistics for the middle of this century ranging over such items as life expectancy, infant mortality, doctors and hospital beds, school enrolments, literacy, newspaper circulation, and ownership of telephones and automobiles. When combined in a health, education, and communication index, these data rank Uruguay ahead of all other Latin American countries in 1950 and 1960, and runner-up to Argentina in 1940 and 1970. in fact, the two countries retain many notable social (but not political) similarities. Chile ranks only between fourth and sixth in those years. See James W. Wilkie and Maj-Britt Nilsson, "Projecting the HEC (Health, Education, and Communication) Index for Latin America Back to 1940." In Wilkie and Ruddle, *Quantitative Latin American Studies*.

    3. In terms of education, the average statistics for the rest of Latin America (excluding Argentina) in the 1960s were similar to those of Uruguay in 1908. See Aldo E. Solari, Néstor Campiglia, and Germán Wettstein, *Uruguay en cifras* (Montevideo: Universidad de la República,

1966), p. 93. With regard to telephone ownership, Uruguay was ahead of countries with considerably higher per-capita GNP in 1965, and in terms of newspaper readership, it was the *fourteenth highest* out of 131 countries. See UNESCO, *Statistical Yearbook 1974,* (Paris: UNESCO, 1974); and Charles L. Taylor and Michael C. Hudson, *World Handbook of Political and Social Indicators,* 2d ed. (New Haven, CT: Yale University Press, 1972).

4. In 1933, the democratically elected president led a bloodless institutional coup against the legislature, which was briefly closed. As a result of a pact with the leader of the majority wing of the opposition, a new Constitution was enacted, which (among other toughened provisions) divided the Senate in half. Each half was assigned to the most-voted faction of the two most-voted parties. At the time of the pact, those factions, of course, were the supporters of the coup. A large part of the president's party, loyal to the progressive principles of deceased President José Batlle y Ordoñez, thereafter boycotted elections, until a later president removed the repressive constitutional features in what became known as a "good coup." At no time did the military play an active role in these events, and the level of repression experienced by the opposition was comparatively mild. See Philip B. Taylor, "The Uruguayan Coup d'Etat of 1933," *Hispanic American Historical Review* 32, no. 3 (August 1952): pp. 301–320.

5. On the plebiscite (which the government, uniquely, lost) see Luis González, "Uruguay, 1980–81: An Unexpected Opening," *Latin American Research Review* 18, no. 3 (1983): pp. 63–76.

6. We do not agree with those who apply the corporatist model to Uruguay, as for example in Martin Weinstein's *Uruguay: The Politics of Failure* (Westport, CT: Greenwood Press, 1975). A critique of Weinstein's position may be found in Charles Gillespie, "The Breakdown of Democracy in Uruguay: Alternative Political Models," Wilson Center Latin American Program, Working Paper no. 143 (Washington, D.C.: 1984).

7. Luis E. González, "Political Parties and Redemocratization in Uruguay," Wilson Center Latin American Program, Working Paper no. 163 (Washington, DC: 1985).

8. See José Pedro Barrán and Benjamín Nahum, *Historia del Uruguay rural*, 5 vols. (Montevideo: Banda Oriental, 1979–1984) by Uruguay's foremost living historians. A summary of its conclusions may also be found in their "Uruguayan Rural History," *Hispanic-American Historical Review* 64, no. 4 (1984): pp. 655–673.

9. The term "informal empire" was applied to Uruguay by Peter Winn in *El imperio informal británico en el Uruguay en el siglo XIX* (Montevideo: Banda Oriental, 1975). A useful economic history of Uruguay is M. H. J. Finch, *A Political Economy of Uruguay Since 1870* (London: MacMillan, 1981). The observation that incorporation into the world economy produced self-sustaining growth in temperate countries, because of more favorable (or less unfavorable) trends in the terms of trade, was made by Sir W. Arthur Lewis, in *The Evolution of the International Economic Order* (Princeton, NJ: Princeton University Press, 1978). This explanation is more convincing than that of theorists such as André Gunder Frank, who has suggested development was possible in those peripheral countries that lacked raw materials and were thus ignored by the predations of foreign investors.

10. This view, expressed by Alberto Zum Felde (see n. 11), ignores the fact that there were significant conservative Colorado and progressive Blanco minorities. See, for example, Carlos Zubillaga, *El radicalismo Blanco* (Montevideo: Arca, 1982).

11. Alberto Zum Felde, *Proceso histórico del Uruguay* (Montevideo: Arca, 1930, 1967). This and all other translations are by Gillespie.

12. Recently, one author has reformulated the classical Colorado view, according to which the Batllista style of development was "anticipatory," in the sense of forestalling popular pressures with reforms and redistribution of the surplus produced by the export sector. See Juan Rial, *Partidos políticos, democracia y autoritarismo*, vol. 1 (Montevideo: Banda Oriental, 1985). A debate on the implications of this thesis may be seen in Rolando Franco, "Batlle: ¿El gran responsable?" *Nueva Sociedad* 16 (1975): pp. 35–47; and an article by M. H. J. Finch that appeared in the same journal in translation with a postscript on the coup (10 [1974]: pp. 38–57). The original English version of Finch's essay was "Three Perspectives on the Crisis in Uruguay," *Journal of Latin American Studies* 3, no. 2 (1971): pp. 173–190.

13. The term was coined by Arend Lijphart in "Consociational Democracy," *World Politics* 21, no. 2 (January 1969): pp. 207–225, in order to describe democratic regimes that allow power-sharing with minorities in segmented societies rather than simple majority rule. Lijphart discusses Uruguay in *Democracy in Plural Societies* (New Haven, CT: Yale University Press, 1977). However, Uruguayan society is not really "segmented" in any reasonable sense of the word.

14. Göran Lindahl provides the best history of the first "Colegiado" in *Uruguay's New Path* (Stockholm: Universitetsforlaget, 1962). There is scant writing on subsequent periods; Philip B. Taylor's *The Government and Politics of Uruguay* (New Orleans, LA: Tulane University Press, 1960) remains a useful source. The economics of the period may be found in Julio Millot, Carlos Silva, and Lindor Silva, *El desarrollo industrial del Uruguay* (Montevideo: Universidad de la República, 1973), while the recent study of the populist politics of progressive President Luis Batlle Berres, by Germán D'Elía, *El neobatllismo* (Montevideo: Banda Oriental, 1984), similarly emphasizes the political economy of import-substituting industrialization.

15. Despite solemn protestations that the excesses of patronage were a thing of the past, a great deal of time was spent in 1985, following the inauguration of the first democratic government since the coup, agreeing on which parties, and which factions of parties, would control which agencies. Patronage, however, is not the only explanation for the attractiveness of those seats; more generally, they confer political power. The Left was given seats on certain boards for the first time.

16. One scholar who has worked on the clientelist aspects of Uruguayan traditional parties is Robert Erle Biles. See his "Political Participation in Urban Uruguay: Mixing Public and Private Ends." In *Political Participation in Latin America*, vol 2, ed. John A. Booth and Mitchell Seligson (New York: Holmes and Meier, 1978). Solari's argument is in his *El desarrollo social del Uruguay en la postguerra* (Montevideo: Alfa, 1967).

17. Of course, the arguments over whether to have a unipersonal presidency or some sort of plural executive were often based on tactical considerations, as when the Blanco leader Luis Alberto de Herrera first favored abolishing the Batllistas' "Colegiado" in 1933; then its restoration in 1951. Interestingly, though, proponents of a return to the plural executive also had an ideological motivation, insofar as they were also anxious to limit the power of a rising leader in the Colorado Party: Luis Batlle Berres. For some, his views were becoming disconcertingly socialistic and, though he did win the 1954 election, his power as leader of the collegial government was limited.

18. See Arthur P. Whitaker, *The United States and the Southern Cone* (Cambridge, MA: Harvard University Press, 1976), ch. 6. Another feature of the presidency of the later Batlle (Luis, nephew of José) was his coolness toward U.S. interests.

19. The most useful summary of Uruguay's electoral legislation regarding both the DSV (known popularly as the Lemas law) and the "closed ballot" is Alberto Pérez Pérez, *La ley de Lemas* (Montevideo: Fundación de Cultura Universitaria, 1971).

20. Principles have at times, however, come first; as when the opponents of Herrera and his support for the 1933 coup broke away from the Blanco Party to found the Independent National Party. The price for such principles was very high for the Blancos. Because of the DSV, it was not until 1958, when the independents returned to the fold, that they were able to win an election.

21. Luis González's reason for arguing that the real (and positive) source of the small number of parties in Uruguay is straight-ticket voting is that this transforms elections into near-analogies to simple majority contests. Since voters above all focus their attention on the presidential race, they frequently end up abandoning minor parties for tactical reasons when they go to the polls. See Luis González, "Political Parties and Redemocratization in Uruguay." Gillespie has not discounted the contribution DSV may make to preventing growth in the number of parties. See his "From Suspended Animation to Animated Suspension: Political Parties and the Difficult Birth of Uruguay's Transition." CIESU-Documento de Trabajo no. 94 (Montevideo, 1985), which is a revised version of a paper presented to the American Political Science Association in 1983.

22. See Dahl, *Polyarchy*, pp. 33–40.

23. See Marcelo Cavarozzi, "La crisis del orden oligárquico y la constitución del estado burgués en América Latina." Paper presented to the 15th Latin American Congress of Sociologists, Puerto Rico, 1981.

24. Marvin Alisky, "Uruguay: Economic Turmoil and Political Stability." In *Political Systems of Latin America*, ed. Martin C. Needler (New York: Van Nostrand, 1970).

25. Perhaps the most significant difference was simply the far higher level of violence in Argentina perpetrated both by guerrillas and right-wing death squads close to the security forces.

26. See Guillermo O'Donnell, "State and Alliances in Argentina," *Journal of Development Studies* 15, no. 1 (1978): pp. 3–33. The precise politicoinstitutional manifestations of the crisis in both countries were naturally rather different.

27. The phrase was coined by Darcy Ribeiro.

28. O'Donnell argues in "State and Alliances" that the prior commencement of industrialization in Argentina represented a "peaceful point in Argentine economic history." Compare this to the

similar account of Javier Villaneuva, "El origen de la industrialización argentina," *Desarrollo económico,* 12, no. 47 (October-December 1972): pp. 451–476. The Uruguayan case is discussed in Millot et al., *Desarrollo industrial.*

29. O'Donnell, "State and Alliances." Argentine productivity, however, generally stabilized at higher levels than did Uruguay's.

30. The share of ranching output exported fell from one-half in 1935–1946 to one-third in 1956–1964. See Instituto de Economía, *Proceso económico del Uruguay* (Montevideo: Universidad de la República, 1969).

31. On the problem of emigration see César Aguiar, *Uruguay: Población y desarrollo* (Montevideo: CLAEH, 1978); and his *Salario, consumo, emigración* (Montevideo: Fundación de Cultura Universitaria, 1981); and Israel Wonsewer and Ana María Teja, La emigración uruguaya 1963–1975 (Montevideo: CINVE-Banda Oriental, 1983).

32. See Charles Lewis Taylor and Michael C. Hudson, *World Handbook.* It is remarkable that the three former states experienced even more serious declines than that of the precarious North Vietnamese wartime economy.

33. See, for example, Germán Rama, "La democracia política," *Enciclopedia uruguaya* 44 (1969): pp. 67–69. This factor was reinforced by the increasingly top-heavy pyramid of age cohorts in Uruguay.

34. Carlos Filgueira, "Imbalance y movilidad en la estructura social: El caso Uruguayo," *Cuadernos de ciencias sociales* 3 (1973): p. 110.

35. This term is widely used in Latin America to refer to professionals, civil servants, teachers, and all those who depend directly or indirectly on the apparatus of the state to make their living. David Rock has defined them as "rentiers, bureaucrats and professional men." See his "Radical Populism and the Conservative Elite 1912–1930." In *Argentina in the Twentieth Century,* ed. David Rock (Pittsburgh, PA: University of Pittsburgh Press, 1975), p. 69.

36. All quotations are from Carlos Filgueira, "Burocracia y clientela: Una política de absorción de tensiones," *Cuadernos de ciencias sociales* 1 (1970): p. 105.

37. Solari, *Desarrollo social,* p. 125 (tenses slightly changed in translation).

38. Sergio L. D'Oliveira, "Uruguay y el mito de los tupamaros," *Military Review* 53, no. 4 (April 1973): pp. 25–43. Even more revealing is the account by Luis Costa Bonino, *Crisis de los partidos tradicionales y movimiento revolucionario en el Uruguay* (Montevideo: Banda Oriental, 1985).

39. The evidence is cited more fully in Charles Gillespie, "Activists and the Floating Voter: The Unheeded Lessons of Uruguay's 1982 Primaries." In *Elections and Democratization in Latin America, 1980–1985,* ed. Paul Drake and Eduardo Silva (San Diego, CA: CILAS, 1986). The radicalization of the Left as one of the "ways out" from a situation of low income among the well-educated has been repeatedly corroborated in the Latin American context. It is therefore legitimate to recognize the general correlation between education and extremism, treating it, so to speak, as a "black box," without specifying the intervening causal processes at work. It should be added, nevertheless, that the most frequent image of the processes at work in such an observed tendency—that of "relative deprivation"—is in fact an excessive and misguided simplification. Apart from merely translating personal misfortune into demands (*reivindicaciones*) and behavior that are in the end merely reactive, individualistic, and "frustrated," relative deprivation may generate a sociotropic attitudinal disposition capable of defining the individual's situation in terms of the structural problems afflicting society as a whole. This does not, to be sure, guarantee the rationality of the political behavior that may result; that is to say, the successful relation of means and ends.

40. See Solari, *Desarrollo social,* pp. 79–82.

41. See D'Oliveira, "Uruguay y el mito."

42. The point is not to suggest that IMF–backed austerity could have improved the situation but to question the possibility of coherently implementing *any* set of policies given the matrix of political constraints.

43. The crisis of the traditional parties was nevertheless relatively successfully stanched in terms of lost votes: Together, they still polled over 80 percent of the vote in 1971.

44. See Gillespie, "Breakdown of Democracy in Uruguay."

45. The military argued that in refusing to lift the immunity from prosecution of a Senator they accused of terrorist links, the Assembly was collaborating with subversion. Moderate politicians felt unable to risk setting a precedent that might easily be used against them under continuing pressure from the military.

46. It should be remembered that the CNT general strike was the major act of resistance to the

military intervention and closing of the National Assembly. From the collapse of that vain effort, to the May 1st Rally of 1983, unions were almost invisible in Uruguay, and strikes were isolated to a handful of plant stoppages. This labor quiescence stands out in comparative perspective; see Paul W. Drake, "Journeys Towards Failure: Political Parties and Labor Movements under Authoritarian Regimes in the Southern Cone and Brazil 1964–1983" (unpublished manuscript, 1983). In the early part of 1981—too late to make much difference—the regime passed a Ley de Asociaciones Profesionales very similar to the new labor law in Chile. In contrast to the previous attempt to co-opt a union movement purged of Communists, the new strategy was to forbid political strikes and allow only unfederated company unions. For a commentary on the issues involved, see Romeo Pérez, "Sindicatos y democracia," *Cuadernos del Centro Latinoamericano de Economía Humana* 20 (October-December 1981): pp. 7–13.

47. Historical details for most of the discussion of the early years of the regime are taken from François Lérin and Cristina Torres, "Les Transformations institutionelles de l'Uruguay (1973–1977)," *Problèmes d'Amérique Latine* 49, Notes et Études Documentaires 4485-6 (November 1978): pp. 9–57.

48. See Luis González, "Transición y restauración democrática." In *Uruguay y la democracia*, vol. 3, ed. Charles Gillespie et al. (Montevideo: Banda Oriental, 1985).

49. Guillermo O'Donnell's earliest treatment was *Modernization and Bureaucratic Authoritarianism* (Berkeley, CA: Institute of International Studies, 1973).

50. This ephemeral group is discussed in Edy Kaufman, *Uruguay in Transition* (New Brunswick, NJ: Transaction, 1979).

51. There exists a large literature on the economic policies of the post-1973 regime, at least compared to the relative absence of analysis of most of their other policies. See Luis González and Jorge Notaro, "Alcances de una política establizadora heterodoxa." Wilson Center Latin American Program, Working Paper no. 45 (1980); Howard Handelman, "Economic Policy and Elite Pressures in Uruguay." American University Field Staff Reports–South America no. 27 (1979), reprinted in Howard Handelman and Gary Sanders, eds., *Military Government and the Movement toward Democracy in South America* (Bloomington: Indiana University Press, 1981); Luis Macadar, *Uruguay 1974–1980: ¿Un nuevo ensayo de reajuste económico?* (Montevideo: CINVE-Banda Oriental, 1982); and Jorge Notaro, *La política económica en el Uruguay, 1968–1984* (Montevideo: CIEDUR-Banda Oriental, 1984).

52. A postmortem on the "Tablita Cambiaria" can be found in Jaime Melo and James Hanson, "The Uruguayan Experience with Liberalization and Stabilization," *Journal of Inter-American Studies and World Affairs* 25, no. 4 (November 1983): pp. 477–508.

53. David Felix has emphasized the "demonstration effect" of developed country living standards and consumption patterns as a major problem for Latin American countries. When they try to liberalize trade, they unleash a tidal wave of luxury imports. See his "On Financial Blowups and Authoritarian Regimes in Latin America." In *Latin American Political Economy*, ed. Jonathan Hartlyn and Samuel A. Morley (Boulder, CO: Westview Press, 1986).

54. For the debate among economists, see Arturo Porzecanski, "The Inflationary Impact of Repetitive Devaluation," *Journal of Development Studies* 11, no. 4 (July 1975): pp. 357–365; and the various comments, replies, and rejoinders in a subsequent issue of the same journal (13, no. 3, [April 1977]: pp. 262–271). In light of the results of the policy, more orthodox explanations of inflation seem ready to return to prominence. See Arnold Harberger, "El rol de los factores fiscales en la inflación uruguaya," *Cuadernos de economía* 12, no. 37 (December 1975): pp. 33–45.

55. See González, "Uruguay, 1980–81. The proponents of the opposing view may be read in Samuel Lichtenstejn, "Le Bloc financier dominant en Uruguay," *Amérique Latine* 5 (Paris: CETRAL, 1981); Gerónimo de Sierra, "Uruguay 1973–1980: Éléments pour un bilan des rapports entre politique économique et régime politique," *Amérique Latine* 7 (Paris: CETRAL, 1981); Unidad de Investigación Latinoamericana, *Uruguay: Dictadura y realidad nacional* (Mexico: FRESU, 1981). Horacio Martorelli offers an alternative Weberian account of the disciplining mission of authoritarian institutions as they perceive their function: see his "La maquinaria de la dictadura en la transición democrática del Uruguay." In his *Transición a la democracia* (Montevideo: Banda Oriental, 1985).

56. See Charles Gillespie, "Democradura or Reforma Pactada? Perspectives on Democratic Restoration in Uruguay." Paper presented to the World Congress of the International Political Science Association, Paris, July 1985. See also Guillermo O'Donnell, "Reflections on the Patterns of Change in the Bureaucratic-Authoritarian State," *Latin American Research Review* 13, no. 1 (1978): pp. 3–38; and his essay, co-authored with Philippe Schmitter, "Tentative Conclusions About

Uncertain Democracies." In *Transitions from Authoritarian Rule*, ed. Guillermo O'Donnell, Philippe Schmitter, and Laurence Whitehead (Baltimore, MD: Johns Hopkins University Press, 1986).

57. González has undertaken an ecological regression analysis of the plebiscite results that shows how opposition to the military split both traditional parties down the middle. See his "Uruguay, 1980–81."

58. Instead of being allowed to use their old names or numbers, each list was randomly assigned a 3-letter code by the Electoral Court.

59. Details on the results of the primaries may be found in Gillespie, "From Suspended Animation to Animated Suspension."

60. Shortly after the coup, Senator Ferreira had gone into exile, whence he conducted an unceasing campaign against the military regime and its human-rights violations. One of his major achievements was to secure an end to U.S. military aid by testimony before the Koch Committee in Congress during 1975. The military were unable to forgive him for this episode in particular.

61. Further details of the events may be found in Charles Gillespie, "Uruguay's Transition from Collegial Military-Technocratic Rule." In *Transitions from Authoritarian Rule*, ed. O'Donnell et al. The military even accepted a pro-Communist list within the Broad Front.

62. On the election results see Juan Rial, *Uruguay, elecciones de 1984: Un triunfo del centro* (Montevideo: Banda Oriental, 1985).

63. France and the United States were Uruguay's political inspiration in the early nineteenth century.

64. Uruguay did not have democratic political institutions prior to independence (largely because this came so early) and did not copy the political practices of the British, into whose "informal empire" it fell during the nineteenth century.

65. Alfred Stepan reports Gallup opinion data that clearly show a major contrast between the attitudes of the upper classes in Uruguay and Chile at this critical juncture of attempted institutionalization of the authoritarian process. In particular, a substantial majority of the Uruguayan upper classes (like the rest of society) were apparently of the view that a more open political process would be good for the economy, according to Gallup. In Chile, presumably because of the far more traumatic memory of the UP government, the upper classes reportedly held exactly the opposite views. See Stepan, "State Power and the Strength of Civil Society in the Southern Cone." In *Bringing the State Back In*, ed. Peter Evans, Dieter Rueschemeyer and Theda Skocpol (New York: Cambridge University Press, 1985): p. 327.

66. See Howard Handelman, "Economic Policy and Elite Pressure." For another interpretation, see M. H. J. Finch, "The Military Regime and Dominant Class Interests in Uruguay, 1974–1981." In *Generals in Retreat*, ed. Paul Cammack and Phil O'Brien (Manchester: Manchester University Press, 1985).

67. For a comparative analysis, see David Collier and Ruth Berins Collier, "The Initial Incorporation of the Labor Movement in Latin America: A Comparative Perspective." Paper presented to the American Political Science Association, New Orleans, September 1985.

68. We therefore differ with Carlos Zubillaga's essay, "El batllismo: Una experiencia populista," *Cuadernos del CLAEH* 27 (July-September 1983): pp. 27–57.

69. On the extraordinary range and independence of Uruguay's pressure groups, see William Berenson, "Group Politics in Uruguay: The Development, Political Activity and Effectiveness of Uruguayan Trade Associations" (Ph. D. Diss., Vanderbilt University, 1975).

70. Indeed, the autonomy of labor was such that one writer has argued that this was the principal cause of the democratic breakdown. See Howard Handelman, "Labor-Industrial Conflict and the Collapse of Uruguayan Democracy," *Journal of Inter-American Studies and World Affairs* 23, no. 4 (November 1981): pp. 371–394.

71. Twenty-six is the figure accepted by a parliamentary committee of inquiry. Most of the disappearances occurred between 1975 and 1978, long after the authoritarian regime had defeated terrorism and established complete control over public order, and a great power of surveillance over civil society, generally. On the Ley de Caducidad (Law of Limitation), which granted the military immunity, see Charles Gillespie and Miguel Arregui, "Uruguay: A Solution to the Military Question?" In *Latin America and Caribbean Contemporary Record VI*, ed. Abraham Lowenthal, (1988).

72. One of the most notable obstacles for the Tupamaros was the lack of any mountainous or wooded hinterland into which they might retreat.

73. For an exploration of these problems see Charles Gillespie, "On the Relationship Between State and Regime: Authoritarianism and Democracy in Uruguay." Paper presented to the

International Society of Americanists, Amsterdam, July 1988.

74. The existence of a plurality of autonomous social groups seems to constitute a "threshold" variable. That is, a certain minimum of such independent groups is clearly necessary, but beyond a certain point more groups may not contribute to democratic stability.

75. On the other hand, comparison between the two authoritarian governments is itself illuminating. From 1933, there arose a government that had the support of sections of both traditional parties, a *dictablanda* with nothing similar to the systematic repression of the military regime after 1973. The latter, in turn, was without major support from the country's traditional political class and had only circumstantial civilian allies.

76. The intricacies of maneuvering involved in Batlle's nomination have been recounted by Milton Vanger in *José Batlle y Ordoñez of Uruguay: The Creator of his Times* (Cambridge, MA: Harvard University Press, 1963. Reprint. Waltham, MA: Brandeis University Press, 1980).

77. Indeed, this view was also shared by the majority of seventy-two leading politicians interviewed by Charles Gillespie during 1984–1985. See his "Party Strategies and Redemocratization: Theoretical and Comparative Perspectives on the Uruguayan Case" (Ph.D. Diss., Yale University, 1987).

78. Emigration is estimated as high as 10 percent of the population.

79. Neither Colombia nor Costa Rica, of course, was democratic.

80. The oil shock came *after* the coup.

81. See Joseph Comblin, *Le Pouvoir militaire en Amérique Latine* (Paris: Jean Pierre Delarge, 1977); and Genaro Arriagada, "Ideology and Politics in the South American Military." Wilson Center Latin American Program, Working Paper, 1980. The military's own account of why they took power is found in: Uruguay, Junta de Comandantes en Jefe, *Las fuerzas armadas al Pueblo Oriental,* 2 vols. (Montevideo: Presidencia de la República 1976–1978).

82. The major similarity of the authoritarian regimes that these coups inaugurated—rule by the military as institution, rather than the delegation of power to Conservative civilians followed by a quick return to the barracks—should not hide their different subsequent paths of institutionalization and erosion. Nor should the similarities in the political forms of crisis prior to each coup be exaggerated. We have already argued that the level of threat to the existing parameters of social organization varied widely in each case, being rather lower in Uruguay than in Argentina, and far lower than in Chile, which was on the brink of social revolution at the time of the military seizure of power. It is important to bear the political dimensions of crisis in such spheres as the party system in mind if we are to make sense of the very different manners by which each authoritarian regime later gives way (or does not give way) to polyarchy once more.

83. We should add three comments about our procedure: (1) in many instances, we would have preferred a finer scale for our judgments, but this might obscure the overall picture; (2) we are certain that in spite of our efforts, time will show that we have erred in at least a few of the assessments (we have far more confidence in the broad analysis than in any of the individual judgments); (3) we shall not consider the evidence related to the present democratic restoration, whose duration has been too short—and its prospects still too arguable—to assign it the same empirical relevance as the other two periods.

84. Luis Eduardo González, "Political Structures and the Prospects for Democracy in Uruguay." (Ph.D. Diss., Yale University, May 1988).

85. Juan Linz, "Democracy, Presidential or Parliamentary, Does It Make a Difference?" Paper prepared for the workshop, Political Parties in the Southern Cone, Woodrow Wilson International Center, 1984.

86. Giovanni Sartori, *Parties and Party Systems: A Framework for Analysis* (Cambridge: Cambridge University Press, 1976).

87. This is the major argument of Luis González, "Political Parties and Redemocratization."

88. Ironically, the failure of Uruguay's authoritarian regime to reverse economic decline (despite insulation from social pressures and with favorable international support) is grounds for optimism as to the future of democracy. Youssef Cohen has argued, on the basis of a time-series–regression analysis of Argentina, Brazil, and Colombia, that bureaucratic-authoritarian regimes raised growth by "half a percent per year." See his "The Impact of Bureaucratic-Authoritarian Rule on Economic Growth," *Comparative Political Studies* 18, no. 1 (April 1985): pp. 123–136. His data, however, do not include the slump of the 1980s, nor Uruguay and Chile, and thus are quite arbitrarily selective.

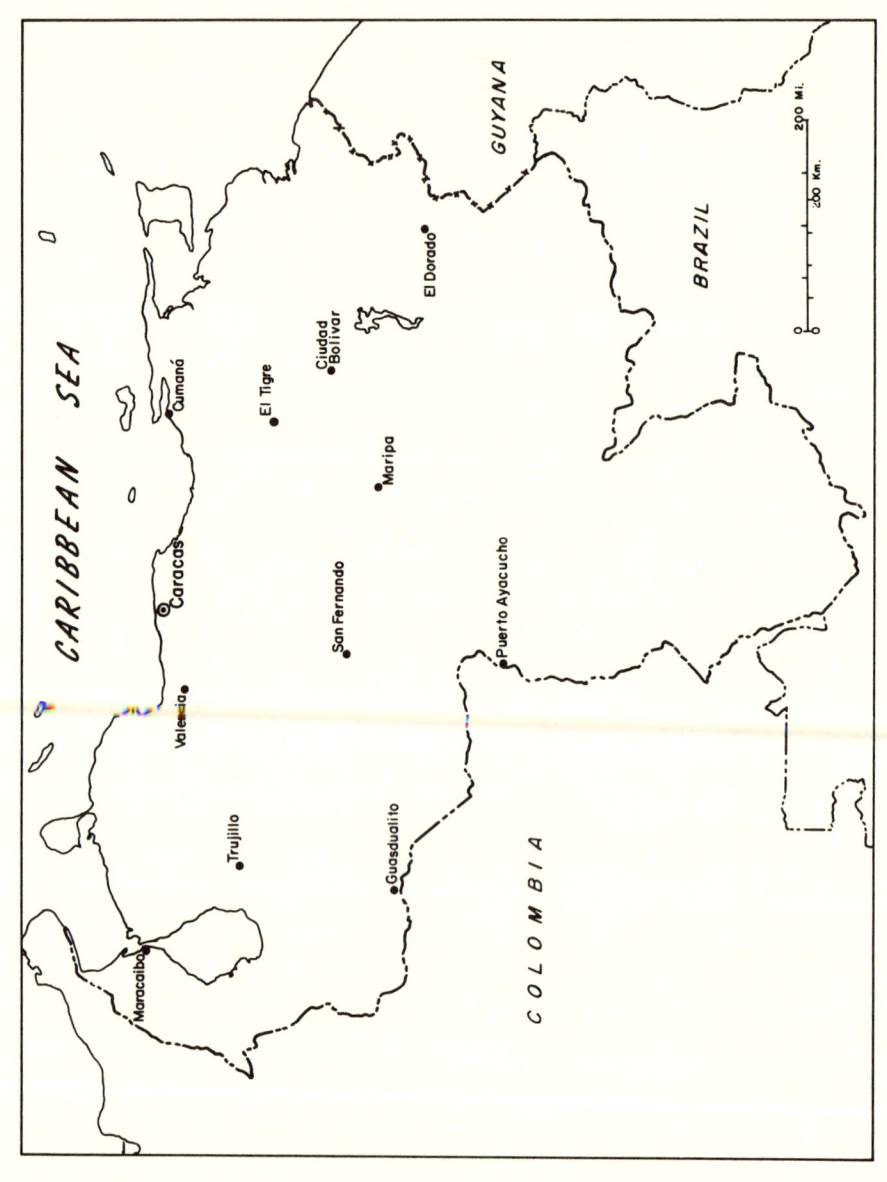

• CHAPTER SIX •
Venezuela: The Nature, Sources, and Prospects of Democracy

DANIEL H. LEVINE

To earlier generations, the phrase "Venezuelan democracy" suggested a quirky sense of humor; at best, a somewhat fragile hope for the future. But once anomalous, democracy is now the expected and customary state of affairs for Venezuelans. Long a model of dictatorship and arbitrary rule, Venezuela now displays an effective democratic political order; the oldest and most stable mass democracy in South America. Since 1958, Venezuelans have built a political system marked by high participation, strong leadership, institutional continuity, and genuine, pervasive competititon. Power has been transferred peacefully in six consecutive national elections, with the opposition party defeating and replacing the government on each of the last four occasions (1968, 1973, 1978, 1983). In a rapidly growing population characterized by youth and high mobility, new generations have been incorporated into the political system, competition established on national lines, and oppositions of Right and Left successfully isolated and defeated.

Democracy in Venezuela may be normal and expected now, but in 1958 it was a new and unaccustomed phenomenon. Before the overthrow of the last military dictatorship in January 1958, only a brief experiment with mass democracy (1945–1948) broke this century's record of authoritarian rule. Prior to 1958, elections were either highly restricted or simply fraudulent, organization curtailed, participation suppressed, and civil liberties subject to capricious violation. Secondary associations were tightly controlled, media censored, and culture-forming institutions (such as schools or churches) authoritarian in structure and projection. On foundations like these, why did democracy emerge in Venezuela; how has it changed over time; and why has it survived and prospered? Why did democracy take the specific form it did? What do its origins and characteristic structures and practices suggest about the future?

The survival and success of Venezuelan democracy are best explained by a combination of powerful mass organizations and strong, skilled leadership. The two go together, and the whole pattern makes sense in terms of the kind of society Venezuela became during this century. The deep social change that petroleum brought to Venezuela made a strong party system possible, creating both a popular base and a generation of potential leaders. Popular needs and experiences fit the goals and plans of emerging leaders very well. Together, the values and ideologies of leaders and rank-and-file Venezuelans, their shared reaction to national experience, and their ability to change creatively as the society evolved are what turned social potential into political reality.

It may be helpful to begin by clarifying a few terms. I use "democracy" as it is defined in this series, Democracy in Developing Countries: a national political system characterized by free and open elections, relatively low barriers to participation, genuine competition, and protection of civil liberties. I use "democratization" in two related senses, each with notable implications for democracy. The first is temporal: Democratization appears as a stage in the creation and maintenance of democracy. Several phases are involved, running from inauguration through consolidation to a transformation to maturity. The second sense of democratization refers to the nature of organized social life and predominant cultural orientations. Democratization here involves the creation, nurturance, and spread of more egalitarian social relations and norms of authority and leadership. These are worked out in associational life, especially through encouraging participation, developing of new sources and patterns of leadership, and generally linking group life to national politics. Ties like these undergird the formal legitimations of democracy with a generalized experience of competition and association in all walks of life, and also through the diffusion of norms of accountability.

These comments suggest that democracy in Venezuela is not well understood as the sole creation of enlightened or supposedly "modern" leaders, whose values are gradually taken up by the benighted masses. Quite the contrary: from the beginning, Venezuelan democracy has rested on an alliance of middle-class leaders with poor and peripheral groups. Throughout its history, Venezuelan democracy has been most firmly sustained by their shared commitment to democracy as a central value.

I go into such detail on the meaning of democracy and democratization because I believe that the issues must be put in positive terms.[1] Democracy is more than just the absence of authoritarianism or military rule: It has sources, dynamics and values of its own. It is particularly important to work on the concepts of democracy and democratization now, when a wave of transition to democracy throughout Latin America challenges common understandings of the process. The urgency of conceptual reassessment is magnified by the limitations and deficiencies of the theories that have dominated analysis for some time.

Over the last few decades, with only minor competition from a now largely discredited cultural determinism, and some criticism from more historically oriented institutional perspectives, scholars working with concepts of dependence and political economy have crafted a set of innovative and convincing explanations.[2] The basic ideas are familiar. The overthrow of democracy and the creation of "new authoritarianisms" was attributed to the elective affinity between an expanding security apparatus, an assertive civil-military technocratic elite, and a development strategy intended to promote capitalism on the periphery through a series of policies spurring industrialization through heavy, long-term investment.[3] Authoritarianism emerges to secure the policies; repression of the popular sector is an integral part of the package.

The problems this literature addresses stemmed above all from the appearance of authoritarianism in the most developed societies of Latin America, especially those in the Southern Cone nations of Argentina, Brazil, Uruguay, and Chile. In these unhappy cases, authoritarian rule became extreme, pervasive, and seemingly permanent in ways rarely seen before. Democracy had long been regarded as the normal concommitant of "development." In light of these theories, it became the exception, an anomaly requiring explanation.

But history did not stop there, and in recent years, these "new authoritarianisms" have decayed. Moreover, the ensuing political opening has been dominated by a traditional liberal agenda, with coalitions, elections, and civil liberties playing a central role in most cases. As scholars and politicians have geared up to assess this process, they have looked once again at the sources of authoritarian rule. In this fresh look, the presumed inevitability of authoritarianism is often played down. Instead, analysis stresses failures of political leadership and organization, which opened the way to military rule. Such failures magnified the general sense of crisis and made arguments about "national security" seem urgent and inevitable to many key groups. But, despite these concerns, democracy remains something of an "empty set" in this body of work. There is little hint of how democratic life is built in open systems, why it is valued by elites and average citizens, and of the ways in which it is reinforced in their daily practice.[4]

As the 1980s got under way, scholars began to study the "redemocratizations" or transitions to democracy occurring throughout the region. In the process, they relied on new concepts: issues of leadership, consensus, institutions, and compromise; and the autonomy of political variables—ideas quite evocative of Venezuelan experience. But, that experience is either absent from these writings or notably distorted.[5] Elsewhere, I have pointed up the significance of building norms of legitimacy, and of the autonomous role of leadership and political organization.[6] Together, these create bonds and shared loyalties between elites and mass publics, which make for enduring forms of power and, thus, make politics effective. Organizations outlive their founders in Venezuela; political commitments can be carried out because the power of strong organization makes implementation possible. Political commitments rest in fundamental ways on shared elite and mass understandings of the lessons of national history. In particular, aversion to dictatorship and fear of the consequences of weakening democracy have made prudence, caution, and willingness to compromise central to the normal politics of Venezuelan democracy at all levels.

These general comments suggest that setting Venezuelan experience against the types and scales of democracy used here yields an enormous sense of dynamism. In the course of this century, Venezuela has moved from authoritarian rule to democracy. Through these years, pressures for democracy and the social base supporting democratic initiatives have grown steadily, as Venezuela's economy, society, and culture continued to change and evolve. At issue in this process is not simply exchanging one sort of regime for another: democracy for authoritarianism. Democracy itself has changed as part of these general transformations, becoming more stable, more competitive, and steadily attuned to a changing society. In the terms used here, Venezuelan democracy has moved from instability through a period of emergent or partial stability, to stability. It has also become steadily more democratic, maintaining high levels of popular participation, while diffusing norms of openness throughout the social order.

• HISTORICAL OVERVIEW: REGIMES AND POLITICS •

The modern history of Venezuela is well documented, and only a brief account is necessary here.[7] It is noteworthy how much of the relevant history is contemporary: Many core institutions and much of the tone and character of modern Venezuelan life are of recent origin. Indeed, in the Latin American context, Venezuela stands out precisely for how little carries over from the colonial period and the nineteenth century to shape the modern scene. There are no great families whose wealth and power span the centuries. The parties that dominated nineteenth century politics left no trace at all. The development of the petroleum industry, from the 1920s on, reworked all aspects of national life: destroying agriculture; spurring massive internal migration; and funding an active state. My account therefore concentrates on this century, with special reference to the post-1936 years. It may be useful to preface the discussion of recent history with brief consideration of several aspects of colonial and nineteenth-century Venezuela, if only to clarify why they survived so little.

Colonial Venezuela was a quiet and unimportant backwater of the Spanish empire. The *audiencia* of Caracas depended, politically and administratively, on more important imperial centers in Bogotá and Mexico. The local economy was based on ranching and plantation agriculture and was generally weak and unproductive. Religion was also weak: The ecclesiastical structures of the Catholic church were largely absent in much of the territory. The colonial period did establish regional and population patterns that have persisted to the present, weighted to the primacy of the capital city and its surrounding area. It also set general relations of dependence on external trade.[8] In these regards, Venezuela differs little from the rest of Spanish America.

The independence struggles with Spain were exceptionally costly. Many campaigns were fought on Venezuelan soil, and Venezuelan soldiers took a leading role in the fighting. The most famous of these was, of course, Simón Bolívar (the Liberator), whose statue (usually equestrian) graces the vast majority of town and city plazas in Venezuela today. The Wars of Independence had several relevant effects. First, they began a series of civil wars and armed conflicts that continued throughout the nineteenth century, wrecked the basis of colonial wealth, and spurred the destruction of what passed for a local aristocracy. Continuous warfare also furthered notable administrative decay and regional fragmentation. Through the nineteenth century, the central state was, for the most part, nominal. Regional warlords held little-checked sway, and their conflicts permanently roiled national life. The role of these armed, regional *caudillos* began to fade only in this century, when a central state and permanent standing army were built after the 1920s.[9]

The long independence wars furthered the decline of Venezuelan aristocracies in another way. Once conflict was under way, masses of plainsmen (*llaneros*) emerged as a formidable cavalry and played a key role in the fighting. Troops like these arose outside the lines of authority sanctioned by the old social and political order. Their initial leader, Paez, made his peace with the old elite, but the presence of large numbers of potential military forces of popular extraction and uncertain loyalty remained a visible and deeply felt threat, erupting time and again in the nineteenth century. The most notable instance came in the Federal Wars (1858–1863), which were especially bitter and destructive.

The fighting and constant upheaval undermined traditional ties throughout rural Venezuela and sparked a process of internal migration that has continued in accelerated ways ever since. Migration initially flowed to the Andean states of Mérida, Táchira, and Trujillo, which were relatively safe havens from the violence endemic in central and plains regions. The growth of Andean states also reflected the emergence of the coffee-export economy. Coffee was well suited to the mountain slopes of the Andean region, much open land was available, and significant production got under way in the mid-nineteenth century.[10]

The accumulation of wealth, population, and power in the Andean region had great significance for the future. At the turn of the century, Venezuela was conquered by an army from the state of Táchira, led by Cipriano Castro and Juan Vicente Gómez. Not long after, the feckless Castro was maneuvered out of office by his lieutenant, Gómez, who remained in power until his death in late 1935. Burgeoning oil revenues allowed Gómez to buy weapons, build a permanent standing army, and lay the bases for the first effective central state apparatus in Venezuelan history. Military and administrative power helped Gómez destroy the enemies of the past, and close the books definitively on nineteenth-century political life.[11] Traditional political parties and military *caudillos* disappeared; political opposition and protest soon began to take new tacks, working to create mass politics and political democracy.[12]

The combination of unchecked state terror and police power with the social changes spurred by petroleum had unexpected effects. The growth of the oil industry soon began reshaping the social and economic landscape, creating new classes and social formations and spurring notable population movement. These new groups and forces had little connection to older elites, or to the social or political structures of the past. Effective repression saw to that, and thus in curious and doubtless unintended ways the Gómez autocracy laid the bases of modern political life, leaving an open field and a growing potential clientele to the organizers of new movements. Most significant among these were the university students and trade unionists who emerged first in the 1920s, and later returned from exile and prison after the dictator's death. After Gómez, political history falls easily into four periods: 1936–1945, 1945–1948, 1948–1958, and the post-1958 years. Each period has a different dynamic, with distinct organizational principles and political methods playing a central role. Table 6.1 summarizes some of the central features of each period.

Transitional Rule: 1936–1945

Gómez was followed in office by his designated successor, General Eleazar López Contreras, who had been his minister of war. López Contreras struggled effectively to keep the lid on change. He repressed incipient trade union and party organization, keeping power in the hands of the army and state machine. Politics remained closed to mass participation. López Contreras was succeeded in turn by his minister of war, General Isias Medina Angarita. Once in office, Medina began a gradual liberalization. Seeking a base of support independent from López, and perhaps influenced by the climate of democratic struggle in World War II, Medina opened the doors to union and political organization. With these changes in the air, an amalgam of groups applied for legal status, and the new party was formally constituted in September 1941 as Acción Democrática (AD; Democratic Action).

AD immediately began to build a comprehensive national party structure, pioneering in developing a new kind of political party in Venezuela: a permanent organization, existing at all levels and integrating many groups into the party structure. All major parties in Venezuela have followed this basic pattern. They are vertically integrated, with strong links binding block and neighborhood to regional and national structures. They are also horizontally integrated, with functional groups like labor, students, professionals, or peasants represented within the party organization. These groups are themselves divided by competing party groups, a state of affairs that underscores the appeal of party as a key affiliation and enhances the independent power of party leaders, who are able to play off one group against another in the name of the party as a whole.[13]

During the Medina period, AD created a vigorous, effective, and close-knit organization. Party organizers helped mobilize and set up industrial and peasant unions; by 1945, AD had defeated competitors (e.g., from the Communist Party) and generally had the upper hand in popular organization. But the limited nature of political change frustrated the party and its leaders. Although organization had indeed grown notably, the political system continued to restrict participation. Indirect elections remained the rule, there was no female suffrage, and in general mass organization yielded little in the way of effective power.

Table 6.1. Regimes, Presidents, Central Political Groups, and Basic Political Methods in Twentieth-Century Venezuela

	Regimes	President	Central Political Groups	Basic Political Methods
1903–1935	Personalist Rule	J. V. Gómez	Police/Army	Force; Terror; Bribery
1936–1945	"Transitional" Military	E. López Contreras (1936–1941) I. Medina Angarita (1943–1945)	Army/Police Bureaucracy	Intramilitary Consultation; Limited Suffrage
1945–1948	*Trienio*	Rómulo Betancourt (Provisional Government) Rómulo Gallegos (1947–1948)	Acción Democrática	Mass Parties; Election
1948–1958	Military	Junta; General Marcos Pérez Jiménez	Army/Police Bureaucracy	Intramilitary Consultation; Terror
1958–Present	Democracy	Provisional Government (1958–1959) Rómulo Betancourt (1959–1963) Raúl Leoni (1963–1968) Rafael Caldera (1969–1973) Carlos Andres Pérez (1974–1978) Luis Herrerra Campins (1979–1983) Jaime Lusinchi (1984–1989) Carlos Andres Pérez (1989–)	Acción Democrática; COPEI; Mass Organizations	Competitive Elections; Political Bargaining; Mass Suffrage

This context helps explain the party leadership's decision to join with young military officers in a conspiracy against the Medina government. They saw this as a chance to initiate rapid and far-reaching change. The coup was launched on October 18, 1945, and after a few days of fighting, a provisional junta was formed with four members from AD, two officers, and one independent civilian. The three years that followed, known in Venezuela as the *trienio,* mark the definitive introduction of mass politics into national life.

The Trienio: 1945–1948

It is hard to overstate the depth of the changes *trienio* politics brought. Organization of all kinds was encouraged and did indeed flourish, especially among labor and peasant groups. In general, barriers to participation were lowered, suffrage was made genuinely universal, extending to all citizens over eighteen, with no restrictions by education, gender, or property. The electorate expanded from 5 percent of the population before 1945 to 36 percent immediately thereafter. Free, direct elections were instituted at all levels, from municipal councils and state legislatures to the national Congress (deputies and senators), and president. New parties were also formed, most importantly the Christian democratic Comité de Organización Política Electoral Independiente (the Committee for Independent Political Organization, or COPEI) and Unión República Democrática (URD), which grouped the non-Communist left wing of forces that had backed Medina.

All sorts of services were extended for the first time to poor and peripheral groups and regions. In these ways, AD's leaders delivered on their promises, and as a result the party strengthened its mass base in spectacular and long-lasting fashion. AD dominated national politics completely, with opposition centered on the extreme Right, represented by the Catholic church, by a range of political parties, most notably COPEI, and by conservative elements in the military.

Expanded participation during the *trienio* must be set against the intense and bitter conflicts that dominated national politics. Conflict stemmed from resistance to AD's radical policies, and from fear that the new regime and its supporters would destroy the previous social order entirely. It is important to realize that while many organizations had been created after 1936, these were mainly popular in composition and radical in orientation. Economic and social elites relied on control of the army and administration to guarantee power and privilege. Popular organizations must have seemed superfluous in a system that rewarded cliques and personal influence more than the capacity to move masses. Religious leaders also failed to build organization, depending instead on nets of elite schools and the sponsorship of other power groups to guarantee their interests.

This situation meant that many sectors were threatened in symbolic and material terms by AD and its regime. There was little trust and no sense of mutual guarantees among major social and political groups. Business generally and the oil industry in particular contested policies favoring labor and restricting company profits. Rural interests resisted land reform and objected vehemently to measures promoting peasant unions and giving them a major voice in implementing rural policy. The Catholic church strongly resisted educational reforms that promoted public schools and restricted the autonomy and likely appeal of church-run institutions. Church resistance led to massive mobilizations and notable public conflict, and generally served as a lightning rod, stimulating and drawing together a broad range of antiregime groups and activities.[14]

This brief review of *trienio* politics suggests that while AD managed in these years to build and secure a mass base, at the same time the party alienated many important power factors in Venezuela. Confident in its vast electoral majorities and secure in its alliance with the military, AD largely ignored such opposition. The party did so at its peril and on November 24, 1948, fell to a military coup: the 3-year experiment in democracy gave way to a decade of bloody dictatorship.

Pérez Jiménez: 1948–1958

Under the leadership of General Marcos Pérez Jiménez, public policy was rolled back across the board: Educational, labor, and agrarian reforms were rescinded, and a new deal was reached with the oil companies, with extensive concessions for exploration arranged on very favorable terms.[15] Military government relied for its public legitimacy on an image of material progress, manifest, for example, in major public-works initiatives. Attempts were made to eliminate all political opposition through a combination of bribery, fraud, and violence. A large secret police force (Seguridad Nacional) hunted down opponents and ran notorious concentration camps.[16] AD maintained an underground organization throughout the dictatorship, supporting clandestine networks and making several frustrated attempts to assassinate military leaders. Nonetheless, as late as mid-1957, the combination of strong economic resources, a powerful police apparatus, and visible public backing by the United States made continued military rule seem a safe bet.[17]

Opposition grew dramatically from that point on, and things fell apart quickly. Several factors converged to undermine military rule. The Catholic church, which had greeted military rule in 1948 as salvation and had long supported Pérez Jiménez personally, moved swiftly to opposition. Through pastoral letters and a series of critical articles in the church's daily paper, *La religión,* Catholic leaders staked out a new position, legitimating opposition to the military among many of its hitherto firmest supporters. At the same time, a general economic downturn combined with notorious corruption (especially in public works) alienated business and stimulated public criticism by professional societies (e.g., engineers, lawyers, and the like).

Confident of his position, Pérez Jiménez called elections for December 1957, but with no warning he scrapped election plans in favor of a plebescite. There would be only one candidate for every office; all Venezuelans over eighteen and all foreigners with more than two years of residence were declared eligible voters. The plebescite was a clear affront and managed to unify and stimulate the opposition. Support within the military proved surprisingly brittle. Concern about the economy, resentment over corruption, and mingled fear of and disdain for the secret police soon resulted in a failed military coup on New Year's Day, 1958. Although the attempt was put down, the dictator's invincible image had cracked. Underground political forces, now united in a *Junta Patriótica,* mounted a wave of demonstrations and street fighting.[18] The regime collapsed in short order. Pérez Jiménez fled the country on January 23, 1958. A provisional government (under mixed military and civilian rule) took over: Elections were scheduled and held at the end of the year.

The Development of Democracy: 1958–1968

Pérez Jiménez was Venezuela's last military ruler. The democracy begun in 1958 has survived and, beyond mere survival, has changed as it has consolidated a hold on national life. Within the history of democracy, a further periodization is possible, marking off the *trienio*, the decade after 1958 (when enemies of Right and Left were isolated and defeated), and the post-1968 years of transformation to maturity. I noted earlier that *trienio* democracy was characterized by sudden change, deep penetration of the party system, and extremely bitter conflict. Political change after 1958 was driven by the particular lessons political actors chose to learn from recent experience. The overthrow of Pérez Jiménez was widely seen in Venezuela as a second chance for democracy, an opportunity to correct past mistakes and thus avoid repeating the political disasters of the *trienio*. The experience of being overthrown, and the corrupt and capricious nature of military rule had a sobering effect on democratic leaders in many camps. In AD, party elites argued that the vast electoral majorities of the 1940s had created a false sense of confidence, making the party ignore the need to bring others along. At the same time, many who had welcomed the coming of military rule (opposition parties, foreign business, and the church) also had suffered under Pérez Jiménez and now sought accommodation with AD.

Elite understandings of the *trienio* were shaped and amplified by the specific character of the transition to democracy in 1958. From the very beginning, the transition was an enterprise built on coalitions. Political parties cooperated, both underground and through pacts forged among exiled leaders. Business and professional groups joined, as did key elements in the military and in popular organizations linked to the political parties. The need to hold such diverse allies together reinforced dispositions to prudent compromise. The inauguration of democracy was relatively sudden, but though the dictator was thrown out, the military institution remained intact. Great effort was expended, in 1958 and after, to woo the officer corps, purging disloyal elements while gradually bringing new generations along. Commitment to free and open elections was present from the outset and was maintained throughout the year in which the provisional government held power.

Of course, this general strategy was not inevitable. Others, pushed, for example, by the Left, stressed the need for more thorough social and economic change and relied on mass mobilization to the exclusion of other methods. But in 1958 and after, key Venezuelan leaders correctly believed that without revolution and firm control of armed force, strategies of that kind were doomed. Moreover, they believed that even under the best of circumstances, democracy is not a likely result of these strategies. Power is either too concentrated in the party running the show (which thus becomes another dictatorship), or conflict is so exacerbated as to make survival simply impossible. Having failed with similar approaches in the past, (i.e., dominance in the *trienio*), the political class learned from experience and opted, this time, for caution.

To the political class, the recent past taught that conciliation, compromise, and prudence were both necessary and desirable if a decent, durable political order was to be built. These lessons were especially critical in the decade after 1958, when the new democracy survived its most direct and severe challenges. The lessons can be summarized as follows: (1) pacts and coalitions; (2) inter-elite consensus; (3) program limitation; (4) encouragement of participation, but controlled and channeled; and (5) exclusion of the revolutionary Left.

Alliances and coalitions were central to the 1958 transition and have remained at the core of political life ever since. A few specific examples may help drive the point home. Before the 1958 elections, the major non-Communist parties (AD, COPEI, and URD) signed two formal agreements. The first, known as the Pact of Punto Fijo, pledged the signatories to respect elections whatever the outcome, to maintain a political truce depersonalizing debate and ensuring interparty consultation on touchy matters, and to provide for sharing political responsibility and patronage. The stress on pacts and coalitions was carried forward after the elections, in coalition regimes led by AD. The party's specific coalition partners changed over time, but the orientation to coalition remained constant. Indeed, the use of coalitions extended beyond national politics to all levels of organized activity: Trade unions and secondary associations generally began choosing leaders by proportional representation, with leadership typically shared among representatives of various parties. Competition within a single group thus replaced older patterns of parallel and conflicting organizations.

The consensus sought through pacts and coalitions was both substantive and procedural. Key political forces essentially agreed to disagree—setting difficult and potentially explosive issues aside to concentrate on more manageable areas where limited, "technical" solutions could be found. Program restriction was central to the process, and its basic outlines were enshrined in a second formal agreement, the Minimum Program of Government. Here, the parties together accepted a development model based on foreign and local private capital, subsidies to the private sector, principles of compensation for any land reform, and a generally cautious approach to economic and social reform. Other key elements of these pacts and agreements aimed at defusing potential oppositions: The military got amnesty for previous abuses and a commitment to modernize equipment and upgrade salaries; the Catholic church got commitments to improved legal status, increased public subsidies, consultation on educational reform, and a general sense of security derived from Christian democratic participation in the coalition government after 1958.[19]

In all these ways, party elites deliberately set out to conciliate old enemies and thereby avoid the kind of intense and relentless opposition that had brought democratic government down in 1948. Reflection on the *trienio* drove two lessons home with special force. First, contrary to much easy rhetoric, there is almost always something left to lose. All-out opposition costs, undermining democratic practices and paving the way for coups and dictatorship. Second, dictatorship has no virtues and, in fact, is likely to prove all the more extreme and repressive in highly mobilized societies like Venezuela. The costs of political carelessness thus grow continuously and must be taken into account at every step. Rómulo Betancourt, founder of AD and president from 1959 to 1963, put it well:

> Interparty discord was kept to a minimum, and in this way leaders showed they had learned the hard lesson despotism gave to all Venezuelans. Underground, in prison, in exile, or living in precarious liberty at home, we understood that it was through the breach opened in the front of civility and culture that the conspiracy of November 24, 1948 of unmistakable regressiveness and supported by some with ingenuous good faith was able to pass—a conspiracy which overthrew the legitimate government of Rómulo Gallegos.[20]

The core agreements were political: Support democracy; band together to resist challenges to its legitimacy and survival; respect elections; and strive in general to institutionalize politics, channeling participation within democratic vehicles and arenas. This had immediate practical consequences; for example, in early clashes between the government and the Left over what counted as legitimate political methods. Specifically, Communists and their allies argued that "the streets belong to the people" and therefore could be used for demonstrations of any kind at any time. President Betancourt's reply marks a watershed in Venezuelan politics:

> The thesis that the streets belong to the people is false and demagogic. The people in abstract is an entelechy professional demagogues use to upset the social order. *The people in abstract does not exist. . . . The people are the political parties, the unions, the organized economic sectors, the professional societies, university groups.* Whenever any of these groups seeks authorization for a peaceful demonstration, there will be no difficulty in granting it. But any time uncontrolled groups go into the streets, on whatever pretext, they will be treated neither with softness nor lenience. For a country cannot live and work, acquire culture and forge riches, if it is always threatened by the surprise explosions of street violence, behind which

the ancient enemies of democracy, totalitarians of all names and colors, seek to engineer its discredit [emphasis added].[21]

Political issues and the search for operative codes of coexistence dominated elite concerns, as the political class made building legitimacy its most immediate and urgent task. As I have shown in detail elsewhere, legitimacy in this case was compounded of agreement on general principles and programs, with larger and critical doses of agreement on procedures.[22] As created in Venezuela after 1958, democracy was both a goal and a means to other unspecified ends: an open-ended set of arrangments founded on common ways of defining "politics" and appropriate political action.

The Constitution adopted in 1961 embodies many of these concepts and is the most most successful and long-lived constitution Venezuela has ever had. The nation's only other democratic constitution (1947) lasted barely one and one half years. Indeed, of the twenty-five constitutional texts adopted between 1811 and 1961, only three (1830, 1854, 1881) endured more than ten years. Of course, none of these was democratic, and most were paper constitutions, whose function, if any, was to screen the everyday practice of arbitrary and capricious governments. The 1961 Constitution is also notable for the relatively nonideological atmosphere of debates during its formulation (a striking contrast with the *trienio* Constitution of 1947) and for its consensual adoption. The Constitution focuses on creating a viable and stable democracy and devotes considerable attention to constructing equitable and workable political procedures.[23]

The overall strategy embodied in these pacts, coalitions, and documents was grounded partly in fear of renewed conflict leading to military intervention, but it also rested on the belief that a political order founded on consensus of this kind was good and proper. Of course, elites are not all there is to politics. Without followers, and especially without mediating structures to organize and mobilize the population, elites are helpless—mere claimants to power and legitimacy. After 1958, barriers to participation were dramatically lowered, and active political involvement facilitated and encouraged. A vigorous and widespread associational life pervades the Venezuelan scene. Participation is high, but, as noted, it is not chaotic or unstructured. Rather, social and political activity of all kinds is channeled through the party organizations and concentrated in a limited range of arenas, especially electoral competition.

The Left was excluded in the Venezuelan transition to democracy in several senses. The parties of the Left were deliberatedly shut out of pacts and coalitions, though they joined in consensual approval of the Constitution. Major party leaders excluded the Left in order to reassure elements in business, the church, and the military, and reconcile them to the new democracy. In any event, the commitment to incremental change embodied in the Pact of Punto Fijo and the Minimum Program of Government obviously excluded the Left's agenda of radical transformation. The Left also excluded itself. Frustrated by the shrinking outlook for major change at home and inspired by the example of the Cuban Revolution, parties on the Left came to believe that revolution was possible in Venezuela.[24] After 1960, they moved quickly to armed opposition, and Venezuela thus became the first major theater of guerrilla war in Latin America after the Cuban Revolution.

The insurrection was easily isolated and defeated. Further, in retrospect it is clear that this failed adventure was decisive in consolidating the coalitions being put together by AD. Pointing to the revolutionary Left (and beyond to Cuba), AD's leaders painted themselves as the only real hope for stability. They thus played skillfully on domestic fears while positioning Venezuela internationally as an alternative to Cuba, seeking and obtaining strong U.S. support. That support also reassured conservative elements and helped isolate diehard military groups, who on several occasions attempted coups in the years just after 1958.

The Evolution of Political Parties

The post-1958 decade was thus devoted to consolidating and defending the new democracy. This was a primary goal, more primary, for example, than any specific economic reform. It was pursued both through alliances and coalitions and through vigorous efforts to isolate and defeat enemies on Right and Left. After 1968, the political game changed considerably, but the spirit of caution and compromise, and the broad commitment to competition and democracy as good in themselves, continued to mark the political process. The 1968 elections were the high-water mark of electoral dispersion in Venezuela. Nine major parties (and countless minor groups) competed for public office, with none gaining more than 30 percent of the vote. But while competition remained high after 1968, fragmentation disappeared. Thereafter, the two dominant parties (AD and COPEI) combined to take over 80 percent of the vote and exchanged power in each subsequent election. Figure 6.1 shows the pattern of voting for president and highlights the precipitous decline of other parties after 1968.

The evolution of competition warrants separate attention. In terms of the periodization sketched out earlier, the decade after 1958 was marked by steady decline for AD, uninterrupted growth for COPEI, and the rise and fall of a number of personalist vehicles or "electoral phenomena." During these years, elections became more competitive, but this competition lacked coherence or enduring structure. There was notable danger of fragmentation and atomization of the party system. The 1968 elections were a decisive turning point. In that year, COPEI took power—the first time an opposition party had ever defeated the government and taken office in free elections. In the subsequent decade, electoral phenomena disappeared, AD rebounded, and COPEI continued to grow, peaking in the 1978 vote. Together, AD and COPEI have pushed their rivals to the political margin. Their joint competition thoroughly dominates the political scene, and the two parties have alternated in power until 1988, when AD's Carlos Andres Perez successfully sought reelection as president succeeding AD's Jaime Lusinchi. Tables 6.2 and 6.3 provide detailed results for presi-

Figure 6.2 Expansion of Electorate and Population, 1941-1983

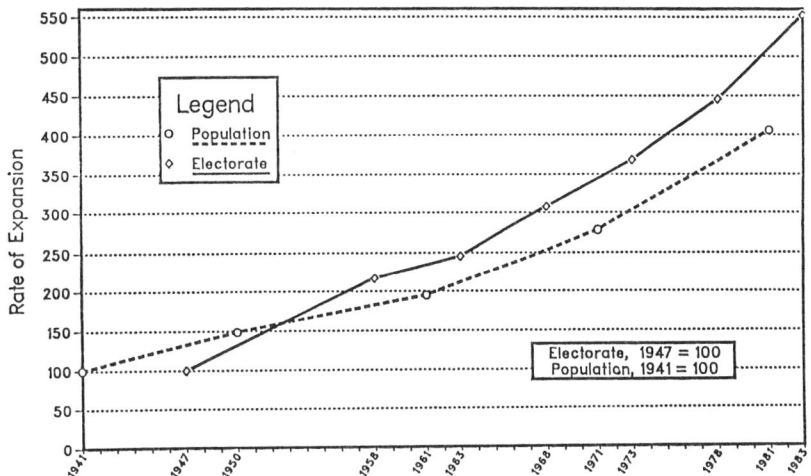

dential and legislative elections through 1983. Table 6.3 also documents the sustained high levels of voter turnout over the years. It is important to emphasize that all this took place in the context of a rapidly expanding electorate, with the number of registered voters growing in each successive election by at least 15 percent, and by margins of 31 and 25 percent in the two most recent elections.

With this account of modern political history in hand, it is appropriate now to look more closely at the nature of Venezuela's major political parties. For almost fifty years, Venezuelan politics has been dominated by AD. Since 1958, the political conflict revolved around competition between AD and COPEI. Other parties have been either short-lived personalist vehicles or permanently marginalized in minor party status.[25] For these reasons, I concentrate here on AD and COPEI and give little attention to the others.

As noted earlier, AD was founded in 1941 and soon took a leading role in the development of mass organization. The party's early base was decisively reinforced during the *trienio*, but organization and electoral predominance decayed together in the decade after 1958. Effective competition from other parties (especially COPEI) kept AD from extending its previous hegemony unchallenged to the new generations of voters now entering the electorate in large numbers. At the same time, ideological and factional disputes caused a series of damaging splits (1960, 1962, 1967) that cut deeply into AD's strength. These were mostly repaired after 1968, as successful organizational and electoral campaigns underwrote the party's remarkable rebound.[26]

COPEI was founded in 1945, as a party narrowly based on somewhat sectarian opposition to the *trienio* regime. Initially, party support was concentrated in traditionally Catholic Andean states. From these origins, COPEI has since grown into a genuinely national party able to compete effectively at every level. The party's steady growth reinforced democracy in several ways. It provided an

Table 6.2. National Results: Presidential Votes, 1947–1983 (percentages)

	AD	COPEI	URD	PCV	FND	FDP	CCN	MEP	MAS	Valid Votes Cast
1947	74.4	22.4	—	3.2	—	—	—	—	—	1,183,764
1958	49.2	15.2	30.7	3.2	—	—	—	—	—	2,610,833
1963	33.4	20.2	17.5	—	16.1	9.4	—	—	—	2,918,913
1968	28.2	29.1	—[a]	—	—[a]	—[a]	—	19.3	—	3,723,700
1973	48.7	36.7	3.1	—	0.2	1.3	—	5.1	4.3	4,375,269
1978	43.3	46.6	—	0.7	—	—	—	—	5.2	5,325,305
1983	56.9	34.6	—	—	—	—	—	3.3	4.2	6,632,374

Sources: Official election returns reported as follows: for 1947, 1958, 1963 in B. Bunimov-Parra, *Introducción a la Sociología Electoral Venezolana.* (Caracas: Editorial Arte, 1968), "Cuadros Anexos"; for 1968 in D. Myers, *Democratic Campaigning in Venezuela: Caldera's Victory* (Caracas: Editorial Natura, 1973), Appendix; for 1973 and 1978 in H. Penniman, ed., *Venezuela at the Polls* (Washington, DC: American Enterprise Institute, 1980), Appendix B. Data for 1983 from: "Los Resultados Electorales," *SIC* 461 (January 1984).

Minor parties (see n. 25) are excluded; hence percentages do not sum to 100.

[a] Coalition of URD, FND, and FDP, yielding vote of 22.3% for one candidate.

Table 6.3. National Results: Legislative Votes, 1946–1983 (percentages)

	AD	COPEI	URD	PCV	FND	FDP	CCN	MEP	MAS	Valid Votes Cast	Turnout % Registered Voters
1946[a]	78.4	13.2	4.3	3.6	—	—	—	—	—	1,402,011	86.5%
1947	70.8	20.3	4.3	3.6	—	—	—	—	—	1,183,764	—
1958	49.5	15.2	26.8	6.2	—	—	—	—	—	2,580,217	92.2%
1963	32.7	20.8	17.4	—	13.3	9.6	—	—	—	2,861,726	90.9%
1968	25.7	24.2	9.3	2.8	2.6	5.3	11.0	13.1	—	3,646,610	93.8%
1973	44.4	30.2	3.2	1.2	0.3	0.8	4.3	5.0	5.3	4,399,765	98.1%
1978	39.7	39.7	1.7	1.0	—	—	—	2.2	6.1	5,281,011	87.6%
1983	49.9	28.7	1.9	1.8	—	—	—	2.0	5.7	6,545,828	87.3%

Source: Official election returns reported as follows: for 1947, 1958, 1963 in B. Bunimov-Parra, *Introducción a la Sociología Electoral Venezolana*. (Caracas: Editorial Arte, 1968), "Cuadros Annexos"; for 1968 in D. Myers, *Democratic Campaigning in Venezuela: Caldera's Victory* (Caracas: Editorial Natura, 1973), Appendix; for 1973 and 1978 in H. Penniman, ed., *Venezuela at the Polls* (Washington, DC: American Enterprise Institute, 1980), Appendix B. Data for 1983 from: "Los Resultados Electorales," *SIC* 461 (January 1984).

Minor parties (see n. 25) are excluded; hence percentages do not sum to 100.

[a] Elections for Constituent Assembly.

alternative focus for popular mobilization, and the party's continued success showed that others could win by playing according to democracy's rules, which had long been identified with unquestioned AD hegemony. As a partner in coalition government from 1959 to 1963, and later as a loyal opposition in Congress and in the nation at large, COPEI gave solid and dependable support to the democratic system.

AD and COPEI share a few key characteristics. Each is a multiclass party, which draws a varied social base together around a central party leadership. The economic and social changes of the interwar period generated enormous social and physical mobility. AD captured these transformations, building a heterogeneous but strongly integrated base. In the next section, I show that the particular pattern of social change in Venezuela strongly enhanced the prospects for broad-ranging organizations of this kind: single-class parties have had little success. COPEI is similar in organizational structure. Indeed, of all the parties that have contested for power with AD, only COPEI has managed to build a durable popular base, drawing elements from all across the social spectrum. Both parties have permanent professional leaders, both are organized across the entire nation and at all levels, and both incorporate functional groups (like unions, students, or professional associations) as wings in the party organization. This structural trait reinforces leadership autonomy and helps explain elite success both in making pacts and coalitions and in selling them to the party faithful. Both AD and COPEI have survived their founders and passed leadership successfully to new generations. COPEI has thus far avoided the divisions that plagued AD after 1958.

To round out this brief review of political parties, consider three final points: the rise and fall of URD; the demise of personalist vehicles; and the problems of the Left. In 1958, URD was the third major party. It played a key role in clandestine opposition to military rule and was a vital coalition partner in the first two AD governments (1959–1963, 1963–1968). The party was founded during the *trienio* and soon fell under the domination of Jóvito Villalba, a former student leader and brilliant orator. Villalba brooked no rivals, and his total control of the party effectively precluded any organizational consolidation. Promising cadres were repeatedly driven out, and opportunities to build a durable organization were wasted. URD declined steadily after 1958 and, for all practical purposes, disappeared by the late 1970s. In any case, the party's strong showing in the 1958 elections (see Tables 6.2 and 6.3) was deceptive, for it rested more on the appeal of its candidate than on the force of the party. URD's candidate in that year was Admiral Wolfgang Larrazábal, the popular former head of the provisional government that had replaced Pérez Jiménez.

Larrazábal later founded his own party and, along with other popular figures, built political vehicles that attracted considerable support in the decade after 1958. But without exception, they disappeared after two elections. In any event, 1968 marks the last time such electoral phenomena played a significant role. Attempts to build similar movements failed utterly in subsequent elections, despite heavy financing and major media campaigns.

The Left comprises a variety of small parties, none of which has ever taken much more than 5 percent of the national vote. Indeed, the history of the Venezuelan Left is one of marginality and frustration. For example, the Communist Party is actually older than AD, but Communists lost the organizational struggles of the 1940s and have remained weak ever since. Leftist strength has been inflated temporarily on several occasions by divisions in AD, but these times, too, have been only fleeting. Serious divisions have also hurt the Left, most notably in 1968, when, in protest against the Soviet invasion of Czechoslovakia, a group of Communist leaders left to form an independent socialist alternative, Movimiento al Socialismo (MAS). MAS has committed itself firmly to mass organization and electoral politics, but the results have been meager thus far. Nonetheless, MAS is the only leftist party to grow between elections and seems to have built a durable place for itself in the political spectrum.

Any summary assessment of Venezuelan democracy at this point must conclude that it has been remarkably successful. In less than three decades, Venezuelans have built strong institutions, tamed the military, and combined high popular participation with social and political stability. There is also strong and universal competition and genuine respect for civil liberties.

This is not to suggest that Venezuela is some sort of earthly paradise. Substantial problems remain, most notably widespread poverty, inequality, and bureaucratic inefficiency.[27] All these stem from decisions taken, in 1958 and after, to postpone reform and avoid rocking the boat insofar as possible. They are the price party elites paid to conciliate the Right and stabilize democracy, and clearly pose a challenge to future leadership generations. But the presence of continuing problems does not invalidate the success achieved. What political order does not have unresolved challenges?

• **THEORETICAL ANALYSIS: FOUNDATIONS OF DEMOCRACY** •

Many explanations have been advanced over the years to account for the unexpected success of democracy in Venezuela. These differ in the factors they make central and in the complexity of the arguments they present. The analysis advanced here has rested thus far on political variables: the goals of leadership; leaders' ability to create and control organizations; and their skill in avoiding crises and making the best of situations. This section carries analysis beyond explicitly political variables to examine the foundations of democracy: specifically, the way in which social, economic, and cultural changes made democracy an understandable and explainable outcome in Venezulea. I begin by disposing briefly of a few common but flawed explanations: (1) money is everything—oil wealth is the true basis of democracy; (2) low demand and low participation made democracy possible, freeing elites from popular pressure; and (3) timing was critical to the success of the whole enterprise.

The vast impact of petroleum on Venezuelan politics and society is undeniable. The state depends utterly on oil revenues, and the economy and social structure are the way they are today as a result of changes beginning almost seventy years ago, and mediated through petroleum's impact on agriculture, industry, migration, city life, and popular culture.[28] All this notwithstanding, it is nonetheless false and misleading to attribute democracy's success mainly to the accident of oil money. The relative abundance petroleum underwrote has obviously helped; it is simpler to pay off and incorporate than to confront, isolate, and defeat. But, oil money makes things easier only for a while. In the long run, money alone is no panacea. Venezuela has had substantial oil income since the 1920s; democracy has flourished only since 1958. The decisions to seek political conciliation and democratic institutionalization were independent of the wealth available. After 1958, money was used in different ways.

The thesis of low demand and low participation rates is equally false. Post-1958 Venezuela is often contrasted with Allende's Chile, where very high levels of demand and activation made conciliation extremely difficult.[29] But such an analysis misreads Venezuelan experience. There has been very extensive activation, mobilization, and organized participation in Venezuelan politics since the 1940s. The open expression of such participation was repressed under Pérez Jiménez, but underground organizations remained alive and blossomed once the dictatorship was gone. Organizations were not created out of thin air in 1958. The nucleus of political parties, trade unions, peasant groups, and associations of all kinds survived military rule and nurtured popular loyalties through difficult and dangerous clandestine work. Demand and participation are simply not low in Venezuela: They are organized, mediated by strong ties to party leaders and structures. In any case, when Venezuelan leaders compare the results of their strategy of postponed demand and stress on institutionalization with the fate of Allende's Chile, they may well feel that theirs has been the better bargain.

Those stressing timing argue that the inauguration (and later consolidation) of democracy are more likely to succeed if they come before mass mobilization and particularly before severe economic crises develop. Highly organized populations hurting from economic crisis are probably not promising candidates for arguments about caution, compromise, and conciliation: Their needs are urgent and short-term. But there are problems with this analysis. Citizens do not always put short-term economic needs ahead of political values. As we shall see, available data on mass attitudes suggests that the reverse is more often true in Venezuela. Moreover, reliance on timing as an explanatory variable avoids a central issue: the role of leadership in managing situations so as to avoid crisis, or at the very least to mitigate its effects and make its burdens seem more equitable and acceptable. Politicians in Venezuela have rarely relied on timing alone: they have always worked to improve the odds for survival.

This is not a justification of pure voluntarism, but simply a recognition of reality. Venezuelan leaders worked hard to build coalitions, defeat the military, and make elections central to political life. They succeeded for many reasons, but not least among these was the high place political tasks took in their agenda. The real question is not timing or desire alone, but rather capability. What allowed leaders to turn desires into reality? The preceding historical review suggests that much of the answer lies in the character of the political parties, which reinforces elite autonomy while giving leaders viable, enduring, and far-reaching tools with which to work.

The limitations of common mythology about Venezuela are clear enough, and it is not hard to see the underlying fallacies. But this done, identification of the social bases of Venezuelan democracy remains a valid and important task. In exploring these foundations, it is vital to avoid simply listing factors. Analysis must specify how and why they go together: why this particular democracy, why here and now? Tocqueville's reflections on the link of associational life to democracy remain a useful guide:

> Is it enough to observe these things separately, or should we not discover the hidden tie which connects them? In their political associations the Americans of all conditions, minds, and ages daily acquire a general taste for association, and grow accustomed to the use of it. There they meet in large numbers, they converse, they listen to each other, and they are mutually stimulated to all sorts of undertakings. They afterwards transfer to civil life the notions they have thus acquired, and make them subservient to a thousand purposes. . . . If a certain moment in the existence of a nation be selected, it is easy to prove that political associations perturb the state, and paralyze productive industry; but take the whole life of a people, and it may perhaps be easy to demonstrate that freedom of association in political matters is favorable to the prosperity and even to the tranquility of the community.[30]

Socioeconomic Development

The social foundations of Venezuelan democracy were laid in the course of the many changes the nation has undergone in this century. Since the discovery and large-scale exploitation of petroleum just before 1920, almost every aspect of national life has altered beyond recognition. Even a thumbnail sketch brings out the enormous depth and scope of change. Over the last sixty years, the population has increased more than six times over. A nation that was overwhelmingly rural and illiterate has moved to the cities and gone to school. In 1920, almost three-quarters of the labor force worked in agriculture; by 1981, less than 15 percent. From 1941 to 1981, the literacy rate more than doubled (see Table 6.4). The population is very young (well over half are under nineteen) and increasingly urban.

National population has expanded by well over 400 percent since the census of 1936. This demographic explosion took off with force after 1941, and has resulted in striking rearrangements of population within the country. Several regions have grown with exceptional speed. Two notable instances are the Federal District (Caracas) and the surrounding central states, whose population has

Table 6.4. Selected Social and Economic Data, 1936–1981

	1936	1941	1950	1961	1971	1981
Total Population	3,364,347	3,850,771	5,034,838	7,523,999	10,721,522	15,628,954
Literacy (% literate over 10 years of age)	—	42.5	51.2	65.2	77.1	88.1
Economically Active Population by Sector (%)						
Agriculture[a]	58	51.3	40.2	29.3	20	14.5
Manufacturing	15	16	10.7	11.7	13.9	17.0
Commerce and Services	25	28.1	28.9	33.3	37.2	39.1
Proportion of GDP by Sector (%)						
Agriculture	21	—	7.9	7.0	6.9	7.0[b]
Mining and Oil	20.8	—	29.8	26.3	16.7	18.1
Manufacturing (including oil-related)	11.7	—	10.0	12.5	12.9	21.5
Construction, Power, Commerce, Services	46.5	—	52.3	54.2	64.5	53.4

Sources: Literacy and Population figures are adapted from data in the following sources: Data for 1936 and 1941 is from *Compendio estadístico de Venezuela* (Caracas: Dirección General de Estadística y Censos Nacionales, 1968), p. 10. Data for 1936 is also drawn from *Noveno censo general de población. Resúmen general de la República, Parte A*. (Caracas: Dirección General de Estadística y Censos Nacionales, 1966), pp. 12–13. Data for 1950, 1961, and 1971 is from *X censo de población y vivienda. Resúmen nacional características generales tomo II* (Caracas: Dirección General de Estadística y Censos Nacionales, 1974), p. 3. Data for 1981 is from *Informe social 1982* (Caracas: Presidencia de la República, 1983), pp. 25, 133.

Employment and GDP figures are adapted from data in the following sources: Terry Karl, *The Political Economy of Petrodollars, Oil and Democracy in Venezuela* (Ph.D. Diss., Stanford University, 1982), p. 132; James Hanson, "Cycles of Economic Growth and Structural Change Since 1950." In *Venezuela: The Democratic Experience*, ed., John Martz and David Myers (New York: Praeger, 1977, p. 68; *Encuesta de hogares por muestreo. Resúmen nacional*, Segundo Semestre, 1981 (Caracas: Oficina Central de Estadística e Informática, 1982), p. 65; and Franklin Bustillos Galvez, *Introducción a la economía venezolana* (Caracas: Libreria Editorial Salesiana, 1978), p. 128.

[a] The figure for Agriculture in 1920 was 72%.

[b] Figure here is for 1980.

risen by 730 percent and 673 percent over the same period. The Andean states, whose nineteenth-century expansion was noted earlier, have grown the slowest of any region. Fifty years ago, less than a quarter of the nation lived in the central states; by 1981, almost 40 percent called this region home, with 15% in the capital itself. In contrast, the Andean region has dropped from almost a fifth to just over 10 percent of the national total.

As a rule, cities have grown faster than rural areas, and bigger cities fastest of all. The countryside has emptied, allowing Venezuela to "solve" its peasant problem by eliminating the peasantry as a social group: There are hardly any peasants left. In the process, once-notable regional differences have blurred as improved transport, communications, and the development of national organizations and media combined to create a truly national society, culture, and market.[31]

There is general agreement that petroleum played a critical role in stimulating these changes and driving them forward. The oil industry shaped modern Venezuela in at least three ways, each of which contributed indirectly to democracy: (1) fiscal and administrative (including the consolidation of the state machine); (2) demographic and social; and (3) economic.

The most immediate and easily visible impact of the petroleum industry was on public finance. Once oil production and export got under way on a substantial scale in the 1920s, official revenue expanded tremendously, and the state was able to pay off foreign debt, stablize the currency, and underwrite an extensive bureaucracy and public-works program. Indeed, since the 1920s, Venezuelan governments have depended on rising petroleum income to solve most of their problems.[32]

As I suggested earlier, the administrative unification of the country combined with the Gómez regime's elimination of old political vehicles to make new kinds of organization possible when the dictatorship finally passed from the scene. It also set in motion and reinforced the very elements of social change that later converged to undergird democracy. With systematic public-health measures, tropical disease declined, and population began the explosive growth that has continued to the present. New roads were built, making travel easier, and the elimination of internal war allowed commerce to grow. Finally, with the growth of commerce and of the public bureaucracy, new middle classes (especially civil servants and minor professionals) began to emerge. Their sons and daughters first surfaced in student politics and later appeared as founders of the political parties.

This brief account shows how hard it is to sort out the direct and indirect effects of petroleum. In the short term, oil underwrote dictatorship by providing the money to pay for a strong state and military. But over the long haul, petroleum created the gravediggers of the old system. The complex and interrelated nature of the process is well exemplified by the fate of agriculture, and by the evolving pattern of economic change generally.

An immediate effect of the oil boom was to distort the structure of agricultural prices and investment and, thus, touch off a massive rural depression. Foreclosures and abandonment of farms were common, the concentration of landholdings was accelerated, and peasants—when not already pulled to oil camps and to the cities by tales of easy wealth—were pushed off the land in great numbers.[33] Until the twentieth century, Venezuela was an agricultural exporting country, but with the advent of petroleum, every line of agricultural production and export dropped sharply. Agriculture's share of GDP sank from over one third in the 1920s to less than one-tenth by 1950: the smallest contribution in all of Latin America.[34]

During the interwar period, times were bad throughout rural Venezuela, and older generations of leaders were discredited, eliminated by Gómez, or simply dead (at home or more likely in exile) of old age. Thus, when young party organizers went to the countryside and to the oil camps in the late 1930s, they found a ready audience. Organizations sprang up everywhere almost immediately after the death of Gómez.[35]

The decline of Venezuelan agriculture is best understood as part of a general restructuring of the national economy. Manufacturing employment increased somewhat since the 1920s, (dropping in the 1940s and then rebounding), while commerce and especially services have grown very sharply. The sectoral composition of Venezuela's GDP has also shifted notably since 1936: The primary sector (including petroleum) has dropped from more than two-fifths to just over 13 percent; the share of the secondary sector has more than doubled (11.7 to 26.5 percent); and the tertiary sector has grown slightly from 46.4 to 56.2 percent.[36]

The overall pattern reflects the emergence of an urban, service-oriented economy. It makes sense in a society that has never "taken off" industrially, relying instead on imports (ultimately paid for by oil) to fill its needs, and on semiskilled service, commerce, and construction jobs to employ its people. Oil revenues have been recycled into the economy mostly through central state expenditures. Historically, these have focused on public works and related efforts in major cities, thereby reinforcing the general trends noted here.

Party System

The political impact of these changes began some time ago and continues to the present. Three points are especially noteworthy. First, the political alliances present at democracy's creation were forged primarily between small-town, middle-class youth and the poor and dispossessed of Venezuela's periphery. These alliances clearly responded to the social changes set in motion by petroleum. But once in power, democratic regimes furthered policies that undercut their own base. The continued growth of public works and education, along with relentless urban expansion, together eliminated much of the social base of the original democratic alliance. This process created a dilemma that seemed critical by the mid-1960s: the ability of democratic political organizations to

Figure 6.1 National Results: Presidential Votes, 1947-1983

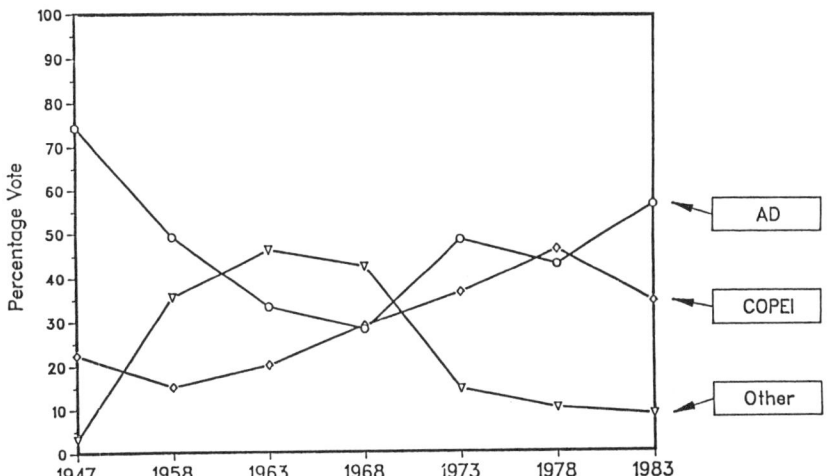

appeal to changing needs and circumstances and to incorporate new generations and groups into the political process in an orderly and enduring way.

The dilemma was solved in several ways. First, as Figure 6.2 shows, the expansion of the electorate has more than matched the growth of the population. This is no mean feat in such a young and rapidly growing country, but the effort was deliberate and consistent. Voting is easy in Venezuela, registration is simple, and barriers to participation are deliberately kept low. But numbers alone are not enough for stability and continuity: Intense organizational effort and new political tactics have also played a central role.

AD and COPEI mounted major efforts to rebuild urban structures throughout the 1960s. They succeeded through a deft combination of effective media campaigns and a careful, deliberate organizational effort. Strong national coordination and overall organizational support helped the major parties push their competitors definitively to the margins. Only AD and COPEI, with strong financial backing from business and government, were able to bear the heavy costs involved in such an effort.[37]

Another factor helps explain the consolidation of electoral politics around AD and COPEI after 1968. Recent research by Venezuelan scholars sheds light on the way partisan ties are created and transmitted over time, and helps explain the success enjoyed by the major parties. Particular stress is given to the specific conditions prevailing at the time new voters enter the electorate (at age eighteen), and also to the cumulative effect of participation in a competitive electoral system. Torres suggests that a first wave of party preferences was laid down in the 1940s and "fixed" strongly during the *trienio*.[38]

The continued inculcation of partisan identities among new voters was undermined by the interruption of open politics under Pérez Jiménez, and further hindered by the confusion and political upheaval (including guerrilla war) of national politics from about 1960 to 1965. These factors had a particularly strong effect on those not already socialized into party identification. But by 1968, accumulated experience, reinforced by new organizational strategies and tactics, began to have an impact, and electoral choice consolidated overwhelmingly around AD and COPEI.[39]

The social, economic, and demographic changes reviewed thus far have an indirect, time-lagged effect on politics. They alter the ground of political action but do not determine particular choices. Indirect effects are very salient, but direct ties between partisan choice and standard demographic traits or social cleavages are hard to establish. The two main parties are quite heterogeneous and draw on remarkably similar social bases. Differences in variables such as sex, literacy, education, income, religiosity, or region have little discernable impact on partisan choice.[40]

Electoral System

The electoral system is quite simple. It was designed to be easy to use (for a largely illiterate and inexperienced population) and has remained substantially unchanged since the 1940s. For example, the parties have long been identified with primary colors (white for AD, green for COPEI), a technique that reinforces the ease of ballot choice. Several features of the system are relevant here, most notably the actual mechanics of voting, the process of candidate selection, and the operation of proportional representation (PR).

Until 1979, when separate municipal elections were instituted, voting for public office in Venezuela occurred only once every five years. To cast a ballot, voters had to make two choices: one for president, by selecting or marking a large card with the appropriate party color or symbol; and another by repeating the operation with a small card, thereby casting a vote for the party's slate for all legislative seats. This included candidates for the Senate and Chamber of Deputies on the national level, and also for state legislative assemblies and municipal councils. Votes for president often involve a coalition of groups around the candidate of a major party; legislative votes are cast for the party alone and thus yield a more accurate reading of levels of party support. I use legislative votes for comparative purposes in this section.

The organization of the ballot and the process of candidate selection constrain voter choice in ways that magnify the power of national party leaders. Top leaders control candidate selection completely and fix the place each candidate receives on the party's slate. Since legislative seats are allocated by PR, location on the list is critical to election. These are closed lists: Voters cannot add to or alter them. Legislative voting is thus an all-or-nothing proposition. Moreover, the structure of voting centers attention on differences between the parties: The names of candidates are often little known.[41]

The transformation of Venezuelan democracy into a system dominated by competition between two heterogeneous and broadly similar political parties deserves careful attention. It is important to realize that this result is not a mere artifact of the electoral system. The kind of PR used in Venezuela allocates seats with minimal distortion and, in fact, makes it relatively easy for minor parties to gain some seats through a national quotient. In any case, the joint dominance of AD and COPEI is clearly rooted in the overall homogenization and nationalization of society and politics described earlier. A review of electoral results by region confirms the decline of regionalism noted earlier. In the seven national elections held since 1947, wherever AD was strong at the outset, it has declined and then rebounded; where it was weak it has come up. The same holds in reverse for COPEI, with the result that each party's vote is broadly similar in all regions, states, and territories. National influences dominate, and vote swings are broadly similar in all areas.[42]

Over the last three national elections, AD and COPEI have together taken a share of the vote that recalls their joint total during the *trienio*. But while *trienio* elections were wholly dominated by AD, in subsequent votes the difference between the two parties' national totals dropped steadily until 1968, when a pattern of alternating victory begins. The data in Table 6.5 show how pervasive competition has become: There are few single-party strongholds left. The decay of political regionalism is reflected in the steady drop of the standard deviation of each party's vote in states and territories, and also in the continuous decline in the standard deviation of the difference between the two. AD and COPEI thus compete evenly and in similar ways throughout the nation. The evolution of vote shares is shown graphically in Figure 6.3.

The importance of elections in Venezuela is not only a matter of their mere existence, or even of the development of a strong two-party system. More fundamentally, elections have served Venezuelans as a central arena for creating political power, legitimating authority, and gradually changing political life. I stress elections and competition so much here because they do make a difference in Venezuela and are strongly valued by elites and mass publics. The legitimate power generated through elections has made effective political decision possible; the regular participation elections provide has let Venezuelans combine high mobilization with order and continuity—no mean feat in today's world.

State Structure

A federalist terminology is one of the few visible heritages the nineteenth century left to Venezuelan political discourse. But the nomenclature of states and territories should not obscure what is in practice a highly centralized system of government and public administration. In theory, the Venezuelan state comprises a balance of powers between legislative, executive, and judicial branches, but in practical terms the executive thoroughly dominates. The 1961

Table 6.5. Competition Between AD and COPEI: Legislative Votes, 1946–1983 (percentages)

	AD–COPEI National Results		AD–COPEI Results in States and Territories					
			AD		COPEI		Difference: AD–COPEI	
	Share of Total Vote	Difference	Mean	Standard Deviation	Mean	Standard Deviation	Mean	Standard Deviation
1946	91.7	65.2	80.9	16.6	10.9	17.1	70	33.1
1947	91.1	50.5	—	—	—	—	—	—
1958	64.7	34.2	55.3	16.9	15.1	13.6	40.2	25.9
1963	53.5	11.9	37.3	11.9	21.7	13.9	15.6	21.8
1968	50	1.5	29.5	7.5	24.8	12.0	4.7	15.1
1973	74.7	14.2	47.7	7.9	28.2	6.4	19.5	10.7
1978	79.4	0.12	42.5	6.1	40.1	5.9	2.1	9.4
1983	78.6	21.2	53.2	7.4	27.9	4.9	25.3	11.3

Sources: Official election returns reported as follows: for 1947, 1958, 1963 in B. Bunimov-Parra, *Introducción a la Sociología Electoral Venezolana.* (Caracas: Editorial Arte, 1973), "Cuadros Annexos"; for 1968 in D. Myers, *Democratic Campaigning in Venezuela: Caldera's Victory* (Caracas: Editorial Natura, 1973), Appendix; for 1973 and 1978 in H. Penniman, ed., *Venezuela at the Polls* (Washington, DC: American Enterprise Institute, 1980), Appendix B. Data for 1983 from: "Los Resultados Electorales," *SIC* 461 (January 1984).

Note: There are a total of twenty-three states and territories that serve as electoral units in Venezuela. Only incomplete returns were reported at this level for the 1947 election.

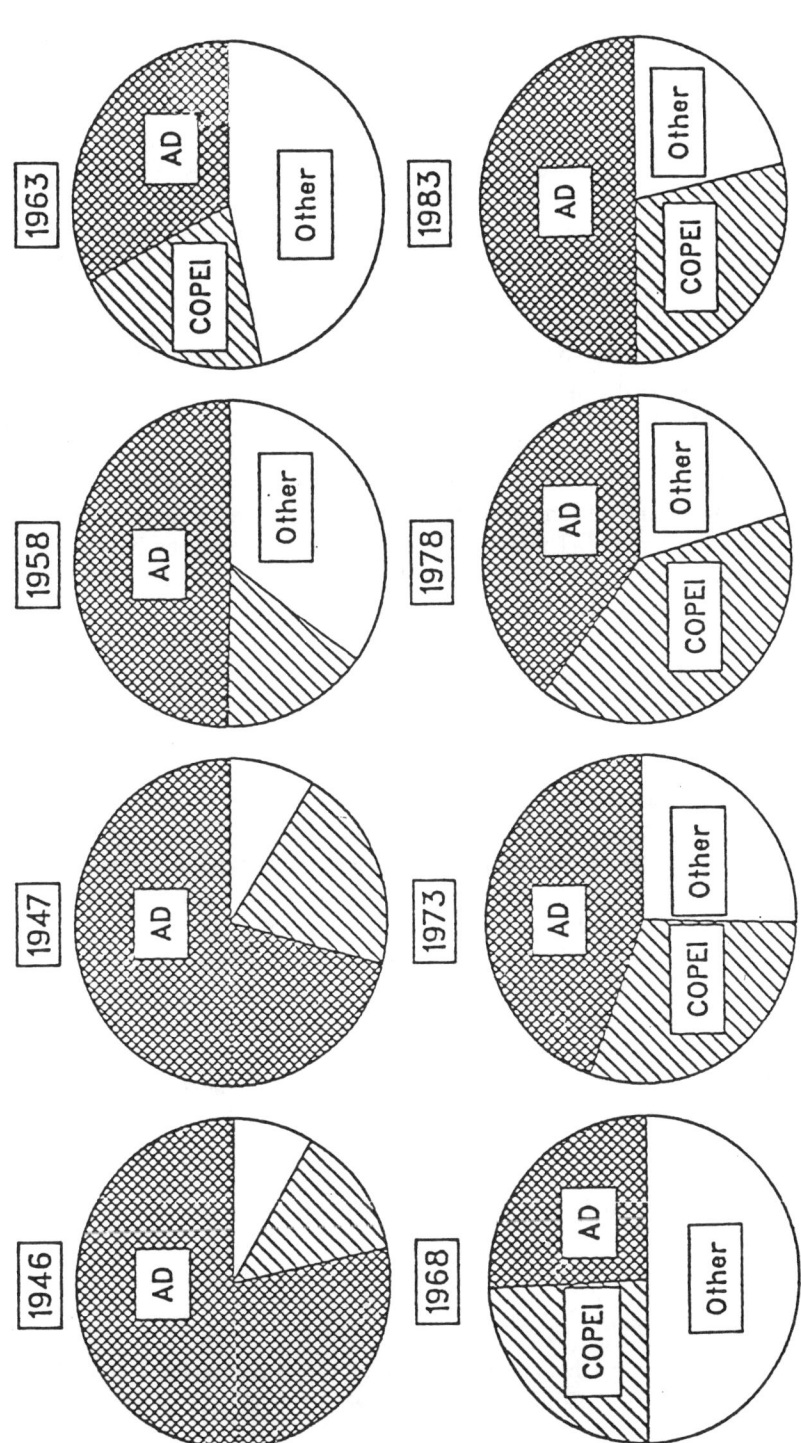

Figure 6.3 National Results: Share of Legislative Votes, 1946-1983

Constitution continued the tradition of a very strong presidency, providing considerable decree powers and a capacity to suspend particular portions of the Constitution, for example, those specifying political or economic rights.[43]

In the national Congress and state assemblies, strong party organization and the power of party discipline bind executive and legislative branches together.[44] Ordinary legislative work is structured around party *fracciones*, chaired by representatives from the party organization. Committees are weak and have few resources with which to sustain an independent position or craft initiatives on their own. States and cities have little autonomy and practically no independent revenues. Further, despite the creation of a series of regional planning organizations, with rare exceptions these have had limited authority and scarce operating resources.

The Venezuelan state has long depended on taxes from the external sector to support its activities. In the nineteenth century, tariffs were the main source of government income, and were regularly mortgaged to secure foreign loans. But, tariff and customs revenues were tiny compared with the income petroleum has brought. Through the modern period, oil money has underwritten growing, and now thorough, fiscal domination by central authorities.[45]

One especially notable way such funds have augmented central state power is by providing the fiscal basis for a series of state corporations and public enterprises. These have grown steadily throughout the democratic period and have given public authorities a set of tools with which to shape economic development, subsidize private capital, pay off political allies, and co-opt enemies. Through a broad range of public or semi-public corporations, the state now holds substantial interests throughout the economy, from agriculture and petroleum to electricity, transport, and tourism.[46]

Governors and mayors are appointed by national political authorities, and, as we have seen, electoral arrangements subordinate local and state contests to national trends and organizational decisions. In recent years, this overwhelming centralization of administrative and political life has stirred much critical commentary in Venezuela. A number of reforms were implemented in 1979 in hopes of promoting popular participation and active citizen involvement in local affairs. These gave greater independence to cities and made municipal elections independent of national voting for the first time since 1958. Municipal elections are now held at a different time. More recently, a Presidential Commission for the Reform of the State was established, charged with crafting proposals to improve public administration and promote citizen involvement in ways that would make Venezuelan democracy more efficient, more accountable, and ultimately more participatory.[47]

Social Cleavages

As we have seen, there is no simple, one-to-one relation between social cleavages and political affiliation. Further, there are no politically significant racial, ethnic, or linguistic splits in Venezuela. Strong religious loyalties may have characterized AD's most vigorous opponents during the *trienio*, but religion is no longer a distinguishing factor in political life. There are also no major religious minorities. Once-powerful regional differences have washed out with the nationalization of the economy, culture, and politics.

Regionalism is of interest here to the extent that regional differences historically encapsulated other dimensions. The initial democratic alliance is a good example: The marriage between small-town youth and the poor masses of the nation's periphery is best understood as a convergence of social groups, not regions. The process is commonly misrepresented by observers who find it anomalous that poor and illiterate people should support democracy in equal or greater measure than do dominant classes.[48] However, it is clear that the poor and dispossessed were present at the creation of democracy and have remained among its firmest backers all along. A similar fallacy underlies a common radical critique, which paints Venezuelan parties as "hegemonic agents," whose primary role is to socialize subordinate classes into the values held by the powerful and, thus, sustain reformist politics and capitalist patterns of development.[49] Why assume that values of this kind appeal only to dominant classes and can only take hold among the poor by manipulation or trickery? There is no reason at all.

Underlying this critique is perplexity over the long-term weakness of independent class organization in Venezuela, and, in particular, the failure of single-class (especially working-class) political parties. But, as we have seen, the specific patterns of Venezuelan social and economic change made heterogeneous political parties especially viable. The party system created out of these transformations has furthered the development of crosscutting cleavages, which over the long haul have helped mitigate political conflict and, thus, contributed to democracy's eventual consolidation.

Has democracy brought democratization, in the sense of greater equity and participation? The extent of democratization in Venezuela in these terms must be assessed in the context of notable continuing social and economic inequalities and strong class barriers. If average people remain very poor and thus heavily dependent on government and party leaders, what does this suggest about the substance of their democratic commitments and practices? Are they (and we) simply victims of an illusion? I do not think so, and in any event, great care is needed in analysis. There is considerable evidence that poor Venezuelans use partisan activity instrumentally. Party organizations are key brokers of jobs and material goods and give average people access to much-needed help, goods, and services.[50] This should come as no surprise; brokerage and influence mediation are what parties do everywhere. Moreover, some dependence of followers on leaders is surely inevitable. In any event, competition and relatively low barriers to organization and action have kept parties and associational life lively and vigorous.[51] Combined with elite and popular commitments to democracy, and with a strong commitment to civil liberties, this has prevented strong leadership from turning into little more than exploitative manipulation. Competition keeps the system open; mass participation keeps it responsive; civil liberties keep it honest.

Political Culture and Associational Life

The Venezuelan mass public places a great value on democracy. Available survey data show consistently strong support for democracy as a political system, and also for the procedural norms and principles of legitimacy on which it is founded.[52] Elections are widely acknowledged as the most legitimate path for political change; there is broad rejection of military or single-party rule and strong support for criticism by opposition parties. Although criticism of governments (as inept or corrupt) increased sharply in recent years, this has no clear impact on evaluations of democracy generally. Discontent with specific policies or leaders is transformed politically into a "throw the rascals out" position.

The data on mass attitudes provide an interesting match with elite values and practices. Elites also stress procedural consensus, compromise, conciliation, and restraint. They recognize limits to action and extend mutual guarantees. Even at the worst moments of the early 1960s, when democratic regimes were threatened both by military coups and guerrilla insurrection, the right of opponents to seek and assume power through elections was acknowledged, and extreme or paranoid views of the opposition were notably absent.[53]

Recent experience suggests that these values remain widespread today. In January 1983, I attended a symposium on the twenty-fifth anniversary of the overthrow of military rule. Academics and politicians gathered in Caracas to discuss the sources and future prospects of democracy. I came to the symposium directly from field work in peasant communities of the western mountains, a guerrilla stronghold during the early 1960s. Among peasants and party leaders alike, I found a common stress on the need for caution, compromise, and conciliation. Politics is taken as the art of the possible in very concrete ways throughout Venezuelan society. There is a keen sense of the limits of what politics can achieve. In particular, there is broad agreement that attempts to get all one's goals, all at once, inevitably lead to disaster by raising stakes, hardening positions, and intensifying conflict beyond any hope of settlement without institutional breakdown. Caution remains the general watchword. Elites and mass publics alike thus take politics as a primary value, and ground legitimacy in conformity to specific procedural norms—above all, elections, civil liberties, and free organization.

All too often, analysis ends here. A collection of values and attitudes is noted, its links to politics are outlined in general terms, and the whole package is labeled "political culture." Such an approach is too static and rests on untenable assumptions about cultural persistence, homogeneity, and impact. As social and economic formations change, cultures also change. Moreover, the link between culture and politics is neither unilinear nor absolutely determining.

Societies and political systems are not passive captives of the culture they inherit: They evolve and change together.

The burden of my argument throughout this chapter has been to establish the independent role of political choices and institutions in shaping change. Obviously, the petroleum industry helped build the modern state, but it is policy decisions taken within that state apparatus that stimulated further demographic, social, cultural, and economic transformations. Mass publics were available and open to new experiences, but deliberate political choices were required to institutionalize this activity, above all through secondary associations, parties, and elections. It is this *linkage* that makes democracy's characteristic principles of legitimacy resonate in all walks of life. Tocqueville's comments on the links between political and civil association are worth quoting at length:

> Civil associations, therefore, facilitate political association, but on the other hand, political association singularly strengthens and improves association for civil purposes. . . . [P]olitical life makes the love and practice of association more general; it imparts a desire of union, and teaches the means of combination to numbers of men who would have always lived apart. . . . Political associations may therefore be considered as large free schools, where all the members of the community go to learn the general theory of association.
>
> But even if political association did not directly contribute to the progress of civil association, to destroy the former would be to impair the latter. When citizens can only meet in public for certain purposes, they regard such meetings as a strange proceeding of rare occurrence, and they rarely think at all about it. When they are allowed to meet freely for all purposes, they ultimately look upon public association as the universal, or in a manner, the sole means which men can employ to accomplish the different purposes they may have in view. Every new want constantly revives the notion. The art of association then becomes, as I have said before, the mother of action, studied and applied by all.[54]

Tocqueville's reflections suggest that if we are to understand the relation between cultural formations and political practice, analysis must take ideas not as some kind of disembodied mental stuff, but rather as norms, concepts, and ways of seeing and making sense of the world, which are part of the fabric of everyday life and routine. They emerge in contexts created by institutions, they are shaped by experience, and they gain organized power through their links to social structure—to the needs and agendas of concrete classes and groups. Institutions are more than just collections of formal legal arrangements. They provide a ground for action as it is experienced, giving members a range of material and symbolic resources, identities, and loyalties, which together shape the meaning and direction of events. Thus, as we stretch common ideas about culture, we must also expand conventional notions about politics beyond the data of parties and government to include the quality of of associational life, and its complex ties with the "high politics" of the nation.

Linkages of this kind provide a concrete basis for the diffusion of shared norms about leadership and legitimate political action. Recall Tocqueville's stress on how free politics and free associational life reinforce one another. It is important to realize that his arguments do not rest on a simple analogy between experiences at different levels, nor does he assume a unilinear causal relation among them. Rather, Tocqueville suggests that associational life elicits and nurtures new sources of leadership and also reinforces general legitimating principles like competition, accountability, and the validity of elections in ordinary practice.

How can associational life in Venezuela be linked clearly, without distortion or romanticization, to the high politics of the state and the political parties? I do not suggest that associations in Venezuela are models of participatory democracy. Nor do I believe that small-group democracy is necessary to maintain democratic politics on the national level. My thesis is more modest and concrete: Associational life flourishes in Venezuela, and the operational norms of most associations are modeled on those common in the political system. Competitive elections are standard practice, the rights of opposition are generally respected, and opposition representatives commonly share in group governance through proportional representation. In all these ways, organizational life reflects and reinforces more general political principles.

Not long ago, I carried out field research on new organizations in Venezuela, especially community groups and cooperatives in peasant and poor urban areas. The general encouragement of associational life helps make experience in group activities self-sustaining and elicits new leaders from hitherto passive populations. Untapped capacities for organization and self-expression are drawn out and then given a chance to spill over from the confines of group life to empower activities in other areas. Such groups take their operative norms from the political system at large and then apply them to the ordinary practice of group life. When I asked one cooperative member how leaders were chosen, his answer was simple and direct: "The group itself chooses through secret voting in a meeting, just like in any election. We choose the most fit."[55]

International Factors

The discussion thus far has pointed up a number of ways in which international factors have helped shape the form, development, and character of Venezuelan democracy. International influences have been both direct and indirect, and manifested through economic, cultural, political, and military mediations.

Venezuela's economy has long been oriented to production for export. As a result, the nature of world markets and the demand for Venezuela's products have played a key role in shaping the development of the national economy, social structure, and political life. The multifaceted impact of petroleum is a particularly telling instance of this general relationship. As we have seen, petroleum underwrote the modern state and set in motion the social and economic changes that lie at the heart of modern Venezuelan life.

Explicitly political and military influences—above all from the United States—have also been noteworthy. As noted earlier, the Eisenhower administration backed the Pérez Jiménez regime strongly. This position stemmed from a general belief that military rule provided the best guarantees for U.S. economic and strategic interests in the area. All this left a bitter taste in Venezuela and contributed strongly to Vice President Richard Nixon's hostile reception in Caracas in early May 1958.[56] U.S. policy changed notably under the Kennedy administration. The new democracy got strong political and diplomatic backing from the United States. This support helped allay conservative fears and restrain potential military conspirators, above all during the shaky early years of the Rómulo Betancourt government.

U.S. fear of the Cuban Revolution was also important. Betancourt and his party had long been firmly anti-Communist, but Fidel Castro's emergence as a radical leader helped them distinguish their program and general orientation all the more firmly from those on the Left. Cuba provided a convenient foil, a telling argument for swaying potential allies. When the likely alternative to AD was no longer the military, but rather something like Castro and his revolution, AD must have seemed considerably more acceptable to conservatives, both at home and in the United States. In any case, under Kennedy, the United States bet heavily on democracy in Venezuela, the kind of bet later administrations have made all too rarely elsewhere in Latin America.

• FUTURE PROSPECTS •

How can the success of Venezuelan democracy be explained in ways that shed light on its own future, and on the implications Venezulean experience holds for other countries? As a beginning, consider that in building a stable democracy, Venezuelans have successfully addressed a series of difficult challenges. For just two of the most noteworthy examples, recall the early isolation and defeat of military oppositions from Right and Left, and the strong move to a two-party system after 1968, which laid to rest fears of party atomization, vote dispersion, and political fragmentation.

My analysis has attributed success above all to the combination of strong party organization, effective leadership, and an evolving democratic political culture. Earlier, I criticized the common notion that Venezuelan democracy rests primarily on the availability of easy money from petroleum. Those earlier comments notwithstanding, it is important to note that most of modern Venezuelan experience with democratic politics has come in the context of an expanding economy, where the central state has enjoyed steady and ever-increasing revenues. Genuine scarcity has been rare.

This review points up at least three potential problems for the future: maintaining organizational strength; transmitting political norms of conciliation and compromise to new leadership generations; and dealing effectively with the ups and downs of the international economy, on which Venezuela depends so heavily. I have already noted the major parties' successful organizational adaptations and pointed out that new leadership generations have taken over in both AD and COPEI, allowing the parties to outlive their founders. The matter of norms and economic policy may be illustrated through a brief look at how the economic crisis of the 1980s has been addressed thus far.

The roots of this crisis lie in the collapse of world oil demand and prices in the early 1980s. The sudden drop in prices for Venezuela's key product brought devaluation, economic stagnation, and a major spurt in unemployment. The enormous oil-price boom of the previous decade had not been an unmixed blessing. There was simply more income than could be absorbed and put to use in any productive way, and the result was extensive scandal and corruption, inflation, and a series of grandiose development plans and spectacularly unproductive investments. The whole process was underwritten by considerable foreign borrowing.[57] Thus, when the bubble finally burst, Venezuela was left not only with expensive and unfinished projects, inflation and unemployment, but also with a heavy burden of private and public international debt.

Dealing with the crisis has been difficult, but thus far the process points up some of Venezuelan democracy's most characteristic strengths. First, instead of rejecting the political system as a whole, voters ousted the administration in power, sending COPEI down to crashing defeat in the 1983 elections. AD came to office facing a very difficult situation but was buoyed by strong support and a mandate for economic and administrative reform. From the outset, the Lusinchi administration began implementing familiar strategies of pacts and coalitions, calling on business and labor to share the costs of required economic adjustments. Pacts included wage and price controls, and a search for guarantees of involvement in economic decisionmaking for major groups. Coalitions were not formalized on the level of cabinet or public administration but nonetheless drew various parties together in regular consultation. Further, it is remarkable that throughout this difficult period, as we have seen, complex proposals for the reform of the state have been advanced, all intended to extend and perfect democracy, not replace it with some hypothetically more efficient form of authoritarian management. Particular governments or policies may be questioned, but democracy as such retains support that is both wide and deep. Further research is needed to detail the intergenerational transfer of norms in the political elite, but these are hopeful signs.

What does all this add up to in policy terms? On the basis of Venezuelan experience, what lessons can be learned, which specific groups promoted, which paths explored? I have stressed the role of strong parties, effective leadership, and dispositions to conciliation and compromise. But extracting reproducible "lessons" from Venezuelan experience is difficult. Structures and strategies cannot simply be transplanted in a mechanical way from one setting to another. Without real social bases and commitments that make sense in context, they are likely to produce little but frustration and failure.

In any event, social and political systems of this kind cannot be created by fiat. Attempts to build parties by decree will produce just empty shells with no power to move the population. Parties of this kind collapse at the first sign of trouble or simply disappear once a particular sponsoring leader passes from the scene. The short and unlamented life of the much-vaunted organizations created by the Peruvian military, after 1968, are a good case in point. The same holds true for pacts and coalitions. Making pacts in a mechanical fashion will surely fail without prior agreement that pacts should be honored, and that compromise and coalitions are proper ways of arranging the business of political life.

I noted at the beginning of this chapter that Venezuela's transition to democracy preceded the current wave of change in Latin America and has led to a remarkably durable and resilient political system. What lessons, if any, does this experience hold for other countries hoping to create or rebuild their own democracies on solid and enduring grounds? Consider once again the main lines of the 1958 transition: It was relatively sudden and without a great deal of violence; the military institution remained intact; and the whole process was managed in a conservative direction by coalitions directed by a professional political class.

A first lesson from all this is clearly the value of institution-building and conciliation. A choice for political methods of this kind at the very least makes it possible to create new ways of acting politically. Recent transitions in Brazil and Spain, and the coalitional efforts of the democratic opposition in Chile suggest the broad appeal of this lesson—a lesson once rejected with scorn by the Chilean Left. Venezuelan experience also suggests that conservatively managed transitions may be more durable. Controlling the scope and pace of change and effectively excluding the revolutionary Left soothes the fears of powerful groups. Once again, recent events in Brazil and Spain confirm this impression, and a sympathetic look at the program of El Salvador's Christian Democrats shows how much their strategy is modeled on an interpretation of Venezuelan experience.

A more general lesson is the need to encourage civilian political organization and spur free associational life. The fact that parties cannot be created by decree does not foreclose the possibility of promoting conditions that let associational life prosper and give party organization a chance to grow. Recall Tocqueville's comments about the way political and civil associations strengthen one another. A final citation from *Democracy in America* reinforces the point:

> A certain nation, it is said, could not maintain tranquillity in the community, cause their laws to be respected, or establish a lasting government if the right of association were not confined within narrow limits. These blessings are doubtless invaluable, and I can imagine that, to acquire or preserve them a nation may impose upon itself severe temporary restrictions: but still it is well that the nation should know at what price these blessings are purchased. I can understand that it may be advisable to cut off a man's arm in order to save his life; but it would be ridiculous to assert that he will be as dextrous as he was before he lost it.[58]

A last lesson from Venezuela is the need to avoid polarization, and the all-or-nothing choices it promotes. Ideological polarization has never been central in Venezuela, but this is no accident. Those advancing polarization were marginalized and defeated; never able to gain a strong popular base. It is essential to find alternatives to polarization, for methods of caution and prudence are difficult to impose in the best of circumstances. The task is harder still when government is harsh and unyielding, and ideological debate sharp, bitter, and never-ending.

All these reflections suggest that the underlying lesson from Venezuela is to take politics seriously. Appreciation of the autonomy of politics, and heightened attention to political values, tools, and needs make it possible for any society to draw more effectively on its own resources and on the strengths of its organized social life in ways that can make democracy more likely. Nothing is forever, but a well-constructed, valued, and carefully managed political order surely has a better chance.

Another look at the social bases of Venezuelan democracy yields lessons that are variations on this theme. The first lesson concerns the extent to which democracy is grounded in the experiences and perspectives of ordinary citizens. A sympathetic look at Venezuelan history suggests that the needs and desires of average people deserve a lot more respect than they commonly get from "expert" observers. A political order that recognizes these needs and perspectives as legitimate and provides a place for their free expression is likely to be more durable, stable, and secure than one founded on force alone, or on a more limited social base. Venezuelan experience gives the lie to arguments about how developing nations cannot "afford the luxury" of democracy. One might suggest that they can afford little else![59]

Recently, many commentators have painted a grim picture of the future of Venezuelan politics. They argue that the political system has ossified into a rigid party oligarchy (*partidocracia*), opposing this to a somehow more genuine "real" democracy. The parties are dismissed as rotten machines for peddling influence and patronage; governments are attacked for their corrupt mismanagement (especially of the economy); and the electoral system is ridiculed for its emptiness and carnival atmosphere. As Baloyra notes, "Judging from these apocalyptic descriptions, one may imagine that the Venezuelan regime survives by an unparalleled act of political will and/or the sheer imbecility of the population."[60]

Such sharp and unrelenting criticism cannot be for lack of accomplishments. Democracy in Venezuela has survived challenges and overcome difficulties fatal in most instances. It has done more than just survive. New kinds of power have been created, and new forms of political practice consolidated and spread throughout the society. Moreover, democratic governments have presided over substantial social and economic changes of all kinds. None of these are as good as they might be in an ideal world, but they are real achievements and warrant careful and respectful attention.

The experience of democracy in Venezuela belies the disdain with which many dismiss "formal" or "bourgeois" democracy as unreal or insubstantial.

Venezuelans of all kinds value democracy *as a value in itself*. Venezuelan democracy may have been just a fragile hope at one time, but that hope rested on a sense of deep and irreversible social change. Rómulo Gallegos, novelist, founder of AD, and elected president in the *trienio*, put the matter well many years ago:

> Dear friend! That this social order will be replaced by another? No question! It is as if astronomical calculations were to show that one day—at a certain hour, minute, and second—the earth would crash with a comet. What good would it be then, to jail the astronomer, and destroy the book where he wrote them down?[61]

• NOTES •

1. I discuss the nature of democracy and democratization, and their implications for group and institutional life in "Paradigm Lost: Dependence to Democracy," *World Politics* 40, no. 3 (April, 1988): pp. 377–394; and in "Religion and Politics: Dimensions of Renewal," *Thought* 59:233 (June 1984): pp. 117–135.

2. Standard treatments of the political economy position can be found in David Collier, ed., *The New Authoritarianism in Latin America* (Princeton, NJ: Princeton University Press, 1979). Guillermo O'Donnell's work has been particularly influential. One very important article is his "Reflections on the Pattern of Change in the Bureaucratic Authoritarian State," *Latin American Research Review*, 12, no. 1 (1978): pp. 3–38. The cultural-determinist position is well represented by Howard Wiarda's much-cited "Toward a Framework for the Study of Political Change in the Iberic-Latin Tradition," *World Politics* 23 (1973): pp. 206–236. Alfred Stepan advances a thoughtful institutional approach in, for example, *The State and Society: Peru in Comparative Perspective* (Princeton, NJ: Princeton University Press, 1978).

3. For a fuller discussion of such regimes, see Collier, *New Authoritarianism*.

4. The late K. H. Silvert described a seminar on "democracy, authoritarianism, and development in the hemisphere" in these terms: "It is amazing how the group can talk endlessly about authoritarianism, endlessly about development, but cannot find five sentences to say about democracy." Silvert, "Coming Home: The United States Through the Eyes of a Latin Americanist." In K. H. Silvert, ed., *Essays in Understanding Latin America* (Philadelphia: ISHI, 1977).

5. This attempted reorientation is apparent in the papers collected in Guillermo O'Donnell, Phillippe Schmitter, and Laurence Whitehead, eds., *Transitions from Authoritarian Rule*, 4 vols. (Baltimore, MD: Johns Hopkins University Press, 1986). The final volume in this work (*Tentative Conclusions About Uncertain Democracies*, by O'Donnell and Schmitter) shows considerable unease with concepts of liberal democracy. Of course, the topic was not created anew with this body of work. Contributors of fundamental importance include Robert A. Dahl, Arend Lijphart, and Juan Linz: See in particular Dahl's *Polyarchy: Opposition and Participation* (New Haven, CT: Yale University Press, 1971); and his more recent *Dilemmas of Pluralist Democracy* (New Haven, CT: Yale University Press, 1982); Lijphart's influential "Consociational Democracy," *World Politics* 21, no. 1 (1969):pp.207–223; and Linz, "Crisis, Breakdown, and Reequilibration." In *The Breakdown of Democratic Regimes*, ed. Juan Linz and Alfred Stepan (Baltimore, MD: Johns Hopkins University Press, 1978). See my "Paradigm Lost" for a full discussion.

6. In particular, see my *Conflict and Political Change in Venezuela* (Princeton, NJ: Princeton University Press, 1973); "Venezuela Since 1958: The Consolidation of Democratic Politics." In *Breakdown*, ed. Linz and Stepan; and "The Transition to Democracy: Are There Lessons From Venezuela?," *Bulletin of Latin American Studies* 4, no. 2 (1985):pp. 47–61.

7. Important sources in English include Robert Bond, ed., *Contemporary Venezuela and Its Role in International Affairs* (New York: New York University Press, 1977); John D. Martz, *Acción Democrática: The Evolution of a Modern Political Party in Venezuela* (Princeton, NJ: Princeton University Press, 1966); and Franklin Tugwell, *The Politics of Oil in Venezuela* (Stanford, CA: Stanford University Press, 1975). Terry Karl's "Petroleum and Political Pacts: The Transition to Democracy in Venezuela," *Latin American Research Review* 22, no. 1 (1987):pp. 63–94, sets Venezuelan experience in the framework of the political-economy school. Judith Ewell's recent *Venezuela: A*

Century of Change (Stanford, CA: Stanford University Press, 1984) is a convenient but flawed overview of contemporary history.

8. John Lombardi explores the nature and impact of colonial history in "The Patterns of Venezuela's Past." In *Venezuela: The Democratic Experience*, ed. John D. Martz and David Myers (New York: Praeger, 1977). For a more detailed treatment, see Lombardi, *Venezuela: The Search for Order, The Dream of Progress* (New York: Oxford University Press, 1982). The development of city hierarchies and demographic patterns is discussed in John Friedmann, "The Changing Pattern of Urbanization in Venezuela." In Lloyd Rodwin et al. *Planning Urban Growth and Regional Development: The Experience of the Guayana Program of Venezuela* (Cambridge, MA: MIT Press, 1969).

9. See R. L. Gilmore, *Caudillism and Militarism in Venezuela 1810–1910* (Athens: Ohio University Press, 1964).

10. On the bases and broad implications of coffee's growth and later decline, see Luise Margolies, "Urbanization and the Family Farm; Structural Antagonism in the Venezuelan Andes"; and William Roseberry, "On the Economic Formation of Boconó." In *The Venezuelan Peasant in Country and City*, ed. Luise Margolies (Caracas: EDIVA, 1979); and also Roseberry's fine *Coffee and Capitalism in the Venezuelan Andes* (Austin: University of Texas Press, 1983). Roseberry shows that the Andean region's share of total national population grew from 10.6 percent at independence to 13.8 percent in 1873 (date of the first official census), to 14.5 percent by the 1890s and 17.9 percent by 1926. See *Coffee and Capitalism*, p. 76. It has dropped steadily ever since.

11. See Gilmore, *Caudillism*. Ramon J. Velásquez discusses the social basis of nineteenth-century militarism and of the Andean triumph in his *La caída del liberalismo amarillo* (Caracas: 1973). See also Domingo Alberto Rangel, *Los andinos en el poder* (Caracas: Talleres Gráficos Universitarios, 1964).

12. Useful sources on the origins of organization include: for peasants, John Powell, *Political Mobilization of the Venezuelan Peasant* (Cambridge, MA: Harvard University Press, 1971); for labor, Steve Ellner, *Los partidos políticos y su disputa por el control del Movimiento Sindical en Venezuela, 1936–1948* (Caracas: Universidad Catolica Andres Bello, 1980); and Charles Bergquist, *Labor in Latin America: Comparative Essays on Chile, Argentina, Venezuela, and Colombia* (Stanford, CA: Stanford University Press, 1986); on students, María de Lourdes Acedo de Sucre and Carmen M. Nones Mendoza, *La generación venezolana de 1928: Estudio de una elite política* (Caracas: Ediciones Ariel, 1967); and for a general overview, Levine, *Conflict*, especially chs. 2, 3, and 8. Juan Bautista Fuenmayor's *1928–1948: Veinte años de política* (Madrid: Editorial Mediterraneo, 1968) reviews early events from the perspective of a founder of the Communist Party.

13. The critical point to bear in mind here is that party ties cut across and dominate those derived from social class alone. This relation of party to class has been criticized by some (e.g., Bergquist, *Labor*) who see it as a betrayal of revolutionary potential. For more detail on the origins of party organization, see Rómulo Betancourt's *Venezuela: Politíca y petroleo*, rev. ed. (Caracas: Ediciones Senderos, 1967), and Levine, *Conflict*.

14. Details on the quality of conflict and oppositions during the *trienio* can be found in Glen L. Kolb, *Democracy and Dictatorship in Venezuela, 1945–1958* (Hamden, CT: Shoestring Press, 1974); Andres Stambouli, *Crisis política Venezuela 1945–58* (Caracas: Editorial Ateneo de Caracas, 1980); and Levine, *Conflict*.

15. On the ideology of the Pérez Jiménez regime, see Freddy Rincón, *El nuevo ideal nacional y los planes económicos-militares de Pérez Jiménez, 1952–1957*, (Caracas: Ediciones Centauro, 1982). On the events leading to its fall, see especially Kolb, *Democracy and Dictatorship;* and Stambouli, *Crisis política*.

16. See José Vicente Abreu, *Se llamaba SN* (Caracas: Editor José Augustín Catalá, 1964). The regime's most infamous concentration camps were located in the Orinoco Delta area, especially at Guasina. See José Vicente Abreu, *Guasina donde el Rio Perdió las 7 estrellas relatos de un campo de concentración de Pérez Jiménez*, ed. José Augustín Catalá, (Caracas: 1969); or the collection, *Documentos para la historia de la resistencia Pérez Jiménez y su régimen de terror* (Caracas: Editor José Augustín Catala, 1969).

17. Pérez Jiménez received the Legion of Honor from the Eisenhower administration in 1954. The full citation of award is reproduced in Kolb, *Democracy and Dictatorship*, p. 142. It is lavish in praise for the dictator and his regime.

18. Kolb's account of the January 1958 events brings out the depth of popular opposition: "In dramatic intensity and popular violence, the events of January 21 and 22 in Caracas, Venezuela can

find a proper comparison only in such a heroic uprising as that of the Hungarian 'Freedom Fighters' of Budapest in 1956 against their Communist overlords. It was a true popular revolution of Venezulan citizens of all ages and social classes, armed with rocks, clubs, home-made grenades, and 'Molotov Cocktails,' against a ferocious and well-trained police force equipped with armored vehicles, sub-machine guns, rifles, revolvers, machetes, and tear gas." *Democracy and Dictatorship,* p. 175.

19. For further detail, see Karl, "Petroleum and Political Pacts," which argues forcefully that postwar changes in the Venezuelan economy created new interests and opportunities and thereby created a structural place for democratization after 1958. She gives special emphasis to the economic underpinnings of the 1958 agreements.

20. *Tres años de gobierno democrático,* 3 vols. (Caracas: Imprenta Nacional, 1962), 1: p. 13. This work is a collection of Betancourt's speeches during his first three years in office. It is a valuable source for the period.

21. *Tres Años,* 1: p. 245.

22. After 1958, Venezuelan politics are guided by four operative norms that set the "rules of the game" for elites and the organizations they controlled: freedom for leaders; respect for the fragility of politics; agreement to disagree; and concentration of politics in a narrow and predictable range of vehicles. For further details and general comments on the nature of legitimacy in Venezuela, see Levine, *Conflict,* especially chs. 8–10.

23. On the 1961 Constitution, see Juan Carlos Rey, "Los 25 años de la constitución y la reforma del estado," *Venezuela 86,* 2 (April–May–June 1986: pp. 25–34, published by the Ministry of Foreign Relations. See also, Rey, "El Futuro de la democracia en Venezuela," (Caracas: Instituto Internacional de Estudios Avanzados, 1986, mimeo).

24. I explore the Left's revolutionary goals in *Conflict,* pp. 47ff. In part, these rested on a generational conflict, pitting exile leaders against those who had run clandestine party networks during the dictatorship. The former tended to support pact-making, conciliation, and exclusion of the Communists from post-1958 arrangements. The latter had worked closely with Communists in mobilizing opposition to Pérez Jiménez and backed broad alliances and more radical transformations. The Cuban Revolution had a major impact on this process, spurring divisions in AD and convincing leftists generally that revolution was indeed possible.

25. For the record, the relevant names of the minor parties are as follows: On the Left are the Partido Comunista de Venezuela (PCV); the Movimiento Electoral del Pueblo (MEP), the largest of the groups derived from divisions in AD; and the Movimiento al Socialismo (MAS). The most significant of the "electoral phenomena" were the Frente Nacional Democrático (FND), the Fuerza Democrática Popular (FDP), and the Cruzada Cívica Nacionalista (CCN). The first was formed to back Arturo Uslar Pietri, a well-known writer; the second gathered around Larrazabal, and the last was organized by supporters of ex-dictator Pérez Jiménez.

26. A brief overview of AD's divisions and of party fragmentation generally in the early 1960s is in John D. Martz, "The Evolution of Democratic Politics in Venezuela." In *Venezuela at the Polls,* ed. Howard Penniman, (Washington, DC: American Enterprise Institute, 1980). I discuss the matter in "Venezuela." In *Competitive Elections in Developing Countries,* ed. Myron Wiener and Ergun Ozbudon, (Durham, NC: Duke University Press, 1987).

27. On the extent of continuing socioeconomic inequality despite petroleum exports, see in particular Vernon Childers, *Human Resources Development: Venezuela* (Bloomington, IN: International Development Research Center, 1974); and Terry Karl, *The Political Economy of Pertrodollars: Oil and Democracy in Venezuela* (Ph.D. Diss., Stanford University, 1982).

28. The depth of U.S. cultural influence (brought in by the petroleum companies) is suggested by the national sport: baseball.

29. In all likelihood, the *trienio* is a more appropriate match for the bitter divisions that characterized Allende's Chile.

30. Alexis de Tocqueville, *Democracy in America,* vol. 2, (New York: Schocken, 1961), p. 143.

31. Population data are derived from the sources cited in Table 6.4., and in n. 10 above. For a more detailed account of demographic transformation, see C.-Y. Chen, *Desarrollo regional-urbano y ordenamiento del territorio mito y realidad* (Caracas: Universidad Católica Andres Bello, 1978).

32. Tugwell details the state's overwhelming dependence on petroleum revenue in his *Politics of Oil.* See also Karl, *Political Economy.*

33. On the agricultural depression, see Margolies, "Urbanization and the Family Farm"; Roseberry, *Coffee;* and Powell, *Political Mobilization.* The decline of rural life and the pull of cities and oil towns is a staple of Venezuelan literature of the period.

34. Karl, *Political Economy,* p. 84.

35. See the sources cited in n. 12 above.

36. The relative share of these sectors over time breaks down as follows:

	1936	1950	1960	1970	1980
Primary	41.8%	38%	36.0%	26.2%	13.8%
Secondary	11.7	17	19.8	19.7	26.5
Tertiary	46.4	45	44.2	54.1	56.2

Figures for 1936 from Rodwin, *Planning Urban Growth,* p. 63. Figures for 1950, 1960, and 1970 from Franklin Bustillos Gálvez, *Introducción a la Economía Venezolana* (Caracas: Librería Editorial Salesiana, 1978) p. 128. Figures for 1980 calculated from data in Ewell, Venezuela, p. 233.

37. The cost of politics rose sharply after 1968, as traditional reliance on mass meetings, parades, and block and precinct work yielded to stress on regular polling and to very lengthy national media campaigns. Both have been packaged and programmed following campaign-management pamphlets and outlines, many of them from the United States. For a more complete discussion of costs, see Penniman, *Venezuela at the Polls;* and my "Venezuela."

38. Arístides Torres, "Familia, fiesta electoral, y voto: Un analisis del origen de las lealtades partidistas en Venezuela," *Revista de estudios políticos* 1 (1982) pp. 47–70.

39. While the end result is clear enough, great care is needed in tracing the dynamics of change and, in particular, in drawing inferences about group or individual choice from aggregate electoral or demographic data. We cannot be sure that change is occuring within identical groups, or if (as suggested here) it stems primarily from the incorporation of new voters. Conclusions about changing bases of individual or group voting decisions are thus unwarranted. The data do not allow us to be certain whether shifts are grounded in changing working-class attitudes, middle-class orientations, or the like. One recent attempt to advance such flawed generalizations is David Blank, "The Regional Dimension of Venezulean Politics." In Penniman, *Venezuela at the Polls.*

40. For the 1978 elections, Robert O'Connor comments, "Demographic variables do not account for the voting intentions of the Venezuelan electorate. If one were to select at random 100 Herrerra [COPEI] supporters and place them in a room, and then repeat this procedure with Pinerua [AD] supporters, the two groups would look very similar." O'Connor, "The Electorate," In Penniman, *Venezuela at the Polls,* pp. 56–90.

41. In mid-1988, after a lengthy period of study and intense national debate, two important political reforms were adopted. Beginning in 1989, mayors and state governors (hitherto appointed by the national executive) will be elected in separate elections. These changes will make it possible for opposition parties to build independent local and regional bases more effectively. Further changes being planned include a move to open party lists, giving voters a chance to select candidates by name. If implemented fully, these and other reforms proposed by the Commission for the Reform of the State will change the way power is organized in the state, in the political parties, and in the electoral process. The whole package of reforms proposed by this commission is intended to spur the decentralization and deconcentration of power, and to make citizen participation easier and more meaningful at all levels.

42. An analysis of the components of variance in votes for AD and COPEI at the state level from 1958 through 1978 confirms the overwhelming dominance of national factors. A more complete account of this analysis is provided in my "Venezuela," which also reports the pattern of regional results in detail.

43. Decree powers have been used extensively; for example, to suspend political guarantees during the insurrectional period of the early 1960s and to give the executive broad authority to regulate the economy.

44. Karl discusses the relative weakness of Congress in "Petroleum and Political Pacts". See also Lynn Kelley, "Venezuelan Constitutional Forms and Realities." In Martz and Myers, *Venezuela.*

45. Petroleum revenues have regularly provided over two-thirds of central state income since 1958. Unlike personal income taxes, such revenues require no public approval, and therefore pose fewer problems in domestic political terms.

46. On the growth of public enterprises, see especially Janet Kelly de Escobar, "Las empresas del estado: del lugar común al sentido común." In Moíses Naim and Ramón Piñango, *El caso Ven-*

ezuela: Una ilusión de armonía, 2d ed. (Caracas: Ediciones IESA, 1985); and Gene E. Bigler and Enrique Viloria, "State Enterprises and the Decentralized Public Administration." In Martz and Myers, *Venezuela: The Democratic Experience,* rev. ed. (New York: Praeger, 1986).

47. On the Commission for the Reform of the State, see Rey, "El Futuro;" and Janet Kelly de Escobar, "Reform Without Pain: The Commission on State Reform in the Lusinchi Administration." Paper presented at the 13th International Congress of the Latin American Studies Association, Boston, October 1986. Initial returns are indicated in note 41 above.

48. Such a position is advanced, for example, in Blank,"Regional Dimension," p. 196; and in John Martz and Enrique Baloyra, *Political Attitudes in Venezuela: Societal Cleavages and Political Opinion* (Austin: University of Texas Press, 1979), pp. 95, 99.

49. This position amounts to explaining *away* the experience of Venezuelan politics. Two recent expositions in this vein are John Peeler, *Latin American Democracies: Colombia, Costa Rica, and Venezuela* (Chapel Hill: University of North Carolina Press, 1985); and Heinz Sonntagg and José A. Silva Michelena, *El proceso electoral de 1978: Su perspectiva histórica estructural* (Caracas: Editorial Ateneo de Caracas, 1979).

50. See Martz and Baloyra, *Political Attitudes,* pp. 70–71; Lisa Peattie, *The View From the Barrio* (Ann Arbor: University of Michigan Press, 1968), chs. 6 and 7; and Talton Ray, *The Politics of the Barrios of Venezuela* (Berkeley: University of California Press, 1969), pt. 2.

51. See Charles Erasmus, "Upper Limits of Peasantry and Agrarian Reform: Bolivia, Venezuela, and Mexico Compared," *Ethnology* 6, no. 4 (1967); pp. 349–380.

52. Enrique Baloyra makes this point strongly in his review of a decade of opinion research: "Public Opinion and Support for Democratic Regimes, Venezuela 1973 to 1983." Paper presented at the Annual Meeting of the American Political Science Association, New Orleans, September 1985.

53. Levine, *Conflict;* and Frank Bonilla, *The Politics of Change in Venezuela,* vol. 2, *The Failure of Elites* (Cambridge, MA: MIT Press, 1970), p. 328.

54. Tocqueville, *Democracy in America,* pp. 139–140.

55. Interview. January 13, 1983.

56. On Nixon's visit, see Kolb, *Democracy,* pp. 182–184.

57. Terry Karl discusses the dimensions and political implications of the current economic crisis in great detail in her *Political Economy.* See also Rey, "Futuro."

58. Tocqueville, *Democracy in America,* pp. 143–144.

59. Przeworski's general comments fit the Venezuelan case well: "The developed capitalist countries owe their stability to institutionalization of intergroup conflict. The belief in the instrumental effectiveness of particular mechanisms for processing such conflicts, accompanied by varying amounts of repression of political activities defined as 'subversive', channels intergroup conflicts into the institutionalized framework. . . . The threat to the stability of democratic capitalist systems comes not from political participation, which for most people involves little more than voting at regular intervals. Rather, the real threat is posed by withdrawals of groups from the electoral process, and a loss of legitimacy of the institutionalized forms of conflict processing." Adam Przeworski, "Institutionalization of Voting Patterns, or Is Mobilization the Source of Decay?" *American Political Science Review* 69, no. 1 (1975); p. 67.

60. Baloyra, "Public Opinion," p. 23.

61. *El Forastero* (Caracas: Ediciones Populares Venezolanos, n.d.).

Reprinted from Jonathan Hartlyn, *The Politics of Coalition Rule*, by permission of Cambridge University Press.

COLOMBIA

• CHAPTER SEVEN •
Colombia:
The Politics of Violence
and Accommodation

JONATHAN HARTLYN

From the perspective of democratic politics, the Colombian case is not easy to categorize. Colombia has experienced tremendous political violence, yet also extensive periods of constitutional civilian rule. In recent decades, it has had moderate patterns of socioeconomic growth and has suffered less decline from the debt crisis of the 1980s than have most other Latin American countries. Yet it continues to have sharp socioeconomic disparities. Since 1958, the country has had a civilian political regime and consistently held elections for all major political offices, though for much of this time under a restrictive political arrangement. Currently, Colombia remains far from consolidating a democratic political regime, though it has undertaken a number of significant political reforms, even as state coherence and basic civil rights are challenged by growing violence from left-wing guerrillas, drug traffickers, and right-wing reaction.

Colombia has experienced many of the same historical, economic, and cultural factors as other Latin American countries: Spanish colonial domination followed by economic dependency on major capitalist powers; a dominant role for the Catholic church; and vastly unequal land-tenure patterns. Yet, given the significant differences in the democratic experiences of various Latin American countries, these factors would appear less significant in explaining the fate of attempts at democracy than others that relate more explicitly to the political process. The latter include the interaction, timing, and sequence of various social, economic, and political variables, and the role of key political elites in certain periods.[1]

In the study of Latin American politics, interest has been shifting increasingly to regime-level and more explicitly "political" variables, in part as a reaction to the failure of economically or culturally deterministic theories to explain changes in political-regime type.[2] Arguments for democratic success or failure based on the restricting impact of levels of economic development, international economic dependency, or (especially) cultural traditions of authoritarianism have often been too broad to distinguish across Latin American cases or to explain changes in countries over time. This is not to deny their (at times overwhelming) importance but to caution against treating them as necessary conditions in most instances.³

This chapter stresses the importance of political factors—parties, electoral dynamics, leaders, statecraft—to the success or failure of Colombia's regimes.⁴ At the same time, it indicates how different structural economic and social factors have facilitated or constrained political processes. Colombia's historical development—particularly the consolidation of its two traditional parties in the context of a relatively weak state; the interaction between its political party system and its evolving economy and class structure; and the successes and failures of political leadership and statecraft—have been crucial in explaining its trajectory in different historical periods. The inability or unwillingness of the traditional parties (and of economically dominant interests) to respond adequately to the dramatic socioeconomic changes of the past several decades is a major cause of the country's current critical period.

Unlike many of its continental neighbors, Colombia has avoided both military rule and chronic political and economic instability since 1958, when the leaders of the two major parties came together to form the consociational National Front. Intense violence between adherents of the two parties in the late 1940s and 1950s, known as *la violencia* (the violence), left 200,000 casualties and led to regime breakdown and military rule. Civilian rule was facilitated by mutual interparty guarantees and the coalition government resulting from party negotiations. As it finally emerged, their National Front agreement established presidential alternation between the two parties until 1974, and bipartisan parity in executive, legislative, and judicial posts. It also required a two-thirds majority for most measures to be approved in Congress. A 1968 constitutional reform led to the partial dismantling of the National Front. It imposed a simple majority vote for most measures in Congress and called for competitive elections at the local level in 1970, and at the national level in 1974. Parity in the judicial branch was maintained; in the executive branch, it was extended until 1978, after which the party receiving the second highest number of votes was to be offered "adequate and equitable" representation by the winning party.

From 1958 to 1986, all governments in Colombia consisted of bipartisan coalitions. In a context of intensifying political and criminal violence, efforts to dismantle coalition rule more fully continued to fail in the late 1970s and early 1980s. Finally, following enactment of a number of decentralizing reforms, including the popular election of mayors (previously appointed by departmental governors, themselves appointed by the central authority), and a landslide Liberal victory in 1986, Conservatives refused participation in the administration of President Virgilio Barco (1986–1990).

Because of the sharp restrictions on majoritarian democracy imposed by the National Front and because the country has been governed for most of the time since the late 1940s under a state of siege,⁵ most analysts have viewed Colombia since 1958 as a qualified democracy, using adjectives such as "controlled";⁶ "oligarchical";⁷ "traditional bipartisan elitist";⁸ "near polyarchy";⁹ or "restricted" (*democracia restringida*).[10] Others have characterized the country from the other side of the democracy-authoritarianism continuum, as "inclusionary authoritarian",[11] or as simply "authoritarian" because of its National Front electoral restrictions.[12] There is also one characterization of the country "in-between" these two, which sees it as in a lengthy (30-year) "transition" from dictatorship to democratic government, accelerated by democratic reforms enacted in the mid-1980s.[13]

In my view, the best characterization of the contemporary Colombian government is that it has been a limited democratic consociational regime, currently in an uncertain process of transformation. It has been consociational because a return to civilian rule in 1958 was inconceivable without mutual guarantees between the major parties, assured by the National Front agreement. Colombia's two major parties represented functional alternatives, though not exact equivalents, to the segmental divisions along religious, ethnic, or linguistic lines, identified in other consociational cases.[14]

The rigid consociational practices (relaxed in the post-1974 period), combined with other restrictions, have limited the regime's democratic nature. Yet the importance of elections for leadership succession, the overall respect for political and civil liberties, and the existence of a judiciary independent of the executive all indicate it is more appropriately considered democratic than authoritarian. In the 1980s, what was increasingly at issue was not only whether the regime could transform itself in a more fully democratic direction, but whether the state (including in particular the judiciary and the police) could regain coherence, and thus capacity to act.[15]

Analyzing the dynamics of the regime's coalition rule and continuing relations between the two traditional parties is central to understanding the moderate political and economic successes of the country in the decades since 1958, and the nature of its current vulnerability and excesses. Contemporary Colombia illustrates the challenges confronted by a consociational regime that finds the political bases of its initial arrangement eroded and must now seek a new political accommodation. The sources of this erosion were the political regime structure (which twice compelled voters to elect a presidential candidate from the opposing party because of the requirement to alternate) and socioeconomic changes that produced a younger, more urban, better-educated population. By the 1970s, these factors generated both a decline in party segmentation (which had initially led to the creation of the National Front) and an expansion of organized societal interests demanding that their voices be heard.

The political realities that led to establishing consociationalism had been superseded, and regime arrangements required transformation. As a consequence, the country would almost certainly have experienced political turmoil in the late 1970s and 1980s. This new, critical juncture in the country's history resulted from: powerful political-electoral incentives for coalition rule to continue; fears felt by the more powerful producer groups; lack of effective social reform or political incorporation; emergence of more significant nonelectoral opposition; increased military autonomy; assassinations of political, labor, and civic leaders; and divisions within the regime over how to address the growing guerrilla threat. The crisis has been further exacerbated by the impact of drug trafficking and other criminal violence on state institutions and on the state capacity to govern. Within the context of the current regime structure, there could be a sharper turn to authoritarianism. An even more intense shift to repression would also almost certainly result from an unlikely, but not inconceivable, military coup. At the same time, consonant with the concept of the regime provided here, evolution toward a more fully competitive democracy is possible within the regime, rather than by its change, though this is not foreseeable in the immediate future.

Colombia is not easily categorized on the summary scale of the volume editors. Should Colombia be placed low in the "democratic" category or somewhere in the "semidemocratic" category? In recent years, has movement been more in the democratic direction, as a consequence of the end of coalition rule and enactment of several political reforms, or more toward authoritarianism, indicated by increased political and criminal violence, including targeted killings of left-wing politicians and activists? Was the National Front ever "stable," and should the regime now be considered "unstable"? Somewhat arbitrarily, I would place Colombia very low in the "democratic" category, between "progressive success" and "mixed success—democratic but unstable" on the 6-point scale used in this book.[16] However, considering that a regime can evolve from the "semidemocratic" to the "democratic" by internal reform (and not necessarily by regime change), Colombia might instead be placed in the "semidemocratic" category, close to the above categories. Either placement highlights the fact that civilian rule has been in place in Colombia since 1958, but with some constraints on its democratic nature and threats to its viability. In the 1980s, Colombia has been shifting further in the partially stable category toward instability, as efforts toward democratic reform have met resistance, and violence has become widespread.

• HISTORICAL REVIEW AND ANALYSIS •

The Traditional Parties, Civil Wars and National Integration

The essential feature of the National Front and post–National Front political regime has been the political dominance of the country's two traditional parties, formed in the nineteenth century. The current political turmoil reflects the difficulty of moving beyond traditional bipartyism and its constraining features. Other key aspects that emerged in the nineteenth century and have had a sustained impact on the country's historical evolution include strong regionalism and a weak state and military. Subsequently, as a result of the nature of Colombia's primary export crop (coffee) and initial industrialization, there was little of the sectoral conflict between the agro-export sector and early industrialists that occurred in some other Latin American countries. Combined with the process of early labor organization, and in conjunction with the established party structure and very limited foreign investment, this meant that Colombia's experience with populism was attenuated. Both political parties became multiclass parties, though the urbanization that accelerated in the 1930s led to a substantial Liberal electoral majority still evident to this day (see Tables 7.1 and 7.2). In addition, these various factors acted to limit the role and autonomy of the state, though there was a strongly centralized presidential system and state ownership of utilities.

With most of the rest of Latin America, Colombia shares a common cultural heritage of Spanish colonial rule. Although not as important a colonial center as Lima (Peru) or Mexico City, Bogotá, the capital, became the center of the viceroyalty of Nueva Granada, which included what is today Colombia, Ecuador, Venezuela, and Panama. The colonial period also bequeathed to the country one of the continent's most powerful and conservative Church hierarchies. The struggle for independence was drawn out (1810–1821), questions of national unity plagued the country, as the efforts of Simón Bolívar to keep Gran Colombia (the old viceroyalty) together failed. Venezuela and Ecuador finally broke away in 1830, and Panama gained its independence in 1903.

Colombia's record of civilian, republican rule in the nineteenth and twentieth centuries cannot be explained primarily by reliance on theories linking postindependence political patterns to a single colonial heritage, though initial problems of integration and legitimacy are certainly associated with its colonial past. Although their origins remain a controversial historical issue, by the 1850s the Conservative and Liberal parties had established themselves, dividing the country politically while promoting a degree of national unity. The parties were capable of generating extensive electoral turnouts as well as mobilizing for violence.[17] They were loose confederations of large landowners and merchants, who possessed considerable autonomy in their region, rather than tight-knit organizations. The country's rugged topography impeded effective national integration and aided the development of a number of regional centers significant to this day.[18]

Ideological differences between the two parties were more significant in the nineteenth century than in the twentieth. In general, the Conservatives were wedded to a view that approximated the previous colonial order, emphasizing close cooperation between Church and state, a strong central administration, and protectionism. The Liberals, more influenced by the industrial, liberal-democratic powers of the nineteenth century, generally argued for federalism, separation of Church and state, and free-trade economic policies.[19] These ideological differences blended with and at times were superseded by more purely personalistic and regional disputes.

That the military establishment was relatively weak and insignificant, in

Table 7.1. Electoral Results for the Legislature, 1935–1986[a]

Year	Liberal %	Conservative %	ANAPO %	Leftist parties[b] %	Total votes	Participation rate[c]
1935	100	—[d]	—	—	430,728	33.4%
1937	100.0	—[d]	—	—	550,726	32.5
1939	64.4	35.1	—	—	919,569	—
1941	63.8	35.7	—	—	885,525	—
1943	64.4	33.8	—	—	882,647	—
1945	63.0	33.6	—	3.2	875,856	38.4
1947	54.7	44.4	—	0.8	1,472,689	56.3
1949	53.5	46.1	—	0.4	1,751,804	63.1
1951	0.6[d]	98.6	—	0.5	934,580	—
1953	—[d]	99.7	—	—	1,028,323	—
1958	57.7	42.1	—	—	3,693,939	68.9
1960	44	41.7	—	12	2,542,651	57.8
1962	35.0	41.7	3.1	19.5	3,090,203	57.9
1964	46.2	35.5	13.1	4.3	2,261,190	36.9
1966	52.1	29.8	17.8	—	2,939,222	44.5
1968	49.9	33.7	16.1	—	2,496,455	37.3
1970	37.0	27.2	35.2	—	3,980,201	51.9
1972	46.3	30.8	19.0	—	2,947,125	36.3
1974	55.6	32.0	9.5	3.1	5,100,099	57.1
1976	52.0	39.1	3.6	4.6	3,265,974	34.5
1978	55.1	39.4	—	4.3	4,180,121	33.4
1980	54.5	38.2	—	4.1	4,215,371	33.8
1982	56.3	40.3	—	2.5	5,584,037	40.7
1984	54.4	39.6	—	2.4	5,654,436	38.0
1986	54.2	37.2	—	4.4	6,909,851	42.9

Source: Jonathan Hartlyn, *The Politics of Coalition Rule in Colombia* (Cambridge: Cambridge University Press), pp. 150–151.
[a]Percentages are of the popular vote. Small percentages for nonleftist minor candidates; blank and void votes are not included. Results are for the House of Representatives for all years, except 1972, 1976, and 1980 (when they are for departmental assemblies), and 1984 for Municipal Councils. (The term for House members was extended to four years beginning in 1970.)
[b]See source for complete listing of these parties.
[c]Participation rate based on estimates by the Registraduria Nacional del Estado Civil of the total number of eligible voters.
[d]Abstained from election.

sharp contrast to other Latin American countries at this time, aided the establishment of the political parties as primary actors. The Colombian elite distrusted Bolívar's predominantly Venezuelan liberation army, and after the breakup of the Gran Colombia federation in 1830, the army was further reduced in size and influence. In subsequent decades, the civilian bands the parties were able to mobilize were often larger than the national army. The army's inability to sustain its overthrow of a civilian government during the 1850s in the face of an armed coalition of Liberals and Conservatives led to further reductions in its size. Thus, as the political parties began to consolidate in the 1850s, the military institution was practically nonexistent. Not until the beginning of the twentieth century did a professional corps of specialized military personnel develop.[20]

In approximate quarter-century cycles beginning in the 1880s, political parties and the state established new institutional arrangements in the face of economic and societal challenges. These arrangements were preceded or surrounded by sometimes intense violence, channeled through the two parties. At the same time, the two-party system helped limit the development of more class-based organizations within the peasantry, the working class, or the middle sectors. Bipartisan coalitions were significant in facilitating major transition points that led to important institutional and constitutional changes in the 1880s, 1910s, 1930s, and 1950s.

The initial postindependence decades of consolidation of the two major political parties were followed first by Liberal dominance (1863–1885) and then by Conservative hegemony (1886–1930). The civil wars of the nineteenth century played a central role in generating population-wide identification with either party. Following the major postindependence conflicts of 1827–1832 and 1839–1842, seven major civil confrontations were fought in the second half of the century: 1851, 1854, 1861–1863, 1876–1877, 1885, 1895, and 1899–1902. Numerous other smaller-scale regional conflicts were also fought during this period. Some 24,600 lives were lost in the civil conflicts between 1830 and 1876, and 100,000 were killed in the turn-of-the-century War of the Thousand Days.[21]

The Liberals emerged victorious at mid-century. Their 1863 Constitution was extremely federalist, secularist, and politically liberal. At least nominal observance of constitutional procedures became more important. Although fraud on the part of incumbents and abstention on the part of opposition groups was common, of the eleven men who occupied the federal presidency between 1863 and 1886, only one attained his post by irregular means. The Constitution's recognition of regional autonomy to some extent, given the central government's inability to extend its control over the entire country, made a virtue of necessity. Federalism and free trade nearly brought Colombia to the brink of economic ruin, destroyed its incipient industrial base, and impeded national integration, submerging the country in crisis.[22]

A centralizing reaction with considerable bipartisan support, known as La Regeneración, followed. This movement, spearheaded by Rafael Núñez,

Table 7.2. Electoral Results for the Presidency 1930–1986[a]

A. 1930–1949

Year	Liberal		Conservative		Total votes	Participation rate
	A	B	A	B		
1930	44.9% Olaya	—	29.1% Valencia	25.9% Vásquez	824,530	n.a.
1934	97.6 López	—	—	—	942,309	n.a.
1938	100.0% Santos	—	—	—	513,520	30.2%
1942	48.5% López	41.3% Arango	—	—	1,147,806	55.8%
1946	32.3% Turbay	26.3% Gaitán	41.4% Ospina	—	1,366,005	55.7%
1949	—	—	100.0% Gómez	—	1,140,646	39.9%

B. 1958–1970

Year	Official National Front	ANAPO	Other A	Other B	Total Votes	Participation rate
1958	79.9% Lleras C.	—	19.8% Leyva	—	3,108,567	57.7%
1962	62.1% Valencia	—	11.7% Leyva	25.9% López M.	2,634,840	48.7
1966	71.4% Lleras R.	28.0% Jaramillo	—	—	2,649,258	40.1%
1970	40.3% Pastrana	38.7% Rojas	11.7% Betancur	8.3% Sourdis	4,036,458	52.5%

C. 1974–1986

Year	Liberal	Conservative	ANAPO	Left	Other	Total votes	Participation rate
1974	56.2% López	31.4% Gómez	9.4% María Rojas	2.6% Echeverri	0.1% Duarte	5,212,133	58.1%
1978	49.5% Turbay	46.6% Betancur	—	2.4% 3 candidates	1.3% Valencia	5,075,719	40.9%
1982	41.0% López	46.8% Betancur	—	1.2% Molina	10.9% Galán	6,815,660	49.8%
1986	58.3% Barco	35.8% Gómez	—	4.5% Pardo	0.6% Liska	7,229,937	n.a.

Source: Jonathan Hartlyn, *The Politics of Coalition Rule in Colombia* (Cambridge: Cambridge University Press), pp. 152–153.

[a] Participation rate based on estimates by the Registraduría Nacional del Estado Civil of the total number of eligible voters.

sought to reestablish the authority of the central state and the Church. The 1886 Constitution, the basic text still in effect to this date, strengthened considerably the powers of the central state and the presidency. The role of the Church was further consolidated by a concordat with the Vatican in 1887. In addition, by the 1890s, the parties had established more formal structures, with party directorates and conventions.[23] By then, though, the Liberals were almost completely excluded from political power. Conflicts regarding Núñez's political and economic reforms, and political exclusion eventually led to one of the longest and by far the bloodiest of the country's civil confrontations, the War of the Thousand Days. It essentially ended in a draw, though the Conservatives retained power.

Oligarchical Democracy

The early 1900s were marked by the emergence from civil war and the loss of Panama. This was followed by the dictatorial government of the Conservative Rafael Reyes, who eventually closed Congress and called for a National Assembly. Reyes reached out to Liberals by including a small number in his cabinet, permitting them representation in the National Assembly, and promoting passage of a measure that would guarantee them representation in future sessions of Congress. Following the civil war, many Liberal leaders rejected violence as a means of promoting their aims or of seeking political office. They sought the adoption of electoral reforms to guarantee proportional representation of the parties and associated economic reforms such as increased sectional autonomy.[24] Violent conflict was followed by consociational practices in an attempt to prevent renewed violence.

Eventually, a bipartisan opposition movement, which flirted with the idea of creating a new party, the Partido Republicano, emerged and led a political struggle to depose Reyes. Supported particularly by merchants and industrialists, the movement never developed a popular power base.[25] However, coming after a period of extensive violence and seeking bipartisan consensus and political demobilization, it foreshadowed the National Front. A Constituent Assembly, established by the Republicanos in 1910, confirmed minority representation in Congress. And in a reform that obviated some of the problems faced by other Latin American democratic (and undemocratic) regimes, it also decreed direct presidential elections for a 4-year term with no immediate reelection.

In contrast to the end-of-the-century years, the period following 1910 was an era of remarkable political stability. Between 1910 and 1949, Colombia had, as Wilde has argued, an oligarchical democracy "of notable stability, openness, and competitiveness."[26] These decades also brought Colombia into far more extensive contact with the outside world. A sustained coffee boom in the late 1800s and early 1900s set the stage for industrialization. Significantly, it incorporated groups from both the Liberal and Conservative parties into the export trade, even as its characteristics helped block development of more radical nationalist politics. Throughout this period, coffee production in the *latifundia* of primarily Liberal landowners eventually came to be challenged by production in small family-owned farms established in the western highlands by colonizers from the predominantly Conservative department of Antioquia. Many of these landowning small growers were less receptive to the radical ideologies that had made inroads in other countries where agrarian wage earners were more prevalent, or where the major landowners were foreigners.[27] That the country's major export product was largely in local hands further inhibited the development of nationalist radical political movements built around opposition to foreign penetration (in contrast, for example, with APRA in Peru).

Economic growth and social differentiation picked up in the 1920s. Led by the coffee boom, an installment of the U.S. indemnification to Colombia for the loss of Panama in 1923, and a rapid increase in foreign loans, GDP grew at an average annual rate of 7.3 percent between 1925 and 1929, primarily as a result of investments in public works and transportation.[28] However, the dramatic economic decline of the late 1920s caught the Conservative government, as it did most governments in Latin America, unprepared. This paved the way for an unprecedented constitutional transfer of power between political parties, as the badly divided Conservatives presented two candidates and the Liberals presented a moderate figure who had some Conservative support. Once inaugurated, the Liberal president formed a bipartisan government but confronted a Conservative majority in Congress. Partisan violence, particularly in rural areas, marked the 1930 elections and intensified during the 1931 elections. It ended as the country mobilized for a brief border conflict with Peru in 1932.

By 1934, a "Liberal Republic" had emerged. Mindful of past Conservative fraud and exclusivism, Liberals employed highly fraudulent elections to place Alfonso López Pumarejo, in any event the only candidate, in the presidency. Conservatives practiced opposition as the Liberals had in earlier years. Electorally, this included refusing to participate in elections (*retraimiento*) in 1934 and 1938, supporting a dissident figure from the other party in 1942, and, ultimately and successfully, presenting their own candidate in 1946 (see Table 7.2).

López's presidency was a period of tumultuous reform and institutional change, known as the Revolution on the March (Revolución en Marcha). Under López, constitutional and legal reforms were enacted to increase the electorate (universal male suffrage) and to modernize and expand the state in the face of the economic challenges of the depression and growing urbanization. López also encouraged legislation to deal with peasant unrest, supported labor organization, co-opted or neutralized dissident political movements from the radical and progressive Left, and struggled against those of the fascist Right. López's reforms were a pragmatic response to "an incipient crisis of the old order." Yet they also served more narrow partisan purposes, consolidating the position of the Liberal Party by limiting the influence of the Church, expanding the electorate in urban areas, and increasing the party's support base within labor.[29]

Significant industrial growth and organization and incorporation of the working class came during this period. Bipartisan participation in the coffee trade also came to be reflected as well in industry. In contrast to other Latin American countries, there was no rupture between industrialists and export-oriented landowners during the 1930s, and none of the Liberal presidents developed a conscious statist industrial policy.[30] In addition, in the early years of unionization, labor was not a very important center for radical activity. This was due in part to low rates of immigration (a focus for anarchosyndicalist movements in many other Latin American countries) and to low levels of foreign investment in these years of initial industrialization. The country's first major labor federation, the Confederation of Colombian Workers (CTC), was founded in 1936 with critical political support from President López.

López, though, met intense opposition from landowners, merchants, industrialists, and leaders from both parties. Opposition from Conservatives, expressed in strongly ideological language, intensified particularly because of the mass dismissals of Conservatives from government. Yet even within his own party, López experienced such intense opposition that late in his term he agreed the country required a "pause" in reformism. López regained the presidency in 1942, in elections pitting him against another Liberal supported by the Conservatives (see Table 7.2). But he now confronted a hostile Congress and an economy buffeted by inflation and lacking, because of the war, needed inputs. After surviving a coup attempt by Conservative military sympathizers in 1944, and in spite of continued labor support, López resigned in August 1945. Besieged by attacks from both Conservatives, led by Laureano Gómez, and Liberals, particularly the populist Jorge Eliécer Gaitán, he hoped his resignation would pave the way for interparty accord.

The parties had managed one peaceful constitutional transfer of power in 1930, though regionalized partisan violence then had only ended with the border war with Peru. They would not be capable of managing a second such transfer.

From *La Violencia* to the National Front

The period 1946–1958 is one of tragic violence and intense drama in Colombian history. The causes of regime breakdown and of *la violencia* remain complex and controversial. I share the perspective that emphasizes the importance of political factors over purely class or economic factors in explaining the breakdown and the initiation of violence, and, ultimately, the establishment of the National Front.[31] At the same time, as argued below, political factors alone cannot explain the evolution of *la violencia* or the successful establishment of the National Front.

The 1946 elections represented the second transfer of power between the two parties in this century and occurred in a mirror image of events in 1930. The Liberal Party was irreparably split, with regional figures, moderate national leaders, and most Liberal CTC labor leaders (as well as Communist leaders pursuing a "Popular Front" strategy) supporting a traditional Liberal candidate. In contrast, many rank-and-file CTC members and Communist sympathizers backed the Liberal populist Gaitán. Just six weeks before the elections, the Conservatives nominated Mariano Ospina Pérez, a far less acerbic and more compromising figure than Gómez, whose candidacy would almost certainly have unified the Liberals.[32] Ospina won, his plurality of votes resulting from the Liberal split (see Table 7.2), and entered office with a bipartisan National Union government (as he pledged he would during the campaign, in spite of Gómez's opposition).

Politicization, polarization, and violence accelerated following the 1946 elections. Although it resembled the violence that followed the 1930 elections, the stakes were higher. Liberals feared that Conservatives, as a minority party, would attempt to consolidate a permanent grip on power by force. Conservatives, mindful of the recent exclusivism by the Liberals in power, feared that if they were to lose the presidency, they would be able to regain it only with great difficulty.[33] With the social and economic changes of the 1920s and 1930s, there were more economically integrated and politically mobilized groups. Party control of the state was more and more crucial, not only for patronage and contracts but also for favorable administrative and judicial decisions. Economic interests and political sectarianism began to reinforce each other, polarizing the country in the opposing figures of Gómez for the Conservatives and Gaitán for the Liberals.

Government-labor relations were reshaped. The CTC, its largest union broken by the interim Liberal government of Alberto Lleras in 1945, attempted a nationwide strike against the Ospina government in May 1947; it failed dismally. Interpreted as part of a Liberal plot to overthrow Ospina's government, it led to further repression and decline of the Liberal labor confederation, and to the encouragement of a new confederation being formed under Jesuit auspices, the Union of Colombian Workers (UTC).[34] The UTC was committed to collective bargaining at the firm level, had a much more centralized organization, and firmly rejected state syndicalism. Given these characteristics, the UTC prospered under Ospina, who saw it as an alternative to the Liberal and Communist-linked CTC. The result, in contrast to the corporatist experience of other Latin American countries, was a labor movement relatively independent from the state, though linked to different political parties and thus divided and neither particularly powerful nor autonomous.

Liberal divisions remained severe. As a result of the 1947 congressional elections, Gaitán emerged as the leader of the party and almost certainly its sole candidate for the 1950 presidential elections. He opposed Liberal participation in Ospina's government, which ended in March 1948. Then, on April 9, the assassination of Gaitán on the streets of Bogotá led to the *bogotazo*—mobs burned commercial buildings, destroyed churches, and attacked government buildings in the capital city; riots spread to other cities. The regime survived, barely. Moderate Liberals, confronted with Ospina's refusal to resign, agreed to reenter the government, which implanted a state of siege. But, moderates in each party were finding it difficult to dissociate themselves from the statements and actions of party extremists without endangering their own position and influence.

The conflict between Conservatives and Liberals became a struggle between the executive and the legislature. In May 1949, the Liberals once again left the government. The following month's congressional elections confirmed their control of Congress, even as the high turnout demonstrated the country's growing polarization (see Table 7.1). Gómez called for Ospina to close Congress, while moderates in both parties established a "Pro-Peace Committee" with industrial, commercial, and financial representation. Ospina proposed postponement of presidential elections by four years and interim bipartisan rule by a four-man government council, with major organs of the state under equal control and a two-thirds majority requirement for legislation. Yet, even as this proposal was being transmitted to the Liberals (by Gómez, who personally opposed it), hard-liners were replacing moderate Conservatives in government. Official repression against Liberals continued. Following Gómez's nomination as the Conservative's presidential candidate and the failure to reach an accord, the Liberals decided to withdraw entirely from the elections they had moved up to November 1949 and began impeachment proceedings against Ospina.[35]

The result was regime breakdown. On November 9, 1949, the president responded to Liberal actions by declaring a state of siege, closing Congress, banning public meetings, and censoring the press and radio. Unopposed, Gómez was elected president. The intensified violence and conflict, though fueled by social and economic changes that had generated significant regional variations, was essentially the result of partisan polarization. What led regional conflicts to spiral into the breakdown of the regime, a "partial collapse" of state authority,[36] and one of the "greatest armed mobilization of peasants . . . in the recent history of the western hemisphere",[37] was the inability of some and the unwillingness of other elements of the top leadership in both parties to negotiate in good faith. With their direct or ambivalent support for the violent activities of their regional party subordinates, given all the other social and economic dislocations and the country's ideologized condition, they soon found they had helped unleash a wave of violence they were unable to control.[38]

The worst casualties were suffered in the earlier years, when the partisan motivation was strongest: An estimated 145,000 deaths are attributable to *la violencia* between 1948 and 1953. Another 25,000 are believed to have been killed between 1954 and 1960.[39] Remarkably, the country experienced healthy economic growth during most of this period, as export crops reached the ports and urban industrial areas were little affected. This may help to explain why reaction against the continued violence grew so slowly under the Gómez presidency.

Under Gómez, censorship tightened, repression against labor increased, and violence against Liberals and Protestants, sometimes with the cooperation of the local clergy, intensified. Additional efforts to establish interparty accords failed. Gómez's government (headed by another figure after his 1951 heart attack) convened a constituent assembly in order to impose a new falangist-corporatist constitution that would free the presidency of most congressional constraints, further centralize power, and convert the Senate into a corporatist body.[40] Yet this constitutional counterreform divided Gómez's own party. Some feared it was a means of perpetuating his followers in office, and others thought it unnecessary or irrelevant in the face of more crucial national issues, including *la violencia*.

Military government and failed populism. Although dictatorial rule (such as by Gómez or by Reyes at the turn of the century) was not unknown in Colombia, direct military rule was uncommon. The country's historical tradition has been largely civilian and republican, if violent and not fully democratic, built around two dominant multiclass parties.

Yet party leaders now welcomed military intervention. Gómez was overthrown by General Gustavo Rojas Pinilla in June 1953, with the active support of many Conservative leaders, particularly former President Ospina, and with the encouragement of the Liberals, many of whose top leaders had fled into exile. Neither Rojas nor the Colombian military, though, had the capability or the inclination to govern the country without civilian assistance. Most of the officer corps, including Rojas, strongly identified with the Conservative Party and sought Church support and approval. Initially, Rojas' goal appeared to have been to stem the violence and broaden and improve the Conservative Party.[41] Rojas' government was staffed heavily with Conservatives, particularly *ospinistas,* and his major economic and political advisers were civilian. Yet, as it became clearer that he was not intending a rapid return to civilian rule but was instead seeking to consolidate and probably prolong his stay in office, opposition began to intensify.

The opposition to Rojas crystalized in the bipartisan movement that led to the National Front. The inability of the Rojas government to end the violence, as well as the fact that groups of insurgents were taking on a more radical revolutionary purpose, helped generate opposition to Rojas among important civilian sectors, and support for restoration of civilian government. Rojas alienated broad sectors of the population by government brutality, incompetence, corruption, and continued press censorship; his Peronist leanings and economic policies gained him U.S. and World Bank opposition. Rojas lost the support of powerful domestic economic actors by his statist and populist economic policies, even as economic transformations during his period in office strengthened those actors' organization and coherence. By the second half of 1956, opposition intensified as the country's economic situation suffered from a sharp drop in world coffee prices.[42]

Rojas' most significant failure, however, was his inability to establish a political movement outside the two political parties. The organizational space already occupied by the political parties and existing labor organizations, as well as domestic implications of the international environment, weighed against his succeeding in creating a corporatist labor organization and a "Third Force" (Tercera Fuerza) political movement. In addition, the Church began to reconsider its active role in partisan politics following Gómez's bitter attacks after his fall from power and in reaction to the horror of *la violencia;* the Church also increasingly distrusted Rojas' government because of its Peronist trappings.[43]

Consociation and transition. Generating a political alternative to Rojas and moving to civilian rule was almost inconceivable without extensive mutual guarantees between the two parties. These were provided through a series of political pacts, eventually enshrined as part of the Constitution by means of a national plebiscite. The Liberal Alberto Lleras sought out Laureano Gómez in his Spanish exile in July 1956. The resulting Declaration of Benidorm and a subsequent Pact of March, signed in Bogotá, called for a return to civilian rule by means of coalition governments. Party opposition to Rojas coalesced around Conservative Guillermo León Valencia as their joint candidate for the 1958 elections.

The growing crisis came to resolution during the "days of May." Following business strikes and middle-sector and student protest, rather than mass mobilization, Rojas finally flew into exile on May 10, 1957. The junta that replaced him formed a bipartisan cabinet, closed Rojas' Constituent Assembly, reestablished freedom of the press, and called for elections to replace itself at the end of Rojas' presidential term in August 1958. While the junta implemented an economic austerity program, party leaders sought to provide assurances to the armed forces that they would be delinked from the attacks on Rojas and his close collaborators. They also continued to work on the mechanisms by which they would provide guarantees to each other in order to insure a transition of power from the military. The major problem, apparent before the fall of Rojas, was a serious split within the Conservative Party; Gómez bitterly opposed the Valencia candidacy.

Tumultuous and complex negotiations ensued. Alberto Lleras traveled again to Spain, and in the Pact of Sitges, he and Gómez agreed to most of the measures of political parity and other mutual guarantees that were eventually approved by the national plebiscite later that year. Every element eventually incorporated into the agreement had been suggested or tried in the late 1940s. However, on his return to Colombia, Gómez threatened to withdraw support from the plebiscite vote. A Pact of San Carlos, agreed to only days before the plebiscite vote (in which 95 percent of those voting aproved the National Front agreement), specified that congressional elections would precede presidential ones, and that Valencia would be the candidate only if congressional lists supporting him gained a victory over Gómez's lists. Gómez's gamble succeeded, but the parties could not agree on a different Conservative candidate. Finally, with Gómez's urging, Alberto Lleras became the presidential candidate only nine days before the elections. The parties agreed to approve a constitutional reform calling for presidential alternation until 1974. The transition effort was marred by several failed coup attempts, including one, successfully beaten back, just two days before the presidential elections. Lleras won an overwhelming victory against Jorge Leyva, a sectarian Conservative candidate (see Table 7.2).

A review of the key events of this period indicates the importance of political factors. These events—such as the fall of Rojas, the Pact of Sitges and the national plebiscite, the Pact of San Carlos and the Valencia candidacy, or the last-minute selection of Alberto Lleras as presidential candidate—indicate that the most difficult problems revolved around reaching inter-elite agreement, not "selling" the accords to the parties' mass following. The various agreements indicated the creativity of the country's political leaders, and their considerable capacity both to negotiate with opposing party leaders and to carry their party followers along. The leaders of the two conflicting parties moved from intransigence and violence to compromise and conciliation; there had been "political learning."

Yet it was not simply a matter of change of will by political leaders. The structural conditions for this alternative in the late 1950s were highly favorable. International actors opposed Rojas and supported initiatives sponsored by domestic political and economic actors. The political parties completely dominated the political landscape, and the idea of bipartisan coalition rule was strongly rooted in historical antecedents. More immediately, the experience of *la violencia* had devastated party leaders, encouraging a compromise that was made even more compelling by the efforts at *continuismo* of Rojas and the fear of incipient radical movements in the countryside. Once the parties were willing to provide guarantees that neither would be excluded from power, their major conflict was resolved. The Church was fully behind the compromise. A more organized and diversified industrial sector had both increased capabilities and greater reasons, beyond the ties of traditional party loyalties, to oppose Rojas. The civilian alternative promised greater stability and economic policies more consonant with their interests than did Rojas' statist and populist policies. Urban and especially rural masses, the primary victims of the bloodshed, had low levels of organization and were largely acquiescent toward an agreement that promised peace.

The transition to civilian rule in Colombia can be viewed as consociational in a descriptive sense, because of the particular political arrangement of the National Front, with its extensive mutual guarantees between the Conservative and Liberal parties. But, it is also consociational in a theoretical sense. These arrangements appear necessary for the transition to occur, and for the regime to persist in its initial years given the nature of the country's two hierarchical, multiclass, historically rooted, and deeply entrenched parties, and the ferocity of the violence in the 1950s. It was difficult to conceive of extinguishing this violence if one party had sought to govern over another.

The Colombian case is somewhat anomalous in Latin America; no other country has had a similar patterning of structured identification and intense violence around two political parties in existence since the mid-nineteenth century. In other Latin American countries, consociational practices and political pacts have probably not been nor are they likely to be, strictly speaking, necessary.[44] However, the Colombian process suggests that forces seeking a transition from military to democratic rule may find consociational pacts helpful in two kinds of situations. To the extent political parties are an important part of a country's social structure, and regime breakdown was associated (in the not too distant past) with their past interaction, consociational mechanisms may provide crucially important mutual guarantees. And to the extent military withdrawal is occurring through gradual steps or by uncertain negotiations with a relatively coherent military institution, opposition unity and thus consociational guarantees may also prove helpful.

In addition, the Colombian case indicates that consociational pacts may be easier when the conflict is over how to agree to "live and let live" (group autonomy) or over how to share divisible goods (patronage). Yet Colombia also illustrates the difficulties of moving to more open and democratic practices from a rigid, constitutionally-enshrined agreement.[45]

Coalition Rule and Uncertain Transformation

The National Front was a pragmatic, though conservative, response to the country's deep crisis. It promised something for all major party groups and economic actors. Yet, different and sometimes contradictory aspects of the agreement and the regime it established generated support among these actors. Liberals regained a share of political power; Conservative *ospinistas* retained a position of influence without the burden of their untrustworthy military allies; and Conservative *laureanistas* (followers of Gómez) regained their position within the party and a chance at political power. The consociational arrangement of parity and alternation soon came to serve the bureaucratic and pork-barrel interests of national and regional party leaders so effectively that few could imagine doing away with coalition rule. The Church could view itself as a force of conciliation for all Colombians as both parties now recognized its privileged position; the military was promised autonomy and respect; and producer groups saw economic policies they favored and the promise of greater access to policy circles. The absence of bitterly contested, ideologized elections and of opposition politics meshed well with the development strategies of foreign-aid advisers and international financial agencies, which encouraged the emergence of a state sector protected from partisan politics. Lacking was any effective, organized presence of different popular groups. They had played no direct role in the regime's creation, and party elites had seen how their mobilization had gotten out of their control. For these groups, the agreement heralded peace and the promise of social reform.

Constrained by these contradictory forces and a restrictive set of political rules, the regime sustained a precarious balance. It generated a set of informal "rules of the game"—increased presidential authority, *ad hoc* decision forums and summit negotiations, secrecy, increased state capacity combined with selective privatization, patron-client and brokerage ties, and government sponsored mass organizations—that allowed it to operate in a context of continual short-term crises. The regime appeared more contingent than consolidated, and its balance became more precarious in the post–National Front period (1978 on). The political parties were seeking to maintain essentially the same political mechanisms they had established in 1958 in a societal structure that had been changed not only by massive population growth, rural-to-urban migration, and industrialization, but also by the very experience of the National Front.[46]

The immobilism generated by the consociational agreement (parity in all branches of government and a required two-thirds majority vote in Congress), and the party factionalization that it further encouraged initially weakened the political parties (one of which had begun the National Front already divided) and led to numerous executive-legislative deadlocks. Combined with a "technocratic" emphasis of certain national leaders, reinforced by international lending agencies, the agreement also increasingly marginalized Congress from many key decisions, leading to increased presidential authority.[47] Congress ceded extraordinary powers to presidents to legislate on specific issues; presidents also legislated after declaring a state of siege or, following the 1968 Constitutional Reform, by declaring a state of national economic emergency. Nominal but only rarely substantive bipartisan participation was assured by the fact that the signatures of the entire cabinet were required on all such presidential decrees. The use of special powers by the president has been common to Latin American presidentialist systems. In Colombia, it took on added importance because of the consociational arrangement, an ironic situation since Colombia is unique among consociational regimes in having a presidential system.

No single institutional forum emerged in lieu of Congress to serve as the locus for bipartisan discussion. Because party factions were sometimes not represented in a cabinet or because ministers identified with a particular faction sometimes were more "technical" than "political," the cabinet—which logically might have served such a function—did so only occasionally. Thus, on specific issues such as agrarian reform or during periods of acute economic or political crisis such as 1965, *ad hoc* decision forums and summit negotiations among top party leaders, many times ex-presidents, were often employed in seeking to break apparent deadlocks. Attempts to create institutionalized decisionmaking structures in Colombia essentially failed. They failed at the congressional level and at a corporatist state-society level. Efforts to establish congressional committee oversight of national development plans were unsuccessful; congressional representatives all sought the patronage advantages of committee membership, even as international agencies and government technocrats feared excessive politicization would result from greater congressional involvement.

Structural pressures from the economy, the influence of international agencies, and the drive to satisfy minimum levels of efficiency led to increasing state capacity in terms of planning, regulating, and investing, though there were important variations from one presidential administration to another. At the same time, in order to avoid potential immobilism or politicization and to seek greater efficiency, or because of concerted efforts by particular producer groups, the regime continued with the historical pattern of selective privatization of certain economic areas and functions (such as the legally private Coffee Federation, which was extensively involved in key pricing and marketing decisions and even in managing state revenues).

Politicians relied extensively on patron-client and brokerage ties to consolidate their electoral position and felt threatened by increased state capacity, which increased the programs and investments channeled through various state agencies and weakened politicians' regional bases of strength. The parties made no serious attempts to institutionalize or to develop auxiliary organizations, even as their ties to the traditional labor confederations weakened. Some popular-sector groups were able to influence policy or attain limited goals by various means, including political ties (through government bureaucrats or through clientelist or brokerage connections with politicians), mass occupations, civic and labor strikes, demonstrations and appeals to the press. Nevertheless, the regime at times employed or condoned the use of undemocratic practices.

There were also ambivalent and only partially successful efforts at government-sponsored organizations of the lower classes. In the end, the National Front did not create loyal popular-sector organizations by corporatist mechanisms, in part because presidential alternation and partisan fears worked against it. The regime sought to pursue more a policy of demobilization and of "divide and conquer" toward the popular sector than one of corporatist mobilization, centralization, and control. The example of the National Association of Peasant Users (ANUC) is telling. ANUC was created by the reformist Liberal President Carlos Lleras (1966–1970) to serve as a "pressure group" in favor of land reform and as a potential mass base for a future reelection bid. With the change to a Conservative administration and retrenchment on agrarian reform, ANUC became radicalized and sponsored numerous land invasions. The government responded by withdrawing financial support, dividing the organization, and repressing the more radical leaders.[48]

"Moderate" economic policies and growth. One factor that has been facilitated by, and also has facilitated, Colombia's consociational regime has been its economic policies. They have been largely "moderate" and relatively continuous, similar to those of countries such as Mexico and Venezuela (until their oil booms in the 1970s), in contrast to the more "pendular" policies of countries such as Argentina, Chile, and Peru. These differences of degree (rather than of kind) have meant that "moderate" countries (at least until the

bonanza and debt crisis of the past decade), while not avoiding economic problems and shifts in policy, have generally avoided extreme populist policies—with high inflation, extreme protectionism, dramatic wage increases, and extensive fiscal deficits—or radical neoliberal ones—brusquely eliminating state subsidies and fiscal deficits, imposing massive devaluations, sharply curtailing wage increases, clamping down on the money supply, and slashing tariffs.[49]

Colombia's economic policies in the past decades have entailed continued attention to variables such as inflation, fiscal deficits, and growth. Facilitated by the nature of its regime, these policies also kept dissenting conservative economic interests within the regime rather than seeking to overthrow it. These policies had some important successes, as the country maintained one of the steadiest growth rates in the region from 1957 to 1981, while, in comparative continental terms, controlling inflation (see Table 7.3). Even in the difficult years of the 1980s, Colombia's record of growth, inflation, and fiscal deficits has been comparatively favorable.

From the 1950s to the 1980s, the country underwent massive economic, social, and demographic changes. It doubled its population and became a substantially younger and more urban country. Significant changes in its labor force resulted from shifts from agriculture toward services and, to a lesser extent, industry. The economy became more diversified and complex, and larger middle-sector groups emerged (see Table 7.4). Improvements in health and education (e.g., life expectancy and literacy rates), though, were not paralleled by im-

Table 7.3. Selected Latin American Countries: Average Growth Rates and Changes in the Consumer Price Index

	Average annual change in real GDP (%)[a] 1957–1981	Standard deviation from the mean (%)[b]	Average annual change in the consumer price index (%)[c] 1958–1980	Standard deviation from the mean (%)[b]
Argentina	3.03	4.7	60.98	98.7
Chile	4.04	4.8	77.22[d]	155.5
Peru	4.17	2.8	17.99	18.8
Brazil	6.94	3.8	37.74	21.5
Colombia	5.15	1.7	14.99	9.2
Mexico	6.37	2.2	8.97	8.9
Venezuela	5.31	1.9	4.60	5.1

[a]A geometric mean calculated from annual percentage change in real GDP (OECD series) in James W. Wilkie and Adam Perkal, eds., *Statistical Abstract of Latin America*, vol. 23 (Los Angeles: University of California at Los Angeles Latin America Center, 1984), pp. 393–409. The assistance of Greg Michaels is gratefully acknowledged.

[b]Calculated from arithmetic means.

[c]A geometric mean calculated from annual percentage change in the consumer price index in International Monetary Fund, *International Financial Statistics Yearbook* (Washington, DC, 1981), pp. 64–65.

[d]For 1964–1980 only.

Table 7.4. Colombia: Demographic and Social Indicators

	Colombia		Average for middle-income countries[a]	
	1960	1978	1960	1978
Total population (millions)[b]	14.5	25.7	—	—
Gross domestic product (per capita)[c]	479	922	—	—
Urban population (%)	48	70[d]	37	51
Labor force (%) in				
agriculture	52	30	58	45
industry	19	23	17	23
services	29	47	25	32
Life expectancy	53	62	54	61
Number enrolled in primary schools as % of age group	77	103	81	97
Adult literacy rate	63	81	54	71
Average annual growth of population (%)				
1960–1970	3.0		2.5	
1970–1980	2.3		2.4	

[a]As defined by the World Bank, comprising fifty-two countries with a per-capita income of over $360 (including eighteen Latin American countries). See World Bank, *World Development Report, 1980* (New York: Oxford University Press, 1980), pp. 110–157.

[b]Figures from James W. Wilkie and Stephen Haber, eds., *Statistical Abstract of Latin America*, vol. 21 (Los Angeles: University of California at Los Angeles Latin American Center, 1981).

[c]From Inter-American Development Bank, *Economic and Social Progress in Latin America* (Washington, DC: 1982), pp. 351, for 1960 and 1980, in 1980 U.S. dollars.

[d]Figure for 1980.

provements of similar scale in the country's vastly unequal income distribution, in part because distributionist policies were rarely formulated, and if formulated, were largely thwarted in implementation.

The regime pursued economic policies akin to those of its continental neighbors in the late 1950s and early 1960s. Thus, it also suffered some of the same kinds of economic and political problems associated with seeking to move beyond initial import substituting industrialization in a period of poor export performance. The consequences of the stop-go economic policies generated by foreign exchange problems, popular-sector pressures, and other factors have been synthesized in the bureaucratic-authoritarian model.[50]

Colombia partially resembled that picture in the 1957–1968 period, as it sought to forge ahead with import-substituting industrialization in a context of low world prices for coffee. Confronted with recurring balance-of-payments problems, the regime applied stabilization programs of differing effectiveness in 1957–1958, 1962, and 1965. International aid (and especially generous U.S. support under the Alliance for Progress) were critical in keeping the economy afloat. The economic problems and growing social discontent that marked the administration of Conservative Guillermo León Valencia (1962–1966) brought the regime to the brink of collapse. In early 1965, a national strike was only narrowly averted; talk of a military coup gradually subsided.

Yet a partial economic shift occurred during the administration of the reformist Liberal president Carlos Lleras Restrepo (1966–1970). A nationalist reaction against IMF demands was followed by pragmatic negotiations leading to the establishment, in 1967, of a new framework for trade and a "crawling peg" exchange rate. The latter sharply reduced political conflicts over devaluation and provided the means for a partial reorientation of the economy from an import-substitution model to one of export promotion.[51]

The change occurred at a much earlier relative stage of Colombia's industrial development than it did in many other Latin American countries. In this way, Colombia avoided some (not all) disastrous experiences in import substitution and did not implement sharply "pendular" policies with their devastating political consequences, as occurred in Argentina, Chile, Peru, and Uruguay. The timing of these changes was fortuitous, for they permitted new exporters to benefit from a booming world economy.

Lleras sought unsuccessfully to create a new reformist coalition of industrialists, workers, and peasant beneficiaries against traditional landowners, while establishing the basis for an active, interventionist state. The legacy of his administration was a stronger state apparatus and a framework for a more efficient economy. However, his aggressive actions generated opposition from politicians concerned about the trimming of pork-barrel funds, numerous producer groups fearful of a more interventionist state, and especially landowners threatened by the encouragement of land reform and peasant associations. The backlash was felt both at election time, when General Rojas' populist Alianza Nacional Popular (ANAPO) movement nearly won, and in the orientation of the subsequent administration.

Conservative President Misael Pastrana (1970–1974), after two years of general economic policy continuity, combined with retrenchment on agrarian reform and co-optive urban policies to prevent further successes for ANAPO, enacted a new development program oriented toward urban construction and further expansion of commercial agriculture and agro-exports. These policies were perceived as having helped to foster higher inflation and were partially abandoned by the incoming administration of Liberal Alfonso López Michelsen (1974–1978). Elected by an overwhelming margin in the first competitive national elections since 1946, López began with a strong reformist orientation, though he also emphasized more conventional strategies focusing on agricultural and manufactured exports. However, his administration was unprepared for the foreign-exchange bonanza that resulted from a boom in coffee prices and the rapid expansion of illegal drug exports. Prudently, though, it borrowed little on international capital markets, permitting the country to postpone and partially mitigate the financial crisis that its continental neighbors faced a few years later as the world went into recession and interest rates climbed.

The country's coffee bonanza ended in 1980, and the administration of Liberal Julio César Turbay (1978–1982) borrowed more extensively both internally and abroad to finance its development program. Yet, affected by the international recession and the economic crises of its neighbors, growth rates flattened, budget deficits mushroomed, industry went into recession, and unemployment grew. These trends continued during the government of Conservative Belisario Betancur (1982–1986). By mid-1984, confronting balance-of-payments problems, Colombia moved to implement an economic austerity program, though one more "moderate" than those adopted by its neighbors. The country's economic difficulties came at a particularly unfortunate period, as the government was seeking a new political reaccommodation and a negotiated peace with the country's major guerrilla groups, even as it confronted increased violence from drug traffickers. By the time Liberal Virgilio Barco (1986–1990) was inaugurated, the country's economy had partially recovered, assisted by increased coffee prices, major investments in coal and oil and continuing dollar inflows from narcotics traffic. Yet, as political violence continued to escalate in the mid-1980s, it began to affect investor confidence and augment capital flight.

The political regime, controlled by a coalition of two factionalized, multiclass, elitist political parties, had inhibited radical policy shifts (in any direction). However, this also meant that even though some elements of the coalition governments had been interested in reformist-redistributive goals, their achievements were quite limited. Presidential alternation (until 1974) and coalition rule (until 1986), as well as the opposition of producer groups represented in both parties, inhibited socioeconomic reform.

One advantage of coalition rule was that the political regime kept conservative opponents to reform within its boundaries (they did not seek out the military), because both reformism and its opposition were channeled through the two-party system. Unlike what occurred in cases such as Argentina, Chile, and Peru, from the perspective of reform opponents in Colombia, the likely political alternative to the reformists was not an even more unsatisfactory populist or radical movement but a more centrist government from within the two parties.[52] This came at the cost, however, of not further democratizing the process in terms of other social groups. Dissent not expressed through the factions of the two traditional parties was viewed with distrust, even as growing segments of the population were looking for a means of expressing new kinds of opposition—transcending traditional party conflicts—in the face of continued coalition rule.

Political tensions. As a result both of the National Front agreement and of the country's massive social changes, many of the factors that helped shape the political regime's establishment and evolution declined in importance. Most importantly, the centrality of the parties in the country's political life declined, even as they maintained their near monopoly in the electoral arena (see Table 7.1). The result was the emergence or the strengthening of nonelectoral opposition—labor confederations independent of the two parties, and civic protest movements. Rather than perceive them as a healthy part of the democratic process, regime leaders viewed them with suspicion. Even more problematic was the growing strength of guerrilla organizations. At the same time, the military gradually dissociated itself from the two parties to become a more coherent, institutional force. The 1960s and 1970s also saw an accelerating centralization and state strengthening, as departments and municipalities lost more and more of their functions and economic resources to the central government and its (ironically named) decentralized institutes.

The growing political problems of the 1970s and 1980s stemmed less from a regime "birth defect" than from the fact that regime leaders were unwilling to respond in time to the country's changing conditions by dismantling the remnants of consociationalism and opening up the political process. The rigid National Front agreement had been necessary to reestablish civilian rule, and *la violencia* had led party leaders to fear popular mobilization. At the same time, the attraction of continued coalition rule, for different reasons, remained high for regional party leaders, major economic groups, and international actors. Under these circumstances, the country would almost certainly have experienced considerable political turmoil in the 1980s. Greatly adding to the sense of political crisis, however, has been the violence and corruption generated by the drug traffic.

Through time, the parties' continued dominance of the electoral arena came to mask significant regime weaknesses. As a result of the National Front agreement, party leaders sought to pursue three principal goals in the electoral process: to generate popular support for the National Front agreement; to defuse continued interparty conflict; and to prevent alternative populist and revolutionary movements from gaining support. These three goals were partially contradictory. Parity and alternation effectively eliminated interparty competition and, thus, a major reason to vote. Yet, mobilizing the vote continued to be important for National Front party leaders: The presence of party factions opposed to the National Front turned each election in effect into a new plebiscite on the National Front. Drops in voter turnout could be (and were) interpreted as a result of the declining legitimacy of the National Front.[53]

Superficially, electoral behavior during the National Front period was not much different from that before. Setting aside the unusual high-turnout elections of the late 1940s and the first elections of the National Front (and controlling for lower participation rates among women after 1957 and among the 18–21 age group after 1976), there were considerable continuities in overall participation rates between the previolence and postviolence periods (see Table 7.1).[54] In addition, party shares, especially in rural areas, have been maintained. Yet, there were significant changes in the pattern and site of abstention after 1958. As the National Front continued, nonsectarianism in government increasingly made attempts to revive the party faithful at election time untenable. The initial high participation rates, further facilitated by relaxing registration procedures, were unsustainable. Especially low participation rates were evident in mid-term elections.

Population growth, massive rural-to-urban migration, and the very experience of the National Front—in which competition at election time was followed invariably by coalition rule and which twice asked Liberals and Conservatives to support presidential candidates of the opposing party—led to declines in party identification. In Bogotá, Liberal party identifiers declined from 50 percent in 1970 to 36 percent in 1982, Conservatives from 21 to 19 percent, while those stating no party preference climbed from 5 to 38 percent. The last tended to be younger, from lower socioeconomic strata, less politically informed, and less willing to express opinions on political issues. This data and other studies suggest that abstention did not reflect a coherent ideological position of regime rejection.[55] Yet, the inability of the traditional parties to motivate the growing urban population to vote did reflect their institutional weakness.

These factors helped create a new and potentially very healthy phenomenon in Colombia: a floating electorate, concentrated in urban areas, mobilizable by different parties and movements. This electorate, as well as many nominal party identifiers, often failed to vote, particularly in urban areas. It first made its appearance in the relatively high-turnout 1970 elections, in which the ANAPO movement of General Gustavo Rojas nearly won (many feel fraud kept the victory from him). In 1970, because of the National Front structure, Rojas could maintain the ambiguous stature of populist opposition figure and of candidate within the Conservative Party; similarly, the ANAPO lists for Congress were also listed under either party rubric; dissident traditional figures could run under the ANAPO banner, yet remain within their party. Another advantage for Rojas was that voters in predominantly Liberal cities had no Liberal presidential candidate for whom to vote. Yet, after its 1970 defeat, the movement quickly faded. The paucity of resources at the departmental and municipal level, obstructionism from other parts of government, and internal divisions all prevented ANAPO from being able to capitalize more fully on the local electoral representation it had gained in 1970.[56]

With the return to competitive elections, the electoral record of opposition movements further deteriorated, though the floating electorate reappeared in 1974. In that year, some Rojas supporters and many Liberal sympathizers who traditionally abstained from voting turned out in large numbers to give Liberal Alfonso López an overwhelming victory. His disappointing administration, though, led to a sharp decline in voter turnout in the 1978 elections. The narrow victory in those elections of the traditional Liberal machine politician, Julio César Turbay, as well as of the party factions that had been participating in government, strengthened the perception that parties or factions could not survive as a "loyal opposition," making regime modification away from coalition rule more difficult.

The political model was stagnating, its legitimacy increasingly in question. The inexorable logic of mobilizing small numbers of voters by distributing public resources in the context of high-abstention elections made politicians reluctant to change the model of coalition rule. If patronage and machine politics is a glue that can help keep otherwise ideologically polarized party systems together (as in Chile), in countries like Colombia where parties are not strongly ideological, the dominance of particularistic, short-term stakes in a political arena with few effective restraints can ultimately impair party coherence and regime legitimacy.

Ironically, with a return to competitive elections, coalition rule made it more difficult for opposition movements, now less able to gain traditional party allies, to win legislative representation. The 1970s were also a more difficult economic context, as higher inflation and economic policy, responding to the unexpected coffee and drug booms, seriously affected middle- and popular-sector urban groups. With a certain deflation of state authority because of drug trafficking, increased corruption, and criminal violence, important nonelectoral opposition made its presence felt.

Although only a small percentage of the country's labor force is organized, key sectors responded to newer organizations independent from the regime or the traditional parties. Both in and out of the public sector, these labor organizations gained adherents at the expense of the traditional labor confederations (the UTC and the CTC), which also distanced themselves from the regime. In 1977, this led to an unprecedented joint national strike by all major confederations, and by the mid-1980s to the merging of numerous labor groups into a single confederation. Further reflecting the economic frustration of urban groups, particularly in smaller cities, and the declining intermediary role of the traditional parties, was the sharp rise in civic movements and protests in the 1970s.[57]

By the late 1970s, the regime confronted a growing challenge from various guerrilla movements. The largest and most important was the peasant-based Revolutionary Armed Forces of Colombia (FARC), with strong links to the Communist Party. Officially formed in 1964, FARC and many of its leaders were spawned by *la violencia*. Another major group was the Movement of the 19th of April (M-19), initially a largely urban movement that took its name from the date of the 1970 elections it felt had fraudulently denied Rojas his victory. It found considerable support among disenchanted middle- and lower-sector groups and professionals who found themselves increasingly squeezed economically in an era of presumed bonanza and apparent large-scale corruption.

President Turbay responded in hardline fashion to the guerrilla challenge. Shortly after he came to office, he enacted a tough Statute on Security using state-of-siege powers. The statute increased the list of crimes to be tried by military justice, substantially augmented the armed forces' powers of arrest, lengthened sentences for crimes like kidnapping and extortion, and prohibited news reports on public disturbances while they were occurring. During his administration, accusations of human-rights violations by the armed forces increased, right-wing death squads (some with military ties) appeared, and in some rural areas large landowners unleashed land-grabbing violence against peasants. The M-19 in particular challenged the administration and was confronted by harsh repression. Its takeover of the Dominican Embassy, with fourteen ambassadors held hostage in February 1980, gained it international visibility. The peaceful resolution of that crisis, however, appeared to reveal the weakness of the guerrillas and the apparent continued ability of Colombian leaders to address difficult situations. And, in late 1981, Turbay moved haltingly toward negotiating a "peace" with remaining guerrillas, even as the theme of peace became a major campaign topic in the 1982 elections because of escalating violence (of all kinds).

Renewed violence and partial accommodation. Conservative President Belisario Betancur seized the issues of "peace" with the guerrillas (amnesty and political incorporation) and of political reforms (democratization) with an intensity and doggedness that surprised everyone. He had been the surprising but convincing victor in the 1982 elections, as his strategy of reaching out to the independent urban vote while also gaining the traditional Conservative "machine" vote succeeded. In some respects, the period was propitious for a peace effort. In addition to a degree of consensus at the level of national political leadership, the M-19 was militarily decimated, other guerrilla groups were weak, and the FARC had let it be known that after decades of rural struggle it was ready to talk.

Theoretically, the combination of an administration committed to increasing democratic access and a guerrilla opposition that clearly represented only a small minority suggested that successful negotiations were possible.[58] Yet, at least five factors militated against success: negative short-term economic circumstances; divisions within the state; an ambiguous negotiating strategy on the part of the administration; lack of unity among the guerrilla groups over whether to give up the goal of seeking state power; and the impact on state coherence of drug trafficking.[59]

The peace process began auspiciously with the approval, in November 1982, of the broadest amnesty law ever passed in the country's history. However, what the next stage should be was not clear. The government finally opted to negotiate truces directly with the various guerrilla groups, a process that ultimately succeeded in 1984. The agreements made no mention of handing over arms, though guerrilla groups promised to halt all attacks and kidnappings. The government, in turn, pledged to implement or seek passage of a variety of political reforms and social programs. Yet, soon after the truce agreements were signed, the administration announced it would have no money for social reforms. The need for economic austerity at this critical moment was especially unfortunate.

From the beginning, the armed forces had indicated their skepticism, which often led to obstructionism. The consensus regarding reform among national political leaders was difficult to translate into concrete action because of occasionally tense relations between a Conservative president and a Liberal-dominated Congress, and between regional politicians fearful of losing their local power base to new political movements and national leaders not fully able to control them. Furthermore, the government's negotiating strategy was not fully thought through, and there was excessive uncertainty regarding its view of the guerrilla groups and its ultimate objective.

In turn, guerrilla groups also played an ambiguous game. This was especially true of the M-19, which had most benefited from the amnesty program but then sought to increase its military capabilities while pressing demands for political concessions on the government. Coordination among guerrilla groups was poor, and even achieving agreement over objectives within some of the groups was increasingly difficult. As a result of these factors and, by mid-1984, of increasing economic problems, opposition to the peace process expanded beyond the military and initially skeptical political and economic groups to include growing sectors of public opinion.

A final complicating factor was the increased violence and corruption engendered by drug trafficking. Narcotics traffic was initially accepted because of the foreign exchange it generated and the jobs it provided. It was also viewed as essentially a consequence of the U.S. demand for drugs. However, it gradually became a more worrisome problem for the Colombian government because of its impact on state institutions, U.S. pressure, increased domestic consumption, and the tactics of drug traffickers seeking to continue doing business, as well as acceptance within Colombian society. The unparalleled assassination of the minister of justice in April 1984, apparently by drug traffickers and weeks after a massive government drug raid, was followed by a government move to implement an extradition treaty for major drug dealers with the United States. Major drug traffickers responded with a combination of bluster (promising at one point to pay off the country's entire international debt if the extradition treaty was repealed), intimidation (bribery and threats), and incredible violence (assassinations of numerous journalists, judges, and other high government officials). Although drug trafficking represented a relatively small percentage of the country's overall economy, and much of the money it generated was kept overseas (in partial contrast to Peru and Bolivia), in the mid-1980s it was clear that its influence was penetrating all sectors of Colombian society. In 1987, a frightened Supreme Court suspended the extradition treaty on a technicality.[60]

The relationship between guerrillas and drug traffickers was complex. At least one major death squad, established by traffickers in response to kidnappings by guerrillas against major drug families, has targetted suspected guerrillas and leftists, sometimes with apparent help from elements of the military. Yet, in remote jungle areas there were also clear instances of collaboration.

Instead of ending the violence, the ultimate result of President Betancur's efforts was even greater violence. Amnestied leaders and other left-wing political figures were targets for assassination, as violence flourished for different reasons in various regions of the country. In June 1985, the M-19 broke the truce, and in November, seeking to regain the political offensive, it took over the country's Palace of Justice (where the Supreme Court and the Council of State are housed). The ensuing military assault resulted in the death of half the country's Supreme Court judges, all of the M-19 participants, and scores of others. The president was left assuming responsibility for a military action many asserted he did not fully control.

Yet, limited political reforms were enacted. The most significant step was a constitutional amendment calling for the popular election of mayors beginning in 1988. It was given added meaning because it was coupled with various fiscal measures to increase the flow of resources at the departmental and municipal levels. Part of the reluctance of the two traditional parties to move beyond coalition rule and part of the frustration of opposition parties and movements lay in the country's extreme political centralization. Other laws were enacted to modernize the electoral system, facilitate entry into civil service for certain public employees, provide a legal structure for political parties, promote regional development, and insure greater access to the media by all political groups. Many of these laws were considerably weakened in passage and others approved with little attention to detail. More far-reaching political reforms, such as multilevel implementation of civil service, effective campaign financing controls, or electoral reforms to provide minority parties more access to legislative posts, were not approved.

A tenuous truce with the largest guerrilla group, the FARC, continued to hold. The opposition party formed by the FARC, the Patriotic Unity (UP), competed in the 1986 elections, gaining a plurality or majority in around a dozen municipalities. Its presidential candidate won a mere 4.5 percent of the vote, though this reflected considerable growth in comparison to previous leftist presidential candidates (see Table 7.2). Similarly, in spite of continued intimidation (including the assassinations of its 1986 presidential candidate and dozens of its activists), the UP also participated in the 1988 mayoral elections.

An overwhelming victory for Liberal Virgilio Barco in 1986 facilitated another significant political event: the formation of a single-party government and return to a "government-opposition" scheme rather than coalition rule.[61] The March 1988 election for mayors could also be viewed as a relative success for the government and for the opposition. In spite of tragic violence before and after, including the kidnapping of the Conservative candidate for mayor of Bogotá, the assassination of the attorney general, and a massacre of nearly two dozen banana workers, election day was peaceful. As machine politicians had feared and others had hoped, in a number of areas elections helped bring new forces into office. Conservatives felt their gamble of refusing government participation to carry out opposition politics was justified. They were able to win victories in a number of major cities with traditional Liberal majorities (in part a result of Liberal factionalism).

Yet, the country's short-term future appeared cloudy. The process of regime transformation promised to continue to be drawn out, resisted, uneven, and violent.

• THEORETICAL ANALYSIS •

Colombia combines a long history of civilian, republican rule with tremendous violence and continuing inequalities. This chapter has argued that the critical factors in explaining the relative success or failure of democratic politics at different junctures have related especially to the party system, the political structure, and political leadership. At the same time, other factors, such as the state structure, the role of producer groups, economic issues, and, to a much lesser extent, features of political culture, have also affected the country's experience with democratic politics.

Party System and Political Structure

Colombia's single most dominant political feature has been its two-party system. As a consequence of how they evolved following independence and a series of bloody civil wars, the two traditional parties from the nineteenth century became "subcultures" in Colombian society. They divided the population but facilitated national integration, impeded the emergence of a strong military institution, and were able to incorporate new social groups and movements into the twentieth century, inhibiting class polarization. When they accommodated each other, democracy of an oligarchical or limited consociational sort prospered; when they did not, political tensions escalated, and bloody conflict often cal tensions escalated, and bloody conflict often resulted.

As argued above, the consociational elements of the National Front agreement appeared necessary for a return to civilian rule in 1958, following *la violencia*. The rigid National Front agreement, though, reflected not only concerns over rekindling party violence but a more general fear of mass mobilization. At the same time, its complex mutual guarantees practically assured governmental immobilism, forcing crisis decisionmaking and limiting the possibilities for political change and social reform.

Both the regime structure as well as societal change blurred party divisions and conflicts. Although the National Front rested on the country's two traditional parties, it had features of both a one-party and a multiparty system. Through the 1970 election, presidential alternation required both parties to agree on an "official National Front candidate," which made the regime appear to be based on a "single" party with hegemonic aspirations. There was no way to express interparty dissent by "voting the rascals out," and each election became in effect a new plebiscite on the National Front. At the same time, party factionalism forced each president to create and recreate an effective governing coalition, making the National Front period resemble a multiparty system. Thus, in these years most of the remaining distinctions between the parties became blurred.

The country's massive urbanization, dramatic improvements in levels of education, and changes in the work force also decreased the centrality of the two traditional parties. In spite of the continued electoral dominance of the two parties, population-wide identification with either began to decline; an independent electorate began to emerge. Most importantly, frustrated by the strictures of coalition politics, opposition increasingly came to express itself outside electoral channels. The apparent electoral successes of the two traditional parties have masked their organizational and leadership weaknesses, and they have been reluctant to move beyond coalition rule even though the social realities that had initially required it have changed. One reason for that has been the logic of brokerage politics in a heavily centralized polity.

Presidentialism and Centralization

The 1886 Constitution, still the country's basic document, provides for a strongly presidentialist and centralized system of governance. Presidential powers increased even more during the National Front years as a way of circumventing the immobilism generated by the requirements of parity and two-thirds majority vote, and as a consequence of the growing importance of the state in the economy. Presidents have also been strong as a consequence of the centralized nature of government. Through the minister of government, the president has named all departmental governors, who, in turn, have appointed all municipal mayors, until the introduction of mayoral elections in 1988. At the same time, over the past several decades, fiscal resources and investment funds the national level.

Electoral incentives for continued coalition rule have remained high. The traditional parties increasingly lost ideological or programmatic content and came to be dominated by regional politicians with almost exclusively brokerage and clientelist motivations. For these politicians, access to patronage, which has meant participation in the executive, was viewed as critical, particularly in the context of high abstention elections (as high as 67 percent), in which small numbers of voters could spell the difference between victory and defeat.

Because of the tremendous benefits that have accrued from control of government, the parties have been unable to negotiate removal of the remaining consociational element in the Constitution (that the party receiving the second highest number of votes be offered participation in government). The Conservatives, in particular, as the minority party, have demanded guarantees that oversight agencies be controlled by the opposing party. Many Liberals, in turn, have feared this could completely paralyze an administration.

However, the country's obvious political crisis and certain decentralizing reforms were sufficient to break finally the constraining mold of coalition politics with the accession of a Liberal administration in 1986. The popular election of mayors, combined with fiscal measures and political reforms, has been a step in the right direction. Following their massive defeat in 1986, the Conservatives felt sufficiently assured by these measures that they were willing to risk serving in the opposition, a step sought as well by national Liberal leaders including the newly elected president. However, the modest reforms that have been enacted and the new opposition politics of the Conservatives may appear to be simply an effort to refurbish an exclusionary bipartisanship, unless they are combined with more vigorous efforts to assure alternative political forces access to power at the local level and adequate representation at the national level. Complicating any such effort, though, has been a dramatic decline in state coherence and state capacity.

State Structure

Historically, the Colombian state has been relatively weak. In the nineteenth century, this was partially a consequence of the early consolidation and power of the two traditional parties. In the twentieth century, the role of the Colombian state in industrialization was limited, as was also true in other Latin American countries where initial export-led growth and incorporation into the world market occurred by means of a product that was nationally controlled.[62] This limited state role, combined with the low level of agricultural-industrial conflict, facilitated the initial incorporation of the working class through party rather than state ties, attenuating the country's experience with populism.

However, the role of the state changed partially during the National Front period. With the assistance of international agencies and the U.S. government, the state's economic and technical capacities increased substantially. At the same time, though, a complex labyrinth of legal requirements on state action evolved, and state employees came to be organized by labor associations hostile to the regime. In addition, the armed forces became more professionalized and developed a corporate identity distinct from the two traditional parties. Although the military has been strongly anti-Communist and opposed many of President Betancur's peace initiatives as excessively generous, its decades of direct conflict with guerrilla groups have also led many in the armed forces to believe that a purely military solution to the guerrilla problem is probably not viable.

The institutional capacities of the judiciary, local governments, the electoral system, and Congress have lagged tremendously behind the state's technical, economic, and repressive agencies. As a consequence of their deterioration (especially that of the judiciary), and of the excessively long retention of the model of coalition rule, the 1980s would almost certainly have been tumultuous in Colombia. However, drug trafficking, guerrilla activities, and criminal violence have dramatically reduced state coherence. Particularly affected has been the judicial branch, as criminal investigations and convictions have essentially been paralyzed. The violence and corruption engendered by drug trafficking has been felt directly and indirectly (by emboldening others who feel they also can act with impunity) throughout all parts of the Colombian state and society; no organized group in society has been untouched.

Consolidating democratic practices will only be possible if state coherence is regained and state capacity augmented. Yet the capacity of central state authorities and national political leaders to act has been limited. Presidents have had very limited success in promoting reform agendas in Congress, as the regional politicians that dominate legislative politics have resisted their efforts. Regional politicians have sometimes formed informal alliances with regional landowners and military commanders to defend what they view as their short-term interests. And, in recent years, presidential efforts to circumvent Congress and promote change have met a surprising obstacle—the judiciary. Numerous executive efforts to reform constitutional and judicial procedures by state-of-siege or other special powers to confront the state's serious institutional deficiencies have been declared unconstitutional. Although in the longer term, restraints on the executive may be viewed as a positive step for democracy, the short-term consequence has been to fuel confusion and further constrain state capacity.

Producer Groups and the Media

If the Colombian state has been weak, organized societal interests have also tended to be weak, though the capabilities of producer associations have extended far beyond those of working-class or peasant associations. Reflecting the country's relatively late integration into the world market, and its somewhat delayed industrialization compared to other major Latin American countries, most producer associations in Colombia have been formed fairly recently, since the 1940s. Only the agricultural, coffee, banking, and some professional associations were founded earlier. And, reflecting the relatively weak state these groups faced, they have not developed a single peak association to represent private-sector interests in Colombia. (The closest approximation, the National Association of Industrialists, is sometimes perceived as a regional pressure group for domestic industrial interests.) By and large, individual associations own sectors.

Producer associations have generally supported civilian rule. As a consequence of the heterogeneity of the two traditional parties, all major producer associations have been bipartisan in makeup, often carefully balancing partisan and regional representation on their boards of directors. The establishment of the National Front was facilitated by the support of industrialists, bankers, and merchants. They perceived that return to civilian rule would assure them greater access and policy influence than had been the case with the military regime, and their interest associations continued to play a supportive role in moments of crisis. In fact, because of its bipartisan nature, coalition rule increased channels of access for producer groups even as it fragmented power across party factions, particularly in periods of a weak presidency. Given their access to policy circles and the regime's overall policy orientation, producer associations have remained supportive of the existing regime. Yet, currently, the increased violence and levels of insecurity have led some regional economic elites to employ paramilitary and other undemocratic tactics and to advocate "military" solutions to the country's guerrilla opposition and growing popular-sector mobilization.

Historically, the country's major newspapers have also supported civilian rule, in part because they have had a clear partisan and sometimes factional identification. Because of interfactional disputes, the newspapers have sometimes provided a glimpse of the country's "invisible politics"; yet, by and large, they have remained supportive of the National Front system, indulged in very little serious investigative reporting, and largely ignored the activities of opposition figures. The directors of the major dailies have also provided discreet behind-the-scenes communications links within their own parties or sometimes between the parties in efforts to settle political crises. In recent years, however, journalists have reported more widely on the activities and views of guerrilla and other opposition figures, though often in the face of government hostility. Those who have reported on drug trafficking, and their editors, have also been the targets of intimidation and assassination. This has severely impaired press freedom and integrity.

Class Structure and the Popular Sector

Colombia has sharp disparities of wealth and income across population groups and regions. These especially affect its relatively small black and Indian populations; as in other less-developed countries, the most serious poverty is found in rural areas. Despite various land-reform laws, land concentration remains extremely high in Colombia. Prior to the lower-growth period of the 1980s, evidence suggested that overall income distribution in the country had remained roughly unchanged from the 1950s, though in the 1970s the poorest and richest groups had gained at the expense of "middle-sector" ones, which include many who identify with the popular sector.[63]

Class differences, as already noted, have not been reflected in the party system because of the historic capability of the traditional parties to incorporate new social groups. From the beginning, the National Front agreement was viewed as a means of mass demobilization, even as the parties sought partial mobilization of their electorate at election time. The avoidance of extreme populist or neoliberal economic policies may also have mitigated mobilization around class divisions. There were ambivalent and only partially successful efforts at state-sponsored organization of the lower classes (corporatism). Attempts at autonomy and greater coordination by popular-sector organizations were met with "divide and conquer" strategies (as noted above in the case of the peasant association, ANUC). This appeared to reflect concern about the potential autonomous capabilities of mass organizations.

By the late 1970s and in the 1980s, the parties lacked substantial links to mass organizations, in contrast to the close ties they had had in the early days of the labor organizations. In these more recent years, a sense of political blockage has led many popular-sector groups to seek nonelectoral channels to express their views. Although still only a small percentage of the country's total work force, organized labor is now somewhat more unified. And civic movements and neighborhood associations are also somewhat stronger than in previous years. They represent the potential for a more substantial democratization of the regime, though whether they will be met by accommodation or by repression and further polarization is far from clear. What does seem clear is that democratic consolidation is highly implausible without some reduction in class disparities.

Political Culture

The impact of political culture on regime type has probably not been very large, and its legacy is ambiguous. Both violence and accommodation have strong historical antecedents in the country, and thus both have significant "cultural carriers" and are available as "options" for core groups at critical moments. There may well be young guerrillas whose parents fought in the days of *la violencia*, and whose grandparents, in turn, were active in the turn-of-the-century War of the Thousand Days.[64] Yet, there are probably just as many, if not more, with the same family legacy who have not turned to violence. This "culture of violence" is certainly inimical to democratic politics, though it also means that since violence has been employed so indiscriminately for such differing objectives, it can be difficult for revolutionary movements to link their use of it to their particular political objectives.

Elitist class distinctions and family background continue to play a role in society and in politics, albeit a declining one. The 1974 presidential election, for example, was between the sons of two former presidents (López and Gómez) and the daughter of General Rojas. Upward mobility, though, is not unknown. One consequence of drug trafficking has been to create a new power group, though its violent tactics and the concentration of wealth in such a small number of people sets it apart from the emergence of coffee, industrial or other influential groups earlier in the country's history.

If societal culture is elitist, political parties and elections gained early legitimacy, and military governments have been few and disappointing. Major producer groups have not been predisposed to jettison democratic rights, which they recognize have given them considerable access to policymaking circles. Yet, as the conspiratorial activities of some regional economic groups in conjunction with paramilitary squads, and the advocacy by others of "military" solutions to guerrilla and popular-sector mobilization indicate, support for democracy is still more instrumental than entrenched across all elements of this crucial group. Among many intellectual groups, influenced both by the country's horrible history of violence without radical social change and by the experience with bureaucratic-authoritarian regimes of the Southern Cone countries, there is strong advocacy of democratic rights as well as of socioeconomic reforms.[65]

Ultimately more important than an ambiguous cultural legacy in determining the evolution of democracy in the country have been the concrete actions of political leaders and other major actors in society in specific structural contexts.

Leadership and Statecraft

The role of political leadership and statecraft in putting together the original National Front agreement in 1957 and 1958 was critical to its success. One could argue there had been "political learning" from the earlier failures to compromise that had led to *la violencia*. The change in behavior and in attitude of major political leaders and Church officials was significant. At the same time, the structure of incentives for compromise was much stronger in the 1950s than it had been some ten years earlier, and this undoubtedly facilitated agreement. Furthermore, fear of uncontrollable popular mobilization (stemming initially from the experience of *la violencia*), the extremely limited role of popular groups in the transition to civilian rule, and the rigid nature of the National Front agreement all discouraged greater political incorporation of the population.

In recent years, in spite of many national political leaders recognizing the need for reform, they have had very limited successes in transforming the political rules. In that sense, statecraft has presently fallen short. Yet, one must also recognize that the structure of incentives (assurances of power, economic benefits, levels of insecurity) for regional politicians and for many economic elites has militated against favoring such changes, even as national leaders have also been constrained by the democratic process in Congress and the Supreme Court.

Development Performance and International Factors

Not graced by natural wealth like neighboring Venezuela, Colombia has pursued an eclectic mix of import-substitution and export-promotion strategies, facilitated by a diversified natural resource base. Its prudent, "moderate," relatively consistent economic policies, controlling inflation and fiscal deficits, have permitted the country to achieve steady economic growth rates, maintained support for the regime among principal economic actors, and helped preclude political cycles of democratic populism followed by military repression. Nevertheless, the country's satisfactory growth record did not generate the kind of economic surpluses for the state that could have facilitated agrarian reform or economic benefits for amnestied guerrillas, as occurred, for example, in Venezuela. In fact, Colombia still suffers from widespread poverty and wealth disparities.

In the early 1980s, Colombia was affected by the international recession, climbing world interest rates, and sharp retrenchment of commercial-bank lending that sunk Latin America into deep financial crisis. The impact of the debt crisis was felt in Colombia somewhat later and to a lesser extent, in part because the country was prudent in its borrowing in the late 1970s. Yet the slow growth of the 1980s reflected the country's worst economic situation since the 1930s. The need for economic stabilization in 1984–1985, at a critical moment in President Betancur's peace plan, was especially unfortunate. Yet violence has continued to increase even as the economy has recovered, suggesting the importance of other factors at work.

The economic recovery of 1986 was fueled by a coffee bonanza and increased sales of coal and oil. Unfortunately, world-market prices for these latter two products dropped just as Colombia was moving into the export market, so expected bonanzas became more ordinary gains in foreign exchange. In the mid-1980s, domestic growth in industry has been achieved primarily by bringing installed capacity to full production, and it would appear likely that the high levels of insecurity in the country will begin to affect investment. Continuing balance-of-payments problems and fiscal deficits may force the current government to cut planned public-investment outlays for programs of rehabilitation in areas of violence over the next few years. There is little question that the economic limits imposed by the debt crisis have had a negative impact on the regime's efforts to seek transformation to a more open system.

International factors, then, have played a mixed role in the country's evolution since 1958. Colombia's overwhelming dependence on the export of raw materials such as coffee has meant a strong vulnerability to swings in commodity prices. These problems have sometimes been at least partially alleviated by international assistance. In the early and mid-1960s, when coffee prices remained very low, the country received aid from the U.S. Alliance for Progress and from international financial institutions. The World Bank, in particular, has played a significant financial and institution-building role.

In more recent years, Colombia's boom in the export of marihuana and then, increasingly, cocaine to the expanding U.S. market appears, on balance, not to have been beneficial. Initially accepted for its generation of foreign exchange (and to a lesser extent employment), the narcotics traffic has dramatically weakened the state as it brought violence, corruption, confrontations with the United States, and a growing drug-consumption problem in Colombia. U.S. agencies combating the drug problem, constrained domestically by civil liberties and environmental considerations, have increasingly "exported" their efforts to producing countries, which often have neither the state capacity nor the resources to address the problem effectively (notwithstanding U.S. pressure). The foreign exchange and employment generated by the drug traffic would not be nearly as important if more significant debt-relief measures and more open trade practices were forthcoming from the industrialized countries. In the meantime, in Colombia, numerous government officials have been victims in the fight against illegal narcotics, even as others have been corrupted by it, and the country's international image has suffered.

• FUTURE PROSPECTS: VIOLENCE AND ACCOMMODATION •

The Colombian state is currently under challenge and the country's limited democratic consociational regime, its legitimacy eroded but its capacity for change not yet exhausted, is in the midst of redefinition and reaccommodation.[66] The current government of President Barco began its term seeking to reaffirm more democratic rules of the game, reclaiming a legitimate role for opposition, opening up the political process, and trying to restore the importance of Congress as a center of national debate. It also was seeking to rebuild state institutions, under challenge from years of neglect and the impact of drug trafficking and other violence. Finally, it was attempting to carry out certain socioeconomic programs, especially in areas of guerrilla activity.

In all three efforts—democratization, state rebuilding, and socioeconomic reform—the administration has encountered serious obstacles. Colombians fear the degeneration of the current state of violence into civil war ("Salvadorization") or reactive repression ("Argentinization"); elements of both are already present. As occurred in Austria and the Netherlands in the 1960s, in Colombia in the 1980s consociational mechanisms have remained in place long after any clear need for them. Unlike the two European cases, though, Colombia is a less developed country with substantial social and economic inequalities, a high degree of violence, and a weak and challenged state.

The inherent biases of consociationalism toward conservative rather than innovative or redistributive policies, combined with its strong possibilities for immobilism and policy incoherence, all point to the difficulty of consolidating democracy in less developed countries from a consociational beginning. Consociational practices in a small number of developing countries often provide a more humane politics than likely alternatives. Yet, their inevitable requirement of considerable elite autonomy and their fear of mass mobilization may inhibit development of broader democratic practices. Some regime elites and their allies may seek to use consociationalism not as a democratic solution but as a means of halting significant democratization by defending privilege. Nevertheless, the possibilities for reform of conservative regimes such as the Colombian —inevitably a gradual and uneven process—may provide better hope than an uncertain revolutionary cataclysm.

There is a growing consciousness in the country that if the route of reform and incorporation is not at least partially taken, the alternative is a continuing spiral of polarization and violence. Yet, the country appears inexorably drawn in that direction. For the longer term, however, there are grounds to hope that the foundation for a more democratic polity are being laid. Certain regime elites have perceived the need to move beyond coalition rule and strengthen democratic processes. The social bases for a more democratic politics are strengthening as a consequence of the emergence of more powerful popular-sector groups. And the economic underpinnings of the country appear solid, as coal and oil are added as significant new exports. Just how intense and how long the spiral of violence will be, and how democratic the outcome, are currently being decided.

• NOTES •

1. In a recent review, Huntington noted that explanations for political democracy tended to revolve around two major sets of variables: those having to do with preconditions and those relating to the nature of the political process. See Samuel P. Huntington, "Will More Countries Become Democratic?" *Political Science Quarterly* 99 (Summer 1984): pp. 193–218. For a critique of historical, cultural, and economic determinants of democracy in light of the Chilean case, see Arturo Valenzula's chapter in this volume.

2. See, for example, the concluding work and many of the articles in Guillermo O'Donnell, Philippe C. Schmitter, and Laurence Whitehead, eds., *Transitions from Authoritarian Rule* (Baltimore, MD: Johns Hopkins University Press, 1986).

3. This is not to deny that one of the more robust statistical findings remains the positive relationship between level of economic development and political democracy. It is only to suggest that, though the social conditions associated with a certain minimum level of economic development may be necessary for political democracy, they are hardly sufficient. We are required to consider more interactive and political processes.

Since there appear to be a number of possible routes to democracy and so many various factors that may impinge on the possibilities of its emergence and consolidation, the absence of one or more of these factors may in part be overcome or "compensated" for by the presence of others. Thus, the search for a *single* rank-ordering of variables or factors is probably wrong-headed. In addition, if enough cases emerge with successful or relatively successful democratic experiences, even though they have the "wrong" cultural, socioeconomic, or class-structure profiles, then the nature of those arguments must be qualified and additional or other factors considered. Colombia would appear to be one such case.

4. In its central approach and for many of its specific arguments, this chapter borrows liberally from Jonathan Hartlyn, *The Politics of Coalition Rule in Colombia* (Cambridge: Cambridge University Press, 1988). Readers seeking a more detailed discussion of a number of the topics discussed here are urged to turn to that source. Other recent book-length analyses of Colombia in English include Robert H. Dix, *Politics of Colombia* (New York: Praeger, 1987); and Harvey F. Kline, *Colombia: Portrait of Unity and Diversity* (Boulder, CO: Westview Press, 1983).

5. The state of siege was usually invoked during the National Front and post–National Front years to address student protests, labor demonstrations, or guerrilla violence. However, especially in the 1960s, it was often retained not so much to restrict civil liberties but to provide the president with special decree powers to circumvent congressional immobilism.

6. Miles Williams, "El Frente Nacional: Colombia's Experiment in Controlled Democracy." (Ph.D. Diss. Vanderbilt University, 1976); and Bruce M. Bagley, "Political Power, Public Policy and the State in Colombia: Case Studies of the Urban and Agrarian Reforms During the National Front, 1958–1974." (Ph.D. Diss. University of California at Los Angeles, 1979).

7. Alexander W. Wilde, "Conversations among Gentlemen: Oligarchical Democracy in Colombia." In *The Breakdown of Democratic Regimes: Latin America*, ed. Juan Linz and Alfred Stepan (Baltimore, MD: Johns Hopkins University Press, 1978).

8. Fernando Henrique Cardoso and Enzo Faletto, *Dependency and Development in Latin America* (Berkeley: University of California Press, 1979), p. 179.

9. Robert A. Dahl, *Polyarchy: Participation and Opposition* (New Haven, CT: Yale University Press, 1971), p. 84.

10. Francisco Leal Buitrago, *Estado y política en Colombia* (Bogotá: Siglo XXI, 1984).

11. Bruce M. Bagley, "National Front and Economic Development." In *Politics, Policies and Economic Development in Latin America*, ed. Robert Wesson (Stanford, CA: Hoover Institution, 1984).

12. Samuel P. Huntington and Clement H. Moore, eds., *Authoritarian Politics in Modern Society* (New York: Basic Books, 1970).

13. See Marc W. Chernick, "Negotiations and Armed Conflict: A Study of the Colombian Peace Process (1982–1987)." Paper presented to the 13th International Congress of the Latin American Studies Association, 1988.

14. Lijphart coined the term "consociational democracy" to describe the politics of countries such as the Netherlands in which actual or potential violence between major societal segments was avoided within an open political regime by means of overarching elite cooperation. See Arend Lijphart, "Consociational Democracy," *World Politics* 21 (January 1969); pp. 207–225; Arend Lijphart, *Democracy in Plural Societies: A Comparative Exploration* (New Haven, CT: Yale University Press, 1977); and Eric Nordlinger, *Conflict Regulation in Divided Societies,* Occasional Papers in International Affairs no. 29 (Cambridge, MA: Center for International Affairs, Harvard University, January 1972). See also Robert H. Dix, "Consociational Democracy: The Case of Colombia," *Comparative Politics* 12 (April 1980): pp. 303–321.

15. Issues of conceptualization of the "state" and the "political regime" are complex and cannot be resolved here. In one sense, a political regime may be viewed as a concrete manifestation of a state. It refers to the structures of governmental rules and processes, including such issues as the basis for legitimacy of rule, patterns of leadership recruitment, mechanisms of representation, and forms and scope of domination and control; see David Collier, ed., *The New Authoritarianism in Latin America* (Princeton, NJ: Princeton University Press, 1979), pp. 402–403. The state is a more general and abstract concept involving a compulsory association that claims control over territory and the people within it; see Theda Skocpol, "Bringing the State Back In: Strategies of Analysis in Current Research." In *Bringing the State Back In,* ed. Peter B. Evans, Dietrich Rueschemeyer, and Theda Skocpol (Cambridge: Cambridge University Press, 1985).

16. See Chapter 1 of this volume, n. 19.

17. See David Bushnell, "Bolivarismo y Santanderismo." In *Política y sociedad en el siglo XX,* Lecturas de Historia no. 3, ed. David Bushnell (Tunja: Ediciones Pato Marino, 1975); for electoral statistics of this early period, see David Bushnell, "Elecciones presidenciales colombianas 1825–1856." In *Compendio de estadísticas históricas de Colombia,* ed. Miguel Urrutia and Mario Arrubla (Bogotá: Universidad Nacional de Colombia, Dirección de Divulgación Cultural, 1970).

18. The western half of Colombia is traversed by three Andean ranges, but the country's highest peaks are located off the Caribbean coast in the Sierra Nevada. South and east from the eastern highlands (*llanos orientales*) are the mostly unpopulated Amazon territories.

19. See Alvaro Tirado Mejía, "Colombia: Siglo y medio de bipartidismo." In *Colombia: Hoy* (Bogotá: Siglo XXI, 1978), pp. 102–130; and Robert H. Dix, *Colombia: The Political Dimensions of Change* (New Haven, CT: Yale University Press, 1967), pp. 231–255.

20. See J. Mark Ruhl, "The Military." In *Politics of Compromise: Coalition Government in Colombia,* ed. Albert Berry, Ronald Hellman, and Mauricio Solaún (New Brunswick, NJ: Transaction Books, 1980), esp. p. 182; James L. Payne, *Patterns of Conflict in Colombia* (New Haven, CT: Yale University Press), pp. 111–133; and Leal, *Estado y política.*

21. Paul Oquist, *Violence, Conflict and Politics in Colombia* (New York: Academic Press, 1980), pp. 21–88; certain dates have been modified in accordance with more customary Colombian historiography, discussed in Helen Delpar, *Red Against Blue: The Liberal Party in Colombian Politics 1863–1899* (University: University of Alabama Press, 1981). Casualty figures are from Payne, *Patterns of Conflict,* p. 4.

22. For a complete compilation and analysis of Colombian constitutions, including the 1863 Constitution, see Diego Uribe Vargas, *Las Constituciones de Colombia,* vols. 1 and 2 (Madrid: Ediciones Cultura Hispánica, 1977). English translations of earlier ones may be found in William Marion Gibson, *The Constitutions of Colombia* (Durham, NC: Duke University Press, 1948). On constitutional procedures and elections, see Delpar, *Red Against Blue,* pp. 15, 96; on the economy, see William P. McGreevey, *An Economic History of Colombia 1845–1930* (New York: Cambridge University Press, 1971).

23. See Delpar, *Red Against Blue,* p. xi.

24. Ibid., pp. 188–189.

25. Christopher Abel, "Conservative Party in Colombia, 1930–1953." (Ph.D. Diss., University of Oxford, 1974).

26. Wilde, "Conversations Among Gentlemen," p. 29.

27. See Marco Palacios, *Coffee in Colombia, 1850–1970: An Economic, Social and Political History* (Cambridge: Cambridge University Press, 1980); F. Rojas Ruiz, "El Frente Nacional: Solución política a un problema de desarrollo?" In *La dependencia externa y el desarrollo político*

de Colombia, ed. Rodrigo Parra Sandoval (Bogotá: Universidad Nacional de Colombia, Dirección de Divulgación Cultural, 1970), esp. p. 109; and Charles W. Bergquist, *Labor in Latin America: Comparative Essays on Chile, Argentina, Venezuela, and Colombia* (Stanford, CA: Stanford University Press, 1986).

28. During this period, Colombia adopted a pragmatic foreign policy of *respice polum*—following the "north star" of the United States—as first stated by Conservative president Marco Fidel Suárez (1918–1922). Colombia essentially maintained a low-profile foreign policy, with close ties to the United States, until the presidency of Belisario Betancur (1982–1986). See Gerhard Drekonja and Fernando Cepeda, "Colombia." In *Teoría y práctica de la política exterior latinoamericana,* ed. Gerhard Drekonja and Juan G. Tokatlian (Bogotá: Fondo Editorial CEREC, 1983); see also Bruce M. Bagley and Juan Tokatlian, "Colombian Foreign Policy in the 1980s: The Search for Leverage," *Journal of Interamerican Studies and World Affairs* 27 (Fall 1985): pp. 27–61.

29. Dix, *Colombia,* p. 85.

30. See Palacios, *Coffee in Colombia;* and Gabriel Poveda Ramos, *Políticas económicas, desarrollo industrial y tecnología en Colombia 1925–1975* Bogotá: Editora Guadalupe, Colciencias, 1976).

31. For a more detailed analysis of the 1957–1958 period and the establishment of the National Front, from which some of the paragraphs below have been taken, see Hartlyn, *Politics of Coalition Rule,* pp. 42–74. A valuable study of the breakdown, which also borrows from the consociational literature, is Wilde, "Conversations Among Gentlemen."

32. See Carlos Lleras Restrepo, *Borradores para una historica de la República Liberal,* vol. 1 (Bogotá: Editora Nueva Frontera, 1975); and John D. Martz, *Colombia: A Contemporary Political Survey* (Chapel Hill: University of North Carolina Press, 1962), pp. 44–46.

33. See Payne, *Patterns of Conflict,* pp. 159–182.

34. Miguel Urrutia Montoya, *The Development of the Colombian Labor Movement* (New Haven, CT: Yale University Press, 1969); and Kenneth N. Medhurst, *The Church and Labour in Colombia* (Manchester, Eng.: Manchester University Press, 1984).

35. Wilde, "Conversations Among Gentlemen," pp. 51–58.

36. Oquist, *Violence.*

37. Eric Hobsbawm, "The Anatomy of Violence," *New Society* (April 11, 1963): pp. 16–18.

38. Other analysts who share this emphasis on the central role of party leadership include Wilde, "Conversations Among Gentlemen"; Gerardo Molina, *Las ideas liberales en Colombia de 1935 a la iniciación del Frente Nacional,* vol. 3 (Bogotá: Ediciones Tercer Mundo, 1977), esp. pp. 251–253; and John C. Pollock, "Violence, Politics and Elite Performance: The Political Sociology of La Violencia in Colombia," *Studies in Comparative International Development* 10 (Summer 1975); pp. 22–50. Oquist, *Violence,* is an excellent study and useful regionalization of *la violencia,* presented under an overall interpretation of the "partial collapse of the state," but it may somewhat exaggerate the extension and coherence of the Colombian state in the 1940s (see Hartlyn, *Politics of Coalition Rule,* pp. 42–48). Useful regional studies of this period include James D. Henderson, *When Colombia Bled: A History of the Violencia in Tolima* (University: University of Alabama Press, 1985); and Carlos Miguel Ortiz Sarmiento, *Estado y subversión en Colombia: La violencia en el Quindío años 50* (Bogotá: Fondo Editorial CEREC, 1985). An excellent study of the latter period of violence is Gonzalo Sánchez and Danny Meertens, *Bandoleros, gamonales y campesinos: El caso de la Violencia en Colombia* (Bogotá: El Ancora Editores, 1983).

39. Oquist, *Violence,* pp. 17–18.

40. Martz, *Colombia,* pp. 147–154; Vernon Lee Fluharty, *Dance of the Millions: Military Rule and the Social Revolution in Colombia, 1930–1956* (Pittsburgh, PA: University of Pittsburgh Press, 1957), pp. 127–135.

41. Dix, *Colombia,* p. 116.

42. For descriptions of this period, see Martz, *Colombia;* Dix, *Colombia;* and Tirado, "Colombia."

43. Daniel H. Levine and Alexander Wilde, "The Catholic Church, 'Politics,' and Violence: The Colombian Case," *Review of Politics* 39 (April 1977): pp. 220–249.

44. In fact, where consociational mechanisms can be viewed as necessary rather than helpful, the overall likelihood of democratic politics may be small, but greater with consociational rather than majoritarian practices (see Lijphart, *Democracy in Plural Societies,* pp. 236–238).

45. For a lengthier discussion of these issues, with contrasts to the cases of Venezuela, Uruguay, and Chile, see Hartlyn, *Politics of Coalition Rule,* pp. 237–243. As is discussed by

Levine in this volume, Venezuela successfully moved from a pact-oriented form of political interaction that facilitated democratic transition in the late 1950s and early 1960s (but that was never as formal or constitutionally established as in Colombia) toward more open interparty competition. In Venezuela, as in Colombia, transition was facilitated by the fact that the electorally stronger party, which had lost power in the 1940s (the Liberal Party in Colombia and AD in Venezuela), subsequently accepted a reduced role in a coalition, in order to assure broad civilian support for the ouster of the military leader and a transition to civilian rule. However, in Venezuela, the role of mass mobilization in this process was greater and "fear" of the masses was not as apparent as in Colombia, reeling from *la violencia*. These two factors may have facilitated the fairly rapid shift to more competitive politics in Venezuela in the mid-1960s.

46. In Hartlyn, *Politics of Coalition Rule,* pp. 75–78, I discuss how the various "rules of the game" emerged in response to three predicaments inherent to the political formula of consociationalism: threatened immobilism; lack of popular responsiveness; and policy incoherence.

The political regime's essential continuity and the only partial constitutional dismantling of the National Front requirements makes it difficult to specify when the National Front "ended" and a post–National Front period "began." National-level competitive elections were first held in 1974, but parity in the executive branch was mandated until 1978. Even after 1978, by constitutional mandate the party receiving the second highest number of votes must be offered participation in government. In 1986, for the first time, the losing party refused to form part of the incoming Liberal administration. The most democratically restrictive administration of this entire period has been that of Turbay (1978–1982) in the "post–National Front period."

47. See Fernando Cepeda and Christopher Mitchell, "The Trend Toward Technocracy." In Berry, Hellman, and Solaún, *Politics of Compromise*. For an analysis of a similar phenomenon in the case of Chile, see Arturo Valenzuela and Alexander Wilde, "Presidential Politics and the Decline of the Chilean Congress." In *Legislatures in Development,* ed. Joel Smith and Lloyd D. Musolf (Durham, NC: Duke University Press, 1979).

48. See Bruce M. Bagley and Fernando Botero, "Organizaciones campesinas contemporáneas en Colombia: Un estudio de la Asociación Nacional de Usuarios Campesinos (ANUC)," *Estudios Rurales Latinoamericanos* 1 (January-April 1978): pp. 59–96; and Leon Zamosc, *The Agrarian Question and the Peasant Movement in Colombia* (Cambridge: Cambridge University Press, 1986).

49. See Jonathan Hartlyn and Samuel A. Morley, eds., *Latin American Political Economy: Financial Crisis and Political Change* (Boulder, CO: Westview Press, 1986).

50. See Guillermo A. O'Donnell, *Modernization and Bureaucratic-Authoritarianism: Studies in South American Politics,* Politics of Modernization Series no. 9 (Berkeley: Institute of International Studies, University of California, 1973); and Collier, *New Authoritarianism*. For an evaluation of the bureaucratic-authoritarian model in the context of the Colombian case, see Jonathan Hartlyn, "The Impact of Patterns of Industrialization and of Popular Sector Incorporation on Political Regime Type: A Case Study of Colombia," *Studies in Comparative International Development* 19 (Spring 1984): pp. 29–60.

51. See Richard L. Maullin, "The Colombia–IMF Disagreement of November-December 1966: An Interpretation of Its Place in Colombian Politics," Memorandum RM-5314-RC (Santa Monica: RAND Corporation, 1967); and Carlos Díaz Alejandro, *Foreign Trade Regimes and Economic Development: Colombia* (New York: Columbia University Press, 1976).

52. Conservatives in Argentina, Chile, and Peru feared, respectively, the Peronists after the Radicals (coup in 1966), the Popular Unity after the Christian Democrats (coup in 1973), and APRA after Acción Popular (coup in 1968); see William Ascher, *Scheming for the Poor: The Politics of Redistribution in Latin America* (Cambridge, MA: Harvard University Press, 1984), esp. p. 221.

53. Elections for Congress, departmental assemblies, and municipal councils are determined by proportional representation, and there is no limitation on the number of lists that can be presented under a party name. In the years that parity was in effect, each party label automatically received one-half of legislative seats; within each party, factional apportionment was determined by the percentage of the vote received.

54. See Rodrigo Losada Lora, "Las elecciones de mitaca en 1976: Participación electoral y perspectiva histórica" (Bogotá: FEDESARROLLO, 1976); and Rodrigo Losada Lora, "El significado político de las elecciones de 1978 en Colombia." In *Las elecciones de 1978 en Colombia,* ed. Rodrigo Losada Lora and Georg Leibig (Bogotá: Fundación Friedrich Naumann, 1979).

55. The data on 1970 is from Miles Williams and Rodrigo Losada Lora, "Análisis de la votación presidencial: 1970," in DANE, *Colombia política* (Bogotá, 1972); on 1982 from Elsa Gómez Gómez, *La elección presidencial de 1982 en Bogotá, Dinámica de la opinión electoral* (Bogotá: ANIF Fondo Editorial, 1982). See also Gabriel Murillo and Miles Williams, "Análisis de las elecciones presidenciales en 1974 en Bogotá" (Bogotá: Universidad de los Andes, Departamento de Ciencia Política, 1975); and Rubén Sánchez et al., "El comportamiento electoral de los bogotanos en las elecciones de 1978" (Bogotá: Universidad de los Andes, Departamento de Ciencia Política, 1981).

56. See Robert H. Dix, "Political Oppositions under the National Front." In Berry, Hellman, and Solaún, *Politics of Compromise*.

57. On labor and civic movements during this period, see Luz Amparo Fonseca, "Huelgas y paros civícos en Colombia." (Tésis de Post-Grado, Universidad de los Andes, Facultad de Economía, 1982); see also Victor Manuel Moncayo and Fernando Rojas, *Luchas obreras y política laboral en Colombia* (Bogotá: Editorial La Carreta, 1978); and Guillermo Perry Rubio, Hernando Gómez Buendía, and Rocío Londoño Botero, "Sindicalismo y política económica," *Coyuntura económica* 12 (December 1982): pp. 176–200.

58. See Chernick, "Negotiations and Armed Conflict."

59. This section is based on Hartlyn, *Politics of Coalition Rule*, pp. 216–235; on interviews with a number of relevant actors in Bogotá, Colombia in June 1986 and April 1988; on Chernick, "Negotiations and Armed Conflict"; and on Ricardo Santamaría and Gabriel Silva Luján, *Proceso político en Colombia* (Bogotá: Fondo Editorial CEREC, 1984).

60. For a useful overview of the drug-trafficking problem, see Richard Craig, "Illicit Drug Traffic: Implications for South American Source Countries," *Journal of Interamerican Studies and World Affairs* 29 (Summer 1987): pp. 1–34.

61. Barco technically complied with the constitutional requirement that "adequate and equitable" participation in government be offered to the party receiving the second highest number of votes by naming three Conservatives to cabinet posts. The Conservatives rejected the positions and entered into what they called "reflexive opposition."

62. See Cardoso and Faletto, *Dependency and Development*.

63. Miguel Urrutia, *Winners and Losers in Colombia's Economic Growth of the 1970s* (New York and Oxford: Oxford University Press, 1985).

64. See Gonzalo Sánchez et al., *Colombia: Violencia y democracia, informe presentado al Ministerio de Gobierno* (Bogotá: Universidad Nacional de Colombia, 1987), p. ??

65. See ibid.

66. These observations are taken primarily from Hartlyn, *Politics of Coalition Rule*, pp. 231–235 and 248–249.

• CHAPTER EIGHT •
Peru: Precarious Regimes, Authoritarian and Democratic

CYNTHIA McCLINTOCK

Since 1980, Peru's government has been democratic. By the definition of democracy in this volume, this regime is the first in Peru's history to deserve the democratic label. For the first time, the franchise has been extended to all adults, and the competition for major positions of government power is entirely open to all political groups. This democratic regime has now survived eight years, crossing the major hurdle of a second consecutive constitutional succession. However, Peru's social, political, and economic problems are very serious, even by Latin American standards. Virtually no Peruvian regime has been widely considered successful for more than a decade; the current democracy cannot be considered stable. Peru thus fits the "mixed success: democratic but unstable" point on the summary scale in this volume.[1]

Peru's history of failure with democracy is not surprising. While many social scientists expected democratic consolidation in Latin America's Southern Cone, they did not in Peru or most other Andean nations. Until 1980, virtually all variables predicted to enhance the potential for democratic consolidation were absent in the Peruvian case. For centuries after the Spanish conquest—until 1968—a relatively small group of descendants from the Spanish, almost exclusively white, ruled a large indigenous Indian population. Ethnic cleavages were reinforced by both economic and geographical cleavages: The country's income distribution was one of the most unequal in the region, and European descendants lived predominantly in Lima, the coastal capital, whereas indigenous Indians lived mainly in the Andean mountains. The inequalities in Peru's social structure prompted, by the 1930s, relatively aggressive challenges to the entrenched elites, who were widely referred to as "the oligarchy." Yet, for almost forty years, when political elites in many other Latin American countries were reaching some sort of accommodation with at least middle-class groups, Peru's oligarchy resisted social and political reforms.

Thus, until 1980 the trappings of democracy in Peru were an illusion. Nominal "democracies" were compromised by excluding the mass political party, Alianza Popular Revolucionaria Americana (APRA), from executive power, and by restricting the franchise to literates, thereby denying political

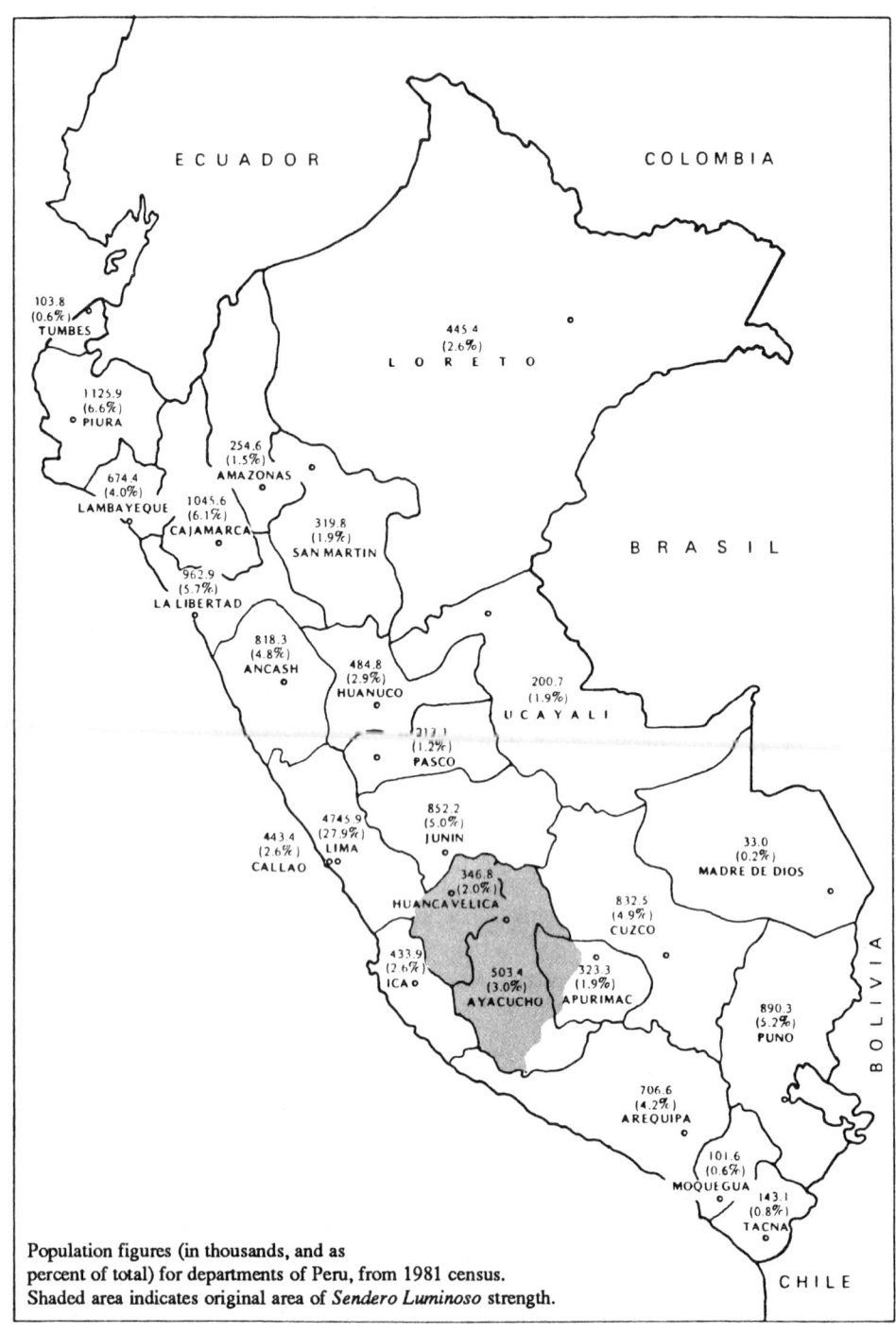

Source: Presidencia de la República, *Peru 1982* (Lima: Presidencia de la República, 1982)

PERU

rights to the bulk of the large indigenous population. About 60 percent of Peruvian adults were illiterate in 1940, and still as many as 40 percent in 1960.[2] Accordingly, in the early 1960s Peru ranked fourteenth among twenty major Latin American countries in the percentage of the population voting.[3] Distorted by these undemocratic features, elections were often won by candidates who were not especially concerned about the welfare of the country as a whole. Indeed, Peru's elected regimes were often less sympathetic to social reform than were various *de facto* (authoritarian) governments.

Peru's authoritarian governments were thwarted, too. While several earned considerable support for a time as a result of their populist and reformist measures, no authoritarian government achieved political institutionalization and long-standing legitimacy. All three major authoritarian governments of the twentieth century ended soon after economic prosperity did.

Will Peru's first real democratic government survive? Considering the propositions in our book about the correlates of democratic government, most analysts would answer no. Many of the key factors expected to enhance the possibility for democratic consolidation are still contradicted by the Peruvian case: The state is weak; economic growth has been dismal; and sharp overlapping subcultural cleavages continue, fueling the flames of guerrilla strife.

However, there are now several factors that do favor democratic consolidation in Peru. Primarily as a result of the far-reaching reforms implemented by the 1968–1980 military government, Peru's class cleavages are not as polarized as they were, and new social groups that endorse democracy are now much more important actors in the political arena. Reflecting on the experience of military rule, these groups, as well as sectors of the traditional elites and the military, seem to have determined—more out of strategic calculations of their own self-interest than from any spiritual commitment—that democracy is their best alternative.

· **HISTORICAL OVERVIEW** ·

Governments in Peru have been more unstable than in any other South American country except perhaps Bolivia. The country's longest period of uninterrupted rule (constitutional or otherwise), the Aristocratic Republic, lasted for only nineteen years (1895–1914). During the twentieth century, the common pattern has been alternation between constitutional and *de facto* rule every five to twelve years. Overall, between independence in the early 1820s and 1985, approximately two-thirds of Peru's presidents have been military, ruling for about 100 of those 160 years. Between 1945 and 1987, Peru's government has been civilian and constitutional half the time, and a military regime half the time.

Peru's colonial experience was harsh.[4] Prior to the Spanish conquest in

1532, Peru was the seat of the Inca Empire, one of the region's greatest civilizations. The Inca Empire was rich and very large. Its territory extended the length of the Andes from northern Ecuador to central Chile, and its population included perhaps 10 million people.[5] Yet less than a hundred Spaniards were able to defeat the Incans, who had been weakened by a leadership struggle. The Spanish *conquistador* Pizarro, betraying a promise, killed the Incan chief Atahualpa, despite the treasure Atahualpa had amassed for Pizarro; this betrayal is highly salient in Andean culture.

Peru became one of Spain's two viceroyalties in Spanish America (the other was Mexico). The Spanish authorities' rule was exploitative and cruel. While the indigenous Indians were not massacred as in Chile, they were drafted to work in the silver and mercury mines of Peru's highlands. Labor conditions were so bad in the mines that mothers would cripple their children to save them from the *mita* (forced labor).[6] By 1600, atrocious labor conditions and new European diseases had decimated the Indian population. The Spanish imposed other hardships as well, forcing the Indians to pay tribute and dispossessing them of much of the best agricultural land, particularly in the highland valleys.

Confronting these conditions, the Indians rebelled frequently. Their stated goal, often, was to restore the Inca Empire. The largest Indian rebellion against Spanish rule was led by Túpac Amaru II in 1780, and gathered substantial support throughout the southern highlands. The Crown repressed the rebellion harshly, killing thousands of Indians.

In the early nineteenth century, as the Latin American independence movement grew, Lima became the center of the Spanish counterattack. Ultimately, it was predominantly foreign forces—Argentine, Venezuelan, Chilean, and Colombian, led by José de San Martín and Simón Bolívar—who brought independence to Peru in 1824. Peru's *criollos* (descendants of the Spanish) apparently feared independence more than did their counterparts elsewhere in the region because, with Lima as the administrative center of Spain's South American colonies, they had received greater political and economic benefits from the Crown. Peru's *criollos* also worried that independence would promote more liberal and egalitarian ideas among the Indian population.

Independence to 1930[7]

As in much of Latin America, the period between independence and the late 1800s was turbulent in Peru. As the country's colonial aristocrats had not participated in the wars of independence, they were displaced from political power by the military leaders of the struggle. For about ten years after independence, these military leaders (or *caudillos*) continued to fight over national boundaries in the Andean region, and then fought each other for power from different regional bases. In Peru's first fifty years of independence, there were thirty-three different presidents, twenty-seven of whom were military officers.[8] Constitutions were written, national congresses were held, but they were all short-lived. A few civilians did become president through indirect congressional selection, but they rarely survived a year.[9]

A major effort to establish a liberal state was not made until 1872, a late date for Latin American countries. The initiative followed Peru's first economic boom; in 1840, Europeans discovered that guano (bird dung) was an excellent fertilizer, and guano sales skyrocketed. Between 1847 and 1878, public expenditures jumped 329 percent.[10] The guano trade was handled inefficiently in a consignment system that benefited a new class of bankers.

Peru's guano entrepreneurs gradually became more and more hostile to what they perceived as the arbitrary mismanagement of the country's new resources by its *caudillo* leaders. Forming the Civilista political party under the leadership of Manuel Pardo, they argued for national integration and export-led economic development. The key means would be railroads and other infrastructure to provide access to Peru's raw materials. In the 1872 "elections," in which 3,778 voters participated, Pardo triumphed.[11]

This liberal experiment was brief. The guano boom was nearing its end; between 1868 and 1872 alone, Peru's foreign debt had quadrupled, and very early in Pardo's term, economic problems became severe.[12] Worse, under the second Civilista president Mariano Ignacio Prado, Peru went to war against Chile in 1879 and was badly defeated. Even worse yet, after the onset of the war, President Prado fled Peru (reportedly with substantial amounts of treasury cash). The Civilistas did not really want to fight the war. They feared that if the Indian peasants were mobilized against the Chileans, the peasants would subsequently turn against them. In 1881, Lima was occupied by the Chilean military. Peace was not achieved until 1883; in the peace treaty, Chile gained important nitrate territories from Peru. The Peruvian military still ponders and regrets its humiliation at the hands of the Chilean military.

Amid the war, Peru's economy and state collapsed. The traditional ruling groups lost all legitimacy. Only the few military men who had tried to fight the Chileans wielded any power. In the first election after the war, in 1885, General Andres Cáceres, who had led peasants against Chileans in Peru's highlands, emerged triumphant.

During the next decade, General Cáceres and his successor, General Remigio Morales Bermúdez, reestablished political order in the country. Perhaps the most pressing problem for the new regime was international creditors' demand that Peru resume foreign-debt service. Through the mediation of U.S. businessman W. R. Grace, an agreement was forged that allowed Peru to reenter international financial markets, but economically the agreement was unfavorable to Peru. To the political opposition, the Grace Contract represented a humiliating surrender to foreign capital. Led by Nicolás de Piérola (who in 1879 had seized power from the Civilistas to try to defend Lima against the Chileans), the opposition also condemned the military governments for failing to build a national state. Military leaders were unable to develop a viable political defense.

In 1895, after the military threatened to thwart Piérola's electoral victory, he came to power in a popular uprising. Although Piérola had been a fiery populist in earlier years, he now forged an alliance with the conservative Civilista party. Piérola's government was the first in Peru's longest constitutional era to date, called the "Aristocratic Republic." The "Aristocratic Republic" endured from 1895 to 1914; after a coup in 1914, the regime was restored in 1915 to survive four more years.

Although suffrage was extended to literate adult males under the Aristocratic Republic, it cannot be deemed democratic by our definition. The literacy clause severely limited the participation of Peru's indigenous peoples, who were, of course, a majority of the population. Although the electorate increased approximately tenfold between 1894 and the early 1900s, still by 1912 only about 10 percent of adult males were registered voters.[13] Electoral participation was also diminished through short registration hours and nonsecret ballots. Fraud was common as well. Moreover, Augusto Leguía, who served as president between 1908 and 1912, and whose inclinations were more populist than most of the other presidents of the period, was exiled in 1913 for several years on political grounds.

The relative longevity of the Aristocratic Republic is widely attributed both to the modernization of the state, initiated by Piérola, and to the export boom between 1890 and 1919. Piérola sought to professionalize the Peruvian military with French military training. He also balanced the budget, stabilized the currency, and rationalized public expenditure.

Partly as a consequence of these policies, Peruvian exports expanded as never before. Between 1898 and 1918, the value of total exports multiplied eight times.[14] Production of sugar, cotton, copper, and oil increased most dramatically. The fortunes that were made in these industries provided the economic base for the political power that was to be wielded for decades by Peru's most elite families, generally referred to in Peru as "the oligarchy."[15]

Peru's oligarchical families formed the core of the Civilista Party at this time. In the early 1900s, the Civilistas split with Piérola's forces, gaining direct control of the state. Between 1900 and 1919, two Civilista sugar magnates became presidents; of twenty-five core oligarchical families who had consolidated their positions at this time, sixteen were represented in Congress, many of them by more than one family member.[16]

There were numerous other effects of the export boom, some of which hurt Peru's indigenous peoples. The growth of employment in manufacturing, mining, and commercial agriculture was robust, and educational opportunities also expanded. However, the new export enterprises often grew by displacing smallholders from their land, and land concentration increased.[17] New mining technologies also at times damaged the ecology of nearby communities. Working conditions in most agricultural and industrial enterprises were abysmal.

In large part as a result of the dualistic character of capitalist expansion in Peru, new social tensions emerged. The oligarchical Civilista Party failed to develop any kind of long-range policy that would ameliorate these tensions, resisting even mild social reforms.

The first crisis for the Aristocratic Republic occurred in 1914, in the midst of Guillermo Billinghurst's term. Billinghurst won the presidency in the 1912 election as the Democratic Party candidate, running on a populist platform when the Civilista Party was in political disarray. Billinghurst sought various reforms, such as the 8-hour day, a minimum wage, and more open and honest electoral procedures. When these proposals were blocked in Congress, Billinghurst called for its dissolution and new parliamentary elections. (Under the constitution of that day, only a third of the Congress had been renewed at the time of Billinghurst's election.) Billinghurst appealed directly to the masses for popular support of his proposal. Frightened and angry, the Civilista political leaders asked the military to oust Billinghurst, and the officers obliged. Apparently, almost all Peruvian elites believed that the coup had been necessary to counter the "disrespectful, insolent and destructive audacity of the lower classes, which were tending to eclipse the ruling class," as one oligarch put it.[18]

New elections were held about a year later, and José Pardo, a sugar magnate, became president. The social tensions to which Billinghurst had tried to respond were becoming worse. Although Peru's raw materials were bringing high prices on international markets, the production of many basic commodities for domestic consumption was displaced, and the prices for these goods rose, too. Inflation was unprecedented. Then, in 1919, with the end of World War I, commodity prices fell, devastating export production and disrupting commerce. Serious strikes erupted; they were repressed by military force.

In the 1919 elections, the Civilistas nominated the planter Antero Aspillaga, a representative of the most conservative Civilista tradition, suggesting the party's political nearsightedness. He was opposed by Augusto Leguía, the former Civilista president who had broken with his party and been exiled for several years. Running as a populist reformer, Leguía gained wide support and swept the elections. However, perhaps fearing that the Civilista-dominated electoral board would try to nullify the results, and that the Civilista-dominated legislature would block his initiatives as it had Billinghurst's, Leguía successfully appealed to the military for a coup on his behalf. The Aristocratic Republic ended.

Leguía, a ruler both populist and authoritarian, governed Peru between 1919 and 1930, an 11-year period called the *oncenio*. Until the last few years of his regime, Leguía enjoyed considerable popular support. He was attentive to the desires of the working class, establishing the 8-hour day and a minimum wage. In Lima especially, the quality of life improved, and employment expanded as huge potable-water, road-pavement, and other important public-works projects were completed. Nor was the peasantry forgotten; the legal standing of peasant communities was restored, and a new Indian affairs bureau began to examine some of the peasants' grievances.

At the same time, however, Leguía was a champion of capitalism. Indeed, his close ties to the United States were a key bulwark of his regime. Leguía's public works were funded in large part by almost $100 million in loans from North American banks.[19] Government revenues doubled during the *oncenio*.[20] Partly in return for this financial support, Leguía welcomed foreign investment. Nor did Leguía damage the economic interests of Peru's oligarchical families. The group that benefited most from the administration was a new one, however, including many relatives and friends of Leguía.[21]

Perhaps especially because of his exile at the hands of the Civilistas, Leguía disdained the democratic rights that they had claimed to uphold. Journalists were periodically detained and deported. The labor movement, the student movement, and peasant rebellions were repressed. Elections were crudely manipulated. Overall, political institutions decayed. Leguía did not try to build a political party or a similar political institution that might have had a long-standing impact on the country.

In 1930, Leguía fell victim to the effects of the worldwide depression, just as most Latin American leaders did. Within a mere three years, export earnings plummeted by more than two-thirds, U.S. bank loans ceased, and many export enterprises fired half their workers.[22] Leguía was overthrown by a Mestizo army commander, Luis Sánchez Cerro.

The APRA Challenge: 1930–1968[23]

The period 1930–1968 in Peru spans the years between the Depression and the Velasco military coup. During this period, Peru became a more socially and politically mobilized country, and many more citizens participated in elections than had previously. But citizens' hopes for social reform through the electoral process were consistently dashed. Several candidates—in particular José Luis Bustamante in 1945 and Fernando Belaúnde Terry in 1963—were elected on the promise of democratic reforms, only to be rapidly overthrown or to retreat from their reformist platform. The most important reason for the political frustration of this era was what might be called the "APRA dilemma." APRA, Peru's first reformist, mass political party, developed before any conservative political parties had been institutionalized and quickly frightened Peru's oligarchy. Soon there was a vicious political circle: Peru's oligarchy refused to accept APRA as a legitimate political party; barred from electoral participation, APRA's behavior was often intransigent and at times even violent; and APRA's antidemocratic actions stiffened elites' resolve to repress the party.

In the wake of the revolutionary social and economic changes of the early twentieth century, radical political currents emerged in Peru. In the early 1920s, a group of students, intellectuals, and journalists called the *indigenistas* gained attention with their writings about the plight of Peru's Indians. In 1924, Haya de la Torre, a former student leader from Trujillo on Peru's sugar-growing north coast, founded APRA. Inspired by the Mexican Revolution, Haya advocated anti-imperialism and reform, but not Marxism. For several years, Haya was a friend of another major Peruvian political thinker, José Carlos Mariátegui, a Marxist and founder of the Peruvian Socialist Party, who was among the first Marxists to emphasize peasant support as essential to revolutionary victory in the Latin American context. In 1928, as Haya's rejection of Marxism became more categorical, the two political leaders' friendship ended. Mariátegui died soon thereafter without having built a strong Marxist movement in Peru.

As the world depression worsened in the early 1930s, Peru's social tensions rose yet further. In part as a result of APRA's stands and in part because of a leadership cult around the charismatic figure of Haya, the party attracted support from Peru's workers, the lower middle class, and students, and it built a permanent base among the sugar workers on the *haciendas* of the north coast. Labor protests became more and more heated. At various times and places, *aprista* militants plotted insurrections (though Haya himself rejected mass violence as an avenue to state power).[24]

In 1931, the most open and probably the most honest election heretofore in Peru's history was held, pitting the Mestizo army commander who had ousted Leguía, Sánchez Cerro, against Haya de la Torre. The franchise was substantially broadened, turnout increased in percentage terms,[25] and electoral procedures were cleaner than ever before.[26] The election was to be the only one in which APRA was allowed to compete for executive power until 1962. It was won handily by Sánchez Cerro, who had enormous popular appeal, probably because of his modest, provincial, lower-middle-class background and Mestizo appearance, as well as his hero status gained through his coup against Leguía. Although oligarchical families began to court Sánchez Cerro successfully before his election, these ties were not evident to the public during the campaign.[27]

APRA's behavior both before and after the 1931 elections was intransigent, alienating both the Sánchez Cerro group and the oligarchy. During the campaign, APRA spokespeople crudely vilified Sánchez Cerro as "an uncultured, illiterate, vain, smelly, dirty, cowardly thief," "a ridiculous, perverse, latent homosexual, mentally retarded and physically an epileptic, a fetid, Black-Indian half-caste," and worse.[28] APRA also denounced the electoral outcome as fraudulent and fervently maintained this position for many years, despite a lack of factual basis for the claim. One of APRA's key slogans was sectarian: "Only APRA will save Peru."

Once in the presidency, Sánchez Cerro quickly allied with oligarchical groups and moved to repress APRA.[29] APRA's entire congressional representation and many other top leaders were arrested and deported, and the party's publications were closed down. Soon thereafter, in July 1932, *aprista* activists rebelled in Trujillo, holding the city for two days. About sixty army officers died in the struggle. In retaliation, when the army regained control of the city, they rounded up and shot between 1,000 and 2,000 suspected *apristas*. Finally, in

1933, Sánchez Cerro was assassinated by an *aprista*. The virulent feud between APRA and the military was on.

After the assassination of Sánchez Cerro, General Oscar Benavides was named president by Congress and ruled for six years, until 1939. Although at first he sought a truce with APRA, he resumed Sánchez Cerro's hard line under considerable oligarchical pressure. For several years, Peru could possibly have been described as in the midst of a civil war.[30] By one estimate, several thousand *apristas* and one hundred non-*apristas* were killed.[31] Most *aprista* leaders were either imprisoned or forced into exile. For their part, *aprista* militants continued to resort to political violence, including shooting the editor of Lima's preeminent newspaper, *El Comercio*, and his wife in 1935. This couple were members of the oligarchical family, the Miró Quesadas; for decades, the family reinforced hostility toward APRA in its paper's features and editorials. During this period also, while Haya de la Torre rejected mass violence as a means to power, he hoped to achieve control through a military coup. *Aprista* leaders sought to infiltrate the army and to identify an officer who would lead a coup and then turn power over to APRA. Needless to say, these *aprista* machinations further fanned the flames of hostility between the party and the military.

Nor did the electoral cause fare well in the 1930s. General Benavides called elections in 1936 but annulled them when the APRA-backed candidate appeared to be winning. Benavides called elections again in 1939, and this time was more careful to put the resources and power of the state behind his favored candidate, Manuel Prado. Benavides was close to numerous members of the Prado family, which was one of the wealthiest in Peru and especially inclined to use its funds for political advancement. Prado won the 1939 election.

Manuel Prado became the only civilian president to complete his elected term between 1919 and 1980. His success was due in good measure to propitious circumstances. As a result of World War II, not only was there strong support for democratic governments from the United States and President Franklin Roosevelt, but world economic conditions improved. Between 1939 and 1945, Peru's exports increased by 60 percent; as a result, the Prado government more than doubled public expenditure.[32] Also, in 1941, Peru emerged triumphant in a border war with Ecuador, reasserting Peruvian authority over several territories. Prado himself was an astute politician, managing at a minimum not to alienate any important group—not the oligarchy, the military, nor APRA.

In 1945, a 3-year period began that was to be Peru's most reformist until 1968. Amid the strongly pro-democratic climate at the end of World War II, the 1945 election was unusually free. APRA was not allowed to run a presidential candidate, but it was permitted to ally with reform-oriented elements in the National Democratic Front, led by José Luis Bustamante.

The National Democratic Front won in a landslide, and APRA gained a majority of congressional seats. But Bustamante was a scholarly lawyer with little political experience and no political base of his own. He occupied a tenuous center between two much stronger poles, the oligarchy on the Right and

APRA on the Left. Although APRA was less militant than in the 1930s, in the more open environment the party was quick to begin new mobilization efforts on the coastal *haciendas* and to orchestrate strikes. In part as a result, wages jumped. The Bustamante government abandoned Peru's traditional economic orthodoxy and enacted price, import, and currency controls.

Facing these new policies as well as a worldwide postwar economic recession, oligarchical families were unhappy indeed. Foreign exchange flowed out of Peru, and elites began a concerted attempt at what is now commonly called economic destabilization. Exports decreased, imports increased, and inflation skyrocketed. Shortages occurred. The economic disarray was complemented by heightened political tensions and violence. *La Prensa*, the country's second most important newspaper at the time, published by a cotton magnate, sought to malign APRA's image.

When one of the paper's managers was assassinated in January 1947, APRA was blamed, though no murderer was ever convicted. The paper's anti-*aprista* campaign was increasingly successful, and Bustamante decided to fire the three *aprista* ministers in his cabinet. A few months later, an indefinite congressional recess was called, through an adroit parliamentary maneuver by rightist elements. In effect, APRA was denied legitimate policymaking participation. To retaliate, Haya de la Torre sought support from Peru's military commanders for a pro-*aprista* coup. At the same time, APRA militants were also seeking an *aprista* revolution. On October 3, 1948, lower-ranking navy sailors rebelled, expecting to undermine the military institution and begin the revolution. Uncoordinated with the APRA leadership, the protest was rapidly repressed, but it exacerbated military suspicions of APRA.

After these events, the Bustamante government declared APRA illegal once again. Yet, to the oligarchs and many sectors of the military, Bustamante's stance toward APRA was still irresolute, and a few weeks later his civilian regime was ended by a military coup.

The military coup of 1948 was led by General Manuel Odría, with the strong support of the oligarchy. Under Odría, the government reverted to extremely harsh persecution of APRA; Haya remained for five years in the Colombian Embassy as a political refugee. Odría also reestablished orthodox liberal economic policies and assiduously courted U.S. investors. Yet he was not an unpopular president; amid the Korean War, Peru's export economy flourished, and Odría was able to launch a large-scale public-works program. However, like Peru's previous authoritarian presidents, Odría did not build a political movement that could withstand new economic pressures. When the export boom ended with the Korean War in 1953, Odría ignored the oligarchy's warnings and refused to cut public spending. Disaffected, agricultural exporters began to fear that Odría intended to perpetuate his rule indefinitely. Political conflict between Odría and various oligarchs erupted, and Odría resorted to authoritarian, gangsterish tactics against them. As more and more elite families withdrew their support from Odría, he apparently saw little choice but to hold elections. After eight years, his regime ended in 1956.

In the 1956 election, the franchise was given to women, and the size of the electorate jumped (see Table 8.1). Still, primarily as a result of the literacy clause, turnout was under 30 percent of adult Peruvians. Former president Manuel Prado won with 45 percent of the vote. Remarkably, Prado came within days of completing his term once again. The economic and social policies of both his administrations were orthodox; no reforms were launched. Yet Prado ameliorated social and political tensions by reaching out further to APRA than most oligarchs wanted. The period was known as La Convivencia for the arrangement between Prado and APRA—legalization of APRA and freedom for the party to organize, in exchange for *aprista* electoral support and moderation of APRA's ideological stands.

As in 1945, the real test of the constitutional regime was over APRA's political power in the upcoming (1962) election. APRA apparently won by the barest of margins over Fernando Belaúnde's Acción Popular, but its 32.9 percent plurality was a shade under the one-third legally required for election. According to the Constitution, Congress would choose among the top three candidates—in this case Haya, Belaúnde, and former dictator Odría. For about five weeks after the elections, the top three candidates debated the electoral outcome and negotiated for the presidency. Then, in July 1962, the military intervened. They ruled for about a year; new elections were held in June 1963 and won by Belaúnde.

Why did the military intervene in 1962? Perhaps the most important factor was its continuing anti-*aprismo*. About three weeks after the election, Haya was

Table 8.1. Voter Participation, 1945–1985

	Estimated Adult Population[a] (Number in millions)	Registered Voters[b] (Number in millions)	(Estimated percent of adult population)	Total Votes[c] (Number in millions)
1945	3.2	0.8	25	0.5[d]
1956	4.0	1.6	40	1.3
1963	4.5	2.1	46	1.9
1978	8.3	5.0	60	4.2
1980	8.7	6.5	75	4.6
1985	10.4	8.3	80	7.6

[a]Twenty-one years and over 1945–1963; eighteen years and over 1978–1985. Figures include illiterates who became eligible to vote in 1980. Source: My approximate calculations from United Nations, *Demographic Yearbook, 1948, 1956,* and *1980* (United Nations: Lake Success, NY), supplemented by Peruvian Census data.

[b]*Source:* Fernando Tuesta Soldevilla, *Peru Político en Cifras* (Lima: Fundación Friedrich Ebert, 1987), pp. 199, 215, 231, 259, 263, 273, and 285.

[c]*Source:* Fernando Tuesta Soldevilla, *Peru Político en Cifras* (Lima: Fundación Friedrich Ebert, 1987), pp. 199, 215, 231, 259, 263, 273, and 285.

[d]Figures available for valid vote only.

informed by the armed forces that he was unacceptable to them as president. The military preferred Belaúnde, who offered social reform without *aprismo*. In a new election, it seemed probable that Belaúnde, whose support had been increasing dramatically, would win. For his part, Belaúnde was opportunistic; he refused to work with Haya or Odría and finally openly called for a coup.

A second key factor was the military's doubt that any of the governments to emerge from the election would be legitimate. While the National Electoral Board and most analysts denied any significant fraud, the voting rolls were in disarray. Moreover, when Belaúnde refused to reach anagreement with Haya, Haya's only alternative was to negotiate with Odría, the most conservative of the three, who had relentlessly persecuted the *apristas* during his administration. An alliance between Haya and Odría did not seem viable. It was after Haya and Odría announced an agreement that the military intervened.

As the military hoped, Belaúnde won the 1963 election. The Christian Democrat, Socialist, and Marxist candidates withdrew from the race, and the bulk of their votes (about 6 to 7 percent of the total) went to Acción Popular rather than to APRA. Whereas APRA called for social reform but was often perceived as sectarian, gangsterish, and out-of-date, Acción Popular called for social reform along with development; Belaúnde seemed "modern" and a model leader for the Alliance for Progress era.

Belaúnde attracted important political constituencies that were newly influential in Peruvian politics. During the 1950s and early 1960s, the Peruvian economy had done very well. With a boom in fishmeal exports and some import-substituting industrialization, new entrepreneurs were gaining economic and political power, undercutting the dominance of traditional agricultural exporters. As communication and transportation into rural areas improved, a new "rural bourgeoisie" appeared in provincial cities. A professional class also emerged; white-collar employment doubled during the 1950s to 15 percent of the work force.[33]

For the first time in Peru's history, the peasantry played a role in the election, despite the literacy clause in the voting law. Belaúnde had campaigned more extensively in the rural highlands than had any previous presidential candidate, and his promise of agrarian reform was salient. His promise was a sign of the times: In the wake of the Cuban Revolution, Peruvian guerrilla groups were going to the highlands "to create another Sierra Maestra," and President Kennedy called for agrarian reform as a major component of the U.S. Alliance for Progress. Although the percentage of the adult population voting in the highlands was still extremely low (under 10 percent in 1963), voters went strongly for Belaúnde—often over 60 percent, versus a nationwide tally slightly under 40 percent.[34]

During his administration, however, Belaúnde failed to fulfil his promises. Agrarian reform was blocked by the oligarchy and by an APRA–Odría coalition in Congress. The highlands guerrilla movement was stopped almost exclusively through armed counterinsurgency, and no major development initiatives were launched in most parts of the highlands. Although Belaúnde had pledged to resolve quickly a 40-year-old dispute with the International Petroleum Company (IPC—a subsidiary of Standard Oil), he stalled until 1968 and then signed an agreement favorable to the company. Belaúnde was also unfortunate to be in office during the end of Peru's export boom and the slowing of economic growth; in the face of a serious balance-of-payments problem in 1967, the government devalued the currency, increasing food prices and alienating the urban poor.

Military Rule: 1968–1980[35]

Although it was not apparent at the time, 1968 was to mark a major watershed in Peruvian politics. The coup by Juan Velasco Alvarado proved very different from earlier coups in Peru, and indeed from almost all previous coups in Latin America. Whereas traditional military *caudillos* had seized power at the bidding of the country's oligarchs, in 1968 Velasco took power as the head of the military as an institution, determined to end the power of the oligarchy. Anti-*aprismo* may have been a factor in the military coup, as APRA was favored to win the upcoming 1969 elections, but the military's commitment to real economic and social reform was the more important element. To this day, the Peruvian military remains the most politically progressive in Latin America.

The Peruvian military developed much more reformist inclinations than other Latin American militaries, in part for very general historical and sociological reasons. Deeply affected by Peru's overwhelming defeat in the War of the Pacific, the Peruvian military has envied the level of national integration achieved by Chile and has doubted Peru's chances to win a second war against Chile if the Peruvian peasantry did not become more patriotic. Especially after the counterinsurgency struggle of the mid-1960s, the military was aware of the economic impoverishment and political subordination of most peasants—just how little stake they had in the Peruvian nation. The military came to believe that, without agrarian reform, defeat in a war with Chile was likely, and renewed insurgencies inevitable. Such beliefs became conventional wisdom in the Peruvian military—but not in other Latin American militaries such as the Salvadorean or Bolivian, whose experiences were similar in some respects—perhaps because the social backgrounds of Peruvian officers are unusually lower-middle-class, Mestizo, and provincial, and perhaps because of the unusually important influence of Peru's national war college, the Center for High Military Studies (CAEM), where instruction often criticized the Peruvian status quo.[36]

While the Velasco coup was thus a response to very deep and long-standing Peruvian problems, it was also a specific reaction to what the military perceived as the almost total failure of Peru's "last, best democratic hope." As noted above, the Belaúnde government failed to implement agrarian reform and failed to nationalize the IPC—both initiatives that the military considered important and overdue. The military came to believe that an important reason for the failure of the Belaúnde government to take action against IPC was that its officials had been bribed by the company.[37] The military officers' anger at the Belaúnde government also mounted with their outrage at the behavior of the United States, which was perceived as at least a nominal ally of Belaúnde. Not only did the U.S. government vigorously back IPC, but it refused to sell Peru F-5 jet fighters and rejected Peru's claim to a 200-mile sovereign off-shore zone for fishing.

General Velasco and his colleagues proclaimed that the goal of the 1968 coup was a bloodless revolution that would ultimately make "real" democracy viable in Peru. The junta did not deem the previous Peruvian political order democratic, but rather a "sellout of the national interest" by "bad politicians" who "acted only to defend the interests of the powerful," and who kowtowed to the United States.[38]

General Velasco was one of the most progressive officers in the coup coalition. As he consolidated his presidential position in the early 1970s, his government expressed more and more interest in dramatic new social designs, in particular workers' self-management, loosely adapted from the Yugoslav experience as well as from Allende's Chile. The government saw itself as a pioneer in the Latin American region, building an entirely new order that was to be a "fully participatory social democracy, . . . in which the means of production are predominantly social property, under the direct control of those whose work generates the wealth; and . . . social, economic, and political institutions [are] directed . . . by the men and women who form them."[39]

Opposition to the Velasco government, though not violent, was considerable, from both the Right and the Left. Peruvian intellectuals tended to dismiss the government's pronouncements as vague and utopian rhetoric that masked corporatist aspirations. They argued that the government's reforms were mere tokens, sops to the masses that would lead not to socialism but to state capitalism, and which would benefit a new industrial bourgeoisie and the military itself.

Ultimately, the Velasco government did not achieve a "fully participatory social democracy," but it did accomplish more than its critics thought it would. The government's highest priorities—to eclipse the power of the United States and the oligarchy—were attained. The IPC was nationalized in a matter of days. The government's agrarian reform was sweeping and provided major benefits to the coastal peasantry in particular. While most of the government's new self-management organizations did not endure into the 1980s, they did capture the political attention of previously marginalized social groups and bring them into the national political arena. It was also true, however, as the government's leftist critics charged, that many of the reforms could have gone further, and that to a considerable degree the structural changes in the state and the economy—for example, the establishment of a large state sector—benefited elites more than the public as a whole.

Although the Velasco government had a rather coherent and viable plan for reform, it did not have a clear *political* agenda. In this respect, the Velasco government resembled Peru's previous military regimes. Officers were undecided whether their government was to last a few years, a decade, or longer. While they claimed to seek a "fully participatory social democracy," this goal often seemed contradicted by their own decisionmaking style, which at the highest levels was closed to input from most social groups and civilians. Although the government was not repressive by Latin American standards—there was no pattern of torture or disappearances—numerous opposition political leaders and intellectuals were deported. Political party activity was severely restricted. In 1974, the government expropriated the country's major daily newspapers. Although the original plan was a complex scheme whereby the newspapers would represent the concerns of various sectors of Peruvian society, within a year or two the papers were mouthpieces for the regime.

While the "fully participatory social democracy" goal would have required that the government hold national elections sooner rather than later, no electoral calendar was specified for almost nine years. Officers apparently feared the disruption of their military institution that would have been entailed by electoral and party politics. The government chose not to establish a political party—a decision that many *velasquista* officers now consider their fatal error. Instead, the agency—National System for the Support of Social Mobilization (SINAMOS)—was established. Amid its own contradictory goals and ideological confusion of the regime's top authorities, SINAMOS was doomed, and it died within a few years.

After 1973, the Velasco government faltered. For various reasons, the economy weakened. Velasco fell ill; intense struggles emerged among different factions of the military. In the wake of rioting in early 1975, almost no group stood up to support the regime. In September, General Francisco Morales Bermúdez ousted Velasco, who died a few years later. In his palace coup, Morales Bermúdez promised to consolidate Velasco's policies but to govern in a less arbitrary fashion.

The economic problems of the mid-1970s grew much more severe in the late 1970s. Between 1971 and 1975, Peru's foreign debt more than tripled, and debt service jumped from about 15 percent of exports in the late 1960s to more than 35 percent in the late 1970s.[40] Petroleum imports soared amid the world's first oil shock, as did food and arms imports, while exports stagnated. When Morales Bermúdez reluctantly sought to refinance Peru's debt, the IMF designed a very harsh stabilization program—indeed, considered too harsh even by most of the IMF's board members.[41] The Peruvian government was angry and tried to evade many of the fund's prescriptions; but, from the perspective of most Peruvian citizens, the government's program was draconian. The sol was devalued by more than 50 percent. In 1978, the real minimum wage plummeted to only 55 percent of its 1973 level.[42] Average daily calorie intake among low-income families fell by 22 percent between 1972 and 1979, to only 62 percent of the internationally recommended minimum level.[43]

Popular protest ensued.[44] Virtually throughout Peru, strikes were intense and frequent. The Morales Bermúdez government tried to repress the popular movements by arresting strike organizers and encouraging the sacking of strike participants, but repression only further fueled social tensions. On July 19, 1977, virtually the entire nation was shut down in a general strike—Peru's first since 1919 and the most massive in the country's history. In response, the Morales Bermúdez government detained an estimated 700 union militants, and companies were allowed to fire about 3,500 workers.[45] While the primary objectives of the strike were at first economic, as strikers faced more serious repression, the demand for democratic freedoms also became prominent. Strikes continued: Another successful general strike was held in May 1978, and the teachers' union was on strike for much of 1978 and 1979.

Confronting such overwhelming opposition, Morales Bermúdez announced a transition to democracy on July 28, 1977, after less than two years in the presidency. Perhaps the most important reason for the military's decision was its own demoralization. Morales Bermúdez felt overwhelmed, trapped between the pressures of the Peruvian people and the pressures of the international financial community.[46] As the economic crisis deepened and popular unrest intensified, the military had become ever more factionalized over the appropriate response. Other factors were important in the military's decision as well. President Morales Bermúdez believed in the viability of electoral democracy for Peru; he established his own political party and ran for the presidency in 1985. U.S. President Jimmy Carter's human-rights policy also persuaded some reluctant officers of the value of military withdrawal.

The New Democracy

In 1978, elections for a Constituent Assembly were held. The elections were honest and free, and 100 Constituyentes were chosen, all from political parties. The 1978 election showed a dramatic shift to the Left in Peru's political spectrum (see Table 8.2). The Marxist Left, which had previously never won as much as 5 percent of the vote, garnered 29 percent of the total valid ballots. This leftward trend was especially pronounced in the highlands and reflected both the gradual impoverishment of this region and political mobilization by the Marxist Left.

A new constitution was proclaimed in 1979. Key new features included enfranchising illiterates and a second-round balloting system. By and large, the Constituent Assembly experience was valuable for Peru's return to democracy. Political leaders from the major parties collaborated effectively in drafting the new Constitution. A major effort was made by both President General Morales Bermúdez and by Haya de la Torre to bury the hatchet between the military and APRA; the effort succeeded.[47]

Table 8.2. Electoral Tallies: 1978, 1980, and 1985 (percentages of valid vote)

	1978 Nationwide[a]	1980 Nationwide[b]	1985 Nationwide[b]
Acción Popular	na	45	7
APRA	35	27	53
Izquierda Unida	29	14[c]	25
Partido Popular Cristiano	24	10	12[d]
Other	12	4	3

Sources: Fernando Tuesta Soldevilla, *Perú Político en Cifras* (Lima: Fundación Friedrich Ebert, 1987), pp. 199, 215, 223, and 231.
[a] For the Constituent Assembly.
[b] For the presidency.
[c] In 1980, the Marxist left parties did not run as a coalition behind one candidate.
[d] Running with an ex-*aprista* faction, as the Convergencia Democrática.

The 1980 elections, the first in which illiterates could vote, were, by our criteria, the first truly democratic ones in Peruvian history (see Tables 8.1 and 8.2). Repudiating the military, the country elected Acción Popular's Belaúnde, the very president whom the military had deposed in 1968. Angry at what they saw as the brutal and unsophisticated behavior of the military, citizens esteemed the statesmanlike character of the former president. In addition, the *aprista* Armando Villanueva was uncharismatic, and the Marxist Left was divided into more than five factions.

Although Belaúnde had campaigned as a Center-leftist, he governed as a Center-rightist. To an even greater degree than during his 1960s administration, he failed to deliver on most of his campaign promises. The major achievements of his second government were restoration of media freedoms and the constitutional transfer of power in 1985. In most other respects, the Belaúnde presidency received low marks from the Peruvian people. The economy deteriorated still further under his government, and Peru was threatened by the most serious guerrilla challenge in its history. Amid the counterinsurgency campaign, the military committed egregious human-rights violations, so many that Peru again did not meet some analysts' criteria for democracy. At the end of the Belaúnde government, more than 55 percent of the respondents in one survey judged the government "one of the worst Peru has ever had" or "a bad government."[48]

In 1985, the charismatic *aprista* candidate Alan García won the presidency in a landslide, receiving more than 50 percent of the valid votes in a contest among four major parties (see Table 8.2). Through the first two years of his 5-year term, President García remained remarkably popular, with an approval rating in Lima of almost 80 percent.[49] Peruvians were especially pleased at the economic upturn of 1986 and 1987. When economic conditions deteriorated again in late 1987 and early 1988, however, the president's popularity plummeted. Citizens were also concerned that, like Belaúnde, García had not been able to check terrorist violence. In mid-1988, for the first time since the establishment of democracy in 1980, coup rumors and presidential resignation rumors circulated in Lima.

• THEORETICAL ANALYSIS •

Why, historically, did democracy fare so poorly in Peru? And why, since 1980, have the prospects for democratic consolidation seemed better, though still uncertain?

Until the 1970s, every variable defined here as affecting democratic outcomes worked against democracy's success in Peru. Because every factor was negative, and real democracy was not even attempted, one factor cannot be isolated as more important than the next. The problems in one area exacerbated the problems in all the other areas, in a kind of vicious circle. For example, Peru's harsh colonial experience both polarized the country's class and ethnic cleavages and badly damaged its political culture. These historical and social problems then raised high obstacles to the development of an effective state and effective leadership. In turn, without a professional state, Peru's development performance was below par for the region. At the same time, economic stagnation had a negative effect on the country's social structure and political culture: Group conflict was exacerbated, and perceptions of political legitimacy were tarnished. Neither the United States nor any other country was sufficiently concerned about the democratic cause in Peru to offer sustained assistance.

Peru's 1968–1980 military government brought about some long-overdue social reforms. In good part as a result, Peru's class structure is less polarized and its political culture more democratic. These changes have made democracy possible in Peru. Its consolidation, however, will probably depend on further changes, in particular the establishment of a more professional state and improved development performance.

Preindependence Heritage

With the possible exception of Mexico, no Latin American country's early history was less propitious for democracy than Peru's. The Spanish conquest, right in the heart of the Peruvian highlands, was traumatic and the subsequent colonial rule brutal. Indigenous peoples' anger and frustration at these events have endured to this day.[50] In the view of many analysts, peasant support for the Sendero Luminoso (Shining Path) guerrillas is due in part to their desire to rid Peru of the Spaniards and return to preconquest traditions.

The Incas were no model for polyarchy either. Rule in the Inca Empire was by decree, and power was based to a large extent on birth. Religion was closely tied to the state. While the Incas were apparently more respectful of human life and local autonomy than the Aztecs in Mexico, democracy was not a political ideal. Their emphasis was on the principles of reciprocity and redistribution.

Class Structure and Political Culture

To the detriment of the construction of democracy in Peru, many features of the preindependence class structure endured for many years. Until 1968, the social science term that was most often used to characterize Peru was "dual." A small, predominantly white, coastal elite held a vast proportion of the country's resources—economic, social, and political—while the Mestizo and Indian majorities held almost none. As Lipset has emphasized, such class polarization tends to produce a political culture that is entirely unconducive to democracy: arrogance and aloofness in the upper class and strong resentment in the lower classes.[51] Fortunately for the democratic cause in Peru, since 1968 the class structure has become much less dual, and the political culture much more democratic.

While the precise figures vary somewhat, virtually every analysis of Peru's income distribution has shown it to be one of the most skewed in Latin America. In 1961, the wealthiest 1, 5, and 20 percent of Peru's economically active population received staggering percentages of the national income: 30, 53, and 67 percent respectively.[52] A mere 100 or 200 families earned the great bulk of property income.[53]

Peru's inordinately skewed income distribution reflected a dualistic, dependent structure of ownership and production. The engine of economic growth was the export sector. Peru's export commodities—primarily cotton, sugar, wool, coffee, oil, and copper through World War II, and subsequently also fish products, lead, zinc, and iron—were produced in relatively large, capital-intensive enclaves. These enclaves were isolated from the rest of the economy, which remained labor-intensive and traditional. Although the agricultural enclaves were owned almost exclusively by Peruvians, as much as 73 percent of mining output and oil production was controlled by foreign firms, based primarily in the United States.[54] In 1968, Peru's "modern," corporate sector generated 67 percent of GDP but employed only 35 percent of the economically active population.[55] While access to business opportunities was not entirely restricted to aristocratic families, the Spanish-descended, pre–World War II clans remained sufficiently predominant that they were almost universally called the oligarchy.

Most of Peru's poorest citizens were, of course, peasants, and from their perspective Peru's gravest problems were land scarcity and land-tenure inequalities. Much of Peru's land is infertile, and the development of new lands has proved difficult on both the country's arid coast and tropical jungle. As a result, land is scarcer in Peru than in any Latin American country except El Salvador.[56] The available land was distributed extremely unequally. In 1961, Peru's Gini index of land distribution was the most unequal reported for fifty-four nations.[57] At that time, an estimated 700 *hacienda* owners controlled more than half Peru's best land.[58]

The dual social structure spawned political attitudes that were antithetical to democracy. Because Peru's elites feared a fully democratic system in which the large indigenous population could participate, voting rights were highly restricted until 1979. Moreover, Peru's elite families collaborated with the military to bar APRA from executive power and to encourage the downfall of non-

aprista reformist presidents such as Billinghurst in 1914 and Bustamante in 1948. While APRA's own commitment to democracy and nonviolence was questionable, elite hostility reinforced *aprista* militancy.

Peru's elites discouraged the lower and middle classes not only from voting but also from organizing. Especially under the authoritarian governments of Leguía and Odría, trade-union organization was repressed. As late as the 1960s, under the nominally democratic first Belaúnde administration, community leaders feared that any attempt to exert pressure on the government could land them in jail.[59] Political control was especially tight on large *haciendas*.

The available cross-national data indicate low levels of both union and party organization in Peru. Only about 7 percent of Peru's economically active population was unionized as of the 1960s, and only about 10 percent of Peru's rural families—versus 40 percent or more of rural families in Mexico, Chile, Venezuela, Colombia, and Bolivia.[60] Whereas approximately two-thirds of a sample of Chilean lower-class settlements considered themselves members of a political party, less than half of a similar Peruvian sample did.[61] In the countryside, a meager 5 to 6 percent of the peasants in various communities reported that they were political party members.[62]

Not surprisingly, in such a context most Peruvians were political skeptics who disparaged Peru's system of government. Unfortunately, no survey directly assessed attitudes about democracy during the 1960s. However, a comparative study in 1965 of lower-class migrant settlements in Lima and Santiago, Chile, when the nominally democratic, progressive Belaúnde government was in power, showed only 20 percent of the Peruvian respondents, versus 60 percent of the Chileans, strongly agreeing that "in general our system of government and politics is good for the country."[63] Only 45 percent of Peruvians, in contrast to 72 percent of Chileans, strongly agreed that "violence should never be the way to resolve political problems." Over 50 percent of the Peruvian respondents said that government officials had given them no help at all—despite the fact that a 1969 survey of peasant's political attitudes found very high levels of political inefficacy and social mistrust.[64] Majorities agreed: "A few have been born to command, others to obey."

The 1968–1975 Velasco government transformed Peru's social structure, and with the changes in social structure came changes in political organization and attitudes. By and large, these changes were advantageous to the establishment of democracy in Peru; however, many obstacles to democracy remained.

The Velasco government expropriated virtually all the major interests of the oligarchy and many key interests of foreign capital. Between 1968 and 1975, the share of Peru's GDP owned by the state catapulted from 13 to 23 percent, and the share of GDP in workers' cooperatives rose from 1 to 10 percent.[65] Wealthy, private capitalists were ousted from agriculture, fishing, and mining—the key oligarchical bastions. The government also nationalized much of the banking system as well as most daily newspapers. With a few exceptions (most notably, the newspapers), the structure of ownership established under the Velasco government endured into the 1980s.

Also, the military government established tariff, exchange, and other policies that promoted industrial development but discouraged agricultural exports. The extractive and manufacturing sectors became the most dynamic sectors of the economy. Manufacturing increased from 23 percent of GDP in 1965 to 28 percent in 1981, a larger increase than in Colombia or Ecuador.[66] The change in exports was even more dramatic, shifting from 60 percent food and agriculture to a mere 20 percent by 1980.

As a result of the reforms of the 1968–1980 period, Peru's "old" oligarchical elites were marginalized not only economically but also politically. For example, though the newspapers were returned to their previous owners in 1980 by Belaúnde, dailies representing oligarchical interests no longer dominated. *La Prensa*, which expressed the interests of agricultural exporters, folded in 1984. *El Comercio* endures but competes against a vast array of more popularly oriented dailies and has only about 15 percent of the market.[67] Perhaps the key to the current political attitudes of the old elite, however, is their suspicion of the military as an alternative to democracy, after the reforms of the Velasco government. The old elite no longer consider the military an ally. If oligarchical preferences—primarily for a free market and favorable conditions for traditional exports—are represented by any Peruvian organization today, it is the conservative political party, the Partido Popular Cristiano (PPC).

A new group of "first families" emerged in Peru. The "new" elite—composed primarily of industrialists and technobureaucrats—are by and large not the children of oligarchs.[68] The new first families have been described as "entrepreneurial," "nationalist," and "developmentalist."[69] They are perceived as "less tied to foreign interests than previous elites, . . . less inclined to rely on interlocking financial networks to assure their wealth."[70]

While no definitive survey of the political attitudes of the new elite has been carried out, considerable evidence is available from journalists' reports of the annual meetings of CADE (Annual Business Executives' Conference),[71] and documentary analysis and interviews by Becker.[72] These reports indicate that most of the new elite holds political attitudes different from the old elite's. Many businessmen are not uncomfortable with a strong state role in the economy; on the contrary, they favor state planning, Andean integration, protectionism, and the like. Perhaps most important, much of the new elite believes that social peace is a *sine qua non* in Peru today. It knows that Peru is on the brink of civil war, and that its economic interests could be devastated in such strife. It fears that a military coup would only exacerbate political tensions. Apparently, in hopes of achieving a national consensus, the majority of the new elite voted for García in 1985.[73]

Another major change in Peru's social structure by the 1980s was a dramatic expansion of the educated middle classes. Both the first Belaúnde government and the military government increased educational opportunities in Peru, and educational levels are now much higher than would be expected on the basis of the economy. Between about 1960 and 1980, secondary school enrolment skyrocketed from 15 percent, about average in the region at the time, to 57 percent—one of the highest in Latin America.[74] The number of university students in Peru multiplied ten times between 1960 and 1982,[75] yielding an enrolment percentage well above the average for the region.[76] Accordingly, about half of Peru's government employees were teachers.[77]

Although the evidence is not conclusive, Peru's new middle classes seem to have gained more economically from the Velasco government's reforms than have all other classes. The military government's reforms did little for Peru's lower classes, but they redistributed income from the top 1 percent and top 5 percent of households to the next 20 percent.[78] This fifth of the population—the winners from the military government's reforms—included white-collar employees, many of whom were employed by the state after the military's reforms.[79] Many small businessmen and merchants were also in this part of the income distribution, as were the wealthiest wage earners in the modern industrial sector and the members of the most prosperous agrarian cooperatives. (Since the late 1970s, however, income distribution has again worsened in Peru, as in many Latin American countries, primarily because of the debt crisis and IMF austerity measures.)[80]

The political attitudes of these middle classes are particularly democratic. According to survey results of the highly respected public opinion firm Datum, the "upper and middle classes"—defined as high-school–educated professionals who earn by the month rather than the day—are consistently more pro-democratic than the lower classes. In most of the surveys, about 15 percent more of the middle classes than the lower classes say that an elected democratic regime is the most appropriate for a country like Peru.[81] The middle classes also appear more democratic on other kinds of political questions, such as the importance of Congress in a democracy.[82]

Considerable numbers of workers and peasants—generally those who were somewhat better-off to start with—gained substantially from the regime's reforms, also. Classes of "middle peasants" and "labor elites" emerged for the first time—with some of these families rising into the top 25 percent of the income distribution. These social classes became politically mobilized, for the most part autonomously of the state (though such autonomy had not been intended by the Velasco government). Gradually, for somewhat complex reasons, these groups came to favor democratic ideas.

Working-class organization grew dramatically. Between 1968 and 1975, the number of recognized trade unions almost doubled, from 2,152 to 4,172.[83] By the early 1980s, about 12 percent of the Peruvian labor force belonged to officially recognized unions, and another 3 percent belonged to unrecognized unions.[84] The trade unions are closely tied to political parties, but not to the state. The largest and most important labor federation, the Confederación General de Trabajadores del Perú (CGTP), is affiliated with the Moscow-backed Communist Party and Izquierda Unida.[85] The second largest, the Confederación

Trabajadores del Perú, is affiliated with APRA.

The Velasco government introduced self-management practices into all industrial enterprises employing more than six workers. About 6 percent of Peru's labor force—some 288,000 workers in about 4,000 enterprises—were incorporated into "industrial communities."[86] These workers received a percentage of the enterprise's profits and shares every year and could participate in enterprise decisionmaking. In the view of most analysts, workers became more politically active and ideologically sophisticated through this self-management experience.[87]

A class of "middle peasants" emerged as a result of the Velasco government's sweeping agrarian reform.[88] The reform devastated Peru's large landowners more than any other in Latin America, except for the Cuban; almost all holdings over 50 hectares were expropriated. Peru's *haciendas* were transformed into cooperatives, run largely by their members, the former workers. These 120,000–odd ex-*hacienda* workers, comprising about 10 percent of all Peruvian farm families and mostly residing on the coast, were the big winners from the reform. Their incomes approximately doubled between 1969 and 1975,[89] enabling many families to become upwardly mobile—establishing homes in provincial cities and sending their children to high school and even to the university. Another 15 percent of (generally highland) farm families also benefited from the reform, though less dramatically. They received some land from expropriated *haciendas* and were no longer obliged to provide semifeudal services to landlords.

Just as in the industrial communities, the members of the agrarian cooperatives became much more politically active and ideologically sophisticated.[90] They not only participated in the new self-management structures—serving on numerous committees and electing their own leaders—but also, in most cases for the first time, formed unions. Survey data showed dramatic increases between 1969 and 1973–1974 in political efficacy, egalitarianism, social trust, and other democratic attitudes.[91] When the state sought to extend greater control over the self-managed cooperatives—dispatching SINAMOS officials and sponsoring a nationwide peasant confederation, the National Agrarian Confederation (CNA), the peasants resisted co-optation. Many cooperative members and other peasants joined the CNA as well as the Marxist Peruvian Peasant Confederation (CCP), but both peasant organizations remained autonomous.

Although labor elites and middle peasants were not particularly active in the popular protests of the late 1970s, which were predominantly Marxist in their leadership and tone, they did become enthusiastic about the democratic transition.[92] They had been listening for years to the Velasco government's calls for a "fully participatory social democracy," and they were engaged in democratic procedures in their self-management organizations. They observed the contradiction between elections and accountability in their workplaces but rule-by-fiat in the nation. Moreover, they came to believe that at the root of the deepening economic crisis was the nature of the military regime.

Thus, popular organizations that grew so dramatically under the Velasco government (as a result both of its social reforms and the new political space it opened for leftist political leaders) used their new strength against his military successor, Morales Bermúdez. In fact, it was the popular organizations—in particular the CGTP, the CCP, and the teachers' union—that were most militant in their opposition to Morales Bermúdez's military government. While at first these organizations primarily protested the regime's harsh IMF–mandated austerity policies, when they confronted severe government repression, they also called for democratic freedoms.

By virtually all indications, every Peruvian social group favored a democratic political regime through 1988. Table 8.3 shows that democratic proclivities, which were considerable in the early 1980s, became overwhelming at the height of Alan García's popularity in 1986, with 88 percent of Lima respondents endorsing democracy over socialist revolution or a military coup. By March 1988, when popular approval of President García had plummeted, 75 percent of a nationwide sample still endorsed the democratic alternative. This percentage approximates the figure for Venezuela, South America's best-institutionalized democracy, where 82 percent of a nationwide sample chose democracy in 1983.[93]

Citizens' responses to other survey questions also attest to their support for democracy. In two 1982 Datum surveys, 73 percent of the respondents believed that Peru's problems could be solved through the democratic system. In 1987, when citizens were asked, "What would you do if tomorrow there were a military coup?" 30 percent responded that they would approve an indefinite general strike.[94]

Citizens' support for democracy is also suggested by their increased electoral participation. Between 1980 and 1985, absenteeism (the percentage of registered voters failing to vote) declined from 18.2 percent to 8.8 percent.[95] In part, the trend was a reflection of more accurate electoral registration, but greater electoral interest was also an important factor. Null votes—which are

Table 8.3. Attitudes Toward Democracy in Peru, 1982–1988

	Preferred Political Regime in Lima				Nationwide
	Feb. 1982	Jan. 1984	June 1986	April 1988	March 1988
Democratic (elected)	66	72	88	81	75
Socialist (by revolution)	16	13	6	10	13
Military (by coup)	11	9	3	7	7
Other, don't know	7	6	4	2	6

Sources: Figures are from Datum polls. The question was: "Which of these types of government do you consider to be the most adequate for a country such as ours?" "N"s are in the 400 to 800 range. *Caretas,* December 13, 1982, p. 22 and *Caretas,* February 20, 1984, p. 24. Data for 1986 and 1988 directly from Datum.

most often a rejection of the electoral process or a mistake—also dropped from 15 to 7 percent.⁹⁶

Yet, some caveats are necessary to our assessment of Peruvians' support for democracy. Although Peruvians endorse "democracy," some do not have polyarchy in mind. In a 1987 Datum survey for Lima, 15 percent of the respondents defined "democracy" exclusively in terms of social equality, and another 8 percent emphasized popular participation. In my nonrandom surveys in coastal cooperatives, more than 60 percent of the respondents defined "democracy" as governmental concern for the people and social justice.⁹⁷ Also, while Peruvians endorse democracy, they may embrace other values more intensely. In a 1986 Apoyo survey in Lima, respondents were asked how much trust they had in a series of values. Democracy scored behind family, work, education, development, religion, the nation, and marriage (in that order).⁹⁸ In another Lima survey, economic growth was valued more highly than democracy.⁹⁹

Still, the dramatic change in democratic attitudes throughout Peru over the last decade has established new parameters for the political choices of Peru's military.¹⁰⁰ Remembering the turmoil of the late 1970s and reading the public-opinion polls in recent years, officers are aware that military rule has been repudiated. They carefully note that, in the 1985 election, former president Morales Bermúdez won under 1 percent of the vote, despite the fact that in various respects his administration had been successful. Military as well as civilian leaders worry that an illegitimate military government would face popular opprobrium and increase citizens' support for guerrilla movements. Officers also remember how severe military factionalization became under their government and doubt the potential for a coherent military regime in the near future.

Perhaps influenced also by the stronger desires for democracy of Peruvian citizens, the behavior of political elites has matured considerably.¹⁰¹ In contrast to the early 1930s, when Haya de la Torre and Sánchez Cerro were the bitterest of enemies, or 1962, when Belaúnde's intransigence facilitated a military coup, Peru's political parties are for the first time putting national goals above partisan ones. On key occasions in recent years, both presidents, Belaúnde and García, have praised opposition party leaders. The tone of the 1980 and 1985 presidential campaigns was high.

Constitutional Structure and Party System¹⁰²

Peruvians' stronger democratic will has been evident in the relative political consensus in the framing of its new constitution, and in the non-factionalization of Peru's party system. While certain aspects of Peru's 1979 Constitution might be questioned in some quarters, no provisions have been widely or strongly condemned. Overall, Peru's constitution has been respected by the country's main political parties; to a certain extent, the parties' endorsement of the constitution can be construed as a pro-democratic pact.¹⁰³

Just as in the past, Peru's post-1979 constitutional system is presidential.

The president is elected for a fixed 5-year term and cannot be reelected. While a prime minister leads the cabinet, he is named by the president and is thus not a functional equivalent to the prime minister in many European regimes. As Linz has argued, a presidential system of this sort is inflexible. During both the Belaúnde and García administrations, five years of an executive and legislature dominated by his party seemed like a very long time. However, at this time, top Peruvian political analysts do not favor changes in the presidential system. For the most part, they fear that a parliamentary system would be unstable and chaotic because Peru's political parties are too loose and undisciplined, and the legislature too unprofessional.

Peru's presidential system concentrates power in the executive, and its legislature is now widely considered too weak. The Belaúnde government actually ruled by decree for about six months during its first year in office, and, between 1980 and 1984, more than two-thirds of all laws were initiated by the executive.[104] Legislative committees tend to be inactive. One reason for the subordination of the legislature to the executive since 1980 has been circumstantial, however; under both the Belaúnde and García administrations, the governing parties controlled a majority vote in both houses of the legislature. To strengthen Peru's legislature, analysts recommend an increase in its resources; mid-term elections that would allow the legislature to reflect changes in public opinion; and possibly the merger of the Chamber of Deputies and the Senate into a single house.

Peru's constitution does, however, provide the legislature with considerable power. It may investigate any matter, and by a simple majority vote the Chamber of Deputies may compel the resignation of any minister or the entire cabinet. The president has no veto power. In these respects, Peru's legislature is stronger than most in Latin America. Indeed, during 1963–1968, when opposition parties controlled it, the legislature was widely considered too powerful and obstructionist. Fears of similar stalemates influenced the makers of the 1979 Constitution to reject mid-term elections.

Of all Peru's political institutions, the judiciary is probably the least effective. In early 1985, when Peruvian elites were asked which institutions functioned the worst, the judiciary was rated third worst, better only than the police forces and social security.[105] In a mid-1970s survey, a mere 14 percent of respondents believed that judicial decisions were based on the law; 70 percent thought they were based on contacts and money.[106] Peru's judiciary has long been wracked by political manipulation, corruption, and underfinancing. The 1979 Constitution sought to strengthen the judiciary, in part by establishing a new Court of Constitutional Guarantees, which would interpret the Constitution just as the U.S. Supreme Court does, but this new court has not been effective. Its justices, like those at other levels, have shied away from difficult decisions, fearing retaliation from the military (on human-rights cases) and Sendero Luminoso (on cases of suspected terrorism).

In contrast, Peru's media are an asset in the democratization effort.

Whereas prior to 1968, oligarchical interests dominated the media, ownership is now extremely diverse, representing very different political views. For example, during 1985–1988, the weekly magazine *Oiga* expressed unusually conservative opinions—so anti-*aprista* that they often appeared to favor a coup—while *El Diario* offered pro-*senderista* views. The center is well represented by the solid, tempered weekly news magazine *Caretas*. Yet, criticisms of Peru's media may be made. Perhaps, some dailies and weeklies are too aggressively partisan. Also, free television time is not provided to the major parties during electoral campaigns; as a result, access to the broadcast medium is extremely disadvantageous to leftist parties, and this is considered unfair and undemocratic by many citizens.[107]

Peru's party system is characterized by some of the features that are considered in this volume to enhance the prospects for democracy, but not by others. Despite proportional representation,[108] the party system is not extremely fractionalized. During the 1980s, there were four major parties: from Right to Left on the ideological spectrum, the PPC, Acción Popular, APRA, and Izquierda Unida (see Table 8.2). While in many countries even a three-party system could pose the problem of a minority presidency—as was due to occur in Peru in 1962 and occurred in Chile in 1970—the dimensions of such a problem were reduced in Peru by introducing into the 1979 Constitution a run-off procedure, in the event that no candidate wins a majority of the first-round vote.

A second feature considered conducive to democracy also applies: Overall, the party system does not reinforce class, ethnic, or regional cleavages. The victorious parties in the 1980 and 1985 elections, the Center-Right Acción Popular and the Center-Left APRA respectively, both enjoyed support from all social classes in all regions, at least at the time of their election.[109] Until 1987, Datum polls showed that while APRA enjoyed more support among lower-class citizens than upper-class, the party maintained the sympathy of 25 to 30 percent of upper- and upper-middle-class citizens. However, in the wake of President García's decision to nationalize private Lima banks, the upper classes felt betrayed by the president and withdrew virtually all their support.

On the other hand, support for the parties at the Right and Left ends of Peru's political spectrum—the PPC and Izquierda Unida, respectively—does not crosscut the nation's social cleavages. In both the 1980 and 1985 elections, the PPC won only 3 to 5 percent in most highland departments, and a 1987 public opinion poll in Lima found that it was supported by 37 percent of the wealthiest citizens, but a mere 4 per cent of the poorest.[110] In contrast, Izquierda Unida's vote in highlands departments has often risen above 40 percent compared to about 25 percent nationwide, and polls regularly show that its support is disproportionately from lower-class voters.[111]

In other respects, Peru's party system does not fit the supposed model for stable democracy. The parties are more ideological than their counterparts in Latin America's long-standing democracies, and the ideological distance between the PPC and Izquierda Unida is vast. Some of the groupings within the

Izquierda Unida coalition would be considered extremist by Colombian or Venezuelan standards; while these groups do not sponsor acts of political violence, they are believed by some Peruvians to condone them. On the Right, PPC's criticisms of the democratic process are at times so strident that the party seems to be calling for military intervention.

Most of Peru's political parties are not deeply institutionalized. By far the best-institutionalized party is APRA, but it has faced serious tensions since the election of García. Many *aprista* veterans consider García insufficiently loyal to the party and worry that he will not favor a party stalwart in the race for the APRA 1990 presidential nomination. Yet APRA has survived a key test of institutionalization—a leadership succession; no other Peruvian party has passed this test to date. The PPC and Acción Popular are personal vehicles for their aging founders, Luis Bedoya and Fernando Belaúnde respectively.

As of 1988, Peru's party system appeared to become less fractionalized, even though charismatic leadership remained a key ingredient in party formation. It seemed likely that, in the 1990 elections, the number of major parties would be three rather than four, representing the Right, the Center, and the Left. The Bedoya and Belaúnde groups were likely to unite under the charismatic leadership of the novelist Mario Vargas Llosa, in a coalition called the Frente Democrático (Democratic Front). While on the Left, the coalition Izquierda Unida has been tenuous since its inception—representing diverse ideological perspectives—it seemed more likely than not that it would hold together through 1990, probably backing the relatively moderate candidate Alfonso Barrantes. Barrantes, who enjoys an excellent record as a pragmatist and conciliator from his 1983–1986 stint as Lima's mayor, is the current frontrunner.

Subcultural Cleavages and Insurrection

Subcultural cleavages have probably been the most important factor in the failed history of democracy in Peru; if the current democratic regime is not consolidated, a primary reason will again be subcultural cleavages. These divisions are sharper in Peru than in virtually any other Latin American country and are more cumulative. Ethnic cleavages are regionally based and closely overlapped by class and religious cleavages. Subcultural cleavage has resulted in civil strife virtually since Peru's inception as a nation and is currently a crucial factor in the Sendero Luminoso rebellion. Since 1980, violence has spiraled; to date, the counterinsurgency efforts of both the Belaúnde and García governments have failed. While both civilian and military leaders know that a military coup is exactly what Sendero wants, disagreements over counterinsurgency strategy could yet end Peru's democracy.

The key subcultural cleavage is between the small group of white descendants from the Spanish conquerors and the indigenous Indian peoples who were conquered and then brutally exploited under Spanish rule. Peru's whites—approximately 12 percent of the population[112]—are likely to be Catholic, residents of the coast (particularly Lima[113]), and relatively wealthy. In contrast, through the 1940s about two-thirds of Peru's population lived in the Andean mountains, and an overwhelming majority of these highland peoples—especially those in the southern highland departments Cuzco, Puno, Ayacucho, Apurímac, and Huancavelica—were impoverished peasants, speaking only Indian languages and adhering more strongly to Incan faiths than Catholicism.[114] Most analysts of Peru considered the white descendants from the Spanish and the indigenous Indian peoples separate "nations," disliking and distrusting each other.

This subcultural cleavage has been exacerbated by Peru's unusually difficult topography. Access between the coast and the Andean highlands—which are steeper and higher in Peru than in any other Andean country except Bolivia—is poor. Unlike the other Andean countries, the capital of Peru is on the coast rather than in the highlands. Thus, whereas the economic and political elites in the other Andean countries are likely to at least visit the highlands occasionally, some of Peru's elites virtually never travel there.

Correlating with this geographical gap is an extremely skewed distribution of productive resources. As of the late 1960s, about 57 percent of the country's GDP was generated in Lima.[115] In the early 1980s, 70 percent of the nation's industrial GDP was concentrated in Lima and 98 percent of all private investment.[116] These dichotomies have sharpened rather than moderated in recent decades.[117]

A major consequence of these inequalities in production is an egregious disparity in regional living standards. Table 8.4 shows that the people of the southern highlands fare worse than those in the central and northern highlands and much worse than those on the coast, especially Lima, on virtually every indicator of well-being—incomes, life expectancy, literacy, medical care, and nutrition. During the last thirty years, indigenous highlands peoples have become steadily poorer—no matter what kind of regime was in power—to the point that their very subsistence was threatened in the early 1980s.[118] In the early 1980s, real highlands farm income was estimated to be about 30 percent less than in 1950.[119]

Why such inequalities? For centuries, the lot of the indigenous Indians was not considered a problem by Peru's governments. The oligarchy's goal was to exclude, not incorporate indigenous Indians into the Peruvian nation. Elites' attitudes were evident not only in their restrictions on the franchise, but also in their reluctance to provide education and other resources to highlands Indians.[120] Interestingly, the military has long been a relatively "brown" profession in Peru—"only" 44 percent of army generals between 1955 and 1965 were born on the coast.[121] It is perhaps in part for this reason that Peru's military leaders were historically more oriented toward social reforms than were civilian presidents.

While the Velasco government's reforms transformed Peru's class structure and political culture, the material benefits to the lower classes were scant. The new middle classes—lower-level professionals, teachers, industrial workers,

Table 8.4. Regional Inequalities

	Annual Farm Income Per Capita (thousands of soles, 1961)	Life Expectancy (years at birth, 1979)	Adult Illiteracy (percentage, 1981)	Without Potable Water (percentage, 1981)	Population Per Physician (1981)	Caloric Intake (percentage of FAO requirements, 1980)
Southern Highlands[a]	3.8	51	45	84	18,000	na
Ayacucho	3.3	51	45	85	16,779	na
Northern and Central Highlands[b]	8.1	57	28	76	8,236	72[e]
Coast[c]	11.2	63	13	48	1,749	na
Lima	30.2	70	5	26	525	96
Fourth World[d]	na	50	57	na	21,124	92

Sources: Consejo Nacional de Población, "Guía demográfica y socioeconómica" (Lima: Consejo Nacional de Población, 1985), p. 1; except, potable water figures from Banco Central de Reserva, "Perú: Indicadores Sociales" (Lima: Banco Central de Reserva, 1986), p. 22; farm income per capita from Richard Webb, *Government Policy and the Distribution of Income in Peru, 1963–1973* (Cambridge, MA: Harvard University Press, 1977), pp. 119–129, and caloric intake from World Bank, *Peru: Major Development Policy Issues and Recommendations* (Washington, DC: World Bank, 1981), p. 35.

[a] Averages for the five poorest southern highlands departments: Ayacucho, Huancavelica, Cuzco, Apurímac, and Puno.
[b] Averages for the three exclusively highlands departments: Junín, Pasco, and Cajamarca.
[c] Averages for the five main coastal departments: Piura, Lambayeque, La Libertad, Lima, and Ica.
[d] Averages for low-income nations in Africa south of the Sahara, from World Bank (vol. 2, 152–155).
[e] Figure is for "northern highlands" only. Exact area is unspecified.

and members of coastal agricultural cooperatives—tended to be Mestizos. As Table 8.4 suggests, the lower classes continued to be composed primarily of indigenous Indians living in the southern highlands. The failure of the Velasco government to help this impoverished subcultural group was a result of several factors. First, the Velasco government's top priority had been to end oligarchical power and wealth, not to aid the poorest of the poor. Second, agrarian reform *per se* could not benefit highlands peasants as much as coastal peasants because of the scarcity and low quality of the land in the mountains.[122] Finally, the military government was unable to redirect public expenditure and investment in favor of the highlands peasantry.

The southern highlands has long been the home base of Peru's rebel movements. Cuzco had been the center of the major Túpac Amaru II rebellion in 1780. Although the guerrilla movements of the early 1960s were led by middle- and upper-middle-class intellectuals from the coast—and in part for that reason were unsuccessful—their activities were primarily in the southern and central highlands. In the early 1980s, the southern highlands department of Ayacucho was the home base of the Sendero Luminoso guerrillas. The strong support for Sendero there was indicated by the high turnout for Sendero-sponsored strikes, and high rates of Marxist voting as well as null and blank voting.[123]

Since 1980, Sendero Luminoso has posed a very severe challenge to democracy in Peru. While Sendero's ideology is Maoist, there are religious and ethnic overtones to the movement. To some *senderista* sympathizers, the struggle is millinerian: The Incan gods have reappeared to battle the Spanish gods, and victory will signify the defeat of the white coastal oppressors and the beginning of utopia.[174] Sendero's membership is estimated at about 5,000 Peruvians, most of whom are young people—the children or grandchildren of peasants—recruited from southern highland universities and, more recently, state universities in Lima. Sendero may be the most sectarian guerrilla movement ever to emerge in Latin America—assassinating political leaders from the Marxist left as readily as those from the right and repudiating the Soviet Union as well as the United States. It may also be the most savage, brutally killing not only political leaders and security personnel but development engineers and peasants whom they deem traitors. Between 1980 and December 1987, guerrillas carried out more than 9,500 violent attacks, and over 10,000 people have died in the political violence.[125]

The Belaúnde government's response to Sendero was ineffective. For almost two years, the government contended that the rebellion was insignificant and tried to ignore it. Not until December 1982–January 1983 did the administration launch a major counterinsurgency offensive, sending the military to the southern highlands. This offensive was bloody: Between 1983 and mid-1985, more than fifty clandestine mass graves were discovered in the southern highlands, with about twenty bodies in each; the number of "disappearances" was estimated at about 2,200; and illegal detention and interrogation centers were established in the zone.[126] The counterinsurgency campaign was exclusively military, with virtually no attention to social, economic, or human-rights problems in the southern highlands. Although many peasants who had been sympathetic to Sendero became frightened and withdrew their support from the movement, violence only increased.

President García's approach differed.[127] Especially during his first year in office, he required a greater respect for human rights from the military. The number of peasant massacres and "disappearances" declined significantly. The García government initiated dialogs with peasant community leaders in key highlands cities; increased economic aid and agrarian bank credit in the southern highlands; and launched a new agrarian reform program in one department, Puno. While these actions seemed to erode Sendero's social base somewhat in the southern highlands, the violence intensified in Lima and some other areas. In 1986 and 1987, the number of civilian authorities and security personnel killed amid the terrorist violence rose sharply: from 35 civilian authorities dead in 1984 to 46 in 1986 and 150 in 1987, and from 82 security personnel dead in 1984 to 106 in 1986 and 228 in 1987.[128]

Why did García's counterinsurgency policy apparently fail? The reasons, of course, are controversial. "Soft-liners" point out that the level of economic aid to the highlands and to Lima's poor was still insufficient, and that human-rights violations—such as the notorious massacre of almost 300 suspected *senderistas* who had mutinied in Lima's jails in June 1986—were still excessive. "Hard-liners," by contrast, propose a more aggressive counterinsurgency policy. There was agreement, however, on several points: not only Sendero but also a second group, the Movimiento Revolucionario Túpac Amaru (MRTA), were wreaking havoc, and both were increasingly able to secure economic resources and peasant support in the coca-growing regions of Peru, where peasants strongly opposed the government's anti-coca programs. Second, intelligence-gathering by security personnel remained woefully inadequate. Third, judicial reform was necessary to assure that prisoners guilty of terrorism would be convicted.

State Structure[129]

If the intensity of Peru's subcultural cleavage is to be reduced, and if the current pro-democratic political culture is to be maintained in Peru, an effective state is essential. Historically, however, the Peruvian state has been unprofessional, clientalistic, and highly centralized in Lima. When the 1968–1980 military government greatly expanded the size of the state, officers' hopes to rationalize bureaucratic behavior were not realized. Indeed, as the challenge of Peruvian economic development appeared ever more daunting in the context of the changes in the world economy in the 1980s, the state seemed to become less and less a rational administrative entity, implementing a cogent economic policy and controlling subversive and illegal actions in its territory; corruption became a more serious problem.

Historically, access to state power has been important to the accumulation and preservation of wealth in Peru.[130] During the "Guano Age" (1840–1879), government officials profited first from licensing guano exploitation to foreign firms and then from transferring the guano consignments to private businessmen. Later, though members of the Peruvian oligarchy were generally not presidents, fortunes were won and lost on the basis of political influence.

In the 1960s and 1970s, the size of the Peruvian state dramatically expanded, from one of the smallest in Latin America to one of the largest. Between 1967 and 1975, public-sector employment almost doubled, increasing from 7 percent of the labor force to 11 percent.[131] By 1981, Peru's public-sector expenditure had soared to 57 percent of GDP, the highest percentage except for Venezuela of the seven largest Latin American countries.[132] State corporations became a major feature of the economic landscape, increasing from twenty-nine in 1968 to 212 in 1984.[133] State enterprises account for about 25 percent of Peru's GDP, one of the highest in the region, and dominate the mining, oil, fisheries, electricity, and banking sectors.[134]

State corporations became a source of patronage. During the Belaúnde government in particular, the salaries of state company officials and workers were extravagant,[135] and in part for this reason the rate of return in public enterprises has been below that in private business.[136] Immediately upon García's inauguration, he launched a "moralization" campaign in the public sector, reducing salaries in state companies and agencies; yet, in the eyes of most Peruvians, political patronage and financial irregularities remain excessive, and state enterprises operated at larger losses in 1987 than in 1985.[137]

Peru's big bureaucracy is an impediment to private investors. Through a simulation exercise, Peru's Instituto de Libertad y Democracia documented that the legal registration of a small clothing factory with two sewing machines would require 289 work-days by professionals, plus more than $1,000 (including several bribes).[138] Faced by such costly bureaucratic hurdles, many—perhaps most—small businessmen ignore the official regulations and enter the so-called "informal sector." "Informals" now dominate many economic sectors.[139]

A further deficiency of the Peruvian state is its centralization. Despite the vast differences and needs among Peru's twenty-four departments, and the poor transportation and communication between many of them and Lima, Peru has not had a federal system of government. The Belaúnde government promoted a set of department-level development institutions—the Corporaciones Departamentales de Desarrollo (Departmental Development Corporations)—but they remained more responsive to directives from Lima than to local authorities.[140] Municipal government exists, but during the early 1980s it controlled only about 4 percent of public expenditure, versus a South American average of over 20 percent.[141] President García has initiated a regionalization project that would yield substantial power over regional development issues to twelve regionally elected entities, but the project has been controversial and its fate is uncertain.[142]

In the 1980s, the challenge of building a professional state that effectively reaches into remote departments has become ever more difficult. First, even low-level development officials are now too fearful of guerrilla violence to work in certain regions. Also, in Peru's prime coca-growing areas, the authority of the state has been undermined by the power and money of drug traffickers. In the context of Peru's sorry economy, it is not surprising that state employees are sorely tempted by drug traffickers' offers.

Peru's state has not directed new expenditures and investment toward the welfare of the country's poorest peoples, the highlands peasantry.[143] To an extraordinary degree, Peruvian public investment has been skewed toward super-scale, extra–high-technology projects. For example, grandiose irrigation projects consumed about three-quarters of the entire agricultural budget during the 1970s, and two-thirds of it during the first three years of the Belaúnde administration.[144] This capital-intensive bias has been criticized from virtually all quarters for numerous reasons: cost ineffectiveness, hugh cost overruns, long gestation periods that are inappropriate in a country with such urgent social tensions as Peru, heavy import requirements, and environmental complications.[145] Meanwhile, relatively inexpensive projects that could benefit larger numbers of poor peasants, such as reforestation, drainage networks, desalinization, and small-scale irrigation have been slighted.

President García achieved some shifts in public expenditure during 1985–1987, but not as much as he had originally promised. In the southern highlands as well as other regions, peasants received more agricultural credit, and the urban poor benefited from a temporary work program.[146] There was a widespread view, both among residents and scholarly analysts, in three provincial cities (Ayacucho, Cuzco, and Trujillo) that I visited during the latter months of 1987 that more money was being spent on local, small-scale development projects than previously. However, overall, public investment remained skewed in favor of super-scale projects on the coast.[147]

Why is Peruvian public expenditure so biased towards large-scale, capital-intensive projects that are often white elephants? In part, the answer is that some state officials continue to take advantage of their positions for financial gain, and that this practice continues to be encouraged by certain businessmen, who seek to get ahead by winning concessions from government officials.[148] Often, the prospect of foreign and domestic funds for a large project stimulates the emergence of a group of contracting firms, who ally with corresponding segments in the bureaucracy. The larger the project, the larger and less noticeable the personal "cuts."

Peruvian public expenditure has been highly skewed toward the military. Not only under Morales Bermúdez but also under Belaúnde, Peru's military expenditures were more than 25 percent of total government expenditures, three times the 8-percent average for the Latin American region and probably higher than in any other South American country between 1975 and 1985.[149] Between

1975 and 1984, the only South American country that might have spent more money for new arms was Chile, for which the available data on military expenditure vary a great deal.[150] The great bulk of the money went for big-ticket items such as fighter jets, rather than for the counterinsurgency effort.[151] Apparently —the data vary considerably—the García government reduced military expenditures dramatically, perhaps by half; as a percentage of GDP, however, Peruvian military expenditures remained high for the region.[152]

It is in good part because of the deficiencies of the Peruvian state that its authority has often been challenged by guerrilla groups. To date, relative to most Latin American militaries, the response of Peruvian officers to guerrilla challenges has been less hardline (in keeping with its overall tendencies toward leftist views).[153] The Peruvian military has never endorsed wholesale repression as the correct state response to subversion. Indeed, to a greater degree than some civilian governments, the Peruvian military has favored social and economic aid for the highlands peasantry. In the 1960s, the Peruvian military looked to agrarian reform as a key component of successful counterinsurgency, and in the 1980s many officers urged dramatic increasees in development aid for the southern highlands. While, especially during the 1980s, human-rights violations were numerous and egregious, they have occurred more out of frustration at Sendero's very effective, clandestine organization than out of any militant right-wing ideology.

Not surprisingly, democracy has not been a traditional concern of Peru's military officers. Officers' primary political concerns have been about effective government rather than democratic government *per se,* as well as about the maintenance of the integrity of the military institution and the attenuation of popular unrest. Accordingly, between 1980 and 1987, the military accepted democracy, making no serious attempt at a coup or at a change in government policy.[154] As noted earlier, officers are sensitive to the unpopularity of their previous government, and to the difficulties that a new military government would face in gaining popular legitimacy without an election. Officers worry that a coup against an elected government would provoke strong protest and possibly civil war. Also, after their twelve years in government, the Peruvian military remained factionalized: Prevailing political attitudes in the army lean toward the Left, while those in the air force and especially the navy lean toward the Right.

In 1988, however, as economic crisis engulfed Peru once again and popular support for democracy eroded, some sectors of the military may have begun to question the efficacy of democratic government and to consider the possibility that a military government would be accepted by a majority of citizens. As the level of guerrilla violence increased in 1988, some officers might determine that Peru is *already* in the midst of a civil war, thereby reducing their fears that a coup would *provoke* a civil war. Still, to govern Peru in the late 1980s is a daunting responsibility. It is at best unclear that the military has any better programs than civilians, and in any case, it can usually lobby the civilian government for its desired program; thus, before risking a coup, officers will probably await the 1990 electoral conjuncture, which promises to be very difficult.

Development Performance

The pattern and rate of economic growth have not been conducive to democratic consolidation in Peru. Economic growth has been sporadic, slow, and unevenly distributed by Latin American standards. Since 1968, when the Peruvian state expanded and began to try to formulate and implement development models, the weakness and inefficiency of the state has been an important factor in Peru's poor development performance.

Historically, the basic problem of the Peruvian economy was its dependence on commodity exports, produced primarily on elite-owned land and mining enclaves. The economy suffered from a high ratio of peasant families for the available land, much of which was of poor quality, and, at least since the post–World War II era, from a labor surplus. Peru's economy often boomed during eras when its exports were valuable on the world market, but the booms were followed by busts. During the boom periods, most governments contracted large foreign debts, which were subsequently difficult to repay. Overall, between the late 1800s and the mid-1970s, per-capita economic growth was only fair in Peru, estimated at slightly over 1 percent a year.[155]

Economic crisis has afflicted both elected and authoritarian regimes in Peru and has been a key factor in the demise of both regime types. The popularity of several authoritarian leaders—in particular Leguía, Odría, and Velasco—lasted almost exactly as long as their governments' economic records were good. Disenchantment with slow economic growth in the 1960s was also a factor in eroding support for the first Belaúnde presidency, and in the 1968 military coup.

Since the 1960s, as Peru's population has exploded, it has become much more urgent that employment opportunities increase and food supplies expand. At the same time, however, especially after 1981, the same economic problems that have afflicted most Latin American countries have hurt Peru, namely heavy debt-service obligations and low prices for its main exports. These problems have overwhelmed the coping capacity of Peru's state. Successive regimes have proclaimed different routes to prosperity, but none have succeeded; indeed, no Peruvian regime was able consistently to implement a coherent development strategy. Table 8.5 shows that Peru's growth rates have been below the average for the region since the 1960s.

As both authoritarian and democratic regimes have failed to sustain solid economic growth in Peru (see Table 8.5), Peruvians have not associated any one regime type with better development performance. In particular, whereas many Latin Americans associate the 1970s military governments with economic prosperity, Peruvians' most recent memory of a military government is that of Morales Bermúdez (1975–1980), when the economy declined at a previously unprecedented rate.

Table 8.5. Economic Growth Rates (Average annual percentages, GNP or GDP, per capita)

	Peru	Latin America and the Caribbean[a]
By Era		
1950–1960	2.9	1.9
1961–1970	2.6	3.2
1971–1980	0.9	3.4
1980–1985	−2.8	−1.6
By Regime		
First Belaúnde government	1.5	2.4
Velasco government	2.0	3.5
Morales Bermúdez government	−1.2	3.0
Second Belaúnde government	−2.8	−1.6

Sources: For 1950–1960, World Bank, *World Tables*, 3d ed. (Baltimore, MD: Johns Hopkins University Press, 1983), Vol. 1, p. 488; for 1961–1970, 1971–1980, and 1980–1985, Inter-American Development Bank, *Economic and Social Progress in Latin America* (Washington, DC: IDB, 1986), p. 152 and Inter-American Development Bank, *Economic and Social Progress in Latin America* (Washington, DC: IDB, 1987), p. 394; for the regimes, Thomas Scheetz, *Peru and the International Monetary Fund* (Pittsburgh, PA: University of Pittsburgh Press, 1986), p. 158, and Inter-American Development Bank, *Economic and Social Progress in Latin America* (Washington, DC: IDB, 1987), p. 394.

[a]For the years relevant to "by regime" for the region as a whole, figures are approximate calculations from data provided by the Statistics and Quantitative Analysis Section of the Inter-American Development Bank.

By 1988, however, an association between economic disaster and democratic government seemed imminent—an association that would bode badly for democratic consolidation in Peru. As Table 8.5 shows, the economic decline under Morales Bermúdez was followed by an even sharper decline under Belaúnde between 1980 and 1985. By 1985, real per-capita incomes were at 1965 levels, the second lowest in South America and only about 60 percent of the Latin American average.[156] For several years, the economy seemed to recover under President García: GDP growth soared to 8.5 percent in 1986 and over 6 percent in 1987, the highest rates in all Latin America for both years; inflation was relatively low; and Peru's poor received a significant share of the benefits.[157] To a considerable degree, however, economic growth was the result of spending Peru's foreign-exchange reserves and strictly limiting debt-service payments; accordingly, when these reserves were exhausted in late 1987 and, not surprisingly, no new international credit was forthcoming, the economy collapsed. In 1988, growth was negative, while inflation exploded and wages plummeted. Now, Peruvians have suffered two consecutive economic failures under a democratic regime, each worse than the last.

The economic decline has meant for the Peruvian people a poverty that has led some recent visitors to compare Lima to Calcutta. In 1984, the legal minimum wage could buy only 20 percent of the food basket necessary for subsistence.[158] In 1979, 65 percent of Peruvian children were estimated to be malnourished.[159] In the slums of Lima (to which many peasants have fled in search of employment and physical safety) and of course in most of the highlands, basic services such as potable water are generally lacking, and accordingly diarrhea remains a major cause of death in children.[160]

Political Leadership

Peru's social and economic problems have long severely constrained the nation's political leaders. Obviously, these problems cannot be solved by one individual. Yet, perhaps just because of the intractability of Peru's problems, citizens are often hungry for a leader who claims that he and his party can wave a magic wand and produce a better Peru. Of course, ultimately these citizens are disappointed by such leaders. Not surprisingly, therefore, in a 1986 survey of the most admired individuals in Peru's history, only one president was on the list of seven men.[161] That president was General Velasco (who perhaps had the "good fortune" to be ousted a year before the onset of economic crisis). The individual at the top of the list was Haya de la Torre, who of course never assumed the presidency. Still, when most Peruvians reflect on democratic failures, they are aware that the problems go much deeper than political leadership.

Because of the severity of Peru's structural problems, Peru's political leaders seemed able to achieve either: (1) social and economic reform on behalf of the nation's impoverished majority; or (2) consensus-building and the maintenance of a liberal political process; but not both. Haya de la Torre seemed to pursue primarily the first goal in his younger days, and then primarily the second. Velasco, of course, pursued exclusively the first goal. Peru's two twice-elected presidents, Manuel Prado and Belaúnde, were both accommodating non-reformists.

Haya de la Torre was a charismatic speaker and a brilliant intellectual. He conveyed a message of salvation and redemption for a suffering people that resonated in the deepest part of may Peruvians' psyche. He was also an institution builder; he nurtured the only political party that has yet survived the death of its founder. Yet, at first, Haya's top priority was not liberal democracy, but reform—even at the expense of constitutional procedures. In part as a result, many critics saw the party as aggressive and sectarian. Subsequently, Haya became more conciliatory. But, choosing to work with Odría during the 1960s, Haya then appeared to have "sold out." Perhaps there were other options available to Haya at these moments; perhaps there were not. The latter interpretation would be suggested by Haya's skillful leadership of Peru's Constituent Assembly in the final years of his life, when he effectively worked for political consensus and a firm foundation for Peru's fledgling democracy.

In a 1988 poll result that bodes badly for Peru's democratic future, Velasco was deemed the best president of Peru since 1950 by a wide margin.[162] Velasco is respected as a social reformer and as a committed, concerned leader who got things done—but without violence. Also, relative to both the Morales Bermúdez regime and the post-1980 administrations, Velasco's 7-year rule was peaceful and prosperous (see Table 8.5). Rightly or wrongly, Peruvians tend to blame the post-1975 economic crisis on Morales Bermúdez, not Velasco.

In sharp contrast to Velasco, Belaúnde was a passive president, both in the 1960s and in the 1980s.[163] In his second administration, Belaúnde's primary goal seemed to be merely a second constitutional succession. He apparently viewed the key means to this goal not so much to be resolving conflict but avoiding it, hoping problems would somehow disappear without his government having to take action that could alienate some important group. For this reason, his administration was often referred to as *desgobierno* (nongovernment). Peruvians were angry that Belaúnde achieved neither economic growth nor greater equity.

President García is an activist, and one of Peru's few presidents to try to achieve both socioeconomic reform and the maintenance of a democratic political process. However, by 1988, his administration was widely considered to have failed also—indeed, in many respects to have been worse than Belaúnde's.[164] Peruvians had held great hopes for García, who is brilliant and charismatic; and so the perceived failure of his administration has a dimension of tragedy. García's apparent conviction that he really could "save Peru" (the decades-old *aprista* promise) gradually tempted him into dangerously wilful decisionmaking. For example, failing even to consult with most of the top leaders of his party, he decided to nationalize Peruvian banks in July 1987. This decision enraged Peruvian businessmen—a group whose support the government needed if its economic strategy were to have any chance of success.[165] For their part, however, García and his closest colleagues tend to blame their administration's failures on the lack of committed, skilled people in the APRA party.

International Factors

International influences have not been decisive in the rise or fall of any Peruvian government. However, at various intervals—perhaps most especially during 1963–1968 and in recent years—international actors have affected the fate of Peruvian governments to a certain extent.

During the twentieth century, by far the most important international actor in Peruvian politics has been the United States. Still, the United States has not had as great an impact on politics in Peru as it has had in many Latin American countries; the United States has never intervened militarily in Peru and did not directly foment any Peruvian military coup. U.S. support was important to various democratic openings in Peru, however, and a penny-wise, pound-foolish U.S. policy toward the 1963–1968 Belaúnde government was one factor in its fall.

At various junctures, the United States encouraged democratic transitions in Peru. Franklin Roosevelt's pro-democratic initiatives contributed to the return of civilian rule in 1939, and to the openness of the 1945 election. The Kennedy administration sharply criticized the 1962 military coup, even withholding recognition from the military regime for almost a month.[166] In the late 1970s, in conjunction with its human-rights policy, the Carter administration provided considerable moral and economic support to the Morales Bermúdez government after it had initiated a democratic opening (see Table 8.6).

However, after democratic regimes have been launched in Peru, U.S. support for democratic principles has seemed to fade. At least prior to 1980, when a new democratic government took actions that were popular but damaging to U.S. economic interests, the United States tended to pursue its economic interests to the detriment of the democratic cause. For example, though the U.S. government was in principle sympathetic to the Bustamante government, the bilateral agenda was topped by the issue of Peruvian debt service.[167] Apparently the United States provided no substantive support to the Bustamante government as the threat of a military coup became severe.[168]

When civilian rule was relaunched in 1963 after Belaúnde's election, the new government was widely considered to be a model Alliance for Progress government: honestly elected and reformist, but not revolutionary. However, when Belaúnde sought to fulfil a campaign pledge to gain nationalistic concessions from the IPC, the U.S. Embassy in Lima criticized the government.[169] After President Kennedy's assassination, when a new agreement between the Peruvian government and the U.S. company had still not been reached, all U.S. aid to Peru was suspended for about a year.[170] The dispute lingered. Although

Table 8.6. U.S. Aid to Peru

	Aid to Peru (millions of current dollars)	Aid to Peru (millions of real dollars[a])	Aid to Peru (percentage of total to Latin America and the Caribbean)
1987	64	na	3
1986	59	16	3
1985	88	27	4
1984	175	56	11
1983	98	33	7
1982	60	21	6
1981	84	31	12
1980	57	23	11
Annual averages:			
1978–1979	70	27	15
1962–1979	38	31	5
1962–1968	44	46	5

Source: Agency for International Development, *U.S. Overseas Loans and Grants: Series of Yearly Data, Obligations and Loan Authorizations FY 1946–FY 1985*, and *FY 1945 – FY 1987* (Washington, DC: AID); includes loans and grants for disaster assistance, economic support funds, PL-480, antinarcotics, Peace Corps, foreign military sales, military-assistance program, and military training; excludes Eximbank loans.

[a]Real values calculated with 1967 = $1.00; from U.S. Department of Commerce, *Statistical Abstract of the United States* (Washington, DC: U.S. Government), Table 763.

the Belaúnde government eagerly sought U.S. aid for public-works projects and the like, actual aid to Peru remained relatively low during these years, only a third to a half of U.S. aid to Chile, for example.[171] Any image of U.S. support for the Belaúnde government was further shattered by disputes over fishing rights and arms sales. U.S. policy toward Peru during this period proved very short-sighted: When the Peruvian military took over in 1968, it immediately expropriated IPC and developed military and fishing relationships with the Soviet Union.

During the 1980s, the United States has effectively communicated a greater concern about Peruvian democracy than it did in the 1960s. However, the commitment to democracy remains tempered by U.S. actions in pursuit of its own immediate interests. During the 1980–1985 Belaúnde government, tensions persisted over trade and transportation rights, as well as over the Peruvian military's enduring relationship with the Soviet Union. With the inauguration of García and a nationalistic stand on Peru's debt service, U.S. aid to Peru declined considerably (see Table 8.6). However, whereas in the 1960s, U.S. Embassy officials in Lima were widely perceived to be puppets of IPC,[172] the officials of the 1980s have not taken aggressive actions on behalf of Peru's creditors. The more sympathetic U.S. attitude would seem to be a result of the overall prodemocratic emphasis of the Reagan administration in recent years, as well as awareness of the fragility of democracy in Peru. Any change in the U.S. attitude on this score would bode badly for democratic consolidation in Peru.

Neither the Soviet Union nor Cuba has played a significant role in Peruvian politics. Of course, Peruvian guerrilla groups have been influenced by Marxist ideology, but neither the Belaúnde nor the García government has found any evidence of Soviet or Cuban aid to Sendero Luminoso. Ironically perhaps, the close relationship between the Soviet Union and the Peruvian military, as well as between the Soviets and some of the Izquierda Unida, reduces any Soviet inclination to aid Sendero. (Sendero itself opposes the Soviet Union as violently as it opposes the United States.)

However, both the Sendero and the MRTA guerillas have gained economic resources from the drug traffickers in the coca-growing areas of the Huallaga River valley and, to a lesser degree, throughout Peru's eastern Andean slopes.[173] Sendero and MRTA activities increased in coca-growing areas in 1987 and 1988 as more coca farmers resisted the U.S.–backed antidrug operations of the García government. Apparently, these activities also helped to fill the guerrillas' coffers.[174] Overall, the international drug traffic is poisonous for democracy in Peru and elsewhere: "Entrepreneurs" flout the law; the police succumb to bribes; and peasants cannot understand why they are asked not to produce such an excellent cash crop.

In recent years, Peru's democracy has been boosted by the rise of polyarchy among the country's neighbors. Since 1983, democratic rule has been in place in every country of the Andean Group (Colombia, Venezuela, Ecuador, and Bolivia, as well as Peru), and also in Argentina, Peru's closest South American ally. No Latin American country wants to be the first to reverse the current democratic trend.

· CONCLUSIONS AND RECOMMENDATIONS ·

For the first time in Peruvian history, the country enjoys a democratic regime, and one with a chance to survive. In contrast to previous eras, some factors are propitious for democratic consolidation in Peru: in particular, the rise of politically organized middle classes and a pro-democratic political culture. Many of the changes in the country's political culture are a result of new political thinking—in particular strategizing about regime alternatives—which occurred during the highly complex and unusual political experiences of the 1968–1980 left-wing military government. In part because of Peruvians' pro-democratic thinking, at key conjunctures the nation's major political parties have stood against a military coup and for political accommodation; by Latin American standards, Peru's party system is not fractionalized.

The consolidation of Peruvian democracy is also favored by the pro-democratic stance of the United States, and by the democratic tides in the region. U.S. policy toward Peruvian democracy has been more sophisticated and sensitive in the 1980s than it was in the 1960s. In the 1980s, the United States has not been as singularly committed to the interests of Peru's international creditors as it was in the 1960s to the interests of the IPC. A continuation of this more long-term, broader outlook by U.S. officials is vital to the consolidation of Peru's democracy. The United States' commitment may be tested in 1990 by the election of Alfonso Barrantes, a Marxist.

Yet, many challenges to Peruvian democracy remain. The indigenous Indians of the remote Andean areas, especially the southern highlands, remain profoundly impoverished, and the cleavage between them and Peru's wealthy, white, Lima-based minority is very deep and extremely long-standing. Since the traumatic conquest of Peru, its indigenous peoples have not trusted white elites, and elites have often taken advantage of Indian peoples. This cleavage—in which region, ethnicity and class converge—has given rise, time and time again, to peasant-backed rebellions. The current guerrilla challenge is the gravest Peru has ever faced, and controversy over how to deal with it could end Peru's democracy.

Peru's colonial experience and its subcultural cleavage have impeded the development of Peruvians' commitment to the nation. Accordingly, some Peruvians try to "get rich quick" rather than to "build Peru." For centuries, the Peruvian state has not been a rational administrative entity; too many officials have considered the "state" as a set of opportunities for graft. In the 1970s and 1980s, as the state expanded and tried to do more, and as Peru's economic problems became more severe, the weakness of the Peruvian state became perhaps the most serious obstacle to Peruvian democracy. Of course, even Latin America's strongest and most professional states have barely coped with the international economic conundrum of the 1980s, and thus not surprisingly the Peruvian state and its leaders have been, essentially, deluged by the crisis. In turn, Peru's disastrous development performance has failed to ease subcultural cleavages and has fueled the nation's guerrilla movements.

It is easy to make recommendations for Peru's democracy but—given the weakness of the Peruvian state—recommendations are hard to implement. President García has called for exactly the same reforms that most political scientists would recommend for Peru: more economic aid for highlands peoples; greater regional autonomy; and more efficient intelligence-gathering. But actually to achieve reform is difficult amid poorly institutionalized parties, when officials fear for their lives, especially if they travel to the highlands, and have so little hope in Peru's economic future that a major concern is the establishment of an economic safety net abroad. I would advance only one recommendation that seems to have been neglected in both Peru and in the United States: the need for greater consideration in antidrug efforts about the effect of these initiatives on peasant support for Peru's guerrillas.

The 1990 presidential elections may prove to be a major test of Peruvian democracy. Whereas both the 1980 and 1985 contests gave clear mandates to relatively centrist candidates, the 1990 race is likely to be a very close, heated contest between the Right and the Left. The Right will probably be represented by the world-class novelist Mario Vargas Llosa, and the Left by Alfonso Barrantes, the former mayor of Lima. To a considerable degree, Barrantes resembles Chile's Salvador Allende: Barrantes has been a politician for many years, and his demeanor is modest and conciliatory; but he is a socialist. It is not clear at this time how Peru's military, the Right, or the United States would respond to Barrantes' election in 1990.

In short, the consolidation of democracy in Peru is at best uncertain. A vicious circle has prevailed, wherein the problems of the country's colonial history and subcultural cleavages have weakened the Peruvian state, which has thereby failed to direct ably the nation's development. In the context of the 1980s international debt crisis, building a more professional state, leading Peru effectively, and improving development performance were difficult—perhaps even impossible—tasks. Peru's failures on these scores in turn exacerbated subcultural cleavages. Yet, there are reasons why Peru's democracy could survive. The popular and elite commitment to democracy—which seem stronger in Peru than almost anywhere else in the region—remains a major advantage.

• NOTES •

I would like to thank the Graduate School of Arts and Sciences at George Washington University and the School of International Affairs at George Washington University for their support of my research on this topic. I am also very grateful to Juan Carlos Capuñay, Luis Deustua, Larry

Diamond, Juan Linz, Martin Scurrah, and Evelyne Stephens for their valuable comments on earlier drafts.
   1. See the Preface, pp. xv and xxvi, n. 19.
   2. Magli S. Larson and Arlene G. Bergman, *Social Stratification in Peru* (Berkeley: Institute of International Studies, University of California, 1969), pp. 363–364.
   3. David Scott Palmer, *"Revolution from Above": Military Government and Popular Participation in Peru, 1968–1972*. Latin American Studies Program Dissertation Series (Ithaca, NY: Cornell University, 1973), p. 9.
   4. On this era, see especially Magnus Morner, *The Andean Past: Land, Societies, and Conflicts* (New York: Columbia University Press, 1985).
   5. Morner, *Andean Past*, pp. 10–25.
   6. Ibid., p. 55.
   7. On this period, see especially Julio Cotler, *Clases, estado y nación en el Perú* (Lima: Instituto de Estudios Peruanos, 1978); David Scott Palmer, *Peru: The Authoritarian Tradition* (New York: Praeger, 1980); Dennis Gilbert, *The Oligarchy and the Old Regime in Peru*. Latin American Studies Program Dissertation Series (Ithaca, NY: Cornell University Press, 1977); Heraclio Bonilla, *Un siglo a la deriva* (Lima: Instituto de Estudios Peruanos, 1980); Morner, *Andean Past*; Carlos Maplica, *Los dueños del Perú* (Lima: Ediciones Ensayos Sociales, 1968); and Manuel Burga and Alberto Flores Galindo, *Apogeo y crisis de la República Aristocrática*, 3d ed. (Lima: Rikchay Peru, 1984).
   8. Palmer, *Authoritarian Tradition*, pp. 36–40.
   9. Ibid.
   10. Cotler, *Clases, Estado y Nación*, p. 94.
   11. Ibid., p. 109.
   12. Ibid., pp. 110–112.
   13. Palmer, *Authoritarian Tradition*, p. 59; Cotler, *Clases, estado y nación*, p. 172.
   14. Cotler, *Clases, estado y nación*, p. 140.
   15. Gilbert, *Oligarchy and Old Regime*. Gilbert carefully identifies various wealthy families, their fortunes, and social networks.
   16. Ibid., p. 55.
   17. For example, in one Puno province, sales of rural properties from Indians to non-Indians increased from 347 between 1896 and 1900 to 1,165 between 1906 and 1910; in Puno as a whole, there were 706 *haciendas* in 1876 but 3,219 in 1915. Morner, *Andean Past*, p. 182.
   18. Cited by Gilbert, *Oligarchy and Old Regime*, p. 69.
   19. Palmer, *Authoritarian Tradition*, p. 63.
   20. Ibid.
   21. Gilbert, *Oligarchy and Old Regime*, pp. 84–9.
   22. Latin American Bureau, *Peru: Paths to Poverty* (Nottingham, Eng.: Russell Press, 1985), p. 32.
   23. Particularly useful works on this era include Frederick B. Pike, *The Politics of the Miraculous in Peru* (Lincoln: University of Nebraska Press, 1986); Gonzalo M. Portocarrero, *De Bustamante a Odría* (Lima: Mosca Azul, 1983); Gilbert, *Oligarchy and Old Regime*; Steve Stein, *Populism in Peru* (Madison: University of Wisconsin Press, 1980); Peter F. Klarén, *Modernization, Dislocation, and Aprismo* (Austin: Institute of Latin American Studies at the University of Texas, 1973); Jane Jaquette, "The Politics of Development in Peru" (Ph.D. Diss., Cornell University, 1971); Larson and Bergman, *Social Stratification*; François Bourricaud, *Power and Society in Contemporary Peru* (New York: Praeger, 1970); Arnold Payne, "The Peruvian Coup d'Etat of 1962" (Washington, DC: Institute for the Comparative Study of Political Systems, 1968); and Howard Handelman, *Struggle in the Andes* (Austin: University of Texas Press, 1975).
   24. Pike, *Politics of the Miraculous*, pp. 158–61.
   25. The 1931 turnout was about 20 percent, almost twice the percentage under the Aristocratic Republic. Latin American Bureau, *Paths to Poverty*, p. 32.
   26. Stein, *Populism*, pp. 197–198.
   27. Gilbert, *Oligarchy and Old Regime*, pp. 96–98; Stein, *Populism*, pp. 101–129.
   28. Stein, *Populism*, p. 166.
   29. One owner of a sugar *hacienda* commented about this time: "[I hope that the repression of APRA will be] bloody, very bloody, and definitively put an end to this damned APRA . . . immediate punishment . . . without waiting for trials and other idiocies." Quoted in Gilbert, *Oligarchy and Old Regime*, p. 103.

30. Pike, *Politics of the Miraculous*, pp. 174–180.
31. Ibid., p. 176.
32. Cotler, *Clases, estado y nación*, p. 256.
33. Latin American Bureau, *Paths to Poverty*, p. 38.
34. Larson and Bergman, *Social Stratification*, p. 383.
35. Valuable studies for this period include: Latin American Bureau, *Paths to Poverty*; Abraham F. Lowenthal, *The Peruvian Experiment* (Princeton, NJ: Princeton University Press, 1975); Cynthia McClintock and Abraham F. Lowenthal, eds., *The Peruvian Experiment Reconsidered* (Princeton, NJ: Princeton University Press, 1983); Cynthia McClintock, *Peasant Cooperatives and Political Change in Peru* (Princeton, NJ: Princeton University Press, 1981); NACLA, "Peru Today," *NACLA Report on the Americas* 14, no. 6 (November-December 1980); Henry Pease García, *El ocaso del poder oligárquico* (Lima: DESCO, 1977); and Alfred C. Stepan, *The State and Society: Peru in Comparative Perspective* (Princeton, NJ: Princeton University Press, 1978).
36. Luigi R. Einaudi and Alfred C. Stepan, *Latin American Institutional Development* (Los Angeles: Rand Corporation, 1971), esp. p. 56; Victor Villaneuva, *El CAEM y la revolución de la Fuerza Armada* (Lima: Instituto de Estudios Peruanos, 1973); Carlos A. Astiz, *Pressure Groups and Power Elites in Peruvian Politics* (Ithaca, NY: Cornell University Press, 1969), p. 143.
37. Adalberto J. Pinelo, *The Multinational Corporation as a Force in Latin American Politics* (New York: Praeger, 1973), p. 150.
38. From the Manifesto of the Revolutionary Government of the Armed Forces, October 2, 1968, reprinted in María del Pilar Tello, ed., *Golpe o revolución? Hablan los militares del '68* (Lima: Sagsa, 1983), pp. 284–285. Velasco communicated a similar message in more colloquial language a few years after the end of his government, in response to a reporter's question about the objective of his government: "[Our goal] was to make Peru an independent country, to change the social structure so that Peru could develop with independence and sovereignty. Not a sold-out nation on its knees. What was it like here? Here the American ambassador ruled! When I became president, the American ambassador had to ask for an appointment and I kept my distance. I kicked out the American military mission. . . . We also routed the oligarchy." Quoted in *Caretas* (Lima) February 3, 1977, pp. 30–31.
39. Juan Velasco Alvarado, *Velasco: La voz de la revolución*, 2 vols. (Lima: Ediciones Participación, 1972), 2: 271.
40. Thomas Scheetz, *Peru and the International Monetary Fund* (Pittsburgh, PA: University of Pittsburgh Press, 1986), p. 184.
41. Ibid., p. 140.
42. Henry A. Dietz, "National Recovery vs. Individual Stagnation: Peru's Urban Poor Since 1978." Paper presented at the 44th International Congress of Americanists, University of Manchester, England, September 5–10, 1982, Table 3.
43. Latin American Bureau, *Paths to Poverty*, p. 67.
44. For more detailed information on this period, see Henry Pease García, *Los caminos del poder* (Lima: DESCO, 1979); Latin American Bureau, *Paths to Poverty*; NACLA, "Peru Today."
45. Latin American Bureau, *Paths to Poverty*, p. 70.
46. Interviews with President Morales Bermúdez, June 1985 and July 1986, and with Ambassador Harry Schlaudeman, January 14, 1986.
47. Interviews with Morales Bermúdez and Schlaudeman. See also Luis A. Abugattas, "Populism and After: The Peruvian Experience." In *Authoritarians and Democrats*, ed. James M. Malloy and Mitchell A. Seligson (Pittsburgh, PA: University of Pittsburgh Press, 1987), pp. 134–135.
48. *Debate* 7, no. 32 (May 1985), 24–28.
49. *Caretas* (January), 19, 1987, p. 22. In contrast, after eighteen months in office, Belaúnde's approval rating had been a mere 40 percent; *Caretas* (February), 14, 1983, p. 21.
50. Manuel Burga, "Indians Against *Mistis*: The Andean Utopia at the Crossroads." Colloquium Abstract Paper. Latin American Program, Woodrow Wilson Center, August 1986.
51. Seymour Martin Lipset, *Political Man: The Social Bases of Politics* (New York: Anchor Books, 1963).
52. Richard Webb, *Government Policy and the Distribution of Income in Peru, 1963–1973* (Cambridge, MA: Harvard University Press, 1977), p. 6.
53. Ibid., p. 85. The shares to the wealthiest were larger in Peru even than in Brazil or Mexico, the two Latin American countries that are perhaps most often described as inegalitarian. See Susan Eckstein, "Revolution and Redistribution in Latin America." In McClintock and Lowen-

thal, *Peruvian Experiment Reconsidered*, pp. 368–369; James W. Howe, *The U.S. and World Development* (New York: Overseas Development Council; Praeger, 1975), p. 215.

54. Rosemary Thorp and Geoffrey Bertram, *Peru, 1890–1977: Growth and Policy in an Open Economy* (New York: Columbia University Press, 1978), p. 212.

55. Ibid., p. 9.

56. Daniel Martínez and Armando Tealdo, *El agro peruano, 1970–1980* (Lima: CEDEP, 1982), p. 39.

57. Charles Lewis Taylor and Michael C. Hudson, *World Handbook of Political and Social Indicators* (New Haven, CT: Yale University Press, 1972), p. 267.

58. McClintock, *Peasant Cooperatives*, p. 73.

59. Handelman, *Struggle in the Andes*, p. 221.

60. Oscar Delgado, "La organización de los campesinos y el sistema político," *Apuntes* 25 (July 1972): p. 86; Astiz, *Pressure Groups and Power Elites*, p. 214.

61. Daniel Goldrich, Raymond B. Pratt, and G. R. Schuller, "The Political Integration of Lower-Class Urban Settlements in Chile and Peru." In *Peruvian Nationalism: A Corporatist Revolution*, ed. David Chaplin (New Brunswick, NJ: Transaction, 1976).

62. McClintock, *Peasant Cooperatives*, p. 162.

63. Goldrich, Pratt, and Schuller, "Political Integration."

64. McClintock, *Peasant Cooperatives*, pp. 156–207. The survey, conducted by a joint Cornell University and Instituto de Estudios Peruanos research team, interviewed 1,581 adults in eighteen rural sites.

65. Bernardo Sorj, "Public Enterprises and the Question of the State Bourgeoisie, 1968–1976." In *Military Reformism and Social Classes*, ed. David Booth and Bernardo Sorj (London: MacMillan, 1983), p. 78.

66. World Bank, *World Tables*, 3d ed., 2 vols. (Washington, DC: World Bank, 1983), 1: 512.

67. *Caretas* (December 1), 1986, p. 31.

68. Compare the list of oligarchical family names in Gilbert, *Oligarchy and Old Regime*, p. 342, with the list of key staff in *The Andean Report* XII, no. 9 (October 1985), pp. 205–207. On a list of 100 key public-sector staff in 1985, at most six or seven of the names were from oligarchical families.

69. David G. Becker, *The New Bourgeoisie and the Limits of Dependency* (Princeton, NJ: Princeton University Press, 1983), pp. 330–355.

70. Abraham F. Lowenthal, "The Peruvian Experiment Reconsidered." In McClintock and Lowenthal, *Peruvian Experiment Reconsidered*, p. 426.

71. *Caretas* (Lima), November 24, 1984 and November 25, 1985; *Debate* 30 (December 1984): pp. 14–18.

72. David G. Becker, "Bourgeois Hegemony and Political Institutions in Latin America: The Peruvian Case." Paper presented at the Annual Meeting of the American Political Science Association, New Orleans, LA, August 29–September 1, 1985.

73. Ibid., pp. 38–40.

74. World Bank, *World Tables*.

75. Presidency of the Republic, *Peru, 1983* (Lima: Presidency of the Republic, 1983), p. 72.

76. James W. Wilkie, *Statistical Abstract of Latin America* (Los Angeles: University of California Press, 1980), p. 123.

77. Latin American Bureau, *Paths to Poverty*, p. 74.

78. Richard Webb, "Government Policy and the Distribution of Income in Peru, 1963–1973." In Lowenthal, *Peruvian Experiment*; Adolfo Figueroa, "El impacto de las reformas actuales sobre la distribución de ingresos en el Perú." In *Distribución del ingreso*, ed. Alejandro Foxley (Mexico City: Fondo de Cultura Económica, 1974). In a study of income distribution in Lima only—by far Peru's richest city—Scheetz found that the wealthiest decile received a staggering 44 percent of the income in 1967, but a moderate 29 percent in the late 1970s. All the other deciles in the capital city gained. Scheetz, *Peru and the IMF*, p. 208.

79. Webb, "Government Policy and Distribution of Income."

80. *Andean Report*, October 1985, p. 169.

81. *Caretas* (Lima), February 20, 1984, p. 24, and other Datum surveys kindly made available to me by Datum.

82. Datum surveys, and also Apoyo surveys reported in *Debate*.

83. Nigel Haworth, "Conflict or Incorporation: The Peruvian Working Class, 1968–1979." In Booth and Sorj, *Military Reformism and Social Classes*, p. 99.

84. Latin American Bureau, *Paths to Poverty*, p. 13.
85. Ibid.
86. Haworth, "Conflict or Incorporation," pp. 101–102.
87. Giorgio Alberti, Jorge Santistevan, and Luis Pásara, eds., *Estado y clase* (Lima: Instituto de Estudios Peruanos, 1977); Evelyne Huber Stephans, *The Politics of Workers' Participation* (New York: Academic Press, 1980); Haworth, "Conflict or Incorporation."
88. For comprehensive data and data sources on the agrarian reform, see McClintock, *Peasant Cooperatives*; and Cynthia McClintock, "Why Peasants Rebel," *World Politics* 37, no. 2 (October 1984): pp. 64–67.
89. McClintock, *Peasant Cooperatives*, p. 226.
90. Ibid.
91. Ibid.
92. By 1980, about 80 percent of the members of coastal cooperatives favored the return to electoral politics. Cynthia McClintock, "The Peasantry and Post-Revolutionary Agrarian Politics in Peru." In *Post-Revolutionary Peru*, ed. Stephen M. Gorman (Boulder, CO: Westview Special Studies, 1982), pp. 12–150.
93. Enrique A. Baloyra, "Public Opinion and Support for Democratic Regimes: Venezuela, 1973–1983." Paper presented at the American Political Science Association meeting, September 1985, p. 17. While the Peruvian results are just for Lima, a small, nonrandom survey I supervised in the highlands city of Huancayo in March-April 1985 indicated that the preference for democracy was high there as well—over 75 percent.
94. Another 2.5 percent approved roadblocks and stone throwing, and 1.2 percent bombs against the military. *Latin America Regional Reports Andean Group*, RA-87-05, June 25, 1987, p. 3.
95. Fernando Tuesta Soldevilla, *Perú político en cifras* (Lima: Fundación Friedrich Ebert, 1987), pp. 199, 223.
96. Tuesta Soldevilla, *Perú político en cifras*, pp. 199, 223.
97. These surveys were applied in October 1987. "N" was 25 in one cooperative near Trujillo, and 15 in a second.
98. *Debate* 8, no. 38 (May 1986): p. 26.
99. Henry A. Dietz, "Electoral Politics During Economic Crisis: Peru 1978–1986." Paper presented at the Latin American Studies Association meeting, Boston, MA, 1986, p. 16.
100. Interviews with military officers, both mine and published. I or a research colleague have interviewed more than 30 military officers on the question of democracy since 1980. See also the numerous interviews in *Caretas* (Lima), January 9, 1984; September 3, 1984; September 17, 1984; January 13, 1986; and February 10, 1986; and in *QueHacer* (Lima), January 1983; October, 1984; April, 1985; also *El Observador* (Lima), July 7, 1983.
101. See especially the presidents' inaugural addresses, and journalists' reports on the 1985 presidential and 1986 municipal elections in *Caretas* and *QueHacer*.
102. Sources for this section include Enrique Bernales, *Crisis política: solución electoral?* (Lima: DESCO, 1980); Roberto Ramírez del Villar and Marcial Rubio Correa, *El rol del parlamento* (Lima: Intercampus, 1981); Pedro-Pablo Kuczynski, *Peruvian Democracy under Economic Stress* (Princeton, NJ: Princeton University Press, 1977); Henry Ruempler, "Anti-Democratic Laws Governing the Military and Opposition Parties in Argentina and Peru" (M.A. Thesis, Georgetown University); Luis Pásara, *Jueces, justicia, y poder en el Perú* (Lima: CEDYS, 1982); Americas Watch, *Abdicating Democratic Authority: Human Rights in Peru* (New York: Americas Watch, 1984); Americas Watch, "Opportunity for Democratic Authority;" and Cynthia McClintock, "The Media and Redemocratization in Peru," *Studies in Latin American Popular Culture* 6 (1987): pp. 115–134.
103. As Levine has emphasized in this volume, party pacts often reflect and reinforce a pro-democratic will.
104. Enrique Bernales, *El parlamento por dentro* (Lima: DESCO, 1984), p. 81.
105. *Debate* 7, no. 33 (July 1985): p. 56. The result of a 1986 survey was similar. *Debate* 8, no. 38 (May 1986): p. 29.
106. Pásara, *Jueces, justicia, y poder*, p. 27.
107. McClintock, "Media and Redemocratization."
108. Both houses are elected by the d'Hondt formula for proportional representation, but Chamber seats are distributed by the vote in each department and Senate seats by the vote in the nation as a whole.

109. For example, in 1980, the victorious Acción Popular slipped below 30 percent of the vote in only two departments, and its share of the vote in four of the five most impoverished southern highlands departments was over 50 percent. Moreover, lower-class voters in Lima were found to be as supportive of Acción Popular as upper-class voters. In 1985, APRA's tally did not dip below 30 percent in any department, and it won over 40 percent of the vote in all five of the poorest southern highlands departments. See Henry Pease García, *Un perfíl del proceso político peruano* (Lima: DESCO, 1981), p. 76; Henry A. Dietz, "Political Participation in the Barriadas," *Comparative Political Studies* 18, no. 3 (October 1985): pp. 323–355; and Fernando Tuesta Soldevilla, *Peru, 1985: El derrotero de una nueva elección* (Lima: DESCO, 1986), p. 32.

110. Pease García, *Perfíl del proceso político*, p. 76; Tuesta Soldevilla, *Peru, 1985*, p. 33; *Caretas*, June 22, 1987, p. 12.

111. Pease García, *Perfíl del proceso político*, p. 76: Tuesta Soldevilla, *Peru, 1985*, p. 33; Datum polls, 1982–1986.

112. Latin American Bureau, *Paths to Poverty*, p. 1.

113. See Einaudi and Stepan, "Latin American Institutional Development," p. 56, on the social backgrounds of Peru's big businessmen.

114. Larson and Bergman, *Social Stratification*, pp. 299, 363.

115. E. V. K. Fitzgerald, *The Political Economy of Peru, 1956–1978* (New York: Cambridge University Press, 1979), p. 93.

116. Asociación Nacional de Centros de Investigación, Promoción Social, y Desarrollo, *Descentralización y desarrollo regional* (Lima: Fundación Friedrich Ebert, 1986).

117. Baltazar Caravedo, *Desarrollo desigual y lucha política en el Perú, 1948–1956* (Lima: Instituto de Estudios Peruanos, 1978), pp. 105–106; Patricia A. Wilson, *From Mode of Production to Spatial Formation* (Ph.D. Diss., Cornell University, 1975).

118. Cynthia McClintock, "Why Peasants Rebel," pp. 59–60.

119. McClintock, "Why Peasants Rebel," p. 61; *Andean Report*, October, 1985, pp. 168–169.

120. Julio Cotler, "Traditional Haciendas and Communities in a Context of Political Mobilization in Peru." In *Agrarian Problems and Peasant Movement in Latin America*, ed. Rodolfo Stavenhagen (Garden City, NY: Doubleday, Anchor, 1970); McClintock, *Peasant Cooperative*.

121. Einaudi and Stepan, "Latin American Institutional Development," p. 56.

122. McClintock, "Why Peasants Rebel," pp. 64–69.

123. Ibid., pp. 54–55.

124. Michael L. Smith, "The Shining Path in Peru." Paper presented at the 1986 International Studies Association meeting, Washington, D.C., March 29, 1986.

125. *Caretas* (Lima), December 29, 1986, p. 17; December 30, 1985, p. 34; and December 30, 1987, pp. 32–35; and *The Peru Report* 1, no. 2 (February 1987), p. 42.

126. Americas Watch, "A Certain Passivity" (New York: Americas Watch, 1987).

127. For further elaboration and documentation, see Cynthia McClintock, "Peru." In *Latin America and Caribbean Contemporary Record*, ed. Abraham F. Lowenthal (New York: Holmes and Meier, forthcoming).

128. *Caretas* (Lima), December 30, 1987, pp. 32–35; December 29, 1986, p. 17; and December 30, 1985, p. 34.

129. Sources for this section include Peter S. Cleaves and Martin J. Scurrah, *Agriculture, Bureaucracy, and Military Government in Peru* (Ithaca, NY: Cornell University Press, 1980); Gilbert, *Oligarchy and Old Regime*; Linn Hammergren, "A Reassessment of the Constraints on Administrative Reform." Paper presented at the 1977 joint meeting of the Latin American Studies Association and African Studies Association, November 1977; and McClintock, "Peru."

130. Gilbert, *Oligarchy and Old Regime*, pp. 26–27.

131. Anthony Ferner, "The Industrialists and the Peruvian Development Model." In Booth and Sorj, *Military Reformism and Social Classes*, p. 44.

132. Inter-American Development Bank, *External Debt and Economic Development in Latin America* (Washington, DC: Inter-American Development Bank, 1984), p. 28.

133. World Bank, *Report on Peru* (Lima: Andean Air Mail & Peruvian Times, 1986), p. 2.

134. Ibid.; and Inter-American Development Bank, *External Debt and Economic Development*, p. 182.

135. Carol Wise, "The Perils of Orthodoxy: Peru's Political Economy," *NACLA Report on the Americas* 20, no. 3 (June 1986): p. 20.

136. Carlos Zuzunaga Flórez, ed., *Las empresas públicas en el Perú* (Lima: Fundación Fried-

rich Ebert, 1985), p. 104.

137. Milton Guerrero, "The Role of Public Enterprises in the Context of Aprista Economic Policies." Paper presented at the Conference on APRA as Party and Government, Institute of the Americas, University of California at San Diego, March 21–22, 1988.

138. Hernando de Soto, *El otro sendero* (Lima: El Barranco, 1986), p. xx.

139. de Soto, *El otro sendero*, pp. xx–xxi.

140. Jaime Althaus et al., *Comunidad, gobierno local y desarrollo provincial* (Lima: Centro Peruano de Estudios para el Desarrollo Regional, 1986).

141. Ibid., p. 21.

142. Gregory D. Schmidt, "Regime-Type, Political Alliances, and Bureaucratization: Explaining Variations in Regional Development Organizations and Decentralized Public Investment in Peru, 1949–1988." Paper presented at the Latin American Studies Association meeting, New Orleans, March 18, 1988, esp. pp. 46–47.

143. Patricia A. Wilson and Carol Wise, "The Regional Implications of Public Investment in Peru, 1968–1983," *Latin American Research Review* 21, no. 2 (1986): pp. 93–116. For example, the 1968–1980 military government allocated less than 7 percent of total public investment to the country's five impoverished southern highlands departments, which contain about 17 percent of the population.

144. Cynthia McClintock, "Agricultural Policy and Food Security in Peru and Ecuador." In *Agrarian Reform in Reverse*, ed. Bruce Drury, Birol Yeshilada, and Charles Brocket (Boulder, CO: Westview, 1987), p. 111.

145. McClintock, "Agricultural Policy," pp. 100–116. For example, the World Bank called Peru's expenditures the grandiose irrigation project Majes a "squandering of public investment funds on a monumental scale"; see *Andean Report*, March 1987, p. 53.

146. Banco Agrario del Peru, "Memoría 1986," (Lima: Banco Agrario del Perú, 1987), p. 38, and Banco Central de Reserva, "Programa de apoyo al ingreso temporal." (Lima: Banco Central de Reserva, 1987).

147. Instituto Nacional de Planificación, "Evaluación de la Inversión Pública 1986" and "Evaluación de la Inversión Pública 1987," both data sets mimeographed by the Instituto Nacional de Planificación in Lima; for 1983–1985, calculations based on data collected personally from the archive of the Instituto Nacional de Planificación.

148. de Soto, *El otro sendero*, and Felipe M. Portocarrero, "The Peruvian Public Investment Programme, 1968–1978," *Journal of Latin American Studies* 14, no. 2 (1982), pp. 433–445.

149. SIPRI, *SIPRI Yearbook* (New York: Oxford University Press, 1987), pp. 168–172, and U.S. Arms Control and Disarmament Agency, *World Military Expenditures and Arms Transfers 1987* (Washington, DC: U.S. Government Printing Office, 1988), pp. 45–80.

150. Compare and contrast data in SIPRI, *SIPRI Yearbook*, and U.S. Arms Control and Disarmament Agency, *World Military Expenditures*.

151. Wise, "Perils of Orthodoxy," p. 24.

152. Compare and contrast the data in U.S. Arms Control and Disarmament Agency, *World Military Expenditures*, pp. 45–80, and International Institute for Strategic Studies, *The Military Balance 1987–88* (Boston: Jane's 1988), p. 196 and 210.

153. For further information and sources for the statements in this paragraph, see Cynthia McClintock, "The APRA Government and the Peruvian Military, 1985–1987." Paper presented at the conference, "APRA as Party and Government: From Ideology to Praxis," at the University of California, San Diego, March 1988.

154. Detailed analysis and documentation of the points in this paragraph and the next are provided in Cynthia McClintock, "The Prospects for Democratic Consolidation in a 'Least Likely' Case: Peru," *Comparative Politics* (forthcoming).

155. Thorp and Bertram, *Peru, 1890–1977*, p. 321.

156. Inter-American Development Bank, *Economic and Social Progress in Latin America* (Washington, DC: Inter-American Development Bank, 1986), p. 394.

157. Scheetz, *Peru and the IMF*, p. 157; *Latin America Weekly Report* (January 15, 1987): p. 1; *Latin America Weekly Report* (December 24, 1987): p. 2; and *Andean Report*, February 1987, p. 19.

158. Maximo Vega-Centeno, María Antonia Remenyi, José Tavara, and Roxanna Barrantes, "Violencia y pobreza: Una visión de Conjunto." In *Siete ensayos sobre la violencia en el Perú*, ed. Asociación Peruana de Estudios e Investigaciones para la Paz (Lima: Fundación Friedrich Ebert, 1985), p. 87.

159. Ibid., p. 91.
160. Carol Graham, "The PAIT in Practice: A Study in Huascar of San Juan de Lurigancho." Unpublished paper, St. Anthony's College, Oxford University, April 1988, p. 20. See also Table 8.4.
161. Apoyo survey, May 1986, p. 26.
162. *Caretas* (Lima), April 4, 1988, p. 52.
163. My assessment is based on documentary materials as well as personal interviews and observation of Belaúnde at conferences.
164. Peruvians' opinions of President García are reported regularly in Peru's news magazines *Caretas* and *Debate*.
165. Francisco Durand, "Los Empresarios y Alianzas Políticas: El Caso del Perú Bajo Alan García." Paper presented at the Latin American Studies Association meeting, March 1988.
166. Jaquette, "Politics of Development," pp. 122–123.
167. Portocarrero, *De Bustamente a Odría*, p. 91.
168. Portocarrero, *De Bustamente a Odría*.
169. Pinelo, *Multinational Corporation in Latin American Politics*, p. 115.
170. Ibid., p. 119.
171. Agency for International Development, *U.S. Overseas Loans and Grants*, vol. 2 (Washington, DC: AID, 1986).
172. U.S. Senate, *Hearings before the Subcommittee on Western Hemisphere Affairs of the Committee on Foreign Relations of the U.S. Senate*, April 14, 16, and 17, 1969 (Washington, DC: U.S. Government Printing Office), p. 96.
173. *Andean Report*, March 1987, pp. 38–39; *Wall Street Journal* (New York), May 1, 1987, p. 23.
174. *Caretas* (Lima), May 30, 1988, p. 32.

COSTA RICA

• CHAPTER NINE •
Costa Rica:
The Roots of Democratic Stability
JOHN A. BOOTH

Democracy involves citizen participation in making and implementing public decisions, but there are many kinds of democracy. Since 1949, Costa Rica has had a constitutional system best described as representative, and a republican (liberal) government with a high degree of correspondence between the actual governance of the system and the formal political arrangements described in its Constitution. Electoral probity has remained very high and regime changes have invariably occurred in accord with the law. Citizens enjoy a degree of participation in public decisions equal to or greater than that in most other Western, liberal constitutional regimes. One may, therefore, justly characterize Costa Rica as a liberal, representative, constitutional democracy.[1]

Peeler correctly observes that liberal democracy denotes "a system very far from true 'rule by the people' [and is] a liberal political system legitimated by the appearance of democracy."[2] Liberal democracy, in Cohen's terms, permits considerable breadth of citizen participation with rather little depth or range;[3] that is, many vote for leaders, but significant, direct popular influence on policy is usually quite modest. In some respects, the depth and range of participation by Costa Ricans are greater than one might expect in a liberal democracy, a fact that could—under sufficient stress—actually imperil the stability of the regime.

• HISTORICAL DEVELOPMENT[4] •

Costa Rica's national myth holds the country unique among Latin American nations because its contemporary political institutions have evolved from a colonial tradition of egalitarian rural life, civilian rule, relatively equal land distribution, ethnic and racial homogeneity, and long-standing electoral integrity. History reveals a more complex reality, substantiating some but not all of the myth.[5]

Spanish conquest of Costa Rica began in 1561, and the colony began to develop after 1575. Colonists settled mainly in the elevated valleys of the nation's center (*meseta central*); they were largely isolated from both coasts by inhospitable terrain, and from the colonial seat of the Kingdom of Guatemala by great distance. Smaller population centers remained marginal: Settlers in Guanacaste (the northwest) were oriented toward Nicaragua; Atlantic coastal cacao plantations eventually failed completely. Spain's Costa Rican colony never developed significant exportable agricultural or mineral wealth and was thus attended to very little by the metropolis and colonial bureaucracy.

Costa Rican colonists brought in only a few slaves to work in the paltry mines; plantations in Guanacaste and the Atlantic region could afford but few slaves. The small indigenous population, heavily exploited for forced labor in the sixteenth century, quickly shrank to low levels, barring development of large *haciendas*. In the absence of sufficient cheap labor, more land than a family itself could work was generally wasted; land ownership was not a source of great wealth and remained rather equally distributed in comparison to other Spanish colonies.[6] By the later colonial era, most Costa Ricans—regardless of their social standing—were subsistence farmers. Much of the wealth and capital that accumulated came from commercial enterprises.

The leveling effect of this poverty and isolation did not prevent status differences. Noble lineage, race, commercial wealth, and ethnicity intertwined to define a status hierarchy topped by a highly self-conscious (albeit poor) creole aristocracy.[7] Even though the relative shared poverty bred a certain egalitarianism of social values among lower-status Costa Ricans, the colony was far from democratic. Participation in governance through the *cabildos* (municipal councils) of Cartago and Heredia (and later Alajuela and San José) was restricted mainly to a political class ascripted from the aristocracy. Early liberal and conservative factions, forerunners of later political parties, emerged within this political class.

Two characteristics of colonial Costa Rica—contrasting with most of Latin America—contributed to later democracy. Costa Rica did not develop a quasi-feudalistic *hacienda* system, in which a creole aristocracy controlled highly concentrated landholdings and exploited Indians and black slaves as elements of plantation economic production. This was partly because of the absence of the large-scale export agriculture that made forced labor systems or slavery profitable elsewhere. Indeed, slavery declined in the eighteenth century because it became cheaper to free slaves and then hire them as laborers than to own them. Disease and forced labor quickly decimated the bulk of the indigenous populace, and the remaining Indians were largely absorbed by extensive racial mixing. By 1800, among Costa Rica's 52,591 persons, only 16 percent were Indian (down from about 80 percent in 1700), 67 percent "Spanish and Mestizo," and 17 percent black (up from 7 percent in 1700).[8]

Second, the colonial era ended without the wars that wracked much of Latin America. Costa Rica, as Guatemala's most remote province, was a dependency of the Viceroyalty of New Spain (Mexico). When Mexico won its independence in 1821, the Central American colonies came with it but declined to join the Mexican Empire. Instead, in 1823, they formed the Central American

Republic, a five-province federation. The four more northern Central American provinces, however, were so torn by civil conflict between liberals and conservatives that the federation collapsed by 1839. Costa Rica largely escaped this civil war because the conservatives took control early on. Internal political conflict remained low in the early federal and national periods, and the first several governments were civilian. The aristocracy governed successfully for some time without militarizing itself. By the time a politicized army developed, Costa Ricans had already developed a habit of civilian rule.

The introduction and rapid expansion of coffee cultivation with the opening of the European market in 1845 brought profound socioeconomic change. Expanding coffee production forged and rapidly expanded a class of smallholding farmers. Late nineteenth-century concentration of coffee exporting, milling, and land ownership consolidated a strong class of coffee planters and importer-exporters. As land ownership became more and more concentrated, a new class of landless agricultural workers appeared. However, a shortage of agricultural labor that persisted until the 1880s kept rural wages high, so that landless Costa Rican peasants were not generally impoverished. Vega Carballo argues that this interdependence among rural classes reinforced the egalitarianism of social values that had developed in the colonial era. "Because peasants and artisans . . . were not mere servile employees or passive instruments of exploitation, . . . it was therefore necessary to elaborate a series of subtle psycho-social, symbolic, and normative ('soft') mechanisms in order to guarantee that they could be persuaded to work."[9]

The social and political aristocracy (most of them now coffee growers) continued to dominate national politics, largely excluding the general public. A brief period of direct elections and expanded popular suffrage (1844–1847) plus the passage of early laws establishing electoral rolls (1848, 1861) revealed an early "preoccupation for organizing the electoral process with great care."[10] Throughout much of the nineteenth century, however, literacy and property ownership requirements and the exclusion of women barred all but about 10 percent of the citizenry from voting. Most elections were indirect. Those with the franchise voted only in the first round of elections to choose electors (usually from the coffee aristocracy) who in turn would choose the office holders. Liberal and conservative elite political factions struggled for power using manipulated elections, fraud, and even military force. By mid-century, military institutions had appeared and had begun to take part in politics. From 1824 to 1899, the average Costa Rican presidency lasted only 2.4 years, 37 percent of the presidents resigned before completing their terms, and another fifth were deposed by coups d'état. From 1835 to 1899, Costa Rica was under military rule over half the time—the generals in the presidency were almost always coffee aristocrats (see Table 9.1).

Further social differentiation came with the development of interest groups and labor organization during the nineteenth century. At first, the government organized certain workers and professionals in order to regulate key trades and

Table 9.1. Characteristics of Costa Rican Presidencies, 1824–1986

Characteristic	1824–1889	1890–1920	1921–1950	1951–1986
Average years per presidency	2.4	3.4	3.8	4.0
(civilian presidents only)	1.5	3.6	3.8	4.0
(military presidents only)	5.8	2.0	—	—
Percentage of period under military rule	44	7	—	—
Percentage of intermim presidencies (not including those resulting from brief absences of constitutional president)	30	11	—	—
Percentage of presidents serving less than one year (excluding interims resulting from absences)	37	22	—	—
Percentage of presidencies ended by resignation	19	22	13	—
Percentage of presidencies ended by coup d'état	19	11	13	—
Average voter turnout as percent of population	—	14	15	—

Sources: Based on John A. Booth, "Representative Constitutional Democracy in Costa Rica: Adaptation to Crisis in the Turbulent 1980s," in *Central America: Crisis and Adaptation,* eds. Steve C. Ropp and James A. Morris (Albuquerque: University of New Mexico Press, 1984), Table 5.1; updated with data from Inter-American Development Bank, *Economic and Social Progress in Latin America: 1987 Report* (Washington, DC: 1987), p. 270; Carlos F. Denton and Olda M. Acuña, *La elección de un presidente: Costa Rica, 1982,* (San José: Instituto del Libro del Ministerio de Cultura, Juventud, y Deportes, 1984); and Roberto Tovar Faja, *Partido Unidad Social Cristiana: Bosquejo histórico* (San José: Litografía e Imprenta LIL, 1986).

thus protect wider societal interests. Between 1830 and 1865, for example, the Costa Rican state created mandatory guilds of miners, ox drovers, port and dock workers, and boatmen. Guilds of medical practitioners and lawyers were also chartered by the state in the 1850s. A second type of organization—mutual-aid societies—proliferated in the last quarter of the nineteenth century as the economy became increasingly subject to international market forces and to the novelty of under- and unemployment. Between 1890 and 1902, there appeared a third type of organization in Costa Rican cities—multitrade self-help guilds. These groups were numerous, though short-lived, but they helped mobilize artisans and laborers directly into politics by promoting the education of their members and by actively supporting presidential candidates.

The dictatorship of Liberal Party chief Tomás Guardia (1870–1882) and his two Liberal successors (1882–1890) laid important foundations for later democratization of Costa Rican politics by greatly expanding public education. Growing literacy and an expanding urban middle class also brought many more Costa Ricans into the political arena. In addition, several new political parties were formed. By the late nineteenth century, such changes and forces had moved to participate in politics a broader public than ever before, much of it dissatisfied with the political elite's decisions.

In the late nineteenth century, economic change accelerated with the construction of a railroad to the Atlantic port of Limón from the capital, San José, and with the accompanying cultivation and exportation of bananas. The railroad and banana industries spread Costa Rica's settlement outside the *meseta central*. The new industries also brought many Caribbean blacks, as well as Chinese, to the Atlantic coastal area; they helped intensify racial discrimination and gave rise to labor conflict. Costa Rica's first recorded labor unrest was a strike by Chinese laborers in 1874. Later came a mutiny by Jamaican blacks in 1879, and a major strike by Italians in 1888. Native Costa Ricans (telegraph workers) struck for the first time in 1883. There eventually followed a series of strikes by Costa Rican artisans and craftsmen in different industries, between 1890 and 1901.

After 1900, Costa Rica's social-class system evolved markedly. The system of yeoman farming ceded still more ground to export agriculture (though the rural middle class persisted). Commerce, services, and manufacturing grew, and urbanization began to accelerate. The aristocratic national bourgeoisie of large coffee farmers, millers, and exporters expanded its investments into commercial and industrial enterprises, while successful new entrepreneurs from outside the coffee industry bought coffee farms. Thus the economic/political elite diversified somewhat but remained generally dominant in politics and strongly opposed to redistributive social reforms.[11] Simultaneously, the growth of new industry created more proletarians, working conditions in traditional trades deteriorated, and the first true labor unions emerged. The banana industry absorbed many workers displaced by coffee production but also bred sharp regional and class tensions, eventually proving fertile ground for labor organization. The increase of popular political participation that had begun in the late nineteenth century not only continued but accelerated in the early twentieth.

Political Liberalization

Costa Rica's first modern political parties arose in the last quarter of the nineteenth century. A key event in this process was the contest for the presidency in 1889, after two decades of Liberal dictatorship under Guardia and his successors. The 1889 contest was between the Liberal Progressives and the Constitutional Democratic Party, which the Catholic church had mobilized to fight the Liberals' anticlerical policies. The Liberal Progressives won and then, in 1891, suppressed the Constitutional Democratic Party. In subsequent elections, the Liberal movement fragmented and gave rise to several personalistic parties/factions that eventually included the National Union Party (Unión Nacional) and the Republican Party (Partido Republicano), which between them would dominate the next several decades of Costa Rican politics.

In 1905, a heated election campaign (with over half the populace now literate) brought the National Union Party's Cleto González Víquez to the presidency on the crest of a substantially increased voter turnout. González Víquez then broke with a tradition of decades by tolerating vigorous opposition and by ensuring a free campaign in 1909. This freedom permitted Ricardo Jiménez Oreamuno to win the presidency by appealing for votes to local peasant leaders (*gamonales*) outside the aristocracy. Once elected, Jiménez Oreamuno secured a constitutional amendment (1913) that instituted direct popular election of public officials, and municipal reforms that permitted the election of *gamonales* to municipal councils.[12] These actions by González and Jiménez (both of liberal orientation and with coffee bourgeoisie backing), between 1905 and 1914, extended the franchise, political participation, and access to public office beyond the aristocracy and convinced more and more of the general public to vote.

The expansion of liberal-democratic institutions and processes in the late nineteenth and early twentieth centuries has been generally attributed to the coffee aristocracy's efforts to consolidate and to protect its political power. Facio and Aguilar Bulgarelli, for instance, argue that the Liberal dictatorship of Guardia led *cafetalero* politicians to promote parties, elections, and suffrage in order to protect their political influence from new dictatorships.[13] Vega Carballo argues that because "visible, frontal, domination 'from above' was inappropriate" under Costa Rica's long-standing condition of relative class equality, the expansion of suffrage in the late nineteenth and early twentieth centuries helped the *cafetaleros* to retain political power as class inequality grew.[14]

> This made possible the implantation in the society of an egalitarian ideology, reinforced by the rhetoric with which the rulers pretended to obtain consensus (and . . . credited themselves for their moderate use of violence and force), in order to continue building the modern Costa Rican Nation-State. . . . Thus it was that, with the passage of time, there emerged "rules of the game" . . . that helped maintain and validate the established order, that regulated and oriented toward defined goals the conduct of the subordinated classes.[15]

The interpretations of Vega, and of Facio and Aguilar, appear to attribute simplistically the liberalization of Costa Rican politics to concerted and self-conscious actions by a unified national bourgeoisie and should, therefore, be regarded with caution at a literal level. There was a *cafetalero* class, but it was quite divided politically (between anticlerical Liberals and pro-Catholic elements, and into various personalistic Liberal factions). What these authors do usefully suggest, however, is that in their various struggles for political and economic influence among increasingly complex class and political forces, bourgeois factions generally distrustful of military dictatorship and inexperienced in the violently repressive means of neighboring nations' elites gradually turned to classical liberal-representative devices.

Economic crisis brought on by World War I led President Alfredo González Flores to impose economic reforms, new taxes, and austerity measures that sharply expanded the state's role in the economy. These policies so angered the coffee aristocracy that it promoted yet another coup and two more years of military rule under the Tinoco brothers. The Tinocos, however, failed to solve economic problems and ruled very repressively as well. An upsurge of popular protest against the regime plus an invasion from Nicaragua by exiled Costa Rican elites toppled the Tinocos from power. Costa Ricans had rejected the military experiment and expressed a strong preference for civilian, constitutional rule.

Expansion of suffrage and improvement of the electoral system continued, in part, because of divisions within the national bourgeoisie and the persistence of class "interdependence." This permitted burgeoning middle- and working-class groups "to expand their interests and open for themselves access to political and economic influence, without by so doing . . . undermining the general system of oligarchic domination."[16] In the two decades following the Tinoco dictatorship, several legal changes occurred in the electoral system: A first national election agency, the Consejo Nacional de Elecciones, was established (1925); parties were given a monopoly on the nomination of candidates for office (1932); the vote became both secret (1928) and obligatory (1936); and the legislature received authority to scrutinize and validate elections (to reduce executive-branch manipulation and fraud). Despite such steps—accepted by the ruling elite as necessary concessions to popular pressure—fraud and executive manipulation of elections continued.[17]

From 1910 to 1950, the number and types of organizations—community groups, cooperatives, labor unions, professional and trade associations, school groups, and many others—expanded rapidly, mobilizing still more Costa Ricans into the political arena, and conveying a proliferating array of demands to the political system. Marxist labor activists formed a Worker's Society in 1909 and helped forge Costa Rica's first central labor organization, the Confederación General de Trabajadores (CGT) in 1913. The CGT sought to develop working-class consciousness, helped promote other unions, supported many strikes, and lobbied the government for accident protection, social security, and retirement programs.

Another important movement began with social Christian activism and eventually merged with the CGT to form Jorge Volio's Reformist Party in 1923. Volio, a devout Catholic, populist, social worker, and supporter of unions, failed in his 1923 bid for the presidency. However, he helped pave the way for later cooperation between the church and the Communist unions in the 1940s and also influenced the social-democratic movement that overthrew this church-labor alliance in 1948. Meanwhile, Ricardo Jiménez Oreamuno, running for a second term on the Republican Party ticket, defeated Volio for the 1924–1928 presidential term. The Reformists forged a coalition with the National Union Party and nominated Cleto González Víquez for his second term. González won the presidency again for the 1928–1932 term, but the alliance saw the Reformist Party peter out as an electoral movement. Ricardo Jiménez led the increasingly dominant Republican Party to victory again in 1932 (his third term); he was succeeded in 1936 by Republican León Cortés Castro.[18]

Considerable labor turmoil in the 1920s, the emergence of a strong leftist intelligentsia, U.S. intervention in Nicaragua (1927–1933), and the onset of the Great Depression in 1929 spawned numerous political and labor groups, the most significant of which was the Communist Party. When labor unrest spread in the banana fields, Communists organized the workers and led the great 1933 strike. The success of the banana strike rapidly expanded the Communist Party's influence. The party founded the Costa Rican Workers' Confederation (CTCR), which quickly became the nation's dominant labor confederation. The CTCR and Communist Party reached their apogee of political power between 1942 and 1948 when the CTCR participated in two governments in coalition with social-Christian forces represented by Archbishop Victor Manuel Sanabria and populist Republican coffee aristocrat and president, Dr. Rafael Angel Calderón Guardia.

Calderón Guardia—a charismatic physician who succeeded Jiménez Oreamuno as the dominant personality in the Republican Party—advocated a social Christian reformism that appealed to depression-impoverished workers as much as it alienated bourgeois groups long allegiant to the party. Calderón pushed a social-security system through the legislature in 1941 and, with the aid of the Communists, enacted a labor code in 1943. The Calderón-Communist alliance, and their reformist policies, engendered several foci of opposition to the government in the early 1940s. The coffee aristocracy, a traditional enemy of redistributive reforms, quickly turned against Calderón. There also developed both conservative and progressive middle-class opposition movements—both strongly anti-Communist. When Republican Teodoro Picado Michalski succeeded Calderón in 1944, he continued the alliance with the Communists. Conservative opposition rallied behind newspaper publisher Otilio Ulate Blanco, who formed a new National Union Party to support his bid for presidency in 1948. Under the leadership of José Figueres Ferrer, other middle-sector forces advocated a revolutionary program of anti-Communist, yet reformist, social-democratic policies.

Partisan violence and terrorism by the social democrats escalated after 1946, fueling labor unrest caused by the post–World War II economic slump. An attempted electoral fraud by the government in 1948 (intended to return Calderón Guardia to the presidency) provided a pretext for Figueres' social democrats to attempt to overthrow President Picado and seize power. There was a short but bloody civil war between the progovernment forces of Calderón and the Communists and Figueres' National Liberation insurgents. With aid and arms from Guatemala and from pro-democratic forces throughout the Caribbean, the rebels defeated the army and Communist troops.

The victorious National Liberation junta ruled for eighteen months, dissolving many unions, outlawing the Communist Party, and enacting economic reforms such as the nationalization of all banks and a major tax on wealth. The junta called a Constituent Assembly to revise the 1871 Constitution and establish what Figueres called the Second Republic. The coffee aristocracy and other conservative elements, angered by the junta's revolutionary-reformist pretensions, won a majority of seats in the Constituent Assembly, blocked the social democrats, and retained most of the 1871 Constitution. The Assembly enacted little change, therefore; its most remarkable act was to abolish the armed forces and to prohibit a standing army. The new constitution also established the Tribunal Supremo de Elecciones (TSE) in an effort to guarantee honest elections and gave full political rights to women and blacks, who had previously been excluded from voting.

Having seen its backing shrink and having failed to implement its revolutionary goals, the frustrated liberation junta turned over power, in 1949, to the victor of the 1948 election, Otilio Ulate. The liberation leaders then transformed their own movement into a political party, the National Liberation Party (PLN). The PLN platform was influenced by founder Figueres' links to Peruvian V. R. Haya de la Torre's APRA, and by the reformism of Volio's party. The PLN accepted most of the social reforms of the Calderón era and promoted increased governmental participation in the economy.

The victory of the liberation insurgents, and their eventual rise to power in the 1953 election, represented a definitive change in the Costa Rican political elite, which had now broadened to include the urban and rural middle sectors. The PLN won the 1953–1958 presidency for José Figueres and has greatly influenced Costa Rican politics ever since. By relinquishing power to Ulate in 1949, and to the victorious opposition party "Unity" coalition after the 1958 election, the PLN reinforced the integrity of elections in Costa Rica. More importantly, it contributed to what Peeler calls the consolidation of a new "democratic regime," or agreement among major political forces to accommodate each other and abide by liberal democratic rules.[19] By 1958, the PLN and a group of conservative parties had thus established an effective working arrangement among major middle-sector political actors and representatives of the national coffee/commercial/industrial bourgeoisie that constitutes the essence of the contemporary Costa Rican polity. Even though the PLN has lost the presidency three times since 1953 (see Table 9.2), it has retained its control of the Legislative Assembly (except for one period, 1978–1982) and has thus imprinted its vision of a new social and economic order even when out of power.

• **POLITICAL INSTITUTIONS, BEHAVIOR, AND BELIEFS** •

The foregoing history sketches the foundation of modern Costa Rican democracy but does not describe how the contemporary polity functions. An examination of political institutions and culture will help to illuminate the factors that sustain democracy in Costa Rica.

Election Administration and Voting Rights

Peeler argues that liberal democracy in Costa Rica (and Venezuela) could not not have survived without something "most untypical of Latin America: honest elections. . . . The establishment of liberal democracies . . . included the creation of powerful, independent agencies to administer the electoral process,

Table 9.2 Election Results, 1946–1986.

Year	Candidates	Party	Vote (1000s)	Percent of Vote	Turnout as % of Populace
1948	Otilio Ulate B.	Unión Nacional	55	54	12.4
	R. A. Calderón G.	Republicano Nacional	45	44	
	other		3	2	
1953	José Figueres F.	Liberación Nacional	123	65	21.0
	Fernando Castro C.	Democrático	67	35	
1958	Mario Echandi J.	Unión Nacional	103	46	19.8
	Francisco Orlich B.	Liberación Nacional	95	43	
	Jorge Rossi Ch.	Independiente	24	11	
1962	Francisco Orlich B.	Liberación Nacional	193	50	29.7
	R. A. Calderón G.	Republicano	136	35	
	Otilio Ulate B.	Unión Naciona	52	14	
	other		3	1	
1966	José J. Trejos F.	Unificación Nacional	223	51	29.4
	Daniel Oduber Q.	Liberación Nacional	219	49	

1970	José Figueres F.	Liberación Nacional	296	55	31.6
	Mario Echandi J.	Unificación Nacional	222	41	
	others		17	4	
1974	Daniel Oduber Q.	Liberación Nacional	295	43	34.0
	Fernando Trejos E.	Unificación Nacional	206	30	
	Jorge González M.	Nacional Independiente	74	11	
	Rodrigo Carazo O.	Renovación Democrática	62	9	
	others		41	7	
1978	Rodrigo Carazo O.	Unidad	419	50	39.5
	Luis A. Monge A.	Liberación Nacional	363	44	
	others		49	6	
1982	Luis A. Monge A.	Liberación Nacional	568	59	42.5
	R. A. Calderón F.	Unidad	325	34	
	others		72	7	
1986	Oscar Arias S.	Liberación Nacional	620	52	46.8
	R. A. Calderón F.	Unidad Social Cristiana	542	46	
	others		22	2	

Sources: Harold H. Bonilla, *Los presidentes*, vol. 2 (San José: Editorial Universidad Nacional Estatal a Distancia, Editorial Costa Rica, 1979), pp. 823–825; John A. Booth, "Representative Constitutional Democracy." In *Central America: Crisis and Adaptation*, ed. Steve C. Ropp and James A. Morris, (Albuquerque: University of New Mexico Press, 1984), Table 5.2; Carlos F. Denton and Olda María Acuña, La elección de un presidente, pp. 117–128; Tovar Faja, *Partido Unidad Social Cristiano*, Inter-American Development Bank, *Economic and Social Progress in Latin America: 1987 Report*, p. 270.

agencies carefully structured to assure that neither the government nor any party could covertly control an election."[20]

The 1949 Constitution gave the TSE "Exclusive responsibility for the organization, direction, and vigilance of acts relative to suffrage, [as well as] independence in carrying out its responsibility."[21] The TSE normally consists of three magistrates and six *suplentes* (substitutes)—expanded during election periods to five magistrates by adding two of the *suplentes*—who are appointed to staggered, 6-year terms by the Supreme Court of Justice. The TSE operates the national Civil Registry (which issues the mandatory national identity cards that also serve as voter registration documents) and maintains electoral lists.[22] Among the key powers of the TSE are to investigate charges of political partiality by public employees, file criminal charges against persons violating electoral laws, scrutinize and validate election results, and control the police and other security forces during election periods so as to "assure that electoral processes develop in conditions of guarantees and unrestricted liberties."[23]

In addition to these constitutional provisions, under electoral law and its own regulations, the TSE monitors political campaign compliance with the law and executive neutrality in campaigns, and allocates the governmental subvention of campaign costs. So scrupulous is the TSE in its conduct of elections that it "has all but eradicated the incidence of fraud in Costa Rican elections. Costa Rica's reputation for fairness and honesty in elections is one of the highest in the world."[24]

Costa Rican citizens eighteen years old or older are required to vote, under mild (but seldom imposed) penalties for not voting. The 1949 Constitution requires the government to register all citizens, to provide representation for minorities, and to make effective guarantees of "liberty, order, purity, and impartiality on the part of government authorities."[25] Almost all eligible Costa Ricans register, and turnout in recent elections has been over 80 percent.[26]

Political Parties[27]

Although Costa Rica's multimember districting and proportional representation encourage the survival of small parties, only two groups effectively vie for the presidency: the social-democratic PLN and the Unidad coalition of centrist and conservative opposition parties that forms for most elections. PLN and Unidad have alternated in power several times. Peeler argues, "It is inconceivable that liberal democracy could have been maintained in [Costa Rica] without . . . the regular practice of alternation of parties in the presidency."[28]

The PLN is the largest and strongest party. Founded in 1951 by José Figueres from his 1948 rebel movement, the PLN became a highly organized, multiclass, permanent party committed to social-democratic ideology and policies. The PLN's major base is in the middle class; it has important links to organized labor through the Confederación de Costarricenses Trabajadores Democráticos (CCTD). All PLN presidents until 1986 came from the liberation junta of 1948–1949—Figueres (1953–1958, 1970–1974), Francisco Orlich (1962–1966), Daniel Oduber (1974–1978), and Luis Alberto Monge (1982–1986). This long dominance of the old guard raised the prospects of generational conflict, but a new generation triumphed when Oscar Arias Sánchez, a young leader groomed in several top party and government posts, won the PLN presidential nomination and the presidency in 1986.

The opposition coalition of Center-Right parties and personalities, including remnants of Calderón Guardia's Republican Party, is presently configured as the Partido de Unificación Social Cristiana (PUSC). The PUSC's constituent parties include supporters and activists from various classes. The coalition also draws on continuing working-class support once won to the Republican Party by Calderón Guardia. In its previous incarnations under the banners of Unidad, Unión, and Unificación, the coalition won the presidency three times: Mario Echandi (1958–1962), José Joaquín Trejos (1966–1970), and Rodrigo Carazo (1978–1982).

Another significant party group has been the leftist coalition known as the Partido Pueblo Unido (PPU) consisting of the old pro-Soviet Popular Vanguard (Communist) Party, the Socialist Party, and the People's Revolutionary Party. Despite involvement in labor unrest since the late 1970s, the leftist parties have generally made moderate, reformist (rather than revolutionary) demands. Electoral support for the Left has come mainly from the Gulf Coast banana regions around Golfito, from San José's working-class neighborhoods, and from some intellectuals and students. Growth of support for the Left was slow but steady through the 1970s, but leftist voting declined in the 1982 and 1986 elections. Because of the leftist coalition's close ties to organized labor, the disastrously unsuccessful 1984 banana strike deeply affected these parties. So, too, did an intense anti-Communist campaign in the national press and Costa Rica's growing difficulties with Sandinista-ruled Nicaragua between 1980 and 1986. In 1985, the Popular Vanguard Party split in two behind competing leaders Mario Vargas Carbonell and party founder Manuel Mora Valverde.

State Structure and Strength

Costa Rican state structure differs notably from that of other Latin American nations in its distribution of authority among branches of government. There are important restraints on executive power, and both the Legislative Assembly and the judiciary enjoy unusual strength and independence relative to the executive. The absence of a standing army greatly strengthens the authority of civil government, and extensive and generally respected social, economic, and civil guarantees provide a framework that facilitates political participation by tates political participation by citizens.[29]

The Costa Rican state is unitary, dominated by a highly legitimate central government. The powers and attributes of the nation's seventy-five municipal (county) governments are modest; the provincial governments are ephemeral.

State power is widely dispersed among the branches of government.

Costa Rica's president serves a single 4-year term, and may not be reelected.[30] The president heads the executive branch, but shares administrative, treaty-making, and other foreign policy, budget-writing, appointment, legislative initiative, and veto powers with his cabinet ministers.[31] The president alone names and removes cabinet members, and is commander-in-chief of the security forces (police and Civil Guard).[32] The president must have the approval of the Legislative Assembly to leave the country.

Costa Rica has almost 200 autonomous administrative agencies, created independently from the central ministries in order to free them from undue political manipulation and increase their technical capacity. They are typically run by independent, appointed boards not subject to presidential removal. Many autonomous agencies provide key public services (electrification, telephones, water and sewer service, agrarian reform, municipal and community development assistance), and they absorb about half the national budget. Fiscal autonomy is assured to many through constitutionally dedicated revenues. Their authority to incur debt was also once extensive but was sharply curtailed in the early 1980s. This occurred because a few powerful autonomous agencies had independently accumulated most of the prodigious public debt that caused Costa Rica's 1980 debt and currency crisis.

The unicameral Legislative Assembly (Asemblea Legislativa) has fifty-seven members elected (proportionally to population) from Costa Rica's seven provinces; its members sit for the same 4-year period as the president. The Assembly's powers include the following: to amend the constitution;[33] legislate; declare war and peace; approve the national budget; levy taxes; ratify treaties; authorize the suspension of civil liberties; impeach and censure high officials; require information from government ministers; and appoint the national comptroller and the justices of the Supreme Court. The Assembly may override an executive veto by a two-thirds vote. In comparison to other Latin American legislatures, the Assembly is quite powerful. Because it makes key national policy decisions and provides extensive pork-barrel funding, citizens and special interests heavily lobby its members.

The seventeen members of the Supreme Court of Justice (Tribunal Supremo de Justicia), appointed by the Legislative Assembly, automatically serve two-year terms unless specifically rejected by the Assembly after the first. The Supreme Court's powers include judicial review of extant and proposed legislation, hearing appeals from lower courts, and appointing lower court judges. The Supreme Court has largely escaped the corruption and lack of independence of other Latin American high courts; it frequently rules against the government and strongly defends individual rights. One example of judicial independence was the Court's overruling of the Figueres administration's granting of a passport to Robert Vesco in the mid-1970s, despite the president's personal involvement in favor of Vesco. Lower Costa Rican courts lack the reputation for honesty and impartiality of the Supreme Court.[34]

Overall, the Costa Rican state has considerable political resources when compared with its Central American neighbors: (1) the absence of a large, politicized army frees fiscal resources, promotes continuity of policy application, and permits political flexibility; (2) a high level of state legitimacy and the political culture's emphasis on compromise and conciliation tend to prevent or reduce the alienation of many interest groups and to ameliorate social cleavages; and (3) policy innovativeness among recent administrations contributes to institutional flexibility and efficacy.

There are also important constraints on state power and resources: (1) decentralized executive authority and checks on the presidency sometimes block efforts to formulate or adjust public policy, especially in times of crisis; (2) the large role of the state in the economy and the large bureaucracy make the government quite subject to political and economic pressures, especially from key public-sector unions; and (3) economically, Costa Rica remains a relatively poor country, and suffers from high dependency on price-elastic commodity exports (coffee, bananas), declining terms of trade, and an enormous foreign debt (well over $2,000 per person). Costa Rica's foreign debt in 1986 was about 90 percent of GDP, almost double the Latin American average of 48 percent.[35]

Church and Media

Through the nineteenth century the sociopolitical role of the church was limited because of Costa Rica's isolation and poverty. In the late nineteenth century, the church increased its political role under the leadership of an activist Jesuit bishop, Monsignor Bernardo Thiel, who advocated fair wages for workers and mobilized a short-lived Catholic party in response to anticlerical reforms by Liberal governments. This led to the expulsion of the Jesuits from Costa Rica, further weakening the church. In the 1940s, activist Archbishop Sanabria promoted labor unions and supported the administration and the sociopolitical reforms of populist President Calderón Guardia and his Communist allies. Later, Sanabria tried to head off the conflict that led to the 1948 civil war. After the war, the church cooperated to some extent with the National Liberation movement's efforts to break up the Communist-dominated union movement. Under subsequent, more conservative archbishops, the Costa Rican Catholic church has not again been able to exercise the political influence of the 1940s.[36]

The press in Costa Rica functions, generally, freely and without censorship. Paid newspaper advertisements are a major form of political discourse in Costa Rica. The state regulates the practice of journalism through a state-sanctioned professional association and restricts ownership of mass media to Costa Rican citizens. A leftist shortwave radio station broadcasting to South America was closed in 1980 after protests from the Argentine government. Debate and discussion in the printed press is very vigorous, and Costa Ricans have unrestricted access to printed material of a prodigious array of ideological and political viewpoints. Ownership of major media is reportedly extremely concentrated among a few persons with very conservative political leanings and with business links to major concentrations of national capital. Media owners have organized and adopted a general editorial line (dominant in most broadcast and print media) supporting the reduction of the state's economic role and criticizing the Sandinista government of Nicaragua.[37]

Political Culture

Costa Rica is a highly participatory society.[38] Although Costa Ricans often characterize themselves as uncooperative, individualistic, and difficult to mobilize, they in fact frequently vote, join and take part in organizations, electioneer and do other party activities, engage in communal self-help activities, discuss politics and community affairs, and contact public officials. They do so at levels higher than many other Third World and Latin American nations, and only slightly lower, if at all, than in the United States and Europe. Although Costa Ricans view themselves as very pacific, the country experiences a fair amount of unconventional and confrontational political participation (demonstrations, strikes, riots). Political violence, however, is low by Central American standards.

In addition to being participatory, Costa Rican political culture has the previously noted, unusual egalitarian traits dating from the colonial era and reinforced by the later nineteenth century's scarcity of agricultural labor. In much of the Hispanic world, long-standing semifeudal agrarian traditions have resulted in elaborate cultural systems of deference. In contrast, two centuries of much greater economic equality imbued Costa Rican popular culture with a sense of the fundamental worth of each citizen, and such traits have persisted despite the subsequent development of great economic inequality.[39] Costa Ricans today manifest little reticence about expressing their opinions to persons of greater status, wealth, or influence. A political scientist recently colorfully illustrated this point thus: "*¡El tico trata de 'vos,' 'mierda,' y 'hijueputa' hasta con el presidente!*"[40]

Costa Ricans tend to behave in a democratic fashion in collective settings, painstakingly hearing all points of view and voting on issues to make decisions. Recent surveys have shown that Costa Ricans generally support democratic civil liberties, though they tend to be intolerant of certain types of participation by critics of the political system. In particular, Costa Ricans generally disapprove of participation by "Communists" despite the long-standing involvement in the nation's politics of the Popular Vanguard Party and its Communist predecessors.

Anti-Communism has been a key feature of Costa Rica's political culture since the late 1940s, in part because of resentment of certain abuses of power and the 1948 electoral fraud during the Communist Party's participation in power from 1942 to 1948. The PLN dismantled much of the Communist-led CTCR and developed competing unions and confederations in order to prevent consolidation of a class conflict–oriented labor movement. However, tolerated under different names, the Communist movement has regained considerable influence in organized labor and has consistently won at least three seats in the Legislative Assembly.

Carvajal's intriguing 1971 survey found some significant differences between Costa Rican mass and elite political values.[41] He reported elites to be much more frequently dissatisfied with the government's management of public affairs (74 percent) than were ordinary citizens (30 percent). A much higher proportion of elites (84 percent) than of ordinary citizens (28 percent) saw a need for basic changes in the Costa Rican political system. Elites were generally more committed to ideological principles than were ordinary citizens and tended to disagree that parties should alternate in office (66 percent opposed it), whereas a majority of the citizen sample (59 percent) favored it. On the other hand, the elite and mass samples more closely agreed in their support for the propositions that parties were the "best instruments of popular representation," and that the "government generally works to improve national conditions." In addition, strong majorities of both samples expressed a sense of satisfaction in voting, and few in either sample favored revolutionary change.

Another prominent trait of Costa Rican political culture is a general striving toward compromise and consensus. Parties to a dispute tend to seek mutually acceptable solutions rather than to hold unswervingly to initial principles or positions, permitting compromise and face-saving on both sides. As practiced by the political elite since 1948, this value has often contributed to innovative public policy designed to co-opt the disgruntled into the system, rather than to defeat and exclude them from it. For example, Costa Rica's victorious National Liberation junta in 1948 retained two of the Calderón Guardia government's most criticized policies, the Labor Code and social security system, in order to mollify the defeated Left. Other examples of innovative compromise between powerful pressures include the successful land reform initiated by the Institute of Land and Colonization in the mid- and late 1970s, and the mixed economy as a whole.

Despite four decades of predominantly peaceful political intercourse, Costa Ricans do occasionally resort to political violence. In the last decade, for example, banana workers, residents of the depressed Atlantic zone, and some landless peasants, when unable to achieve their objectives through other means, have occasionally employed strikes and violent confrontation. The violence (sometimes including limited small-arms fire) has on some occasions been premeditated, both by protesters and by police.

Unlike in neighboring nations, however, government response to protest and confrontation has generally been moderate. The Costa Rican government tends to employ force cautiously and to seek compromise in its place. Such moderation has usually defused violence and contained conflict to the original issue. Despite the growing frequency of violent conflict in recent years, the press and politicians of almost all parties have tended to disavow violence as unacceptable for political discourse. Thus, even when violence occurs, it is rarely extolled even by extremist parties and is generally regarded as exceptional and warranting special efforts to resolve its causes.

Even though both parties to the 1948 conflict employed terror, it had so long been absent from the national scene that several terrorist incidents since 1980 have shocked Costa Ricans. In spite of its recent rise, terrorism remains rare in Costa Rica, especially in comparison to other Central American societies. Both right- and left-wing terrorist groups seem to lack a significant popular base. However, Costa Rican terrorists have been nurtured by international contacts with other Central American revolutionaries and counter-revolutionaries, who are numerous in Costa Rica because of its large exile communities.

Despite a recent rise in political violence in Costa Rica, general popular support for national political institutions remains strong. In 1971, Carvajal found broad support for the Costa Rican governmental system and for elections, regardless of levels of political activity or education.[42] Even more interesting, Seligson and Muller traced Costa Ricans' levels of diffuse or general support for their political system across a national crisis in the early 1980s.[43] They reported that, before Costa Rica's severe 1980 economic crisis (which prompted a 70-percent devaluation of the currency and very high inflation), "levels of system support were very high by any standard of comparison, [and] fell from 79.7 percent in the high category to 70.2 percent." However, the percentage expressing "low support" for the system barely increased (from 2.3 to 3.7 percent), "even though negative incumbent evaluations had more than tripled between 1978 and 1980." Three years later, after a new government had responded to the economic crisis, "positive incumbent evaluations had risen from less than one-third in 1980 to over two-thirds in 1983, and negative evaluations had dropped from one-third to only five percent."[44] Seligson and Muller concluded that because Costa Rica's political system enjoyed a high level of political legitimacy (as measured by their index of diffuse support), it was able to weather a severe crisis of political effectiveness without becoming unstable.

• STATE, SOCIOECONOMIC STRUCTURE,
AND DEVELOPMENT •

The premise shaping the development of the Costa Rican economy from 1948 through 1982 was that unfettered capitalism causes undesirable and destabilizing socioeconomic dislocations and inequalities. The state therefore constrained the free market through social guarantees, regulation of business, and public ownership of certain means of production. Furthermore, the state has sought to promote economic development through joint ventures with private capital and through public investment in production, while also attempting to redistribute income to the middle class and poor.

Such policies led to a steady expansion of the state's role in the economy. Among public-sector monopolies are banking, insurance, telephone and electrical service, railways, ports, and oil refining. There is heavy state involvement in urban mass transit, and alcohol and banana production. The Costa Rican government extensively regulates exports, imports, agricultural production, environmental contamination, consumer prices, and public health and welfare. The government provides extensive, subsidized services in health care and higher education. The public-sector share of GDP in 1970 was about 20 percent and had risen to about 28 percent by 1983. The expansion of public-sector ownership was accompanied by a trebling of the public sector's share of employment between 1950 (when it was 6.1 percent) and 1985 (19.1 percent). Privatization of public assets and controls on state spending and employment since 1983 have no doubt reduced the public-sector share of GDP to some degree.[45]

The Costa Rican private sector has continued to flourish, partly in symbiosis with the state. However, criticism of the growth of the state sector—both domestically and from abroad—has escalated sharply in the last decade. Such criticism from the Right focuses on the allegedly stifling weight of the state bureaucracy on productive individuals and firms, and on deficit spending, excessive regulation, the inefficiency of state enterprises, and public ownership of potentially profitable enterprises. Critics from the Left denounce growing corruption, inequality, and the misdirection of services away from the needy poor and toward both middle-sector supporters of the major parties and public employees.

A prominent (and for Latin America, quite distinctive) feature of Costa Rica's development from 1948 until 1980 was the steady and broadly felt improvement of popular well-being. Income redistribution and improved delivery of public services to the poor increased popular living standards and decreased income inequality in Costa Rica between 1948 and 1980.[46] As Table 9.3 reveals, income distribution from 1961 to 1971 shifted away from the top quintile of the population (its share dropping from 60 to 51 percent), moved markedly toward the middle three quintiles (from 34 to 44 percent), and declined somewhat for the poorest quintile. Since 1971, the middle three quintiles' share has remained static, that of the richest quintile has recovered somewhat to about 53 percent, and the share of the poorest quintile has eroded substantially, to less than 4 percent.[47]

Because of the Costa Rican state's economic role and national elites' consistent promotion of social welfare, Costa Ricans have the lowest infant mortality and disease rates and the highest literacy, life expectancy, and caloric intake of all Central American countries.[48] These measures of well-being significantly improved during the 1960s and 1970s (see Table 9.4). In addition, a land-reform program in the 1960s and 1970s redistributed some land to landless peasants, but it appears to have had little impact on the substantial inequality in the countryside that is reflected in the poorest quintile's declining income share.

Despite complaints by the Right that the mixed-economy model stifled

Table 9.3. Income Distribution in Costa Rica: 1961, 1971, 1977, 1983 (by quintiles of income earners)

Quintiles	Percent of national income earned			
	1961	1971	1977	1983
Poorest 20 percent	6.0	5.4	3.6	3.9
Second quintile	7.8	9.3	8.4	8.5
Third quintile	9.8	13.7	13.5	13.8
Fourth quintile	16.4	21.0	21.1	20.3
Fifth quintile	60.0	50.6	53.4	53.0

Sources: Victor Hugo Céspedes S., "Evolución de la distribución del ingreso en Costa Rica" (Ciudad Universitaria Rodrigo Facio: Universidad de Costa Rica, Instituto de Investigaciones en Ciencias Económicas, November 1979), Table 6; and Victor Hugo Céspedes, Alberto di Mare, and Ronulfo Jiménez, *Costa Rica: La economía en 1985* (San José: Academia de Centroamérica, 1986), p. 73.

growth, GDP in Costa Rica during the 1960s and 1970s grew at an average rate of over 6 percent per year (the third highest in Latin America). GDP per capita (in constant dollars) nearly doubled during the same period, substantially better growth than in any other Central American country.[49] However, in 1980, the Costa Rican economy entered a severe economic crisis. Declining terms of trade, high levels of imports, and excessive foreign public debt brought about a default on foreign obligations, a dramatic devaluation of the *colón* (from 8.6 to 50 to the dollar), and a severe recession.

In order to reorganize its debt, Costa Rica was forced by the IMF to adopt a severe austerity program in 1981, curtail imports and deficit spending, and reduce the central government budget. Private-sector forces have taken advan-

Table 9.4. Selected Indicators of Socioeconomic Change

	Selected indices of change[a]			
		Costa Rica		Other lower-middle income countries
	1927	1960	1980	1980
Per-capita GDP ($)	—	780[b]	1430	850
Percent literate	66	84[c]	90	59
Infant mortality (per 1000 births)	—	83	27	95
Life expectancy at birth (years)	—	62	73	57
Percentage of economically active population in				
Agriculture	63	51	29	55
Industry	12	19	23	17
Services	7	30	48	28
Percent urban	20	37	44	33

[a]World Bank, *World Development Report 1983* (New York: Oxford University Press, 1983).

[b]Estimate based on Inter-American Development Bank, *Economic and Social Progress in Latin America: 1987 Report* (Washington, DC: 1987), p. 426.

[c]Estimate based on Mavis Hiltunen de Biesanz et al., *Los costarricenses* (San José: Editorial Universidad Nacional Estatal a Distancia, 1979), p. 399.

tage of this external pressure to successfully promote divestiture of profitable public-sector enterprises and reduced social spending.

The PLN government of Luis Alberto Monge (1982–1986) accepted some externally imposed curtailment of the economic role of the state and some reduction of social services in order to cut the country's fiscal deficit. His successor, Oscar Arias Sánchez, followed similar policies in the first half of his administration. Debt service grew as a percentage of the budget, while spending on education and other social services was curtailed. Government deficits dropped from over 8 percent of GDP in 1980 to an average of around 3 percent in the mid-1980s, and central government expenditures have contracted modestly in relation to GDP between 1980 and 1986.[50] Neither Monge nor Arias, however, has accepted dismantling of the social-democratic regime extant since 1949. Overall, since 1982, the PLN–led social democratic public philosophy appears to have been modified by a somewhat more *laissez faire* economic model that constrains service delivery in order to serve the austerity program (especially the external debt).

Organizational Demands[51]

Costa Rica is distinguished by its high level of formal organization. Costa Ricans take part in many groups, and through them make demands of the government. A 1973 national survey found that Costa Rican family heads reported a mean of 1.5 organizational memberships each.[52] Two-thirds of the sample reported having held office in some group, and about 60 percent attended with medium frequency. About 56 percent reported having engaged in at least one project to improve their communities, an activity that frequently brought people into contact with public officials.

The tendency to organize is not new in Costa Rica. The government organized guilds of key artisans as early as the 1830s; independently organized guilds of professionals and mutual-aid societies began to appear in the 1950s, community-improvement groups by the 1880s, and modern labor unions in the early twentieth century. Government-promoted cooperatives, health, nutrition, and community-improved groups have proliferated since 1950. In 1977, the Ministry of Labor and Social Security estimated there to be 417 unions with 132,000 members, and 327 cooperatives in Costa Rica.[53] Thus, Costa Rica abounds with organizations, and many of them—especially business and producer groups, unions, cooperatives, and self-help groups—make demands on the government. The Costa Rican government has traditionally responded favorably to group pressure. A 1973 nationwide survey of organizations and their projects in over 100 communities found that a substantial majority had received some form of outside assistance, usually from the national or municipal governments.[54]

Costa Rican organizations usually initiate their demand by contacting the competent authority through regular channels, sometimes with the help of a local notable with political contacts or prestige, later followed by higher appeals if unsuccessful. If such efforts fail, groups sometimes escalate demands through confrontational tactics such as demonstrations, small acts of civil disobedience, or consumer or employee strikes. The government generally responds to such confrontation with study and compromise to defuse the conflict.

Organized labor constitutes an important but divided interest sector.[55] Overall, only about 19 percent of the work force was organized in unions and professional associations in 1977.[56] Government policies have fragmented, and restrictive laws have hobbled the labor movement since the 1948 defeat of the Calderón-Communist populist alliance.[57]

As of the late 1970s, 40 percent of the nation's unions remained unaffiliated with any central labor organization. Among them are several large, powerful, independent unions that represent teachers, telephone/electrical-system workers, health/hospital employees, bank workers, and public-works ministry employees. Such unions have pressed middle-sector demands on the government and shaped public policy to favor such middle-class elements as public employees.

At the same time, four major confederations divided the rest of the unionized work force. The Christian Democratic Confederation had about 4 percent of the organized work force. The social-democratic, CCTD—affiliated with the American Institute for Free Labor Development and the Interamerican Regional Labor Organization—had about 16 percent, and a CCTD splinter known as the Authentic Confederation of Democratic Workers (CATD) another 8 percent.[58] CATD and CCTD leaders have close links to the National Liberation Party. Their public employee and skilled-trades unions generally press moderate, wage- and job-oriented demands.

The Communist-dominated General Confederation of Workers (CGT)—built since the CTCR was dismantled in 1948—and other Communist-led unions united, in 1980, into the Unitary Confederation of Workers (CUT), which represented about a third of the organized work force.[59] Strongly oriented toward class struggle, the CUT has, since 1981, called several major banana-worker strikes; each has involved violence. These strikes not only failed to win wage gains, but caused the United Fruit Company, the nation's largest banana producer, to decide to abandon banana production in the Golfito area in 1984. This disaster precipitated a leadership struggle that split the CGT in 1985 and appears to have cost unions a loss of membership.

Another type of labor organization is "solidarity associations," which had some 40,000 members in about 230 groups as of the early 1980s—around 8 percent of the total work force. Solidarity-association employers make modest profit-sharing contributions to the associations, which employees use mainly as credit unions. Solidarity associations arose out of a private-sector initiative informed by conservative social Christian theory in the late 1940s. Dominated by the businesses rather than by workers, their principal political objective is "helping detain the advance of the popular movement directed by the Popular

Vanguard [Communist] Party."[60] Solidarity associations thus undercut class-conscious labor organization, reduce labor conflict, and raise productivity by promoting patron-employee "cooperation."

Another class of interest/pressure groups is the associations (colleges) of professionals, which are much more widespread than in the United States. These groups, chartered by the state (rather like U.S. state bar associations), officially represent their members' professional interests in the public-policy arena. They also serve as pressure groups for their members and have been important vehicles representing middle-sector interests.

Business pressure groups are numerous, and several exercise great influence over national economic policy. The Costa Rican Management Association, the National Association for the Promotion of Enterprise, the Chamber of Commerce, the Chamber of Industries, and the National Union of Chambers represent private capital (or important subsectors of it). They strongly support business interests and have recently lobbied to reduce public-sector participation in the economy. Business interests exert considerable influence, apparently because entrepreneurs both contribute to and otherwise support political candidates of the PLN and the Unity coalition, and because entrepreneurs often serve in public posts. Business organizations lobby the executive and legislative branches heavily.

In summary, Costa Rica has numerous clearly articulated and heavily involved pressure groups making demands on the government and in some cases even competing for power. There is a general tendency for associational cleavages to be crosscutting, rather than mutually reinforcing. This has permitted the state and elites, especially since 1950, to reduce overt interclass competition for influence and benefits, despite the existence of effective political organizations representing lower-class, middle-class, and bourgeois interests. Because the 1950–1980 period was one of economic growth and relative prosperity, these mobilized interests were all favored (to varying degrees) by the growth of the Costa Rican state. The economic crisis of the early 1980s, however, raised prospects for increased class conflict as both the national economic pie and state resources shrank.

Class Structure

Costa Rica's social structure has evolved rapidly since the onset of coffee exportation in the mid-nineteenth century. The population, one of the most rapidly growing in Latin America for much of the period since independence, rose from 60,000 in 1821 to 472,000 in 1927 to 2,330,000 in 1982. The capital city grew during the same period from a village to a modern city with over one-fourth of the nation's population. The overall percent of the populace residing in urban areas climbed from 37 to 44 percent between 1960 and 1981.

Seligson points out that urban growth in Costa Rica stemmed in considerable measure from displacing smallholders as the spread of coffee production led to rapidly increased concentration of land ownership. Indeed, curves of urban growth and coffee exports are strikingly similar. Coffee also caused peasants displaced from the *meseta central* to colonize open peripheral lands, beginning the dispersion of the population throughout the national territory. This process culminated within the last two decades in the exhaustion of cultivable public land available for colonization.[61]

The growth of exporting and importing and of urban centers brought increases in the service, manufacturing, and other sectors of the economy in the late nineteenth and early twentieth centuries. By 1927, one worker in eight labored in industry, and one person in nine lived in San José. As towns and new economic activities developed, there appeared multiple new interests, many of which became mobilized into politics conflicting with the politically dominant coffee aristocracy, especially when Costa Rica's economy suffered from world recessions. Industrial and service sectors have continued to expand throughout the twentieth century. By the 1980s, almost one person in four worked in manufacturing, and only 29 percent remained in agriculture (see Table 9.4).

The assumption of new roles by the state during the 1940s at the beck of the burgeoning labor movement—roles expanded by the post–civil war governments—swelled the size of the government and made public employees a key political and economic force. The public sector (central government plus autonomous bureaucracies) grew from about 17,000 employees (6 percent of the work force) in 1950 to 102,000 (15 percent) by 1976, and to 160,000 (19 percent) in 1985.[62] By the early 1980s, the service sector made up almost half the work force, and two persons in seven lived in San José.

The benefits of the expanded political power of the middle class since 1950 are compellingly reflected in the data on the changing distribution of income between 1961 and 1971 (see Table 9.3). The middle 60 percent of income earners increased its share notably between 1961 and 1971, while the share of the poorest fifth declined only modestly. The segment benefiting the most was the middle quintile, whose 1971 share of national income increased by 40 percent. The middle three quintiles, one may safely assume, correspond to the segments of the populace represented by the numerous labor unions, professional associations, and professional colleges discussed above. Most heavily represented in the poorest quintile are landless and land-poor peasants.

As in most developing countries, income inequality coincides with the huge gap between town and country. The social groups earning higher incomes reside disproportionately in the metropolitan area of San José and in the larger towns and cities. In a 1973 study, family heads in the metropolitan area reported income levels 4.8 times greater than residents of the rest of the nation. Similarly, family heads in communities larger than 4,500 inhabitants reported 5.2 times greater incomes than those residing in smaller (mainly agricultural) communities. Such state services as health-care facilities, public transportation, electricity, and potable water were also skewed sharply in favor of metropolitan-area residents.[63] A 1979 study reported that three-fourths of Costa Rica's poorest families lived in rural areas, and that about two-thirds of these were rural nonfarm families (landless peasants).[64]

Moreover, it is within the rural sector that inequality in Costa Rica remains most extreme. The spread of coffee cultivation in the mid-nineteenth century created a large population of smallholding peasants, but in the late nineteenth and early twentieth centuries there occurred great concentration of land ownership, coffee production, milling, and exportation in the hands of the emergent class of coffee capitalists. This greatly increased the percentage of landless peasants. Since then, the proportion of landless peasants has increased further, to about one-fourth in 1963. Some of the excess rural populace has been absorbed in the cities, but even so three-quarters of 183,000 persons working in agriculture in 1963 either had no land at all or less than two acres. A vigorous land-reform program in the 1960s and early 1970s distributed some 50,000 hectares to thousands of peasants, reducing the share of landless and land-poor peasants somewhat (to an estimated 72 percent by 1973).[65]

However, despite Costa Rica's land-redistribution efforts in the 1970s, Seligson reports that the Gini index of land-distribution inequality *rose* slightly (from 78.9 to 79.6) between 1963 and 1973, leaving land distribution in Costa Rica among the most unequal in Latin America. An even more ambitious land-redistribution program was undertaken in the mid- and late 1970s, but its impact is not yet known. Seligson concluded that land concentration and the impoverishment of peasants continues in Costa Rica despite government efforts to arrest it.

> [I]t is the peasantry that bore the cost of economic development in the past and continues to do so in the present. Therefore, it is on the peasants' back that the coffee aristocracy and growing middle class ride. . . . To the extent that there has been economic development in Costa Rica, it has been a product of the ability of the elites to extract an even greater surplus from the underlying peasantry, while at the same time restricting the peasantry from partaking of the benefits of that developed society.[66]

These two trends—the shrinkage of the peasantry and increasing rural inequality and poverty—raise interesting questions for Costa Rican democracy. On one hand, the relative decline of the peasantry might be expected to reduce the overall significance of peasants as a potential political force. On the other hand, increasing rural poverty has led to unrest and peasant rebellion in many nations, especially in neighboring Central American countries.[67] Moreover, in a country whose economy is based on export agriculture, most other economic sectors and the state live on resources that depend on the peasantry for production. Although it is difficult to assess concretely, the potential for problems of agriculture and the peasantry to affect Costa Rican political stability should not be lightly dismissed.

By way of summary, the breakdown of social classes described by Biezanz and colleagues in the late 1970s is useful:[68]

- Half the upper class consists of an elite of roughly 1 percent of the population, earning about 10 percent of the national income and made up of aristocratic families descended from the conquerors. The other half consists of 1 percent of the population, earning a like amount of income but lacking aristocratic family connections. The wealth and income of both groups derive from large landholdings, especially in coffee production, from import-export and other commercial enterprises, and from industrial investments.
- The upper middle class, perhaps 5 percent of the population, includes merchants, industrialists, larger landholders, and prosperous professionals, whose earnings make up 10 percent of national income.
- The lower middle class, of perhaps 15 percent of Costa Ricans, consists of small-business owners, poorer professionals (such as most teachers), upper-level white-collar employees, and "relatively prosperous small farmers."[69] I estimate that their share of national income is roughly 20 percent.
- Roughly 50 percent of Costa Ricans fall into the working class, which earns between 40 and 45 percent of national income. In this class are steadily employed proletarians, some white-collar and most blue-collar public employees, manual laborers, smallholding peasants, and service workers.
- The lower class, made up of roughly one-quarter of the population, earns only about 7 percent of national income. Among its members are landless and very land-poor peasants (except banana workers), domestic servants, unskilled urban laborers, street vendors, and others in the urban informal sector, including beggars, prostitutes, and bootblacks.

Racial and Religious Cleavages

Costa Rica is fairly homogeneous racially, culturally, and religiously, because its original indigenous and black populations were almost completely assimilated into the predominant Mestizo population.[70] However, there is some tendency to overstate racial and ethnic homogeneity and to overlook discrimina- homogeneity and to overlook discrimination in Costa Rica.

A substantial proportion of the nation's 3-percent black populace resides in the Atlantic coastal area, where Jamaican blacks originally were brought as railroad and banana workers and today make up about a third of the total population. There developed pronounced racial discrimination and marked tensions between blacks and whites in that area. Since the loss of the United Fruit Company banana plantations in the 1930s—when blacks were not permitted to follow the company and jobs to the Pacific coast—the region and its population have been mired in poverty.

Many blacks today still speak English, do not share the culture of Latin Costa Rica, and resent the hispanization of their education since 1948. There are three times as many Protestants (15 percent) in the Atlantic zone as in the nation as a whole (5 percent); blacks are far more frequently Protestant than are Hispanics. Average income, economic status, employment, service delivery, and educational attainment of Atlantic-zone residents are all sharply below national averages.[71] *De jure* discrimination no longer exists in Costa Rica, but cultural biases against blacks are common.

The overlapping of racial, religious, linguistic, cultural, and economic cleavages—aggravated by discrimination—may well contribute greatly to the outburst of rioting that shakes the Atlantic coastal city of Limón every few years.

International Pressures and Constraints

Costa Rica, without a standing army, has pursued a foreign policy of pacifism and qualified neutrality since 1950.[72] On the one hand, this has meant advocating peaceful resolution of international disputes, mediating between other Central American states in conflict, seeking international assistance (especially from the Organization of American States) when its national security was threatened, and resisting long-standing U.S. efforts to expand its national security forces.[73] On the other hand, Costa Rica has generally aligned itself with the United States in international fora and supported the Western alliance.

During the 1970s, Costa Rica acted more independently of the United States (though it remained quite friendly); it renewed diplomatic ties with Cuba and overtly supported the insurrection against the Somoza regime in neighboring Nicaragua. But as Rojas notes, Costa Rica's support for the Sandinistas during the insurrection (1977–1979) had very clear costs in terms of "important allies and links in the international environment."[74]

However, the United States has won increased Costa Rican cooperation with U.S. policy against Nicaragua since 1981, though the Costa Rican policy shift partly predated the Reagan administration. President Carazo cooled down Costa Rican–Nicaraguan relations in 1980–1982, and the Monge administration intensified support for the United States and opposition to Nicaragua. President Monge reconciled such pro–U.S. and anti-Sandinista policies with his declared posture of Costa Rican neutrality by arguing that Costa Rica remained neutral with respect to armed conflict affecting other states, but not to moral, political, or ideological problems represented by the Sandinista regime.[75]

Monge administration policymakers (and leaders of the PUSC opposition) clearly regarded the Sandinista government as undesirable because of its Marxist ideology, its political organization, and its growing military power.[76] Thus, rather than build a costly army in violation of long-standing tradition, the Monge administration accepted considerably escalated U.S. military assistance for its Civil Guard after 1982, including a U.S.–run training program. U.S. military assistance to Costa Rica rose from zero in 1980 to $2.5 million in 1983, and to $10 million in 1985.[77] Costa Rica also harbored an important part of the anti-

Sandinista guerrilla forces backed by the United States and permitted U.S. authorities to set up a Voice of America radio station forty miles from Nicaragua. This precarious policy package placated Washington and provided a modest counterweight to the Nicaraguan armed forces, but it also risked losing control over national territory to the Contras and an escalated conflict with Nicaragua.

The upshot of these changes was essentially threefold: First, Costa Rican democracy became less secure both from without (because of increased regional turmoil and Nicaragua's growing military strength) and from within (because of the presence of anti-Sandinista Contra forces and their domestic impact). Second, the strengthened Civil Guard, while useful to manage the Contras, developed increased potential to threaten the security of civilian governments by introducing a new power contender in the Costa Rican polity. However, increased militarization and escalating tensions with Nicaragua received little popular support in Costa Rica in the early and mid-1980s. When Oscar Arias adopted a pro-peace platform in his presidential campaign, he came from behind to win the 1986 election. Continuously monitoring public opinion, Arias subsequently pushed hard for the Central American peace accord signed in Guatemala in August 1987. Success of the accord would remove the major internal and external justifications for increased military spending. Ultimately then, the Contra presence and conflict with Nicaragua appear to be greater short-term problems for Costa Rican democracy than is a resurgence of militarism. The Central American peace process held forth promise for addressing both.

Another possible international effect on Costa Rican democracy involves economic policy. From 1946 to 1975, Costa Rica received $208.5 million in U.S. economic assistance. From 1970 to 1981, there was a net inflow of foreign assistance of $523 million.[78] This aid and extensive public borrowing from foreign private lenders boosted the growth rate in the 1970s but built up $2.246 billion in public external debt by 1981 (a seventeenfold increase over the 1970 level)—an amount almost equal to a year's GNP.[79] Deteriorating terms of trade, a decline in the Central American Common Market, regional political tensions, and capital flight brought on the 1980 default on foreign obligations and caused a severe economic slump. In 1986, after three years of slow recovery, real GDP remained 8.3 percent below the 1980 level.[80]

In order to weather this crisis, Costa Rica required massive balance-of-payments aid, new credit, and a reorganization of its debt package. The IMF successfully pressured Costa Rica to implement a radical economic austerity program (curtailed imports and reduced deficit spending) and reorganized the debt package. The United States also sharply stepped up aid to Costa Rica; for example, U.S. balance-of-payments grants exceeded $1 million per day in the 1984–1985 budget. Such massive assistance has helped Costa Rica recover from the recession and lowered unemployment, and moderated the harsh effects of the adjustment program. For a while such U.S. aid made collaboration with U.S. Central American policies more palatable for Costa Rica. By 1987, however, the election of Arias, Costa Rican public opinion, the Iran-Contra sandal, and faltering U.S. support for the Contras contributed heavily to Costa Rica's assumption of leadership in the Central American peace negotiations.

In sum, Costa Rica's economic-development options (especially potential redistributive programs) have been sharply curtailed by the debt crisis and the externally imposed recovery plan. Reduction of the public sector and curtailed social-service spending may gradually undermine an important source of popular support for democracy. The social and developmental programs of the governments since 1948 created and co-opted a substantial middle and working class. Under present economic policies and the heavy debt load, the national income pie has shrunk and, though recovering, will grow more slowly than in the past. Income distribution has become more unequal, and the government will be stingier with the poor in the future because of the burden of foreign debt. Such changes could well increase class conflict in Costa Rica.

• THEORETICAL ANALYSIS •

Liberal democracy in Costa Rica developed over the course of centuries. During the colonial era and nineteenth centuries many Latin American nations developed export-oriented economies based on militarily enforced, feudal, or forced-labor systems that exploited Indians and blacks. Their polities were dominated by the beneficiaries of that system—a landowning aristocracy that ruled by military power. In contrast, Costa Rica's isolation, emergent racial homogeneity, and poverty bred relative economic equality, a tradition of and taste for civilian rule, weak military institutions, and egalitarian social values. When coffee production eventually permitted the Costa Rican social aristocracy to accumulate capital, and economic inequality grew in the late nineteenth century, it did so during a labor shortage that made landowners dependent on scarce rural workers. This circumstance restrained the bourgeoisie's political and economic power and reinforced existing egalitarian social norms. This interdependence among economic classes was reinforced by the organization, enfranchisement, and political mobilization of emergent middle-class and working-class interests.

Two remarkable political leaders (Ricardo Jiménez Oreamuno and Cleto González Víquez) developed elections and expanded popular suffrage as mechanisms for the coffee aristocracy's accommodation of popular power in the first third of the twentieth century. As evolving class structures and economic crises impoverished many Costa Ricans after 1910, an ethic of social reformism (informed by social-Christian, social-democratic, *Aprista,* and Marxist movements) developed within the Costa Rican political elite. When Calderón's populist reformism and burgeoning class conflict led to the 1948 civil war, José Figueres' middle-class National Liberation movement emerged to eventually bind both electoral integrity and social reformism into the modern Costa Rican political system.

From 1948 until the early 1980s, the commitment of the political elite (now expanded to include middle-class elements) to a social-democratic political philosophy expanded the economic role of the state, redistributed income toward the middle sectors, ameliorated some of the effects of poverty, and strongly supported electoral probity. Political institutions also served the consolidation of democracy. The Costa Rican Constitution decentralized state authority, leaving the executive relatively constrained, and the courts and legislature relatively powerful compared to most Latin American polities. The abolition of a weak and defeated army, in 1949, has strengthened civilian institutions and freed economic resources for the state; while the state's expanding economic role from 1948 until 1982 increased the size of the national economic pie and markedly increased the middle sectors' share. Two major, moderate, multi-class partisan groups, the PLN and the Unity (presently PUSC) party coalition, alternate in power and manifest commitment to the post-1949 constitutional rules of the game.

The Costa Rican populace is highly politically mobilized, but many associational cleavages crosscut one another. Organized labor has been divided and hamstrung by deliberate policies of the state and political elite. There are, however, powerful public-sector unions that can immobilize the state and have considerable, though rarely exercised, potential to press their demands on the government. Class structures are characterized by extreme inequality between the landed and landless in agriculture and between the capital and hinterland. However, State policies have attenuated the destabilizing implications of this inequality. The lower class, mainly the dispersed and politically disorganized landless peasantry, receives some attention from the state in the form of social-welfare and land-reform programs. A large middle sector (about half the population) has benefited from redistributive public policies and programs.

Costa Rica's political culture has contributed significantly to the maintenance of democracy. Costa Ricans and their organizations generally engage in pacific demand-making, and the state has had a tradition of acquiescing to such demands. Political elites and masses share considerable commitment to the liberal system of parties and clean elections. There exists a strong tendency toward popular loyalty to the political system, regardless of disapproval of momentary incumbents. Though present, political confrontation and violence are very mild by regional standards, and the state reacts to them with moderation and conciliation.

Costa Rican political culture developed egalitarian social values, preference for civilian rule, and a drive for consensus and conciliation, while the configuration of the class system required upper-class co-optation of increasingly mobilized middle- and working-class elements, which gave rise first to electoral democracy and later to redistributive social policies. The high degree of political organization and participation among the populace and special interests is modulated by crosscutting allegiances and by a wide dispersion of effective power within and outside the state. One can hardly overstate the importance of this situation, variously described by Costa Rican scholars as the "neutralization of classes"[81] or the "interdependence of classes."[82]

• PROSPECTS FOR COSTA RICAN DEMOCRACY •

Costa Rica's configuration of class structures, state institutions, public policy, and popular and elite political culture has created a system of stable liberal democracy without parallel in Latin America. The economic crisis of the early 1980s has proved the stability of the Costa Rican polity. Despite a plunge in economic activity and employment and soaring inflation that sharply lowered the standard of living of most Costa Ricans, the 1982 and 1986 national elections took place normally, and power passed peacefully from Carazo's Unity government to the successive PLN governments of Monge and Arias. Costa Rica's 36-year-old liberal democracy, however, is probably not invulnerable. Uruguay and Chile provide grim reminders that neither age nor tradition guarantee the survival of liberal democracies. Several potential threats to the stability of Costa Rican democracy can be identified.

External pressures (supported by certain internal entrepreneurial interests) brought on by the 1980 debt crisis have weakened the social-democratic public ideology that prevailed in Costa Rica from 1948 through 1982. The state's role in the economy has diminished, and social-welfare programs have shrunk. The Costa Rican state thus became weaker in domestic resources and now enjoys less autonomy vis-à-vis external actors than it did before the onset of the crisis.

These changes have reversed a decades-old trend of reducing income inequality and improving popular living standards. In the short run, public support for the political system has remained high, but it is still too soon to judge fully the lasting effects of increasing poverty. One might reasonably conjecture, however, that should programs benefiting key, highly organized middle- and working-class groups collapse, class conflict could grow. The sharp recent increases in rural inequality and the diminishing income share of the very poor also hold potential for growing political conflict. This is especially so given the political power of key vested interests: Key public-sector unions control essential public services, and pressure groups wield sufficient power to block policy reforms in the legislature. On balance, the ability of a now weaker Costa Rican state to contend with intense competing policy demands or a policy stalemate appears limited. This situation could easily lead to an increased use of governmental or private repression to curtail demands. Such an increase in either conflict or repression could weaken public support for national institutions.

In the early 1980s, growing Costa Rican animosity toward Nicaragua, encouraged by the United States, exploited by domestic actors for their own political reasons, and fed by old rivalries, also raised a potential threat to Costa Rican democracy. By 1985, anti-Communist rhetoric in the Costa Rican press had risen to unprecedented levels, anti-Nicaraguan rhetoric was intense, and rightist groups had attacked peace demonstrators and the Nicaraguan Embassy. There had also appeared discussions of "anti–Costa Ricanism" (strikingly similar to 1950s commentary about "un-Americanism" in the United States). However, no official persecution of suspected "subversives" occurred, and the election of Oscar Arias and the Central American peace accord of 1987 began to ameliorate such trends.[83] Xenophobia and anti-Communism can be used to justify repression and the denial of civil liberties essential to democratic participation; both attitudes remained strongly present in Costa Rica in the 1980s.

Distaste for Sandinista rule and fear of growing Nicaraguan military power have contributed to some strengthening of Costa Rican military and paramilitary forces. The expansion and partial militarization of the Civil Guard could also affect prospects for the stability of the Costa Rican liberal, constitutional system. Costa Rica has not built a large or powerful army in the 1980s, but the increased strength of the Civil Guard and the rise of paramilitary forces do raise the possibility of disruptive new players in the political game and a greater potential for repression of citizens. By the late 1980s, there were signs that paramilitary forces had begun to wane and that the Central American peace accord could help control military growth.

Were Nicaragua to invade Costa Rica, the former's immediate advantage in a head-to-head military confrontation (*ceteris paribus*) would be enormous. In such a clash, however, Costa Rica could expect direct military help from the United States and other regional powers. Thus, Nicaragua would probably eschew any significant direct military action against Costa Rica. Nicaragua might, however, assist subversive elements on the radical Left within Costa Rica to retaliate for Costa Rican assistance to the anti-Sandinista Contras. The prospect of such subversion succeeding seems small, indeed, but its presence could justify repression and restrictions of civil liberties by the Costa Rican government. The Central American peace accord of 1987, signed by both Costa Rica and Nicaragua, barred both countries from aiding the other's rebels and thus had potential for reducing the principal sources of conflict between them.

Finally, in a moment of increased class conflict, popular unrest or terrorism, elites—either from the Right or Center—could overthrow a constitutional regime in an effort to restore order and pursue particular policy objectives. In fact, such an event would be most similar to what happened in the 1948 civil war. In such a situation, especially if resistance from popular organizations developed, there could be considerable violence, and democracy could be permanently destroyed. Among Costa Rican economic and political elites there are those who would benefit substantially from reduced democracy, curtailed political participation, and the reduction in benefits for the working and middle classes that could represent. Indeed, Daniel Oduber mentioned in a 1979 lecture series that, while president, he had been encouraged several times to suspend the Constitution and impose certain desired, but frustrated, policy initiatives through a dictatorship.[84]

External actors and forces can influence the Costa Rican liberal democratic regime. Costa Rica's huge foreign debt was managed, after 1980, largely by rescheduling, new borrowing, and austerity, but had nonetheless doubled by 1987. Foreign countries such as the United States and European nations helped ameliorate immediate threats to Costa Rican democracy from the debt by granting assistance and loans on generous terms. Such aid, however, may have only postponed an ultimate reckoning in the form of a general economic collapse that could undermine the regime. Future foreign efforts should seek to eliminate or greatly reduce Costa Rica's debt in order to enhance the long-term stability of the political system.

Foreign governments, especially the enormously influential United States, may also enhance or impair the survival of Costa Rican democracy by their geopolitical behavior. Abatement of U.S. pressure on Costa Rica to support anti-Sandinista rebels, to increase hostility toward Nicaragua, and to militarize would help curtail forces that could undermine democracy. International efforts to support the 1987 Central American peace accord and the Contadora peace process (such as the awarding of the Nobel Peace Prize to president Arias in October 1987) could help reduce regional tensions that have placed great strains on Costa Rican democracy. However, because of U.S. involvement in the Contra war and because opposition by the United States has been the major obstacle to the Contadora process, a major change in U.S. foreign policy in Central America would be necessary to maximize the prospects for the survival of Costa Rican democracy. As the Reagan administration neared the end of its second term there were signs that Congress and regional powers might impose such a dramatic shift on U.S. policy in Central America, but the situation remained very volatile, and the implications for Costa Rica remained obscure.

In conclusion, given the Costa Rican tradition of popular participation in politics and the society's degree of organization (especially class-based groups), the turbulent Central American and world economic environments, the shrunken resources of the Costa Rican state, and increased coercive potential in the society all raise certain threats to an otherwise remarkably stable liberal democracy. The range and breadth of participation in politics in Costa Rica today are extensive, but its depth is not. Should regional conflict or economic change harm the interests of major mobilized groups in Costa Rica, one might reasonably expect citizens in the future to demand deeper (more meaningful) influence on public decisions. That would likely place them in conflict with extant elites, sharpen interclass conflict, increase political turmoil, and strain many of the multiple factors that have contributed to liberal democracy in Costa Rica.

• NOTES •

1. See John A. Booth, "Representative Constitutional Democracy in Costa Rica: Adaptation to Crisis in the Turbulent 1980s." In *Central America: Crisis and Adaptation,* ed. Steve C. Ropp and James A. Morris (Albuquerque: University of New Mexico Press, 1984).

2. John A. Peeler, *Latin American Democracies: Colombia, Costa Rica, Venezuela* (Chapel Hill: University of North Carolina Press, 1985), pp. 5–6.

3. Carl Cohen, *Democracy* (New York: Free Press, 1973), pp. 8–27.

4. This section is drawn mainly from Booth, "Representative Constitutional Democracy," pp. 158–176; and John A. Booth, "Costa Rican Labor Unions." In *Latin American Labor Unions*, ed. Gerald W. Greenfield and Sheldon L. Maram (New York: Greenwood Press, 1987).

5. Lowell Gudmundson discusses the myth in detail in his *Costa Rica Before Coffee: Society and Economy on the Eve of the Export Boom* (Baton Rouge: Louisiana State University Press, 1986), pp. 1–24.

6. Elizabeth Fonseca, *Costa Rica colonial: La tierra y el hombre* (San José, Costa Rica: Editorial Universitaria Centroamericana, 1984); see also Gudmundson, *Before Coffee*, pp. 25–87.

7. See Carlos Meléndez, "Bosquejo para una historia social costarricense antes de la independencia." In V. de la Cruz et al., *Las instituciones costarricenses del siglo XIX* (San José, Costa Rica: Editorial Costa Rica, 1985), pp. 42–43 (my translation).

8. Ibid., p. 44; see also Mavis Hiltunen de Biesanz et al, *Los costarricenses* (San José: Editorial Universidad Nacional a Distancia, 1979), ch. 2.

9. José Luis Vega Carballo, *Poder político y democracia en Costa Rica* (San José: Editorial Porvenir, 1982), p. 30 (author's emphasis, my translation).

10. Ibid., p. 88; see also Johnny Alfaro Ramos et al., *La evolución del sufragio en Costa Rica*. (Licenciatura thesis in Law, Facultad de Derecho, Universidad de Costa Rica, 1980), pp. 39–40.

11. Jacobo Schifter, "La democracia en Costa Rica como producto de la neutralización de clases." In Chester Zelaya et al., *¿Democracia en Costa Rica?: Cinco opiniones polémicas* (San José: Editorial Universidad Nacional Estatal a Distancia, 1978), pp. 197–200.

12. Vega Carballo, *Poder político*, p. 96; and Samuel Stone, *La dinastía de los conquistadores* (San José: Editorial Universidad de Costa Rica, Editorial Universitaria Centroamericana, 1975), p. 223.

13. See Oscar Aguilar Bulgarelli, "Evolución histórica de una democracia." In Zelaya et al., *¿Democracia en Costa Rica?, pp. 42–46*.

14. Vega Carballo, *Poder política*, p. 30.

15. Ibid., p. 30.

16. Ibid., p. 95.

17. Ibid., pp. 97–98.

18. Harold H. Bonilla, *Los presidentes*, vol. 2 (San José: Universidad Nacional Estatal a Distancia, Editorial Costa Rica, 1979), pp. 823–825.

19. Peeler, *Latin American Democracies*, pp. 72–76.

20. Ibid., p. 113.

21. *Constitución política de la República de Costa Rica* (San José: Asamblea Legislativa, 1978), Article 99 (my translation).

22. Ibid., Article 104.

23. Ibid., Article 102.

24. Charles D. Ameringer, *Democracy in Costa Rica* (New York: Praeger, 1982), p. 51.

25. *Constitución*, Article 95.

26. Only convicted felons are excluded from voting. Ibid., Articles 90–95; Ameringer, *Democracy*, p. 58; Mitchell A. Seligson and Edward Muller, "Democratic Stability and Economic Crisis: Costa Rica, 1978–1983," *International Studies Quarterly* 31 (1987): pp. 307–309, fig. 1.

27. See Burt English, *Liberación Nacional in Costa Rica: The Development of a Political Party in a Transitional Society* (Gainesville: University of Florida Press, 1971); and Peller, *Latin American Democracies*, pp. 43–142.

28. Peeler, *Latin American Democracies*, p. 113.

29. See, for example, U.S. Congress, *Country Reports on Human Rights Practices* (Washington, DC, February 2, 1981), pp. 391–96.

30. The provision for no reelection does not effect presidents elected prior to 1969. It has for some years been the object of an unsuccessful push for constitutional amendment by Daniel Oduber Quiros, who became president after 1969.

31. E.g., at least one cabinet member must also veto a bill for the veto to take effect.

32. *Constitución*, Articles 130–140.

33. Amendment is by a two-thirds vote of total membership in each of two successive annual sessions of the Legislative Assembly.

34. *Constitución*, Articles 152–167; Ameringer, *Democracy*, p. 53.
35. Based on data in Inter-American Development Bank (hereafter IADB), *Economic and Social Progress in Latin America: 1987 Report* (Washington, D.C., 1987).
36. James Backer, *La iglesia y el sindicalismo en Costa Rica* (San José: Editorial Costa Rica, 1978), pp. 83–220.
37. Interviews and conversations with Costa Rican social scientists, and personal observations, August 1985 and August 1987.
38. Booth, "Representative Constitutional Democracy," Table 5.3
39. See Biesanz et al, *Los costarricenses*, pp. 30–39.
40. "The Costa Rican says 'vos' [thou—the familiar second person pronoun], 'shit,' and 'son of a whore' even to the president." All are common locutions in Costa Rica.
41. Mario Carvajal Herrera, *Actitudes políticas del costarricense* (San José: Editorial Costa Rica, 1978), pp. 137–173. He sampled 100 party and group leaders and 305 citizens from three municipalities.
42. Ibid., pp. 166–167.
43. Seligson and Muller, "Democratic Stability," passim.
44. Ibid., pp. 319–322.
45. Victor Hugo Céspedes, et al., *Costa Rica: la economía en 1985* (San José: Academica de Centroamérica, 1986), pp. 59, 78.
46. Seligson and Muller, "Democratic Stability," pp. 13–16.
47. Victor Hugo Céspedes S., *Evolución de la distribución del ingreso en Costa Rica* (Ciudad Universitaria "Rodrigo Facio": Instituto de Investigaciones en Ciencias Económicas, Universidad de Costa Rica, 1973), Table 6.
48. Booth, "Representative Constitutional Democracies," Table 5.4.
49. Victor Bulmer-Thomas, "Economic Development over the Long Run—Central America since 1920," *Journal of Latin American Studies* 15 (November 1983): pp. 269–294.
50. IADB, *1987 Report*, pp. 268–275, 437–438; Victor Hugo Céspedes et al., *Costa Rica: La economía en 1985* pp. 77–85.
51. (Material in this section is drawn from Booth, "Representative Constitutional Democracies"; from my "Democracy and Citizen Action in Costa Rica: The Modes and Correlates of Populuar Participation in Politics." (Ph.D. Diss., University of Texas at Austin, 1975); and Booth, "Labor Unions."
52. Booth, "Democracy and Citizen Action", pp. 89–105.
53. E. Lederman et al., "Trabajo y empleo." In *Costa Rica contemporánea*, vol. 2, ed. Chester Zelaya (San José: Editorial Costa Rica), Tables 26, 27, 30.
54. John A. Booth and Mitchell A. Seligson, "Peasants as Activists: A Reevaluation of Political Participation in the Countryside," *Comparative Political Studies* 12 (April 1979): passim.
55. Backer, *La Iglesia*, pp. 13–28, 135–207.
56. See Booth, "Labor Unions;" and Lederman et al., "Trabajo y empleo," Table 27.
57. Schifter, "La democracia," pp. 171–240.
58. Lederman et al.'s 1977 statistics (Table 29) from the Ministry of Labor and Social Security vary somewhat from these, taken from 1979 Ministry of Labor data summarized in Booth, "Labor Unions."
59. Booth, "Labor Unions;" see also Lederman et al., "Trabajo y empleo," Table 29.
60. Gustavo Blanco and Orlando Navarro, *El solidarismo: Pensamiento y dinámica social de un movimiento obrero patronal* (San José: Editorial Costa Rica, 1984), p. 298.
61. Mitchell A. Seligson, *Peasants of Costa Rica and the Development of Agrarian Capitalism* (Madison: University of Wisconsin Press, 1980), ch. 6.
62. Ibid.; statistics on the public sector from Lederman et al., "Trabajo y empleo;" Tables 7 and 8; and Céspedes et al., *La economía en 1985*, p. 79.
63. Booth, "Democracy and Citizen Action," fig. 2.2, 2.3, and 2.4.
64. Biesanz et al., *Los costarricenses*, p. 247.
65. Seligson, *Peasants of Costa Rica*, pp. 23, 147; work force data from Lederman et al., "Trabajo y empleo," Table 4.
66. Quote from Seligson, *Peasants of Costa Rica*, p. 48; see also ch. 6.
67. John A. Booth, "Toward Explaining National Revolts in Central America: Socioeconomic and Political Roots of Rebellion." Ms., July 1986; revised version of a paper presented at the 44th International Congress of Americanists, Manchester, England, 1982.
68. Biesanz et al., *Los costarricenses*, pp. 245–251. The impact on income distribution and

classes of the economic crisis of the 1980s, which substantially lowered income levels for at least two thirds of Costa Ricans, has not yet been fully assessed.

69. Ibid., p. 246.
70. Ibid., p. 274.
71. John A. Booth et al., *Tipología de comunidades, vol. 2: Estudio para una tipología de comunidades* (San José: Dirección Nacional de Desarrollo de la Comunidad, Acción Internacional Técnica, 1973), passim.
72. Fracisco Rojas Aravena, "La percepción de la crisis centroamericana y la administración Monge Alvarez." (Heredia, Costa Rica: Universidad Nacional, Escuela de Relaciones Internacionales, 1984), pp. 69–70.
73. *CRISIS* 1 (Spring 1985?): pp. 2–6.
74. Rojas Aravena, "La percepción," p. 61.
75. From statements by Luis Alberto Monge Alvarez, in ibid., p. 35.
76. See, for instance, ibid., passim.
77. *CRISIS* 1 (Spring 1985?): p. 4.
78. World Bank, *World Development Report 1983* (London: Oxford University Press, 1983), Table 15.
79. Ibid., Table 16.
80. Victor Bulmer-Thomas, *The Political Economy of Central America Since 1920* (New York: Cambridge University Press, 1987), Table 11.6.
81. Schifter, "La democracia."
82. Vega Carballo, *Poder político.*,
83. Author's observations based upon visits to Costa Rica in August 1985 and 1987, and on an informal of survey of Costa Rican press for several years.
84. Daniel Obuder, Lecture series. Escuela de Relaciones Internacionales, Universidad Nacional Autónoma. Heredia, Costa Rica, August 1979.

• CHAPTER TEN •
The Dominican Republic: Mirror Legacies of Democracy and Authoritarianism

HOWARD J. WIARDA

Among Latin American nations, the Dominican Republic has been one of the most unfortunate and least successful in its efforts to develop a system of stable democratic rule.[1] In its 150 years of independence, the authoritarian tradition and legacy have been powerful, and the democratic weak. In all that time, the Dominican Republic has enjoyed only twenty-five years, or one-sixth of its history, under what can loosely be called "democratic government", and one-third of those years have come within the last ten. Democracy in the Dominican Republic, when it has existed at all, has been weak, tenuous, unstable, and uncertain—and that remains the case under the present democratic regime.

A democratic breakthrough has occurred, nevertheless, and one would be wrong either to overestimate its importance or to underestimate it. Dominicans still sometimes exhibit rather ambivalent feelings about democracy, but there can be no doubt that there has been a significant shift toward democratic rule. This change is related to other, broader transformations in Dominican society: greater affluence; a larger middle class; economic development; changing political culture; and changes in the international environment. The shift is therefore not limited to a change in political institutions at the top but is based on profounder and deeper alterations in that often unfortunate nation. For this reason it would be very difficult for the country at this stage to revert to its more authoritarian and repressive traditions. That could now be accomplished only with such bloody repression, à la Pinochet in Chile, that it would be very difficult to bring off, but not impossible. That is why, while democracy is established and now even more institutionalized than ever before in Dominican history, its future is not entirely certain, cannot be taken for granted, and bears close scrutiny.

Few North Americans would disagree with the definition of democracy employed in this book, which after all derives from and is close to the Lockean, Madisonian, Anglo-American understanding and tradition.[2] In Latin America, however, where historic political roots lie in a Thomistic-Suárezian and, later, Rousseauan tradition, a somewhat more ample and broader definition must be used.[3] In Latin America, the pluralism that exists is usually more controlled and

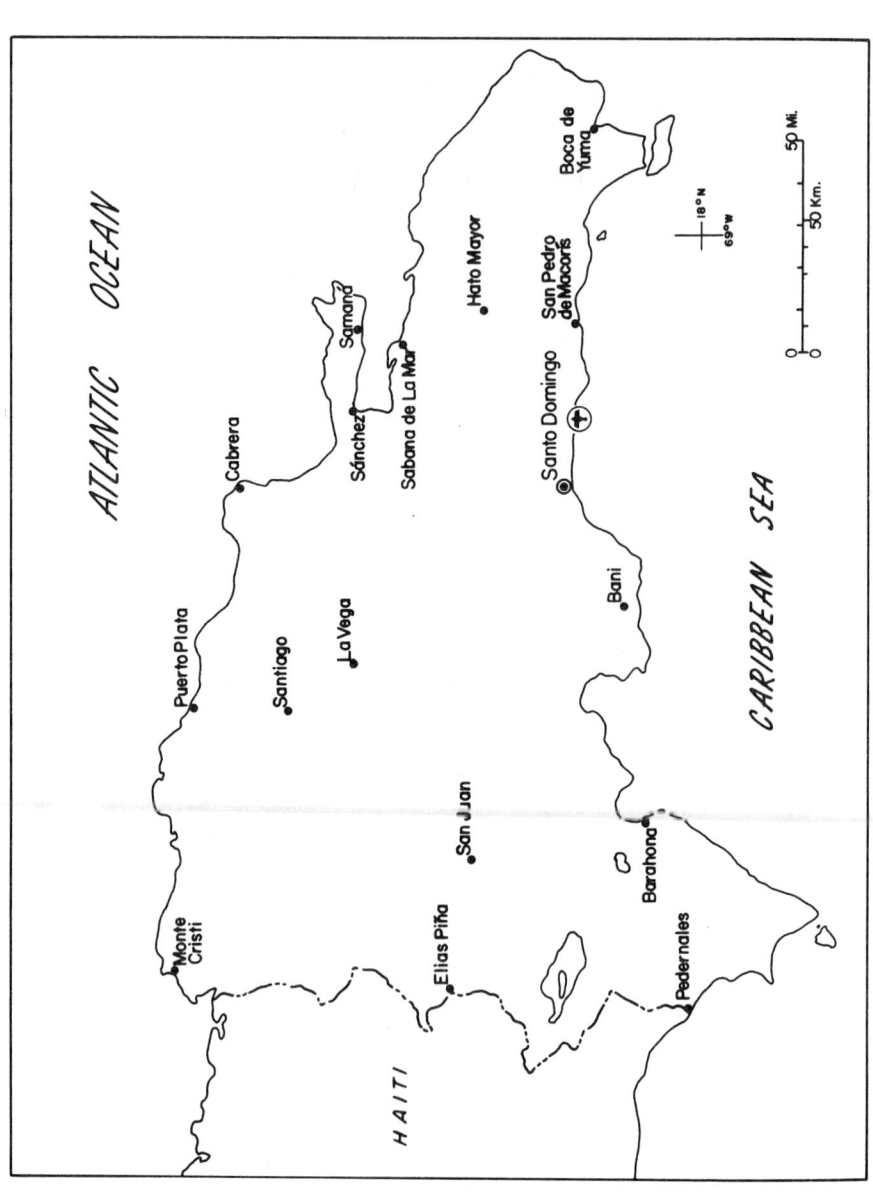

THE DOMINICAN REPUBLIC

limited than is the unbridled and virtually anarchic competition of U.S. interest-group pluralism.[4] "Participation" is also understood somewhat differently, often in organic, corporate, and group terms as much as through the individualistic form of participation—"one-man-one-vote"—of the United States.[5] Similarly, civil and political liberties are often defined differently from the U.S. understandings, or with distinctive nuances, or with a different sense of priorities than is true in the Anglo-American tradition.[6]

These differences of meaning are crucial because they lie at the heart of the Dominican Republic's efforts to achieve democratic rule. Historically, Dominicans have imported forms of democracy derived from the Anglo-American tradition, including constitutions that were simply translations into Spanish of the U.S. Constitution, which have not always worked very well in the Dominican context. When democracy failed to work or produced anarchy and breakdown, Dominicans reverted to their other, authoritarian, historic tradition. *Never* in history have the Dominicans been able to find a formula that blends these two traditions, or one that takes into account their own, somewhat distinctive meanings of democracy. Today, the quest for such a formula goes on, which is why we must remain both hopeful and at the same time somewhat skeptical about the permanence of the present democratic system in that country.

· HISTORICAL OVERVIEW ·

The Dominican Republic is a nation of nearly 6 million people on 19,386 square miles (48,464 square kilometers) of territory.[7] It occupies the eastern two-thirds of the island of Hispaniola, the second largest (next to Cuba) of the string of islands rimming the Caribbean Sea. The Dominican Republic, Catholic, Spanish-speaking, and Hispanic, shares Hispaniola with French-speaking Haiti, which the Dominicans are wont to portray as black and "African."

The Dominican Republic has a per-capita annual income of about $1,200. The country has experienced impressive economic growth in the last twenty years and is no longer among the poorest of the Latin American countries. It is now about 55 percent urban, reflecting the recent growth of the manufacturing, commercial, and service sectors. Literacy has climbed to about 70 percent. The changes in the last two decades in terms of the modernization of virtually all areas of life have been nothing short of remarkable.[8] These changes have laid the basis for the emergence of a more democratic system.

It has not always been this way. Indeed, the Dominican Republic has one of the most chaotic and disruptive histories in all of Latin America. This history has strongly shaped not only the nation's development, or, properly put, the absence sometimes thereof, but also its attitudes toward democracy.

The Colonial Past

At the time of Columbus's landing on the island in 1492, Hispaniola ("little Spain," the name the Spaniards gave to it) was peopled by the Taino and Arawak Indians. Neither had very large or complex societies, compared to the vast Aztec, Mayan, and Inca civilizations that the Spaniards would later find on the mainland.[9]

The Spaniards established the first permanent European settlement in the New World on Hispaniola, calling it Santo Domingo. Here the first university, the first cathedral, and the first monastery in the Americas were founded. It was on Hispaniola that the first Spanish social experiments in colonial rule were carried out.[10]

Before its arrival in America, Spain had had considerable experience with conquest and colonization. The reconquest of the Iberian Peninsula from the Moors had just been completed the same year that Columbus discovered America, and the Spanish conquest of America may be looked on as almost a continuation of that reconquest. Indeed, quite a number of the hierarchical and authoritarian practices and institutions that Spain carried to America were reflections of the same institutions recently established in Iberia.[11] The "democracy" of Spain's middle ages—the system of representation by estates, the autonomy of cities, the rule of law—had been eliminated by the sixteenth century in favor of absolutism and authoritarianism; and it was this later, or "Hapsburgian," model that was carried over to the New World.[12]

On Hispaniola, the Spaniards established the practices and institutions of imperial rule that would later be extended to the rest of the Americas. The Spaniards conquered and subjugated the native Indians. They milked the colony of its gold and silver. They forced the Indians to work in the mines under inhuman conditions that resulted in rapid decimation of the native population. More or less simultaneously, a *hacienda* or slave-plantation system was established in which the Indians were obliged to perform exhausting manual labor.[13]

The Spanish colonial system represented a whole way of life—political, social, military, religious, legal, and intellectual, as well as economic. This system was imposed on Hispaniola during the sixteenth century, and it remained the dominant pattern for centuries thereafter. It remains strongly present today, representing an alternative to the current and emerging liberal-democratic system. It therefore behooves us to know more about that system and why it has been so long-lasting.

The Hapsburgian system, in all its manifestations, was a rigid, top-down, hierarchical, and authoritarian system that still has powerful echoes in the Dominican Republic.[14] Politically, it was a system of absolutist authority proceeding from all-powerful king to captain-general to local military conqueror *cum* oligarch. Each unit in the hierarchy exercised absolute authority, allowing for no challenge or questioning from below. There were no hints of democracy or grassroots participation.

Socially, the system was similarly rigid and hierarchical. The Spanish conquerors occupied the highest place in the hierarchy. There was a very small "traditional middle class," often Mestizo or mulatto, of soldiers, artisans, and craftsmen. At the lowest levels, as serfs or virtual slaves, was the native Indian population. As the Indians began to die out, the Spaniards began to import African slaves to do manual labor. Importing African slaves did not change the social structure of the colony, however; it only meant substituting one lower class for another. The basic two-class system was thus established and remained intact. It was reinforced by racial criteria, so that the class barriers to social advancement became virtually impossible to overcome.

The economy was similarly exploitive, mercantilist, and feudal. A small elite milked the colony dry for its own benefit and that of the Spanish Crown. Almost nothing was reinvested in the colony for internal development; that would not have been in accord with the mercantilist philosophy then prevailing. The religious, legal, and educational systems established under the Spanish colonial system were similarly hierarchical and authoritarian. There was no preparation in self-rule, let alone democratic self-government.[15]

Since that was the prevailing mode, it should not be surprising that the Spanish colonial structure was established in this fashion in the early sixteenth century. What is surprising is that it lasted so long: through three centuries of Spanish colonial rule, on into the independence period of the nineteenth century, and even to the present. For even now, the sixteenth-century Spanish model of a bureaucratic-authoritarian state serves as an alternative to the liberal one, a top-down system that has by no means disappeared from the Dominican consciousness.

The first half-century, 1492–1550, was the "glorious" period of Spanish colonial rule on Hispaniola. After that, the colony was ignored and abandoned and became bedraggled. The population declined, the more enterprising Spaniards went off to the richer colonies of Cuba and the mainland, and Hispaniola went into a centuries-long depression from which it is still recovering. It became a run-down and backward way station in the vast Spanish empire. Important for our purposes is the fact that its main institutions also declined: the church; the university; the *hacienda*.[16] From this point on, Hispaniola would face the problem not just of overcoming its authoritarian Spanish past but also of creating institutions—any institution—to fill the void. The colony of Hispaniola was characterized chiefly by disorganization, by what Dominicans would later refer to as a *falta de civilización* ("lack of civilization"). Not only did the island lack any liberalizing and democratizing institutions, it lacked any institutions at all on which a viable postindependence political order could be based.

The second problem is the island's strategic location, commanding two key passageways into the Caribbean: that between North and South America; and that between the Isthmus of Panama and Mexico and Western Europe or North America. This important strategic location means that Hispaniola has been frequently shelled, occupied, and pressured by the larger powers. In the colonial period, the Dutch, British, and French all sought to wrest control of the island from Spain. The French eventually succeeded, in the eighteenth century, in taking the western third of the island from Spain and converting it into a valuable sugar colony based on slave labor, from which the later independent nation of Haiti sprang. In the independence period, Spain and France again, then Britain, Germany, the United States, and the Soviet Union all sought to conquer the island, secure bases there, or use the island as a pawn in larger global power struggles. Never would the Dominican Republic be able to develop autonomously. Rather, it was always caught up in, and always a pawn of, these larger international struggles, which served further to retard its possibilities for democratic progress.[17]

The Independence Period

At the end of the eighteenth century Spanish Hispaniola was a bedraggled backward colony, with nowhere near the wealth, the importance to Spain, nor the institutional base of a Mexico, a Peru, or an Argentina, for example. It had neither the strong church, strong oligarchy, or strong *hacienda* system of a more traditional or conservative society nor the nascent liberal or liberalizing institutions of a more democratic and modernizing one. Indeed it is the absence of any institutions of any sort that would now plague its life as an independent nation.

Dominican independence was set in motion by events occurring outside its borders. In 1795, as a result of the wars in Europe precipitated by the French Revolution, Spanish Hispaniola was ceded to France. Soon, the first of a series of slave revolts broke out in Hayti (as Haiti was spelled before its independence) aimed at overthrowing white, French colonial oppression. The rebellion and upheaval soon spread to the Spanish end of the island. French Hayti achieved its independence, but in 1809 Spanish-speaking Hispaniola was reunited with Spain.[18]

In 1821, the Dominican Republic declared its independence, but before independence could be consolidated, Haitian columns again overran the entire island. Haitian rule, 1822–1844, was cruel and barbarous, and it left an indelible mark on the Dominican Republic. The Haitians freed the slaves but also burned the plantations, slaughtered the cattle, drove out the Hispanic elements, and provoked social and political chaos. Hispaniola had always lacked, since 1550, an organizational infrastructure; now, whatever institutions it did have were largely wiped out. The once-proud colony reverted to a more primitive form of existence.[19]

The twenty-two years of Haitian occupation, and continued Haitian raids and incursions after that, gave rise to a further development important to the main theme of this chapter: a widespread desire for strong authoritative (if not authoritarian) rule as a way—as Dominicans viewed it, the only way—of keeping out the Haitians. Haiti's rule had not only been destructive, but it was also by a black nation that the Dominicans viewed as "African," "uncivilized," and "barbaric." Henceforth, they would make strenuous efforts to expand their military and secure strong, authoritarian rule. Dominicans might admire democracy and representative government in the abstract, but in their own country they felt authoritative rule was necessary to preserve an entire white, Western, Hispanic way of life. In the mid-nineteenth century, when racial theories were still in vogue and long before the Civil War settled the issue in the United States, these were powerful and compelling arguments in Dominican eyes.[20]

As Haitian rule proved increasingly corrupt and inefficient in the early 1840s, sentiment among the Dominicans for independence increased. A group of secret societies was organized that led the independence fight. These societies were infused with the ideals of republicanism and of the French Revolution. Led by the charismatic Juan Pablo Duarte, the Dominicans not only threw off Haitian rule in 1844 but also adopted a liberal and democratic constitution patterned after that of the United States. It provided for separation of powers, civilian control over the military, an independent legislature and court system, regular elections, and a long list of civil and political rights.[21]

From this point on, there would be two political and constitutional traditions in Dominican history. The first, the authoritarian, was older and well-established. It went back to the island's "golden era" in the sixteenth century. It would continue to dominate for at least a century and a quarter of Dominican independent life, strengthened by fears of Haiti and the absence of strong institutions. It was powerful in the army, the church, the rural areas, the traditional landed class, and the rising business and commercial elites. But alongside this tradition, competing with it and even occasionally coming to power for short-lived stretches, was a liberal and democratic tradition. It remained for a long time a minority strain in the Dominican Republic but gradually gained strength, especially in the urban areas, among intellectuals and a part of the middle class, and eventually among students, workers, some businessmen, and some peasants. From then on, Dominican politics would have to be viewed not as a single hierarchical, "Hapsburgian" pyramid, but as two competing paradigms and ways of life, existing side by side, seldom overlapping or intermingling, touching sometimes but usually locked in mortal combat, rivals to control the pinnacles of power and the state system from which money, influence, patronage, public policies, and spoils all flowed.[22]

The first problem with liberal democracy in the Dominican Republic, when independence was achieved in 1844, was that it bore absolutely no relation to underlying Dominican social or political realities. To this point, Dominicans had had no experience whatsoever in democratic self-government. None of the measures contained in the Constitution had any grounding in Dominican experience or realities. The realities that did exist—the church, the landholding system, the class structure—were hardly supportive of democratic governance. On the contrary, a liberal constitutional framework had been superimposed on a social structure that was still cast in authoritarian molds. It could not possibly last or work.[23]

The second problem is that Dominicans did not all or necessarily want democracy, or want it all that much. They admired liberal representative government (what they knew of it) in the abstract and as it worked in the United States. But they were not fully convinced of its efficacy in the Dominican Republic. The Dominican Republic was too unorganized, too chaotic, too "uncivilized" for democracy to work; it had no existing democratic institutions. On top of that, Haiti's assaults continued intermittently all through the later 1840s, 1850s, and 1860s. Only a strong government and a strong military, Dominicans reasoned, could repel the Haitians and provide a degree of domestic order.[24]

The third problem was underdeveloped socioeconomic conditions. In 1844, the Dominican Republic was about 98 percent illiterate and 90 percent rural. There was practically no middle class. The economy was run down and had been devastated further by the Haitian occupation. The social and economic base, to say nothing of the political traditions, on which a viable democracy could be based were simply not present.

Hence a recurring pattern developed in Dominican history. A new liberal-democratic element would rise up every generation (1840s, 1870s, 1900s, 1920s, 1960s, 1980s). With high expectations and with great flurry and romance, they would launch a new democratic opening that ordinarily lasted from a few weeks to a few years. The democratic elements would prove inept or unable to solve the country's immense, underdevelopment-related problems and, hence, in the absence of a strong institutional structure, would quickly be replaced by authoritarian men-on-horseback. The authoritarians would stay in power for extended periods of twenty to thirty years, until the next generation of liberal democrats rose up. The question we face today in the Dominican Republic is whether this cycle has finally been broken, or whether it will repeat itself.

Within months of taking office, Duarte and his fellow democrats were replaced by military authoritarians. Duarte himself was weak and incompetent, he lacked any administrative experience, and the only semi-strong institution in the country was the independence army. For the first thirty years of the Dominican Republic's independent life, in fact, two rival men-on-horseback, Buenaventura Báez and Pedro Santana, alternated in the presidency. Báez served five times as president, and Santana four. Both men were preoccupied with holding the infant and underinstitutionalized country together—as well as with reaping profits out of the public treasury for themselves. Both strove to ward off Haiti's assaults, which meant developing a larger army and searching for an outside "protector." Spain, France, and the United States were all approached with protectorate plans, and from 1861–1865, Spain reoccupied the country. But Spain was also driven out, and the country reverted to its familiar chaos alternating with strong-arm rule. The Haitians were in fact kept at bay during these thirty years, but that success came at some sacrifice of national sovereignty and with the further cost of continuing complete lack of institutionalization of democratic government.[25]

In the 1870s, there was a second brief interregnum of democratic rule under Ulises Espaillat. Espaillat promised to administer the nation's finances honestly and to govern constitutionally. Espaillat was in the tradition of Duarte, long on ideals but weak on practical realities. He proved unable to manage the contentious forces in the nation, especially the regional *caudillos* and their private ragtag armies, and soon fell from power. He was succeeded by another dictator, Ulises Heureaux.

Heureaux governed for seventeen years, from 1882 to 1899. He was a corrupt and brutal tyrant, but he was able to govern. As had the Báez and Santana regimes, his strong-arm rule did manage to keep the Haitians out. But Heureaux was not just a bloody dictator. He was a new breed of authoritarian who provided both stability and development. In this, he was very much like Porfirio Díaz in Mexico and was part of the same Latin American preoccupation, so widespread at that time, with a positivist philosophy of order and progress.[26]

Under Heureaux, the Dominican Republic took off economically for the first time. The developmentalist accomplishments of Heureaux and, later, Trujillo were due as much to international business cycles as to the policies of these authoritarian rulers; but they did provide a climate of stability in which investment increased and the economy could flourish, and they made sure they received the credit for the accomplishments. In the 1880s and 1890s, new roads were built, telephones introduced, dock facilities built. The population increased, foreign capital began to pour in, lands under cultivation increased, the first manufacturing was introduced, exports increased. The tempo of economic life quickened and a new business and middle class began to grow. Prosperity expanded; some real national infrastructural development went forward. But note: All these accomplishments came about under authoritarian auspices, not democratic. Another plus was thus added to the arguments for Dominican authoritarianism: Not only did authoritarianism help preserve peace and keep Haiti away, but it also seemed to be responsible for progress and prosperity.[27] Meanwhile, Heureaux had piled up an immense foreign debt.

Following Heureaux's assassination in 1899, disorder and instability again set in. In 1905, Ramón Cáceres came to power, ushering in another of those brief interregnums of well-meaning democratic rule. The economy was in ruins, and democracy again fell victim to *caudillismo* and the feuds among the rival elites. Cáceres was also assassinated, and the country again fell back into chaos.

Meanwhile, the U.S. presence in the Dominican Republic had been growing incrementally. European creditors had been threatening to use gunboats to collect unpaid debts; hence in 1905, under the Roosevelt corollary to the Monroe Doctrine, U.S. tax officials had been sent in to administer the country's customs receipts and to help pay off its large foreign debts. In 1907, U.S. Marines were sent in to protect the customs agents. In 1909 and again in 1912, the Marine contingent was increased. In 1916, faced with continued instability and also the outbreak of World War I, President Woodrow Wilson authorized the Marines already on the island to assume control. The full-scale occupation lasted from 1916 to 1924, though the Marines' presence was actually a full decade longer.

Although this interpretation will doubtless be controversial, the U.S. Marines' occupation may be looked at in terms comparable to the rule of the "order-and-progress" dictators that came before and would come after. Albeit at first, the occupation forces tried to work through the local political institutions, eventually they tired of the effort, suspended the Constitution, and ruled by decree—as a long line of Dominican dictators had done. The Marines disarmed the population, stripped the regional *caudillos* of both their irregular private armies and their source of funds (the local customs house), and created a centralized constabulary to maintain order. Moreover, the progress brought by the Marines was considerable. Not only did they introduce baseball and chewing gum, they also built highways, water systems, docks, telephone lines, sewerage systems, bridges, and other infrastructural projects. In all these ways, the Marines' rule was remarkably similar to that of Heureaux. It could be added that neither Heureaux nor the Marines were hesitant to use force and repression against those who opposed them.[28]

Following the Marines' withdrawal the pendulum again swung briefly to the democratic side. A new constitution was drawn up, largely drafted in the U.S. Embassy and following closely the U.S. model. In the elections of 1924, supervised by the Marines, Horacio Vásquez was elected president.[29] Vásquez presided over another of those brief democratic interruptions in what otherwise has been a long authoritarian tradition. But Vásquez, in 1928, illegally extended his term of office, thereby undermining his government's legitimacy, which, since it had been established by the U.S. occupation forces, was shaky to begin with. Vásquez became sick, further weakening his hold. He neglected to create a political party, and the nation's institutional infrastructure, after the Marine occupation, was almost nonexistent. In 1929, the world market crash occurred, and in 1930, the bottom dropped out of the Dominican economy. Plotting by the elites and *caudillos* was renewed. That same year, General Rafael Trujillo, head of the Marine-created National Guard, seized power; he would rule for the next thirty-one years and add some further ingredients to the long tradition of Dominican authoritarianism.

The Trujillo Era

The dictatorship of Generalissimo Rafael Trujillo, 1930–1961, was a far more complete or "total" dictatorship than anything the Dominican Republic had seen up to this point. Trujillo began his rule as a rather typical man-on-horseback, but, using modern organizational, technological, and informational techniques, his dictatorship eventually came to resemble the totalitarian regimes of Europe in its repressiveness and extent of centralized control.[30]

Trujillo dominated all areas of Dominican national life. He controlled the armed forces and turned them into an instrument of internal occupation and repression. He created a single party to serve as the political machinery of his dictatorship. He dominated and controlled, privately or through the state, about 50 percent of GNP. He stamped strict controls on all group and associational life: trade unions, businessmen, professional associations, etc. He created a vast national spy network and introduced, after World War II, technologically proficient terror, torture, and surveillance techniques. He controlled education and the media. With those forces he could not absolutely control, such as the church or the U.S. Embassy, he worked out mutually supporting arrangements. No group or institution could remain independent of Trujillo's control.[31]

Several aspects of Trujillo's dictatorship merit particular attention in this context: First, he absolutely eliminated whatever early stirrings of democratic rule—nascent political parties, interest groups, and the like—had begun to emerge in the early part of the century and in the 1920s. By the end of the long Trujillo era, there was no foundation—no leaders, no institutions—on which a new democratic order could be based.

Second, Trujillo was, like Heureaux, an order-and-progress dictator. He presided over a period of unprecedented economic growth. Although enriching himself in the process, he built roads, bridges, public buildings, curbs, docks, highways, and more. He greatly expanded agricultural production and exports. Manufacturing, commerce, and industry also expanded several times over. Per-capita income more than doubled, though it remained terribly unevenly distributed. The stability and discipline of his regime attracted foreign investment. Trujillo did not stay in power for thirty-one years by blood and terror alone; rather, there were real economic accomplishments of the regime, and not all the profits ended up in the dictator's foreign bank accounts.[32]

Third, the development and modernization that occurred were closely related to the kind of regime Trujillo's was. Beginning in the 1930s in the underdeveloped society of that time, the Trujillo dictatorship was also rather primitive, limited largely to political and military controls. But in the more developed nation of the 1950s, Trujillo's controls could also become more complete and pervasive in dominating civil society. As the regime took on more and more "totalitarian" characteristics (thought control, mass indoctrination, technologically efficient terror), it also became more and more problematic that democracy could be built in its aftermath.

Fourth (and related), the regime became more explicitly corporatist and bureaucratic-authoritarian. Trujillo was a man of action and certainly not an intellectual or institutional innovator; but his advisers were caught up in the wave of corporatist sentiment that swept Europe in the interwar period, and they gradually introduced more and more modern corporatist features into the regime. These included organic-integralist ideas and the sectoral organization of society and representation. Similarly, by the 1950s, the regime was no longer just a personalist dictatorship but had become more and more bureaucratic-authoritarian. In this regard (though not in others), the Trujillo regime was like the regime of Generalissimo Francisco Franco in Spain. That is, it always remained a personal dictatorship, and no one ever had any doubt where ultimate decisionmaking authority resided. But under the impact of societal and economic modernization, both these regimes also became more complex and sophisticated over the years, necessitating modern bureaucratic structures to go along with the personalist dictatorship. A bureaucratic-authoritarian model thus grew up along side of but did not supplant the older system of one-man rule.[33]

Finally, because Trujillo's rule was so total, its collapse provoked a near-total vacuum. In terms of democratic institutions, the Dominican Republic was only slightly more advanced in 1961, when Trujillo was assassinated, than it was in 1844, when independent life began. It had developed some institutions in the interim, but very few were democratic. There were no democratic political parties operating in the country (though there were numerous exile groups), no autonomous associations or economic interest groups, no independent press or judiciary, no experienced democratic leaders, no practice in democratic ways. After 127 years of independence, the authoritarian tradition remained dominant, and the democratic one was pitifully weak. That would change dramatically, however, in the period after 1961.

Democratizing the System

Following Trujillo's assassination, the Dominican Republic went through another of those brief democratic interims that has traditionally followed the collapse of dictatorship. But conditions had changed: The country was more affluent, more socially differentiated; the United States (fearing another Cuba) poured in economic aid. Democratic forces were far stronger than ever before, in part because the blood and excesses of the Trujillo regime had thoroughly discredited the historic authoritarian model. Had Trujillo ruled more moderately and not been so greedy or cruel, the historic authoritarian model, tempered by paternalism, might have been able to hang on. Instead, Trujillo had ruled as a tyrant, had overstepped the bounds of permissible behavior that a long tradition of Iberian and Latin American political theory had established for "just princes," and therefore by his own doing had helped justify his people's "right to rebellion."[34]

The rebellion that came, however, was not limited to a circle of elites at the top. The original assassination plot was limited to elite elements, but almost immediately it spilled over into popular demonstrations.[35] This change was related to other, vaster changes that had occurred in Dominican society during the long Trujillo era. A sizable middle class (perhaps 20 percent of the population) had emerged, there was a large working class in the capital city, students and others had been mobilized, and rapid urbanization had resulted in a large unemployed *lumpenproletariat* in the capital's downtown streets, who could be recruited for political demonstrations. In the years 1961–1965, a veritable "explosion" of political participation occurred, which meant in long-range terms that the country could never go back to its earlier, "sleepier," semifeudal past.[36]

Initially, Trujillo's son and heir, Rafael, Jr., or "Ramfis," tried to continue his father's regime. But societal pressures built up, and in November 1961, he resigned the military position he had held and fled the country—along with virtually the entire Trujillo family. For the next two months, a former Trujillo puppet, Joaquín Balaguer, tried to preserve continuity by agreeing to share power with a Council of State, but in January 1962, he too was forced into exile. The Council of State, without Balaguer, continued in power.[37]

In the meantime, the United States had become heavily involved in internal Dominican affairs. The United States was interested in a democratic outcome in the Dominican Republic, but its main concern, in the immediate aftermath of the Cuban Revolution, was to prevent a "second Cuba" in the Caribbean. To this end, the United States had pressed the Trujillos to liberalize and even attempted to push them out of power, but not precipitously or in a way that would upset stability or lead to a Castroite takeover. Strenuous efforts were made to control the post-Trujillo transition, in contrast to the post-Batista transition, which the United States had not controlled. The dilemma for U.S. policy was captured by President John F. Kennedy: "There are three possibilities in descending order of precedence: a decent democratic regime, a continuation of the Trujillo regime, or a Castro regime. We ought to aim at the first, but we really cannot renounce the second until we are sure that we can avoid the third."[38]

The Council of State ruled during 1962. It carried out some modest reforms and prepared the way for elections in December. The elections were won by a two-to-one margin by Juan Bosch and his populist Dominican Revolutionary Party (PRD). Bosch was a socialist, a democratic, and a charismatic but mercurial leader who had lived in exile for over twenty years. His base of support was workers, peasants, and young people. He sought to bring a democratic revolution to the Dominican Republic and to carry through much needed social reforms. But Bosch ran into the implacable hostility of the Dominican military, the church, and the economic elites. The country became polarized. The U.S. Embassy also became suspicious of his socialist orientation. Bosch's personal idiosyncrasies and his and his party's inexperience of governing also weakened his position. After only seven months in office, Bosch's government was overthrown by a military coup.[39]

Power then returned to the conservative elite and upper-middle-class elements who had governed under the Council of State. But the new regime proved to be corrupt, inefficient, and repressive. It could no longer, after the explosion of participation of the previous two years, return to the more traditional and "sleepier" politics of the past. Resentments began to build up among the trade unions, the middle class, and intellectuals. Even the business community became disillusioned with the existing government. Meanwhile, the PRD plotted to stage a constitutionalist and democratic comeback.[40]

The explosion came in April 1965. A PRD–led popular and middle-class–based revolution resulted in toppling the government. It was on the verge of defeating also the regular armed forces. At that moment, fearing the revolution would be taken over by Castro-Communists, the United States intervened. In the next few weeks, the United States sent in 22,000 troops, occupied the country, quashed the revolution, and installed an interim government. The democratic revolution in the Dominican Republic, which had as its goal the restoration of Bosch to the presidency and the government that had been ousted in 1963, was thus snuffed out by the greatest democracy on earth. The irony was not lost on the embittered Dominican people; anti-Americanism increased.[41]

By 1966, the contending forces in the Dominican civil war had been pacified, new elections were scheduled, and the bulk of the U.S. forces had been withdrawn. The winner of the 1966 presidential election was Joaquín Balaguer, the shrewd political leader who had once been a puppet president under Trujillo. He presented himself as an efficient administrator (in contrast to Bosch), as a populist, and as a peacemaker to a population now fed up with upheaval. Balaguer ruled for the next twelve years. Although it may be characterized as semidemocratic or pseudodemocratic, his regime was in the tradition of Santana, Báez, Heureaux, and Trujillo; it merits close scrutiny.[42]

Balaguer was, to begin, a deft politician. He cleverly played off contending political forces, meanwhile enhancing his own power. This was no mean feat in the more complex and pluralistic society that the Dominican Republic had become.[43]

Second, he presided over a period of unprecedented economic growth. Largely fueled initially by money from the United States, the Dominican economy achieved such increases as to be dubbed the "Dominican miracle." The economic and social development of the Balaguer era gave rise to a general economic quickening that affected all areas of the national life, and it helped swell further the size of the middle class.

Third, Balaguer used repression, albeit selectively. His was not a bloody regime as Trujillo's had been. Rather, he was careful to stay within constitutional bounds. He was not averse to having the police and armed forces use repressive tactics, including "disappearances," especially against PRD labor leaders and political organizers; but he managed to avoid the violence being associated with him personally. Instead, Balaguer quietly went about depoliticizing the population, lowering the decibel rate, avoiding confrontations, and calming down the country from the frenetic politics of the early 1960s.[44]

Fourth, Balaguer's regime was, therefore, more in the long traditions of Dominican *dictablandas* (soft dictatorships) as opposed to *dictaduras* (hard dictatorships). His was a regime that blended constitutional precepts and considerable freedom with tempered authoritarianism, as contrasted with Trujillo's bloody excesses. Balaguer provided order, stability, and discipline but without going beyond the generally acceptable standards of Dominican society. He was also a builder and developer of his nation. For these reasons, his regime remained popular; Balaguer still has widespread popularity today, as witness his return to power in 1986, after an 8-year absence, in a genuinely fair and competitive election. He represented one of the two main streams in the Dominican political tradition—the authoritarian one, now blended with various democratic overlays—and was careful not to overstep the boundaries of permissible behavior. He did not become a tyrant; he was not discredited as a leader. A Balaguer or Balaguer-like option, therefore, was a possibility for the Dominican Republic, however undemocratic or pseudodemocratic it might be. That occurred in 1986, and, given the country's opposing democratic and authoritarian traditions (which Balaguer deftly and sometimes incongruously reconciles), it could well be a possibility for the future.

Nonetheless, by 1978 Balaguer's earlier regime had run its course. Balaguer himself was older and feebler. He had a less-firm control on the levers of power. The bloom was off the economic "miracle." Democratic pressures were again rising, as they have periodically in Dominican history, but this time they were stronger and were coming at shorter intervals.

In the 1978 election, Balaguer faced a formidable foe in the person of Antonio Guzmán of the PRD. The PRD was both populist and the best-organized political party in the country. Guzmán was clearly ahead in the balloting when the armed forces, still fearful of Bosch's party from past experiences, stepped in to try to secure a Balaguer victory. This time, the United States intervened on the part of the democratic forces, putting immense pressure on the regime and threatening to cut off all aid. The ballot count resumed, and Guzmán and the PRD emerged victorious. Since 1978, the Dominican Republic has been governed democratically.[45]

Guzmán represented the right wing of the PRD, and he served until 1982. Even with Guzmán's suicide (widely attributed to the uncovering of corruption in the regime and perhaps even in his family) in the closing weeks of his administration, constitutional procedures were followed. His successor, Salvador Jorge Blanco, also of the PRD, was inaugurated. Both Guzmán and Jorge carried out significant social reforms, though within a context of increased economic difficulties and austerity. Both respected freedom and civil liberties, both ruled democratically. This was, in short, a reassertion, once more, of the country's alternative and democratic tradition, long submerged or popping out only temporarily, but now in full blossom.[46]

Guzmán and Jorge provided eight years of uninterrupted, PRD–led, democratic rule. It was the longest continuous period of democracy in Dominican history. Both presidents took steps to curb the military, to respect human rights, to rule constitutionally, and to provide for social and economic reform. Democracy appeared more strongly consolidated than ever before. But both these presidents were hamstrung by deteriorating economic conditions in the late 1970s and early 1980s that forced unpopular austerity measures, by rising corruption within the large state bureaucracy, and by patronage demands pushed by the PRD's own stalwarts.

In 1986, the PRD put up an unpopular candidate, Jacobo Majluta, who was tainted with the earlier corruption, while an opposition coalition nominated the venerable Balaguer. Balaguer was legally blind and quite infirm, but again his appeal—based on populism, efficiency, prosperity, and a blending of the traditions of democratic and strong rule—proved attractive. Juan Bosch was also a candidate and, though finishing a distant third, drew votes from the PRD. Balaguer won the election by a narrow margin; indeed, the margin was so narrow and sufficiently questionable that the vote count was temporarily halted, and the military threatened to annul the results. Eventually, after considerable machinations involving the armed forces, the U.S. Embassy, and the outgoing PRD government, Balaguer was declared the victor.

Currently, the Dominican Republic has a democratic system that could be called "emergent" and only partially stable. But it also shows tendencies toward being only semidemocratic and perhaps even, depending on the definitions and criteria used, partially authoritarian.

Hence, the questions we must ask ourselves are whether the present democratic system will be permanent, or if it too will prove but temporary. Has authoritarianism been eliminated or superseded; has democracy now finally achieved majoritarian support; or will we continue to see an alternation between the two? Alternatively, have the Dominicans now achieved, in the system of Balaguer, something of a fusion between the two, a formula for blending and reconciling these two powerful, alternative forces in their long political history? If so, they will have hit on a formula that the country has long sought, and which other Latin American countries have also long tried to achieve. Should that formula work, the Dominicans will have developed a genuinely indigenous, developmentalist framework—an achievement whose significance would reach far beyond the small island of Hispaniola and that would be of interest to many other Latin American and Third World nations.[47] Unfortunately, because of Balaguer's infirmity and the country's continued severe economic problems, it seems unlikely that in the Dominican Republic this formula will achieve any greater success than have others in the past.

• THEORETICAL ANALYSIS OF THE HISTORICAL PATTERN •

Having traced the historical evolution of the Dominican polity, we now turn to a dissection of it. That is: What are the major social, economic, cultural, historical, political, and external factors that account for the major historical developments reviewed above? Our purpose is to explain the transitions to and from democratic rule, to and from authoritarian regimes, as well as the periods of persistence of democratic and/or authoritarian rule. So as to facilitate comparative analysis as well as to determine which of the general theoretical variables concerning democratic development are especially salient, we focus here on the following nine variables: political culture; historical evolution; class structure; ethnic and religious cleavages; state structure and strength; political institutions; political leadership; development performance; and international factors.

Political Culture

Most Dominicans believe in democracy—at least in the abstract. That is, they are supportive of representative government, constitutionalism, regular elections, and basic human and civil rights. Moreover, such democratic sentiment has been growing in the Dominican Republic and, by this time, may even represent majoritarian opinion. The problem is not that Dominicans are natural "Fascists" or that they love authoritarianism. The problem is simply that they are not convinced, given their chaotic history and absence of institutions, that democracy works well or as intended in the Dominican context.[48]

The Dominicans have had considerable experience with democracy, and most of it has not been good. Duarte was a romantic idealist who was quickly overthrown; the same is true of Espaillat in the 1870s. Cáceres was a good president, but under his rule U.S. customs agents and Marines came in, and the Dominicans lost their sovereignty. Vásquez ruled ineffectively in the 1920s and paved the way for Trujillo. Bosch was similarly ineffective as a political leader and later launched a revolution that produced chaos, bloodshed, and U.S. intervention. Guzmán killed himself, and Jorge's regime was plagued by corruption and economic contraction. Democracy does not, in the Dominican Republic, have a great and glorious history.

The Dominicans are suspicious of democracy for some other, quite sound reasons. The history of repeated Haitian invasions in the nineteenth century, and the continuing fear of Haitianization of Dominican culture and society even today, has led them to think that only strong, authoritarian regimes can withstand Haitian pressures. Second, the Dominicans know their own sad history well, especially the historic absence of institutions, the chaos, the disorder. From their point of view, only a strong government can keep this underinstitutionalized country from fragmenting and falling apart. Third, Dominicans look at the success stories in their history and ask who provided the most progress, the most development. The answer is, again, not the democrats but authoritarian or authoritarian/paternalist rulers like Heureaux, Trujillo, and Balaguer. These men all were, quite literally, builders of their country. In Dominican eyes, it is not the democratic but the authoritarian regimes that are associated with success. Democratic legitimacy has been difficult to build and sustain because the performance of the democratic governments has been weak, while that of the authoritarians has been strong, and also because of the lingering suspicions of the inadequacies of democratic rule.

These sentiments have been present even more broadly within the political elite, historically, than among the mass of the population.[49] It is the elites that most fear Haitianization—by which they no longer mean invasion from Haiti but rather the rising up of their own lower (and darker) classes. It is the elite that requires order, stability, and discipline for its economic profit-making. And it is the elite, especially its *nouveaux riches* elements, who have been most strongly supportive of Trujillo and Balaguer. In this sense, support for authoritarianism has a class base—though it should also be emphasized that *all* within the elite, those on the Left as well as on the Right, tend to prefer top-down rule. The question we must wrestle with now is whether in the present circumstances elite interest in order and stability is best served by supporting authoritarianism or democracy. Increasingly—and it is a very significant departure—elite sentiment has swung around to support moderate democratic regimes.[50]

The other complicating factor is the politicization of social and economic life. In the Dominican Republic, this has not reached an acute stage as yet, but it is increasing. Under the impact of the "revolution of rising expectations," social and economic relationships are increasingly being related to political issues and posed in political terms. Questions of employer-employee relations, state-owned enterprises, class relations, etc., are being increasingly politicized. To the degree this trend is emerging, it does not augur well for stable, moderate democracy.

A more democratic political culture has thus emerged in recent years in the Dominican Republic, but it is still tenuous. Democratic beliefs and values—in particular the legitimacy of democratic institutions and practices—are stronger than before, but they are still unevenly held and not held all that strongly even by those who profess them. In past times of crisis, Dominicans have abandoned democracy and opted for an authoritarian solution, or for some blend of strong central control coupled with considerable individual freedom. This is particularly true among the political elites, whose commitment to democracy may be quite fickle. nor is it clear at this stage how strongly Dominican social institutions—the church, the armed forces, religion, family, clan, community, work life—are conducive to or supportive of democratic values. The alternative authoritarian tradition is still strong, and it could at some point make a comeback.

Historical Evolution

The Dominican Republic felt the full force of Spanish colonial administration, strongly authoritarian in all its aspects, during its first fifty years (1492–1550); but after that the colony was largely ignored by Spain. Colonial neglect did not assist the Dominican Republic to develop nascent democratic institutions, however; instead, it resulted in the absence of institutions of any sort. Hence, at the time of independence, the Dominican Republic had neither the liberal institutions of a democratic polity nor strong traditional institutions derived from the colonial era, which might have provided stability during the transition to independent nationhood. This institutional vacuum accounts in large measure for the country's alternation after independence between chaos and authoritarianism.

Although independence from Spain came relatively peacefully, the subsequent twenty-two–year Haitian occupation was not only oppressive but also destructive of those few institutions the country had left: the church, the *hacienda*; the landed oligarchy; the university. The conditions under which the Dominican Republic ultimately achieved independence were bloody and destructive, not peaceful and gradual. Moreover, the country had had no opportunity or training in democratic self-government, and there had been no opportunity for a system of more competitive politics to develop prior to independence.

Furthermore, when independence finally was achieved, the Dominicans adopted an inappropriate constitutional framework. In essence, they took the U.S. constitution, translated it into Spanish, tacked on the French Bill of Rights, and made no effort to develop a constitution reflective of indigenous traditions. Shortly thereafter, when democratic government was overthrown, a constitution was adopted that provided a more authoritarian form: powerful executive; weak Congress and courts; special position for the armed forces, and so on. Although the Dominican Republic has had by this time nearly thirty constitutions in its life as an independent nation, in fact there has been an alternation between two main forms: one liberal and democratic; and the other Caesarist or Bonapartist. Never has the country developed a constitution that reflected an indigenous design or tradition, and never has it fashioned a stable and lasting formula for governance that effectively reconciles its democratic and its authoritarian currents.[51]

In sum, the nation never had the opportunity to acquire experience with democratic institutions prior to independence. Political competition began before there were any well-grounded institutions to handle such competition. Nor were democratic institutions adapted to the country's unique conditions, built upon, or integrated with its cultural and historical traditions.

Class Structure

The Dominican Republic has a rigid class structure, reinforced by racial criteria. Racially, the country is about 5 percent white, about 60 percent mulatto, and about 35 percent black. Those at the top of the pyramid are both wealthy and white, or light mulatto. The middle class is chiefly mulatto. The lower classes tend to be black and darker mulatto. Race and class are thus closely intertwined. The divisions between the classes are both clear and deep; in addition, Dominicans are very conscious of racial background and class ground and class positions.[52]

Historically, the white ruling class has dominated the presidency, the cabinet, and the highest positions of governmental authority. Land, commerce, industry, banking, and the learned professions have similarly been dominated by this same element.

In the last fifty years, the mulatto middle class has emerged as a major and new force. The middle class now numbers about 20 to 30 percent of the population. Its avenues of social mobility have included the armed forces, the university, smaller-scale business, and the bureaucracy. Trujillo emerged out of this mulatto middle class and brought along with him into power fellow mulatto middle-class officers, as well as civilian sycophants. Because of this, some authors see the long Trujillo era (1930–1961) as effecting a class and racial change in the Dominican power structure: from white elitist rule to increasingly mulatto middle-class rule.[53]

The middle class has emerged as a dominant force in Dominican national affairs—some would say *the* dominant force. The middle class is now preeminent in many of the country's leading institutions: the bureaucracy; the church; the university; the military officer corps; political-party executive committees; the trade-union leadership. While this class has become numerically far larger and influential in all these institutions, it also remains deeply divided on social and political issues. It is dependent on the state for jobs, favors, and contracts; it is also dependent on foreign capital and therefore cannot be considered a strong, autonomous, or indigenous bourgeoisie. It is likely that this element will emerge (and perhaps it already has) as a force for moderation and stability, but so far there are few signs of a happy, liberal, stable, middle-class society emerging in the Dominican Republic.[54]

The working class has similarly grown in size in the last half-century, but it is weakly organized and dependent on the state. Only about 8 to 9 percent of Dominican workers are unionized, and there is an immense pool of unemployed laborers, whom employers can hire if workers become too demanding. Moreover, the unions are deeply divided between Communist, Socialist, Christian Democratic, and U.S. Embassy–sponsored movements. Organized labor is by now a force to be reckoned with in Dominican society, but by itself it cannot—unlike some other groups—determine political outcomes.[55]

The peasant element is numerically the largest but politically the weakest of all Dominican groups. There are now peasant cooperatives and peasant political organizations, but these tend to be small and not very effective as interest groups. Neither they nor the trade unions are entirely free to organize independently of the state or employers. The distribution of land is very unequal, with most of it concentrated in the hands of civilian or military elites, but there is a large class of peasant smallholders and subsistence farmers. The Dominican countryside thus remains backward and semifeudal, dominated by patron-client relationships, though it is also increasingly socially differentiated.

On balance, the social and class structure of the Dominican Republic does not augur well for democracy. However, the growth and affluence of the middle class—and therefore the possibilities for stable democracy—are far greater now than they were a generation ago.

Ethnic and Religious Cleavages

For the Dominican Republic, ethnic and religious cleavages are not a major problem. In fact, in these areas the country is quite homogeneous. Catholicism is the religion of over 90 percent of Dominicans. While many do not actively practice their religion, and while Protestant sects have grown significantly in recent years, religion has not been a major source of societal cleavage. Indeed, one can say, given the divisiveness of Dominican history and its class structure, that religion and a Catholic political culture help provide the cement that holds the country together and gives it national identity.[56]

Nor is ethnicity a major divisive issue. Although the Dominican Republic has a social system in which race and class are mutually reinforcing, the country has remained remarkably free of racial hatred or racially inspired violence. Prejudice does exist with regard to darker-skinned persons, and Dominicans are very conscious of racial backgrounds and features. But there has never been a race war nor is there intense racial bitterness. There are no black-power movements in the Dominican Republic, nor anything resembling apartheid or "Jim Crow" laws. Rather, the Dominican system has been one of gradual assimilation: of blacks into the mulatto category and of mulattos into the "white" or upper classes. In this sense, prejudice is as much cultural as racial, and therefore it is possible to move up in the social-racial scale. Money, education, clothes, and position are all "whiteners" in the Dominican Republic.

The country's other ethnic groups are small and numerically insignificant. There are small communities of Chinese, Lebanese, Japanese, North Americans, Jews, and Western Europeans. To varying degrees, these elements have been integrated into Dominican society and into the political class. Most of the foreign communities, however, maintain a considerable degree of separate existence. They are not generally bothered by the Dominicans (though there have been instances of occasional friction), and they themselves have not pushed for separate power. The numbers involved in these foreign communities are simply insufficient for serious ethnic cleavage or conflict to develop.

The Dominican Republic is, therefore, more or less homogeneous religiously, culturally, and ethnically. Whatever subcultural cleavage exists is not centralized around two or three but dispersed among numerous small groups. Nor has subcultural cleavage resulted in separatist terrorism or civil strife.

State Structure and Strength

The Dominican state system has historically been weak. It performed few functions; it was not always able to preserve stability or maintain public order. The biggest change came with the Trujillo era. Trujillo built up enormously both his own power and that of the central state. He divested the country's regions of their residual power; he built immense new ministries that reached into more and more areas of national life. He greatly increased the size and strength of the armed forces, using them as an instrument of his dictatorship. The economic-control mechanisms of the central state were also greatly strengthened during the Trujillo era, both to increase the power of the dictatorship and to enrich the ruling family. By the end of the Trujillo era, the Dominican Republic was a far more centralized system—militarily, politically, and economically—than it had been before.[57]

The extensive role of the state in the economy, and of state ownership, has roots in and derives from the Trujillo era. Not only did Trujillo centralize economic decisionmaking, he also used his dictatorial control to amass immense personal wealth. When he was killed, the vast Trujillo holdings were taken over by the government. These included factories, airlines, steamship companies, sugar mills, and land holdings—the total amounting to about 50 percent of Dominican GNP. At the time (1961), the Dominican Republic had the second-largest state sector in all of Latin America, behind only Marxist-Leninist Cuba. This was achieved through inheritance, not expropriation.[58]

The large Dominican state sector has major social and political consequences. The state corporations have become, over the last quarter-century, gigantic patronage and employment agencies: corrupt, bloated, and inefficient. Another consequence is that the private accumulation of wealth has come to depend in large part on having a position in or access to the state. The immense size of the state sector has also meant it is virtually impossible for private entrepreneurs to compete in the same economic areas. Finally, because of the sheer size and numbers of persons employed by the state, social and cultural groups and voluntary associations have little check on state power, nor can they retain much of an autonomous existence. The sinecures, jobs, and opportunities for enrichment through the state sector help explain why the electoral and, sometimes, extra-electoral struggle to control it has been often heavily suffused with violence and fraud.

Turning from the state's economic functions to its more manifestly political ones, we find a mixed record in maintaining public order. The Dominican state has not only been authoritarian historically, but it has also—particularly its military and security forces—often been arbitrary. Opposition politicians and groups have frequently been intimidated, beaten, repressed, and even killed. At times, the security forces have operated outside governmental control, engaging in terrorist activities and settling political and other scores with or without the supervision or even knowledge of the political authorities. In most circumstances, the state has been able to control protest movements and riots, often using violent methods to do so, but there is that unforgotten instance in the 1965 revolution, when a ragtag people's army defeated the regular military apparatus and caused its disintegration. Overall, the assessment is that military repression has frequently had a negative effect on democratic institutions; further, that it has sometimes tipped the balance between civil and military authority away from the former.

The armed forces as an institution deserve special mention in this context.[59] The military has long been extremely suspicious of democratic movements and of civilian control. Civilian "meddling" in the affairs of the armed forces has often been answered by military involvement in politics. The military tends to think of itself as a special institution with special obligations, above the Constitution. It is also a major avenue of social mobility for ambitious middle class Mestizo youths, and it is frequently a means to achieve wealth and power, often illegally, on a grand scale. The armed forces therefore occupy a special place: They think of themselves as a proud and professional institution, but their performance has often left a great deal to be desired, and they are often resented and hated by the civilian population. Hence, the potential for conflict between military and civilian authorities or amongst rival factions within the military remains great. The efforts of recent civilian democratic governments to change these corrupt and repressive practices remain of uncertain effect.

Summing up, we can say that the authority of the national state has been effectively established in the Dominican Republic. Indeed, the power of the state has gone beyond an effective minimum: State power is heavily concentrated and centralized; the state has immense power over the economy; and the state is not always effectively limited by autonomous intermediate groups. Nor has the state always been able to maintain order and national security by democratic means. The armed forces frequently operate above "mere" civilian control and are not fully committed to democratic principles.

Political Institutions

Despite the large number of constitutions promulgated in Dominican history, in fact the constitutional tradition has been quite continuous. The large number of constitutions relates to the Dominican practice of promulgating a new basic law every time there is an amendment or even a modest change in constitutional wording or procedures. But actually, all the constitutions have duly provided for separation of powers, a presidential system, basic human rights, and so on. The difference has been in the different emphases given these provisions. Recall that the Dominican Republic has two major political and constitutional traditions: one more authoritarian and the other more democratic. But the differences even between these two traditions have not been all that great. The more authoritarian constitutional tradition provides for a stronger executive, a significant role for the armed forces, wide emergency powers, and, at least historically, a special position for the Catholic church. But even in the Dominican Republic's authoritarian tradition, provision is made for a congress and a judiciary, though not usually on a coequal and independent basis. The country's democratic constitutional tradition, by contrast, provides for a somewhat weaker executive, a stronger congress and court system, subordination of the armed forces to civilian control, separation of church and state, fewer emergency powers, and a more extended list of human, political, social, and economic rights.

The problem in Dominican constitutional history, as we have seen, has been to reconcile these conflicting traditions, both of which have considerable resonance in Dominican national history. And it is interesting that, in their provisions for a strong executive, for example, these two traditions are not all that far apart. Both the supporters of the one point of view and the supporters of the other have come to recognize a certain validity in the other group's position. It is therefore especially significant that in the most recent Dominican constitution, that of 1966, a major effort was undertaken to blend the authoritarian and the liberal traditions. The executive remains powerful, but Congress and the judiciary are elevated in importance and have achieved some greater degree of independence. Human rights are emphasized, but there is also provision for the exercise of broad emergency powers. The position of the armed forces remains ambiguous. Importantly, both the authoritarian government of Balaguer, which promulgated this constitution, and the democratic regimes that succeeded him after 1978 have been able to live with and function within—not always happily or comfortably but so far without repudiating the basic law—this constitutional framework.[60]

The Dominican political-party system has historically served to perpetuate and reinforce the country's deep divisions. The parties in the past tended to be the personal followings and/or machines of one or another family, clique, and clan. To an extent, many of them have these same characteristics today. But since the Trujillo period, more broad-based and ideological movements have emerged, and there is some evidence now of greater continuity and permanence to the parties. The Center-Left is dominated by the PRD, the country's best-organized political party. There is a small Communist Party and several other small groups on the far Left.[61] Bosch's Party of National Liberation (PLN) has been gaining in strength.

The Center-Right was long dominated by the Reformist Party, the personal machine of President Balaguer. It was caudillistic, devoid of ideology, and poorly organized. The weakness of the party system on the Center-Right is due in large part to the fact that this social element, led by wealthier and middle-class Dominicans, has historically had other routes to power open to it besides popular appeals and elections: family and interpersonal connections or even a military coup, for example. The Christian Democratic Party had also long tried to lay claim to the center of the political spectrum. In addition, there are a number of farther-Right and other personalistic parties, who may present candidates form time to time. For the 1986 election Balaguer managed a merger of the Reformist and Christian Democratic parties into the Partido Reformista Social Cristiano (PRSC) which represented a wedding of his machine with the ideology and organization of the Christian Democrats. Hence overall, the trend has been away from temporary and personalistic factions and toward a more broad-based and lasting party system centered around two relatively moderate parties: the PRD, somewhat to the left of Center, and PRSC to the right of Center.

Since Trujillo's demise in 1961, the Dominican press has been remarkably free. It consists of four vigorous dailies in the capital city, over 100 radio stations (a large number for a country so small), and seven commercial television stations. Freedom of the press has been generally respected; the press has taken on an active political role in presenting alternative viewpoints and, overall, has been one of the great bulwarks of Dominican democracy in recent years.[62]

Political Leadership

At the end of the Trujillo era, the Dominican Republic faced an almost complete vacuum of political leadership. Trujillo had concentrated all power in his own hands and had taken pains to ensure that other leaders would not come to power. Many potential leaders were killed or jailed; others were forced into exile where they lost contact with the realities of their own country. By the end of Trujillo's 31-year rule, the Dominican Republic had practically no leaders with domestic political experience, and none with experience, so important in the modern world, in international agencies, banks, and lending institutions. This lack of leadership showed up immediately in a succession of short-lived post-Trujillo governments.[63] To a considerable extent, the Dominican Republic's repeated failures of democracy may be attributed to the lack of vision, ingenuity, and political skills on the part of its democratic leaders.

It takes a long time to build up cadres of political leaders, and in the last twenty-five years the Dominican Republic has come a long way. Within the parties, the private sector, the state-owned enterprises, and the professions there is now a corps of trained and experienced leaders who can run the government. That marks a major change from the Dominican Republic's earlier experiment with democratic government in 1963, when Juan Bosch could not find enough trained persons to man the cabinet, let alone all the other agencies that needed to be staffed.[64]

The general assessment is that the quality, skill, effectiveness, and innovativeness of leadership, and of democratic leaders in particular, has improved greatly in the last quarter-century. More and more, leaders have become committed to democratic processes, not always or necessarily because they are committed to democracy *per se,* but because they see now democracy as providing coherence, order, stability, and continuity to the polity. However, since the Dominican Republic's political system is based strongly on patronage and has a patronage-intensive style of politics, U.S. standards of honesty and probity in managing public accounts cannot always be taken for granted.

Development Performance

Unfortunately for the proponents of Dominican democracy, it has been the country's authoritarian leaders who have been the most successful in providing for national economic growth. Heureaux, Trujillo, and Balaguer: these are the presidents credited with being the Dominican Republic's great builders. It is they who built the roads and highways, the port facilities, the transportation systems, the curbs and sewerage systems, the bridges and public buildings, the water supplies and electrical grids. It is these authoritarian presidents who are given credit for the great spurts of national economic growth. Under Balaguer, for example, the Dominican Republic's growth rates averaged 6 to 7 percent per year and in some years were in double digits—right up there with the miraculous growth rates of Japan, West Germany, and Brazil. Many Dominicans still consider the Balaguer regime as the best government they ever had. (This is less true for Trujillo; his regime is now too far back for most Dominicans to remember, and he was too brutal). These accomplishments help explain Balaguer's continuing popularity today.

By contrast, the country's democratic leaders have not been very successful developers. Juan Bosch's regime, in 1963, was so chaotic and disruptive that little in the way of economic development could or did take place. Guzmán was inaugurated in 1978, when the Balaguer "miracle" was already in decline, and when the second oil shock (1979) devastated the Dominican economy. Jorge Blanco was forced to preside over such a severe austerity program that it cost the PRD significant political support and undermined the possibilities for social reform. Jorge Blanco had campaigned on the promise that he would bring economic as well as political democracy to the Dominican Republic, but the world economic downturn, which began in 1979 and continued—and worsened—thereafter, prevented him from carrying out these ambitious goals. It is not possible to say, therefore, that Dominican economic growth under democratic rule has been sustained and reasonably well distributed. The rapid growth has come under authoritarian governments; development under democratic regimes has been inconsistent and uneven.

On the other hand, the socioeconomic changes since the early 1960s (the end of the Trujillo era) have been impressive and indicate how much broader and more propitious the socioeconomic base for democracy is now as compared with earlier. Literacy has increased from 50 to 70 percent. Per-capita income is triple what it was in 1960. The country is 65-percent urban and 35-percent rural, just the reverse of what it was thirty years ago. What might be termed the "participatory population" (those involved in the money economy, who are informed, who vote, etc.) is also far higher. The manufacturing and industrial sectors are far larger, and, as indicated, there is more wealth and a larger middle class. Because of these changed socioeconomic conditions, the Dominican Republic is becoming a country where a more open and democratic system may become the rule rather than just an occasional interlude.

International Factors

Historically, it has been the next-door Haitian threat that has led Dominicans to prefer strong and authoritarian governments as the only way to preserve their independence as a nation. By now, the Dominican Republic has achieved military parity and even superiority vis-à-vis Haiti, and the populations of the two countries are now also about equal, between 5 and 6 million in each. Currently, the Dominican "great fear" is of Haitianization internally; that is, a rising-up of their own lower classes, who tend to be darker. In modern times, this has served as a main rationalization for authoritarian rule.

The Dominican Republic remains highly dependent internationally.[65] It is dependent economically on the prices, or quotas, that the large importers—mainly the United States—will pay for its exports, chiefly sugar. Since world sugar prices are so low (about 5 cents per pound, way below production costs), the state of the Dominican economy is especially perilous. It is vulnerable to changing world-market prices, to changing consumer habits (the preference for artificial sweeteners), and to the quotas set by the major importers. The country is also heavily dependent on the United States for capital, foreign aid, investment, technology, and other markets.

The Dominican Republic lies within what the United States considers its sphere of influence. It is close to Cuba and Puerto Rico and commands the key passageways into the Caribbean, to the Panama Canal, and to the entire isthmus of Central America. Because of its key strategic location, the Dominican Republic has long been buffeted about in international crosswinds, as a pawn of the major powers of which the United States is only the most recent.[66]

The United States' interests in the Dominican Republic are primarily strategic, which means its attitudes toward Dominican democracy have often been ambivalent. The United States long supported the Trujillo dictatorship, since it assumed that Trujillo would best support its interests in the area. When Castro came to power in neighboring Cuba, the United States reasoned that right-wing dictators like Batista or Trujillo, rather than preserving stability, might instead provide the conditions under which communism would flourish. Hence, the United States moved to depose Trujillo and install a moderately conservative regime, which would enable the United States to control the Dominican transition in a way that it had not controlled the Cuban.

The United States supported Bosch (but only half-heartedly), and there is some evidence of U.S. involvement in his ouster. In 1965, the United States intervened militarily to put down the PRD–led democratic revolution. The United States subsequently supported Balaguer with mammoth amounts of economic assistance in the late 1960s; but then turned around and supported his opponent in the 1978 elections. Since 1978, the United States has been supporting the existing democratic governments, since they are perceived as best preserving stability and U.S. security interests in the country. It is, so far as the support of democracy is concerned, a spotty record. The United States' main interests are strategic, and it is not always the case that democracy was viewed as best securing that priority.

Summing Up

The Dominican Republic has not had a long, consistent, or particularly happy experience with democratic government. There is now a clear pattern of evolution toward democratic rule; but the historical experience has not been particularly auspicious. In this section, we try to explain and summarize the country's overall degree of success (or lack thereof) with democratic government, cutting across the preceding analysis of discrete developments and abstracting from them the most important explanatory factors. We try to offer some summary judgments of the general historical, cultural, social, economic, and political factors that have been most important in determining the country's overall degree of success or failure with democratic government.

Dominican political culture historically has not been conducive to democratic rule. We consider this a very important explanatory factor. Dominican political culture, inherited from Spain, has been absolutist, elitist, hierarchical, corporatist, and authoritarian. Democracy has been a more recent addition to the Dominican tradition and, up until recently, was neither very popular nor deep-rooted. In many areas and institutions of Dominican national life, the authoritarian tradition and practices persist.

Spanish colonial rule left the Dominican Republic with no experience in democratic rule. Equally damaging to the Dominican democratic possibilities were Haiti's continuous assaults and occupations, after independence had initially been achieved. That left the Dominicans not only without democratic experience but downright fearful that weak institutions, which they equated with democracy, would lead to complete destruction of the nation.

Dominican class structure, reinforced by racial criteria, has been rigid and immutable. There is a certain fluidity in Dominican society because of its mixed racial character, and because prejudice is more cultural than racial. Nevertheless, class and race have served as virtually insurmountable obstacles to egalitarianism and greater democracy.

Ethnic and religious cleavages have not been particularly important in hindering democracy. The Dominican Republic is rather homogeneous on both these scores. We would not, in the Dominican case, judge this to be an important factor in explaining democracy or its absence.

The Dominican state structure has historically been weak, so weak that it actually retarded the possibilities for democratic growth. More recently, the state structure has become larger and stronger but not so much so as to have a major damaging effect on democracy. We judge the Dominican state system to be relatively neutral so far as its impact on democracy is concerned.

Two political traditions, authoritarian and democratic, coexist in the Dominican Republic, and these are reflected in the country's political structures and two main constitutional traditions. Now an effort is being made to combine and reconcile these two conflicting traditions. An emerging political-party system in which the two main parties are close to the middle of the political spectrum, coupled with a free and vigorous press, have added further to democracy's possibilities.

The country's political leadership has been thin—and kept purposely so by its authoritarian leaders. The democratic leadership has not been experienced or skillful. Now that is changing, as a cadre of able and experienced leaders has emerged—a development that augurs well for future democratic development.

The Dominican Republic has generally been more successful in achieving economic development under authoritarian regimes than it has under democratic ones. Many Dominicans therefore associate progress with authoritarian rule. By the same token, they tend to associate incompetence, inefficiency, lack of progress, and now even austerity with democracy. Over the long run, these associations will probably change, but they remain a difficult factor for the country to overcome.

The Dominican Republic is both a dependent nation economically, and one that lies within the U.S. sphere of influence. It is unlikely the country can quickly break out of its dependency relations, though it has by now considerably diversified its economic base and trade relations. Nor is it certain the country would be better off that way. Existing within the U.S. orbit strategically has produced mixed results for Dominican democracy, though in the present circumstances it appears that U.S. strategic interests and those of Dominican democracy may be meshing.

The most important factors overall in explaining Dominican democracy or its absence would thus seem to be political culture, decolonization (by which we mean the Haitian experience), class structure, political structure, and international (dependency) factors. Important—but less significant than these others as explanatory variables—would seem to be political leadership and development performance. Of less importance or even irrelevance in the Dominican case would seem to be ethnic and religious cleavages and state structure and strength. These last factors either are not salient to the Dominican case, or else their effects were the reverse of what the general theoretical model for all developing nations hypothesized.

These same factors, in more or less the same order of importance, have influenced the present, more optimistic prognosis for democracy in the Dominican Republic.

1. Dominican political culture is now far more supportive of democratic rule. Admiration for authoritarianism and authoritarian solutions diminished significantly because of the repression of the Trujillo experience; and support for representative, democratic government has increased significantly. In addition, the international political culture, with its enthusiasm for democracy and human rights, is now more supportive of Dominican democracy.[67]

2. The possibilities for Haiti's continued assaults have now been minimized, as the Dominican Republic has achieved military and population parity with Haiti. Indeed, one could say this factor has all but been eliminated as a contributory cause of the retardation of democracy in the Dominican Republic.

3. Class structure remains crucially important but there are now ameliorating effects. There is more general affluence, and the standard of living has increased appreciably in the last two decades. The now sizable middle class,

while not the rock of stability and democracy that some writers predicted,[68] has emerged as a balancing force in the political arena, oriented toward preserving stability and a moderate, middle-of-the-road government.

4. The political structure also shows some hopeful signs. Especially encouraging are the present Constitution (which achieves a working balance between the nation's more democratic and its more authoritarian aspects); the political-party system's evolution toward the moderate middle; the growing strength and autonomy of associational life; and the sheer persistence of and practice under existing democratic institutions.

5. The international environment has also become more promising. The Dominican Republic has managed to renegotiate some of its ties of dependence, particularly its relations with the United States. In addition, the United States has come to see that its strategic interests can best be served by supporting and identifying with moderate democratic governments. In addition, on a global level, democracy is the goal toward which almost all nations and peoples now aspire.

In addition to these major factors, it can also be said that Dominican leadership is now better and broader than it was, and that the developmental performance and overall achievements of the two most recent democratic governments are viewed—relatively speaking—more favorably than before.

All these factors add up to a considerably altered set of conditions now, as compared with the past, that point toward a more favorable situation for democracy in the Dominican Republic today than at any time in history. The societal base, the cultural environment, the political structure, and the international setting all provide a foundation on which democracy may be enabled to both thrive and endure.

• FUTURE PROSPECTS AND POLICY IMPLICATIONS •

The preceding discussion seems to indicate a more optimistic conclusion regarding the future prospects for democracy in the Dominican Republic. To a point, such a conclusion can be justified. But democracy still hangs by some terribly weak threads in the Dominican Republic. Dominican democracy remains subject to buffeting by a variety of crosscurrents; threads could snap and break at just about any time. Democracy is firmer than before, and the overall societal conditions more supportive of it, but that by no means rules out the possibility for extrademocratic elements staging a takeover.

Three themes command our special attention in this final section. The first is the impact of the world economy on the prospects for Dominican democracy. The world economic recession that began in 1979 and deepened thereafter has had a devastating effect on the Dominican economy. The Dominican Republic is going through the worst economic slump since the Great Depression of the

1930s. Unemployment is up, social problems are mounting, per-capita income is declining, and there are fewer and fewer pieces of the economic pie to hand out to more and more clamoring groups. The country has been forced to carry out a severe austerity program that, in 1983, produced large-scale food riots, which were met by police repression. The country's economic problems are undermining the viability of its recently established and still-fragile democratic institutions.[69]

It has been the case historically that when the bottom drops out of the Dominican economy, the bottom has usually dropped out from under the political system as well. It should be understood that we are talking here of the possibilities for undermining not just the government of the moment but an entire system of more-or-less moderate, more-or-less democratic, more-or-less prudent and centrist politics built up with so much difficulty over the past twenty-five years. That is what makes the present economic crisis so serious: It has the potential to subvert and destroy an entire set of democratic political institutions that, with much nurturing, have grown, developed, and become better-institutionalized in the quarter-century since Trujillo.

A second major theme requiring analysis is the ongoing Dominican search for an appropriate developmental formula. Earlier, when Dominican authoritarianism was still both in bloom and in power, I suggested that such a formula would likely mean joining the country's corporatist-authoritarian and democratic traditions.[70] Subsequently, I have suggested that few Latin American nations would likely make it to being full-fledged democratic systems, but that the best we could probably hope for was a transition from a "closed" (authoritarian, top-down, nonparticipatory) to an "open" (more pluralist, freer, more competitive, quasi-democratic) corporatist regime.[71] Understandable at the time it was written, when Latin American corporatism and bureaucratic-authoritarianism were still in full flower and power, the prognosis may have been unduly pessimistic.

It is still my view that countries such as the Dominican Republic need to find a formula to blend and somehow reconcile their authoritarian and democratic traditions. They need to devise a framework in which their organic, integralist, and corporatist forms can be joined with their liberal and democratic preference. They need, in short, to be able to blend their Thomistic-Suárezian-Rousseauan traditions with the Lockean-Jeffersonian one.[72] But given the recent transitions to democracy in so many Latin American countries and the obvious strength of democratic sentiment, in the Dominican Republic as elsewhere in Latin America, one can now be more optimistic about the prospects for a more firmly based and solidly institutionalized system of democracy there. Our expectations can now be enhanced to encompass not just a more open corporatist system, but a full-fledged democracy. Dominican democracy must still reach its accommodation with and adjust to the currents of organicism, corporatism, and Bonapartism still strongly present in Latin America—that is, it must be indigenous and genuinely Latin American and not just imported—but we can now be more optimistic that it will be real democracy nonetheless.

The third and last concluding theme concerns whether the Dominican Republic is, in the present circumstances, reverting to its earlier authoritarian, quasi-democratic, and paternalistic basis. Recent criticisms of the existing Dominican government have suggested precisely that point. These criticisms suggest that in the use of authoritarian methods against rioters in the spring of 1983, in the use of patronage by the government to secure its hold on power, and in the use of strong executive power, the Dominican Republic was returning to its historic authoritarian and *caudillo* forms.[73] The 1986 reelection of Balaguer gives rise to the same disturbing thought.

Some of these trends toward tightened controls are in fact under way, but another interpretation may be given to them besides the one given by critics. One may concede that the government's tactics in some of these instances have been questionable (and we do not have the space to discuss these here in detail), but without drawing the same inference as do the government's foes. For one may also see these steps as an attempt by a democratic Dominican government to adjust realistically to that other, more historic, organic-corporatist-authoritarian Dominican tradition. In the use of patronage, in the employment of executive power, and in government assistance to trade-union, peasant, and professional associations, we see attempts by a manifestly democratic regime to accommodate and reconcile itself to that other tradition. One cannot govern democratically in the Dominican Republic without such accommodation. Historically, when the one Dominican Republic that is liberal and democratic has tried to govern entirely without the other Dominican Republic that is not, that has been a formula for instability and anarchy. One can remain a democrat while also recognizing realistically that to prevent national breakdown and the historic pattern of alternation between democratic and authoritarian rule, compromise and reconciliation between these "two families" of beliefs and sociologies is absolutely necessary. That is also what the reelection of Balaguer seems to indicate.

Hence, in the long run, it is the great independence hero Bolívar, not Saint Thomas and Suárez on the one hand nor Locke on the other, who provides the model for Latin American, including Dominican, democracy.[74] Bolívar recognized Latin America's profound democratic aspirations, yet he also recognized realistically the powerful centrifugal forces tearing the continent apart and forcing it to opt for authoritarianism. Hence, he fashioned a formula that combined democratic rule with strong leadership, that incorporated certain Rousseauan and organic forms into a liberal-constitutional arrangement. It is a formula still valid today, one from which both the Latin American nations undertaking a democratic transition and those on the outside who are encouraging them in that direction can profitably learn.

Among the policy recommendations directed toward the industrialized countries (especially the United States) that emerge from this study, therefore, the following would seem to be of particular, overall importance:

1. Provide economic relief (aid but especially trade) so that the current economic crisis not only does not undermine the economy but is prevented from tearing down democratic political institutions
2. Provide assistance to democratic political groups in ways that relate to Dominican needs and aspirations and are not based on ethnocentric notions
3. Exercise patience and understanding, so that Dominican efforts to find a developmental formula uniquely their own, which combines and seeks to reconcile their conflicting traditions, which responds to and builds upon their own historical experience rather than that of others, are not met with knee-jerk rejection and hostility
4. Reorient U.S. strategic interests in ways that support moderate democratic regimes rather than disrupt them[75]

• NOTES •

Iêda Siqueira Wiarda commented on an earlier draft of the manuscript.

1. For some comparative perspectives that also put the Dominican Republic in context see Howard J. Wiarda and Harvey F. Kline, eds., *Latin American Politics and Development*, 2d rev. ed. (Boulder, CO: Westview Press, 1985).

2. See the preface to this volume; and also Robert Dahl. *Polyarchy: Participation and Opposition* (New Haven, CT: Yale University Press, 1971).

3. Richard Morse, "The Heritage of Latin America." In *The Founding of New Societies*, ed. Louis Hartz (New York: Harcourt, Brace, Jovanovich, 1964).

4. Juan Linz, "An Authoritarian Regime: Spain." In *Mass Politics*, ed. E. Allardt and S. Rokkan (New York: Free Press, 1970), pp. 251–283.

5. For further discussion, see Howard J. Wiarda, *Corporatism and National Development in Latin America* (Boulder, CO: Westview Press, 1981).

6. Howard J. Wiarda, "The Struggle for Democracy and Human Rights in Latin America: Toward a New Conceptualization," *Orbis* 22 (Spring 1978): pp. 137–160.

7. Ian Bell, *The Dominican Republic* (Boulder, CO: Westview Press, 1981); Howard J. Wiarda and Michael J. Kryzanke, *The Dominican Republic: Caribbean Crucible* (Boulder, CO: Westview Press, 1981).

8. See the annual reports of the Inter-American Development Bank, *Economic and Social Progress in Latin America* (Washington, DC: IDB, yearly).

9. On the Indian background, see Samuel Hazard, *Santo Domingo, Past and Present* (New York: Harper and Row, 1873); and Frank Moya Pons, *Historia colonial de Santo Domingo* (Santiago: Universidad Católica Madre y Maestra, 1974).

10. Lewis Hanke, *The First Social Experiments in America* (Cambridge, MA: Harvard University Press, 1935).

11. The best study is Lyle N. McAlister, *Spain and Portugal in the New World, 1492–1570* (Minneapolis: University of Minnesota Press, 1984).

12. McAlister, *Spain and Portugal*; also Sidney Greenfield, "The Patrimonial State and Patron-Client Relations in Iberia and Latin America: Source of 'The System' in the Fifteenth Century Writings of the Infante D. Pedro of Portugal." Occasional Papers Series no. 1 (Amherst: Program in Latin American Studies, University of Massachusetts, 1976).

13. Hanke, *First Social Experiments*.

14. Donald Worcester, "The Spanish American Past: Enemy of Change," *Journal of Inter-American Studies* 11 (1969): pp. 66–75; Magali Sarfatti, *Spanish Bureaucratic-Patrimonialism in America* (Berkeley: Institute of International Studies, University of California, 1966).

15. Charles Gibson, *Spain in America* (New York: Harper and Row, 1966); C. H. Haring, *The Spanish Empire in America* (New York: Harcourt, Brace and World, 1963).

16. Moya Pons, *Historia colonial*.

17. A classic statement in Alfred Thayer Mahan, *The Interest of American Sea Power, Present and Future* (Boston: Little, Brown, 1898).

18. Rayford W. Logan, *Haiti and the Dominican Republic* (New York: Oxford University Press, 1968).

19. Franklin J. Franco, *Los negros, los mulatos y la nación dominicana* (Santo Domingo: Editora Nacional, 1969); Carlos Larrazabal Blanco, *Los negros y la esclavitud en Santo Domingo* (Santo Domingo: Postigo, 1967).

20. Antonio Sánchez Valverde, *Idea del valor de la Isla Española* (Santo Domingo: Editora Nacional, 1971); Miguel Angel Monclús, *El caudillismo en la República Dominicana* (Santo Domingo: Editora del Caribe, 1962).

21. Julio G. Campillo Pérez, *El grillo y el ruiseñor: Elecciones presidencialies dominicanas* (Santo Domingo: Editora del Caribe, 1966).

22. The same theme has been struck for other countries; see Raymond Carr, *Spain, 1808–1939* (Oxford: Clarendon Press, 1966); and Jacques Lambert, *Latin America: Social Structures and Political Institutions* (Berkeley: University of California Press, 1967).

23. Glen Dealy, "Prolegomena on the Spanish American Political Tradition," *Hispanic American Historical Review* 48 (1968): pp. 37–58.

24. Sánchez Valverde, *Idea del valor*; Monclús, *El caudillismo*.

25. Selden Rodman, *Quisqueya: A History of the Dominican Republic* (Seattle: University of Washington Press, 1964); Sumner Welles, *Naboth's Vineyard: The Dominican Republic, 1844–1924*, 2 vols. (Washington, DC: Saville Books, 1966).

26. Miguel Jorrín and John Martz, *Latin American Political Thought and Ideology* (Chapel Hill: University of North Carolina Press, 1970).

27. Harry Hoetink, *The Dominican People, 1850–1900: Notes for a Historical Sociology* (Baltimore, MD: Johns Hopkins University Press, 1982).

28. Bruce J. Calder, *The Impact of Intervention: The Dominican Republic During the U.S. Occupation of 1916–1924* (Austin: University of Texas Press, 1984).

29. Welles, *Naboth's Vineyard*. Welles was the chief U.S. official involved in these events.

30. Howard J. Wiarda, *Dictatorship and Development: The Methods of Control in Trujillo's Dominican Republic* (Gainesville: University of Florida Press, 1968).

31. Jesús de Galíndez, *The Era of Trujillo* (Tucson: University of Arizona Press, 1973); Germán Ornes, *Trujillo: Little Ceasar of the Caribbean* (New York: Nelson, 1958).

32. Robert D. Crasswelder, *Trujillo: The Life and Times of a Caribbean Dictator* (New York: Macmillan, 1966).

33. Wiarda, *Dictatorship and Development*, ch. 9.

34. Lawrence E. Rothstein, "Aquinas and Revolution." Paper presented at the Annual Meeting of the American Political Science Association, Chicago, September 2–5, 1976.

35. Bernard Diederich, *Trujillo: The Death of the Goat* (Boston: Little, Brown, 1978).

36. Samuel P. Huntington, *Political Order in Changing Societies* (New Haven, CT: Yale University Press, 1968), p. 407.

37. For two contrasting views of these events, see John Bartlow Martin, *Overtaken by Events: The Dominican Crisis from the Fall of Trujillo to the Civil War* (New York: Doubleday, 1966); and Howard J. Wiarda, *Dictatorship, Development, and Disintegration: Politics and Social Change in the Dominican Republic* (Ann Arbor, MI: Xerox University Microfilms Monograph Series, 1975).

38. Quoted in Arthur M. Schlesigner, Jr., *A Thousand Days: John F. Kennedy in the White House* (Boston: Houghton Mifflin, 1965), pp. 769–770.

39. Martin, *Overtaken by Events*; Wiarda, *Dictatorship, Development, and Disintegration*.

40. Howard J. Wiarda, "Trujilloism Without Trujillo," *The New Republic* 151 (September 19, 1964): pp. 5–6.

41. The best studies are Piero Gleijeses, *The Dominican Crisis* (Baltimore, MD: Johns Hopkins University Press, 1978); Abraham F. Lowenthal, *The Dominican Intervention* (Cambridge, MA: Harvard University Press, 1971); José Moreno, *Barrios in Arms* (Pittsburgh, PA: University of Pittsburgh Press, 1970); and Jerome Slater, *Intervention and Negotiation* (New York: Harper and Row, 1970). Revisionist interpretations include Howard J. Wiarda, "The United States and the Dominican Republic: Intervention, Dependency, and Tyrannicide," *Journal of Inter-American Studies* 22 (May 1980): pp. 247–260; and Michael J. Kryzanek, "The Dominican Intervention Revisited: An Attitudinal and Operational Analysis" (unpublished paper).

42. Michael J. Kryzanek, *Political Party Opposition in Latin America: The PRD, Joaquín Balaguer and Politics in the Dominican Republic 1966–1973* (Ph.D. Diss., University of Massachusetts, Amherst, 1975); also Howard J. Wiarda and Michael J. Kryzanek "Dominican Dictatorship Reconsidered: The Caudillo Tradition and the Regimes of Trujillo and Balaguer," *Revista/Review Interamericana* 7 (Fall 1977): pp. 417–435.

43. See G. Pope Atkins, *Arms and Politics in the Dominican Republic* (Boulder, CO: Westview, 1981).

44. Michael J. Kryzanek, "Diversion, Subversion, and Repression: The Strategies of Anti-Regime Politics in Balaguer's Dominican Republic," *Caribbean Studies* 1 (1977), and 2 (1977).

45. Michael J. Kryzanek, "The 1978 Election in the Dominican Republic: Opposition Politics, Intervention and the Carter Administration," *Caribbean Studies* 19 (1979).

46. Wiarda and Kryzanek, *Dominican Republic*.

47. Howard J. Wiarda, *Ethnocentrism in Foreign Policy: Can We Understand the Third World?* (Washington, DC: American Enterprise Institute for Public Policy Research, 1985).

48. Sánchez Valverde, *Idea del valor*; based also on interviews conducted by the author in the Dominican Republic in 1962, 1964–1965, 1966, 1969–1970, 1972, 1977, and 1978.

49. Interviews (see n. 48). For a report on some of these interview results see Howard J. Wiarda, *The Aftermath of the Trujillo Dictatorship: The Emergence of a Pluralist Political System in the Dominican Republic* (Ann Arbor, MI: Xerox University Microfilms, 1967).

50. See Juan Bosch, *Composición social dominicana* (Santo Domingo: Libraría Nacional, 1970).

51. Howard J. Wiarda, "Constitutions and Constitutionalism in the Dominican Republic: The Basic Law within the Political Process," *Law and Society Review* 2 (June 1968): pp. 385–405.

52. Pedro Andres Pérez Cabral, *La comunidad mulata: El caso socio-político de la República Dominicana* (Caracas: Gráfica Americana, 1967).

53. Marvin Goldwert, *The Constabulary in the Dominican Republic: Progeny and Legacy of United States Intervention* (Gainesville: University of Florida Press, 1962).

54. Wiarda, *Dictatorship, Development, and Disintegration*, ch. 10.

55. Howard J. Wiarda, "The Development of the Labor Movement in the Dominican Republic," *Inter-American Economic Affairs* 20 (Summer 1966): pp. 41–63.

56. James A. Clark, *The Church and the Crisis in the Dominican Republic* (Westminster, MD: Newman Press, 1967).

57. Wiarda, *Dictatorship, Development, and Disintegration*, chs. 16–17.

58. *Ibid.*

59. Howard J. Wiarda, "The Politics of Civil-Military Relations in the Dominican Republic," *Journal of Inter-American Studies* 7 (October 1965): pp. 465–484.

60. Wiarda and Kryzanek, *Dominican Republic*, ch. 7.

61. Wiarda, *Dictatorship, Development, and Disintegration*, ch. 13.

62. *Ibid.*, ch. 14.

63. See the numerous comments in Martin, *Overtaken by Events*.

64. Wiarda, *Dictatorship, Development, and Disintegration*, ch. 16.

65. Jan Knippers Black, *The Dominican Republic: Politics and Development in an Unsovereign State* (Boston: Allen and Unwin, forthcoming).

66. G. Pope Atkins and Larman C. Wilson, *The United States and the Trujillo Regime* (New Brunswick, NJ: Rutgers University Press, 1972).

67. Michael J. Kryzanek, *U.S.-Latin American Relations* (New York: Praeger, 1985).

68. John J. Johnson, *Political Change in Latin America: The Emergence of the Middle Sectors* (Stanford, CA: Stanford University Press, 1958); W. W. Rostow, *The Stages of Economic Growth* (Cambridge: Cambridge University Press, 1960).

69. See the monograph-length report prepared by the author for the Inter-American Development Bank, *Latin America at the Crossroads: Debt, Development, and the Future* (Boulder, CO: Westview Press, 1985).

70. Howard J. Wiarda, ed., *The Continuing Struggle for Democracy in Latin America* (Boulder, CO: Westview Press, 1980); also *Corporatism and National Development*.

71. Howard J. Wiarda, "The Political Systems of Latin America: Developmental Models and a Typology of Regimes." In *Latin America*, ed. Jack W. Hopkins (New York: Holmes and Meier, 1985).

72. Richard M. Morse, "The Challenge of Ideology in Latin America," *Foreign Policy and Defense Review* 5 (1985): pp. 14–23.

73. See, for example, José Oviedo, *Las formas políticas del eterno retorno* (Santo Domingo: Instituto Tecnológico de Santo Domingo, 1985).

74. See especially Vicente Lecuna and Harold A. Bierck, eds., *The Selected Writings of Bolívar,* 2 vols. (New York: Colonial Press, 1951).

75. Howard J. Wiarda, "Updating United States Strategic Policy: Containment in the Caribbean Basin." Paper presented at a conference, Containment and the Future, National Defense University, Washington, DC, November 7–8, 1985.

• CHAPTER ELEVEN •
Mexico: Sustained Civilian Rule Without Democracy

DANIEL C. LEVY

Alone of the countries examined in this volume (and exceptional in the series, Democracy in Developing Countries) Mexico has had no significant twentieth-century experience (and precious little prior experience) with democratic rule. Instead, Mexican politics has displayed considerable disdain for the public competition and accountability integral to liberal democracy. Nevertheless, Mexico merits inclusion in our comparative study for three reasons: (1) the nation's overall importance; (2) theoretical insights distinguishing the bases of democratic and stable civilian rule; and (3) notable if uncertain democratizing developments in recent years. The first reason is obvious; this chapter will focus on the others, especially the second reason.[1]

The dominant theme here is that many factors commonly associated with good prospects for democracy have been present in Mexico without promoting that result. Moreover, the very achievement of Mexico's major political success—stability—has presented obstacles to democratization. Naturally, observers have long realized that democracy and stability are empirically and analytically separable. But a strong tendency lumps the two together as one desired outcome. Many of the hypotheses orienting this comparative project illustrate this tendency. Although distinct measures are developed for democracy and stability, democratic stability appears as the key dependent variable.

Among recent attempts to explore difficulties in achieving democracy and stability together, some have concentrated on why democracies fall. For other nations discussed in this volume, but not Mexico, we can analyze democratic periods, democratic breakdown (or consolidation), and "redemocratization." Another line of inquiry concerns the conditions under which authoritarian regimes become democratic.[2] But the literature on that process deals overwhelmingly with military regimes—typically very exclusionary and coercive—and to a limited extent with narrow personalistic regimes. Unlike either "bureaucratic-authoritarian" or personalistic rule, Mexico's authoritarianism has much of the institutionalization, breadth, forms, pacts, and legitimacy often associated with democratic government.

In fact, many factors associated with democratic stability have promoted,

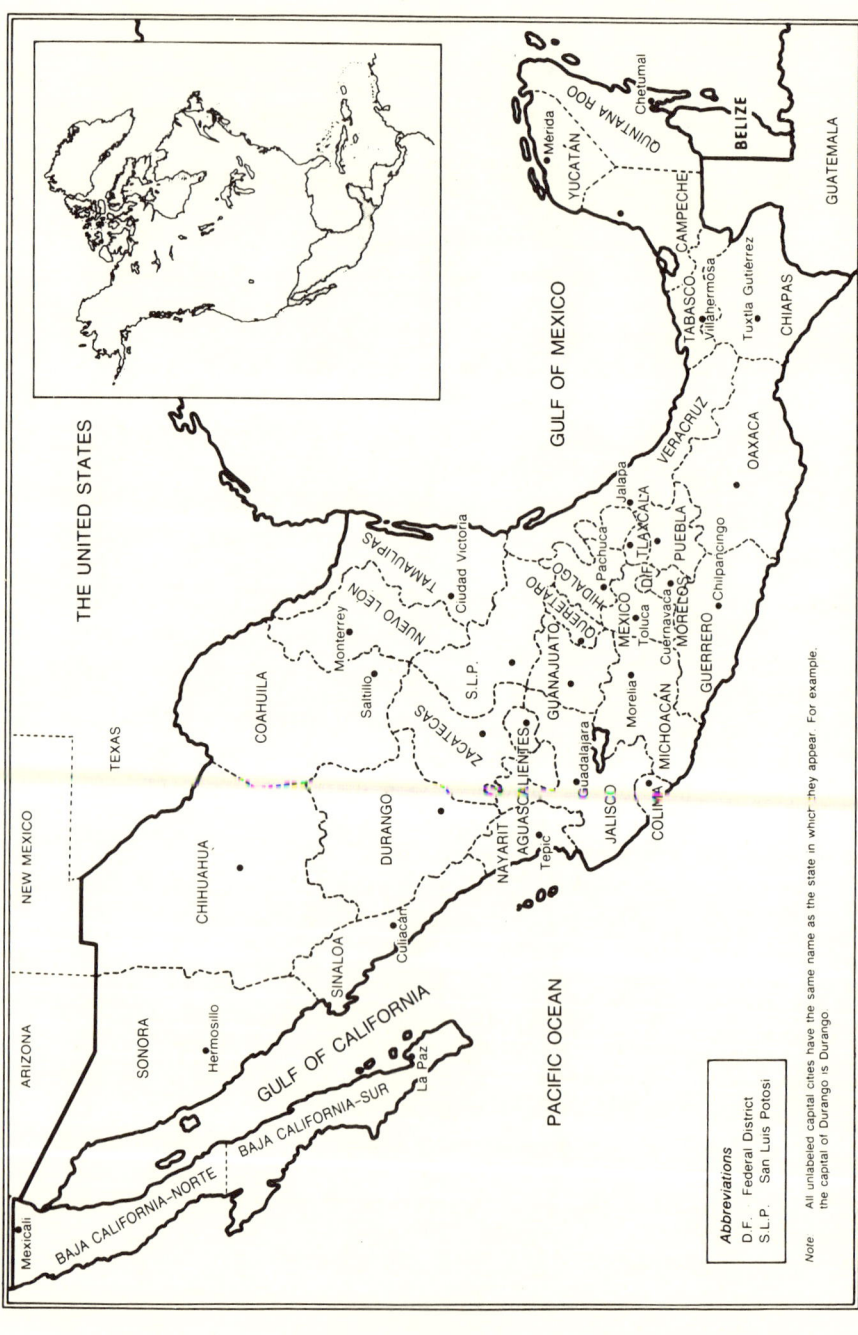

Reprinted from Daniel Levy and Gabriel Szekely, *Mexico: Paradoxes of Stability and Change*, 2d ed., by permission of Westview Press.

in Mexico, a civilian authoritarian rule that has managed the most impressive political stability in all Latin America regardless of regime type. No other major Latin American nation has sustained civilian rule throughout the postwar period; Mexico's predates that period. In terms of our measures of stability, no regime in the region matches Mexico's in durability and legitimacy built through periods of change, conflict, and challenge. Despite recent developments, including increased challenges and decreased support, efficacy, and effectiveness, Mexico has ranked in the category of stable polities, albeit bordering on partially stable. Unlike Latin American systems that are partially stable because they have not consolidated new regimes, Mexico's difficulty concerns erosion of previous consolidation.

Assessments of stability have been clearer than assessments of democracy in Mexico. The latter have been excessively influenced by dominant paradigms in comparative politics in general and Latin American studies in particular. An irony is that interpretations of Mexican politics have changed so much while the system itself has remained remarkably stable. In line with burgeoning literature on political development, Mexico was typically depicted in the 1950s and most of the 1960s as incompletely but increasingly democratic. Probably the most cited work emphasized an evolution toward Western democracy in rising interest-group activity, participation, inclusiveness, national identity, legitimacy, and functional specialization, alongside declining personalism. Mexico fell short on its citizenship base and leadership selection largely because the regime had pursued "suitable social and economic conditions" before democratic goals, but those conditions had made Mexico ready for democracy.[3] Subsequently, however, Mexico was almost consensually depicted as authoritarian, with democratic tendencies not ascendent. Linz's seminal work on authoritarianism was widely employed by Mexicanists, and Mexico was even overzealously tied to bureaucratic authoritarianism. Recently, interpretations of complex blends of authoritarianism and pluralist forces have been developed.[4]

From 1945 to 1985, Mexico ranked between third and seventh among twenty nations on the best-known (if controversial) ratings for Latin American democracy.[5] Mexico ranks much lower in this volume, however, as all the other cases except Chile currently fit our basic definition of democracy. Mexico falls far short on three elements of democracy, though some qualification is pertinent in each case: (1) Mexico has lacked meaningful and extensive competition among organized groups for major government office, though competition is increasing; (2) participation does not reliably extend to leadership selection through fair elections, though neither is that element entirely absent and elections are regular; and (3) civil and political liberties have been insufficient to guarantee the integrity of competition and participation, but they have been significant and variable rather than minimal. Similarly, Mexico falls into the lowest category (failure/absence) in this study's six-part "summary scale" of democratic experience because there has been no extended period of democracy, and little immediate prospect for it. However, democratic space has increased in recent years, and the future is far more uncertain than it has been for decades.

Regarding this study's classification of democratic stability, Mexico comes closest to the "hegemonic party" system. The dominant party does not tolerate genuine challenges (i.e., alternatives) to its rule, it claims almost all subfederal posts, and electoral fraud is common. Still, the party does not regularly take the high vote percentage cited for hegemonic systems. More broadly, our overall definition of democracy is heavily weighted toward electoral dimensions, long a weak area for Mexico. Thus, the Mexican case shows some significant features of "semidemocracies," including substantial room for expression, and suggests that hegemonies are not necessarily the least democratic of authoritarian nations.

This chapter identifies basic roots of Mexico's complex system of stable civilian rule without democracy, and more specifically considers the editors' hypotheses about stable democracy. Finally, it analyzes prospects for democratization and the role the United States might play.

First, however, a preliminary qualification must be inserted here. This chapter was written before the 1988 electoral campaign took shape and hurtled towards an exciting, unprecedented finish. In the election's immediate aftermath, no serious observer has more than questionable ideas about most of the implications for democracy. What is clear is that the elections were the most competitive in spirit and result of any in modern Mexican history and that they vastly increased uncertainty about the future of Mexican politics. Even if Mexican politics undergo transforming changes, however, it will be important to understand the long-standing reality that preceded (and undoubtedly would help shape) those changes.

• AN UNDEMOCRATIC PAST: REVIEW AND ANALYSIS •

Mexico's political heritage is authoritarian. There is less democratic precedent to analyze than in any other country considered in this volume; viable democratic rule has been virtually absent. A point highlighted by Wiarda in the Dominican case is particularly relevant in the Mexican case: Democratic experiments historically proved ineffective, in contrast to certain authoritarian periods.

Great precolonial civilizations, such as the Aztec, presaged a pattern of relatively strong authoritarian rule. Spain's centuries-long rule was similar in that respect. Some observers see not only precedent but causal roots in these experiences. According to Octavio Paz, the Aztec *tlatoani* introduced impersonal, priestly, institutional rule, and colonialism introduced Arabic-Hispanic reverence for the personal *caudillo:* "I repeat: there is a bridge that reaches from *tlatoani* to viceroy, viceroy to president."[6] And much has been made of the contrast between authoritarian and "liberal" colonizations by Spain and England, respectively.

Independence (1821) brought neither democracy nor stability. Federalist-centralist conflicts were among the most important. The lack of stability crippled hopes for economic growth, which in turn contributed to further instability. Despite examples of autonomous local rule, liberal projects were weak. Liberal rule was extremely short-lived, as was the presidency of Valentín Gómez Farías in the 1830s, until the Reform (1855–1876). The Reform is probably the closest Mexico has come to democracy. It featured a belief that democracy (however restricted) was compatible with stability and growth; a liberal constitution; substantial liberties; some significant elections; and some socioeconomic mobility and educational expansion alongside attacks on large landholders, including the church. On the other hand, the Reform was limited in mass inclusiveness and hostile to Indian communitarianism. Yet, democracy often begins with public contestation restricted to certain groups. Mexico's liberal experiment failed because it could not build sufficient strength. French imperial intervention, though eventually beaten back, was debilitating. Mostly, liberal democratic forms were used by antidemocratic forces. Regional *caciques* used decentralized authority to block reform. As it often has in Latin America, Congress represented *cacique* and other oligarchic interests in conflict with a liberal executive.[7] The weakness of liberal experiments with decentralized political authority would not go unnoticed by twentieth-century leaders.

Always fragile, the Reform faded after leader Benito Juárez's death (1872). A split over the 1876 presidential succession opened the way for a military coup. Porfirio Díaz became supreme dictator. For the first time, independent Mexico achieved political stability and economic growth. The regime was repressively authoritarian: Gone were free elections; diminished was freedom of the press. Commonly for Latin America, some democratic formalities were preserved, but Díaz's reference to Congress as his herd of tame horses was indicative of the basic realities. The *porfiriato*'s positivist notions of progress through permanent evolution, accompanied by economic growth without distribution and political stability without democracy, offer broad historical parallels to the contemporary regime.

Among factors ultimately bringing down the *porfiriato* (1910), contemporary optimists about democracy might speculate on both repressiveness and economic growth leading to calls for democracy; but the main reason for the regime's fall was its unwillingness to allow political mobility among the elite. In any case, Díaz's fall was precipitated by his quickly inoperative pledge not to seek reelection in 1910. Francisco Madero held Díaz to his rhetoric about free elections, and Díaz's attempts at electoral fraud were his end. Madero won Mexico's uniquely free (if still limited) election and became president (1911–1913). He led those whose agenda was "a return to '57," the Reform constitution, and "free suffrage, no reelection." Considerable democracy blossomed. For example, Congress was autonomous of the executive and the scene of powerful debates among very antagonistic forces. Division of power (federalism) and separation of power (including judicial review) were important for Madero.

But such democratization proved largely irrelevant for Mexico. Democratic, competitive structures did not lead to the destruction of Porfirian forces including *caciques,* governors, bureaucrats, the military, and a partially revitalized church. Madero even appointed former Díaz aides to government positions, while he tended to exclude revolutionary groups. In other words, this democratic leader, so popular in 1911, neither destroyed the old order nor constructed a viable new one. Although a good deal of the literature on transitions to democracy stresses the need for pacts among elites, probably the major weakness in Madero's approach, reflected in his inattention to socioeconomic problems, was failure to strengthen democratic forces by adding a mass base. Of course, whether Madero could have successfully done so is unknown. After his assassination (covertly aided by the United States), other leaders would incorporate the masses—undemocratically.

Years of revolutionary warfare among various armies brought mass mobilization and, especially, death and destruction. By 1916, a million Mexicans had died, and nearly as many had emigrated. Compared, for example, to Emiliano Zapata's peasant army and its demands for land reform, Venustiano Carranza's ultimately victorious constitutionalists were not committed to fundamental socioeconomic change. In subsequent years, some observers would even question whether a real revolution had occurred. In any case, the revolution would become a symbol of mass involvement, progressive change, and nationalism, skillfully manipulated by the regime to bolster its legitimacy. By 1940, the revolution would be "institutionalized," the fragile stability forged since 1916 safely deepened. Two crucial factors in building this postrevolutionary stability were pacts among those elites not destroyed by the revolution, and organized integration of mass groups.[8]

President Carranza only partly recognized these two necessities, but he accepted provisions that gave the 1917 Constitution strong mass appeal as a legacy of the revolution. These included a minimum wage, an 8-hour workday, workman's compensation, land reform, and notable nationalist measures. Equally significant, the Constitution ambiguously blended democratic aspirations with authoritarian realities: popular sovereignty; free elections; guarantees for individual rights; federalism; separation of powers; and a potent national government in general and presidency in particular.

Between them, Carranza's two powerful successors, Alvaro Obregón and Plutarco Elías Calles extended the state's ties to and control over mass agrarian and urban labor interests. Yet, when their terms ended (1928), the regime's stability was still much in doubt. All three presidents had plotted to rule beyond their constitutional terms; two had been assassinated. Major groups still competed violently; and none was powerful enough to end the nation's political stalemate.

At this point, Mexico experienced two moments of great political leadership, the kind in many ways associated with democratic consolidation. The leadership that stabilized Mexico's civilian rule would be undemocratic in means (not unusual in democratic consolidations) but also in ends. First, Calles engineered a grand pact among elite power-holders. Convincing them that without compromise they faced defeat or endless uncertainty, he brought them to support creation of a civilian institution (the party) that would centralize authority for the regime on the basis of bargains, including elite circulation through peaceful means. Second, ironically, Calles' successor had to block his personalistic attempt to regain and perpetuate his rule.[9] Although Calles had the edge among elites, Lázaro Cárdenas fortified the incorporation of the masses, as he won their allegiance not only to himself but to the regime. Critically, however, Cárdenas was not responding to autonomous demands from below. His modes were corporatist; he was in fact a proclaimed opponent of bourgeois democracy.

By the time the immensely popular Cárdenas peacefully relinquished power to a moderate successor (1940), the regime was sufficiently institutionalized to pave the way for more than a quarter-century of maximum strength and stability, followed finally by increasing weaknesses but not instability.

• CIVILIAN RULE WITHOUT DEMOCRACY •

This section analyzes four topics identified as crucial to democratic development. For each, I explore how basic features have evolved and operate, how they serve civilian stability but not democracy, and what challenges have recently emerged in Mexico.

State-Society Relations

State relations with mass groups approximate "state corporatism" much more than pluralism.[10] The regime has significant control over organizations that bring the masses into the system. Participation and interest-group demands are seriously limited. In fact, much of the Mexican population is unorganized and politically "marginal"; it does not express discontent, or it asks for help from a political mediator without demanding rights. Even formal, organized groups often react to more than participate meaningfully in policy formation.[11]

Encapsulating mass organizations obviously is antithetical to democracy. It also greatly limits the democratizing option available in Venezuela's *trienio* when the AD party could organize peasants and workers. Those groups have already been organized in Mexico, into an undemocratic party. On the other hand, the early incorporation of mass groups has promoted stability. It has given the regime a wide base, which has been used to boost the regime's autonomy from business. Mainly, however, incorporation has made organized dissent on the Left extremely difficult. Such dissent threatens other regimes, particularly when mass mobilization leads to elite fears and military coups. The Mexican regime has repeatedly been able to effect austere economic policies that would bring revolt in other nations.[12] Thus, the regime's mass base has sustained civilian rule even while it has been undemocratic. Additionally, because major threats have been forestalled in Mexico, the regime has been able to use less repressive force than have many other authoritarian regimes in Latin America.

As one of two major organized mass groups (the peasantry is the other), labor verifies the pattern of state corporatism. Labor power, including access to rewards, is concentrated in one dominating union, the Confederation of Mexican Workers (CTM), which Cárdenas carefully grafted onto the official party. Crucially, labor was incorporated and granted benefits from above, more than independently organized for the conquest of rights.[13] Labor leaders have helped make Mexican unions "moderate" but neither autonomous nor democratic. Occasionally, when independent labor movements have threatened to become powerful, the regime has resorted to severe repression (as in the late 1950s); but usually the regime has relied on the undemocratic internal structure of organized labor and its ties to the regime.[14] A big challenge has emerged, however, with the economic crisis of the 1980s. As Waisman points out in this volume, Argentine labor corporatism worked to give the government support only as long as the workers reaped the benefits of redistribution. In Mexico, the regime has long carefully funneled benefits to organized labor, but real wages have recently plummeted.

However formidable, corporatist controls are far from complete. Even official trade unions often bargain hard for benefits, and some leaders have increased their criticism of regime policies. Further, independent labor movements have precedent and recently became usually active, at least until economic setbacks in the 1980s. Attention has focused on the electrical workers' Tendencia Democrática and parallels for telephone workers, miners, and teachers. Third, the CTM's share of the organized work force is diminishing, and the regime's economic opening of the 1980s could further weaken it.

Whereas qualifications must be made to a corporatist view of state-labor relations, such a view is fundamentally inappropriate for state-business relations. Reasonable scholarly debate exists over past relations. Some "peak" business associations have been established by government, mandatory in inclusiveness, and dependent (on government) in matters ranging from subsidies to leadership selection. But a good case can be made that domestic business, even including older associations such as the Confederation of Industrial Chambers and the National Chamber of Manufacturing Industry, has long worked with government because of mutual self-interest and "inducements" more than coercion and "constraints"; has been economically strong and politically able to influence regulatory, trade, and other policies; and has expressed a "sectorial consciousness" involving some "adversary relationship with political elites."[15] In any case, this more pluralist view holds for newer associations, such as the Entrepreneurial Coordinating council and the Mexican Employers' Confederation, and increasingly for traditional ones. The economic populism of President

Luis Echeverría in the early 1970s weakened state-business ties by scaring and alienating business and by hurting the economy. Today, harsh and repeated business criticism of the regime simultaneously jeopardizes political stability and shows considerable freedom of expression.

Juxtaposition of business and labor relations with the state illustrates how the balance between freedom and corporatist controls usually depends on social class. Consider highly educated groups. Granted, dependency on the state goes far beyond what is found in the United States in terms of employment opportunities and professional associations. But intellectuals and other professionals have been much freer than workers to control their affairs and even to criticize the government. Despite the potential corporatist tie of depending almost fully on the state for income, Mexico's public universities have substantial though circumscribed autonomy from government. Furthermore, groups within the public universities have considerable freedom of expression and power to affect institutional policies, as the massive and successful student demonstrations against academic reforms proposed in 1986 illustrate.[16] Private universities, holding roughly 15 percent of the nation's more than 1 million enrolments, add significantly to state-society pluralism.[17]

What, then, of the infamous events of 1968, when the government killed hundreds of protesting university students? The slaughter was a watershed in views about Mexican democratization: It convinced many of the regime's unalterably repressive nature. But my view is that limits on protest are not so fixed. Behavior that lies within the "logic" of this authoritarian system is not inevitable behavior; at other times, other Mexican leaders have been more tolerant. To be sure, the student protests of 1968 were unprecedented for the widespread questions they so actively raised about the lack of democracy in Mexico. And 1968 serves as a chilling and restraining reminder of the state's possible violent response to protest, a response much more commonly visited on poorer groups.[18]

One rule demarking zones of permitted and unpermitted freedoms can be identified as central to Mexico's exclusion from the democratic category: Organized dissent that poses a realistic alternative to the regime is forbidden. Violations usually bring harsh repression along with co-optation. Even this formidable restriction leaves some room for pluralism and, especially, individual freedoms.[19] Religion provides an example of both the restrictions and the possibilities. After the revolution broke the church's tremendous political-economic power, a *modus vivendi* allowed it considerable autonomy in religious cultural-educational affairs—beyond what the Constitution ostensibly permits. In turn, the church has not been allowed the opposition voice heard in Brazil, Chile, Nicaragua, and elsewhere in Latin America—though some Mexican church leaders have recently supported opposition party calls for democratization with free elections. Meanwhile, individuals are free to worship (or not) as they please, and several religious and ethnic minorities have significant group autonomy. Mexico has no official religion.

Of course, some such societal freedoms (e.g., private schooling and freedom to travel) lack a direct political component or offer opportunity for the privileged only. Nonetheless, evidence of increased vibrancy and inclusiveness in political life abounds. As president, Echeverría criticized the nation's basic development model. Under José López Portillo (1976–1982), Mexico enjoyed an unusually open (though still partly managed) debate over whether to join the GATT. Under Miguel de la Madrid (1982–1988), the freedom to advocate alternative policies reached new heights, though presidential claims that policy was often made through popular consultations were mere pretense. The 1988 electoral campaign then opened considerably more space for free expression.

While this tendency to use the increasing democratic space has been most evident among privileged groups (as in middle-class organizations on environmental issues), it also extends to popular sectors. A basic factor has been disenchantment with government, particularly given the consequences of continued economic crisis. (A catalyst was the earthquakes of 1985; the government appeared impotent in reacting.) Some see scars and challenges that go beyond 1968 and could promote "an initial democratization of Mexico's political institutions."[20] Individuals have formed associations to deal with urban problems such as homelessness, tenant conditions, schooling, and other public services. Although spontaneous association has considerable precedent in Mexico, one wonders whether a new era has begun. Recent behavior can be contrasted to Fagen and Tuohy's well-known depiction of "depoliticized" urban life, where management substitutes for politics and most people believe that government should or will handle their political affairs.[21] The new vibrancy in Mexican politics alters traditional state-society patterns associated with stability; indeed, it has resulted from both the state's success in modernizing and diversifying society and from its declining legitimacy.

My points about societal freedom—its limits and growth—are illustrated by analysis of the media. First, outright repression and censorship exist. Despite the pluralism apparently offered through the multiplicity of outlets, mostly private, dependence on government is insured through official control of newsprint and the need for licenses. Mostly, however, smooth state-media relations reflect overlapping elite interests. Mutual interests on "macro" orientations such as growth and stability without major redistribution are supported by "micro" support through government advertising revenue, corrupt stipends for reporters, and the like. In return, government has counted on fairly favorable reporting and a lack of the information a citizenry needs for responsible democracy with accountability. Where the media come closest to escaping such restrictions, we tend to see elite pluralism. Most independent publications, including newspapers (e.g., *Uno Más Uno* and *La Jornada*), magazines (e.g., *Proceso* and *Nexos*), and academic books are not only expensive but appeal to the educated minority. Electronic media are much safer in content. Television's conservative banality is crucial. Thus, the most vigorous areas of contestation are the ones that reach the least inclusive audience. Additionally, considerable room exists for fundamental Marxist critiques of the immutable state but much less for practical critiques including policy alternatives.[22] Where coverage of such alternatives is found, it is often in the cautious form of citing what various officials and others have said, avoiding in-depth analysis.

Nevertheless, coverage of true dissent is increasing. Repression of the nation's leading independent newspaper in 1976 has been followed by the greatest media freedom contemporary Mexico has known. It has included investigative reporting and public opinion polls concerning increased cynicism about government, and prominent calls for widespread democratization. All this, however limited, contributes to a new era of democratic challenge.

Government Centralization

In turning now from state-society relations to the structure of the government, we turn from elements intrinsic to democracy to elements hypothetically associated with democracy. That is, a system with widespread freedoms and pluralism is more democratic than one in which state corporatism rules society, whereas decentralized governments can exist in undemocratic systems and centralized governments can exist in democratic systems.

The editors have hypothesized a strong association between decentralization and democracy. The Mexican case is perhaps supportive of the hypothesis, but only indirectly, as it combines centralization with the absence of democracy. Much clearer is that centralization—geographically and in the presidency—has been crucial to civilian stability. As González Casanova's classic analysis showed, Mexico's antiliberal government structure must be viewed in historical context. Mexico City–based presidentialism with a hegemonic party ended military and legislative conspiracies as well as divisively unstable rule by regional and other *caudillos*. "Respect for the balances of power would have been respect for the conspiracies of a semi-feudal society."[23]

Establishing central authority and national identity and security is a major problem for new nations. Mexico was unsuccessful in the nineteenth century. Into the 1920s and even 1930s, regional and village strongmen ruled outside the grasp of Mexico City. Such decentralized power had nothing to do with democracy; nor did the ensuing geographical centralization of power. Although aided by transportation and communication advances, a key was decisive political leadership by the likes of Obregón, Calles, and Cárdenas. Overcoming centrifugal antidemocratic forces is often a prerequisite to democratic consolidation. In Mexico, it proved crucial to stability but not democracy.

Mexico formally has a federalist structure with thirty-one states (plus the Federal District), which in turn are divided into over 2,000 supposedly free municipalities. State political structures parallel the national except that their legislatures are unicameral. In practice, a range of daily and other activities are handled by states, and the federal government usually intervenes only when conflicts are not locally contained. However, the very infrequency of explicit interventions reflects (as we saw in state-labor relations) ongoing national government control over basic policy. In essence, presidents appoint the official party's gubernatorial candidates and depose troublesome governors. National cabinet ministries have delegates in each state, and stationed military officers represent national authority. States have very limited funds and depend on the national government for most of them. Similarly, municipalities depend on states and the national government regarding leadership and funds, and funds are very unevenly disbursed; most municipalities lack income beyond very small appropriations and fees from licenses and fines. Political careers have been made in Mexico City, not at the grassroots.

Electoral patterns have illustrated the centralized hold.[24] First in 1958, then in 1967, and especially since the 1977 reform, several opposition victories have been allowed at the municipal level. But the opposition has not gained a single governorship. And the official party still holds roughly 95 percent of the municipalities. Sometimes, as after the leftist victory in Juchitán, Oaxaca, the regime uses violence to oust the municipal opposition. Usually, the centralized party-government structure itself limits the importance of municipal opposition victories.

Centralization has recently come under strong attack, however. Disaffection runs especially high in the industrial north, though Mexico does not face the separatist threats that undermine stability in some Third World nations. Many Mexicans consider decentralization necessary for increased participation and democratization (suggesting some parallel to what Hartlyn finds for Colombia). Decentralization in implementation and, more controversially, in decision-making is increasingly linked to regime effectiveness and stability as well. Latell even portrays a fundamental split between "federalists" and "centralists." The former include many business and conservative opposition party leaders joined by a minority of government officials. President de la Madrid, while duly citing the historical necessity of centralization, called it "a grave limitation": "Centralist mentalities have become obstacles that distort democracy."[25] His administration claimed to have expanded municipal autonomy and increased access to local resources. In its 1988 campaign, the official party made decentralization a major theme.

But obstacles to decentralization remain enormous. Centralization goes beyond political to economic and social realms; economic crisis makes it hard to invest in decentralization; party leaders, governors, and many other government official have vested interests in centralization; political traditions carry weight. Overall, decentralization involves risks. Even if overcentralization now threatens stability, sudden decentralization might threaten it more.

Centralization of power in Mexico City has meant centralization of power in the presidency. Constitutional provisions about the separation of powers within the federal government have had no more impact than provisions about the division of powers between federal and state governments. Mexico achieved stability not by defying authoritarian tendencies toward the enormous concentration of authority in one leader but by limiting the leader's term. Apt are references to Mexico's "king for six years." The president has been central to policymaking, agenda setting, conflict resolution, key appointments, control over the party, and so forth. He heads a vast network of federal agencies (employing 17 percent of the nation's workforce), including many "parastatals."[26]

Cardoso even called the Mexican president perhaps more powerful than any Southern Cone military president.[27] Such assessments probably underestimate three factors, however. One is the comparative limits of the Mexican state's control over society; the Mexican president can be no more powerful than his government. Second are the terrible disorders, rivalries, and duplications rampant in the Mexican federal bureaucracy. Third is the erosion of presidential strength in the last two decades, reflected in increasing attacks on presidents, once unthinkable, and widespread beliefs about the failures of at least the last three presidents. In fact, the last presidential "giant" was Miguel Alemán, who left office in 1952.

The presidency nonetheless has remained very powerful, largely because Congress and the judiciary have been so weak. Congressional debate and opposition continued into the 1920s but died with regime consolidation. Although token opposition reappeared in 1940, executive initiatives have been approved unanimously or overwhelmingly. A function of Congress has been to show the rule of law in legitimizing executive action. Since the 1970s, however, political reform has expanded opposition representation, and one sees some coalition building, revelations about unpopular government actions, and greatly expanded debate.[28] The opening has included the appearance of cabinet officers to answer questions posed by the legislative opposition. Still, the legislature has lacked the openness or, especially, the power found in democracies. I must add, however, that the opening may well have grown dramatically in 1988. Opposition parties gained nearly half the seats in the Chamber of Deputies (as Table 11.1 will show) plus its first Senate representation, and vigorous protests were seen. However cloudy the prospects for policymaking power remain, unprecedented openness seems certain.

The judiciary has played a more important role than has the legislature (until recently) but also a limited one. It has been a place for privileged actors to protect their interests even against executive initiatives, particularly in the case of landlords working against land reform. Although it has handled disputes among citizens, it has not limited executive authority by interpreting the Constitution or executive actions. Nor has it, for example, yet dealt seriously with electoral fraud. No parallel has emerged for the liberalization occurring in the legislature. "Judicial reform" refers basically to speeding up the decisionmaking process. It has not referred to increasing autonomy from the executive.[29]

Given common patterns of both Latin American politics and Mexican history from independence until roughly the 1930s, however, the main reason that government power is centralized in the presidency is that the military is subordinated. In the postwar era, only Costa Rica rivals Mexico in degree of subordination. Outside Mexico, subordination is generally associated with the establishment and defense of democracy, as in Costa Rica. But Mexico produced no Figueres, no democratic rule. Nonetheless, skilled political leadership was crucial in establishing civilian supremacy.

Presidents Obregón, Calles, and Cárdenas, themselves revolutionary generals (like all presidents until 1946, at least nominally) adeptly timed and executed measures to subordinate the military. These included: purges and other forced retirements and transfers (which minimized loyalty to given officers); welcome opportunities for corruption within the service and for business employment outside it; dependence on government salaries and social security; professionalization; cuts in military funding; creation of a viable political party; and incorporation of mass organizations into civilian structures. And since 1946, all presidents have been civilians.

Since the institutionalization of the regime, there have been no coups or serious threats of coups. The military has not been a powerful interest group blocking policies it does not like and forcing others. Its share of government expenditures has been famously low. The military has not been integrated with the civilian Right. All these factors distinguish Mexico from most of Latin America and help us understand the nation's stability.

Some signs of increasing military strength have recently appeared in role, stature, funding, modernization, and appointments of retired generals.[30] Still, a major change in the military's role remains very unlikely. The civilian regime would probably have to weaken so much as to need continual assistance to quell protests over austerity or electoral fraud. To this point, the Mexican military has loyally sustained rather than threatened civilian rule, but its loyalty is not to democracy.

The Party and Electoral Systems

Integral to both state corporatism and centralization is the dominance of the Institutional Revolutionary Party (PRI). The editors hypothesize that deeply institutionalized competitive parties are conducive to stable democracy. The PRI is deeply institutionalized. It has held power longer than any other party in Latin America and has reached widely into society. Yet this institutionalization has been conducive to a distinctly undemocratic stability. It has helped to encapsulate groups and to preclude alternative institutionalized parties.

From independence until the revolution, parties were mostly political clubs. The elections in which they participated "were not a mechanism of popular voting but a legitimization of military force."[31] Of seventy-one governments (1823–1911), only seventeen were elected by constitutional norms. Even these involved indirect elections, open balloting, and so forth. The elected president almost always came from the incumbent party or group. Nonetheless, all new governments felt obliged to seek popular-constitutional legitimization through elections. Again, democratic ideology is juxtaposed to undemocratic reality.

Even after the revolution, parties continued to be weak, transitory, dependent on a single leader, without mass bases, and multitudinous. Then, however, a new party, continually juggled and deepened from 1929 to 1946 (when it became the PRI), replaced anarchic conflict and made elites play by institutionalized and legal rules. From 1929 to 1933, the number of parties dropped from fifty-one to four.[32] Mass organizations were incorporated. Civilian rulers built a strong institution that could organize and distribute resources, thus helping to subordinate the military. Such developments are often associated with transitions to democracy, but in Mexico, competition among elites did not encompass open public contestation, and mass incorporation was corporatist.

Not surprisingly, then, the PRI has not concentrated on the functions expected of democratic parties. Its main mission has been neither to aggregate nor to articulate demands. It has not truly competed for power. Although it has always been—until now—"in power," the PRI has not had a major role in policymaking. Instead, it has concentrated on other party functions but has directed them to the service of the government of which it is really a part (even though party and government personnel are formally distinct). These functions include mobilizing support for the regime; suppressing dissent; gathering and manipulating information; distributing welfare and patronage; engaging in political socialization and recruitment; handling particularistic grievances; and providing an ideological rationale for government action. Unlike what one expects of democratic party systems, PRI's hegemonic rule has sustained socioeconomic inequalities, and the PRI wins its largest vote from the least privileged groups.

But the PRI has stumbled into critical difficulties. Once more, we see where new challenges to political stability suggest increased hopes for democratization. So integral is the PRI to the regime that all the regime difficulties already cited (e.g., the beleaguered presidency and the need for decentralization) are PRI difficulties as well. In fact, the PRI is crucial to the overall crisis of the "political class" that has so adeptly managed key aspects of Mexico's postrevolutionary affairs.[33] The party is not legitimizing the regime as it once did. Very high abstention rates (roughly 50 percent in 1979 and 1985) and the PRI's declining share of the votes cast illustrate the problem (see Table 11.1). In fact, PRI's decline suddenly accelerated in 1988 when even official tallies gave the party only a slim majority in the presidential vote and in congressional seats. One could imagine the PRI as the "party of pluralities," flanked by a powerful Right and Left. PRI's invincibility appears shattered.

PRI's crisis is a culmination of both relatively sudden problems, such as the imposition of austerity, and long-run problems. Perhaps a party built to handle a basically rural and uneducated society is ill-equipped for modern Mexico. Perhaps a party established without true democratic functions finds itself unprepared to compete openly for citizen support.[34] Efforts to reform the PRI naturally produce further tensions within the party.

In truth, most PRI reforms (at least until now) have been aimed less at democratizing *per se* than at reviving legitimacy and combating opposition parties.[35] Probably the most ambitious (pre-1980s) reform attempt, undertaken by PRI president Carlos Madrazo in the mid-1960s, envisioned primaries and some separation of party from government. It was beaten back by vested PRI interests. In 1986, a new "democratic tendency" was immediately denounced by party and labor leaders as disloyal, selfish, and misleading—since PRI is continually perfecting its democracy. Whatever its motives, the movement at first carefully stressed its party credentials and limited its call for reform. But from the outset it proposed increased dialog within the party and with groups outside it, and it challenged the key practice of presidential appointment of successors by suggesting that "precandidates" resign ministerial posts and campaign openly before the public. Even before it split from the PRI to run against it in 1988, the movement had received well over a year of extraordinarily extensive, daily media coverage, as it has energetically carried its message around the country. Nevertheless, during that time, de la Madrid followed traditional practice by handpicking the PRI's next candidate for president, and therefore the next president, Carlos Salinas de Gortari.

If democracy has been weak within the PRI, it has also been weak in the party system overall. Granted, opposition parties have existed and some have expressed considerable dissent. But until recently, they have served mostly to legitimize PRI–regime rule. In fact, opposition parties were largely government-created in the 1940s and 1950s. Co-optation was the norm at least until the 1970s.

On the Left, legal parties have usually been tied to the left wing of the PRI. The Popular Socialist Party, historically connected with mainstream labor, is the main example. Since the 1970s, however, independent leftist parties have arisen. The Communist Party, formed in 1919 but denied electoral registration from 1945 to 1979, has been the major party in recent socialist coalitions. But at least until 1988, the coalitions repeatedly split (as on whether to join rightist parties in pressing for free elections). Moreover, even when united, the electoral Left has had very little mass appeal.[36] This weakness reflects the lack of an organized independent Left in Mexican society, particularly given the state corporatism encapsulating labor and the peasantry. But in 1988 Cuauhtémoc Cárdenas (son of the revered ex-president) led dissident leftist PRI members into a powerful coalition with mostly leftist parties (although perhaps the campaign was as "populist" as "leftist"). The official count gave the coalition a startling second place with over three in ten votes. If (but it is not an easy if) the coalition could be solidified at local levels, and show itself not to be primarily a personalistic or protest phenomenon, Mexico could take a major step toward multiparty democracy.

As Table 11.1 shows, the Right has had a much stronger sustained electoral presence, concentrated almost fully in one party. The National Action Party (PAN), formed in 1939, has functioned mostly as an institutionalized opposition, not pressing seriously to defeat the PRI. Recently, though, a significant

Table 11.1. Electoral Support for the PRI and the PAN, 1946–1985 (Official Tallies)

YEAR	% of Vote for Presidency		% of Vote for Chamber of Deputies		Seats in Chamber of Deputies		
	PRI	PAN	PRI	PAN	PRI	PAN	OTHER
1946[a]	78	—[b]	—	—	143	4	0
1952	74	8[b]	—	—	154	5	2
1958	90	9	—	—	152	6	3
1961	—	—	90	8	172	5	1
1964	89	11	86	12	175	20[c]	15
1967	—	—	83	12	176	20	16
1970	86	14	80	14	178	20	15
1973	—	—[d]	70	15	189	25	20
1976	99	—	80	9	196	20	22
1979	—	—	70[e]	11	296	43	61
1982	72	16	69	18	299	51	50
1985[f]	—	—	65	16	289	41	71

Sources: Pablo González Casanova, *Democracy in Mexico* tr. Danielle Salti (London: Oxford University Press, 1970), pp. 199–200; Secretaría de Gobernación, *Diario Oficial*, various; Comisión Federal Electoral; Dale Story, "The PAN, the Private Sector, and the Future of the Mexican Opposition." In *Mexican Politics in Transition*, ed. Judith Gentleman (Boulder, CO.: Westview Press, forthcoming), Table 11.3, drawing on various sources.

a. 1946 was the PRI's first year; PRI forerunners had claimed 98% and 94% of the vote in the 1934 and 1940 presidential elections, respectively.

b. The PAN was not the major opposition winner.

c. Since 1964, opposition seats have been based on outright district victories but overwhelmingly on PR; I show the total figures.

d. The PAN did not field a candidate.

e. Starting in 1979, the new PR procedure took effect; I report the simple plurality vote rather than the separate, but quite close, PR vote.

f. Preliminary results for 1988 show the PRI claiming just over half the presidential vote (51%) followed by the leftist Cárdenas coalition with nearly one-third of the votes (31%) and the PAN with just over one-sixth (17%), and claiming 260 of 500 Chamber seats (with 139 for the leftist coalition and 101 for the PAN).

portion of the party has favored all-out competition in a democratic setting. Joined by the independent Left, the PAN advocates honest elections. It takes the lead in championing federalism and the separation of powers. Unlike the PRI, it selects candidates rather openly. Like the PRI and the opposition in general, however, the PAN usually fails to offer specific alternatives to PRI–government policies. Indeed, its ideology (including links to Catholic thought) has usually been ambiguous, though a business orientation is increasingly marked. The PAN's appeal is limited to certain regions, particularly in the north and urban areas, and to privileged groups. It does not even run candidates in many districts around the nation. It does not attract a major portion of labor or the peasantry the way, for example, some Christian-democratic parties have done (e.g., in Chile and Venezuela). Much of its vote has been a protest vote.

Opposition parties have gained more freedom and importance with the reforms inaugurated in 1977 and modified in 1986. Previous electoral reform had been very limited. Universal suffrage was achieved in 1954 and 1973 reforms on a 1918 base. Since 1963, the regime has reversed a 1929–1954 trend that greatly inhibited opposition-party formation and representation. The 1977–1986 reforms went much further with democratization. They allowed parties to register more easily and granted public funds and free media time. Most dramatic, however, was the procedure for modified proportional representation in the Chamber of Deputies. While 300 seats were still determined by plurality vote by district, first 100 and then 200 seats were open to a PR system; whereas the 100 were reserved for minority parties, the 200 were not, but then the majority party was restricted to a 350-seat maximum.[37] Even critics on the Left and the Right have generally acknowledged that the electoral system now provides more freedom, information, exposure, and alternative positions. Indeed, the 1988 elections indicated how profound the changes facilitated by the reform might be.

Why the opening? Mostly, the regime tried to arrest its declining legitimacy and respond in a controlled way to cries for democratization. Moreover, the regime wanted to make sure that dissent is institutionalized, not spontaneous.[38] Possibly, the regime also hoped to strengthen the electoral Left a bit to offset the PAN's growth. Nonetheless, to understand the regime's purposes is to understand that it still contemplated no full-blown democratization. Thus, several "reform" provisions aimed at insuring the PRI a legislative majority even were it to gain fewer than half the votes; a major problem is continued PRI dominance on the electoral body that supervises elections. Additionally, certain PRI leaders have blocked measures such as imposing reform on states.[39]

The regime's disposition to increase freedom, choice, and competitiveness in the party system without democratically risking its rule has been verified in recent elections. Those of 1979, 1982, and 1983 were unusually clean. Opposition strength increased to where, in 1983, it captured mayoralties in five state capitals. Putting the best face on it, regime and PRI leaders claimed proof of competitiveness. Led on by presidential pledges to honor electoral results, and by foreign press and governmental attention stimulated by recent democratization in Latin America, many looked toward imminent elections for much further democratization (including opposition governorships). How unrealistic they appeared in the 1984–1987 period. Resorting to an unspecifiable but apparently ample degree of fraud, the PRI took all cities in question in 1984, and all governorships in the next two years. Regime officials denounced critics of the elections for promoting foreign models at the expense of national sovereignty.

The regime would strengthen oppositions but, unlike true democratizers of the Betancourt stripe, not to the point that those oppositions could win.[40] For the real function of Mexican elections is still not to select parties, leaders, and policies through open choice, but rather to offer the hope, mobility, and regularized renewal necessary to maintain support for the regime.

Increasingly, however, voices are being raised against ratifying rather than democratic elections. Protest intensified with the 1986 Chihuahua elections. Hunger strikes, roadblocks, demonstrations, boycotts, and repeated denunciations ensued. The bishop ordered church closed one Sunday (though the Vatican overruled him). Clearly, protest was not limited to the PAN. Nor was it transient. On the contrary, the imposed PRI rulers in Chihuahua have had a hard time. Nationally, civic groups, religious leaders, and independent leftist parties joined the PAN in an unprecedented national alliance. They focused their attention on one issue—free elections. They established a National Forum for Effective Suffrage. They made specific proposals, including ones dealing with electoral financing and supervision. The regime, they said, "has for many years paralyzed national democratic development."[41]

And all this preceded the 1988 elections. Pressures for free and honest elections have become (and will likely remain) stronger than ever before. In fact, debate over fraud brought Mexico near a constitutional brink in 1988 as repeated large demonstrations and severe confrontations emerged over ratifying the reported results, access to stored ballots (blocked by the military), and calls for immediate new elections. So hard did major oppositions press their claims that some believe the regime ultimately bought acquiescence largely by committing itself in negotiation to more democratic procedures in future elections. In sum, prospects for free, clean elections are stronger than ever, but they are still uncertain.

Performance and Support

Until the 1970s at least, Mexico's strong civilian rule brought widely envied economic success and societal support. Like many nations in Latin America, Mexico relied heavily on import substitution. Unlike others, Mexico achieved average annual economic growth of over 6 percent from 1940 to 1970, and held its inflation low (under 5 percent annually) in the latter half of the period.

Economic growth promoted enormous social change. Today, roughly two-thirds of the population live in urban communities of 2,500 or more. Only about one-third of the labor force remains in agriculture. A large middle class has developed, though it is still dwarfed by the lower class. Mexico has pulled itself to an average position among the larger, relatively developed Latin America nations with its 65-year life expectancy at birth, its infant mortality rate of fifty-six per 1,000 live births, its 83-percent adult literacy, and its dramatic improvements in caloric intake, access to primary schools, and energy consumption.[42] In turn, the regime has used economic growth in playing a prominent if selective role in social modernization. Even amid socioeconomic crisis in 1986, the president could point out that 86 million school textbooks were distributed free that year, while one in three Mexicans was in school, and that, from 1970 to 1986, the average number of years of schooling for the over-fifteen population had doubled (from three to six).[43]

Of course, even official national figures show not just progress but underdevelopment. Moreover, these figures obscure regional and class inequality, both tragically high in Mexico. Such outcomes have been consistent with Mexico's striking internal contrasts in the distribution of power and freedom. In fact, government policies have contributed to inequalities. Promotion of capital-intensive industrialization has brought severe problems for rural Mexico and for employment of the less privileged. Hyperurbanization often means urban dwellers also suffer from a lack of piped water and sewage systems, and from increasing water, soil, and air pollution. Government social expenditures and services have been very unequally directed, in ways that reward some potentially dangerous groups while repressing and marginalizing others. Health benefits for unionized workers are a good example. Consistent with Mexico's elite pluralism, a wide network of private organizations, including schools, universities, and hospitals are available for the privileged.[44] Consequently, economic successes under civilian rule have been compatible with what a World Bank study called one of the world's worst profiles of income distribution.[45] As Table 11.2 shows, the profile did not improve even during decades of growth and selective mobility.

Table 11.2. Income Distribution in Mexico, 1950–1977[a]

Income Group (deciles)	Percentage of Income Earned		
	1950	1963	1977[b]
1–2 (lowest 20 percent)	4.7	3.5	3.3
3–5	12.7	11.5	13.4
6–8	23.7	25.4	28.2
9–10 (highest 20 percent)	58.9	59.6	55.1

Source: Daniel C. Levy and Gabriel Székely, *Mexico: Paradoxes of Stability and Change*, 2nd ed. (Boulder, CO.: Westview Press, 1987): Table 5.6, based on data from ECLA for 1950 and 1963, and Mexico's Secretaría de Programación y Presupuesto for 1977.

a. Similar but even more extreme data are reported in Werner Baer, "Growth with Inequality: The Cases of Brazil and Mexico," *Latin American Research Review* 21, no. 2 (1986): p. 198.

b. 1977 is the last year for which data are available. Although debate exists over whether distribution improved in the immediately ensuing years, it has certainly worsened in the last few.

Thus, or at least thus far, hypotheses linking economic growth to the likelihood of democratic government are not supported in Mexico. Nor does Mexico fit the bureaucratic-authoritarian notion that dependent industrialized development leads at a certain point to instability followed by military rule. Instead, Mexican economic and social modernization has long reinforced stable, undemocratic civilian rule. Still, significantly, such modernization has also increased pressures for democratization.

However much long-term socioeconomic modernization brings pressures, it is probably the recent economic reversal that has most clearly brought pressures. Economic crisis dominated the 1980s. Many see its roots in policies designed for political, not economic, efficiency that built support from business, the middle class, organized labor, and even less privileged groups: protracted import substitution; a variety of credits and subsidies (e.g., for energy, universities, public transportation); low taxes; and bloated public employment. Unfortunately, the government's income increasingly failed to meet its expenditures and huge borrowing resulted. Added to all this, world oil prices fell sharply. And so, Mexico came to face a foreign debt of over $100 billion, blocked and even negative growth, inflation rates of roughly 100 percent, and socially devastating declines in employment and real wages.

No one knows how much economic disaster will undermine political strength. What we do know is that careful manipulation of the fruits of economic success has long been associated with political strength and high support levels. That manipulation long helped sustain a myth of continual progress, which provided legitimacy. In fact, Mexicans have taken pride in their political system and credited it for many of the social and personal material successes they have seen, despite cynicism about politicians and low evaluations of the daily performance of government. Even much of the Left has granted legitimacy for the regime's progressive record in some socioeconomic and particularly nationalist matters.[46]

A decline in long-standing legitimacy is illustrated by attitudes toward corruption; perhaps an increasingly modernized society has decreasing tolerance for it. In any case, corruption is a target of broadly rising popular discontent with a struggling system. And corruption is a target because it recently exceeded vaguely institutionalized limits, under President López Portillo. Thus, de la Madrid made what appeared to be the most serious in a line of presidential commitments to curb corruption. Some measures were taken, such as requiring financial statements from top government appointees and punishing a few ex-officials. By virtually all accounts, however, the clean-up campaign was disappointing. Explanations are varied but, historically, corruption has figured in the regime's performance and legitimacy. We have already seen that opportunities for corruption helped bring the military under civilian control. Additionally, corruption has provided some flexibility in an often unresponsive bureaucracy. It has provided an incentive for major and minor actors to seek rewards within the system and to rely on the peaceful turnover of personnel. It has provided glue for many implicit political pacts among elites and has been integral to patron-client and state-society relationships.

Whether corruption on the Mexican scale is compatible with significant democratization is uncertain. I think it is not. At the same time, corruption is illustrative of factors that may now increasingly undermine legitimacy even as the system has not yet found satisfactory alternatives, democratic or otherwise.

· **THEORETICAL ANALYSIS** ·

I have tried to show how several factors commonly associated with democratic stability have in Mexico long contributed to stable civilian rule that is not democratic. I have referred throughout to this study's hypotheses about democracy, but I now summarize the argument in the explicit context of those hypotheses. A major problem in so doing is that the hypotheses deal with factors that contribute to democracy, whereas Mexico is not a democracy. Repeatedly, we identify where Mexico has lacked a characteristic associated with democracy, but that offers only indirect evidence to sustain the hypothesis.

Political Culture and Legitimacy

We have seen that political legitimacy in Mexico has been high, though diminishing. Mexicans have been remarkably accepting of their political system. Whether because of a national trait of stoicism, or the fear of disorder, or belief in the regime's positive orientations, Mexicans have at a minimum not rebelled even when their aspirations have been long frustrated, and many have maintained pride in their system.[47]

With respect to democratic values, works on Mexico's "national character" have often depicted hierarchical, authoritarian, submissive, and other undemocratic inclinations. They suggest that such character traits help promote Mexico's authoritarian politics; political culture both explains and legitimizes the political system. On the other hand, most social scientists have been either skeptical or hostile to such interpretations. I am inclined to the Purcells' position: Political culture appears to reinforce the system but it is "striking how much of Mexican politics can be comprehended by a model of the rational political actor."[48] Others argue that the political culture is basically at odds with the political structure. They find that Mexicans support participation and dissent and oppose censorship.[49]

If evidence on deep values remains inconclusive, evidence on behavior is not. Mexico's regime has not been precariously superimposed on a society filled with democratic practices. The society never was so constituted, and the revolution brought new and strong but mostly undemocratic institutions. State corporatism goes hand-in-hand with hierarchical, authoritarian rule inside mass institutions such as unions. And it goes hand-in-hand with limited mass participation, encapsulated and restricted to official channels; patrimonial networks;

and petitions rather than aggregated demands. Allowing for recent signs of increased grassroots participation, the rule has been to hope that government acts. Efficacy increases with socioeconomic status, however.[50] Participation by elites is much freer and more influential, but elite institutions (media, intellectual publications, businesses, private schools, and universities) often operate undemocratically. Pluralism exceeds democracy.

Yet elites display a behavioral norm hypothesized (in this book and elsewhere) to be powerfully associated with democracy. This is the disposition to compromise. Ongoing politics confirm our historical (postrevolutionary) evidence of flexibility, bargaining, moderation, restraint, and pacts that avoid "fights to the finish."[51] In Mexico, acceptance of such norms has contributed to regime consolidation and stability without democracy. First, though elite pacts in democracies often limit mass participation, Mexico's corporatist mass inclusion is distinctly antidemocratic. Second, the restraint in the elite pacts has covered the exclusion of open, organized competition for rulership.

Overall, my view is that the Mexican case presents interesting information on the relationship between political culture and democracy, but not information that strongly confirms or disconfirms major project hypotheses.

Historical Sequences

Mexico scores low on the historical dimensions associated with democracy. Mexico lacks sustained, successful democratic precedents. In fact, it has had few experiments with democratic government. If the present regime has precedents, they are chiefly authoritarian. Where it democratizes, it innovates.

Moreover, Mexico has not followed Dahl's favored route of early liberal contestation followed by mass incorporation.[52] Rather, Calles, Cárdenas, and others adeptly incorporated mass organizations into a corporatist system. If elite pacts in nations like Venezuela have limited the masses' ability to obtain socioeconomic benefits, Mexico's pacts excluded democracy. Mexico's pacts were aimed at controlling masses mobilized by the revolution and established viable, perhaps ingenious, alternatives to open elite contestation for power. Such is the conventional scholarly wisdom on sequences, which I accept. However, if one were to highlight the persistent marginality of unorganized Mexico and perhaps the rise of new groups, or if one were to reserve "inclusiveness" for a more independent mass participation, then Mexico might rank low on that dimension. In that case, recent political reforms expanding contestation, coupled with longer-standing and expanding personal freedoms, might then give some sense of liberalization preceding inclusiveness.

Class, Ethnic, and Religious Cleavages

Key hypotheses on class structure and cumulative cleavages do not suggest favorable conditions for democracy in Mexico. The distribution of wealth is terribly unequal, as data on income show. Despite massive land reform, large agribusiness and an impoverished, massive peasantry divide the land very unequally in terms of both the size and desirability of plots. Mexican agriculture is not characterized by middle-class farming. Moreover, many cleavages are cumulative. A common disadvantaged profile would include low-income, Indian-Mestizo, peasant, and rural south.

Indians form the largest ethnic minority, perhaps 10 percent of the population (depending on definition), though ethnic diversity is largely determined by the "European-Indian" mixes among Mestizos. The revolution brought some respect for Indian identity, and pockets of self-governance exist (with some direct democratic selection of leaders and policies). Mostly, however, the Indian population continues to be either marginalized or integrated into a servile underclass, despite some mobility for individuals. In turn, the "rule of law" and the state are often seen as oppressive alien forces by Indian communities. Of interest are increasing signs of ethnically based political demands.[53] Overall, however, Indian distinctiveness hardly translates into pluralist politics.

The regime has been effective in defusing the destabilizing potential of great societal diversity and cumulative cleavages. One way has been to grant autonomy to groups and institutions (e.g., religious) that avoid mainstream politics. This, of course, fits Linz's now classic notion of authoritarian regimes.[54]

Second, the regime handles much of its politics in ways that cut across class cleavages—not on basic distributive policies but on symbolic and organizational ones. Symbolically, it has successfully used nationalism even if the concept means somewhat different things to different groups. Organizationally, it has structured itself on "vertical" patron-client relationships. This reinforces hierarchy and other undemocratic societal norms. The "formation of horizontal alliances based on common class interests is impeded" and the relationships serve "to maintain the separation between ideology and its social base."[55]

Third, as noted earlier, the regime has been sophisticated in managing privileged groups differently from other groups. Allowing for important flexibility, and other qualifications, state relationships with mass organizations are corporatist, whereas state relationships with elite groups are much more pluralist. But autonomous elite organizations have not usually been run democratically, nor, perhaps more to the point, have they pressured for democratization. Instead, they have normally accepted a stable nondemocracy that has granted them considerable material reward and a substantial if restricted degree of freedom.[56]

State Structure and Strength

Although state strength is a necessary condition for democratic stability, it is not sufficient. Lack of strength may doom a democratic experiment, but in Mexico state strength has meant the stability of an undemocratic system.

Building authority was a historic accomplishment of the postrevolutionary regime. The regime's stability is unique in both historical and comparative perspective. The regime has centralized power, maintained order, and preserved civilian rule. It has created an adept political class, while controlling mass groups and excluding organized challenges to its rule. Nonetheless, the state has not been the nearly omnipotent political force that much of the literature on Mexican authoritarianism has depicted. Its power has been limited by business and the middle class, and it has had to work out deals and make compromises with organized labor and even with less privileged groups. We have seen, for example, that the state lacked the capacity to tax sufficiently to pay for the political bargains it struck. A further qualification is that the regime's legitimacy and strength have substantially weakened in recent years.

One element in the regime's political strength was its early and sustained control over key parts of the economy. Unaccompanied by great bureaucratic professional autonomy from partisan politics, such statism is hypothesized to diminish prospects for democracy. However, it is simply impossible to know whether a causal relationship holds in Mexico, though the idea is in vogue in some business circles. What is clearer is that statism promoted civilian stability. It provided populist legitimacy; the nationalization of oil (1938) is a notable example. And it gave the regime tremendous political leverage.

Even though the Mexican economy has for the most part been privately owned, the state has owned such sectors as oil, mining, electricity, railroads, and, since 1982, banks. It has been heavily involved in regulation, subsidies, public investments, public credits, and so forth. It has established institutions such as the Central Bank (1925), the National Development Bank (1934), and a tremendous network of parastatal agencies. Measures such as the public expenditure's share of GDP show even a recently expanded state role (22 percent in 1970 to 44 percent in 1983).[57] But de la Madrid undertook a reversal. Citing counterproductive political effects of statism but concerned chiefly about economic crisis and inefficiencies, the president repeatedly cut state expenditures, employment, and subsidies. He sold off many state enterprises and brought Mexico into the GATT. His selection of Salinas de Gortari as his successor was apparently aimed at sustaining this historic change in economic policy. The consequences for democratization remain uncertain.

Political Structure and Leadership

The structural reality of Mexico's undemocratic civilian rule has been overwhelmingly centralized. Mexico's has been a presidential system with only limited roles for the judiciary, the legislature, and state and local government. More liberalism, though still restricted, has been evident regarding the rule of law, freedom of the media, and other liberties. But the party system was long characterized by PRI hegemony and integration with the regime. The PRI has generally been pragmatic. It has been at least somewhat inclusionary and has built a multiclass base. It has kept the vote for extremist parties very small. Yet, like other successes of the centralized party-regime, these have served civilian stability without democracy. Earlier interpretations of a political structure purposefully or ineluctably evolving into liberal forms have proved naive. On the other hand, the recent ineffectiveness of centralized forms has raised interesting speculations about future changes in Mexico's political structure.

Like the political structure, political leadership in postrevolutionary Mexico has proven unusually effective, and this effectiveness has been crucial to sustaining civilian rule without democracy. In fact, leadership and structure have been intertwined. Leaders have created and respected structures strong enough to condition behavior but flexible enough to allow for change and continual leadership.

Mexico takes second place to no nation in the skill and will of leadership to build a viable civilian system out of a past characterized mostly by weak political rule. I have highlighted the formative leadership acts of Carranza, Obregón, Calles, and Cárdenas in establishing legitimate, inclusive, centralized, civilian rule. Their acts provide powerful evidence for those political scientists who have championed the resurgence of "politics" and "choice" as major variables in studies of development. For example, Almond and Mundt write that a rational prediction from coalition theory would have pointed toward a military coup in the 1930s, but Cárdenas pulled off the "most striking" leadership success discussed in their volume featuring choice in a number of nations.[58] But unlike leaders in the Venezuelan case or in contemporary Argentina, Brazil, and other Latin American nations, Mexico's civilian leaders have not acted out of a commitment to democracy. On the contrary, some Mexican leaders have been hostile to democracy as a foreign, unworkable model, whereas others have been indifferent, and still others see democracy as an ideal too risky for Mexico today. Yet another view, however, is that realities have changed to where blocking democratization has become too risky.

Political learning has been crucial to Mexico's civilian success, but: (a) most of its leaders have not set democracy as their goal; and (b) the lessons have been undemocratic ones. Again, unlike Venezuela, with its *trienio,* not to mention Argentina, Brazil, and (at an extreme) Uruguay, Mexico has not had a modern liberal experiment that made headway before failing. Mexico would have to look back to the Reform for even a mixed record with liberal politics; the Madero interlude at the beginning of the revolution represents more recent failure. Most of the nineteenth century and the first two revolutionary decades suggested to elites the impracticality of decentralized systems and the dangers of excessive competition among elites. The revolution also impressed on them the need for elite pacts to forestall devastating actions by the masses.

By definition, an institutionalized system does not require continual acts of great formative leadership. Instead, Mexico managed to create a strong political class. This class has boasted many of the traits of successful professions: comparative autonomy, status, authority, and power; and control over training and rites of entry. Since the 1940s (with due qualifications for the deterioration elaborated above), Mexico's leaders have shaped politics in ways largely associated with establishing or even the smooth functioning of democracy. Yet for each aspect, the shaping has been distinctly undemocratic. The party has incorporated and legitimized but has also encapsulated. Sexennial rule has guaranteed mobility, turnover, renewal, and flexibility, but not public choice of leaders. Leaders have denounced disloyalty to the system and violence against the system, but have regarded some democratic dissent as disloyal and have used violence against peaceful dissenters. They have contained conflicts and managed crises enviably, but their tools have been predominantly undemocratic. Formative leaders shrewdly forged pacts among conflicting elites, and subsequent leaders have continually bargained, compromised, and disciplined themselves and their followers to accept less than optimal outcomes. Such procedures have excluded democratic opponents, limited mass participation, and often worked against mass material interests. Leaders have also subtly varied their approaches (depending on time, place, policy field, and constituency) in ways that show a greater sensitivity to and understanding of the public than most authoritarian regimes have, but such sophistication is not synonymous with democracy. Thus, we see corporatism mixed with pluralism, repression with cooptation and acquiescence, and continuity with flexibility.

Development Performance

Political leadership also played a major role in establishing Mexico's decades of high growth with low inflation. Legitimacy, stability, and incentives were crucial, though so were repression and sanctions. Why did sustained growth (inconsistency and reversal are recent phenomena) not produce democracy?

One explanation concerns Mexico's failure to attain the kind of sustained growth hypothesized to promote democracy, growth whose fruits are well distributed. Mexico's have been horribly maldistributed. A middle class has grown, but its commitment to democracy remains debatable (as it does in comparative politics generally), and much of Mexico's middle class has been dependent on the state. Moreover, the rise of the middle class has not been part of a generalized equalization of wealth or a broad movement involving coalitions with mass groups. In fact, a second possible explanation for the lack of democratization is that the growth argument is by itself irrelevant to democracy, or even that growth may serve the interests of reigning undemocratic regimes. In Mexico, growth has contributed to the legitimacy and power of such a regime. It has allowed it to manipulate, reward, and claim credit.

A third explanation, compatible with the first two, is that growth can help efforts at democratization (perhaps is even vital to them) but is just one factor and therefore insufficient.[59] I am inclined to believe that changes brought about by sustained growth in Mexico eventually promote pressures for broad democratization, that they in fact have contributed some to liberalization. In short, there is much to conventional development theses about an association between growth and social change, and between both and the chances for democracy.[60] Still, chances are far from certainties and it is difficult to gauge effects. The record shows that decades of growth produced comparatively limited pressures for democracy in Mexico, and more limited results. The strongest calls for democratization have come since growth was reversed.

To sum up, growth may well increase the chances for democracy eventually, but for a long time it may well shore up almost any regime. After all, the fall of Latin American authoritarian regimes, like Latin American democracies, has been tied to economic failure more than success. In Mexico, growth has been integral to the stability of civilian authoritarian rule.

International Factors

As with so many other variables in this comparative study, international factors hypothesized to be conducive to democratic stability have, in Mexico, long been conducive to stability without democracy. For one, Mexico has not been a significant target of external subversion since the regime consolidated power. But such fortune is much more likely to sustain than to create democracy. Second, the major source of diffusion—given realities of geography, continual back-and-forth migration, trade, investment, and cultural and media might—has long been the United States, a democracy. Third, Mexico has been a recipient of extraordinary foreign assistance from the United States and other democracies, though the emphasis is recent. Whereas the second and third realities are postulated to have democratizing influences even on undemocratic systems, Mexican leadership has limited the degree of political dependency and influence that accompany economic dependency on the United States.

Protecting itself from leftist subversion has been one reason for Mexico's progressive foreign policy. The only Latin American nation not to break diplomatic relations with Communist Cuba, Mexico was never targeted the way Bolivia, Venezuela, and others were. Comparatively sympathetic to the Sandinistas and to the guerrillas in El Salvador, Mexico again achieved an at least tacit agreement that leftists outside Mexico would not encourage independent leftists inside.

Into the bargain, such progressivism has enhanced legitimacy by demonstrating independence of the United States. Given a historical legacy of military conquest (costing Mexico much of her good land) and an ongoing contrast of wealth and culture, it is not surprising that Mexicans would feel alienation as well as respect for their neighbor. Something seen as a U.S. model—and liberal democracy as defined in this book fits here—is not simply seen positively. Moreover, to the degree that the United States has leverage stemming from its might, its priority for Mexico has been stability, not democratization. So, despite the fact that it has depended on the United States for almost two-thirds of its imports and exports, roughly 80 percent of its tourism, and roughly

70 percent of its foreign investment, Mexico has maintained a notable degree of independence from U.S. influence.[61]

• PROSPECTS AND POLICY IMPLICATIONS •

However much cited variables may have contributed to sustaining civilian stability without democracy, Mexican politics is changing. Of course, it has constantly changed, and one of the strengths of the system and its leadership has been the flexibility to modify a stable system. The question here is whether contemporary changes will add up to more than adaptation within a nondemocracy. In an important sense, factors that have reinforced stability have blocked democratization. That does not prove, however, that they will always do so. Nor does it suggest that instability is likely to produce democracy.[62] Major change is a necessary but insufficient condition for democratization.

Positive Prospects for Democratization

Numerous political uncertainties represent some hope for democratization. First, the erosion of undemocratic practices opens at least some possibility of democratic alternatives and strengthens opposition voices. Second, the regime's realization that traditional bases of stability are endangered can stimulate liberalizing moves aimed at protecting stability. Third, some of the uncertainties themselves involve a degree of opening. To be sure, the second and third points involve liberalization rather than transformation toward a democracy, as defined here. Nevertheless, just as Mexico has enjoyed several aspects of democracy, so it may increase the degree of democracy. Moreover, continued liberalization may, in turn, increase the pressures for such practices as free elections among truly competitive alternative parties. In fact, one can imagine the 1988 elections reinforcing many factors considered here as favorable to democratization.

The following recapitulates some of the major recent political changes that involve uncertainties. Regarding state-society relations, the degree of freedom (e.g., media freedom) has expanded. Middle-class, business, and even grassroots popular groups have organized more autonomously and become much more critical of the regime. Regarding centralized regime power, the presidency has been tarnished, the legislature is increasingly a forum of debate and dissent, and perceptions are widespread that geographical centralization is excessive, and that significant decentralization must somehow be achieved. Regarding the party system, the PRI (like the political class overall) has lost much of its strength, while an independent Left has appeared and the independent Right has grown substantially. For the middle class in particular, elections have become times of delegitimation more than popular affirmation. Pressures for honest elections are strong, perhaps undeniably so in the aftermath of the 1988 elections. The party and electoral reforms inaugurated in the 1970s have helped open the system significantly but have not settled the issue of how far the opening will go. Regarding the regime's performance, legitimacy has eroded and the economy—long central to the regime's strength—has fallen into crisis. Economic opening, even if ultimately successful in purely economic terms, might well reduce the regime's tools of control.

Political reform, uncertainty, and (regime) weakness have contributed to increased calls for democratization. Such calls are not new, of course. For years, some observers argued that democratization was necessary for socioeconomic development and, therefore, for political stability. These observations have not fared well, but perhaps they are valid in the long run. Or perhaps circumstances have changed enough in Mexico that they are now becoming valid. At any rate, previous calls for democratization have not been nearly as widespread and sustained as today's. Nor did they enjoy the degree of free space for development that dissenters now have.

Naturally, proponents of democratization are not united. They do not hold identical views of what democracy means, nor how to pursue it (though the broad coalition formed, in 1986, reinforced in 1988, around the banner of truly free elections is significant). Voices on the Right argue in terms partly consistent with major hypotheses of this project: a highly centralized state with massive power concentrated in an unchecked presidency, which exercises extensive corporate controls over society and the economy, is incompatible with democracy. By contrast, most of the Left argues that democratization requires a large and revitalized state assuming a central role in economic policy and social change. But many on the Right want merely a return to a successful undemocratic state that grants concessions to business, suppresses labor, and so forth. And many on the Left couple demands for a revitalized state with demands for increased autonomy of societal organizations and for internal democratization within labor unions, neighborhood organizations, and other institutions. Finally, one may question the sincerity of certain democratic banners on both the Right and the Left. For some, such banners are but a tool in the play for power. For others, democracy is a worthy pursuit, but principally a means toward higher priorities. Thus, some business leaders see democracy largely as a way to weaken government and achieve growth and profits, and some intellectuals see democracy as a means of mass mobilization to achieve better socioeconomic distribution and, eventually, socialism.

Another way to see hopeful signs for democratization is to focus on the many ways in which Mexico ranks high on variables associated with democracies. In terms of our variables, my thesis has been that Mexico shows that many of the variables are compatible with a civilian rule that is effective, stable, and undemocratic. That thesis has allowed, however, that Mexico's high standing on some of the variables may have built certain pressures for democratization. The notion of "zones" of lower and higher probabilities for democracy may be useful in assessing Mexico's future. Economic growth, industrialization, urbanization, the growth of a middle class, increased education and other indices of rising expectations among even the poorer classes, the persistence of at least formal structures of liberal government, growing if still inconclusive evidence of some political cultural affect for democracy—these and other factors put Mexico in a higher zone of probability for democracy than would have been the case even a couple of decades ago.[63]

Recent research on transitions to democracy also suggests some hopes for democratization in Mexico, though O'Donnell rightly labels Mexico "a type by itself" (largely because the regime is so institutionalized). First, authoritarian regimes constantly evolve. Second, transitions usually occur through evolution, not sudden overthrows. Third, democracy usually results from stalemate and dissensus, not from a clear plan based on consensus. Fourth, these transitions usually begin with elite calculations and initiatives, not independent mass mobilization. When the regime initiates liberalization, it runs risks of losing the initiative amid rising expectations and mobilizations, but it can sometimes control the pace of change, experiment, retreat, and so forth. Fifth, democratization often emerges from situations with seemingly low probabilities for it.[64] In sum, the lack of a clear or massive movement toward democracy in Mexico does not preclude democratization. And the experimental, evolutionary, regime-led notion of transition could allow further societal liberalizations involving press freedom, criticism (short of organized mass alternatives to the regime), and party and electoral reform. Reform within the PRI, expanded representation for oppositions, and opposition victories in localities and even states could occur without immediate threat to the regime's rule. Nor after the shock of 1988 does it seem naive to speculate on even the transfer of national government to the opposition, or at least on opposition appointments to cabinet positions.

The Brazilian case is particularly interesting for speculations on Mexico.[65] Brazilian authoritarian rule was comparatively long and economically successful on its own terms, with massive inequalities. Repression was comparatively limited in the years prior to transition. In fact, constitutional forms persisted almost throughout the dictatorial period, and the limited term of the presidency proved significant. Elections took on increasing importance even as the regime manipulated the rules. Transition was stimulated by long-term factors, but an economic downturn critically undermined support for the regime. Nonetheless, unlike some other cases, democratization was not precipitated by mass mobilizations but by elite accommodations. In short, the Brazilian case illustrates how democratization need not be an all-or-nothing proposition. This fact can make the prospect less threatening for the Mexican regime, which realizes that some political changes are necessary.

Negative Prospects for Democratization

But the factors that point away from full-blown democratization remain weighty. This is especially evident if we refer to democratization as a transition toward democratic government and not just further liberalization. Obviously, transformation is less common than continuity. Beyond that, Mexican authoritarianism has been uniquely long-lasting and institutionalized. Unlike other authoritarian regimes, Mexico's has always justified itself as permanent (albeit evolving) rather than transitory *en route* to democracy.

Whereas factors commonly associated with democracy are found in Mexico, others are not. Mexico lacks significant experience with democratic government (though I would emphasize the potential importance of increasing experience with liberalizing politics). Despite its declining legitimacy, the regime has not been discredited in the dramatic way that sometimes leads to democratic transitions (e.g., in Argentina) or that leads major actors to value democracy as an alternative system of rule. Not all the rising criticism of the Mexican regime concerns its lack of democracy. The political-cultural attachment of the masses to democracy is questionable, and elites have given uncertain evidence of such attachment. Opposition parties, indeed organized oppositions in general, have usually been limited. Corporatist controls have precluded both independent mass-based institutions (unions or parties) and sudden mobilization of the unorganized. The state retains a large role in politics and the economy. And poverty remains widespread, wealth painfully concentrated.

Prospects for any liberalization are also limited because of the risks of transition.[66] Fear is a central notion in the relevant literature; in Mexico, the fear of transition has dominated the perceived need for or benefits of transition. To be sure, even before the 1988 elections some in the regime, as well as critics, believed that the system required major changes. President de la Madrid spoke repeatedly of how changes in demographics, urbanization, education, communications, and class structure have created "a new vigor in society," a greatly expanded "civil society" that requires political changes. As in Colombia, a widespread perception is that conditions that called for structures of restricted, stable civilian rule have been superseded. But, also as in Colombia, powerful political incentives are built into the status quo. Even the "soft-liners" within the Mexican regime have focused on modernizing measures (including liberalizing ones) that would not produce a liberal democracy. Cornelius writes that the regime, and indeed the elites in general, regard two-party or multiparty competition for and alternation in power as an alien concept.[67] "Democracy" has meant the PRI as the "party of majorities," with opposition voice allowed. Some argue that a return to economic normalcy is all that is required for politics to return to normal. And many, whatever their ultimate hopes, believe that times of great economic change, and of some inevitable political change, require steadying reliance on established political structures and practices.

Crucially, fear of transition is not limited to the regime or even the elites overall. As Monsiváis has emphasized, the regime has succeeded in portraying alternatives to it as disasters, as fascism, communism, or anarchy.[68] Anarchy is perhaps particularly frightening to many Mexicans, perhaps because of the nation's history. Consequently, another point about democratization in nations like

Venezuela is relevant in Mexico, again with a twist. As Levine writes in this volume, a major reason for Venezuela's democratic stability is that citizens realize they "can afford little else," given authoritarian alternatives. In Mexico, many citizens have found that they could well afford something other than democracy: Their system has provided them with relative social peace and political tranquility, economic growth, mobility, selective rather than pervasive repression, a degree of political liberty, and substantial national pride.

In sum, the prospects for democracy are brighter than they have been since the revolution. And yet, they are very uncertain. The prospects for stability are perhaps dimmer than they have been for several decades. And yet, they are bright, remaining brighter than the prospects for democracy. Such contrasts reflect the way Mexico's strong, undemocratic political system has long functioned.

U.S. Policy

If democratization merits increasing serious attention, but democracy still appears only a possibility in Mexico, what should the United States do? The conventional scholarly wisdom has been: not much. I concur.

I do not believe that all attempts by one nation to encourage democracy in another are wrong, but I do believe that several demanding criteria ought to be present. They usually are not. First, a viable alternative to the present regime must exist. Second, that alternative should be more democratic than the present regime. Third, a rather limited role by the foreign nation should have a high probability of making a substantial positive impact.

None of these conditions has characterized the case of Mexico and the United States, although the first two points could be debated in light of the 1988 elections. Much of this chapter has concerned why no viable alternative to the regime has been organized. Leading opposition parties and groups have not proved their democratic credentials. And even if U.S. policymakers believed a viable and democratic alternative existed, their efforts would likely have either an insignificant or negative impact. For one thing, the Mexico–U.S. relationship is particularly sensitive, given historical, geographical, economic, and cultural realities. For example, President Wilson's military interventions and threats in the early revolutionary years contributed to turmoil, not democracy, and left a legacy of mistrust about the democratic giant to the north. In the early 1980s, perceptions that Ambassador John Gavin and U.S. Republican Party leaders supported the PAN probably hurt that opposition party, as the PRI identified it with a still-arrogant, interfering neighbor.

Beyond the particular sensitivities of Mexico–U.S. relations lie broader obstacles to government efforts to encourage democracy. Whitehead concludes that in peacetime, the overall international role in democratization is subordinate; U.S. efforts in Latin America have with reason been viewed as "showcase" and short-term.[69] Whether or not the United States deserves any credit for the wave of Latin American democratization in the 1980s, its clearest successes have come in protesting grievous human-rights abuses; such abuses have been less characteristic of Mexico than of the bureaucratic-authoritarian regimes. Moreover, this comparative study of Third World democracies reminds us of the variability, complexity, and uncertainty of the conditions that promote democracy. In any event, particular cases present their own dynamics, as we have repeatedly seen for Mexico. Even if we could identify clearly the factors associated with democracy, we would be left with a standard research-policy question: How do we move from the present to the desired future? Rallying cries of the U.S. Right and simplifications by both Democratic and Republican administrations to the contrary, we know little about this.

In reality, U.S. pressures have not concerned democratization, or most other aspects of Mexican domestic politics, as much as Mexican economic and foreign policy. Again, we really do not know what economic and foreign policies, against which the United States has brought pressure, have been identifiably associated with the stability of Mexico's civilian rule. Regarding foreign policy, for example, the United States should therefore recognize that Mexico has based its foreign policy not on naive leftist notions or anti-Americanism but on sober judgments about its own security from external threats and from domestic delegitimation. If U.S. pressure can "work"—in the sense of influencing Mexican foreign policy, and if times of Mexican economic weakness make some such influence possible—impacts on Mexico's political stability may be negative.

A more reasonable course for the United States is to support Mexico's political stability. This can be done in the hope that stability will allow for democratization, but mostly in the realization that instability is even less likely to produce democratization, and that stability is important on other grounds. If these admittedly debatable assumptions are accepted, several oft-cited measures to support stability make sense. Some, such as easing terms on debt payment, reducing protectionism, and providing economic aid, are not particular to Mexico but have special relevance there. Others are more particular to Mexico, such as guaranteeing the safety valve of migration and not discouraging tourism and investment by portraying Mexico as too lenient with drug dealers and Communists. Moreover, the United States should temper the arrogance that views Mexico's troubles as the simple result of poor policy, not to mention political-cultural backwardness. Instead, the United States should respect the successes of the Mexican political system and the enormous difficulties and dilemmas of meeting present challenges. And the United States should realize that many of these challenges result from factors for which Mexico is not solely responsible, such as excessive U.S. bank loans, high U.S. interest rates, and fallen oil prices.

None of this is to deny the U.S. government a right to express critical opinions about Mexican politics, including its markedly undemocratic aspects, but advocacy and heavy pressure are different matters. Nor is it to ignore the possible positive impact on democratization of some private actors. For example, recently increased foundation aid to academic institutions and scholarship recipients seems legitimate and hopeful, though effects would typically be indirect, long-term, and difficult to gauge.

To conclude, the possibilities of external influence on democratization are limited—and largely negative. And there is much to lose. Things can get worse. Regarding U.S. self-interest, this should be clear from the stability, markets, labor, resources, and so forth, that Mexico has provided. For Mexicans, there is also much to lose. On the political side, even restricted degrees of freedom and liberalization count. Unparalleled stability stands out more in Mexico. There is also much to criticize and work for politically. Democratization is a prime example, but perhaps major improvements remain less likely than major losses.

Should Mexico continue to liberalize and even democratize without shattering its stability, it will have achieved a truly historic and magnificent political feat. Our understanding of the conditions for Third World democracy would be profoundly affected. For most of the century, however, Mexican reality has shown how many conditions conducive to sustained civilian rule can have neutral or even negative implications for democracy.

• NOTES •

I thank John Bailey and Gabriel Székely, as well as their series editors, for the comments on drafts of this chapter.

1. Mexico's population, over 80 million, ranks second in Latin America and eleventh in the world; its economic size ranks roughly fifteenth among market economies; and its geography makes its fate vital for the United States. I use democracy in the sense of a desired result, democratization as movement in that direction, and liberalization as movement in terms of at least increased freedoms.

2. On breakdown, see Juan Linz and Alfred Stepan, eds., *The Breakdown of Democratic Regimes* (Baltimore, MD: Johns Hopkins University Press, 1978). On democratization, see Guillermo O'Donnell, Philippe C. Schmitter, and Laurence Whitehead, eds., *Transitions from Authoritarian Rule: Prospects for Democracy* (Baltimore, MD: Johns Hopkins University Press, 1986).

3. Robert Scott, *Mexican Government in Transition* (Urbana: University of Illinois Press, 1964), pp. 16, 300–301.

4. See, for example, the citations and analysis in Daniel C. Levy and Gabriel Székely, *Mexico: Paradoxes of Stability and Change,* 2nd ed. (Boulder, CO: Westview Press, 1987), ch. 4.

5. Kenneth F. Johnson and Philip L. Kelly, "Political Democracy in Latin America," *LASA Forum* 16, no. 4 (1986): pp. 19–22, has the most recent data and points the reader to earlier sources.

6. Octavio Paz, *The Other Mexico: Critique of the Pyramid,* tr. Lysander Kemp (New York: Grave Press, 1972), pp. 102, 111. Some Indian villages enjoyed self-government in the precolonial and colonial eras.

7. See, for example, Juan Felipe Leal, "El estado y el bloque en el poder en México: 1867–1914," *Latin American Perspectives* 11, no. 2 (1975): p. 38.

8. A standard work on the integration is Arnaldo Córdova, *La formación del poder en México,* 8th ed. (Mexico City: Serie Popular Era, 1980).

9. Two major accounts are Tzvi Medín, *Ideología y praxis político de Lázaro Cárdenas* (Mexico City: Siglo XXI, 1976); and Wayne A. Cornelius, "Nation Building, Participation, Distribution: Reform Under Cárdenas." In *Crisis, Choice, and Change: Historical Studies of Political Development,* ed. Gabriel A. Almond, Scott C. Flanigan, and Robert J. Mundt (Boston: Little, Brown, 1973), p. 394, 429–462.

10. I use the terms as elaborated in Philippe C. Schmitter's widely cited "Still the Century of

Corporatism?" In *The New Corporatism*, ed. Frederick Pike and Thomas Stritch (Notre Dame, IN: University of Notre Dame Press, 1974), pp. 93–105.

11. On political marginality, see Pablo González Casanova, *Democracy in Mexico*, tr. Danielle Salti (London: Oxford University Press, 1970), pp. 126–134; on reacting, see Susan Kaufman Purcell, *The Mexican Profit-Making Decision: Politics in an Authoritarian Regime* (Berkeley: University of California Press, 1975).

12. See Evelyn Stevens, *Protest and Response in Mexico* (Cambridge, MA: MIT Press, 1974), pp. 276–277, on how activists have been unable to attract mass followings. On the consequences of early incorporation, see Robert R. Kaufman, "Mexico and Latin American Authoritarianism." In José Luis Reyna and Richard S. Wienert, *Authoritarianism in Mexico* (Philadelphia: ISHI, 1977), pp. 220–221.

13. See, for example, Jesús Silva Herzog, *La revolución mexicana en crisis* (Mexico City: Ediciones Cuadernos Americanos, 1944), pp. 22–34; and for a similar point on peasants, see Gerrit Huizer, "Peasant Organization in Agrarian Reform in Mexico." In *Masses in Latin America*, ed. Irving Louis Horowitz (New York: Oxford University Press, 1970), pp. 445–502.

14. Raúl Trejo Delarbre, "El movimiento obrero: Situación y perspectivas." In *México, hoy*, 5th ed., ed. Pablo González Casanova and Enrique Florescano (Mexico City: Siglo XXI, 1981), pp. 128–130.

15. Dale Story, *Industry, the State, and Public Policy in Mexico* (Austin: University of Texas Press, 1986), pp. 105, 195. See also John J. Bailey, *Governing Mexico: The Statecraft of Crisis Management* (London: MacMillan, forthcoming), ch. 6.

16. On intellectuals, see Roderic A. Camp, *Intellectuals and the State in Twentieth-Century Mexico* (Austin: University of Texas Press, 1985); on public universities, see Daniel C. Levy, *University and Government in Mexico: Autonomy in an Authoritarian System* (New York: Praeger, 1980).

17. While this case cannot settle the debate over whether national political democratization requires democratizing society's associational life, it is pertinent that Mexico's mass-based organizations are notoriously undemocratic. For example, both labor and peasant elections are controlled and corrupt. Practice varies among the associations of more privileged classes; many media, intellectual, and student associations are far from open and free. See, for example, Camp, *Intellectuals*, p. 225.

18. See especially Sergio Zermeño, *México: Una democracia utópica: El movimiento estudiantil del 68* (Mexico City: Siglo XXI, 1978). My views and further citations are found in Levy, *University*, pp. 28–33, 39–41.

19. In Frank Brandenburg's apt label for the regime, "liberal Machiavellian," "liberal" refers to tolerance more than the Dahl/O'Donnell-Schmitter sense of contestation. Brandenburg, *The Making of Modern Mexico* (Englewood Cliffs, NJ: Prentice Hall, 1964), pp. 141–165. Disturbing evidence of intolerance has long come from brutal repression of peasant actions and, recently, from reports about human-rights abuses including torture.

20. Jorge G. Castañeda, "Mexico at the Brink," *Foreign Affairs* 64 (Winter 1985–1986): p. 293.

21. Richard Fagen and William Tuohy, *Politics in a Mexican Village* (Stanford, CA: Stanford University Press, 1969).

22. Levy and Székely, *Mexico*, ch. 4.

23. González Casanova, *Democracy*, p. 68.

24. Alvaro Arreola Ayala, "Elecciones municipales." In *Las elecciones en México: Evolución y perspectivas*, ed. Pablo González Casanova (Mexico City: Siglo XXI, 1985), pp. 330–336. While some observers find local political participation minimal, others see competition within the PRI that includes citizen support for political wings or for candidates proposing popular policies (e.g., improvement of water or electrical systems).

25. Brian Latell, *Mexico at the Crossroads: The Many Crises of the Political System* (Stanford, CA: Hoover Institution, June 1986), pp. 23–25; Miguel de la Madrid, *Los grandes problemas nacionales de hoy* (Mexico City: Editorial Diana, 1982), p. 139.

26. Bailey, *Governing*, ch. 4. See also, on presidential power, Jorge Carpizo, *El presidencialismo mexicano*, 3d ed. (Mexico City: Siglo XXI, 1983).

27. Fernando Henrique Cardoso, "On the Characterization of Authoritarian Regimes in Latin America." In *The New Authoritarianism in Latin America*, ed. David Collier (Princeton, NJ: Princeton University Press, 1979), pp. 42–43.

28. Kevin J. Middlebrook, "Political Liberalization in an Authoritarian Regime: The Case of Mexico." In O'Donnell, Schmitter, and Whitehead, *Transitions from Authoritarian Rule: Latin America*, p. 140.
29. Norman Cox, "Changes in the Mexican Political System." In *Politics in Mexico*, ed. George Philip (London: Croom Helm, 1985), p. 20; Scott, *Mexican Government*, pp. 267–271.
30. A prominent recent source is David Ronfeldt, *The Modern Mexican Military: A Reassessment*. Monograph Series 16 (La Jolla, CA: Center for U.S.–Mexican Studies, University of California at San Diego, 1984).
31. Gustavo Ernesto Emmerich, "Las elecciones en México, 1808–1911: Surfragio electivo, no reelección?" In González Casanova, *Elecciones*, pp. 54–64.
32. Luis Javier Garrido, *El partido de la revolución institucionalizada 1929–45* (Mexico City: Siglo XXI, 1982); González Casanova, *Democracy*, p. 34.
33. This class has been comparatively distinct from the nation's economic elites, despite greatly overlapping interests. Martin C. Needler has compared it to the East European "new class" described by Djilas, except that it has been more legitimate and effective in its ownership of state power. See Needler, *Mexican Politics: The Containment of Conflict* (New York: Praeger, 1982), pp. 131–133. Intertwined with the official party, the political class has lacked career service and merit characteristics, but its strength has been tied to its politicization. Recently, however, the class's coherence has been weakened by a surge of technocrats who rise to high posts based on special educational credentials rather than apprenticeship with the party, elective office, public universities, mass organizations, and so forth. See, for example, Roderic A. Camp, "The Political-Technocrat in Mexico and the Survival of the Political System," *Latin American Research Review* 20, no. 1 (1985): pp. 97–118. Additionally, economic opening and diminishing ratios of state expenditures to GDP could mean diminished resources to reward and sanction (e.g., through subsidies and protectionism).
34. Bailey, *Governing*, ch. 7.
35. Implemented reforms have been limited to measures such as selecting candidates with local appeal and varying selection methods. PRI candidates for some 1984 municipal posts were selected after open party assemblies or secret votes rather than just by appointment from above. See Cox, "Changes," p. 28. The PRI has issued some statements critical of government economic policy.
36. On leftist weaknesses and platforms, see, for example, Barry Carr, "The PSUM: The Unification Process on the Mexican Left 1981–1985." In *Mexican Politics in Transition*, ed. Judith Gentleman (Boulder, CO.: Westview Press, forthcoming).
37. Congressional opposition parties unanimously voted against the 1986 legislation, calling it more marginal maneuvering than democratization. For details on the 1977 reform, see Luis Villoro, "La reforma política y las perspectivas de democracia." In González Casanova and Florescano, *México, hoy*, pp. 355–357. On the 1986 reform, see Juan Gerardo Reyes, "Iniciativa de MMH al Congreso," *Excélsior* (November 4, 1986). PR was first authorized in 1963, but the opposition could barely qualify.
38. Villoro, "Reforma," pp. 355–357; and Middlebrook, "Political Liberalization," pp. 126–128. Middlebrook concludes (p. 143) that the regime operated "from a position of strength." That is true in comparison with many transitions in Latin America, but his own analysis properly identifies challenges to which the Mexican regime felt compelled to respond.
39. Some states then chose reform anyway. See Jorge Madrazo, "Reforma política y legislación electoral de las entidades federativas." In González Casanova, *Elecciones*, pp. 293–302.
40. Terry Lynn Karl, "Petroleum and Political Pacts: The Transition to Democracy in Venezuela." In O'Donnell, Schmitter, and Whitehead, *Transitions: Latin America*, p. 217.
41. Advertisement in *Proceso* (September 1, 1986). On Chihuahua, see, for example, Francisco Ortiz P., "Baeza, acorralado," *Proceso* (June 8, 1987).
42. 1980 data from Bela Belassa, et al., *Toward Renewed Economic Growth in Latin America: Summary, Overview, and Recommendations* (Washington, DC: Institute for International Economics, 1986), pp. 56–57. For 1985, see Inter-American Development Bank, *Economic and Social Progress in Latin America, 1986 Report* (Washington, DC: IDB, n.d.), p. 314 (on Mexico); see also Table 1.1 herein.
43. Miguel de la Madrid Hurtado, "Cuarto informe de gobierno," *Comercio Exterior* 36, no. 9 (1986): p. 760.
44. See, for example, Daniel C. Levy, *Higher Education and the State in Latin America:*

Private Challenges to Public Dominance (Chicago: University of Chicago Press, 1986), pp. 114–170.

45. World Bank, *World Development Report, 1980* (Washington, DC: World Bank, 1980), pp. 156–157.

46. Gabriel A. Almond and Sidney Verba, *The Civic Culture* (Boston: Little, Brown, 1963); Ann L. Craig and Wayne A. Cornelius, "Political Culture in Mexico: Continuities and Revisionist Interpretations." In *The Civic Culture Revisited*, ed. Gabriel A. Almond and Sidney Verba (Boston: Little, Brown, 1980), p. 375. See also Fagen and Tuohy, *Political*, pp. 38–39, 136–137.

47. The three respective explanations of acceptance are emphasized in, for example, Paz, *The Other*, Fagen and Tuohy, *Politics*, and Almond and Verba, *Civic Culture* (1963). Observers are divided on whether there has been a significant increase in civil disturbances.

48. Susan Kaufman Purcell and John F. H. Purcell, "State and Society in Mexico: Must a Stable Polity Be Institutionalized?" *World Politics* 32, no. 2 (1980): pp. 204–205. See Craig and Cornelius, "Political," pp. 341, and 385–386, fn. 35, on the different positions. A prominent recent example of the causal political-cultural approach, bitterly denounced in Mexico, is Alan Riding, *Distant Neighbors: A Portrait of the Mexicans* (New York: Knopf, 1985).

49. John Booth and Mitchell Seligson, "The Political Culture of Authoritarianism in Mexico: A Reexamination," *Latin American Research Review* 19, no. 1 (1984): pp. 110–113. The authors report uniformly strong democratic values, though less among women, the less-educated, and the working class than in the middle class. But their data come from developed urban areas known for dissent from the PRI–regime. Also, expressed values do not seem quite so at odds with the system when one acknowledges that it permits some degree of free expression, demonstration, etc.; it does not permit organized alternatives, and the one issue on which the authors report a majority of undemocratic responses was on critics seeking office. Craig and Cornelius, "Political," pp. 348–350, report conflicting data regarding "working-class authoritarianism." Finally, the *New York Times*, November 17, 1986, reported that a poll of 1,576 Mexicans showed "envy" of U.S. democracy and economic strength, but in fact only 16 percent cited democracy as the main point.

50. Rafael Segovia, *La politicización del niño mexicano*, 2d ed, (Mexico City: El Colegio de México, 1982); Craig and Cornelius, "Political," p. 369. Family socialization and interrelations are often described as intolerant and undemocratic. However, the introduction of more participatory educational practices (e.g., Montessori schools) may have a democratizing influence.

51. In a sense, then, elites have developed a degree of "trust" in their pacts even though interpersonal trust is low. On the generally low degree of trust in Mexican society, see Craig and Cornelius, "Political," p. 372.

52. Robert Dahl, *Polyarchy: Participation and Opposition* (New Haven, CT: Yale University Press, 1971).

53. Guillermo Bonfil Batalla, "Los pueblos indígenas: Viejos problemas, nuevas demandas." In González Casanova and Florescano, *México, hoy*, pp. 100–107.

54. Juan J. Linz, "Totalitarian and Authoritarian Regimes." In *Handbook of Political Science*, vol. 3, ed. Fred I. Greenstein and Nelson W. Polsby. (Reading, MA: Addison-Wesley, 1975).

55. Respective quotations from Larissa Lomnitz, "Social Structure of Urban Mexico," *Latin America Research Review* 16, no. 2 (1982): p. 69; and Purcell and Purcell, "State and Society," p. 226.

56. Elite autonomous organizations do not usually serve as "training grounds" for democracy. The public university is the best example of a substantially autonomous organization that has trained most of Mexico's (undemocratic) political elite. Relevant skills are the ability to mobilize and manipulate mass groups, bargaining, and leadership.

57. Bailey, *Governing*, Table 6.1.

58. Gabriel A. Almond and Robert J. Mundt, "Crisis, Choice, and Change: Some Tentative Conclusions." In Almond and Mundt, *Crisis*, pp. 635, 637.

59. The Mexican case is pertinent to the ongoing debate about the role of oil in Venezuela's success with democracy. Levine's chapter in this volume is certainly accurate in asserting that oil is not enough. Mexico was one of the world's top producers in the 1920s and has been again recently. In fact, oil may have helped save Mexico's undemocratic system. But it may also contribute to pressures for democracy and, as in Venezuela, oil and growth could potentially help democratic rule consolidate.

60. Perhaps Mexico's unequal socioeconomic development has facilitated autonomous political participation for some privileged groups alongside mobilized participation by mass groups.

See Samuel P. Huntington and Joan Nelson, *No Easy Choice* (Cambridge, MA: Harvard University Press, 1976). Such a view appears consistent with this chapter's corporatist-pluralist contrasts.

61. I give my views on how Mexico's foreign policy has contributed to stability and on the growing challenges that policy faces in "The Implications of Central American Conflicts for Mexican Politics." In *Mexico's Political Stability: The Next Five Years,* ed. Roderic A. Camp (Boulder, CO.: Westview Press, 1986), pp. 235–264.

62. On prospects for stability, see especially Camp, *Political Stability.*

63. Whether "success" by itself would ever undermine an authoritarian regime, particularly a well institutionalized one, is an interesting but perhaps remote question. More pertinent is whether success sets the general conditions for democracy to the point that crises (economic disaster, military defeat, scandal) leading to instability, or at least turmoil, may in fact lead to democratization.

64. Guillermo O'Donnell, "Introduction to the Latin American Cases," pp. 5, 15; and Luciano Martins, "The 'Liberalization' of Authoritarian Rule in Brazil," p. 72, both in O'Donnell, Schmitter, and Whitehead, *Transitions: Latin America;* and, especially, O'Donnell and Schmitter, *Transitions From Authoritarian Rule: Tentative Conclusions About Uncertain Democracies* (Baltimore: Johns Hopkins Press, 1986), pp. 48–72; also, Alfred Stepan, "Paths Toward Redemocratization: Theoretical and Comparative Considerations." In O'Donnell, Schmitter, and Whitehead, *Transitions from Authoritarian Rule: Comparative Perspectives,* pp. 72–74.

65. See Lamounier's chapter in this volume, and also Martins, "Liberalization," pp. 72–74.

66. The theoretical argument is developed in Adam Przeworski, "Some Problems in the Study of the Transition to Democracy." In O'Donnell, Schmitter, and Whitehead, *Transitions,* pp. 47–63; and in O'Donnell and Schmitter, *Transitions,* pp. 7–16, 48–49.

67. Wayne A. Cornelius, "Political Liberalization in an Authoritarian Regime: Mexico, 1976–1985." In Gentleman, *Mexican.*

68. Carlos Monsiváis, "La ofensiva ideológica de la derecha." In González Casanova and Florescano, *México, hoy,* p. 315. This underscores Przeworski's point ("Some Problems," pp. 50–53) that perceptions of alternatives as well as of the present regime are critical to choices about pushing for transition.

69. Laurence Whitehead, "International Aspects of Democratization." In O'Donnell, Schmitter, and Whitehead, *Transitions: Comparative Perspectives,* pp. 20, 44. Whitehead also writes (p. 43): "Mexico provides a particularly significant litmus test of American priorities. Does it not remain an open question in that country how much democracy of the conventional liberal democratic variety would be tolerable to Washington policymakers?" It does, but when will Mexico put the United States to that test?

• The Contributors •

LARRY DIAMOND is senior research fellow at the Hoover Institution, Stanford University. He is the author of *Class, Ethnicity and Democracy in Nigeria: The Failure of the First Republic*, and numerous articles on democracy in developing countries, Nigerian politics and development, and ethnicity, class formation, and democracy in Africa. During 1982–1983 he was a Fulbright visiting lecturer in Nigeria at Bayero University, Kano. He is now organizing and editing a comparative study of political culture and democracy in developing countries.

JUAN J. LINZ is Pelatiah Perit Professor of Political and Social Science at Yale University. He has written dozens of articles and book chapters on authoritarianism and totalitarianism, fascism, political parties and elites, and democratic breakdowns and transitions to democracy, in Spain and in comparative perspective. His English-language publications include *Crisis, Breakdown and Reequilibration*—Volume one of the four-volume work, *The Breakdown of Democratic Regimes*, which he edited with Alfred Stepan—and "Totalitarian and Authoritarian Regimes" in the *Handbook of Political Science*. From 1971 to 1979, he chaired the joint Committee on Political Sociology of the International Sociology and Political Science Associations. In 1987, he was awarded, in Spain, the Premio Principe de Asturias in the Social Sciences.

SEYMOUR MARTIN LIPSET is senior fellow at the Hoover Institution and Caroline S. G. Munro Professor of Political Science and Sociology at Stanford University. He has published widely on various themes in comparative political sociology. His many books include *Political Man, The First New Nation, Revolution and Counterrevolution, The Confidence Gap* (with William Schneider), and *Consensus and Conflict*. He has served as president of a number of academic bodies, including the American Political Science Association, the

Sociological Research Association, the International Society of Political Psychology, and the World Association for Public Opinion Research.

CARLOS H. WAISMAN is professor of sociology at the University of California at San Diego. He is the author of *Modernization and the Working Class: The Politics of Legitimacy* and *Reversal of Development in Argentina: Postwar Counterrevolutionary Policies and Their Structural Consequences,* as well as numerous articles on politics, social structure, development, and foreign debt in Argentina and in Latin America. Currently, he is researching economic policies and political processes under authoritarian rule in Argentina during the 1970s and early 1980s.

BOLÍVAR LAMOUNIER is director of the Instituto de Estudos Econômicos, Sociais e Políticos de São Paulo (IDESP) and professor of political science at the Catholic University of São Paulo and the São Paulo State University. Among his many authored, edited, and coedited works in Portuguese are *Political Parties and Democratic Consolidation in Brazil* (with Rachel Meneguello), *How Democracies are Reborn* (with Alain Rouquié and Jorge Schwarzer), *Political Science in the 80s, The Future of the Opening: A Debate* (with José Eduardo Faria), and *Parties and Elections in Brazil* (with Fernando Henrique Cardoso). He has been a member of the Brazilian Presidential Commission for Constitutional Studies and the Academic Council of the Woodrow Wilson International Center's Latin America Program, as well as several other Brazilian commissions and international scholarly panels.

ARTURO VALENZUELA is professor of government and director of Latin American Studies at Georgetown University. Among his many publications are *Political Brokers in Chile, The Breakdown of Democratic Regimes: Chile, Military Rule in Chile: Dictatorship and Opposition* (edited with J. Samuel Valenzuela), and *Chile: Prospects for Democracy* (with Mark Falcoff and Susan Kaufman Purcell). He is now working on *The Origins of Democracy: Theoretical Reflections on the Chilean Case* and *By Reason or By Force: The Pinochet Dictatorship* (with Pamela Constable).

CHARLES GUY GILLESPIE is assistant professor of Latin American politics at the University of Wisconsin, Madison. He has written widely on political parties, democratic breakdown, redemocratization, civil-military relations, and the prospects for democratic consolidation in Uruguay, Brazil, and the Southern Cone of Latin America. In 1984–1985 he coedited the three-volume *Uruguay y la democracia*. He has recently completed a book on party strategies and redemocratization in Uruguay and is now writing about elite pacts in democratization, and the U.S. role in promoting democracy in Latin America.

LUIS EDUARDO GONZÁLEZ is a researcher at the Centro de Informaciones y Estudios sobre Uruguay (CIESU) and teaches at the Centro Latinoamericano de Economía Humana and at CIESU-FLACSO in Montevideo. He also directs the Department of Public Opinion of Equipus Consultores Asociados, an Uruguayan consulting firm. He has published several articles on political parties and redemocratization and has completed a book on the role of political leaders and electoral systems in democratic consolidation in Uruguay. He recently organized an international conference in Uruguay on the role of political institutions in democratic consolidation and is now participating in a comparative study of the evolution of democratic values in post-transition Brazil and the Southern Cone.

DANIEL H. LEVINE is professor of political science at the University of Michigan. He is the author of *Conflict and Political Change in Venezuela, Churches and Politics in Latin America, Religion and Politics in Latin America: The Catholic Church in Venezuela and Colombia,* and *Religion and Political Conflict in Latin America*. In addition, he has published a wide range of articles on democracy, politics, religion, and social and cultural change in Venezuela and in Latin America generally. He is now working on a book tentatively titled *Popular Voice in Latin American Catholicism*.

JONATHAN HARTLYN is associate professor of political science at the University of North Carolina, Chapel Hill. He is the author of *The Politics of Coalition Rule in Colombia* and numerous articles on development and democracy in Colombia. Recently, he edited with Samuel A. Morley *Latin American Political Economy: Financial Crisis and Political Change*. He is now writing a book on democratic politics in the Dominican Republic.

CYNTHIA MCCLINTOCK is professor of political science at George Washington University. Her published works include *Peasant Cooperatives and Political Change in Peru, The Peruvian Experiment Reconsidered* (coedited with Abraham Lowenthal), and numerous articles on agrarian reform, peasant rebellion, and political change in Peru. She is currently engaged in comparative research on redemocratization in Peru.

JOHN A. BOOTH is professor and chair of the Department of Political Science at the University of North Texas. In addition to his book, *The End and the Beginning: The Nicaraguan Revolution,* he has coedited and contributed to *Political Participation in Latin America,* Volumes 1 and 2 (with Mitchell Seligson), *The Politics of San Antonio: Community, Power and Progress* (with D. R. Johnson and R. J. Harris), and *Elections and Democracy in Central America*. He has published many other articles and chapters on politics, labor unions, income distribution, political participation, political violence, political culture, and U.S. policy, with a particular focus on Central America.

HOWARD J. WIARDA is professor of political science at the University of Massachusetts at Amherst and resident scholar and director of the Center for Hemispheric Studies at the American Enterprise Institute in Washington, DC. He is also a research associate at the Center for International Affairs at Harvard University. He has been editor of the journal *Polity* and director of the Center for Latin American Studies at the University of Massachusetts, and was a lead consultant to the National Bipartisan (Kissinger) Commission on Central America. His extensive publications on Latin America, Southern Europe, developing nations, and U.S. foreign policy include: *Corporatism and Development: The Portuguese Experience, The Continuing Struggle for Democracy in Latin America, Latin American Politics and Development* (with Harvey F. Kline), *Corporatism and National Development in Latin America, Human Rights and U.S. Human Rights Policy, Politics and Social Change in Latin America, Ethnocentrism and American Foreign Policy, Rift and Revolution: The Central American Imbroglio, In Search of Policy: The United States and Latin America,* and *New Directions in Comparative Politics.* He is now completing for the Twentieth Century Fund a book titled *The Democratic Revolution in Latin America.*

DANIEL C. LEVY is professor of educational administration and policy studies and of Latin American studies at the State University of New York at Albany. He is author of *University and Government in Mexico: Autonomy in an Authoritarian System, Mexico: Paradoxes of Stability and Change* (with Gabriel Székely), and *Higher Education and the State in Latin America: Private Challenges to Public Dominance,* and editor of *Private Education: Studies in Choice and Public Policy.* His articles focus on the politics of Latin American universities, Mexican politics, and nonprofit organizations. Currently, he is conducting research on U.S. foundation and official assistance to Latin American universities and research centers.

• Acronyms •

ACF: "Adelante con fé" ("Forward with faith," Uruguay)
AD: Acción Democrática (Democratic Action, Venezuela)
ANAPO: Alianza Nacional Popular (National Popular Alliance, Colombia)
ANUC: Asociación Nacional de Usurios Campesinos (National Association of Peasant Users, Colombia)
APRA: Alianza Popular Revolucionaria Americana (Popular American Revolutionary Alliance, Peru)
ARENA: Aliança Renovadora Nacional (Alliance for National Renewal, Brazil)
BA: bureaucratic authoritarian regime
CADE: Conferencia Anual de Directores Empresas (Annual Business Executives' Conference, Peru)
CAEM: Centro de Altos Estudios Militares (Center for Advanced Military Studies, Peru)
CATD: Confederación Auténtica de Trabajadores Democráticas (Authentic Confederation of Democratic Workers, Costa Rica)
CCP: Confederación de Campesinos del Perú (Peruvian Peasants Confederation, Peru)
CCTD: Confederación de Costarricenses Trabajadores Democráticos (Democratic Workers Confederation, Costa Rica)
CGT: Confederación General de Trabajadores (General Confederation of Workers, Costa Rica)
CGTP: Confederación General de Trabajadores del Perú (General Confederation of Peruvian Workers, Peru)
CNA: Confederación Nacional Agraria (National Agrarian Confederation, Peru)
CNT: Convención Nacional de Trabajadores (National Workers' Convention, Uruguay)

COMASPO:	Comision de Asuntos Políticos (Armed Forces Political Affairs Commission, Uruguay)
COPEI:	Comité de Organización Política Electoral Independiente (Committee for Independent Political Organization, Venezuela)
COSENA:	Consejo de Seguridad Nacional (National Security Council, Uruguay)
CTC:	Confederación de Trabajadores de Colombia (Confederation of Colombian Workers, Colombia)
CTCR:	Confederación de Trabajadores Costarricenses (Costa Rican Workers' Confederation, Costa Rica)
CTM:	Confederación de Trabajadores Mexicanos (Confederation of Mexican Workers, Mexico)
CUT:	Confederación Unitaria de Trabajadores (Unitary Confederation of Workers, Costa Rica)
DINA:	Dirección de Inteligencia Nacional (National Bureau of Intelligence, Chile)
DSV:	double simultaneous vote
FA:	Frente Amplio (Broad Front, Uruguay)
FARC:	Fuerzas Armadas Revolucionarias de Colombia (Revolutionary Armed Forces of Colombia, Colombia)
GATT:	General Agreement on Tariffs and Trade
GDP:	gross domestic product
GNP:	gross national product
IMF:	International Monetary Fund
IPC:	International Petroleum Company (Peru)
M-19:	Movimiento del 19 de Abril (Movement of the 19th of April, Colombia)
MAS:	Movimiento al Socialismo (Socialist Movement, Venezuela)
MDB:	Movimento Democrática Brasiliero (Brazilian Democratic Movement, Brazil)
MRTA:	Movimiento Revolucionario Túpac Amaru (Túpac Amaru Revolutionary Movement, Peru)
PAN:	Partido Acción Nacional (National Action Party, Mexico)
PCU:	Partido Comunista de Uruguay (Communist Party, Uruguay)
PDS:	Partido Democrático Social (Social Democratic Party, Brazil)
PIT:	Plenario Intersindical de Trabajadores (Inter-union Workers' Plenary, Uruguay)
PLN:	Partido de Liberación Nacional (National Liberation Party, Costa Rica)
PMDB:	Partido do Movimento Democrático Brasileiro (Party of the Brazilian Democratic Movement, Brazil)
PPC:	Partido Popular Cristiano (Popular Christian Party, Peru)
PPU:	Partido Pueblo Unido (United People's Party, Costa Rica)
PR:	proportional representation

PRD:	Partido Revolucionario Dominicano (Dominican Revolutionary Party, Dominican Republic)
PRI:	Partido Revolucionario Institucional (Institutional Revolutionary Party, Mexico)
PRSC:	Partido Reformista Social Cristiano (Reformist Social Christian Party, Dominican Republic)
PUSC:	Partido de Unificación Social Cristiana (Social Christian Unity Party, Costa Rica)
SINAMOS:	Sistema Nacional por Mobilización Social (National System for the Support of Social Mobilization, Peru)
TSE:	Tribunal Supremo de Elecciones (Supreme Electoral Tribunal, Costa Rica)
UDN:	União Democrática Nacional (Democratic National Unity, Brazil)
UP:	Unidad Popular (Popular Unity, Chile)
UP:	Unión Patriótica (Patriotic Unity, Colombia)
URD:	Unión Republica Democrática (Democratic Republican Union, Venezuela)
UTC:	Unión de Trabajadores de Colombia (Union of Colombian Workers, Colombia)

· Index ·

ARENA (Aliança Renovadora Nacional) (Brazil), 113, 116
Acción Democrática (AD) (Venezuela), 16, 21, 252, 254-256, 258, 260-261, 264-265, 271-273, 277, 281-282, 285, 465
Acción Popular (Peru), 346-347, 352, 362-363
Aguirre Cerda, Pedro, 168
Alberto de Herrera, Luis, 210
Alemán, Miguel, 471
Alessandri, Arturo, 17, 167-168, 170
Alessandri, Jorge, 168, 170, 184
Alfonsín, Raúl, 33, 46, 99, 100, 101, 104
Alianza Nacional Popular (ANAPO) (Colombia), 313, 316
Alianza Popular Revolucionaria Americana (APRA) (Peru), 21, 335, 342-348, 351-352, 354-355, 358, 362-363, 374, 395
Allende, Salvador, 18, 25, 98, 168-169, 171, 182, 184, 185, 187-188, 193, 238, 266, 349, 378
Alliance for Progress (Peru), 347, 375
Alvarez Armellino, Gregorio, 224
Anarchists (Argentina), 65, 66, 70
April Package (Pacote de Abril), 113
Argentina, 2, 4, 6-9, 20, 23, 28, 123, 129, 176, 200, 214, 226-227, 401; authoritarianism, 63, 70-71, 81; class, 39, 41, 65-68, 70-73, 75, 77, 79, 81-82, 86, 88-91, 93, 95, 103; communism, 70, 77-80; corporatism (state), 29, 71-72, 75-78, 80, 84, 89, 95, 100; democracy, 52, 59, 62-65, 68-70, 79, 83-87, 89, 91-94, 96-101, 103-104; development, 42, 62, 76, 97-98; economy, 3, 43-44, 46-48, 51, 61-62, 64, 71-76, 78, 80-85, 88, 92, 99-101; elections, 67, 70, 94, 104; electoral reform, 62, 64, 67; elites, 64-68, 75-77, 79, 83-86, 91, 94-96; ethnicity, 90-91; foreign debt, 49, 83, 100-101; immigration, 59, 61, 64-67, 79, 84, 88, 90; industrialization, 62, 65, 70, 74-75; inequality, 65, 87-88; intelligentsia, 81-82, 85, 94, 98, 103; judiciary, 92, 96; labor, 62, 66-67, 70-74, 78, 80, 84-85, 93, 99, 103; legitimacy, 65, 67, 69-71, 74-75, 83, 85, 88, 94; liberalism, 73, 79, 89; military, 32-33, 70, 73, 77, 79-81, 83-85, 92-94, 98-102; military coups, 61, 63, 69, 71-72, 75, 82, 84, 93, 98-99; participation, 35, 62-63, 65-67, 69, 71, 86-87; parties and party system, 21, 68-69, 82, 94-95, 97, 104; Peronism, 70-72, 75, 77, 80-81, 83, 86-87, 92-93, 95-96, 100, 102, 104; political culture, 10, 12-13, 86-87; political leadership, 16, 18, 96-97; praetorianism, 73, 85, 94, 99, 100; protectionism, 70-71, 74-78, 80, 84-85, 89; repression, 65, 71, 80-83, 89, 98, 102; state, 27, 63, 73, 92; unemployment, 78, 82, 103; and the United States, 50, 76-77, 83, 98-99
Arias Sánchez, Oscar, 399, 407, 414, 417-418
Armed Forces Political Affairs

505

Commission (COMASPO) (Uruguay), 225
Army of National Liberation (Costa Rica), 15
Aspillaga, Antero, 341
Atahualpa (Peru), 338
Austral Plan (Argentina), 100
Authentic Confederation of Democratic Workers (Costa Rica), 408
Aztecs, 353, 462

Báez, Buenaventura, 430-431, 436
Baker Plan, 238
Balaguer, Joaquín, 435-440, 446-449, 454
Balmaceda, José Manuel, 165-166
Barco, Virgilio, 292, 314, 320, 329
Barrantes, Alfonso, 363, 377-378
Batista, Fulgencio, 28, 435, 449
Batlle y Ordóñez, José, 17, 210-211, 228, 231
Bedoya, Luis, 363
Belaúnde Terry, Fernando, 17, 50, 342, 346-349, 352, 355-356, 360-361, 363, 366-367, 369, 371-376
Benavides, Oscar, 344
Betancourt, Rómulo, 258, 281, 477
Betancur, Belisario, 314, 318-319, 323
Billinghurst, Guillermo, 341, 355
Blanco Party (Uruguay), 20, 210-213, 218, 223-225, 230, 235
Bolivia, 2, 6, 28, 162, 179
Bolívar, Simon, 4-5, 250-251, 295, 297, 338, 454
Bordaberry Arocena, Juan María, 19, 217, 219-221
Bosch, Juan, 49, 435, 437-438, 446-449
Brasil, Assis, 121-122
Brazil, 2, 5-8, 20, 77, 98, 221-222, 283, 489; authoritarianism, 111, 123, 137, 143, 149-151; bureaucracy, 119, 124, 149-150; civil society, 36, 128-129, 135, 150-151; class, 39, 120, 123, 132-136, 140; clientelism, 132, 141, 144, 151, 153; colonial rule, 117, 127, 133; communism, 123-124; congress, 26, 120, 124, 150-153; constitution, 119-120, 122, 135; corruption, 132-133; coronéis, 120; democracy, 52, 111-112, 116-117, 122, 124-125, 128-130, 133-134, 137, 139-147, 149-153; democratic breakdown, 111, 125, 140-141, 153; democratic transition, 124; economy, 47, 51, 114-116, 119, 121, 124, 130-131, 133-137, 140, 144-145, 148-151, 153; elections, 112-116, 118, 120-122, 124-125, 140-141, 143-144, 148, 152; electoral court, 121-122, 143; electoral college, 111, 114-115; elites, 117, 123, 128, 130, 142-144, 146-147; empire, 116, 123, 128, 133, 137, 138 (table 3.2); Estado Novo, 14, 20, 123-124, 128, 137, 138 (table 3.2), 141; ethnic and national cleavages, 41, 123, 136-137, 152; First Republic, 119-121, 133, 137, 138 (table 3.2); foreign debt, 49, 115, 132, 145, 149; inequality and poverty, 3, 40, 44, 123, 125, 133-136, 141-143, 145, 147-148, 151; judiciary, 118, 120, 129, 137; labor, 119, 133, 135-137, 140, 153; legitimacy, 4, 112-116, 121-122, 128, 130-133, 137, 142, 144, 148, 151, 153; New Republic (Nova República), 19, 40, 111, 132-133, 139 (table 3.2), 142, 146-147; military, 32-34, 48, 112-113, 117, 119, 124-125, 128-130, 132, 134-135, 139 (table 3.2), 140, 144-145, 150; monarchy, 117-119; oligarchy, 120, 137, 144, 152; political culture, 12, 14, 121, 123, 128-129, 133-134, 141-144, 151; political leadership, 19, 120, 124, 140-141, 148; parties and party systems, 23, 25, 28, 113-117, 120, 124-125, 129, 137, 140, 149-153; populism, 125, 143, 148, 153; proportional representation, 121-122, 125, 140, 152; regionalism, 136, 140, 151; representation, 122-123, 134-135, 143-144, 146-147, 151; repression, 113, 115, 129; revolution of 1930, 121, 128, 137, 138 (table 3.2); social mobility, 136-137, 146; social mobilization, 125, 132-133, 140-143, 150; state, 29, 126-127, 150; state building, 112, 116-120, 129-130, 137, 150, 152; and the United States, 50, 137

Broad Front (Frente Amplio) (FA) (Uruguay), 213, 217-218, 220, 224-226, 230, 237-238
Bulnes, Manuel, 15, 163, 179-180
Bustamente, José Luis, 342, 344-345, 355, 375

Cabildos, 3
Cáceres, Andres, 339
Cáceres, Ramón, 431, 439
Calderón Guardia, Rafael Angel, 394-395, 399, 401, 403, 415
Calles, Plutarco Elías, 464-465, 469, 472, 481, 484
Carazo, Rodrigo, 413, 417
Cárdenas, Lázaro, 465-466, 469, 472, 474, 481, 484
Cardoso, José Pedro, 471
Caretas (Peru), 362
Carranza, Venustiano, 464, 484
Carter, Jimmy, 50, 351, 374-375
Castro, Cipriano, 251
Castro, Fidel, 281, 449
Castro, León Cortés, 394
Catholic Church; in Argentina, 11, 72, 77, 92; in Brazil, 123, 150; in Chile, 164-165, 174, 178; in Colombia, 291, 295, 300-301, 305-306, 308; in Costa Rica, 391-393, 401; in Dominican Republic, 442-443, 445; in Mexico, 467; in Peru, 363-364; in Uruguay, 229; in Venezuela, 250, 254-255, 258
Caudillos, 6, 179; Dominican Republic, 431-432; Mexico, 462, 469; Peru, 338-339; Uruguay, 212; Venezuela, 251
Center for High Military Studies (CAEM) (Peru), 348
Central American Peace Accord, 418-419
Central American Republic (Costa Rica), 388-389
Chaco War, 6
Chamber of Commerce (Costa Rica), 409
Chamber of Deputies (Peru), 361
Chile, 4, 6-8, 26, 103, 209, 266, 283, 339, 348, 355, 370; authoritarianism, 175; class, 38-39, 176-178, 181; Civil War of 1830, 162-163; cleavages, 164, 167; colonialism, 162, 172-173; conservatives, 173, 150, 190; congress, 160, 163, 165-166, 171, 183-186, 199; constitutions, 159-160, 162-163, 167, 173, 183, 190-192, 195, 199; Council of State, 191-192; Decree Law, 190; democracy, 160, 165-166, 170-172, 175-177, 194; democratic breakdown, 43, 46, 48, 160-161, 171, 182-187; democratic evolution, 42, 174, 178-182; democratic prospects, 52, 161, 198-200; economy, 3, 44, 47-48, 163-165, 167, 177, 185, 194, 200; education, 159, 164; elections, 159, 161, 163-165, 168, 170-171, 184, 196-199; electoral reform, 165, 182; elites, 162-164, 174, 176, 180-181; foreign aid, 184; ideology, 171, 183-184; independence, 162; inequality, 171; judiciary, 190; labor, 166; the Left, 161, 171, 182-185, 188, 194-196; legitimacy, 163, 165-166, 171, 176, 190-191, 196-197; liberals, 164-165, 173; military, 31-32, 162-163, 167, 180, 185, 192-193, 198-200; military junta, 159-160, 166, 189-191, 197; military rule, 159, 188-189, 193-194, 199; National Guard, 163-164; national identity, 179; parliamentary system, 166-167, 187, 199; participation, 160-161, 181-182; parties and party system, 21-22, 24, 28, 159, 166-171, 183-187, 194-199; plebiscite, 196-200; polarization, 161, 169, 185, 195-196, 199; political culture, 11-14, 174-176, 188; political leadership, 15-18, 179, 186-187; presidentialism, 24-25, 170, 186-187; press, 159; radicalism, 184; repression, 159, 188, 195; social structure, 175; "Socialist Republic," 168; state, 29, 179-180, 189; and the United States, 50, 168, 174, 184
Christian Democratic Confederation (Costa Rica), 408
Christian Democratic Party (Chile), 168-169, 183-185, 187, 194-196
Christian Democratic Party (Dominican Republic), 446
Christian Democratic Party (Peru), 347

Christian Democratic Party (Uruguay), 224
Christian Democratic Party (Venezuela), 258
Civil Society (Comparative), 35-37
Civilista Party (Peru), 339-342
Cleavages (Comparative), 37-42
Colombia, 6, 8, 22, 231, 490; authoritarianism, 293-294; civil wars, 297; class, 38-39, 325-326; coalition rule, 317; colonialism, 291, 295; congress, 300, 304, 309, 318; consociationalism, 293, 300, 306-309, 315, 321, 329; constitutions, 292, 297, 300, 305-306, 309, 320; democracy, 51, 291-294, 318, 329-330; development performance, 327-328; drugs, 48, 294, 313-315, 317-319, 328; economic policies, 46, 305, 310-314; economy, 48, 292, 297, 300-301, 308, 310, 328; elections, 292, 296 (table 7.1), 298-299 (table 7.2 and 7.3), 301, 306, 315-317, 320-322; foreign debt, 301, 327-328; guerrillas, 317-319; international factors, 328; judiciary, 26, 293, 317, 319-320, 323-324; labor, 302-303, 317, 326; legitimacy, 315-317; media, 37, 325; military, 295, 297, 308, 318, military rule, 305-306; national assembly, 300; oligarchical democracy, 300-302; opposition, 305, 314-316; pacts, 306; parties and party systems, 20-21, 24, 292-295, 297, 300-309, 314-316, 320-322; polarization, 303-304; political culture, 12, 326-327; political leadership, 15-16, 307, 326-327; political reforms, 320; political violence, 303-304, 314, 320, 329-330; presidentialism and centralization, 322-323; producer associations, 324-325; regionalism, 294; repression, 294, 304; state, 27, 30, 294-295, 310, 313, 323-324; and the United States, 50, 301, 305, 319, 323, 328
Colorado Party (Uruguay), 20, 210-213, 217-219, 223, 225-227, 230-231, 235
Comite de Organización Política Electoral Independiente (COPEI) (Venezuela), 21, 254, 260-261, 264, 271-273, 282
Commission for the Reform of the State (COPRE) (Venezuela), 30-31, 276
Communist Party (Argentina), 70, 78, 89, 103
Communist Party (Chile), 39, 166-169, 195-196, 198
Communist Party (Costa Rica), 393-394, 399, 402, 408-409
Communist Party (Dominican Republic), 446
Communist Party (PCM) (Mexico), 474
Communist Party (Peru), 357
Communist Party (Venezuela), 265
Communist Party of Uruguay (PCU), 217, 223-224, 237-238
Confederación de Costarricenses Trabajadores Democráticos (CCTD) (Costa Rica), 398, 408
Confederación General de Trabajadores (CGT) (Costa Rica), 393
Confederación General de Trabajadores del Perú (CGTP), 357-359
Confederación Trabajadores del Perú (CTP), 357
Confederation of Colombian Workers (CTC), 302-303
Confederation of Industrial Chambers (CONCAMIN) (Mexico), 466
Confederation of Mexican Workers (CTM) (Mexico), 466
Consejo Nacional de Elecciones (Costa Rica), 393
Conservative Party (Argentina), 16, 62, 65, 68-69, 77, 86, 92, 95-97
Conservative Party (Chile), 22, 164-166, 178, 180-181
Conservative Party (Colombia), 20, 292, 295-308, 310, 312-314, 316, 318, 320, 322-323
Constituent Assembly (Colombia), 300-306
Constitutional Democratic Party (Costa Rica), 391
Contreras, Manuel, 193-194
Convención Nacional de Trabajadores (Uruguay), 220

Convergencia Democrática (Uruguay), 224
Corporaciones Departamentales de Desarrollo (CORDES) (Peru), 368
Costa Rica, 2, 4, 8, 26, 175, 231, 471; associations and interest groups, 389-390, 393, 407-409; civil society, 35-36; class, 38-39, 389-392, 409-412, 416-417; cleavages, 412-413; colonialism, 387-389; communism, 402-403; constitution, 392, 394-395, 398, 416; democracy, 387-389, 395, 411, 415; democratic prospects, 417-419; economy, 3, 48, 389-391, 401, 404-407, 414-415; education, 389; elections, 389, 391-395, 396 (table 9.2), 398; elite, 389, 391, 395, 403, 416-417; foreign debt, 49, 401, 406, 414-415, 417, 419; foreign policy, 413-414; inequality, 40, 392, 410-412; international pressures, 413-415, 419; judiciary, 400; labor, 393-394, 408-409; legislative assembly, 395, 400; legitimacy, 399, 404; media, 401-402; military, 33, 394-395, 413-414, 418; participation, 392, 402; parties and party system, 391, 393-394, 398-399; political culture, 11-13, 402-404, 416; political leadership, 15-17; political violence, 402-404; poverty, 388; race, 391, 412-413; reforms, 392, 394; Second Republic, 394; socioeconomic development, 44, 46, 389, 405-406; state, 29, 399-401, 404-407, 416; and the United States, 50, 393, 413-415, 417-419
Costa Rican Management Association (ACOGE), 409
Costa Rican Workers' Confederation (CTCR), 394, 402
Council of the Nation (Uruguay), 222
Court of Constitutional Guarantees (Peru), 361
Criollos, 338
Cruzado Plan, 19, 136, 148
Cuba, 2, 28, 98, 260, 281, 413, 427, 449, 486

Cuban Revolution, 48, 52, 81, 98, 125, 184, 259, 281, 347, 435

da Fonseca, Deodoro, 119
Days of May (Colombia), 306
de la Madrid, Miguel, 468, 470, 474, 479, 483, 490
de Miranda, Francisco, 4
de San Martín, José, 338
Declaration of Benidorm, 306
Democracy (comparative), 1-2, 5, 8-52
Democracy, consociational and majoritarian, 151, 211, 292-293, 306-307, 329
Democratic alliance (Brazil), 115, 148
Democratic Party (Peru), 341
Depression (1930s). *See* Great Depression.
Díaz, Porfirio, 431, 463-464
Dominican Republic, 2, 8; authoritarianism, 423, 426, 429-433, 436-437, 439-440, 451; civil society, 36; class, 427, 434-435, 440-442, 450; ethnic, racial, and religious cleavages, 41, 427, 441-443, 450; colonialism, 426-428, 440-441, 450; constitutions, 429, 432, 441, 445-446; corporatism, 433-434; corruption, 445; democracy, 423, 425, 429, 431-434, 437-441, 447-449; democratic prospects, 449-455; economy, 48, 425, 431, 433, 436, 444, 449, 452-453; elections, 435, 437-438; elites, 434, 439-440; foreign policy, 448-449, 452; Haitian rule, 428-430; independence, 429-430, 441; inequality, 3, 40-41, 44, 426; institutional weakness, 428, 433, 440; international pressures, 428, 448-449, 452; labor, 442; legitimacy, 432, 439; military, 31, 430, 433, 437, 444-445; parties and party system, 23, 446; political culture, 9-12, 14, 429-430, 439-440, 450-451; political leadership, 15, 447, 450-451; political violence, 433, 436, 444-445; press, 37, 446-447; socioeconomic development, 430, 447-448, 451; state, 27, 29, 443-445, 450;

Trujillo era, 432-434, 443-446; and the United States, 49-50, 425, 428-432, 434-437, 439, 449, 451-452, 454-455
Dominican Revolutionary Party (PRD), 435-438, 446, 448-449
Don Pedro, 4
Double Simultaneous Vote (DSV) (Uruguay), 23, 212-213, 217, 227, 238
Drug trafficking, 48, 319, 328, 376
Duarte, Juan Pablo, 429-431, 439

Echandi, Mario, 399
Echeverría, Luis, 467-468
Ecuador, 2, 6, 26, 295, 344
Eisenhower, Dwight D., 280-281
Ejército Revolucionario del Pueblo (ERP) (Argentina), 28
El Comercio (Peru), 344, 356
El Diario (Peru), 362
El Salvador, 283
Entrepreneurial Coordinating Council (CCE) (Mexico), 466
Erro, Enrique, 220
Espaillat, Ulises, 431, 439

Falklands/Malvinas War. *See* Malvinas/Falklands War.
Fascism, 11, 20, 71, 78-80, 123-124
Federal Party (Argentina), 96
Federal Wars (Venezuela), 251
Ferreira Aldunate, Wilson, 224-225
Figueiredo, João Baptista, 114-115
Figueres Ferrer, José, 15-16, 394-395, 398-400, 415
Figueroa, Emiliano, 167
France, 428-430
Franco, Francisco, 20, 112, 434
Frei, Eduardo, 168-169, 183-184
Frente Amplio (FA) (Uruguay). *See* Broad Front.
Frente Democratico (Democratic Front) (Peru), 363
Frente Liberal (Brazil), 115

Gaitán, Jorge Eliécer, 302-303
Gallegos, Romulo, 285
Gallinal, Alberto, 223

García, Alan, 18, 30, 46, 52, 352, 356, 359-363, 367-370, 372, 374
Gavin, John, 491
Geisel, Ernesto, 113-115, 145
General Agreement on Tariffs and Trade (GATT), 238, 468, 483
González Videla, Gabriel, 168
González Víquez, Cleto, 16, 391, 393
González, Flores Alfredo, 392
Goulart, João, 19, 111, 125, 128, 140
Grace, W. R., 339
Gran Colombia, 5, 295, 297
Great Britain, 209
Great Depression; in Argentina, 18, 61-62, 68-70, 76, 80, 84; in Chile, 17, 168; in Costa Rica, 393; in Peru, 342-343; in Uruguay, 48, 214-215 (table 5.1), 231
Gómez Farías, Valentín, 463
Gómez, Juan Vicente, 251-252, 269-270
Gómez, Laureano, 302-306
Guardia, Tomás, 390-392
Guatemala, 394
Guzmán, Antonio, 437, 439, 448

Haiti, 2, 428-431, 439-440, 448-451
Haya de la Torre, Victor Raúl, 342-344, 346-347, 351, 360, 373, 395
Heureaux, Ulíses, 431-433, 436, 439, 447
Hispañola, 426-428

Ibañez, Carlos, 167-168
Incas, 338, 353, 366
Inequality. *See* Cleavages.
Institutional Revolutionary Party (PRI) (Mexico), 27, 472-473, 476-477, 483, 487, 489-491
Instituto de Libertad y Democracia (Peru), 368
International Factors (comparative), 47-50
International Monetary Fund (IMF), 99-100, 219, 313, 350, 406, 414
International Petroleum Company (IPC) (Peru), 348-349, 375-376
Intransigent Party (Argentina), 103
Irarrazaval, José Manuel, 17, 165

INDEX 511

Italy, 79
Izquierda Unida (Peru), 357, 362-363, 376

Jiménez Oreamuno, Ricardo, 17, 392-394
Jorge Blanco, Salvador, 437, 448
Juárez, Benito, 463

Kennedy, John F., 281, 347, 375, 435
Korean War, 345
Kubitscheck, Juscelino, 132, 141, 144

La Prensa (Peru), 345, 356
La Regeneracíon (Colombia), 297
La Religión (Venezuela), 255
La Violencia (Colombia), 292, 302-305, 315, 326
Lacerda, Carlos, 141
Larrazabal, Wolfgang, 264
Leftist Radical Party (Chile), 187
Leguiá, Augusto, 17, 27, 340-341, 343, 355, 371
Leigh, Gustavo, 190-191
Leyva, Jorge, 307
Liberal Party (Chile), 22, 169
Liberal Party (Colombia), 20, 292, 295-308, 310, 313-314, 316, 318, 320, 322-323
Liberal Party (Costa Rica), 390-392
Liberal Progressive Party (Costa Rica), 391
Liberal Republic (Colombia), 301
Liberal Republic (Costa Rica), 17
Lleras Restrepo, Carlos, 310, 313
Lleras, Alberto, 303, 306
López Contreras, Eleazar, 252
López Michelson, Alfonso, 313, 316
López Portillo, José, 468, 479
López Pumarejo, Alfonso, 301-302
Lusinchi, Jaime, 17, 260, 282

Madero, Francisco, 463-464, 484
Madrazo, Carlos, 474
Majluta, Jacobo, 438
Malvinas/Falklands War, 7, 33, 83
Mariátegui, José Carlos, 343
Maurras, Charles, 11

Medici, Emílio Garrastazú, 114, 132
Medina Angarita, Isias, 252, 254
Méndez, Aparicio, 222
Mexican Employers' Confederation (COPARMEX) (Mexico), 466
Mexico, 2, 8-9, 388; associations, 468; authoritarianism, 462, 490; centralization, 469-472; civil society, 35-36; class, 478, 481-482, 485; cleavages, 481-482; colonization, 462; constitution, 464; corporatism, 465-467, 481; corruption, 479-480; democracy, 52, 459, 461-464, 477, 480-487; democratic prospects, 487-493; dissent, 465-469; economy, 44, 48, 477-480, 483; elections, 462-463, 470, 472-477; elites, 463-465, 481, 484; federalism, 469-470; foreign debt, 479; foreign policy, 486-487, 492; inequality, 3, 478; international pressures, 486-487; judiciary, 471; labor, 466; legitimacy, 461, 464, 468, 476, 480-481, 483, 486, 488; media, 37, 468-469; military, 32-33, 464, 471; parties and party system, 472-477, 487-488; political culture, 10-11, 480-481; political leadership, 15, 464-465, 483-485; political reform, 471; political violence, 466; presidency, 471; religion, 467; repression, 468; revolution, 3, 38; socioeconomic development, 43, 479, 485-486; stability, 461-462, 469, 482-483, 492; state, 27, 29-30, 465-469, 482-483; students, 467; and the United States, 486-487, 491-493
Military (comparative), 31-35
Minas Gerais (Brazil), state of, 7, 120-121
Minimum Program of Government (Venezuela), 257-259
Monge Alvarez, Luis Alberto, 399, 407, 413, 417
Montt, Manuel, 163-164, 179
Mora Valverde, Manuel, 399
Morales Bermúdez, Francisco, 350-351, 359-360, 369, 371-373
Morales Bermúdez, Remigio, 339

Movement of the 19th of April (M-19) (Colombia), 317-320
Movimiento al Socialismo (MAS) (Venezuela), 265
Movimiento Revolucionario Túpac Amaru (MRTA) (Peru), 367, 376

National Accord for Transition to Democracy (Chile), 195
National Action Party (PAN) (Mexico), 474-477, 491
National Agrarian Confederation (CNA) (Peru), 358
National Association for the Promotion of Enterprise (ANFE) (Costa Rica), 409
National Association of Peasant Users (ANUC) (Colombia), 310
National Bureau of Intelligence (DINA) (Chile), 193-194
National Chamber of Manufacturing Industry (CANACINTRA) (Mexico), 466
National Democratic Front (Peru), 344
National Endowment for Democracy, 198
National Forum for Effective Suffrage (Mexico), 477
National Front (Colombia), 292-294, 302, 305, 307-310, 314-316, 321-325
National Liberation Junta (Costa Rica), 403
National Liberation Party (PLN) (Costa Rica), 394-395, 398, 401-403, 407-409, 415-417
National Party (Uruguay). *See* Blanco Party.
National Security Council (Uruguay), 220, 222, 225
National System for the Support of Social Mobilization (SINAMOS) (Peru), 350, 358
National Union (Colombia), 303
National Union Party (Costa Rica), 391, 393-394
Naval Club Pact (Uruguay), 225, 227
Neves, Tancredo, 19, 111, 115, 148
Nicaragua, 28, 388, 392-393, 399, 402, 413-414, 417-418
Nixon, Richard, 281

Nueva Granada, 295
Nuñez, Rafael, 297, 300

Obregón, Alvaro, 464, 469, 472, 484
Odría, Manuel, 345-347, 355, 371, 373
Oduber Quirós, Daniel, 399, 418
Oiga (Peru), 362
Orlich, Francisco, 399
Ospina, Pérez Mariano, 303-305

Pacheco Areco, Jorge, 19, 213, 223, 229
Pact of March (Colombia), 306
Pact of Punto Fijo (Venezuela), 257, 259
Pact of San Carlos (Colombia), 306-307
Pact of Sitges (Colombia), 306-307
Panama, 295, 300
Panama Army School of the Americas, 231
Paraguay, 2, 6, 11, 48, 52
Paraguayan War (Brazil), 119
Pardo, José, 341
Pardo, Manuel, 339
Parque Hotel talks (Uruguay), 225-226
Partido de Unificación Social Cristiano (PUSC) (Costa Rica), 399
Partido Popular Cristiano (PPC) (Peru), 356, 362-363
Partido Pueblo Unido (Costa Rica), 399
Partido Reformista Social Cristiano (PRSC) (Dominican Republic), 446
Partido Republicano (Colombia), 300
Partido Revolucionario Institucional (PRI) (Mexico). *See* Institutional Revolutionary Party.
Partido Social Democrático (PSD) (Brazil), 115, 125, 140
Party for Democracy (Chile), 196
Party of National Liberation (Dominican Republic), 446
Party of the Brazilian Democratic Movement (PMDB), 113-115, 142
Pastrana, Misael, 313
Patriotic Unity (UP) (Colombia), 320
People's Revolutionary Party (Costa Rica), 399
Peronist party (Argentina), 21, 63, 68, 82, 84, 86, 92-94, 96, 104
Perón, Isabel, 82

INDEX 513

Perón, Juan, 7, 18, 20, 31, 63, 70-72, 75, 77-82, 84, 89, 97, 123, 189, 228
Peru, 2, 4, 6-7, 162, 179, 302; Aristocratic Republic, 340-342; associations, 359; authoritarianism, 337, 371; class, 38-41, 337, 353-357, 362-364; colonialism, 337-338, 353; constitutions, 346, 351, 360-361; corruption, 361; democracy, 335, 349, 351-354, 358-360, 363, 366, 370, 374; democratic breakdowns, 335; democratic prospects, 376-378; economy, 46-48, 339-341, 344-345, 347-348, 354-357, 369, 371; education, 356-357; elections, 337, 340, 342-347, 350-352, 359-360, 378; elites, 335, 340, 345, 356, 360, 362, 364; ethnic cleavage, 335, 341, 343, 363, 377; foreign debt, 49, 399, 350, 357, 372, 375-376; guerrillas, 347, 352, 366-367, 370, 376; independence, 338-339; Indians, 335, 338-340, 342, 364, 366, 377; inequality, 3, 40-42, 44, 363-367; international factors, 374-377; judiciary, 361; labor, 351, 357-358; legitimacy, 339, 347, 370; media, 37, 344, 350, 356, 361, 362; military, 33-34, 339-341, 343-352, 356-360, 364, 367, 369-371, 376; military coups, 48; participation, 35-36; parties and party system, 21, 23, 342-343, 350-351, 355, 361-362; peasants, 347-348, 358; political culture, 11-12, 14, 353-360, 374, 377; political leadership, 17-18, 373-374; presidentialism, 25, 361; reform, 341, 348-349, 358; repression, 342-343, 350-352; socioeconomic development, 367-368, 371-373; state, 27, 29-30, 367-371; and the United States, 342, 347, 349, 351, 353, 366, 374-378
Peru-Bolivia Confederation, 162, 179
Peruvian Peasants' Confederation (CCP), 358-359
Peruvian Socialist Party, 343
Picado Michalski, Teodoro, 394
Piérola, Nicolás de, 339-340
Pinochet Ugarte, Augusto, 11, 13, 20, 31-32, 159, 161, 180, 188-199, 223, 227, 423
Pérez Jiménez, General Marcos, 49, 255-256, 264, 266, 272, 281
Pérez, Carlos Andres, 260
Pizarro, Francisco, 338
Plenario Intersindical de Trabajadores (PIT) (Plenary Workers' Union) (Uruguay), 225
Political culture (comparative), 9-14
Political institutions (comparative), 19-27
Political leadership (comparative), 14-19
Popular Front (Chile), 168-171
Popular Socialist Party (PPS) (Mexico), 474
Popular Unity (Chile). *See* Unidad Popular.
Porfiriato, 463
Portales, Diego, 162, 173
Portugal, 2, 4, 127
Prado, Manuel, 17, 344, 346, 373
Prado, Mariano Ignacio, 339
Prieto, Joaquin, 162-163, 173
Protestants, 304, 413, 443
Punta del Este Conference, 238

Quadros, Jânio, 19, 125, 128, 141

Radical Party (Argentina), 16, 21, 62-63, 65-70, 83, 86, 90, 92, 94, 96-97, 99, 101, 103-104, 176
Radical Party (Chile), 164, 166, 168-171, 176, 178, 181, 183-184
Reagan, Ronald, 376, 413, 419
Reform of 1912 (Sáenz Peña Law, Argentina), 16, 65, 67, 97, 176, 181
Reformist Party (Costa Rica), 393
Reformist Party (Dominican Republic), 446
Republican Party (Costa Rica), 391, 393, 399
Revolutionary Armed Forces of Colombia (FARC), 317-318, 320
Reyes, Rafael, 300, 305
Roca, Julio, 96
Rojas Pinilla, Gustavo, 36, 305-306, 313, 316, 326
Roosevelt, Franklin D., 344, 374

Sáenz Peña Law. *See* Reform of 1912.
Sáenz Peña, Roque, 16, 97
Salazar, António de Oliveira, 20
Salinas de Gortari, Carlos, 29, 474, 483
Sanabria, Victor Manuel (Archbishop), 394, 401
Sánchez Cerro, Luis, 342-344, 360
Sanguinetti Cairolo, Julio María, 229
Santa Cruz, General Andrés, 162
Santana, Pedro, 430-431, 436
Sarney, José, 19, 46, 115, 136, 148, 153
São Paulo (Brazil), 7, 115, 119-121
Sendero Luminoso (Shining Path) (Peru), 42, 353, 361, 363, 366-367, 370, 376
Seregni, Líber, 224
Social Christian Unity Party (PUSC) (Costa Rica), 416-417
Socialist Party (Argentina), 39, 65-66, 68
Socialist Party (Chile), 168-169, 185, 195
Socialist Party (Costa Rica), 399
Socialist Party (Peru), 347
Socialist Party (Uruguay), 224
Socioeconomic development (comparative), 42-44
Somoza Debayle, Anastasio, 11, 28, 49, 189, 413
Soviet Union, 98-99, 265, 366, 376, 428
Spain, 5, 79, 90, 112, 250-251, 283, 306, 430, 462
Spanish Civil War, 78-79
State structure and strength (comparative), 27-31
Stroessner, Alfredo, 11, 52, 89

Tercera Fuerza, 306
Thiel, Bernardo, 401
Tinoco, 392-393
Tomic, Radomiro, 169, 184
Tocqueville, Alexis de, 267, 279-280, 283
Trejos, José Joaquín, 399
Tribunal Supremo de Elecciones (TSE) (Costa Rica), 395, 398
Trujillo, Rafael, 27, 29, 31, 37, 49, 432-436, 439-440, 442-444, 446-449, 451, 453
Trujillo, Rafael, Jr., 435
Tupamaros (Uruguay), 28, 209, 217, 219
Turbay, Julio César, 313-314, 316-318
Túpac Amaru II, 338, 366

Ulate Blanco, Otilio, 394-395
UN Economic Commission for Latin America (ECLA), 51
União Democrática Nacional (UDN) (Brazil), 124, 140-141
Unidad Popular (Popular Unity Coalition) (Chile), 18, 169, 185, 187, 192, 238
Union of Colombian Workers (UTC) (Colombia), 303
Union of the Democratic Center (Argentina), 96, 104
Unión Republica Democrática (URD) (Venezuela), 254, 264
Unitary Confederation of Workers (CUT) (Costa Rica), 408
United States, 6, 10, 15, 24, 47-51; and Argentina, 50, 76-77, 83, 98-99; and Brazil, 50, 137; and Chile, 50, 168, 174, 184; and Colombia, 50, 305, 328; and Costa Rica, 50, 393, 413-415, 417-419; and Dominican Republic, 49-50, 425, 428-437, 439, 449, 451-452, 454-455; and Mexico, 486-487, 491-493; and Peru, 50, 339, 342, 344-345, 347, 349, 353, 366, 374-378; and Uruguay, 50, 231, 238; and Venezuela, 255, 260, 280-281
Uruguay, 2, 4, 6-9, 20, 26, 119; authoritarianism, 220-226, 239; civil society, 35, 228-229, 234, 236; civil wars, 207; class, 38-39, 41, 216-217, 221, 228, 234; cleavages, 229; clientelism, 212; constitutions, 220, 222-223, 225, 232; corruption, 219, 233; coup of 1973, 219-220, 231-233, 235-237; democracy, 52, 207, 209, 213, 222, 224, 232-233, 237-238; democratic breakdown, 46, 214-220, 231-237; democratic transition, 226-227; economy, 3, 44, 46-47, 210, 214-216, 221, 224, 226, 238; elections, 217-218, 224-225, 230; electoral system, 207, 212-213; foreign debt, 49, 215, 221, 238; foreign policy, 212; human rights, 229; international factors, 227, 237; judiciary, 230, 236; labor, 217, 220, 225, 228; legislature, 220, 238-239; legitimacy, 219, 222, 224, 226, 234; military, 33-34, 48, 218-226, 232-233,

INDEX 515

235-236, 239; opposition, 211, 224; parties and party system, 21-23, 210-213, 217-218 (table 5.3 and 5.4), 219-220, 222-225, 230, 233, 235-238; polarization, 216, 218, 232; political culture, 11-14, 223, 227-228, 233; political leadership, 17-19, 230-233, 236; presidentialism, 25, 238; press, 37, 207, 230, 236; radicalism, 28, 232; reforms, 211; socioeconomic development, 42-43, 207, 231, 236; state, 27, 29, 210, 229-230, 235; and the United States, 50, 231, 238

Valencia, Guillermo León, 306-307, 312
Vargas, Getulio, 7, 14, 20, 121, 123-125, 128-129, 137, 141, 153, 189, 228
Vargas Carbonell, Mario, 399
Vargas Llosa, Mario, 363, 378
Vásquez, Horacio, 432, 439
Velasco Alvarado, Juan, 12, 17, 36, 348-350, 355-359, 364, 366, 371, 373-374
Venezuela, 2, 8, 28, 295, 359, 491; associations, 249, 254, 266-267, 270, 279-280, 283; authoritarianism, 247-249, 253 (table 6.1), 258; civil society, 35; civil wars, 251; class, 269, 277; cleavages, 276-278; colonialism, 250-251; Congress, 254, 276; Constitution (1961), 259, 276; corruption, 255-256, 282; coups, 254, 256, 260; democracy, 22, 247-249, 253 (table 6.1), 258-259, 265-267, 273, 277; democratic prospect, 281-285; democratic transition, 249, 256-257, 260, 283; economy, 48, 250-251, 256, 280, 282; elections and electoral system, 247, 254, 256-257, 260-261, 262-263 (tables 6.2 and 6.3), 264-265, 272-273, 274 (table 6.5), 284; elites, 256-259, 278; foreign debt, 269, 282; inequality, 40, 277; international factors, 280-281; left, 259-260, 264-265, 281; legitimacy, 249, 255, 259, 278; military, 32-34, 255-256, 258; participation, 252, 254, 259, 266; parties and party system, 39, 247-248, 252, 254, 260-265, 267, 270-272, 277, 284; petroleum (oil boom), 247, 250-251, 255, 265-267, 269-270; polarization, 283-283; political culture, 12-13, 258, 278-279; political leadership (political class), 15-16, 18, 248, 257-259, 265-267; proportional representation, 272-273, 280; regionalism, 273, 277; repression, 249, 251-252, 255; socioeconomic development, 43-44, 46, 267-270; state, 27, 30, 273, 276; trienio, 253 (table 6.1), 254-255, 258, 261, 271, 273; and the United States, 50, 255, 260, 280-281
Vesco, Robert, 400
Villalba, Jóvito, 264
Villanueva, Armando, 352
Volio, Jorge, 393, 395

War of the Pacific (1879-1883), 6, 165, 179, 348
War of the Thousand Days (Colombia), 297, 300, 326
War of the Triple Alliance, 6
Wars of Independence (Venezuela), 251
Wilson, Woodrow, 432, 491
Workers' Party (PT) (Brazil), 142
World Bank, 305

Yrigoyen, Hipólito, 16, 97

Zapata, Emiliano, 464
Zorilla, Juan José, 220